CHURCHILL'S SPANIARDS

Continuing the Fight in the British Army, 1939–1946

Séan F. Scullion

Helion & Company

Helion & Company Limited
Unit 8 Amherst Business Centre
Budbrooke Road
Warwick
CV34 5WE
England
Tel. 01926 499619
Email: info@helion.co.uk
Website: www.helion.co.uk
X (formerly Twitter): @Helionbooks
Facebook: @HelionBooks
Visit our blog at helionbooks.wordpress.com

Published by Helion & Company 2024
Designed and typeset by Mach 3 Solutions (www.mach3solutions.co.uk)
Cover designed by Paul Hewitt, Battlefield Design (www.battlefield-design.co.uk)

Text © Séan F. Scullion 2024
Maps by Michael Heald, of Fully Illustrated (https://fullyillustrated.com)
© Séan Scullion 2024
Illustrations © as individually credited
Cover: Churchill image by Michael Heald, of Fully Illustrated.

Every reasonable effort has been made to trace copyright holders and to obtain their permission for the use of copyright material. The author and publisher apologise for any errors or omissions in this work, and would be grateful if notified of any corrections that should be incorporated in future reprints or editions of this book.

ISBN 978-1-804515-33-4

British Library Cataloguing-in-Publication Data.
A catalogue record for this book is available from the British Library.

All rights reserved. No part of this publication may be reproduced, stored in a retrieval system, or transmitted, in any form, or by any means, electronic, mechanical, photocopying, recording or otherwise, without the express written consent of Helion & Company Limited.

For details of other military history titles published by Helion & Company Limited, contact the above address, or visit our website: http://www.helion.co.uk

We always welcome receiving book proposals from prospective authors.

Contents

Lists of Illustrations ... iv
List of Colour Plates ... ix
List of Maps ... x
Chronology ... xi
Glossary ... xxi
Acknowledgements ... xxiii
Foreword ... xxvii
Preface ... xxix

1 'The First Summer After and The Last Summer Before' ... 35
2 'Brave New World' ... 57
3 'My Country' ... 92
4 'Vagabonds' ... 115
5 'See You In Hell' ... 155
6 'Wonderful Way to Go' ... 184
7 'Flying Through The Smoke' ... 217
8 'Did You Make It Safe?' ... 242

Appendices
I No. 1 Spanish Company, Nominal Roll Dated 5 December 1942 ... 269
II List of SCONCEs ... 278
III 50 Middle East Commando List Summary ... 284
IV Spaniards on the Nominal Roll of D Squadron, 1st Special Service Regiment in the Summer of 1942 ... 291
V Spaniards in the SAS During The Second World War
VI List of Spaniards known to have died whilst serving in the British Army, recorded by the Commonwealth War Graves Commission ... 294
VII List of Enlisted Spaniards in the British Army 1939–1946 ... 296

Bibliography ... 338
Index ... 350

Lists of Illustrations

A lorry of goods and Spanish Republicans at the French border. (Agustín Roa Ventura archive)	41
A group of Spaniards at Le Bacarès camp, 1939. (Agustín Roa Ventura archive)	43
Women, children and the elderly at a *Centre d'Accueil*. (Agustín Roa Ventura archive)	44
A group of Spaniards in a camp in Algiers, 1939. (Antonio Obis archive)	46
A pass for Eduardo Tamarit. (Eduardo Tamarit Archive)	49
A group of Spaniards in one of the *RMVE*s. (Manuel Surera archive)	51
Francisco Geronimo in *Légion Étrangère* uniform. (Francisco Geronimo collection)	53
Attestation d'Identité of Antonio Obis. (Antonio Obis archive)	55
Group of No.185 Spanish Labour Company, early 1940. (Jesús Gallindo collection)	60
Three members of No.185 Spanish Company. (Antoine Nieto Sandoval)	61
Jesús Velasco and 'Bob' Parkins, 1940. (Jesús Velasco collection)	62
List of names handed to the captain of the Polish ship leaving St Nazaire. (Jesús Velasco collection)	63
José García Flores. (José García Flores collection)	68
Spanish *Légionnaires* in the North African desert. (Augusto Pérez Miranda collection)	69
Spaniards pose taking a rest during their training. (José García Flores collection)	69
Franksa Kirkegarr cemetery. (Agustín Roa Ventura collection)	71
No.1 Spanish Company football team, 1940. (José García Flores collection)	75
Section of No.1 Spanish Company, Plymouth. (Jesús Velasco collection)	77
Members of No.1 Spanish Company. (José García Flores collection)	78
Members of No.1 Spanish Company. (Rodrigo Haro collection)	78
Members of No.1 Spanish Company with a Senior Non-Commissioned Officer. (Rodrigo Haro collection)	79
Rodrigo Haro and Selina Gardner's wedding, 1943. (Rodrigo Haro collection)	80
Rodrigo Haro late in the war. (Rodrigo Haro collection)	81
Members of No.1 Spanish Company, 1944. (Agustín Roa Ventura collection)	82
Members of No.1 Spanish Company before the liberation parade in Le Nebourg in 1944. (Jesús Velasco collection)	83
A team from No.1 Spanish Company, Rouen area 1944. (Rodrigo Haro collection)	83
Leclerc's 2nd Armoured Division in Paris. (Agustín Roa Ventura collection)	84
Von Cholditz under escort by Spanish troops. (Agustín Roa Ventura collection)	85
Members of No.1 Spanish Company in Normandy. (Agustín Roa Ventura collection)	86
Members of No.1 Spanish Company loading trucks, October/November 1944, Belgium. (Rafael Treserras collection)	87
Carrying out forestry tasks, Belgium, late 1944. (Jesús Rodriguez collection)	88
Resting between forestry shifts, winter 1944/45. (Jesús Rodriguez collection)	88

The entrance of the chateau at Romedenne today. (Author's collection)	89
At the entrance to the chateau at Romedenne. (Augusto Pérez Miranda collection)	90
Outside the chateau, summer 1945. (Rodrigo Haro collection)	90
Senior Non-Commissioned Officers of the No.1 Company. (Pioneer Corps Association Archives)	91
Members of SCONCE IV at Thame House. (Augusto Pérez Miranda archive)	97
Sergeant Manuel Espallargas. (Manuel Espallargas collection)	98
Corporal Augusto Pérez Miranda. (Augusto Pérez Miranda archive)	99
Francisco Alapont. (José García Flores collection).	101
Three students at the Wireless Training School at Fawley Court. (José García Flores collection)	102
Members of No.1 Spanish Company take a rest. (José García Flores collection)	105
Pass issued to Jesús Velasco, 1942. (Jesús Velasco collection)	106
Commendation for Good Service to Sergeant Manuel Espallargas. (Agustín Roa Ventura collection)	111
Parachute wings of José García Flores. (José García Flores collection)	112
José García Flores. (José García Flores collection)	113
Spanish *legionnaires*, Syria. (Francisco Geronimo collection)	118
Spaniards of the 6e REI, Syria 1941. (Manuel Surera collection)	120
Jaime Trill. (Fernando Esteve collection)	121
Spaniards unloading a truck, Syria, 1940. (Miguel Martínez collection)	122
Orders for the 2nd Battalion Queen's Royal Regt, 1941. (Surrey History Centre)	125
Spaniards in No.50 Middle East Commando, Egypt. (Joaquín Fajardo collection)	126
Rowing training on the Bitter Lakes. (Miguel Martínez collection)	128
Carrying out training amongst reeds near the Bitter Lakes. (Miguel Martínez collection)	129
Manuel Sánchez, Middle East Commando. (Fernando Esteve collection)	130
Resting below the Great Sphinx at Giza. (Manuel Surera collection)	132
Range training, Crete, late 1940. (Miguel Martínez collection)	133
Spaniards in the garrison in Crete. (Manuel Surera collection)	133
No.50 Middle East Commando on Crete, early 1941. (Manuel Surera collection)	133
Manuel Surera's No.50 Middle East Commando pass, Crete, 1941. (Manuel Surera collection)	134
Awaiting embarkation for an operation on Crete. (Francisco Geronimo collection)	135
'Living off the land' three men plucking a duck. (Manuel Surera collection)	137
Spaniards pose with Mr and Mrs Carreno in Egypt. (Miguel Martínez collection)	138
The ground looking south on the bend of the road near Beritiana. (Philip Brazier)	140
POW documents for Joaquín Fajardo. (Joaquín Fajardo collection)	144
Joaquín Fajardo and Basilio Marín with other POWs. (Joaquín Fajardo collection)	145
Allied POWs including Spaniards. (Joaquín Fajardo collection)	146
Joaquín Fajardo and Manuel Barroso during their time as POWs. (Joaquín Fajardo collection)	147
Fajardo and Francisco Lumbrera. (Joaquín Fajardo collection)	149
Braulio Heras stops for a cigarette. (Manuel Surera collection)	149
In camp in Egypt after returning from Crete, 1941. (Miguel Martínez and Francisco García Garrigos collection)	151
Manuel Surera in Middle East Commando uniform. (Manuel Surera collection)	151
Francisco Geronimo after his 11 months spent escaping and evading on Crete. (Francisco Geronimo collection)	152

Moisés Trancho Bartolomé. (Joaquín Fajardo collection)	153
Enrique Bernárdez's pass on the cruiser, *Miguel de Cervantes*. (Enrique Bernárdez collection)	158
The harsh conditions for internees in camps in North Africa. (Agustín Roa Ventura collection)	161
Fausto and Teodosia García in Orán. (Fausto Miguel García collection)	163
Agustín Roa Ventura's good conduct certificate. (Agustín Roa Ventura collection)	164
Spaniards shortly after their arrival in Djelfa. (Antonio Obis collection)	165
Spaniards interned at Djelfa with their camp guards. (Family archives of Joaquín Chamero Serena & Eliane Ortega Bernabeu)	166
Spaniards held at Djelfa stand outside their accommodation tent. (Antonio Obis collection)	167
Internees during the building of accommodation huts in Djelfa. (Antonio Obis collection)	168
Eduardo Tamarit amongst tomato plants at Djelfa Camp. (Eduardo Tamarit collection)	168
Spaniards with villagers in Djelfa, 1943. (Antonio Obis collection)	171
Eduardo Tamarit's pay book. (Eduardo Tamarit collection)	173
Officers of 91 Pioneer Group in Algeria. (Hubert Cole collection)	175
Corporal Agustín Roa Ventura, in Hussein Dey. (Agustín Roa Ventura collection)	176
Eduardo tamarit with two colleagues from 361 (Alien) Pioneer Company, 1945. (Eduardo Tamarit collection)	178
Antonio Obis, North Africa, 1944. (Antonio Obis collection)	179
Members of 361 (Alien) Pioneer Company at Sudbury. (Miguel Martínez collection)	180
361 (Alien) Pioneer Company rest between shifts at Branston. (Antonio Obis collection)	181
Antonio Obis with two comrades shortly after arriving in Britain. (Antonio Obis collection)	181
Two Spaniards from 361 (Alien) Pioneer Company. (Antonio Obis collection)	181
Spaniards from 361 (Alien) Pioneer Company, 1945. (Eduardo Tamarit collection)	182
Agustín Roa Ventura towards the end of the war. (Agustín Roa Ventura collection)	183
Spaniards on parade after their escape from Crete in 1941. (Manuel Surera collection)	185
A group after carrying out training or about to deploy on a mission. (Fernando Esteve collection)	186
Middle East Commandos in 1st Special Service Regiment. (Manuel Surera and Francisco García Garrigos collection)	187
Manuel Surera, early 1942. (Manuel Surera collection)	188
Basilio Santiago of 1st Special Service Regiment. (Manuel Surera collection)	188
Waiting to be collected for a patrol with the LRDG. (Manuel Surera collection)	189
Francisco Revuelta at the end of the war. (Francisco Revuelta collection)	191
Justo Balerdi, radio operator in 2nd SAS Signals. (The SAS and LRDG Roll of Honour 1941–47)	194
Ángel Camarena and Francisco Geronimo shortly after joining the SAS. (Francisco Geronimo collection)	195
Francisco Geronimo's POW card. (Francisco Geronimo collection)	199
2nd SAS members of the Italian Detachment, Wivenhoe, October 1945. (Francisco Geronimo collection)	204
Privates Simpson and Ramos and Sergeant Guscott pause during Operation BRAKE II. (Robert Hann collection)	207
Ralph Ramos and Sergeant Guscott with partisans. (Rafael Ramos collection)	208
Members of the *Alleato* Battalion. (Dr Grizi Collection)	209

Ralph Ramos training partisans prior to the attack on the LI German Mountain Corps. (Dr Grizi Collection)	209
Villa Rossi today. (Author's collection)	210
Members of Operation TOMBOLA including Justo Balerdi. (Francisco Geronimo collection)	211
The grave of Justo Balerdi in Milan. (Author's collection)	212
Ralph Ramos and Francisco Geronimo in Rome at the end of the war. (Francisco Geronimo collection)	213
Members of 2nd SAS from Operation TOMBOLA, October 1945. (Francisco Geronimo collection)	213
Francisco Geronimo in Rome with, on the right, the author in the same location. (Francisco Geronimo collection and Author's collection)	214
Ángel Camarena during Operation ARCHWAY. (Martin Tate)	215
Front cover of the Thanksgiving Service programme held in Colchester for 2nd SAS. (Francisco Geronimo collection)	216
Queen's Royal Regiment transfer book, summer 1943. (Surrey Heritage Centre Archive)	218
Josep Vilanova MM, Crete, early 1941. (Fernando Esteve collection)	220
1/5 Battalion, Germany 1945. (Fernando Esteve collection)	223
Victory Parade in Berlin, July 1945. (Fernando Esteve collection)	223
Corporal Fernando Esteve, Germany, 1945. (Fernando Esteve collection)	224
Fernando Esteve. He fought in British Army uniform from August 1940 until mid–1946. (Fernando Esteve collection)	225
Grave of Lucío Sauquillo Echevarría, Hermanville Cemetery. (Paul Woodadge)	229
José María 'Joe' Irala. (https://www.paradata.org.uk)	230
Arnhem main Drop Zone X-ray today. (Author's collection)	231
Hartenstein Hotel today. (Author's collection)	232
Grave of Trooper 'Joe' Irala. (Author's collection)	234
Grave of Guardsman Marcial Fernández. (Author's collection)	235
Three key officers of the AUBE Mission, Bill Probert, Pascual Gimeno, Marcel Bigeard. (Alfonso Canovas collection)	238
Newspaper cutting from the 1980s about the liberation of the Ariège in 1944. (Alfonso Canovas collection)	239
Alfonso Canovas, Saverdun, 2004. (Alfonso Canovas collection)	241
Joaquín Fajardo at the end of the war. (Joaquín Fajardo collection)	248
361 (Alien) Company, 1945. (Manuel Surera collection)	249
Antonio Obis at the end of the war. (Antonio Obis collection)	251
Juan Francisco Fernández Caballero, parachute training, early 1945. (Juan Francisco Fernández Caballero collection)	252
Fernando Esteve, chef at Le Caprice in St James. (Fernando Esteve collection)	253
José García Flores and Juliet Constance's wedding day, 1947. (José García Flores collection)	254
Ralph Ramos and Libuše Kodešová's wedding day, 1945. (Rafael Ramos collection)	255
Frank Williams and Laura Bravo's wedding day, 1946. (Francisco Geronimo collection)	255
Augusto Pérez Miranda and his wife Carmen in Trafalgar Square, 1947. (Augusto Pérez Miranda collection)	256
A small protest in Trafalgar Square shortly after the Second World War. (Fernando Esteve collection)	259

Agustín Roa Ventura and Antonio Vargas lay a wreath in Whitehall, 1958. (Agustín Roa Ventura collection)	260
Protestors in Trafalgar Square, 1960. (Agustín Roa Ventura collection)	262
Agustín Roa Ventura, Trafalgar Square, July 1960. (Agustín Roa Ventura collection)	262
Inside cover of a booklet from the Spanish Ex-Servicemen's Association, 1960. (Agustín Roa Ventura collection)	263
1963 protests about the plight of prisoners held by the Franco Regime. (Agustín Roa Ventura collection)	264
Reunion of *Los Reclutas* at Martínez Restaurant. (José García Flores collection)	265
Leaflet from the Spanish Ex-Servicemen's Association, 1975. (Agustín Roa Ventura collection)	266
Spanish Ex-Servicemen's Association on Whitehall before moving to the Cenotaph to lay a wreath. (Agustín Roa Ventura collection)	267
The Spanish Ex-Servicemen's Association hands in a letter at No.10, 1975. (Agustín Roa Ventura collection)	267
Three Spanish members of No.50 Middle East Commando take a rest below the Sphynx. (Miguel Martínez collection)	348
Other ranks in the No.1 Spanish Company queue up for a meal in Belgium. (Augusto Pérez Miranda collection)	349
Members of the Spanish Ex-Servicemen's Association on Whitehall, October 1975. (Agustín Roa Ventura collection)	349

List of Colour Plates

The Spanish Ex-Servicemen's Association Badge. (Courtesy of Mike Heald)   i

The standard of No.1 Spanish Company embroidered with the words '1940 until Victory'. Note the red and green diamond with a yellow 'S' in the middle which is the badge the company wore on its arm. Also note the Spanish Republican flag colours in the lace on the left. (Courtesy of Royal Logistics Corps Museum collection)   ii

Commando service certificate of Joaquín Fajardo. All commando trained personnel were issued with a certificate for their loyal service, signed by Bob Laycock. (Courtesy of the Joaquín Fajardo collection)   ii

Front cover of one of the Spanish Ex-Servicemen's Association Newsletters. It was produced in London and issued to all members. (Courtesy of the Agustín Roa Ventura collection)   iii

Front cover of the booklet *Franco's Prisoners Speak* published in December 1960 by the Spanish Ex-Servicemen's Association. (Author's collection)   iv

Miguel Bon's (Michael Montgomery) Alien registration card. Bon served in No.1 Spanish Company, was trained as a SCONCE and settled on the south coast of England. (Courtesy of the Miguel Bon collection)   v

Alien registration card for Antonio Obis. (Courtesy of the Antonio Obis collection)   v

José García Flores who served in No.1 Spanish Company and Royal Signals became naturalised in 1948. (José García Flores collection)   vi

A protest in London showing solidarity with the miners of Asturias. (Agustín Roa Ventura collection)   vii

Frank Williams (Francisco Geronimo) on the left and Alan Cooper (Ángel Camarena) relaxing at home in Cardiff in the 1970s. (Francisco Geronimo collection)   viii

Agustín Roa Ventura and his wife Matilde Díaz with his lifelong friend Antonio Vargas in the 1980s. (Agustín Roa Ventura collection)   viii

List of Maps

1	Spain, showing the cities and towns where many of the Spaniards in this book came from. (Artwork by Mike Heald)	xxxii
2	Britain, showing the locations where many of the Spaniards in this book were based or consequently lived. (Artwork by Mike Heald)	xxxiii
3	*La Retirada* and the Franco-Spanish border. (Designed by Mike Heald)	37
4	French Internment Camps, *CTE*s, France 1940 and the German Invasion. (Artwork by Mike Heald)	65
5	The Middle East. (Artwork by Mike Heald)	116
6	The Battle for Crete. (Artwork by Mike Heald)	142
7	Camps and locations in North Africa. (Artwork by Mike Heald)	156
8	SAS Operations in France. (Artwork by Mike Heald)	197
9	SAS Operations in North Italy. Operations GALIA, BRAKE II and TOMBOLA. (Artwork by Mike Heald)	206

Chronology

1914–1935

4 August 1914:	Spain unofficially declares 'benevolent neutrality' during the First World War.
1914:	Commonwealth of Catalunya is declared.
1917:	The 'Crisis of Spain'. The Spanish Government is threatened by the military *Juntas de Defensa*, a political movement organised by the Regionalist League of Cataluña and a socialist general strike.
1917–1923:	Period of *Pistolerismo* (gun violence) where Spanish employers hired people to face up to or kill trade unionists.
1921:	Rif War begins after the Disaster of Annual on 1 July 1921. France joins in 1924.
13 September 1923:	*General* Miguel Primo de Rivera *coup d'état* and subsequent dictatorship.
8 May 1925:	The landings at Alhucemas Bay in Morocco bring about the final stages of the Rif War which ends in 1926.
July 1927:	Spanish Morocco declared officially pacified.
29 October 1929:	Wall Street stock market crash takes place.
28 January 1930:	Following unrest and a lack of support from the army, *General* Miguel Primo de Rivera resigns. Unrest builds across Spain.
14 April 1931:	The Second Republic is proclaimed after municipal elections on 12 April. The monarchy falls and Alfonso XIII goes into voluntary exile.
28 June 1931:	Republicans call general elections.
9 December 1931:	Republican Constitution announced. The Republic announces that it will concentrate on three areas: agrarian reform, statutes of autonomy for Cataluña and the Basque Country, and an emphasis on educational and cultural policy.
10 August 1932:	*General* Sanjurjo's *pronunciamiento* known as the *Sanjurjada* becomes an abortive coup – the *Sanjurjada*.
29 October 1932:	José Antonio Primo de Rivera founds the *Falange Española*, the Spanish Falangist movement.
30 January 1933:	Hitler is appointed Chancellor of Germany.
20 March 1933:	Dachau, the first Nazi concentration camp opens.
5 November 1933:	The Basque Country votes overwhelmingly in a referendum to become independent (97 percent of votes cast in favour).
19 November 1933:	Clear victory to the right and the administration led by Lerroux and *Confederación Española de Derechas Autónomas* (*CEDA*, the Spanish Confederation of Autonomous Right-Wing Parties).
2 August 1934:	Adolf Hitler becomes *Führer* of Germany.

6 October 1934	Armed miners' rebellion in Asturias and a separatist rebellion in Catalunya are quashed by the army.
16 March 1935:	Hitler announces the start of German rearmament contrary to the Treaty of Versailles.
15 September 1935:	Nuremberg Laws are enacted in Germany, removing citizenship from Jews.

1936

20 January:	King George V dies at Sandringham.
16 February:	In Spain, elections are won by the *Frente Popular* (a coalition of left-wing political parties).
7 March:	Germany reoccupies the Rhineland.
7 May:	Italy annexes Ethiopia.
17–18 July:	Military rebellion begins against the Spanish Government in North Africa and Spain.
19–20 July:	Military uprising is defeated in Madrid and Barcelona.
1 August:	The Olympic Games open in Berlin.
1 October:	Franco is invested as *Caudillo* (Leader) of Spain after being named *Generalissimo* (Supreme Commander) in September.
1 October:	The first International Brigades formed.
25 October:	Rome-Germany Axis formed.
7 November:	Rebel Nationalist ground attack on Madrid begins.
18 November:	Germany and Italy recognise Franco's Government as the legitimate government of Spain.
18 November:	The Franco-Mussolini Pact is signed.
11 December:	Edward VIII abdicates as King of The United Kingdom. George VI becomes monarch.

1937

6 February:	The Battle of Jarama, south-east of Madrid, starts and continues for most of February resulting in a stalemate.
7 February:	Málaga is taken by Rebel Nationalist Forces.
8 March:	The Battle of Guadalajara. Italian troops are defeated by Republican forces.
26 April:	The bombing of Guernica takes place.
12 May:	George VI is crowned in Westminster Abbey.
17 May:	Dr Juan Negrín becomes Republican Prime Minister.
12 June:	Huesca offensive takes place by the Republicans but is abandoned on 19 June.
19 June:	Bilbao taken by the rebel Nationalist forces.
23 May:	The *Habana* arrives in Southampton from Bilbao. It has on board 3,840 Basque refugee children, 80 teachers, 120 helpers, 15 catholic priests and two doctors.
6 July:	The Battle of Brunete begins. It ends 26 July.
26 August:	Santander taken by rebel Nationalist forces.

21 October:	Gijón falls. Rebel Nationalist forces put an end to their campaign in the North.
14 December:	Battle of Teruel begins.

1938

22 February:	Battle of Teruel ends with a Nationalist victory and the recapture of Teruel.
12 March:	German Army crosses the border into Austria to annex the nation to Nazi Germany.
10 April:	Edouard Daladier becomes Prime Minister of France.
15 April:	Catalunya is cut off from the rest of Spain by the Nationalists.
2 May:	Daladier issues his decree regarding refugees and asylum seekers in France.
July:	Mauthausen concentration camp is built in Austria.
July:	The *Esko-Etxea* is established in London for Basque refugees.
5 July:	Agreement is made regarding the withdrawal of foreign troops from Spain. Ignored by Italy and Germany.
11 July:	The French government pass a decree that extends the duties enforced by law onto the rights of foreigners under asylum for the 'general organisation of the nation in times of war.'
25 July:	Battle of the Ebro begins with Republican crossing of the Ebro River.
21 September:	Withdrawal of the International Brigades announced.
30 September:	Munich Agreement signed.
12 November:	The Daladier government publishes a decree on the setting up of holding centres for 'undesirable' foreigners.
16 November:	Battle of the Ebro ends with Nationalists pushing the Republicans back across the Ebro River.
23 December:	Nationalist Catalunya offensive begins.

1939

21 January:	The first reception centre is opened at Rieucros in France for 'undesirable' foreigners.
26 January:	Barcelona falls to the Nationalists.
6 February:	The French Government accepts the reception of Republican Spaniards and groups them into five main camps in the Eastern Pyrenees, near the border with Spain.
10 February:	Catalunya falls to Nationalist troops.
26 February:	Britain and France recognise Franco's Government.
15 March:	Germany invades Czechoslovakia.
28 March:	The SS *Stanbrook*, captained by Archibald Dickson, sets sail for North Africa with 2,638 people on board.
28 March:	Madrid taken by Nationalist forces.
April:	Internment camps in North Africa are established.
1 April:	Republican armies surrender. Franco declares the war over.

12 April:	French Government sends out a ruling extending to all male foreigners (between 20 and 48 years of age and entitled to the right of asylum) to serve in the French Army or the War Ministry in one role or another as *Prestataires Militaires Étrangers* (foreign workers pressed into military service).
5 May:	In France, authorities in camps start to identify potential workers on behalf of the Ministry of Employment.
9 May:	Spain leaves the League of Nations.
20 June:	The *Préfecture d'Alger* reports on newly arrived Spanish refugees and where they are interned in the country.
23 August:	Germany and the Soviet Union sign the Molotov-Ribbentrop Pact. This is a neutrality treaty that agrees to the division of spheres of influence.
1 September:	Germany invades Poland, and the Second World War begins.
1 September:	France passes a further decree confirming that all 'foreigners' coming from enemy countries will be interned.
3 September:	Britain and France declare war on Germany.
9 September:	The British Expeditionary Force (BEF) starts arriving in France.
12 September:	The Soviet Union invades Poland.
End December:	No.185 Spanish Labour Company is formed in Gurs Camp, south-west France to support the BEF.

1940

13 January:	Other foreigners given the right to asylum in France are allowed to join elements of the French armed forces.
15 April:	1e BMVE arrives in Beirut from France. It becomes 11e BE at the end of the month based in Baalbeck.
6 May:	Spaniards serving in the *13e DBMLE* land in Norway.
10 May:	Germans launch their offensive in the west of Europe. Chamberlain resigns as British Prime Minister; Churchill takes over and forms a coalition government. On 13 May he states in the House of Commons that 'I have nothing to offer you but blood, toil, tears and sweat.'
26 May:	Operation DYNAMO (the evacuation of the BEF from Dunkirk) begins. It ends 4 June 1940.
17 June:	After establishing his cabinet, *Maréchal* Pétain announces a ceasefire.
18 June:	*Général* de Gaulle makes his appeal for resistance on BBC Radio.
20 June:	Spaniards in the 13e DBMLE arrive in Portsmouth.
22 June:	The armistice is signed between Vichy France and Nazi Germany. France is to be divided into an occupied zone and a free zone.
25 June:	The armistice comes in effect across France.
27 June:	*13e DBMLE* arrives at Trentham Park.
28 June:	*Général* de Gaulle is recognised as 'Leader of all Free Frenchmen, wherever they may be' by Britain.
29 June:	*Général* de Gaulle visits Trentham Park. Spaniards in the *13e DBMLE* there carry out a sit-down protest.
July:	The first Spaniards, who have escaped from the French Army in Syria, arrive in the Middle East and join the British Army. No.50 Middle East Commando starts to be formed.

1 July:	Stand-off at Avonmouth railway station as Spaniards are allowed to stay in Britain. Approximately half of the *13e DBMLE* leaves for Vichy North Africa.
3 July:	The Royal Navy launches Operation CATAPULT and sinks or seizes ships of the French fleet in the Algerian ports of Mers-el-Kébir and Orán.
17 July:	Spaniards sign up to join the British Army at Westward Ho!
31 July:	Major George Young and Captain Harry Fox-Davies interview the Spaniards at Moascar, Egypt, with a view to them joining the Middle East Commandos.
6 August:	The first Spaniards arrive at Mauthausen-Gusen concentration camp.
Mid-August:	The Battle of Britain begins.
September:	No.1 Spanish Company is established at Westward Ho!
16 September:	No.1 Spanish Company moves to Plymouth.
27 September:	*Groupes de Travailleurs Espagnols/Étrangers* are established following a law by René Belain, Minister of Work and Industrial Production for the Vichy Regime.
5 October:	The Spaniards in No.50 Middle East Commando complete their training.
15 October:	No.51 Middle East Commando is formally established with Spaniards serving amongst its ranks.
23 October:	Franco and Hitler meet at Hendaye.
9 November:	The code name Operation FELIX is assigned by the OKW (*Oberkommando der Wehrmacht*) for the capture of Gibraltar.
24 November:	No.50 Middle East Commando embarks for Crete.
2 December:	The first Spaniards from No.1 Spanish Company are recruited to train as SCONCES for the SOE. SCONCE I starts training soon after.

1941

19 January:	British troops begin attacks on Italian held Eritrea in East Africa.
25 January:	Franco's Foreign Secretary, and brother-in-law, Ramón Serrano Suñer delivers a message to Nazi Germany regarding pre-conditions of entering the war.
1 February:	Force Z (containing Nos.7, 8 and 11 Commandos) under the command of Colonel Bob Laycock leaves the Isle of Arran. It arrives in Egypt 7 March 1941.
12 February:	Franco meets with Mussolini in Bordighera reiterating the support he needs to enter the war. As a consequence, Hitler realises that Spain has essentially priced itself out of the war.
March:	Vichy France reconstitutes *Compagnies de Travailleurs Étrangers* into *Groupements de Travailleurs Étrangers*.
13 March:	In Britain, SCONCES I and II complete their SOE training and are put on immediate standby for potential operations in the Iberian Peninsula.
20 March:	No.1 Spanish Company provides a Guard of Honour at Millbay Station during the visit to Plymouth by their Majesties the King and Queen.
21–23 March:	The 'Plymouth Blitz' takes place. Three members of No.1 Spanish Company are killed.

28 March:	D Battalion formally formed at Geneifa, Egypt, as part of Layforce.
6 April:	Germany, Italy and Hungary invade Yugoslavia, thus starting the Battle for Greece.
7 April:	SCONCE IV is praised for its abilities and hard work.
21 April:	Greece capitulates to Germany. Commonwealth troops withdraw to Crete.
20 May:	The Battle of Crete begins after Germany launches an airborne assault on the island (Operation MERKUR).
26 May:	A & D Battalions of Layforce arrive in Suda Bay to join the battle for Crete.
1 June:	Lieutenant Colonel George Young, commanding officer of D Battalion, Layforce leads the surrender of the troops at Sphakia to the Germans.
8 June:	British and Free French forces invade Syria.
Mid-June:	Hitler decides to postpone Operation FELIX.
19 June:	No.1 Spanish Company moves to Redruth, Cornwall.
21 June:	Germany invades Russia (Operation BARBAROSSA).
14 July:	Vichy France signs an Armistice with Britain; the armistice ends the fighting in Lebanon and Syria.
September:	No.1 Spanish Company moves to Wiltshire and works with New Zealand Forestry Companies until 1943.
17 October:	*El Hogar Español* at 22 Inverness Terrace, London opens its doors.
30 October:	President Roosevelt approves the first tranche of Lend Lease aide to the Soviet Union.
November:	Operation FLIPPER, failed operation to capture or kill Rommel in North Africa, takes place.
7 December:	Pearl Harbour is attacked by Japan which declares war. The US president declares war on Japan the following day as does Britain.
11 December:	Germany and Italy declare war on the United States.

1942

14 January:	Operation POSTMASTER: a successful SOE operation on the Spanish island of Fernando Po, off West Africa in the Gulf of Guinea.
19 January:	Japan invades Burma.
21 January:	*Generalleutnant* Erwin Rommel launches his offensive on Cyrenaica.
25 January:	The *Casal Català* for Catalan refugees is established in Hamilton Terrace, London.
15 February:	Singapore falls to the Japanese.
28 March:	British commandos carry out the spectacular raid on St Nazaire (Operation CHARIOT).
17 April:	French *Général* Henri Giraud escapes from Königstein Fortress near Dresden.
22 May:	Francisco Geronimo is able to escape from Crete thanks to the SOE (Force 133).
26 May:	The Battle of Gazala takes place. Rommel out foxes the British. At Bir Hakeim, the Free French of the *13e DBLE* carry out a valiant defence. Many Spaniards are amongst the *Légionnaires*.
10 June:	Free French forces evacuate Bir Hakeim.

17–21 June:	The siege of Tobruk opens. The town was eventually taken by Rommel.
1–17 July:	The First Battle of El Alamein takes place.
19 August:	The Allies carry out a failed raid on Dieppe (Operation JUBILEE). D Squadron of 1 Special Service Regiment takes part which contains over 20 Spaniards.
23 August:	German troops reach the suburbs of Stalingrad.
13–14 September:	Operation AGREEMENT takes place. A failed commando raid on Tobruk.
18 October:	Hitler issues the Commando Order, stipulating that commandos encountered by German forces should be executed immediately.
23 October:	The Second Battle of El Alamein opens.
3 November:	Rommel's army is forced to retreat from El Alamein.
8 November:	Operation TORCH starts. Allied landings take place all along the coast, from Morocco to Tunisia.
11 December:	337 (Alien) Pioneer Company is formed in Algiers. Many of its members are Spanish.
24 December:	*Amiral* Darlan is assassinated in Algiers eventually making way for the more Allied friendly French regime of *Général* Giraud in North Africa.

1943

14–24 January:	The Allied Casablanca Conference takes place.
2 February:	The Battle of Stalingrad ends with the surrender of the German 6th Army.
19–24 February:	Rommel's *Afrika Corps* defeats US forces at the Battle of the Kasserine Pass. By this time, Spaniards are fighting behind enemy lines as part of Operation BRANDON for both the SOE and the OSS.
April:	Spaniards who have been interned in North Africa are given opportunities to serve in the Allied armies by the Inter-Allied Mission.
28 April:	Spaniards leave Djelfa concentration camp by train to Boufarik. 361 (Alien) Pioneer Company is established the following day.
13 May:	2nd SAS raised at Philippeville, Algeria. On the same day the German and Italian armies surrender in Tunisia.
June:	The majority of Spaniards from No.1 Spanish Company who have been training with the SOE and been held at high readiness are released back to the company.
July:	Spaniards from 1 Special Service Regiment transfer to the Pioneer Corps, infantry or SAS.
10 July:	The Allied invasion of Sicily takes place (Operation HUSKY). The 'Axis forces evacuate' by 17 August 1943.
21 July:	Three Spaniards who have served in No.50 Middle East Commando transfer to 1/5 Battalion Queen's Royal Regiment (West Surrey).
Summer:	The No.1 Spanish Company starts training for D-Day.
9 September:	The Allies land at Salerno, south of Naples (Operation AVALANCHE).
7–11 October:	Allied actions on the Volturno River, north of Naples, result in Private Josep Vilanova from 1/5th Battalion Queen's Royal Regiment (West Surrey) being awarded the Military Medal.

28 November:	The Allied Tehran Conference takes place. The Allied invasion of Western Europe is decided upon for 1944.
December:	No.1 Spanish Company moves to Bournemouth. Spaniards start to undergo SAS selection in Philippeville, Algeria.
24 December:	General Dwight D. Eisenhower becomes Supreme Allied Commander Europe.

1944

12 January:	Churchill and de Gaulle meet in Marrakech.
17 January:	The final battle for Monte Cassino in Italy begins.
22 January:	The Allies land at Anzio (Operation SHINGLE).
March:	2nd SAS arrive in Britain at the end of this month.
18 March:	Mount Vesuvius erupts.
9 April:	Spaniards in 2nd SAS carry out a two-week parachute training course at RAF Ringway, Manchester.
18 May:	Monte Cassino is finally captured.
June–August:	SOE trained Spaniards are used in France pre and post D-Day as wireless operators.
6 June:	D-Day takes place. The Allied landings in Normandy begin. 12th (Yorkshire) Parachute Battalion parachutes into Normandy at 0100. Private Lucío Sauquillo Echevarría dies on 13 June 1944 of his wounds received during the invasion.
8 June:	1/5th Battalion Queen's Royal Regiment (West Surrey) land in Normandy. Spaniards are in A Company.
22 June:	The Battle of Kohima finally ends in a British victory.
3 July:	The Battle for Imphal ends in a British victory.
9 July:	The Allies capture Caen.
4–15 August:	Five Spaniards take part in Operation DUNHILL V, an SAS operation in France.
5–31 August:	Operation RUPERT, another SAS operation takes place in Northern France. Parachutist Justo Balerdi takes part in this operation.
15 August:	Operation DRAGOON takes place. The Allies land in southern France.
8 August:	AUBE mission (an SOE operation), troops parachute into the Ariège near the Pyrenees.
14 August:	No.1 Spanish Company lands in Normandy.
17–25 August:	Three Spaniards take part in Operation TRUEFORM II, near Rouen.
19 August:	The AUBE mission captures Foix. Sergeant Alfonso Canovas is awarded the Military Medal.
21 August:	The 'Falaise Pocket' in Normandy is finally closed.
25 August:	Paris is liberated by Free French forces. Amongst them are members of *La Nueve*, the *9ᵉ Compagnie* of the *Régiment de Marche du Tchad*, part of *Général* Leclerc's French 2nd Armoured Division.
September:	Two Spaniards who are part of 2nd SAS take part in Operation LOYTON.
3 September:	The Allies liberate Brussels.
17 September:	Operation MARKET GARDEN begins.

20 September:	Trooper 'Joe' Irala is fatally wounded in Oosterbeek. He dies two days later.
2 October:	The Warsaw Uprising is finally crushed by the Germans.
14 October:	Three Pioneer companies (361, 362 and 363) embark from Algiers for Britain. On the same day *Feldmarschall* Rommel commits suicide. The three companies arrive in Glasgow two weeks later.
27 November:	No.1 Spanish Company moves to the Brussels area. By this stage it is augmented by Spaniards from 361 Pioneer Company.
16 December:	The German Ardennes offensive begins.
27 December:	First parachute drops take place for the 2nd SAS in Northern Italy for Operation GALIA.

1945

13–26 January:	Operation BLACKCOCK takes place, driving the German 15th Army out of the Roer Triangle.
17 January:	The Soviet army occupies Warsaw.
27 January:	The Soviet army liberates Auschwitz and Birkenau concentration camps.
31 January:	Operation BRAKE II begins. Three members of 2nd SAS set off on foot through enemy lines to meet up with Operation GALIA. One of the three is Parachutist Rafael Ramos. It eventually links up with Operation GALIA on 12 February.
3 February:	Manila is entered by US troops. General MacArthur enters the city four days later and the city is liberated on 23 February.
4–11 February:	The Yalta Conference takes place to discuss the post-war organisation of Germany and Europe.
13 February:	The RAF and USAAF bomb Dresden.
4 March:	Operation TOMBOLA begins in Northern Italy, a 2nd SAS operation near Regio Emilia which has three Spaniards in it. Ramos joins the operation from Operation GALIA on 17 March.
16 March:	The Battle for Iwo Jima ends.
25 March:	Operation ARCHWAY crosses the Rhine into Germany. Two Spaniards take part.
28 March:	1/5th Battalion Queen's Royal Regiment (West Surrey) crosses the Rhine at Xanten.
April 1945:	The majority of Spaniards taken prisoner during the Battle of Crete are liberated from camps in Germany and Poland.
15 April:	No.1 Spanish Company is moved south of Charleroi. Bergen-Belsen concentration camp is liberated.
24 April:	Operation TOMBOLA ends. Balerdi is killed in action during the operation, Ramos is awarded the Military Medal for his actions on the night of 27 March.
28 April:	Benito Mussolini and his lover are executed near Milan.
30 April:	Hitler commits suicide in his bunker in Berlin.
2 May:	The Soviet Army takes Berlin. On the same day all fighting ceases in Italy.
3 May:	1/5th Battalion Queen's Royal Regiment (West Surrey) enters Hamburg.

4 May:	The Germans surrender to Field Marshal Montgomery at Lüneburg Heath.
5 May:	Mauthausen concentration camp is liberated by US troops. Several thousand Spaniards are freed.
7 May:	*Generaloberst* Alfred Jodl signs the unconditional surrender of Germany in Reims, France.
8 May:	Victory in Europe Day. The Allies officially mark the end of the war in Europe.
21 June:	The Battle of Okinawa ends.
26 June:	The United Nations Charter is signed in San Francisco.
17 July:	The Potsdam Conference begins, it ends 2 August.
21 July:	1/5th Battalion Queen's Royal Regiment (West Surrey) takes part in the Victory Parade in Berlin.
26 July:	Winston Churchill resigns as Prime Minister after a resounding Labour victory at the general election and Clement Atlee becomes the new Prime Minister.
6 August:	The USA detonates an atomic bomb over Hiroshima. It explodes a second over Nagasaki on 9 August 1945.
15 August:	Victory over Japan Day. Imperial Japan surrenders.
17 September:	No.1 Spanish Company returns to England and is based in Chard, Somerset.
December:	2nd SAS is disbanded.
31 December:	Last diary entry for No.1 Spanish Company in Chard as well as for 361 (Alien) Pioneer Company.

1946–1975

December 1946:	The General Assembly of the United Nations adopts Resolution 39.
17 November 1952:	Spain is admitted into UNESCO.
27 August 1953:	Spain signs a Concordat with the Vatican.
23 September 1953:	The Pact of Madrid is signed followed by the United States-Spanish Defence, Economic Aid and Mutual Defence Assistance Agreements coming into effect.
14 December 1955:	Spain is permitted to join the United Nations.
Early 1960:	The Spanish Ex-Servicemen's Association is founded in London.
10 July 1960:	The Spanish Ex-Servicemen's Association organises a protest in London against the visit of the Franco Regime Foreign Minister, Fernando María Castiella.
December 1960:	The booklet *Franco's Prisoner's Speak* is published by the Spanish Ex-Servicemen's Association.
23 July 1969:	Franco names Juan Carlos Borbón as his successor (he later became King Juan Carlos I following Franco's death).
8 June 1973:	*Almirante* Carrero Blanco is named Prime Minister of Spain by Franco.
20 December 1973:	Carrero Blanco is assassinated with a car bomb by ETA.
19 October 1975:	The Spanish Ex-Servicemen's Association carries out a wreath laying at the Cenotaph and delivers a letter to No.10 Downing Street.
20 November 1975:	Franco dies, and Juan Carlos I is proclaimed King of Spain.

Glossary

1 SSR	1st Special Service Regiment
13ᵉ DBMLE	*13ᵉ Demi-Brigade de Montagne de la Légion Étrangère*
AMPC	Auxiliary Military Pioneer Corps
BEF	British Expeditionary Force
BIA	*Bataillon d'Infanterie de l'Air*
BMVE	*Bataillon de Marche de Voluntaries Étrangers* (Foreign Volunteer Marching Battalions)
BVE	*Bataillon de Volontaires Étrangers* (Volunteer Foreign Marching Battalion)
CAFRE	*Comisión Administrativa de Fondo de Ayuda a los Refugiados Españoles* (Administrative Commission for the Foundation for Help to Spanish Refugees)
CIA	*Compagnie d'Infanterie de l'Air*
CNT	*Confederación Nacional de Trabajo* (Spanish Anarchist Party)
CTE	*Compagnies de Travailleurs Étrangers* or *Compagnies de Travailleurs Espagnols*
DCRE	*Dépôt Commun des Régiments Étrangers* (Foreign Légion Training Depot)
DCRMVE	*Dépôt Comun des Régiments de Marche de Volontaires Étrangers* (Foreign Volunteer Marching Regiments' Training Depot)
Demi-Brigade	*Demi-Brigade* (half-brigade) is a peculiarly French military unit title supposedly being for a (usually) three battalion unit – literally half of a brigade. *Demi-Brigades* were first created in 1793 by the First French Republic in place of the 'Royalist' term *Régiment*. Although abolished in 1803 by First Consul Bonaparte and the term *Régiment* restored, *demi-brigade* continually reappeared thereafter for many units that were *hors-ligne*, that is those not in the sequential numbering of units in the army's order of battle.
EVDG	*Étrangers Volontaires pour la Durée de la Guerre* (Foreign Volunteers for the Duration of the War)
ETA	*Euskadi Ta Askatasuna* (armed Basque nationalist and far left separatist organisation)
FTP	*Francs Tireurs et Partisans* (communist-led resistance group)
GHQ	General Headquarters
LRDG	Long Range Desert Group
MC	Military Cross
MI(R)	Military Intelligence (Research) Branch at GHQ
MEF	Middle East Forces
MEW	Ministry of Economic Warfare
MP	Member of Parliament

MP	Military Police
NAAFI	Navy Army and Air Force Institute
NATO	North Atlantic Treaty Organisation
NCO	Non-Commissioned Officer
NJC	National Joint Committee for Spanish Relief
NZ	New Zealand
OBE	Order of the British Empire
OSS	Office for Strategic Service
PIAT	Projector Infantry Anti-Tank
PME	*Prestataires Militaires Étrangers* (Foreign Workers Pressed into Military Service)
POW	Prisoner of War
Pronunciamiento	Spanish Army rebellion or *coup d'état*
PSOE	*Partido Socialist Obrero Español* (Spanish Socialist Workers' Party)
PT	Physical training
QM	Quartermaster
RCP	*Regiment de Chasseurs Parachutistes*
REI	*Régiment Étrangers d'Infanterie* (Foreign Infantry Regiment)
REME	Royal Electrical Mechanical Engineers
RMVE	*Régiments de Marche de Volontaires Étrangers* (Foreign Marching Volunteer Regiments)
RQMS	Regimental Quartermaster Sergeant
RSM	Regimental Sergeant Major
RV	Rendezvous
RUR	Royal Ulster Regiment
SAS	Special Air Service
SERE	*Servicio de Evacuación de Refugiados Españoles* (Spanish Refugee Evacuation Service)
SFF	*Secteur Fortifié de Flandres* (The Flanders Fortified Sector)
SIS	Secret Intelligence Service
SNCO	Senior Non-Commissioned Officer
SNCF	*Société Nationale des Chemins de Fer Français* (French National Railway Company)
SOE	Special Operations Executive
SSgt	Staff Sergeant
STS	Specialist Training Centre
WO2	Warrant Officer Second Class
WO1	Warrant Officer First Class
UNESCO	United Nations Educational, Scientific and Cultural Organisation

Acknowledgements

During the course of the eight years researching and writing on the subject of Spanish Republicans who served in the British Army during the Second World War, it has been an absolute joy to meet so many people and study such excellent material. Consequently, I have a large number of people to thank while undergoing this journey of discovery. Families continue to get in touch on a regular basis and my horizons are continuously expanding. So, it is my hope that the testimonies and photos you read and see in this book will give you the opportunity to connect with these men and their families. Without much of their help, this book would simply not have happened.

It would be remiss of me not to start by thanking two people who were at the beginning of my journey. Firstly, *mil gracias* to my lifelong friend Óscar Luís Fernández Calvo who obtained for me a second-hand copy of Daniel Arasa's book many years ago and sparked my interest in this totally unknown subject. ¡*Eres un campeón!* Secondly, to Daniel Arasa himself for his kind encouragement.

For the amazing and thought-provoking book cover, maps and simply fantastic work on the photos in this book I must thank Michael Heald of Fully Illustrated. Mike is the proud grandson of Manuel Surera who served in the Middle East Commandos. Thanks for your sheer hard work and dedication Mike, it has made a huge difference!

It also goes without saying that historian and author Dr Richard Baxell has supported me greatly in this journey. To be able to find connections with his work and see so many parallels between aspects of British and Spanish history have brought many aspects to life. Sir Paul Preston has been utterly charming in his support for my project too and his generosity has been such a breath of fresh air. If someone had told the younger me in July 1986 while attending events in London commemorating 50 years since the start of the Uprising in Spain (and where I met Sir Paul) that I would be writing a book on the subject, I would never have believed them!

In the study of *La Retirada* and the plight of Spaniards in France and beyond, I have many to thank. To Professor Bob Coale from the Université de Rouen for his many excellent exchanges and also for the opportunity to be involved in the conference in Rouen and Paris entitled *Historia y memoria de los republicanos españoles en la Segunda guerra mundial, 1939–1945* – a huge honour. For invaluable information on 185 Spanish Labour Company in France I must thank Luís Garrido for his excellent research and enthusiasm along with Jesús N. Galindo Sánchez for the great photos. My thanks must also go to Olivier Vermesch for sharing his work on Spaniards who fought at Dunkirk in the North of France in the summer of 1940. Carlos Hernández de Miguel who has written extensively on Republican exiles deported to Mauthausen and other locations has also been very generous with his time. Finally, I must also thank Professor Diego Gaspar Celaya from the Universidad de Zaragoza for his suggestions, thoughts and friendship.

A great deal of support has also come from like-minded groups and individuals keen to tell these unknown stories. One of these groups in the Fighting Basques Project where Guillermo Tabernilla and Pedro Oiarzabal have not only been extremely encouraging and generous with their time, but have also become good friends. Coupled with them I must also thank The Association for the UK Basque Children and Manuel Moreno in particular.

Getting into some of the tricky contents of documents, files and sifting through countless archives and websites to get to the detail needed to tell many of the stories in this book has been a labour of love. For much of this, and especially for chapters four and six, I must thank Phil Williams. Phil is extremely proud of being the grandson of Francisco Geronimo who served in the Middle East Commandos and 2nd SAS. What an amazing man he was! Thankyou Phil, for your steadfastness, comradeship, humour and sheer hard graft. Asher Pirt has also aided me greatly in tracking key information down for these chapters and forms part of an elite group of people who are very knowledgeable about the Special Forces.

Without the baseline material of regimental numbers and enlistment details I would have not been able to track down over 1,000 Spaniards who feature in this book. As all Spaniards were at some point part of the Royal Pioneer Corps, I am so grateful that the Royal Pioneer Corps Association has been extremely generous in passing on key information on the Spaniards who served. Thanks to John Starling and Norman Brown you can see the list of names of these men at the back of this book. I must also thank the RLC Museum for their support as well, in particular Sam Jolley, Collections Manager there.

With the story of No.1 Spanish Company, I am grateful for much information from many families. In no particular order I must thank: Antonio Suárez Martínez, Begoña Rubio, Bonnie Grenham, Brian San Felix, Francisco Haro (for the amazing photographs), John Munn, John Vistuer (for the brilliant family stories), Joseph Luque, Julián Rodriguez, Mike Tresserras, Sara García (for the extensive post-war information), Shaun Montgomery, Michael Velasco (for his father's memoir), Philippe Olive and Victor Asensio (for the information on his grandfather Manuel Espallargas). I am also grateful to Steven Balagan for the work he does on his excellent website on wargaming and Spanish military history. It was via this that I was able to contact some families and start the ball rolling on many lines of enquiry. An apology if I have missed any families that recently contacted me.

Bernard O'Connor has also been very generous with his time on the topic of Spaniards in the SOE. I must also thank the SOE Forum where they have been very supportive with a wealth of knowledge. Kate Vigurs and Helen Fry have also given up much of their time in tracking down specific pieces of information and pointed me in the right direction on many occasions. Also, to María Sardà Villardaga for her Spanish insights and Alan Judge, Pierre Trivelle and Nick Fox for their support.

In telling the story of Spaniards in the Middle East Commandos I must thank Tony Fajardo in particular. Tony was the first person I interviewed fully for my research and has given sage advice and helped clarify many things as I have got further into the detail. I must also thank all the families of Spaniards who served in the Middle East Commandos who have given up so much of their time: Elvira Curlew, Fernando Esteve (for the excellent photos), Father Ricardo Morgan, Graham Renshaw (for the excellent extra information), Joseba Trancho, Laura Loechel, Professor Miguel Martínez Lucío (for his patience and extensive photo archive), Pierre Barrosso, Saskia Lara, Susana Hidalgo and Mike Heald. I must also thank the Royal Marines Historical Society, the Commando Veterans Archive and the Imperial War Museum. Finally, I need to give sincere thanks to O'Mark Roberts regarding the Middle East Commando Archive which he very kindly passed into my safekeeping.

With the Spaniards who served in the SAS, I must firstly thank the families who have been very generous: Dionisio Cooper and Caryl Bingham for the amazing stories of Ángel, Christine Ramos (for the great stories of her father Ralph), Cliff Colman, Phil Williams (of course!), Hayley Shaw, ex-lance-corporal X QGM, author of *The SAS and LRDG Roll of Honour 1941–47* and Robert Hann. I am also truly indebted to the French SAS Association, Jean-Philippe Courtois, Philippe Get, Danielle Meier, Michele Becchi (for the Dr Grizi collection) and Tim Williams for their support and time.

Many people have also helped me in finding information on Spaniards in North Africa. Principal amongst these has been Eliane Ortega Bernabeu, a stalwart in getting the story out of the Spaniards interned in camps in North Africa. Jorge Marco, from the University of Bath has been very generous with his time also, especially on information regarding Spaniards and the OSS. I must also thank Richard Normington, grandson of Hubert Cole who commanded a company of Spaniards in Algeria. Families whose relatives were in North Africa have also been very supportive: Anita Fernández, Begonia Tamarit, Elena Olloqui, Julie (granddaughter of Enrique Bernárdez), Rhys Roberts, Rob García, Celia Villalanda and Ricardo Obis in particular – thanks you for your many chats about life after the war in the Midlands and your faith in letting me tell your father's story.

Jason Canovas has been justifiably proud of his grandfather and has been very helpful in filling in many gaps. Paradata and the Airborne Museum have provided great help. I would also like to thank Paul Woodadge who has not only taken a few photos for me for this book but has also given me airtime on his excellent WW2TV YouTube Channel. Philip Brazier has also helped greatly with photos of Crete. The Surrey History Centre has also been very supportive in providing information on the Queen's Royal Regiment. The Society of Army Historical Research was also very generous in allowing me to present my first paper in 2021 as part of their centenary commemorations – many thanks, Dudley Giles.

One of the biggest things that has helped get the story of these Spaniards out there more into the public domain has been the many podcasts I have participated in and are available online. I first began speaking on podcasts with Alex and Peter on the History's Most Podcast. This was at the earlier stages of my research, and I was spurred on to delve even deeper into it consequently. I then extended the story by discussing things further with Angus Wallace on his WW2 Podcast which in turn helped me talk to others about my research. Paul Woodadge then allowed me to speak on his excellent WW2TV YouTube Channel which meant that even more families got in touch. This then made me come to the decision to write a book about Spaniards serving in the British Army. But the biggest breakthrough was to follow in 2021 when I was invited to be on the We Have Ways of Making You Talk Live with Al Murray and James Holland. I had just joined social media and the message was now passed to a far wider audience. Shortly after, I was grateful to be able to talk on History Hack with Zack White. Some interest in Spain then meant that I was soon speaking to Sergio Murata on his *Niebla de Guerra* Podcast which got interest going more there ¡*Gracias Sergio*! Speaking on the *Sobremesa* Podcast with Alan and Eoghan was brilliant especially as a later episode of theirs was with Professor Sir Paul Preston! I then spoke on the History Rage Podcast with Paul Bavill and Kyle Glover which I greatly enjoyed as it helped me talk about wider aspects of the story.

A sincere thanks must also go to the We Have Ways of Making You Talk community and in particular Al Murray and James Holland. They have done a great deal to widen the knowledge and understanding of the Second World War through their podcast and I have had the privilege of presenting at their festival three times now. In doing so, it has become clear that the story of Churchill's Spaniards is intrinsically linked to the wider story of the Second World War as well as that of the traditions and customs of the British Army. Getting the story to a wider audience has been amazing – thanks!

The publication of this book also coincides with me stepping down as Secretary of the Royal Engineers Historical Society. It would therefore be remiss of me not to thank the members of the committee, the Royal Engineers Museum and particularly the support of Major General Mungo Melvin CB OBE.

Many historians and academics have also been very supportive and given up their time to help me. Dr Peter Caddick-Adams was particularly helpful in supporting me with approaching publishers – thanks Peter! Dr David Abrutat has been massively encouraging and supportive as have Professor Tom Buchanan, Dr Saul David, Dr Robert Lyman, Paul Beaver, Joaquín Montañés and Luís Monferrer Catalán who has shared a great deal of his knowledge with me. I must also thank Dr Mark Thompson for his expert advice, Francisco Carpintero, Steve Hopkins, Pablo Azorín, Nick Lloyd (for some excellent exchanges), Jenny Grant and Juan José Ortiz Cruz for their help in tracking down elements of detail only they would know about. I could not also fail to mention the assistance I have received from William Chislett (my father did know you!), Carlos Hernández, Dan Parry, Carlos at GEFREMA, my good friends Nips Adams and Mike Owens, Iain MacGregor, Dr Wendy Ugolini for her encouragement, Tom Vardle (keep going Tom!), Andy Rawson, Professor John Tregoning, Professor Íñigo Fernández, Dr Ghee Bowman for his unfailing support, Stuart Bertie and Helen Tabor of Helen Tabor Photography for the publicity , as well as New Model Army for keeping me on track with their music for over thirty years! Finally, a massive thanks and *enhorabuena* to Dr Antonio Muñoz Sánchez (the work you do with Peter Gaida on Spanish Slave Workers is truly inspirational).

One of the greatest things about this journey has been that I have been approached to help other people with their projects and endeavours. It was a pleasure to write the foreword of the latest book by Joaquín Montañés and David Lopez Cabia's recent novel. Being involved in both projects was very humbling and hugely rewarding. Finally, I must thank Freedom Press for allowing me to place a short article on Spanish anarchists in the British Army.

The archive of Agustín Roa Ventura has helped me greatly over these last few years. A huge thanks must go to his two daughters Vida and Linda and his niece Leonor in particular who has kept me going during the dark moments. I very much hope that the archive will be disclosed in the future for further projects and be made more widely available.

I must also thank the Spanish Embassy for helping me with the launch, the Instituto Cervantes for supporting my project, the National Army Museum, Imperial War Museum, RLC Museum and RE Museum for kindly agreeing to support the book and finally the British Spanish Friends for their backing. The Helion team have also been amazing, and I have learnt a great deal. Finally, if I have omitted someone or a family that has been in contact, can I thank you most sincerely.

Two people who have been fundamental to keeping me going and on track with the writing of this book have been my brother Simon and my lifelong friend Richard Warrick. Thanks for your patience and perseverance!

Lastly, I must remember my mother Shirley fondly (and who would have been my staunchest critic!) and I am eternally grateful to the four most important women in my life – Beki, Maria, Chris and Eva. I love you!

Séan F. Scullion

Foreword

In his account of Spanish Republicans in France between 1939 and 1955, *Beyond Death and Exile,* Louis Stein recounts how *Général* Charles de Gaulle was notoriously fond of asking members of the Resistance how long they had been fighting the Nazis. The expected reply was always, 'Since June 18, 1940, *Général*'. Yet in September 1944, in recently liberated Limoges, the Free French leader received a rather different response from a *colonel* in the Communist wing of the Resistance, the *Franc Tireurs et Partisans*: 'With respect, General, before you. I fought the Germans during the war in Spain.' For the *colonel*, and for other Spanish Republican exiles and the volunteers from around the world who had fought alongside them, the liberation of Europe was a direct continuation of the struggle that had begun with the military uprising in Spain in July 1936.

The July coup was the latest in a long history of Spanish *pronunciamientos,* or military revolts. Initially the two sides in the conflict, the left-wing Republicans and right-wing Nationalists (or *Nacionales*) were fairly evenly matched, but that changed dramatically with Hitler and Mussolini's decision to send help to the military rebels. Nazi Germany and fascist Italy provided vital aircraft to transport *General* Franco's elite troops of the Army of Africa across the Strait of Gibraltar onto the peninsula, where they were able to head rapidly north, brushing aside the poorly armed militias' efforts to stop them. In response, anti-fascists from around the world flocked to Spain to support the government and both Mexico and the Soviet Union provided military support. Meanwhile, the western democracies, desperate to avoid a wider European conflagration chose not to come to the Republic's aid. Instead, a 'non-intervention agreement' was created to which Britain, France, Germany Italy, Portugal and the USSR all signed up. However, it soon became apparent that the agreement strongly favoured the Rebel Nationalists and was very much, as the Labour peer Lord Strabolgi declared, 'a malevolent neutrality'. Abandoned by the western democracies, the Spanish Republic struggled on desperately for nearly three more years. While the Republicans scored the occasional successes, the momentum was overwhelmingly with *General* Franco's forces. They slowly ground down the defenders, capturing the Republican zone in northern Spain by October 1937 and splitting the remaining Republican territory in half during a huge offensive in the spring of 1938. The following year, with the international volunteers withdrawn and the Republican forces exhausted, Franco triumphantly declared victory on 1 April 1939.

Fearful of the fate that awaited them under a Franco dictatorship, in what became known as the *Retirada* some half a million Spanish refugees fled north through Catalonia, seeking safety in France. Instead, the refugees were seen as fugitives and callously thrown into 'internment' camps, cordoned off with barbed wire and lacking food, fresh water and shelter from the elements. In despair, many elected to return to Spain despite the risks; yet for former Republican soldiers, who were under no illusion as to the fate that awaited them, this was not an option. Following the outbreak of the Second World War, many were strong-armed into French labour battalions or into military service. By early 1940 there were perhaps 60,000 Spaniards in the French war machine, many of them in the *Légion Étrangère* (the French Foreign Legion). Famously, the first Allied tanks to enter Paris in August 1944 were driven by exiled Spanish Republicans in *Général* Leclerc's Second French Armoured Division. The tanks bore the names of Guadalajara, Teruel, Brunete and other battles from the Spanish Civil War painted proudly on their sides.

What is perhaps less known is that more than 1,000 Spanish Republicans served in the British Army. The experiences of these exiled soldiers are the subject of this ground-breaking and inspiring new study by Séan Scullion, a British Army officer who grew up in Spain. Building on Daniel Arasa's *Los Españoles de Churchill*, published in the early 1990s, it is the first study of its kind in English. It benefits enormously from a wealth of material – much of it unpublished – released during the last 30 years that was not available to Arasa.

During the eight years that the author researched this book, he has unearthed details on 1,072 Spaniards who served in the British forces, over 500 of whom were in Britain at the end of the Second World War. As the author recounts in absorbing detail, Spaniards served throughout the European theatre, as well as may other places many in elite units such as the Commandos and alongside the Long Range Desert Group in North Africa. A number also fought with the SOE, enthusiastically following Churchill's edict to 'set Europe ablaze' and over a dozen served in the SAS. As is often the case with military histories, the book contains a seemingly limitless number of military abbreviations and acronyms. Fortunately, the author has included a useful glossary to decipher them all. There are also a number of helpful maps and photos, a chronology and the appendices include an invaluable annotated list of the Spaniards who served in the British forces.

As the author explains, the admittance of Spaniards into British forces seems to have required a certain amount of adjustment on both sides, particularly because many Spaniards spoke little or no English. Fully aware that they risked being returned to Spain if captured, some Spaniards pretended to be Gibraltarians. Others tried to pass themselves off as French, though not always successfully. One Spaniard when asked his name replied 'Bonjour!' and the British Army enlistment clerk dutifully recorded him as Private 13803102, Jacques Bonjour. Many anglicised their names, though as the author reveals, suggestions put forward by Spaniards such as 'Francis Drake' and 'Walter Raleigh' did not always meet with British Army approval!

While there seems, initially at least, to have been a certain amount of ingrained prejudice against the Spaniards, British officers soon came to recognise that the former Republican combatants could be every bit as good as British soldiers. They particularly excelled at commando work and some British troops allegedly hated doing night exercises with the Spaniards, as they were invariably much better at keeping silent. The book is awash with stories of the Spaniards' acts of fortitude and bravery, whether they were fighting at Narvik in 1940, behind enemy lines, or in the liberation of Europe following D-Day in June 1944. A number were decorated, such as Private Josep Vilanova, who was awarded the Military Medal for showing 'great courage and daring' during the fighting in Italy in 1943. Sadly, as the author's painstaking research reveals, all too many were killed in action.

Most of the Spanish soldiers seem to have been extremely proud of having served in the British Army. Like many former members of the International Brigades, they were generally positive about their experiences, particularly compared to the fighting in Spain or in the *Légion Étrangère*: they had better food, uniforms, decent arms, plenty of ammunition and were (relatively) well paid. Several hundred Spaniards were offered British citizenship after the war, though not all were so lucky. And all were understandably bitterly disappointed that the allies did not go on to liberate Spain following the defeat of Franco's friends, Hitler and Mussolini. Just as the western democracies had refused to come to their aid during the civil war, so they were left high and dry at the end of the Second World War. Clearly, and understandably, the author has great sympathy with their plight and this book is as much a homage to them as a history. As he explains, 'this book hopes to repay the debt we owe these men by telling their story.' He movingly – and entirely fittingly – ends with a quote from one of the brave Spaniards who were part of the long fight against European fascism from 1936 to 1945: *Ellos hicieron la historia y ellos se merecen el tributo del autor.*

Richard Baxell
May 2024

Preface

Spaniards are capable in thinking in terms not of themselves but of the generations who will follow them. That girl is dreaming of a time when Spain will be free again. Not in her lifetime but some day.[1]

On 20 November 1975 came the announcement on Radio Televisión Española: *Españoles, Franco ha muerto*. With this, a tearful Carlos Arias Navarro, President of the Spanish Government, announced to the whole world the end of a dictatorship that had gripped Spain for 39 years. For Spaniards, Franco's death was a turning point in its modern history. As a schoolchild in Spain at the time, I remember it well. Not just because people were anxious to find out what the ailing health of the *Caudillo* was over those tumultuous final months, but also because I got several days off school.

Many miles away in London, only a month prior to Franco's death, a group of Second World War veterans had gathered in Whitehall. In the softening October sun, they stood solemnly upright, dressed in their smart blazers, shiny shoes and with medals hanging from their chests. At the front, at the feet of one of them, was a wreath adorned with the Spanish Republican colours that read 'TO THE MEMORY OF THE SPANIARDS WHO GAVE THEIR LIVES IN THE FIGHT FOR FREEDOM 1939–45.' What were smartly dressed Spanish Republicans wearing British Second World War medals doing at the Cenotaph? These men were, in fact, members of the Spanish Ex-Servicemen's Association. Men who had served as soldiers in the British Army in North Arica, in the Middle East, on Crete as well as in France and Germany. But how and why did all of this come about?

When my good friend Óscar Luís Fernández Calvo sent me a second-hand copy of Daniel Arasa's book entitled *Los Españoles de Churchill* I was totally taken aback by its content and intrigued at the same time. Not soon after, I managed to contact Daniel Arasa who told me that yes, Spanish Republicans had served in the British Armed Forces during the Second World War and that a far more thorough study was needed, especially now that archives had opened up more and a great deal of further information was available. I resolved to do just that, but I had a great number of questions: How was it that so many Spaniards served in the British Armed Forces during the Second World War? Where did they come from exactly? What were their journeys? Which theatres of war did they serve in and what operations did they take part in? What units did they serve in? Were there any families I could speak to about it? Where could I get other information? Armed with Arasa's book and a few other starting points, I decided to set out on a journey of discovery and find out as much as I could on Spaniards who served in the British Army during the Second World War. So began my eight year quest that has taken me from Norway to the depths of Africa and from Gibraltar to the Far East. I have had the real privilege of meeting many families who are justly proud of what these men achieved. To tell their story is amazing, a

---

1 N.E.A. Briggs, 'France Grapples with Spanish Refugee Problem,' *The Daily Record* (Long Branch, New Jersey), Monday 20 February 1939, page 2.

story that hopefully provides an insight into an aspect of the Second World War that most do not know anything about.

For those Spanish Republicans who served in the British Army during the Second World War, many had gone through epic journeys and experienced severe hardships. These were men who had been born in a Spain that had declared 'benevolent neutrality' in The Great War, and they were probably still at school when Spain underwent the dictatorship of Primo de Rivera in the 1920s. They had been teenagers in a Spain that saw the flight into exile of its Royal Family and the birth of a Spanish Republic in the early 1930s, only to go through a turbulent period that resulted in a bloody civil war – the prelude to the Second World War. Fighting for the Spanish Republic, these Spaniards were forced into exile in France in 1939, joined the French armed forces or labour companies and then suffered many more privations as the war progressed. By not long after Churchill became Prime Minister, several hundred had already joined the British Army in Britain and in the Middle East. The next wave of Spaniards joining the British came in late 1942 after the liberation of thousands of Spanish Republicans from camps in North Africa. By the war's end, over 500 were in Britain still serving and awaiting their demobilisation. In many cases, one could argue that Spanish Republicans like these ended up fighting in three wars: the Spanish Civil War, then for the French and then for the British. Some even talk about living under up to *cinco banderas* (five flags) covering the Spanish Republic, France, Free France, Britain and finally Spain later in their lives – several were in uniform and fighting for 10 years. It could be argued that those who served in the British Army were the lucky ones. But this does not mean that their story is less worthy of the telling. Many had been victims that converted themselves into combatants and worked tirelessly to continue fighting against fascism, something that we must not forget.

In this book are Spanish Republicans involved in virtually all aspects of the fighting that the British Army carried out in the Second World War. As has rightly been argued by many, the Spanish Civil War was in fact part of the same conflict. Nevertheless, at the outbreak of the Second World War itself in 1939, many had already learnt a great deal about Blitzkrieg and were battle hardened as a consequence. The much-used quote by Camus stating that 'Men of my generation have had Spain in our hearts … It was there that they learned … that one can be right and yet be beaten, that force can vanquish spirit, and that there are times when courage is not rewarded.'[2] was in fact turned on its head by 1945 as Spanish Republicans were to discover that '… one can be victorious and yet be wrong.' The survival of the Franco Regime would be a very bitter pill to swallow for many, but despite this, their spirit was not vanquished, and their courage was rewarded as soldiers in the British Army. Many would crave their homeland and 'Freedom for Spain', something that most would not experience until after Franco's death in 1975.

Whether it was as personnel supporting the BEF in France or fighting for survival during the dark days of Dunkirk in 1940, Spanish Republicans were continuing the fight virtually from the outset. Their paths crossed with that of many key figures including Kim Philby and Ian Fleming as they became agents of the Special Operations Executive. Spanish Republicans served in British units in the Middle East and in the deserts of North Africa, in operations behind enemy lines and in front of them. They fought in the elite SAS in Northwest Europe and Italy and as soldiers on the beaches of Normandy in June 1944. Some gave the ultimate sacrifice in the airborne forces in Arnhem. Spanish Republicans fought in the streets of German towns in 1945 and were present at the Allied Victory Parade in Berlin that July.

As we commemorate 50 years since the publication of the mighty volume by Pedro Pons Prades entitled *Republicanos Españoles en la Segunda Guerra Mundial*, it is difficult to imagine that so much has occurred since to tell the story. Yet, people are still not aware of so many hidden aspects.

---

2 Albert Camus, *L'Espagne Libre* (Paris: Calman-Lévy, 1946), preface.

The historiography of exiled Spanish Republicans fighting in the Second World War has been a well-trodden path, but a great deal more needs to be told and is still being uncovered. To date, I have uncovered 1,072 Spanish Republicans who served in the British Army, all are listed in the appendices of this book, and I am certain there are still many more to discover. As I have delved deeper into the topic, I have learnt that numerous Spanish Republicans served with distinction. Many spoke of being proud of their service in British Army uniform and how they had assimilated to life in the British military despite their political differences. These Spaniards Republicans, in fact, brought about another facet to the rich history and traditions of the British Army.

Sadly, none of the Spaniards featured in this book are with us any longer, so the responsibility now falls on us to discover more about their stories and to re-tell them. *El deber de contar* (the obligation to tell the story) has for so long been an aspect of keeping historical memory alive. It is therefore important that we tell the story of these men, so they do not fade into the dark recesses of history. This book hopes to tell their story, a story of Spanish Republicans 'continuing the fight' against fascism during the premiership of Winston Churchill, beyond the Spanish Civil War in British Army uniform.

Séan F. Scullion

xxxii CHURCHILL'S SPANIARDS

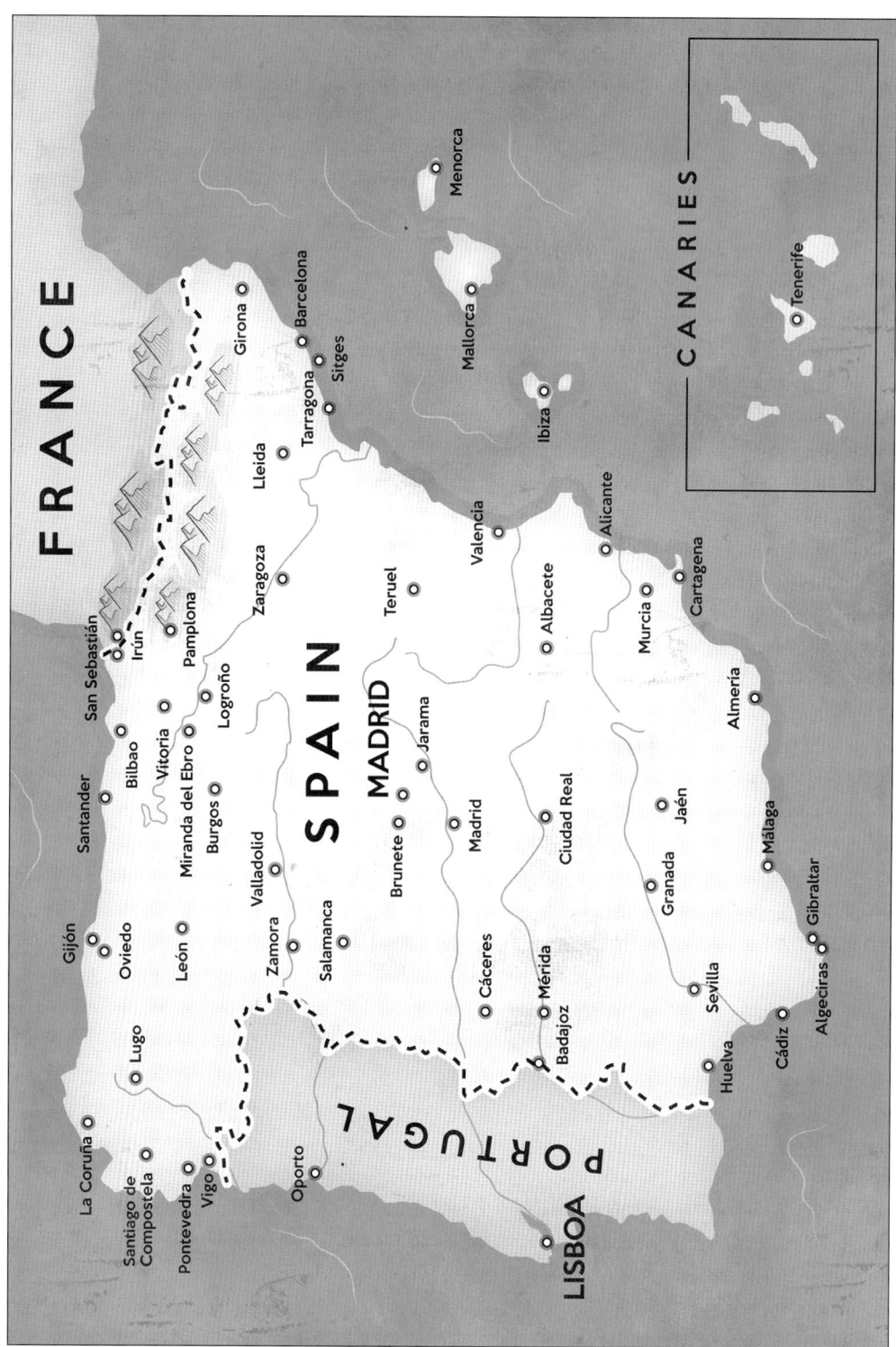

Map 1 Spain, showing the cities and towns where many of the Spaniards in this book came from. (Artwork by Mike Heald)

PREFACE xxxiii

Map 2 Britain, showing the locations where many of the Spaniards in this book were based or consequently lived. (Artwork by Mike Heald)

Chapter 1

'The First Summer After and The Last Summer Before'

Shoulder to Shoulder in France and Beyond

> I passed in front of the French flag. One more step and I was no longer in Spain. One more step and I found myself in France at 4.30pm on February 12th, 1939.
>
> Jaime Trill[1]

For the Spaniards in this book and the countless others who were to be in exile after the Spanish Civil War, their story of service in foreign armies began when the defeated Republican Army found itself in southern France at the beginning of 1939. This followed a torrid and incredibly violent period in Spain's history, where the country had undergone huge changes during the first decades of the twentieth century, only to suffer a civil war between 1936 and 1939, which was fought over the soul of Spain itself. In France in 1939, and following internment in the camps set up by the French authorities, numerous Spaniards decided to join the French armed forces as foreign volunteers rather than be returned to Spain or remain imprisoned. When France declared war on Germany in September 1939, many of the Spaniards remaining in France became members of Foreign Labour Companies (*Compagnies de Travailleurs Étrangers* or *Compagnies de Travailleurs Espagnols – CTEs*).[2] Several were to remain detained in France after the German invasion of May and June 1940, some at the behest of Franco.[3] Those who were sent overseas ended up in North Africa or the Middle East as soldiers serving in the *Légion Étrangère* or in *Bataillons de Marche de Voluntaries Étrangers* (*BMVE*s, Foreign Volunteer Marching Battalions). Many others who found themselves in foreign parts were interned in camps set up later by the Vichy regime. It was therefore to be the defeat of France in June 1940 that would witness the first wave of Spaniards joining the British Army.

---

1 James Trill, *Biography of a Spanish Soldier 1939 – 1946*, Private Papers of J. Trill, Imperial War Museum collection, document 3705, p.12.
2 Vincent Parello, 'Les Compagnies de Travailleurs Étrangers (C.T.E.) en France à la fin de la Troisième République,' in *Bulletin Hispanique*, (Bordeaux: Presses Universitaires de Bordeaux, 2016), pp.233–250.
3 Diego Fonseca, 'What was Franco's Role in the Deportation of 10,000 Spaniards to Nazi camps?' in *El País*, Madrid, 26 April 2019. <https://english.elpais.com/elpais/2019/04/26/inenglish/1556272970_468527.html>. Accessed 12 December 2020.

The Soul of Spain

The men who served in the British Army during the Second World War were born into a Spain in turmoil. When Britain declared war on Germany on 4 August 1914, Spain's Government declared 'benevolent neutrality' and thus did not participate in the bloody war that followed. By the later stages of the Great War, Spain was undergoing its period of '*Pistolerismo*' (gun violence) where the proliferation of several armed groups (composed of *pistoleros*) took place, further dividing parts of the country. The lines between the *Las dos Españas* were being drawn. On one side were the deeply conservative forces of the monarchy, the military, the Catholic Church and industrialists; on the other was Spanish radicalism encompassing a wide range of groups spanning from anarchism to liberalism, which had been encouraged by the industrialisation and recent social mobilisation Spain had offered. The country's neutrality between 1914 and 1918 had also led to a big increase in its industrial production; and so, by the early 1920s, the country was suffering from social unrest and violence, especially in Barcelona, an industrial heartland. Much of the mistrust from industrialists was borne from the inability of the Spanish liberal state to deal fully with the matters of the day, thus leading them to take matters into their own hands and turn to the army.

On 13 September 1923, *General* Miguel Primo de Rivera took power through a coup d'état. It was not a huge surprise given what had been happening in the country. In North Africa, the Spanish Army had suffered a humiliating defeat in 1921 at Annual in north-east Morocco adding to the upheaval back at home. But after support from France, the Rif War (fought against the Berber tribes of the mountainous Rif region of northern Morocco) was over by the end of 1926. Some even thought things seemed to be turning a corner until the Wall Street stock market crash of October 1929. The subsequent global economic crisis that followed exacerbated a political and economic disaster in Spain. Unemployment soared and regional nationalists demanded more autonomy. Following unrest and a lack of support from the army, *General* Miguel Primo de Rivera resigned on 28 January 1930. The Second Republic was proclaimed on 12 April 1931 after municipal elections, and Spain's King, Alfonso XIII, went into voluntary exile. Elections soon followed, and a Republican Constitution was announced on 9 December 1931. Despite promising wide-ranging changes in agrarian reform, autonomy for some of the regions as well as educational and cultural changes, the more extreme elements felt that the Republic overpromised and underdelivered. On the right, changes were resisted wholeheartedly. It was a disastrous combination, summarised years later by Franco's brother-in-law, Ramón Serrano Suñer, who said '… the truth is, we Spaniards couldn't stand each other.'[4] Extremism in politics grew across Europe. Hitler was appointed Chancellor of Germany on 30 January 1933. In Spain, the pendulum swung back to the right on 19 November 1933 when the *Confederación Española de Derechas Autónomas* (Spanish Confederation of Autonomous Right-Wing Parties, the CEDA) won the elections. Much of what had been established by the Republic was swept aside. An armed miners' rebellion in Asturias was violently quashed in October 1934 by the Army of Africa led by a young general, Francisco Franco Bahamonde.

---

4 David Mathieson, *Frontline Madrid, Battlefield Tours of the Spanish Civil War* (Oxford: Signal Books Limited, 2014), p.3.

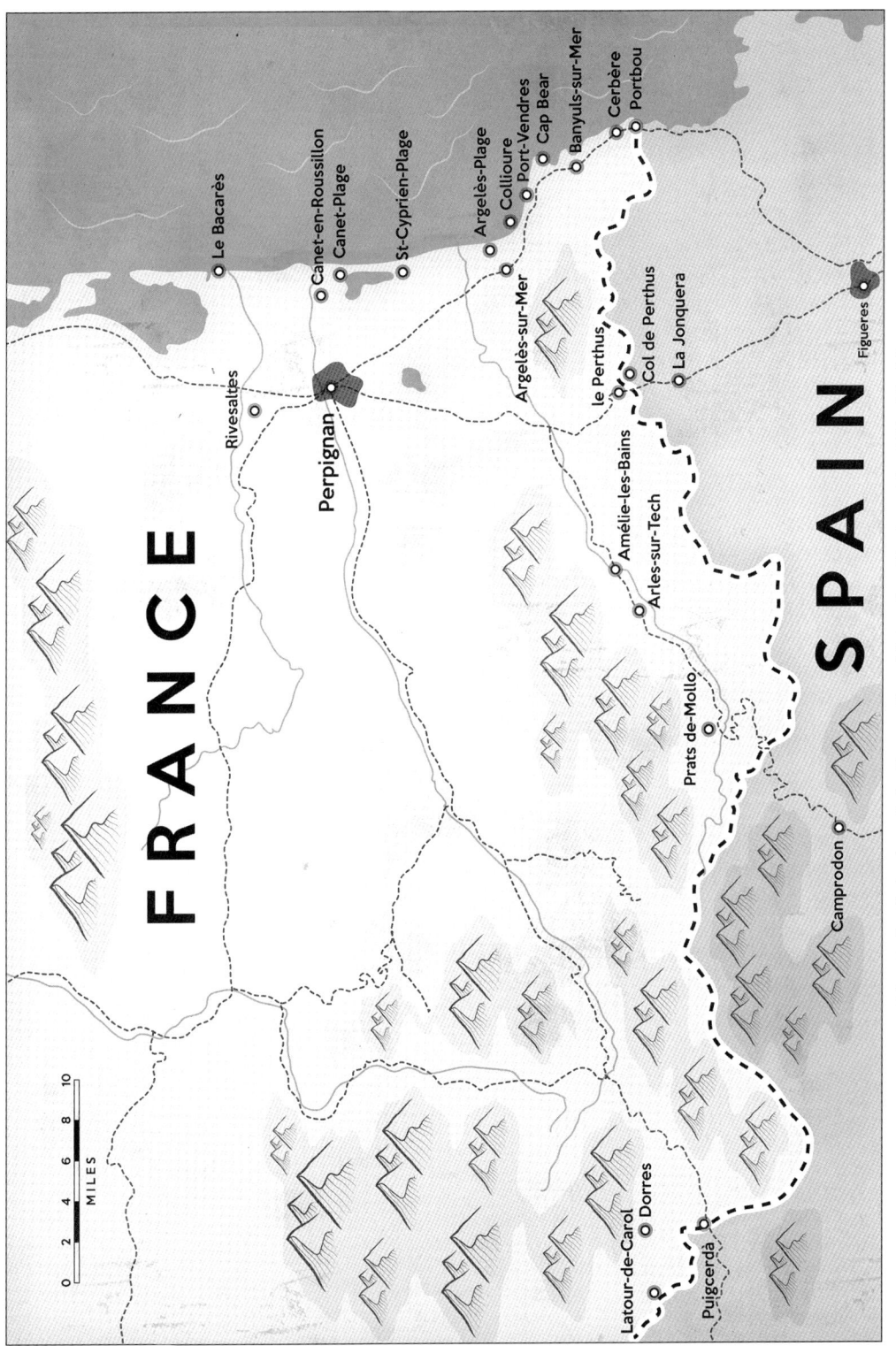

Map 3 *La Retirada* and the Franco-Spanish border. (Designed by Mike Heald)

The country swung back to the left on 16 February 1936 when the *Frente Popular* (a coalition of left-wing political parties) won the elections. Some three weeks before in Britain, King George V had died at Sandringham. The following month, Nazi Germany reoccupied the Rhineland and by May Italy had annexed Ethiopia. Not everyone saw the Spanish Civil War coming though when some officers of the Spanish military High Command declared a coup d'état on 17 July 1936. The plotters had underestimated the popular enthusiasm for the Republic in the country and, following the defeat of the rebels in Madrid and Barcelona (and the support gained by Franco from Italy and Germany), the country tumbled into an inevitable civil war. On 1 October 1936 Franco was invested as *Caudillo* (Leader) of Spain after being named *Generalissiomo* (Supreme Commander) in September. By early November 1936 Madrid was under siege. The following two and a half years saw both sides fighting to the death in several battles. Franco's Rebel Nationalist forces started to gain the upper hand in 1937 after defeating Republican forces in the north which was highlighted by the atrocities at Guernica on 26 April 1937 carried out by the German Condor Legion. The Republican Army tried to take the initiative at Brunete and later in Teruel, but Franco's centralised command and continued support from Germany and Italy coupled with the policy of non-intervention led by Britain enabled him to push on ominously towards the total victory he craved for.

La Retirada and into France

Between 1936 and 1939, during the Spanish Civil War, there were five main movements of Spanish Republicans across the border into France. The first took place at the end of August 1936 when the province of Guipúzcoa in the north was attacked by *General* Mola's troops resulting in thousands fleeing across to France.[5] Refugees presented themselves at Hendaye and crossed the International Bridge. The French Government immediately put into practice the policy which they hoped would become standard practice, namely to disperse those recently arrived in France across other parts of the interior. But it is worth bearing in mind that many of those who crossed the border into France subsequently returned to Spain via the Catalan part of the border, further east.

The final subjugation of the north and the Nationalist seizure of Bilbao, Santander and Gijón between June and October 1937 produced a second wave of refugees from the Civil War. This resulted in some 125,000 refugees fleeing to France by ship to various ports.[6] The majority would return to Spain later across the Pyrenees or via the Eastern end of the Pyrenees through Cataluña.[7] Of note during 1937, was the evacuation of Basque children from the Iberian Peninsula which

---

5 There have been many debates on exact numbers which have differed from 10,000 to 20,000 for this first wave. The same occurs with the other four. I have based my figures for all five movements of Spaniards on the in-depth study carried out by Diego Gaspar Celaya, *La Guerra Continua. Voluntarios Españoles al Servicio de la Francia Libre (1940–1945)* (Madrid: Marcial Pons Historia, 2015).
6 Diego Gaspar Celaya, *La Guerra Continua. Voluntarios Españoles al Servicio de la Francia Libre (1940–1945)* (Madrid: Marcial Pons Historia, 2015), p.73.
7 From June 1937, ships sailed to the French ports of Bordeaux, Paulliac, Le Verdon-sur-Mer, La Pallice, Saint Nazaire and Nantes as well as numerous others. Louis Stein, *Beyond Death and Exile. The Spanish Republicans in France, 1939–1955,* (London: Harvard University Press, 1979), chapter 1, footnote 15.

brought nearly 4,000 children to Britain as refugees from the war.[8] In total, some 33,000 children would be evacuated from Spain during the period from 1936 to 1939.[9]

In 1938 the rebel Nationalists pressed hard in the first half of the year and retook Teruel which sits between Zaragoza and Valencia. There were very heavy losses on both sides and Franco now turned his attention on the central Pyrenees as well as the push to the Mediterranean. The Nationalist forces reached the Mediterranean coast by 15 April 1938. The end of fighting in the Pyrenees on 16 June 1938 resulted in a further movement of people over the mountains into France.[10] Soon after, the Republicans opened the Battle of the Ebro which continued from July to November 1938. This was the last major Republican offensive of the war and was defeated, leading to the Nationalist push across the Segre River and the Cataluña Campaign which opened on 23 December 1938. The writing was now on the wall for the Republic, and it was only a matter of time before it would be defeated. Between January and February 1939 some 450,000 civilian and military refugees crossed into France and were then held in French internment camps.

Despite a considerable amount of experience in dealing with Spanish refugees entering France between 1936 and 1938 and the measures adopted by the French Government, it was impossible for it to be prepared for the nearly half million or so Spanish refugees that crossed the Pyrenees at the beginning of 1939. In April 1938 with a reasonable amount of agreement between most political groups in France, as well as a strong xenophobic sentiment that had begun in the early 1930s, the French Government decided to implement a series of measures to force the overwatch and repression of foreigners that found themselves in French territory. And thus, on 2 May 1938, the decree dealing with foreigners was adopted. It said:

> Any foreigner referred to … who in the interest of order or public security, should be subject to more strict surveillance measures than those dictated in the previous paragraph, will be required to reside in camps whose designation will be made by decree.[11]

Commonly known as the Daladier Decree, it authorised French Prefects to place refugees and asylum seekers under house arrest. The French Government then published a decree on 11 July 1938 that extended the duties enforced by law onto the rights of foreigners under asylum for

---

8 <https://www.basquechildren.org/colonies/history>. Accessed 20 March 2021. 'Public opinion was outraged by the bombing of Guernica 1937, the first ever saturation bombing of a civilian population. The Basque Government appealed to foreign nations to give temporary asylum to the children, but the British Government adhered to its policy of non-intervention. The Duchess of Atholl, President of the National Joint Committee for Spanish Relief, took up the campaign to urge the Government to accept the Basque children and finally, permission was, reluctantly, granted. However, the Government refused to be responsible financially for the children, saying that this would violate the non-intervention pact. It demanded that the newly formed Basque Children's Committee guarantee 10/- per week for the care and education of each child [in 1936 the average wage of a farm labourer was around 30/- per week]. The children left for Britain on the steamship the *Habana'*on 21st May 1937. Each child had been given a hexagonal cardboard disc to pin on his clothes with an identification number and the words *'Expedición a Inglaterra'* printed on it. The ship, supposed to carry around 800 passengers, carried 3,840 children, 80 teachers, 120 helpers, 15 catholic priests and 2 doctors. The children were crammed into the boat, and slept where they could, even in the lifeboats. The journey was extremely rough in the Bay of Biscay and most of the children were violently seasick. The steamer arrived at Southampton on 23rd May.'
9 Diego Gaspar Celaya, *La Guerra Continua. Voluntarios Españoles al Servicio de la Francia Libre (1940–1945)* (Madrid: Marcial Pons Historia, 2015), pp.74–76.
10 Diego Gaspar Celaya, *La Guerra Continua. Voluntarios Españoles al Servicio de la Francia Libre (1940–1945)* (Madrid: Marcial Pons Historia, 2015), p.84, totalling around 25,000.
11 <http://pages.livresdeguerre.net/pages/sujet.php?id=docddp&su=103&np=780>. Accessed 12 June 2021.

the 'general organisation of the nation in times of war.'[12] On 12 November 1938, the French Government went further still and authorised the construction of camps to house those under suspicion. Therefore, by 1939, despite the chaos that was taking place, the French had already put in place the skeleton measures required to disarm and initially house those who crossed the border into their country.

In January and February 1939 thousands passed over via four main crossing points on the Mediterranean side at Portbou to Cerbère, La Junquera to Le Perthus, Camprodón to Col d'Ares to Prats de Mollo and Puigcerdá to Latour-de-Carol-Osséja.[13] On the French side of the border indecision and a hardening of government policy on immigrants had led to a series of hurried exchanges between the Minister of the Interior, Albert Sarraut, and a handful of other ministers and prefects who effectively gave the order to close the border on 26 January. The border was only formally opened for civilians on 28/29 January, for wounded on 31 January, with most military refugees allowed in soon after. The fighting men were not permitted to enter France until 5 February, although many had crossed clandestinely before that date. Before being let through, they were searched and disarmed. Then as they were watched over by the ever-present *gendarmes* and *gardes mobile*, they were marched off, with no idea of what their final destination might be. At the end of this march, they were herded into a series of hurriedly set up barbed wire enclosures.[14] On the Spanish side, Figueras was evacuated, and crowds pressed the border area. The *New York Times* correspondent, Herbert Matthews described the scene around five kilometres from the French border:

> There are not ten square yards anywhere near roads that have not their refugees. Every side road, every field, and even the hills are swarming with unhappy thousands who are gradually finding their way to La Junquera. There by the thousands they wait patiently or stand in lines to get food that the international commission is sending from France.[15]

Cleto Sánchez Monterrubio ended up joining the British Army via the *Légion Étrangère* in Syria. Sánchez was from Azuaga in southern Extremadura and volunteered to join the Republican Army at the outbreak of the Spanish Civil War. He served in the 1st Battalion of the 104th Brigade and was then attached to the 31st Division before fighting in the Battle of the Ebro and was a part of the withdrawal through the Pyrenees. In his memoirs he said:

> It's from there that we began to withdraw, some days more some days less. But what was for sure was that we were retreating every day going along the high mountains of the Pyrenees until we got to the border. We passed the border at a place called Septfonts and it was there that the Colonel told us that we had lost the War and according to him we would get on a boat in Marseille and return to Spain to carry on fighting. But when the 13th of February 1939 came, and we arrived in France we knew that we would never go back to Spain and fight.[16]

---

12 *Loi du 11 juillet 1938 sur l'Organisation Générale de la Nation pour le Temps de Guerre, July 13th, 1938*, 8330.
13 On 9 March 1939, the Vallières Report stated that around 440,000 had crossed the frontier. 210,000 of these were civilians, 220,000 were from the Republican Army and at least 10,000 were injured. See also, Louis Stein, *Beyond Death and Exile, The Spanish Republicans in France, 1939–1955,* (London: Harvard University Press, 1979), Chapter 1, footnote 91.
14 Geneviève Dreyfus-Armand, *El Exilio de los Republicanos Españoles en Francia*, (Barcelona: Ediciones Crítica, 2000), p.44–46.
15 Louis Stein, *Beyond Death and Exile. The Spanish Republicans in France, 1939–1955,* (London: Harvard University Press, 1979), pp.27–28.
16 Cleto Sánchez Monterrubio, *Memorias de Tres Banderas,* unpublished memoir. Cleto Sánchez was a member of No. 50 Middle East Commando and wrote a short memoir.

A lorry loaded with goods and Spanish Republicans is stopped as it approaches the French border. (Agustín Roa Ventura archive)

Two weeks later the final elements of the Republican Army in Cataluña crossed into France with Nationalist forces hot on their heels. Between 9 and 11 February, most of the Republican Army in the eastern region of Spain had crossed into France. Two days later, the last Republican soldiers were able to escape, with them were around 5,000 International Brigade members who had decided to keep on fighting even though the Brigade had been disbanded in 1938. Testimonies of the experiences from this time are some of the most harrowing of the Spanish Civil War – fear, the cold, long marches, extreme fatigue, bitter sadness and uncertainty. Despite their ordeals, there were many that saw a disciplined army crossing the border, but for numerous soldiers it was hard to grasp the reality. For them the war was over – they were no longer soldiers but refugees. Scattered and broken units crossed over the border and the final elements of the rearguard approached the border near Prats de Mollo. A further 12,000 'refugees' emerged from the mountains near Col d'Ares on 14 February.

50 days later and the Spanish Civil War was over. But before that, the final group of some 12,000 Republican refugees was able to get away by ship from the eastern coast of Spain from places such as Alicante and Cartagena and escape to northern Africa.[17] This last move should be

---

17 For more information about the evacuation of exiled Spaniards using the Stanbook from Alicante to Orán see Juan B. Vilar, ¡Ay de los vencidos! El exilio y los países de acogida (Madrid: Ed. Eneida, 2009), p.74 and Juan

regarded as the fifth and last large exodus of Spanish Republicans at the end of the Spanish Civil War. Amongst the many that were able to escape in this last wave were many from the Republican Navy, including *Almirante* Miguel Buiza who left on 5 March 1939 along with the majority on the Republican Fleet to stop these elements falling into Franco's hands.[18] As well as the Republican Fleet around 6,000 to 8,000 managed to escape from the south-east of Republican Spain across to North Africa to places like Orán on the Algerian coast.

Into the Camps

Opinion had been divided in France regarding support for Republican Spain during the Spanish Civil War. The non-intervention pact and divisions in the French press had all contributed to the mixed messages coming from the French population as Republicans streamed across the border. Once across, the refugees had to undergo a selection procedure and were then relocated to temporary camps known as *Centres d'Accueil* (Reception Centres).

The first *Centre d'Accueil* had been opened on 21 January 1939 in Rieucros. The first camp to open, only a little further north along the coast, was Argelès-sur-Mer on 1 February 1939. Due to the large number of refugees arriving between 5 and 9 February, another camp was opened in Saint-Cyprien. Both were for refugees crossing the border through Le Perthus and Cerbère. In the areas surrounding Vallespir and the Cerdaña the camps of Arles-sur-Tech and Prats de Mollo were additionally opened.[19] The camps were guarded by the French police as well as Moorish and Senegalese colonial troops of the French Army. Soon after arrival, the refugees started to suffer malnutrition and overcrowding as well as lack of hygiene and water contamination caused by the presence of human detritus on the beaches. All these factors led to scabies, dysentery, and the death of a great many. Cholera outbreaks were common because of the conditions most had endured for weeks. Starvation was commonplace. Severe overcrowding in the camps of Argelès-sur-Mer, and Saint-Cyprien obliged the French Government to establish another camp at Le Barcarès situated in the region of the eastern Pyrenees along the coast from Argelès-sur-Mer.

Despite the establishment of camps to house the Spaniards, conditions remained difficult with hunger prevailing for most who had already endured so much. Juan Torrents Abadía (later known as John Colman), from Barcelona was involved in left-wing politics from an early age. He served as a policeman in the Catalan Government and served at the Aragón Front before crossing over to France in early 1939. In an Imperial War Museum interview in his thick Catalan accent, he later recalled:

> The French tried to stop us at the beginning but couldn't ... it was really something that ... they [the refugees] organised and built things with corrugated iron and whatever they could find. The first time they brought in a lorry full of bread into the compound there ... people just ran at them. The second time, the lorries stood outside the wire and they threw the bread over the wire. But one thing was that women and children were not there ... only men in those camps.[20]

B. Vilar, 'La Última Gran Emigración Política Española. Relación Nominal de los Militantes Republicanos Evacuados de Alicante en el Buque Inglés Stanbrook con Destino a Orán en 28 de Marzo de 1939,' in *Anales de Historia Contemporánea*, (Murcia: Universidad de Murcia, 1983), No. 2, 1983.
18 Hugh Thomas, *The Spanish Civil War* (London: Penguin Books, 2001), p.877.
19 Enrique Moradiellos, *El reñidero de Europa. Las dimensiones internacionales de la guerra civil española* (Barcelona: Ediciones Península, 2001), pp.239–240.
20 John Colman (Juan Torrents Abadía), IWM Interview, Catalogue Number IWM 17730, 27 December 1997.

A group of Spaniards at Le Bacarès camp in the spring of 1939. (Agustín Roa Ventura archive)

Little by little, new camps were erected in other districts such as Adge in Hérault for Catalans and Bram in the Aude for the more elderly refugees. Of interest, was the camp established at Gurs in Béarn (inland from Bayonne). This was designated for Basque refugees, members of the Republican Air Force and members of the International Brigades. Judes (Septfonds) was a camp for specialised workers for the war effort (specialised being a vague and undefined term).

Despite the desperate situation people found themselves in, there were some good stories. Many that crossed were welcomed by French families that were able to accommodate them in their own homes. Constancia de la Mora who had been a key member of the Republican Press Department during the Spanish Civil War and was married to *General* Cisneros, the commander of the Republican Air Force, was rescued at the border by an unknown French family as groups of people around her were separated. One of the biggest disappointments for those escaping Franco's troops was this separation of men, women and families upon arrival on the French side of the border. Others were also able to track down family members who were already in France and join them or were collected at the border. But the policy for most women, children, elderly, sick and injured was clear – that they ended up in *Centres d'Accueil*. Most of these were situated further inland in France and tended to be abandoned factories, old convents, old barracks, schools, prisons or churches that the French civil authorities were in control of.

It was the men of working age who would be incarcerated in internment camps.[21] The definition of these camps has always been a contentious topic as nobody could, or would, categorise them

---

21 Eduardo Pons Prades, *Republicanos Españoles en la Segunda Guerra Mundial*, La Esfera de los Libros S.L.,

Women, children and the elderly are fed in a *Centre d'Accueil* near the border with Spain.
(Agustín Roa Ventura archive)

properly. Some called them concentration camps, which is the term that was found in the French press. Others defined them as internment camps, or even shelters since they described the occupation of them as temporary. After a few weeks, the level of organisation in the camps improved, resulting in better conditions for those held in them. Once interned, Spaniards worked together to improve their circumstances. Many were forced to build the very shelters they were to live in. Camp life was cold, wet and dreary with few facilities. Despite this, many activities such as theatrical and music events began to take place in the camps. However, there were still places that were no go areas in some camps where prostitution and racketeering were rife.

2003, pp.32–33. According to Pons Prades, the most important camps were in the region of Perpignan: Saint-Cyprien (80,000), Argelès-sur-Mer (65,000) and Le Bacarès (35,000). Others were established further inland: Agde, Hérault (18,000), Gurs, Basse Pyrenées (16,000), Vernet y Noé, Haut-Garonne (15,000), Rieucros for women, Vernet d'Ariège, a punishment camp for men (12,000), and Mazères also in Ariège (5,000). There were other camps for 'chosen' refugees: the Judes (Septfonds) Camp, Tarn et Garonne (20 to 25,000) and the Fort of Collioure which was the first prison for punishment (500 to 1,000 men).

By the spring of 1939 the French Ministry of the Interior had also started to put together lists of political suspects of those they designated as dangerous or undesirable because of their type of service in the Republican Army or in the International Brigades, and place them in specific camps. Several Spaniards and *Internationales* (former members of the International Brigades) were interned in the Collioure fortress, south of Argelès-sur-Mer. Upon arrival, those to be interned were told, in no uncertain terms, that 'He who breaks the rules will be punished'.[22] Similarly, the former prison camp of Vernet d'Ariège was used to accommodate anarchists belonging to the *Columna Durruti*.[23] Women who were categorised as requiring punishment by the French authorities were instead sent to Rieucros. The buildings in Rieucros later served during the Second World War as prisons to intern women of different nationalities who had specific military and political significance, such as anti-fascists from central Europe, and French communists and anarchists.

In March 1939, as tensions rose across Europe, the French Government decided it had to make the most of this immense number of Spaniards housed in the camps and so, on 5 May 1939, an Interior Ministry note said that it wanted to 'Transform this unorganised and passive rabble of refugees into useful elements for the nation …' Consequently, the military authorities running the camps started to identify potential workers on behalf of the Ministry of Employment. Each French *département* produced reports on those who could be used in agriculture and other areas.

North Africa

In North Africa the 12,000 or so Spanish refugees that arrived in March 1939 into French territory were received mainly in Algiers, Orán and Tunis. Algeria had been a French colony from the beginning of the nineteenth century and in 1848 was incorporated into France as a *département* and a part of the French Second Republic. It was to be largely those Spanish Republicans who were either from the Republican military or more politically active that were able to get to the North African coast. It seemed that their arrival was initially greeted in a more positive way than those who crossed the Pyrenees due to the resident Spanish communities that were already in the region. But most were kept on their ships until the relevant French colonial authorities were able to decide how to deal with them. Once off their ships, just as in France, these groups were classified and then held in camps. Initially, the authorities had wanted to turn the refugees away, but they were forced to come up with a plan, and by May 1939 new camps were established that allowed many of the refugees in the Algiers area to disembark.

Women, children, and whole families tended to be housed in locations surrounding the city of Algiers such as Carnot, Orléansville and Molière. Men who were deemed to be of a higher socio-professional ranking were moved to Cherchell, 70km south of the city. The French authorities did not have a plan for these Spaniards *per se*; they knew that at some point they might come in handy, but in the meantime they were kept isolated where they were. Ex-Republican combatants were placed in separate camps. Opened in April 1939, Camp Moránd at Boghari in the *département* of Algiers was opened specifically for more than 3,000 Spanish refugees and here temperatures regularly rose above 50°C and living conditions were very harsh close to the Ouarsenis Mountains.[24] Those who arrived in Tunis that were mainly from the recently arrived Republican Fleet plus

---

22 IWM interview with John Colman, 27 December 1997, IWM 17730.
23 The *Columna Durruti* was the largest anarchist military unit formed during the Spanish Civil War. It was headed by Buenaventura Durrutin and was fully militarised and merged into the Republican Army in 1937. Durruti had been killed at the Madrid front in November 1936.
24 Harry Alexander, 'Oral History interview with Harry Alexander.' <https://collections.ushmm.org/search/catalog/irn504525> (25/05/2018), accessed 10 December 2019.

A group of Spaniards in a camp in Algiers shortly after their arrival in 1939. (Antonio Obis archive)

2,000 or so others; they were housed in Maknassy Camp or the nearby Gasa Camp (for the men) or in Kasserine for the women and children.

Once war was declared in September 1939, most of those who had been held were moved to Colomb-Béchar Camp in southern Algeria where they were integrated into the *8ᵉ Régiment de Travailleurs Étrangers*. Members of this regiment were, in essence, press ganged into joining it from the camps. This regiment was made up nearly entirely of Spaniards and had 12 companies with the majority of the Spaniards being ex-Republican Navy. Initially *8ᵉ Régiment* was used for working on roads and building new military facilities. The members of the *Régiment* continued to be used for labouring tasks and a large number were used to build the infamous Trans-Saharan railway line, they would also work across Morocco and southern Tunisia.

Although Camp Moránd at Boghari was probably the most infamous camp of the many established by the French in North Africa where Spaniards were held, also notorious amongst the camps in Algeria was Djelfa Camp. This latter had been set up in the Ouled Hills near to the village of El Djelfa and had received its first groups of French communists in 1939. The camp was positioned next to the oasis where there was a small settlement. Cold and wet conditions prevailed for much of the year because of the altitude and isolation of the location. Harry Alexander, a German national of Jewish origin who fled to France through Italy in 1940, joined the resistance and was later imprisoned at Argelès-sur-Mer. He remembered his arrival at Djelfa and the reception by Caboche, the camp commander:

> You all came here to die. It's a matter of time. Some will live a little longer, some won't, but you all came here to die. That is my job and I am good at my job.[25]

In April 1941, the French at Djelfa were replaced by Spaniards along with members of the International Brigades, German Jews, Poles and some Italians. Their move to Djelfa was for

---
25 Archives Nationales d'Outre-Mer, Aix-en-Provence. Harry Alexander, 'Oral History interview with Harry Alexander.' <https://collections.ushmm.org/search/catalog/irn504525> (25/05/2018), accessed 10 December 2019.

varying reasons. Some had been arrested for political views that were contrary to fascism and others were from camps in France, or had been transferred from other parts of Algeria itself. The number of Spaniards in Djelfa steadily grew to about 500 by the middle of 1942. A new wave of arrests made by the Vichy Regime meant that many from mainland France were now interned in the camp subsequent to their initial detention.

One of the Spaniards sent to Djelfa at this time was Agustín Roa Ventura. A tall, thin man originally from Almería but brought up in Barcelona, he had been heavily involved in the youth wing of the anarchist *Confederación Nacional de Trabajo (CNT)* during the Civil War. In the summer of 1942, he had been arrested in France and sent to Vernet d'Arriège following his escape from Spain and subsequent internment in Saint-Cyprien and Le Bacarès. Of his arrival at Djelfa he later commented:

> They did not give us clothes or bedding at all. We were still carrying our poor refugee bags; a bit less than we had left Spain with. In the early hours, the forty-five men who had just arrived were sheltering in their places in one of the two huge tents to settle down in …[26]

As well as those who escaped to North Africa, between 1939 and 1940 nearly 30,000 managed to emigrate elsewhere, mostly to South America, to countries such as Chile, the Dominican Republic, Argentina, Venezuela, Colombia and Cuba. Some 4,000 also managed to get to the Soviet Union.

The French War Machine

On 12 April 1939, and linked to the 1938 decrees, the French Government set out a ruling that extended to all male foreigners between 20 and 48 years of age and entitled to the right of asylum, to serve in the French Army or the War Ministry in one role or another as *Prestataires Militaires Étrangers* (*PME* – Foreign Workers Pressed into Military Service). This was primarily due to a lack of skilled workers but also the need to expand the armed forces quickly now that war seemed inevitable. Spaniards in France therefore now had six options: [27]

1. Volunteer to return to Spain. For many this was not actually an option, although thousands did. This was because many were on hit lists due to the units they had served in, or were political enemies of the Franco Regime. Many returned to Spain because they felt they had no option due to family reasons.
2. They could try to emigrate to a third country, mainly ones located in Latin America such as Mexico. This was difficult because they needed to have sufficient funds. Many were helped to do so however.
3. Sign a contract as employees, either in the agricultural or industrial sectors to compensate for the shortage of workers in the country as France went onto a war footing.
4. Volunteer to join *Compagnies de Travailleurs Étrangers* (*CTEs* – Foreign Labour Companies) employed by the French War Ministry to carry out a myriad of tasks in support of the defence of France ranging from working in arms factories or on the Maginot Line, to carrying out works on roads, railways and pipelines.

---

26 Agustín Roa Ventura, *Los Años de mi Vida 1942–1950, Contribución histórica sobre el proceso de los españoles fuera y dentro de España*, Libro IV, unpublished, p12.
27 Diego Gaspar Celaya, *La Guerra Continua. Voluntarios Españoles al Servicio de la Francia Libre (1940–1945)* (Madrid: Marcial Pons Historia, 2015), p.130.

5. Volunteer to serve for a period of five years in the *Légion Étrangère* (the Foreign Legion). As foreigners they were eligible to volunteer to join the *Légion*, foreigners were not permitted to join the French Army, (as French citizens were not permitted to join the *Légion*) but the *Légion* was in essence a way for foreigners to join the French Army as part of a 'foreign' unit that served overseas.
6. Become volunteers in the newly formed *Régiments de Marche de Volontaires Étrangers* (*RMVE* – Foreign Marching Volunteer Regiments) *'pour la durée de la guerre'* (the duration of the war). *RMVE*s were a means by which the French Army was able to recruit more foreign citizens in the 1930–40 period. It was similar to the *Légion* in many ways but with different terms of service and pay.

Compagnies de Travailleurs Étrangers

The first 79 *CTE*s were established between April and June 1939 (53 on 20 April and 26 on 13 June). Before long, around 40,000 Spaniards were working in agriculture and in factories. Volunteering for a *CTE*, an *RMVE* or the *Légion Étrangère* represented a viable solution for socialist, anarchist and communist refugees who were afraid to go back to Spain to face retaliation. But the French armed forces were keen to make the most of the opportunity to not only start emptying the camps but also to use the readily available labour as *PME* in the *Compagnies de Travailleurs Étrangers* (which were more like *Compagnies de Travailleurs Espagnols* as there were so many Spaniards and they were such a high percentage of the personnel).

The structure of a *CTE* comprised some 250 labourers (this was generally 220 Spaniards and 30 French, who would be two officers, eight Senior Non-Commissioned Officers, eight Junior Non-Commissioned Officers and 12 soldiers). It would be commanded by a French reservist officer with a Spanish officer as his deputy. When war was declared in September 1939, there were upwards of 20,000 Spaniards in *CTE*s. By mid-November there were 25,000 in 102 *CTE*s and by December there were 180 *CTE*s on the establishment. On the eve of the invasion of France, 55,000 Spaniards were serving and at the disposal of the French armed forces.[28] By the time the Armistice was signed in June 1939, over 200 *CTE*s existed, meaning that there were, on paper, some 56,500 Spaniards available.[29] These were distributed as follows: 93 were attached to the French Army, 52

---

28 Diego Gaspar Celaya, *La Guerra Continua. Voluntarios Españoles al Servicio de la Francia Libre (1940–1945)* (Madrid: Marcial Pons Historia, 2015), pp.150–153.
29 Testimonies of Spaniards in these 200+ *CTE*s exist for the following (Pedro Pons Prades, *Republicanos Españoles en la Segunda Guerra Mundial*, pp.36–37):
CTE 7,8,9 and 10 formed in Argelès-sur-Mer in April/May 1939 and initially sent to the French/Italian Alps;
CTE 25, 26, 27 and 28 formed in Gurs in October 1939 and initially sent to the Maginot Line;
CTE 30, 31 and 32 formed in Septfonds in November 1939, also initially sent to the Maginot Line;
CTE 33 and 34 formed in Saint-Cyprien in November 1939 and also initially sent to the Maginot Line and soon after to the area of Verdun;
CTE 43, 44 and 44 formed in Agde in June 1939 and initially sent to the French/Italian Alps;
CTE 54, 55, 56, 57 and 58 formed in Mazères in April 1939 and sent to the eastern end of the Maginot Line;
CTE 63, 64, 65, 66 and 67 were also formed in Septfonds in December 1939 and sent initially to Yonne and Aube;
CTE 103, 104 and 105 formed in Septfonds at the end of 1939 and 114, 114, 116, and 117 from Saint-Cyprien in the North between the western point of the Maginot Line and the Channel Coast;
CTE 133 and 137 formed in Septfonds in January and sent initially to the French/Italian Alps;
CTE 160 formed in Saint-Cyprien in February 1940 and sent to the Indre;
CTE 191 which was formed very late in mid-June 1940 from other depleted CTEs, and which ended up in the Corrèze in central France.
Olivier Vermesch, *Les Espagnols de l'Opération Dynamo: Les Compagnies de Travailleurs Étrangers Dunkerque*,

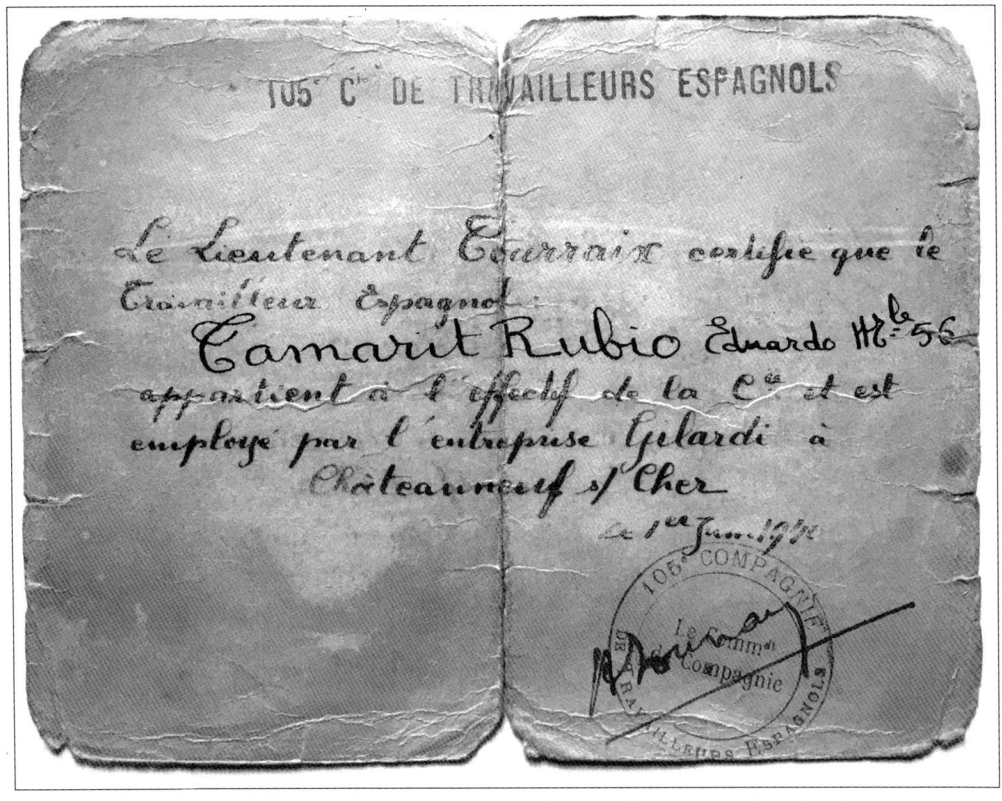

A pass for Eduardo Tamarit who served in *105ᵉ Compagnie de Travailleurs Espagnols*. (Eduardo Tamarit Archive)

were placed under the command of French territorial commands, 18 were with the artillery, 17 attached to the French Air Force, four were with logistics units and one with an engineer unit, one was also detached to the BEF. Forty-three were transferred to the Armaments Ministry, 23 transferred to various forestry services, 20 to gunpowder and explosive factories, 16 to the French regions, seven to the Agricultural departments of several French *départements*, five to the *Compagnie des Eaux et Forêts*, four to the *Société Nationale des Chemins de fer Français* (*SNCF*, the French National Railway Company), one to Saint Nazaire (*Loire-Atlantique*), and 14 others to unspecified locations.[30]

Overall, the intention was that *CTEs* worked in the French interior rather than in border areas and no more so than in the Armament Ministry. However, some of these *Compagnies* were employed in border areas so that work could begin apace on the necessary fortifications in these regions. By November 1939, the following *CTEs* made up of Spaniards were working within French Army Group Sectors:[31]

---

mai-juin 1940. 2020, pp.3–4. <https://atf40.1fr1.net/t10452-compagnies-de-travailleurs-etrangers-espagnols-1939-1940>. Accessed 12 February 2021.

30 Diego Gaspar Celaya, 'Premature Resisters. Spanish Contribution to the French National Defence Campaign in 1939/1940,' *Journal of Modern European History*, Volume 16, 2018, Issue 2, pp.203–224.

31 Olivier Vermesch, *Les Espagnols de l'Opération Dynamo : Les Compagnies de Travailleurs Étrangers Dunkerque, mai-juin 1940,* 2020, p.5, <https://atf40.1fr1.net/t10452-compagnies-de-travailleurs-etrangers-espagnols-1939-1940>. Accessed 12 February 2021.

French Army Group	Sector	*Compagnies de Travailleurs Espagnols*
1st and 7th	Flandres	51 52 53 59 71 72 73 & 84
2th	Ardennes Meuse	74 75 76
4th	Lorraine	22 23 24 25 26 27 30 31 32 33 (this Army Group had up to 19 *CTE*)
5th	Bas Rhin Lorraine	28 29 58 77
6th	Alpes	Dauphiné-Savoie 1 to 12, 18 to 21, 34 to 37, 78 to 83, 86 to 95 Haute Provence-Alpes Maritimes 13 14 15 38 39 40

Régiments de Marche de Volontaires Étrangers and the *Légion*

Even though it had only been a few months since they had last fought, many Spaniards decided to join the French Army, although the only way to do this though was through the *Légion Étrangère*. Recruiting teams from the *Légion* toured the camps in the south of France to raise recruits. However, many of the interned Spaniards were unwilling to join, primarily due to the harsh reputation of the *Légion* and the required five-year contracts on offer. Despite an increase in numbers joining the *Légion*, the French Army, realising that they still had a recruiting problem, established the *Régiments de Marche de Volontaires Étrangers* (*RMVEs* – Foreign Volunteer Marching Regiments, i.e. non-French combat regiments). In all three regiments were established, *21ᵉ*, *22ᵉ* and *23ᵉ Régiments de Marche de Volontaires Étrangers*, and the foreigners who volunteered for service with them were given the official title of *Étrangers Volontaires pour la Durée de la Guerre* (*EVDG* – Foreign Volunteers for the Duration of the War) similar to the *Légion*, although this did not give them the same status as being *Légionnaires*. Despite this, many of the officers in the *RMVE* were reservists from the *Légion* and had received their training at the *Légion* training depot in Sidi Bel Abbès in Algeria. The colours used were the red and green of the *Légion* as well. Originally called *1ᵉ*, *2ᵉ* and *3ᵉ RMVE*, in order to avoid confusion with the *1ᵉ*, *2ᵉ* and *3ᵉ Régiments Étrangers d'Infanterie* from the *Légion Étrangère* (*REI* – Foreign Infantry Regiment), these newly formed regiments were renamed, *21ᵉ* and *22ᵉ RMVE* on 28 and 25 February respectively and *23ᵉ RMVE* was renamed on 31 May 1940.

Most Spaniards who joined the *RMVEs* would go through training at the camp at Le Bacarès on the Mediterranean coast near the French-Spanish border which had formerly been an internment camp. This was called a *Dépôt Comun des Régiments de Marche de Volontaires Étrangers* (*DCRMVE* – Foreign Volunteer Marching Regiments' Training Depot). Training lasted three months and consisted of individual activities followed by specialist training in machine guns, pioneer training and communications et cetera depending on what part of a battalion the recruits were to be put in. Further training also took place at Larzac, which was broken into four parts – ranges, field craft, combat exercises and night exercises.[32] *21ᵉ RMVE* finished at Larzac in April 1940 and *22ᵉ RMVE* started their final training there on 18 April. *23e RMVE* was formed on 31 May 1940 and was sent directly into combat in Picardie. Most Spaniards who fought in *21ᵉ*, *22ᵉ* or *23ᵉ RMVEs* and survived would be imprisoned after the Armistice in June 1940.

Further individual foreign volunteer battalions were also established. The *1e Bataillon de Marche de Volontaires Étrangers* (*1ᵉ BMVE*) was established on 1 March 1940 in Le Bacarès Camp. The battalion was sent to the Middle East in April and landed in Beirut on 15 April 1940, moving

---

32 Diego Gaspar Celaya, *La Guerra Continua. Voluntarios Españoles al Servicio de la Francia Libre (1940-1945)* (Madrid: Marcial Pons Historia, 2015), pp.205–207.

A group of Spaniards in one of the *RMVEs*, most probably *23ᵉ RMVE* or *1ᵉ BMVE*. (Manuel Surera archive)

inland to Baalbeck the following day. It was then integrated into the *6ᵉ REI* and renamed the *11ᵉ Bataillon de Volontaires Étrangers* (*11ᵉ BVE*). It consisted of 19 officers, an officer cadet, 80 warrant officers and senior NCOs, and 729 other ranks who were almost entirely Spanish. Unlike the battalions from the *RMVEs* in France, *11ᵉ BVE* would not be disbanded after the Armistice signed in June 1940. One of the Spaniards in this battalion was Private Moisés Trancho Bartolomé (see more below), an athletic, well-built Basque renowned for his footballing prowess, who had fought in the Barakaldo Battalion during the Spanish Civil War, he had crossed to France with another 10 Spaniards. Here he joined the *122ᵉ CTE* before escaping again and volunteering to join *1ᵉ BMVE* at Le Bacarès.

Spaniards were to volunteer to join the ranks of the *Légion Étrangère* in their largest numbers from February 1939 to June 1940. Most of them enlisted at the main recruiting centre for southern France in Perpignan close to the French-Spanish border. There were also some who joined the *Légion* directly in North Africa. The usual route was for those who volunteered to go from their respective camps in south-east France to Perpignan where they would be transferred to the main *Légion* training depot (*Depot Commun des Régiments Étrangers – DCRE*) at Sidi Bel Abbès in Algeria. Once there, they would go through basic training before being posted to their respective unit. To get to Sidi Bel Abbès they would have to travel by ship to Orán from Marseille. At Marseille they were housed at Fort St Jean, an imposing mediaeval fortress, before embarking, and once in Orán they were moved by train to Sidi Bel Abbès. Another Spaniard who decided to join the *Légion* and travelled to North Africa to carry out his training was Francisco Geronimo from Málaga. A born fighter, he was posted to Syria and joined the *6ᵉ Régiment Étranger d'Infanterie* in early 1940.

Due to the large numbers of new recruits into the *Légion*, an alternative training pipeline was established via the training depot in Sathonay (*Dépôt Métropolitain de la Légion Étrangère de Sathonay*) which was set up on 2 September 1939 and had initially been based at Vancia, north of Lyon. Due to the avalanche of new recruits the *Dépôt* had to be expanded and split between the camps at Sathonay and La Valbonne. Recruits were initially registered at Sathonay via Vancia where they got their uniforms and then went to Valbonne for their training. Most of the Spaniards that went through Sathonay went into the *11ᵉ REI* or *12ᵉ REI*.

A.D. Printer, who had volunteered for the *Légion* for the duration of the war but who was able to escape to the United States after the summer of 1940 said:

> Even from their fellow volunteers the Spaniards met suspicion. Most of the others, having been residents or refugees in France, spoke the language and understood the people. The only French contacts the Spaniards had had before they came to the Légion were the Garde Mobile or the Senegalese in the concentration camps at Gurs and Le Vernet. In order not to be lonely, they formed cells which were against the spirit of the Légion and which isolated them still more. For the officers and for the noncoms, the Spanish *Légionnaires* were a nuisance. They did not fit in. They had been members of a popular party; now they were subjected to the ironclad discipline of a mercenary unit. They brought with them their typical Spanish individualism. They brought, too, their great sense of personal dignity, which was constantly trampled upon in the units where German sergeants and veteran French colonials had formed the outlaws of Europe into soldiers. Most of the left-wing extremists had preferred to remain in the concentration camps. Those who joined the Légion were loyal young soldiers of the Republic, professionals of the Spanish army, a few intellectuals and tradesmen.[33]

Attracting Spaniards as well as many other nationalities into the *Légion Étrangère* or *Bataillons de Volontaires Étrangers* also brought a series of clashes between traditionalists and those wanting to give support to these recent arrivals. But the decision to allow foreign volunteers to join in such numbers had two consequences for the *Légion*. Firstly, that politics was brought into the mix and, as the war went on and the Gaullist/Vichy struggle continued (especially after the capitulation of France in the summer of 1940), it was clear that there were many divisions amongst *Légion* members, especially the officer corps. Secondly, many of these new recruits, who had signed up for five years or *pour la durée de la guerre*, were not as amenable to traditional *Légion* methods of

---

33 Douglas Porch, *The French Foreign Legion. A Complete History of the Legendary Fighting Force* (New York: Skyhorse Publishing, 2010), p.449.

Francisco Geronimo in *Légion Étrangère* uniform shortly after enlisting. (Francisco Geronimo collection)

indoctrination. As a consequence, the relationship between the *Légion* and many of its new recruits would be marked by friction and distrust.[34] For many *Légion* officers, men of the left also posed a serious threat to the *Légion* esprit de corps. Many were also certain that the Spaniards only joined the *Légion* to get out of the internment camps and had no desire to soldier for France, or for the *Légion*. Nevertheless, by the end of 1939 an estimated 3,052 Spaniards had joined the *Légion*'s ranks. This was a large number and made up 27.7 percent of those recruited in 1939 although it only made up 8.2 percent of the *Légion* strength overall.[35] These figures do not include those Spaniards who served in the *RMVEs* who numbered some 2,709, making up over 40 percent of their combat strength.[36]

Many argued, however, that the *Légion* had to be more flexible in its approach as it recruited more volunteers, and not immediately see every Spaniard as 'either a communist or an anarchist, to be handled with the same affection as a box of dynamite.'[37]

By the time war was declared in September 1939, the *Légion* had to restructure and set up new units because of the large number of volunteers wanting to join (around 64,000 by the middle of October 1939).[38] On 1 October 1939, the *6ᵉ REI* was formed in Homs, Syria and the *11ᵉ REI* was established in La Valbonne with many of its troops coming from *4ᵉ REI* in Morocco and from volunteers and reservists. *12ᵉ REI* was set up soon after in La Valbonne too. On 1 March 1940 the *13ᵉ Demi-Brigade de Montagne de la Légion Étranger* (*13ᵉ DBMLE*, later *13ᵉ DBLE* of the *Légion Étrangère*) was established in Sidi Bel Abbès and consisted of fused elements making up two battalions. By the end of the Phoney War (which lasted between September 1939 and May 1940 and consisted of very little action from the Allies and Germans), seven regiments of the *Légion* were involved in operations and Spaniards were to be found in most of them.

The Battle for France

By the time the invasion of France came in May 1940, exiled Republican Spaniards were fully integrated into the French armed forces and were even supporting the BEF. *21ᵉ RMVE* had been sent to the Northern Sector of France, at Verdun, in May and faced the German onslaught suffering a number of casualties, especially on 8 and 9 May. *22ᵉ RMVE* was sent to Alsace on 6 May but was soon moved to Marchélepot on the Somme to defend the approaches to Paris. Here it suffered huge losses but fought over the course of several days in early June. It managed to keep the Germans at bay but was eventually overwhelmed on 6 June. Many of the surviving Spaniards taken prisoner would end up in concentration camps and perish there. Elements of *23ᵉ RMVE* were sent to Picardie, where on 7 June it fought in the Battle of Soissons and later at Pont-sur-Yonne. When the Armistice was signed on 22 June 1940 the *RMVEs* were disbanded because their members had enlisted *pour la durée de la guerre*. Many Spaniards were either able to escape in some way, were killed in action, hospitalised, or taken prisoner. Those in the *CTEs* would not fare much better.

---

34 Douglas Porch, *The French Foreign Legion. A Complete History of the Legendary Fighting Force* (New York: Skyhorse Publishing, 2010), pp.441–443.
35 André-Paul Comor, *L'Epopée de la 13e Demi-Brigade de Légion Etrangère, 1940–1945*, (Paris: Nouvelles Editions Latines, 1988), p.27.
36 Douglas Porch, *The French Foreign Legion. A Complete History of the Legendary Fighting Force* (New York: Skyhorse Publishing, 2010), pp.448–449.
37 Douglas Porch, *The French Foreign Legion. A Complete History of the Legendary Fighting Force* (New York: Skyhorse Publishing, 2010), p.449.
38 Diego Gaspar Celaya, *La Guerra Continua. Voluntarios Españoles al Servicio de la Francia Libre (1940–1945)* (Madrid: Marcial Pons Historia, 2015), p.211.

In Flanders alone, several hundred would be killed as the battle raged, and moved further west towards the coast and the eventual evacuation at Dunkirk.

By the end of the summer of 1940, those who survived in France after the Armistice were given three choices by the Vichy Regime:

- They could still be repatriated back to Spain;
- They could formalise their work in agriculture or in industry in Labour Companies and Labour Groups;
- Or they could volunteer to join the *Organisation Todt*.[39]

Most chose the second option and were therefore permitted to remain in France, mostly in the Vichy Zone. On 27 September 1940, René Belain, Minister of Work and Industrial Production for the Vichy Regime, introduced a law covering aliens aged between 19 and 54. Those unable to return to their own countries could be recruited into Labour Groups. These men would receive no salary, but their families had the right to have some financial aid from the government. Because of this, the Vichy Regime decided to re-establish the *CTEs*, this time calling them *Groupes de Travailleurs Espagnols* and by 1943 31,000 out of the 37,000 men in the *CTEs* were Spanish. It is thought that some 15,000 Spaniards recruited through this means ended up working in the *Organisation Todt* and several thousand were used in the construction of the Atlantic wall, with several hundred sent to the Channel Islands, which were occupied by the Germans. One of these latter was Antonio Obis Campo who was placed into *159ᵉ Compagnie de Travailleurs Espagnols* in the south of France and would later be sent to Djelfa as forced labour. Later in the war, after the Allied landings in

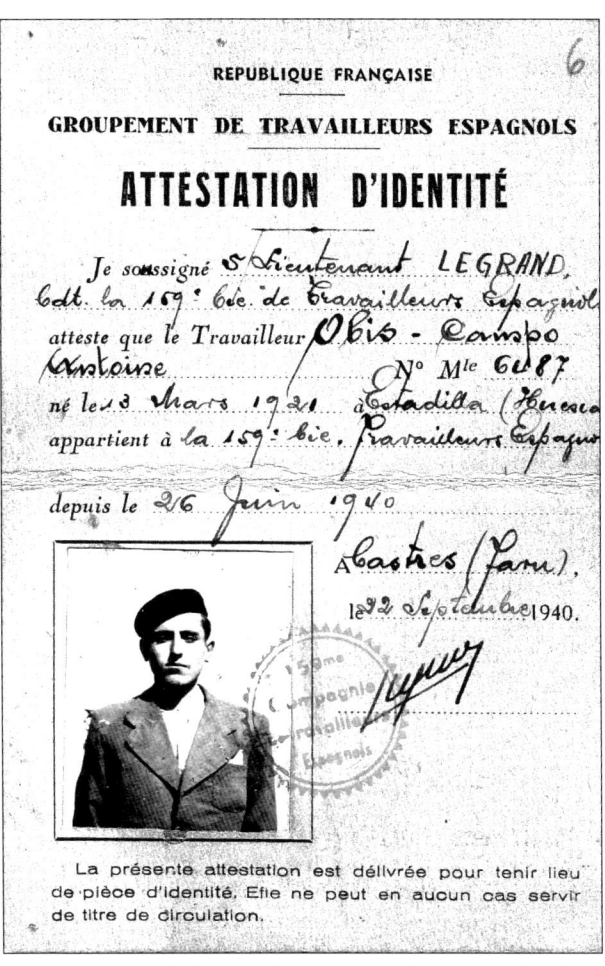

The *Attestation d'Identité* (Identity Card) of Antonio Obis who was a member of *159ᵉ Compagnie de Travailleurs Espagnols*. (Antonio Obis archive)

---

39 The *Organisation Todt* was a civil and military engineering organisation named after its founder Fritz Todt who was an engineer and senior member of the Nazi Party. *Handbook of the Organisation Todt*, MIRS, London, dated March 1945, Ike Skelton Combined Arms Research Library Digital Library, <https://cgsc.contentdm.oclc.org/digital/collection/p4013coll8/id/1457>. Accessed 21 November 2022.

Normandy in June 1944 and the subsequent operations in the Low Countries and Germany, many Spaniards were mixed in with German POWs and consequently 226 of them ended up in Hall o'the Hill Camp, near Chorley in Lancashire, where most remained until their final release in 1946.[40]

Up until the capitulation of France in the summer of 1940 the chances of being forcibly returned to Spain were not high. But when Franco and Pétain met at Montpellier on 13 February 1941, a list of 800 Spanish Republican 'Delinquents and Political leaders' was prepared by the Spanish Ambassador in Paris. The German Gestapo and the Vichy Government arrested many of the people on this list and they were delivered to Franco's Nationalists or tried in French courts. One of these, Luís Companys, who was President of the Catalan Republican Government, was handed over to Franco and executed. Other Spanish Republican leaders were prohibited from leaving France. However, the mass return of Spanish exiles to feel the full force Franco's 'justice' was not initially officially permitted by Vichy.

What is certain however, is that Pétain was more cooperative with the Germans in this respect, than with his friend Franco. Despite never truly understanding how the impetus behind the deportation of Spanish prisoners was fully reached, it is known that on 25 September 1940 an order from the Gestapo addressed to the authorities of the Third Reich in occupied Europe was issued. This specified how the German authorities in occupied territories were to proceed regarding the 'red' Spanish fighters or *Rotspanienkämpfer* as they were known.[41] As they were officially stripped of their POW status they lost their protection under the Geneva Convention. On top of this, the Vichy Government delivered thousands of Spanish Republicans to camps as forced labour in German factories. Over the months following the setting up of the Vichy Regime, over 9,000 Spaniards were deported to the Reich's concentration camps, the majority to Mauthausen-Gusen in Austria, but some would end up in camps such as Dachau as well.[42] A few hundred arrived by 6 August 1940 but the first major transports of Spanish prisoners arrived in the middle of 1941.[43] It is estimated that a little over 5,000 of these deportees perished by the end of the war. Mauthausen-Gusen concentration camp sat on the top of a huge granite quarry situated near the confluence of the Elbe and Danube rivers. The Nazi concentration camps to which Spaniards were sent were very different from the French camps of 1939. The French camps were hastily thrown together while the German ones were well-planned extermination centres.

By the beginning of 1941, many of the men who were left in the Vichy zone in France joined the resistance and became members of the *maquis*, especially so in areas close to the Spanish border. Sadly, many others were essentially back to where they had started in the internment camps in the south of France or worse still were POWs, slave labour, or even in Nazi concentration camps. The war still had a long way to run and Spaniards would have an opportunity to serve in the British Army soon enough.

---

40 Richard Cleminson, 'Spanish Anti-Fascist 'prisoners of war' in Lancashire, 1944–46,' *International Journal of Iberian Studies*, volume 22, number 3, 2009, DOI: <10.1386/ ijis.22.3.163/1>.
41 Diego Gaspar Celaya, 'Premature Resisters. Spanish Contribution to the French National Defence Campaign in 1939/1940,' *Journal of Modern European History*, Volume 16, 2018, Issue 2, p.208.
42 José Playà, 'Los 9.161 Españoles Deportados a Campos Nazis: Sus Nombres y sus Historias,' *La Vanguardia*, Barcelona, 5 May 2020, <https://www.lavanguardia.com/cultura/20200505/48973724359/registro-online-espanoles-campos-concentracion-nazi.html>. Accessed 12 June 2021. Mauthausen Concentration Camp Memorial website. <https://www.mauthausen-memorial.org/en/Gusen/The-Concentration-Camp-Gusen/Prisoners/Spanish-Republicans>. Accessed 29 December 2021.
43 David Wingeate Pike, *Spaniards in the Holocaust, Mauthausen, the Horror on the Danube*, (London and New York: Routledge, 2000), pp 2–8. José María Naharro-Calderón, *Ante el Horror … Los Campos de Concentración Devant l'Horreur … les Camps de Concentration*. Archivo de la Frontera, Nota de lectura, 2015.

Chapter 2

'Brave New World'

A Very Colourful and Full-Blooded Addition – The Number 1 Spanish Company

> Throughout their service with the British Army, they wore the Corps badge with pride, and their loyalty is evidenced by the Spanish standard, embroidered with the words '1940 until Victory'.[1]

A fascinating and little-known addition to the British Army came in the summer of 1940, with the formation of No.1 Spanish Company of the Auxiliary Military Pioneer Corps (AMPC). The company would be the only unit made up entirely of Spaniards to serve in the British Army for a significant part of the war. Most of the Spaniards in this company came from the French *Légion Étrangère* who had fought in Norway, those who were in France in April to June 1940 plus some who had escaped Spain via Gibraltar and other routes. Members would serve with distinction with over 100 carrying out training with the Special Operations Executive (SOE), and some being involved in SOE type operations towards the end of hostilities. Over the course of the war, the company spent most of its time on the British mainland before deploying to Normandy in 1944 and ending the war in the Ardennes, before returning to England and being disbanded in early 1946. Members of the company would undergo many trials and tribulations: escaping from France, fighting in Norway, leaving the *Légion Étrangère*, the Blitz, and training for the SOE. The company also played its part in operations after D-Day but it would also be betrayed by one of its own. Many of the Spaniards in it would settle down in the United Kingdom after demobilisation in 1946, but it would be in France that this Anglo-Spanish relationship would begin, and last until the end of the war. To understand the origins of No.1 Spanish Company we must turn to the stories of individuals in the *13ᵉ Demi-Brigade de Montagne de la Légion Étrangère* (*13ᵉ DBMLE*) and No.185 Spanish Labour Company which supported the BEF in France in 1940.

No. 185 Spanish Labour Company

Antonio Grande and Jesús Velasco were amongst those original members of No.185 Spanish Labour Company in France and would join No.1 Spanish Company after signing up for the AMPC at Westward Ho! on 24 July 1940. It is through Grande's account *Number One Spanish*

---

[1] W. A. Green, 'The Early Days,' in Major E. H. Rhodes-Wood, *A War History of The Royal Pioneer Corps 1939–1945* (Aldershot: Gale & Polden Ltd, 1960), p.76. Converted electronically by Norman and Paul Brown, www.royalpioneercorps.co.uk

Company. Memorias de Antonio Grande[2] and Jesús Velasco's personal memoirs, along with the interviews carried out by Daniel Arasa in the 1980s that we know such a large amount about the establishment of No.185 Spanish Labour Company and life in it. However before looking at either of their accounts, we need to understand some of the background of the requirement for manpower for the BEF and the establishment of the various 'Alien' Labour Companies that were to support it.

According to *A War History of The Royal Pioneer Corps 1939–1945*, General Headquarters (GHQ) in France had, by the end of 1939, realised that labour requirements for the BEF would be 220,000 men.[3] Given this huge requirement, it was clear that the British would have to turn to foreign sources of labour. Some work had already been done on this with overseas territories in Malta and Cyprus but it had proven difficult to raise the requisite amounts of men. Three sources were therefore looked at during a meeting on 12 December 1939: (i) *Prestataires*,[4] (ii) Italians, who were not *prestataires*, and (iii) men of the Spanish International Brigade. As these *prestataires* had no officers or NCOs it would be necessary to have some staff supervising them. The men taken on strength would be organised into formed bodies and treated as soldiers in regards to pay, clothing, et cetera. The men of the Spanish International Brigade, however, were being treated as prisoners of war and required guarding. The British Military authorities ended up deciding to make use of all three groups and soon after No. 185 Spanish Labour Company was functioning under the command of the then Captain R.D. Smith MC (in fact according to French Records this was 21 January 1940).[5] By 27 December 1939 the War Office had approved the use of *prestataires* and Italians.

13802597 Antonio Grande's story was typical of the Spaniards who ended up in the British Army. An athletic man who would later become a Physical Training Instructor in the British Army, Antonio was born in 1917 in the province of Albacete and had been brought up in the small town of Minaya which sits between the city of Albacete to its southeast and Madrid to the northwest. He came from a humble background and his father died young leaving his mother to support a young family. Like many, he had been excited by the arrival of the Republic in Spain in 1931 and, in common with others of his age, when the Spanish Civil War broke out, he enlisted in the Republican Army. It would not be long before he was fighting at the Madrid front around Buitrago protecting the Lozoya River, which supplied the capital. By the end of the war, Grande had risen to the rank of lieutenant but had to surrender with the rest of his unit when the capital itself surrendered on 29 March 1939. After this, he was moved to a POW camp in Valladolid in north-central Spain and then to another camp in Extremadura close to the Portuguese border where, with other prisoners, he stripped barbed wire and filled in trenches. He was moved again six months later, this time to the Pyrenees to be part of a labour force to build a new barracks. From his new camp, he could see France and the coastal town of St Jean de Luz. By the middle of January 1940, Antonio and another prisoner had decided to make an escape. Crossing the border on 14 January they were held at Ainoha, south-west of St Jean de Luz and next to the Spanish border, then ended up in Bayonne from where they were transferred to the camp at Gurs. Grande takes up the story:

---

2   Antonio Grande Catalán, *Number One Spanish Company. Memorias de Antonio Grande* (Alicante, Editorial Club Universitario, 2002).
3   W.A. Green, 'The Early Days,' in Major E.H. Rhodes-Wood, *A War History of The Royal Pioneer Corps 1939–1945* (Aldershot: Gale & Polden Ltd, 1960), p.20.
4   See above for an explanation of *Prestataires*.
5   Luís Garrido Orozco,' La Odisea de los Aviadores de la 185 Compañía de Trabajadores Extranjeros (I), Icaro,' *Boletín Informativo de La Asociación de Aviadores de la República*, Nueva época, nº 125, abril 2018, (Madrid: Publicación cuatrimestral, 2018).

> A couple of weeks after our arrival about ten in the morning ... we saw some outriders arrive escorting some Humber cars ... out popped some colonels who went to the camp offices. About two or three hours later and the loudspeakers announced that Spanish volunteers between the ages of 20 or 30 and who were willing to work for the British Armed Forces in France should go to the camp office.[6]

Other members of No.185 Spanish Labour Company talk about being 'recruited by the British' and that they were well treated. Members of the company – Emilio Borrás Castell, Antonio Llorens White and Joaquín Cardenal Atence – all mention being:

> ... very happy with the English, that treated us a lot better than the French. We ate well, slept in bunk beds, the toilets were good, and we even got cigarettes with our pay.[7]

The 250 members of the company were moved to Brittany by train and housed initially in railway wagons. In the account of Miguel de Miguel Montañés, they were eventually moved to a twelfth century Benedictine monastery called Blanche Couronne between Saveney and La Chapelle Launey near Saint Nazaire on the southern Brittany coast west from Nantes.[8] Saint Nazaire had been famous for shipbuilding and in 1942 would be synonymous with Operation CHARIOT, the commando raid that was carried out at a heavy cost. This attack would ultimately put out of action the only dry dock capable of servicing the German pocket battleship *Tirpitz*. Sadly, many exiled Republican Spaniards would be employed as slave labour to rebuild the docks after the attack.

Upon No.185 Spanish Company's arrival, its members were provided with work clothes, given armbands marked 'BEF Allies', to ensure they were not stopped by the French or military authorities, and issued with military identification. They soon started to get into a routine and were paid every Thursday. This meant that they were consequently given some free time, something which most of them had not had for over a year. The company was divided into 10 groups of 25 and worked in warehouses and railway sidings that were linked to the newly constructed storage areas. Also located in the area at the time were No.4 Railway Labour Company (later No.231 Labour Company) and No.31 Labour Company. The Spaniards' company was eventually to come under No.4 Group although it was not fully in the British chain of command since the company was 'on loan' from the French Army.

The company commander, Captain R.D. Smith MC, was greatly respected by the Spaniards who saw him as a father figure and able to get the best out of them. The day-to-day running of the company was carried out by an ex-Spanish Republican Air Force lieutenant, Joaquín Ferrándiz Boj, who had been a Polikarpov pilot during the Spanish Civil War. Despite the difficulties of language, the Spaniards worked hard with their British counterparts, and were often to be found singing and happily carrying out the tasks in hand. As a consequence, many friendships were made. One of these was between Jesús Velasco and Robert Parkins, who was serving in one of the nearby infantry battalions. Despite not knowing each other's language, they did their best to communicate in pidgin French! The two would remain lifelong friends.

From the end of February 1940 some Spanish families were allowed to move to the area and were lodged in different local towns and villages such as Le Bourg, La Guyonnière, l'Hôtel Fourré, le Goulet and Le Landron (some 19 wives and 22 young children). These families had been separated

---

6 Antonio Grande Catalán, *Number One Spanish Company. Memorias de Antonio Grande* (Alicante: Imprenta Gamma, 2002), p.51.
7 Daniel Arasa, *Los Españoles de Churchill* (Barcelona: Editorial Armonía Poética, 1991), p.15.
8 Luís Garrido Orozco, *Des Républicains Espagnols á La Chapelle-Launay. Janvier–Juillet 1940.* <http://enenvor.fr/eeo_actu/wwii/des_republicains_espagnols_a_la_chapelle_launay_janvier_juillet_1940.html>.

A group photo of part of No.185 Spanish Labour Company taken in early 1940 at La Chapelle-Launay or at Savenay, near St Nazaire. Captain R.D. Smith MC is in uniform in the centre of the front row. (Jesús Gallindo collection)

Three members of No.185 Spanish Company standing outside their initial accommodation. Two of the four men are known. First on the right is Antonio Nieto Sandoval Díaz, who had been a fighter pilot in the Republican Air Force, and second from the left is Joaquín Ferrándiz Boj. (Antoine Nieto Sandoval)

on their arrival in France in early 1939. Spaniards and British would spend time together in the evenings socialising and drinking and eating in local cafes. This would sadly all come to an end in June with the arrival of the Germans in the area.

According to Antonio Grande and to the testimony of Miguel de Miguel Montañés, shortly before 18 June orders came through from GHQ that they were to destroy the stores inside the warehouses they had been working in and pour acid on the uniforms and other stores in them so they would not fall into the Germans' hands.[9] With tears in his eyes, Captain Smith told his men that the evacuation of all British troops in the area would take place immediately and that everyone else would have to fend for themselves. The men of the company were shocked, saddened and now began thinking about how they could survive yet another disaster having only been out of Gurs for some six months. Jesús Velasco's testimony goes on to say that many felt they had also been abandoned by their officers.[10] Both Velasco and Grande were keen to get to England by ship and it was not long before over 20 others joined them. Their first issue was how to get hold of all relevant uniforms and equipment to blend in. Given the nod by Captain Smith before his departure, they returned to the warehouses and recovered some uniforms. They were then approached by Joaquín Ferrándiz Boj who tried to persuade them to hand themselves over to the Germans when they arrived. Despite this, the group still decided to set off and did so in a body moving towards St Nazaire town. En route they were able to jump onto a truck but sadly were turned back when an officer found out they were not British. By now it was getting dark, and they gathered in a small wood outside of town which they had approached on foot. From there they managed

---

9 Antonio Grande Catalán, *Number One Spanish Company. Memorias de Antonio Grande* (Alicante: Imprenta Gamma, 2002), pp.56–60.
10 Jesús Velasco Zapico, *Una Vida Española, a Personal Family Memoir, 1915–1995*. Unpublished memoir. Author's collection and copyright.

Jesús Velasco and 'Bob' Parkins pose for a photo in Saveney. (Jesús Velasco collection)

to infiltrate themselves into St Nazaire despite a brush with some *gendarmes*. There was incessant bombing of the centre and port area as the skies were lit up with searchlights and they decided to spend the night in a barn near the harbour.

The next morning there were only 13 of the group who still wanted to go – the others had disappeared in the night. The group was up early, got into their uniforms and noticed units of men marching down to the port. Forming up into a squad they proceeded down to the harbour where thousands of people were trying to embark, and the ships were taking on military personnel first. When they got to the quayside there were a lot of Poles waiting to board and who were being transferred to the larger ships by launch. 13802594 Emilio Borrás Castell, who would later be in the No.1 Spanish Coy, told Daniel Arasa:

> It was around the 18 of June. We had managed to put on our British uniforms and had gone to St Nazaire. When we arrived at the port, we could desperately see that close to the mouth of the harbour were the last boats in a convoy that had just set sail. We shouted out and waved our arms and, surprisingly, one of the ships stopped to wait for us. We were picked up by a launch and we climbed up the rope ladder up to deck. It was the Polish ship 'Lechistan'.[11]

This was very much the case and can be backed up by Polish accounts.[12] The 13 Spaniards decided that they would fight to stay on board whatever happened. The atmosphere amongst them was tense as they boarded, and one of the group even burst out crying, saying that it was a suicide mission. They were approached by a Polish officer who spoke to them in English and was surprised that they were Spaniards. Nevertheless, he soon realised that they were in fact ex-Spanish Civil War veterans, and he could see why they were there, having been in Spain during the Spanish Civil War himself as a journalist, and said he would support them. They were called to see the ship's captain who was given a handwritten list and he then radioed to the mainland and was able to get confirmation that they were members of No.185 Spanish Company. The captain said that he would not do any more until they set sail. Bombs were by now falling in the harbour area at quite a rate.[13]

The handwritten list of 13 names handed to the captain of the Polish ship leaving St Nazaire. The list is: 1. Jesús Velasco Zapico, 2. Pedro Belenguer Ferrandez, 3. Antonio Grande Catalán, 4. Emilio Borrás Castell, 5. Miguel Lozano Aro, 6. Francisco Conesa Barreda, 7. Pedro Herreras Catalán, 8. Teodoro Fernández Ario, 9. Amancio García Pérez, 10. Joaquín Cardenal Atance, 11. Manuel Solís Fernández, 12. Valeriano Beclés Barreda, 13. Emilio López Gómez. (Jesús Velasco collection)

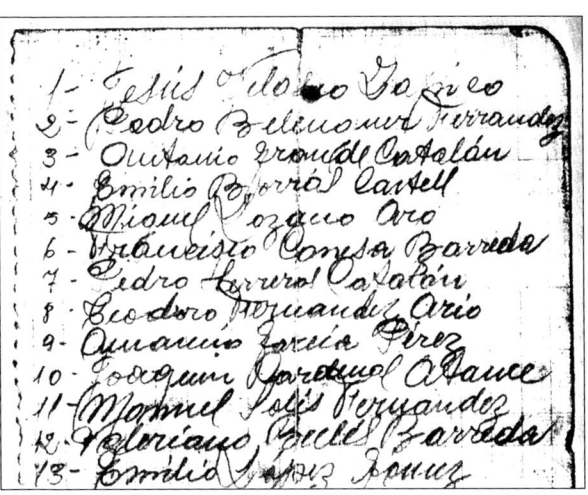

---

11 Daniel Arasa, *Los Españoles de Churchill* (Barcelona: Editorial Armonía Poética, 1991), p.16.
12 Ksawery Pruszyński, *Polish Invasion* (Edinburgh: Birlinn Publishers, 2010), pp.3–4. 'Some greatcoats and caps did double duty. Mixed with Poles, some Spaniards jumped into the British launch. The forage caps with Polish eagles looked odd on the heads of olive-skinned Castillians, but there was no time for racial study.'
13 Jesús Velasco Zapico, *Una Vida Española, a Personal Family Memoir, 1915–1995*. Unpublished memoir. Author's collection and copyright.

The crossing seemed to take forever, but the Spaniards were treated well by their Polish comrades who welcomed them as they ate and rested during the journey. By 20 June, they had arrived in Plymouth and were anchored up in the bay and were soon met by local police at the quayside who accompanied them to Citadel Barracks in the City, home of a Royal Artillery Regiment, where they were warmly welcomed. Over the next month, members of the Royal Artillery Regiment often did collections for their 'Spanish friends' and Grande soon volunteered the group to help out in the kitchen – much to their surprise. By the end of July, the Artillery Regiment had been posted overseas and the Spaniards were sent to Westward Ho! and signed up for the AMPC.

But what of the remaining Spaniards in No.185 Spanish Labour Company? Sadly, the majority ended up in labour companies or worse. Antonio Llorens White, who had also been a Republican pilot, tried to leave Blanche Couronne in a lorry:

> Our lorry travelling turned north so we could embark closer to England, but the roads were congested by French forces in utter disorder harassed by the German Air Force as well as by abandoned or destroyed machinery. I decided to escape alone and, on my journey, came across an abandoned vehicle with plenty of fuel in the tank. I hotwired it and set off back to the monastery we had just left and stayed there. The Germans arrived a few days later.[14]

Not knowing where to go, most of the Spaniards in the company stayed put. Some were hidden by locals, but before long the French authorities were forced to gather the Spaniards together in the main square in La Chapelle-Launay and the majority were then imprisoned in a camp in La Berthelais, not far away from La Chapelle-Launay. Within a few weeks a large number of these men were sent back to Spain, arriving in Irún, just across into Spain, on 10 July. They were then imprisoned in the renowned concentration camp in Miranda de Ebro, between Vitoria and Burgos. This camp had been set up in 1937 during the Civil War and was not eventually closed until 1947. On 2 August, these men were transferred to the Miguel de Unamuno camp in Madrid, and from here many were sent to penal colonies in Morocco. Others would be tried and condemned to lengthy terms of imprisonment. Joaquín Ferrándiz Boj was sentenced to 12 years detention but was released in January 1942. Antonio Llorens White suffered a similar fate.

Meanwhile, in the north of France, several *CTEs* were supporting the Allied effort in its defence. By May 1940 a total of eight *CTEs* were part of the *Secteur Fortifié de Flandres* which included the Dunkirk area.[15] This was a total of some 2,000 men of whom approximately 1,400 were Spaniards. Prior to the evacuation of Dunkirk, some Spanish members of the *CTEs* further inland were able to put up stiff resistance as they took up arms (according to the French regulations, they were not supposed to be armed).

There was one occasion when the Spaniards did fight under their own Republican flag. Manuel López, a former teacher from Extremadura, was part of a *CTE* digging fortifications near a small chateau near Tourcoing, Lille which came under constant German artillery fire. Abandoned by their French officers, some 100 Spaniards decided to take up arms. The German infantry opened fire on the besieged men. The Spaniards seized four machine guns and distributed rifles among themselves. With these weapons and a moderate supply of ammunition they offered a stubborn resistance. One of the men suddenly disrobed and unwrapped a large Spanish Republican flag from around his body. The flag was quickly secured to a pole and hung from a balcony. By nightfall,

---

14 Daniel Arasa, *Los Españoles de Churchill* (Barcelona: Editorial Armonía Poética, 1991), p.17.
15 Olivier Vermesch, *Les Espagnols de l'Opération Dynamo : Les Compagnies de Travailleurs Étrangers Dunkerque, mai-juin 1940*, 2020, p.11. These *CTEs* were – 9, 15, 59, 116,117, 118 and 253 and 254. Apart from 59, 253 and 254 all the *CTEs* were made up of Spaniards.

'BRAVE NEW WORLD' 65

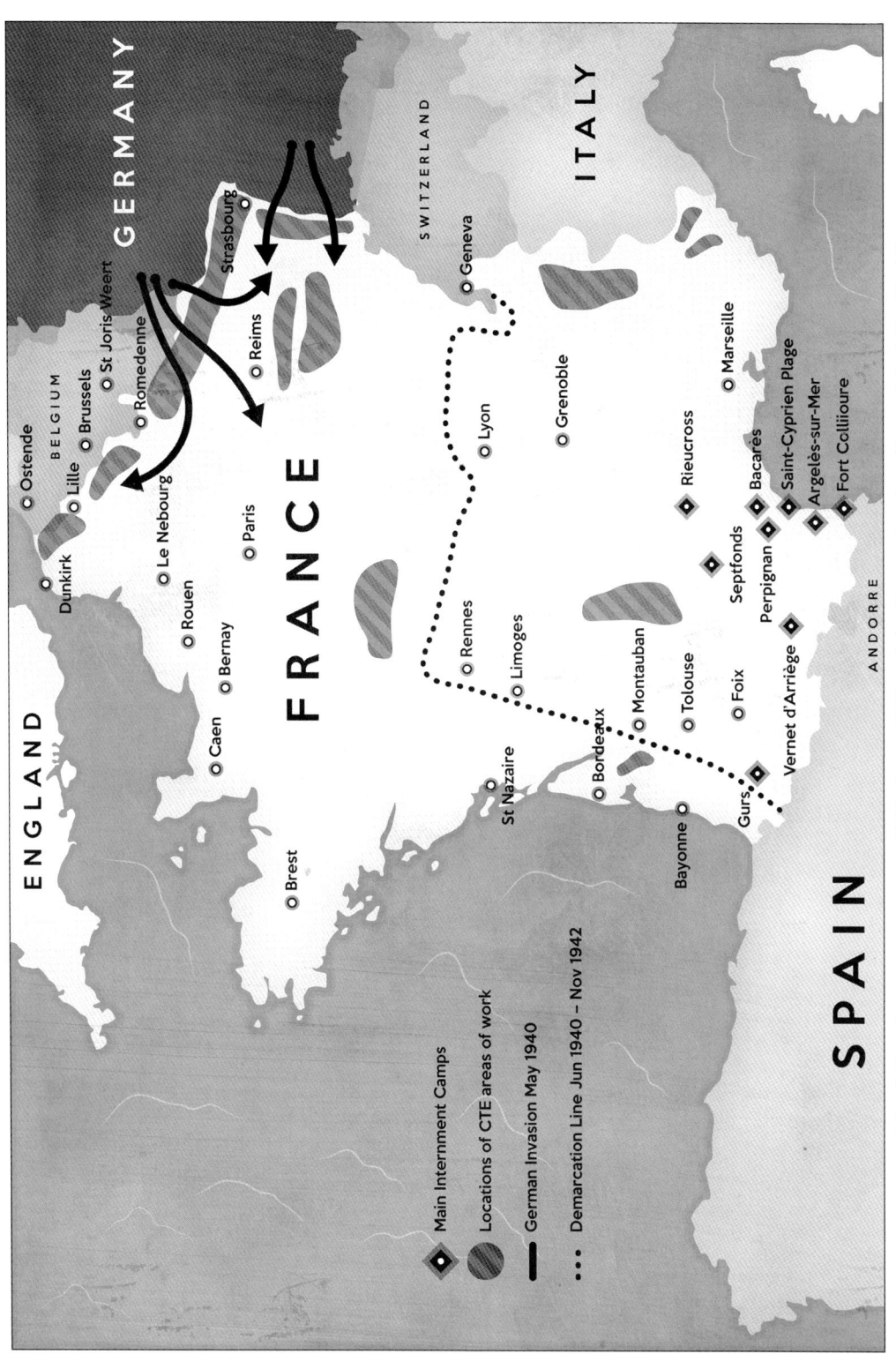

Map 4 French internment camps, *CTEs*, France 1940 and the German invasion. (Artwork by Mike Heald)

three of the machine guns had jammed and ammunition was in short supply and a mere 30 men remained able to resist. The young captain who had been elected commander had been a former medical student in Madrid and was now wounded in both his arm and his thigh. Before the Spaniards could hold a council, the Germans made a desperate assault and entered the building and the Spaniards were forced to surrender. The German officer leading the assault inquired as to the nature of the flag of these die-hard defenders, and he could barely believe the answer he was given. A short time later the Spaniards were transported to a prisoner of war camp near Yser. The following night five of them, including Manuel López, managed to escape. Probably the strangest commentary of this episode came at the end of May 1940, when the main Nationalist radio station in Barcelona broadcast a German bulletin which recounted the day-long resistance of a unit that had held up the advance on Dunkirk, and identified the fighters as Spanish refugees.[16]

Back in Dunkirk, by 4 June the *CTE*s of the *Secteur Fortifié de Flandres* had surrendered to the Germans as part of the French force that had defended the series of positions around the port and beach. Many Spaniards had tried to get to the beach to get on boats but were unable to get on board. But a few hundred were fortunate and were able to get away by a number of means, including small rowing boats. One of these was José Oliveira Avidaño who was in *117ᵉ CTE* and would later write about his time in France:

> ... we searched for a lifeboat and in it we hid water bottles, oars and all that we thought necessary with the idea of getting it on the water when the tide was up as the beach was busy and the boats were far from the shore. The 6 or 7 of June, I cannot remember the exact date. From early on in the day the bombing got worse on ships and that morning merchant and navy ships were sunk. Amongst these tragic events we saw our chance to get out to sea. But fate was against us as the tide was low and our boat was quite far from shore. With the use of some tree trunks we managed to roll our boat to salvation ... but we had no compass to navigate with ... Two others joined us from the company ...[17]

Avidaño, who in 1939 had been held in St Cyprien internment camp on the Mediterranean coast and near the Spanish border, would reach the English coast and arrive at Margate a few days later. In June 1940, most of these few hundred Spaniards who were able to escape the area around Dunkirk would be sent back to France a few weeks afterwards as the French continued their fight against the Germans until an Armistice was signed on 22 June. Along with many others, Avidaño was taken to Pentonville prison and eventually returned to France via Portsmouth. Once in France, he was injured and evacuated by ship to Plymouth before being sent from Bristol, with other French troops, to Casablanca where he was interned and forced to work on the construction of the notorious Trans-Saharan railway.

Arthur Joscelyne who was one of the many hundreds of Britons who crossed the English Channel as part of Operation DYNAMO (the evacuation of Dunkirk) would also recall, when interviewed in 1986 by the Imperial War Museum, that during his return to the English coast in the middle of the Channel:

> ... there was a barge's dinghy with about a dozen dark skinned fellas you know who couldn't speak hardly English at all! They were part of the Spanish Labour Corps and they had tacked onto this boat with all these English soldiers on board and they were doing all the work and

---

16 Louis Stein, *Beyond Death and Exile. The Spanish Republicans in France, 1939–1955* (London: Harvard University Press, 1979), pp.120–121.
17 José Oliveira Avedaño, 'Españoles en la Segunda Guerra Mundial,' *Revista Historia y Vida,* no.106, pp. 22-25.

rowing like mad, pulling as hard as they could go … and these soldiers were all sitting back letting them pull it! Another little incident that stuck in my mind, one of these Spaniards had got a small suitcase and you know, he held on to that suitcase as though his life depended on it … and I always asked myself 'I wondered what was in that suitcase? He's got something and would not let it out of his sight'. It was obvious that there was something valuable in it![18]

The fate of many Spaniards hung in the balance after the fall of France. Several months later, when Franco and Pétain met in Montpellier in February 1941, a list of 800 Spanish Republican 'delinquents' (who were mostly Republican political leaders), was prepared by the Spanish Ambassador in Paris. The German Gestapo and Vichy Government arrested many of those on this list and they were handed over to the Nationalists or tried in French courts. Luís Companys, President of the Catalan Republic was among those handed over to Franco by Pétain – and executed. Other Spanish Republican leaders were prohibited from leaving France. However, the mass returning of Spanish exiles to Franco's justice was not permitted by the Vichy Government. Instead, it delivered thousands of Spanish Republicans to German concentration camps and as forced labour in German factories. At the conclusion of the Armistice most of the men and women together with the survivors of the battles in the north of France returned to the same camps from which they had volunteered only a few months before.

As has been already mentioned, the establishment of *Groupes de Travailleurs Espagnols* (*GTE*s) by the Vichy Regime meant that many Spaniards were still held or their movement severely restricted. The *GTE*s were much larger, discipline was harsher and many commanders were openly collaborationist. At this stage, the choice given to Spanish Republicans was very narrow: they could enlist in the *CTE*s or for other German work voluntarily or be assigned arbitrarily. German commissions visited the camps and explained that volunteers would receive far better treatment than those who had fought in the service of France. This, of course, was not true – those who ended up in the *Organisation Todt* found themselves living virtually in conditions of slavery and being forced to assist the Germans. At Bordeaux, for example, over 2,000 of the 6,500 foreigners who built the German submarine base were Spaniards.[19]

Many were able to escape into the shadows and become part of the resistance against the Nazi regime. The *maquis* were originally made up of those Frenchman and Spaniards escaping work in Germany or on the Atlantic wall. Soon thousands of people sought to leave France, including Frenchman seeking to join de Gaulle, foreign refugees and downed or escaped Allied airmen soldiers. Here began the development of an intricate network of escape routes that extended from Belgium to Morocco or Portugal. French and Spaniards worked closely in the operation of many of the networks. It seems entirely likely that some of the Belgium to Portugal networks were in operation in the autumn of 1940. Certainly, the Vichy French authorities were aware of this activity from the outset and made strenuous efforts to close it down.

Général de Gaulle was fond of asking the *maquis* how long they had been in the resistance. He often expected a standard response such as 'Since the 18th of June 1940, *mon Général*.' When he visited Limoges in September 1944 after it was liberated, the *Général* asked the question of a *colonel* of the *Francs Tireurs et Partisans* (*FTP*). He was surprised by the reply 'With all respect, *mon Général*, before you, I fought the Germans during the war in Spain.'[20]

---

18 Imperial War Museum interview with Arthur William Joscelyne, recorded 23 April 1987, IWM 9768.
19 Bassins des Lumieres, <https://www.bassins-lumieres.com/en/discover/place-of-history#3/1>. Accessed 15 August 2023.
20 Pierre Bertaux, *Libération de Toulouse et de sa Région* (Paris: Hachette, 1973), p.90.

Narvik and the *13ᵉ DBMLE / DBLE*

As well as coming from No.185 Spanish Labour Company, many of the members of No.1 Spanish Company had served in the *13ᵉ Demi-Brigade de Montagne de la Légion Étrangère* (*13ᵉ DBMLE*), which was later renamed the *13ᵉ Demi-Brigade de la Légion Étrangère* (*13ᵉ DBLE*). This *demi-brigade* was based in northern Africa and consisted of two parts: a battalion in Fez, Morocco (recruited from the *Légion Étrangère* training depot (*Dépôt Commun des Régiments Étrangères*) and the *1ᵉ Regiment Étranger d'Infanterie* (*REI*) and the other in Sidi Bel Abbès in Algeria (made up of personnel from the *2ᵉ*, *3ᵉ* and *4ᵉ REI*). The *Demi-Brigade* was formed in early 1940, with a total strength of 2,322 men.[21] A large percentage of the *Légionnaires* were Spanish.

José García Flores (on the right) joined the *Legion Étrangère* in 1939 and served in Sidi Bel Abbès before going to Norway. (José García Flores collection)

At the end of the war, 13809776 Agustín Roa Ventura, who later served in 361 (Alien) Company of the Pioneer Corps in North Africa and the United Kingdom shared a house with Manuel Espallargas. They became good friends, and he was later able to give a full account of what the Spaniards did when they fought in the *Légion* in Scandinavia through Manuel's testimony to him. Such accounts help us to fully understand the many frictions that took place during 1940. Agustín would later write extensively about these actions and would recount the story of these men on many occasions.[22]

---

21 Diego Gaspar Celaya, *La Guerra Continua. Voluntarios Españoles al Servicio de la Francia Libre (1940-1945)* (Madrid: Marcial Pons Historia, 2015), p.219. Over the years several figures have been quoted on the subject of how many Spaniards were in the *13ᵉ DBLE*. According to *Général* Béthouart, 500 Spaniards disembarked in Bjervik, but other accounts have quoted up to 1,200 Spaniards in Norway, although most say around 600 Spaniards.
22 Agustín Roa Ventura, *Los Años de mi Vida, Personal Papers, 1942–1950, Contribución Histórica Sobre el Proceso de los Españoles Fuera y Dentro de España,* Libro IV, pp.90–97. Agustín Roa Ventura, 'La Batalla de Narvik,' *Historia y Vida,* No.119, pp.120-125.

A group of Spanish *Légionnaires* move their pack animals through the North African desert. (Augusto Pérez Miranda collection)

Spaniards pose for the camera while taking a rest during their training to become full members of the *Legion Étrangère*. (José García Flores collection)

In mid-February 1940 the first and second battalions of the *13ᵉ DBMLE* were moved by ship from Orán to Marseille and then moved to Larzac to receive further training. In April, the *Demi-Brigade* moved to the Belley region on the Swiss border to be trained in mountain warfare, and over the course of several weeks they carried out training exercises and mountain warfare training. The initial plan of the French was to support Finland in its fight against Russia, which had invaded in November 1939; but the end of Russo-Finnish hostilities in March 1940 caused the cancellation of these preparations by Britain and France. However, the operation was relaunched on 9 April and the target this time was Norway. The Spaniards (in what was now called *13ᵉ DBMLE*) were eager to fight. On the same day, Germany had invaded Denmark and Norway. Denmark put up little resistance (it surrendered six hours after the Germans crossed the border), but Norway fought back, and the objective of the Franco-British troops was to aid Norwegian resistance. Extra troops were now added to the *13ᵉ DBMLE* and they were soon readying themselves. On 15 April the troops arrived at Brest and embarked eight days later on the *Ville d'Argel*, bound for Norway.[23]

En route the *Ville d'Argel* collided with another ship and they were landed in England, crossed the country by train to Edinburgh, where the troops embarked for their final destination. The French expeditionary forces landed on the Haafjelder Peninsula after a 12-day crossing on 6 May 1940 and swiftly successfully attacked the Germans at Bjervik, taking the town on 13 May, before moving on to Narvik. One of the scouts of the *13ᵉ DBMLE* was *Légionnaire* Manuel Espallargas, who was born on 26 June 1909 in Alcorisa, Aragón, and who had been told shortly before crossing into France in 1939 that his wife had been shot in Spain by the Franco Regime. Manuel enlisted in the *Légion* in Tarbes and signed up for five years being integrated into the *1ᵉ REI*.[24] He would later become 13802514 Sergeant Manuel Espallargas of No.1 Spanish Coy, receive a Certificate for Good Service in the King's Birthday Honours and carry out SOE training.[25] It is said that it was in Norway that the performance of the Spanish *Légionnaires* in the campaign caused French officers to change their opinion of them. These were men who had fought on the Madrid and Aragón fronts and were used to the intensity of the conflict ahead. One witness to these actions was *Capitaine* Pierre-Olivier Lapie, who was decorated with the *Croix de Guerre* for his bravery in Norway:

> … the Spaniards saw on those tortuous tracks something similar to their own lands. They jumped from one side to the other like tigers and never seemed to tire out. If there were officers who were apprehensive about having these Spanish Republicans in the *Légion*, believing they were communists, they were now proud and happy with their fighting spirit. An example was the case of a young Spaniard who attacked and captured a German machine gun position in Elvegaard.[26]

This young man was the small, determined and physically tough, Manuel Espallargas who led a small team up the mountain fighting for 10 hours to take the position from the Germans. As

---

23 André-Paul Comor, *L'épopée de la 13e Demi-Brigade de Légion Etrangère, 1940–1945*, (Paris:Nouvelles Editions Latines, 1988), pp.40–45.
24 Victor Asensio Pérez, *Un Alcorisano en la II Guerra Mundial*, 2021 (manuscript in the Author's collection). Victor is the grandson of Manuel Espallargas and has written and self-published three short articles on his grandfather.
25 No.1 Spanish Company War Diary entry for 11 Jun 1943 reads: Sergeant M Espallargas, awarded Certificate for Good Service in the King's Birthday Honours. Agustín Roa Ventura, *Los años de mi vida, Personal Papers, 1942–1950*, pp.93–94.
26 Agustín Roa Ventura, *Los años de mi vida, Personal Papers, 1942–1950*, p.93.

The Franksa Kirkegarr cemetery where many Spaniards who died in the fighting in Norway are buried (Agustín Roa Ventura collection)

they continued to advance to higher peaks, they were attacked from the air and eventually met up with Norwegian partisans. Over the course of these days, many Spaniards lost their lives and were buried in the Franksa Kirkegarr cemetery.

Charles Favrel who served with the Spaniards in Norway also remarked:

> For them, the legion had not been a choice, but a requirement accepted with a heavy heart, a bad moment to get over by making common cause with their companions. Resolved to remain men, they refused therefore to allow themselves to be poured into the mould of unconditional obedience. In addition to this, their combat experience caused them to reject the traditional conceptions of the Prussian system implanted at Sidi Bel Abbès for a century. Tenacious and courageous, reluctant to accept sacrificial missions, their idea of war was to kill and not to be killed stupidly! They were not traditional legion timber, the docile blind executors of the order given by the superior.
>
> The officers' prejudice changed when they began to appreciate the soldier equalities of the men, and later Spaniards were chosen for the hardest tasks. These young Spanish volunteers were famous for their skill as machine gunners and for their marching ability. They were not, as a rule, good shots with light arms lacking the phlegm that is essential. They loved the feel of steel in their hands – their great pocket-knives and the four-edged bayonets of the French army.[27]

---

27 Douglas Porch, *The French Foreign Legion. A Complete History of the Legendary Fighting Force* (New York: Skyhorse Publishing, 2010), p.450.

However, worrying news from France prompted the expeditionary corps to withdraw from Norway. The Spanish *Légionnaires* were landed at Brest to head for Rennes to reinforce other French troops but arrived too late. It was here that they would meet up with French officers who had not fought in Norway and still held very prejudiced views on the Spaniards. They were also surprised by the French officers' unwillingness to fight, and the Spaniards soon held a 'soldiers' commission' (a meeting of the NCOs and men without officers present) deciding that they were willing to fight till the death. Three days later they departed by train for Brest and arrived at the port witnessing similar scenes to what they had seen and experienced at the end of the Civil War over a year before. They left on a French ship passing the burning wrecks of ships sunk in the harbour and were back in England on 20 June.

Upon their return, the *Légion Étrangère* soldiers were held at Plymouth until 27 June before being sent to billets at Trentham Park, near Stoke-on-Trent. Prior to this, 29 Spaniards had been imprisoned for failing to muster.[28] Pretty much all of their new officers had joined them from France and tensions were high. During their week on board ship in Plymouth a great deal of anguish went through the Spaniard's minds as their loyalty was pulled two ways. Should they stay in France and end up being part of Vichy France, knowing that they would probably be sent back to Spain, or should they side with the emerging Free French under de Gaulle or should they follow their own path in some way? An initial order to send the *Demi-Brigade* to North Africa was cancelled.

On 29 June, the *13ᵉ DBMLE* was visited by de Gaulle in an appeal to it to join the Free French forces.[29] Some joined de Gaulle, but most of the *Demi-Brigade* decided to stay loyal to the newly forming Vichy Government. During his visit, some 300 Spaniards carried out a silent sit-down protest for which they were imprisoned in Stafford Prison.[30] The tall and distinctive 13802444 Francisco Balagué, who would later be promoted to sergeant in No.1 Spanish Company and be trained by the SOE, later told Daniel Arasa when interviewed by him:

> General de Gaulle came to visit us. When the Spaniards found out … we passed around instructions to show our disdain for the French: we would throw down our weapons and sit down when the order was given to present arms. That is what we did. De Gaulle and the French and British officers who accompanied him stopped in their tracks, surprised by our attitude. The Military Police took us by lorry to Stafford Prison … a British officer arrived there and spoke perfect Spanish and we told him we were willing to join the British Army but not continue in the French Army.[31]

Later in July, Colonel Wedgwood (MP for Newcastle-under-Lyme) would talk about the plight of the Spaniards:

> … They are interned in great numbers to-day in Stafford Gaol, and I suppose in other prisons. They were members of the French Foreign Legion. They fought at Narvik; they came back from Narvik and were sent to Brest; and they came back from Brest to England. At Narvik and Brest they saw the relations that exist between the British soldiers and British officers.

---

28 André-Paul Comor, *L'Épopée de la 13e Demi-Brigade de Légion Etrangère, 1940–1945* (Paris: Nouvelles Editions Latines, 1988), p.83.
29 Nicholas Atkin, *The Forgotten French: Exiles in the British Isles, 1940–44* (Manchester: Manchester University Press, 2003), p.123.
30 André-Paul Comor, *L'Épopée de la 13e Demi-Brigade de Légion Etrangère, 1940–1945* (Paris: Nouvelles Editions Latines, 1988), p.83.
31 Daniel Arasa, *Los Españoles de Churchill* (Barcelona: Editorial Armonía Poética, 1991), p.29.

They are now interned because they declined to remain under French officers who were Petainists. They are unable to fight for the cause which they love so well under British officers who would treat them as soldiers and not as criminals.[32]

The *13ᵉ DBMLE* was disbanded on 1 July 1940: 636 officers and *Légionnaires*, loyal to the Vichy Government – from an original total of 1,619[33] – took the train to Avonmouth near Bristol, from where they embarked for North Africa. The 300 Spanish *Légionnaires* who mutinied were directed by the British police to the port city but opposed their embarkation at the railway station. *A War History of The Royal Pioneer Corps 1939–1945* takes up the story:

> Arrangements had been made for their return to Spain but, since Spain was for obvious reasons the last country they wanted to go to, the men had refused to embark at Avonmouth. Their French military officers thereupon contacted the French Military Mission in London for instructions and received orders that one in every three should be shot 'pour encourager les autres'. At this stage the British authorities intervened, relieved the French officers of their command, and after an interval of indecision sent the men to No. 3 Pioneer Corps Training Centre at Westward Ho![34]

Lieutenant Gabriel Brunet de Sairign, from a French noble family, had fought in Narvik and Brittany. He decided to side with de Gaulle over the 23 to 25 June 1940 period and noted in his diary: 'Shameful armistice. What will North Africa do? Repatriation is being talked about, perhaps Morocco. Discipline impossible: the Spaniards are leaving.' On 1 July he witnessed the departure of those leaving on their way to Avonmouth: 'Emotions at the station as the colonel said goodbye. Everyone is making excuses. We all know that Morocco will not fight. Almost everyone is motivated by personal questions.'[35]

The incident at Avonmouth certainly came to public attention and is something where many of the families I have interviewed talk of the Spaniards' willingness to fight and not to leave Britain. The Spaniards knew what their fate would probably be, and they were determined to stay in Britain and fight as members of the British Army if at all possible. On the evening of Wednesday 10 July 1940 Colonel Arthur Evans (MP for Cardiff South) during a debate on refugees stated:

> The other day I had a conversation with a gentleman who had had practical experience in the Spanish War, an experience which I am happy to say he is now placing at the disposal of the authorities of this country. He had occasion, I believe, to go down to Avonmouth to settle a dispute which had taken place between a number of Spaniards comprising a company of French Foreign Legion, who wished to stay in this country and fight on the side of Great Britain, and who were being placed in a difficult position because of the attitude of their French officers. In conversations accompanied as he was by a Spanish-speaking officer from the War Office, he satisfied himself that if those Spaniards had been allowed to enlist in a British foreign legion or in an alien company of the Pioneers, and officered as they wished to be

---

32 Hansard Volume 362: Refugees, debated on Wednesday 10 July 1940. <https://hansard.parliament.uk/Commons/1940-07-10/debates/513c14f4-f07b-48c8-bf14-f863b62ffa58/Refugees?highlight=spaniards%20pioneers%20corps#contribution-cfe94ba1-8e93-499e-bf95-fa0ef7663819>.
33 Douglas Porch, *The French Foreign Legion. A Complete History of the Legendary Fighting Force* (New York: Skyhorse Publishing, 2010), p.473.
34 Major E H. Rhodes-Wood, *A War History of The Royal Pioneer Corps 1939–1945* (Aldershot: Gale & Polden Ltd, 1960), p.76.
35 Robert Gildea, *Fighters in the Shadows – A new History of French Resistance* (London: Faber & Faber, 2015), p.28.

officered, by experienced British officers who had served in France, they would be prepared to render further valuable services to our cause. In conclusion, I want to earnestly ask the Under-Secretary to persuade the War Office to look into this question again. We have in this country many units, some large and some small, composed of aliens; we have Poles, Czechs, Spaniards, Germans, and Austrians who have already enlisted as British soldiers in the British Army. I feel that the force could be organised into one single body as a foreign legion, reinforced by friendly aliens in this country, who have been subject to careful examination by MI5 and encouraged could thus be given to these people, who, although their national flag has been lowered in their own country, are prepared to come in our side and continue to fight for victory.[36]

This was a debate that would continue for some time. A vast movement of foreign nationals arriving in Britain during this period presented a dilemma to the British Government. Many of those Britons who had fought in the International Brigades in the Spanish Civil War were already on watch lists and as the fear of Fifth Columnists increased, coupled with the arrival of so many in the summer of 1940, the Government was put into a huge quandary. The No.1 Spanish Company, which would soon be established, was the only sub-unit of its kind in the British Army (i.e. made up solely of Spaniards) that served for almost the whole duration of the war. But by 1942 with a shortage of manpower for the British Army, many of the aliens that had fled to Britain and many others liberated in regions like North Africa (where well over 500 Spaniards would volunteer to join the British Army in early 1943 after Operation TORCH) were accepted as volunteers and became members of the British Army.

The majority of the Spaniards who crossed over from the *Légion Etrangère* would sign up on 17 July 1940. By the summer of 1940 these were truly battle-hardened fighters who, in some cases, had fought continuously for years. A typical example is that of 13802368 Francisco Martínez from Almería, who had fought in the *Carabineros* from 1938 during the Spanish Civil War. In March 1938 his brigade was moved to the Ebro front after fighting at Brunete in the summer of 1937. On the Ebro the brigade became part of the X Corps to defend the area of Tamarite de la Litera to Vértice Viñaza. In the Nationalist push to the coast, it suffered many losses and was eventually moved to Lérida. After Republican Spain was cut in two, it was moved to the Bellvís Division and on 25 July 1938 attempted to cross the river at Amposta but failed. When the Nationalist attack on Cataluña came, the brigade was in the 56th Division of the XII Army Corps based in the area of Serós and soon after started a withdrawal to the Pyrenees. Francisco then crossed over to France and subsequently joined the *Légion Etrangère* because he wanted to keep on fighting against a common enemy.

When enlisting, some of the Spaniards who joined from the *Légion* did not use their real names at first and of course the language barrier caused many issues. In the summer of 1940, one soldier replied upon being asked for his name by a British Army enlistment clerk with '*Bonjour!*', so he was down on the records initially as 13803102 Private Jacques Bonjour!

The Number 1 Spanish Company

No.1 Spanish Company was fully established in September 1940 at Westward Ho! with now Major R.D. Smith MC as the Officer Commanding, and with Captain B. Le Grand as the Second in Command, Company Sergeant Major WO2 A.T. Wells and the Company Quartermaster

---

[36] Hansard Volume 362: Refugees, debated on Wednesday 10 July 1940. <https://hansard.parliament.uk/Commons/1940-07-10/debates/513c14f4-f07b-48c8-bf14-f863b62ffa58/Refugees>.

Members of No.1 Spanish Company football team in Plymouth in 1940 (José García Flores collection)

Sergeant WO2 L.A.A. Dieudonna. An intensive period of training followed as the company settled down and the Spaniards in it got to work with their new weaponry and equipment. On their sleeve they wore a small diamond-shaped patch which divided vertically green (left as you look at it) and red with a golden 'S' overall in the middle. According to the Company Diary, by 16 September there were 207 Spaniards in the Company as it moved to Plymouth as part of 6 Group. This increased by mid to late 1941 when more Spaniards joined via other means and routes bringing the number closer to 250. Training soon commenced, and the Company was put to good use straight away, working on the building of defences along the South Coast as well as other tasks. In the little spare time available, they were able to take part in sport and soon set up a football team.

Not all the Spaniards in the Company were *Légionnaires* though, and between the end of 1940 and the autumn of 1941 an additional 40 Spaniards volunteered to join the Company. Several were Spaniards who had already been in Britain for some time, but others had travelled far to get to Britain and join up. The Royal Pioneer Corps archives show that Spaniards volunteered to join up in places like Euston and Holloway, in London, Glasgow, the Isle of Man and Northampton. 13805984 Francesc Dalmau i Norat and 13805986 Antonio Jornet were amongst these later arrivals and had both gone through a great deal to get to England.

Francesc Dalmau had escaped across to France at the end of the Spanish Civil War and had decided to continue his medical studies in Montpellier. Despite this, he decided to return to Spain and was immediately arrested and detained, passing through various internment camps before being sent to the Punta del Carnero camp near Cádiz, where he was put to work on road building in Punta Carnero itself. He managed to escape in the autumn of 1940 and when he got to La Línea de la Concepción he swam across to Gibraltarian water, climbed onto an unoccupied anchored ship and was picked up soon after. After a cup of tea and some questioning, he declared he wanted to join the British Army because, to him, it was the closest he could get to fighting Franco. He was soon on a ship bound for Canada and eventually arrived at Liverpool from where he travelled to London and volunteered to join the AMPC.

Joining the company on the same day was Antonio Jornet who had also managed to escape from an internment camp and get to Gibraltar. Once there, he was able to get onto a British merchant ship as a member of the crew. Setting off, the ship was part of a convoy which was attacked by German U-boats and the ship Jornet was on was sunk. As the members of the crew got onto the lifeboats a German U-boat came to the surface and members of its crew stood on the submarine's deck saluting them, a scene loaded with huge emotion in the middle of the Atlantic Ocean. The surviving crew was picked up by a Portuguese ship which dropped them off in Lisbon, from where they were moved to Gibraltar. Antonio travelled by sea as he feared being detained if he travelled overland through Spain. In Gibraltar Antonio joined Francesc Dalmau as well as 13805985 José Llons Fontanillas and 13805989 Victoriano Mateo and they then travelled to Britain via Canada, eventually enlisting on 27 October 1941 in Euston to become members of No.1 Spanish Company. Another to join late was José Robba who was originally from Gibraltar and whose family had moved to Britain at the beginning of the war.[37]

Plymouth and the South-West

While many Spaniards from the Company were being trained as SCONCEs (see Chapter 3, later) the remaining members were busily engaged in many other tasks. In January 1941 the Company joined 10 Group, continuing to be based in the Plymouth area.[38] On 20 March the Company supplied a Guard of Honour at Millbay Station on the occasion of the visit to Plymouth by their Majesties the King and Queen. But sadly, that night and the following evening, Plymouth was the target of German bombing. In what would later be called the 'Plymouth Blitz' the city was heavily bombed at the end of March and during April. The Drill Hall where the Spaniards were accommodated received a direct hit and initially one Spaniard was known to have been killed, another was missing and three were wounded. But it was consequently discovered that there were actually three who had lost their lives (13802426 José López from Toro to the west of Valladolid, 13802400 Francisco Gómez from Orihuela near Alicante, 13802384 Eladio Zamora from Cuenca) and five had been injured. All three dead were buried at Weston Mill Cemetery in Plymouth. Their deaths were reported in *The Spanish News Sheet* on 3 and 10 April 1941.[39] The Spaniards were also involved in many rescues in the city over the following days. As a result of all billets for the company being destroyed, they were evacuated to Saltash where they took over accommodation previously used by the Somerset Light Infantry. By April they had moved back to Plymouth and were based at Marshills Camp. Then in June 1941 the Company was split up and spread out, working under 56 Group on ammunition resupply, roads and agriculture with sections in Redruth, Bodmin, Washaway and Holsworthy.

In September the Company was moved to Biddestone, near Chippenham in Wiltshire, and became part of 37 Group. It was here that the Company started its long association with forestry. In particular, the Company worked with 14th and 15th New Zealand Forestry Companies which had arrived in Britain shortly after the summer of 1940.

---

37 Eric Canessa, *They Went to War – The Story of Gibraltarians who served in His Majesty's Forces in World War II away from their homeland* (Gibraltar: Eric Canessa, 2004), pp.174–175.
38 TNA, WO 166/5440. Pioneer Corps, 10 Group War Diary.
39 *The Spanish News Sheet*, edited by the International Commission for War Refugees in Great Britain, 1940–45, British Library, system number: 013943647. UIN: BLL01013943647.

Men of No.1 Section of the No.1 Spanish Company at Marshills Camp in Plymouth. (Jesús Velasco collection)

14th New Zealand Forestry Company was initially commanded by Captain O. Jones, and then later by Major D.V. Thomas, after Captain Jones left to join the RAF, where he took up aerial photograph interpretation work. The Company was sent to Grittleton in Wiltshire, where it built a New Zealand type mill, which cut its first log on 31 January 1941.[40] In April 1941 a detachment moved to Burbage to start cutting in Savernake Forest and to finish the construction of a sawmill there. Not surprisingly the small resident herd of deer suffered some antipodean poaching! In May, yet another detachment moved to Calne to take over logging and sawmilling operations at Bowood Forest from 11th New Zealand Forestry Company. New mills were built by the Company near Hungerford and at Wickwar, south-east of Swindon. Additionally, they secured a light English type mill and converted it into a portable model to cut up large top logs for pit props. All these operations were interspersed with periods of military training. The 14th Company received two prominent visitors in 1941. One was Peter Fraser, the New Zealand Prime Minister who received many requests from men who wanted to transfer to the New Zealand Division in the Middle East, none of which were ever granted. The other was from Queen Mary, who came to take tea with the officers and some of the other ranks. Later she returned the compliment and invited members of the Company for tea. The 14th Forestry Company was deployed to North Africa in 1943.

K.O. Tunnicliffe, who served in the New Zealand Forestry Company, recorded in his diary for 14 September 1941 that 'members of the No.1 Spanish Company have started work on labouring jobs already.'[41] This continued for the next year or so as the Spaniards built up their experience and confidence. By the end of 1942, the company had some of the Spaniards who had been seconded to SOE return to it. The Nominal Roll in Appendix I provides a list of all those who were now in the company, with the exception of any who remained with the SOE or had been posted elsewhere. It gives a fascinating insight into the backgrounds of the men in the company.

---

40 Peter McKelvey, 'New Zealand Foresters at War,' *The New Zealand Journal of Forestry*, February 2001.
41 Major K.O. Tunnickliffe MBE, 14th Forestry Company, New Zealand Engineers, Private Diaries.

Members of No.1 Spanish pose while working with 14th New Zealand Forestry Company. (José García Flores collection)

Members of No.1 Spanish Company rest on a bulldozer as they carry out forestry work. (Rodrigo Haro collection)

Spaniards pose, with a Senior NCO keeping an eye on them, in between forestry shifts. (Rodrigo Haro collection)

One of the Spaniards who would continue to work in forestry after the war was 13802423 Rodrigo Haro. A rugged and hard working man, Haro was born in March 1908 at Calle de Las Tiendas, Turre, Almería to Alonso Haro González and Francisca Hernández Haro. During his time in No.1 Spanish Company, he was part of a team that operated a mobile sawmill at various locations in south-west England. While stationed at Charfield, Gloucestershire, he met Selina Gardner from Scotland at an army dance in Wotton-under-Edge, near to Charfield. This was probably at the Swan Hotel, as research has shown that this was the hotel where army dances were primarily held. Rodrigo and Selina married in Kilwinning, in Ayrshire, south-west of Glasgow, in 1943 while they were on leave, and after the war they would settle there.

Probably the saddest event in the history of No.1 Spanish Company was the stabbing of 13802477 Antonio Gutierrez by 13802438 Juan Cano in November 1943; Gutierrez died of his wounds. But the incident was not a clear-cut case of murder. The courts-martial in Truro uncovered that Gutierrez had in fact been threatening to kill Cano for some time and following other testimonies from members of the company, it was also discovered that he had been threatening other members as well. Further investigation also showed that on the day of the stabbing, Gutierrez had said that he was going to kill Cano 'now' which provoked Cano to defend himself. The final verdict was that Cano killed Gutierrez in self-defence. Despite being found not guilty, Cano would unfortunately be medically discharged in 1944 because of his fragile mental state.

Rodrigo Haro and Selina Gardner's wedding in Kilwinning, 1943. (Rodrigo Haro collection)

Rodrigo Haro towards the end of the war. (Rodrigo Haro collection)

Normandy, La Nueve and Until Victory

It was not long before the much-awaited preparations for D-Day itself were being put in place. The build-up was a stark contrast to so many of the battles in which the Spaniards had fought on the Republican side during the Civil War, when the preparations, and indeed the equipment, was nowhere near as thorough nor as well resourced. By now, command of the Company by Major R. D. Smith MC, who had previously commanded No.185 Spanish Labour Company in France, had passed to Major A.L. Chapman MC – an Argentine rancher who after joining the company rose swiftly through the ranks, was commissioned and became affectionately called *El Comandante* by the company. Chapman was ably assisted by Captain L. de Lara, a French wine merchant, who had the happy knack of obtaining vital commodities such as food and stores by 'devious' means which were, however, 'vital' for the company's well-being.[42]

Members of No.1 Spanish Company pose for a photo shortly before deploying to Normandy. (Agustín Roa Ventura collection)

The Company was initially intended to be deployed to Normandy a few weeks after the main landings in June, but this was delayed once the second Mulberry Harbour was destroyed in a storm, and it was not until 14 August 1944 that it landed in France. The members of the company were immediately struck upon arrival by the immensity of the Mulberry Harbour. The Company soon got to work in Bernay where it was employed in loading and unloading supplies. From here the Company moved to the Rouen area where it continued to not only load stores but was also used for public order and for guarding POWs. One of the first tasks the Company was involved with was a liberation parade. For many, returning to France was bitter-sweet: on the one hand, they were glad to be part of the Allied advance into Europe but on the other, memories of time spent in France had been tinged with sadness about their internment and their poor treatment.

---

42 Major E.H. Rhodes-Wood, *A War History of The Royal Pioneer Corps 1939–1945* (Aldershot: Gale & Polden Ltd, 1960), p.76.

Members of the company prepare for the liberation parade in Le Nebourg in 1944. (Jesús Velasco collection)

A team from No.1 Spanish Company has a group photo before it gets ready to queue for a meal. Photo probably taken in Rouen area. (Rodrigo Haro collection)

Men and vehicles from Leclerc's 2nd Armoured Division arrive in the centre of Paris. (Agustín Roa Ventura collection)

Another group of Republican Spaniards would show immense bravery during August 1944. The *9e Compagnie* of the *Régiment de Marche du Tchad*, part of Leclerc's French 2nd Armoured Division was nicknamed *La Nueve* (the New). The company consisted of 160 men under French command, 146 of whom were Spanish Republicans. The commander was *Capitaine* Raymond Dronne and the Spaniard Amado Granell served as his lieutenant. After landing in Normandy with the division during the night of 31 July/1 August, it was quickly thrown into the fighting. By 23 August it had reached the south-west of Paris at Croix-de-Berny. Given direct orders by Leclerc himself, Dronne and the company set off for the city along with elements of the *501ᵉ Régiment de Chars de Combat* and it had entered the city centre via the Porte d'Italie by the evening of 24 August. Crowds were soon out on the streets and by half past nine that evening the force was outside the Hôtel de Ville. During the afternoon of 25 August, the German garrison surrendered, and *General* von Choltitz was held prisoner by Spanish soldiers until he was handed over to a French officer. The following day, Allied troops entered Paris in triumph. Spanish soldiers participated in the Victory Parade, with four half-tracks chosen to form *Général* de Gaulle's escort along the Champs-Elysées, and they paraded near a banner of the Spanish Second Republic. The company would continue to fight for the rest of the war although its achievements were forgotten soon afterward, however interest has been revived more recently.

After stopping briefly around La Nebourg, near a Calvados distillery, No.1 Spanish Company was on the move again, this time further north as Montgomery's 21st Army Group moved towards Belgium. It passed Lille and Valenciennes and came to a stop at Saint Joris Weert, near Brussels. In the end, the company would spend the rest of the war in Belgium. The Company was reinforced in November 1944 by 50 or so members of 361 Pioneer Company which was also almost entirely made up of Spaniards, and which had been dispatched from North Africa the previous month. The company would now concentrate on the role it had done the most of – forestry. Much of the

General von Cholditz is escorted away after initially being guarded by Spanish troops in the city centre. (Agustín Roa Ventura collection)

wood cut during the following months would be used in supporting defensive positions during the Battle of the Bulge and in the myriad of necessary tasks when the Allies crossed the Rhine in 1945.

Despite a fright during the Germans' Ardennes Offensive of December 1944 and January 1945, the company did not need to be relocated and continued with the job in hand. In April 1945 it was moved to Romedenne, south-west of Charleroi and not far from the French border, and the role of Company Sergeant Major was assigned to a Spaniard – the much respected 13802518 José Jurado. Here they occupied an old chateau on the outskirts of the village. This gave the company a great base for accommodation and allowed the Spaniards an opportunity to hold parades and events.

The end of the war certainly came as a bit of a surprise to the company, but they remained working on forestry and were given the odd bouts of leave to go to Brussels or other nearby towns. According to some accounts, the company was stood by to deploy to the Far East, but this did not materialise before Japan's surrender in August.[43] By July the company command had changed again, and Major L.H. De Lara was the new Officer Commanding.

On 16 September, the company was moved to Ostend for embarkation for Britain and once back in Britain, it moved to Chard in Somerset on 17 September. Here it continued working and was employed in demolishing camps and searchlight sites. The company's final War Diary entry had it still in Chard on 31 December 1945 with detachments at Sidmouth, Cotleigh, Axminster and Stoneybridge.

Members of No.1 Spanish Company were mainly demobilised in March 1946 and given permission by the British authorities to remain and settle in the United Kingdom. Some also

---

43 Antonio Vargas Rivas, *Guerra, Revolución y Exilio de un Anarcosindicalista* (Almería: privately published, October 2007 second edition), Part 2, Chapter 3.

Members of No.1 Spanish Company pose next to an anti-aircraft battery in Normandy. On the right is Augusto Pérez Miranda. (Agustín Roa Ventura collection)

Members of the company load trucks with wood which has just been felled ready to be taken to the front line. Photo taken in October/November 1944 in Belgium. (Rafael Treserras collection)

state that members of the company took part in the Victory Parade in Taunton in the summer of 1946.[44] Because it had been in the United Kingdom for some considerable time, many members of the Company had already set down roots and would remain in the country for the rest of their lives. Men of the company had gone through countless trials and tribulations, and many would continue in the struggle for recognition of Spanish Republican exiles, becoming members of the Spanish Ex-Servicemen's Association 15 years later. But as *A War History of The Royal Pioneer Corps 1939–1945* says: 'Throughout their service with the British Army they wore the Corps badge with pride, and their loyalty is evidenced by the Spanish standard, embroidered with the words "1940 until Victory."'[45]

---

44 Antonio Vargas Rivas, *Guerra, Revolución y Exilio de un Anarcosindicalista* (Almería: privately published, October 2007 second edition), Part 2, Chapter 3.
45 Major E.H. Rhodes-Wood, *A War History of The Royal Pioneer Corps 1939–1945* (Aldershot: Gale & Polden Ltd, 1960), p.76.

Standing outside the on-site Guard Room while carrying out forestry tasks in Belgium in late 1944. Far right is Jesús Rodriguez, in the middle next to the tent is the soon to be Sergeant Antonio Grande. (Jesús Rodriguez collection)

Spaniards rest between forestry shifts during the winter of 1944/45. (Jesús Rodriguez collection)

'BRAVE NEW WORLD' 89

Photograph of the entrance of the chateau at Romedenne today. (Author's collection)

Jesús Rodriguez on the left stands with two other Spaniards at the entrance to the chateau at Romedenne. (Augusto Pérez Miranda collection)

Men stood outside the chateau after a long day in the forest in the summer of 1945. (Rodrigo Haro collection)

'BRAVE NEW WORLD' 91

The Senior Non-Commissioned Officers of No.1 Company. Standing from left to right are Sergeants Solome, Delgado, Roy, Iovina, Grande, Poole, Green, Rangera and Jurado. Sitting, left to right, Sergeant Espallargas, Company Quartermaster Sergeant Staff Sergeant Walker, Company Sergeant Major WO2 Gibbs and Sergeant Izquierdo. This photo was taken in the summer of 1943, shortly before CSM Gibbs was posted out of the company and when a large number of Spaniards returned to the company having been detached to the Special Operations Executive. (Pioneer Corps Association Archives)

Chapter 3

'My Country'

Spaniards in the SOE – The SCONCEs

> The British authorities knew that if Hitler had invaded Spain, and Franco had put up a fight we would have been willing and ready to fight the Germans once more, even if it meant helping a traitor.
>
> Francisco Balagué[1]

No sooner had No.1 Spanish Company been established in the autumn of 1940, than its members were whisked off to train for the SOE. Across a nearly three year period, over 120 Spaniards would go through SOE training. While many did not get through all the training and selection courses, several would be on standby on many occasions, ready to deploy on operations into the Iberian Peninsula and later elsewhere. The SCONCES (the codename given to the Spaniards) would go through many challenges. A few, however, would take active roles in operations in France in 1944 and in other locations, but most would return to No.1 Spanish Company and serve in it until the end of the war.

Establishing the SCONCES

A few months after its establishment, on 2 December 1940 No.1 Spanish Company was visited in Plymouth at Millbay Drill Hall by a Major Hugh Quennell, who was head of H Section of the SOE, which covered the Iberian Peninsula as its area of responsibility.[2] Following the fall of France, planning was taking place for potential operations behind enemy lines in Spain and Portugal. It was soon realised that the only immediate source of Spaniards serving in the British Army was No.1 Spanish Company. The first batch of 32 Spaniards started their training immediately, and over the course of the next 18 months some 120 Spaniards would enter training at the various SOE training establishments. The training and potential use of the Spaniards involved a plethora of people working in the Secret Intelligence Service (SIS) amongst who were Ian Fleming and Kim Philby.

It is worth explaining what was going on in Spain and the plans and actions which were carried out by the British to ensure that Spain was prevented or dissuaded from entering the war. If they were successful then Britain might still have had to carry out operations in the Iberian Peninsula

---

1 'Fought in Spanish Civil War, French Foreign Legion and for Britain,' *Henley Standard*, 29 September 1989.
2 Bernard O'Connor, *Blowing up Iberia: British, German and Italian Sabotage in Spain and Portugal during the Second World War* (Bedford: Bernard O'Connor, 2019), p.35.

to disrupt a potential invasion of Spain by Germany. Key to ensuring Spain's neutrality was the appointment of Sir Samuel Hoare, former Foreign Secretary, as British Ambassador who arrived in Spain in May 1940. He was given the principal task of putting in place plans as to how such Spanish neutrality could be ensured. On 12 June, Spain decided to switch its stance to 'non-belligerence' to replace the neutrality it declared on 4 September 1939. It was obvious that Franco was now weighing up his options. The weapon of a policy governed by economics was also established by Britain, but this would not be enough. At the same time, it was soon discovered that there was a need to 'strengthen elements in Spain desiring to maintain neutrality.' The question at this stage for Churchill and Britain was: how could this be achieved?[3]

Hugh Quennell, who had been a partner in Slaughter and May, a London legal firm, was appointed by Sir Frank Nelson to head up Section H and Quennell soon got to work, recruiting members of his team many of whom also came from Slaughter and May. Spain was now to be categorised as '23-Land' and Portugal as '24-Land'. Prior to Quennell's visit to Plymouth, Hitler and Joachim von Ribbentrop, Germany's Foreign Secretary, had met with Foreign Minister Ramón Serrano Suñer at Hendaye railway station on 23 October to discuss the conditions for Spain to join Germany and Italy in the war. Disagreements dominated seven hours of talks and Hitler had decided to give only vague guarantees that Spain would receive territories in Africa. That summer, following Operation DYNAMO, the evacuation of the BEF and French forces from Dunkirk, and the fall of France in June, Britain and her Empire had announced it would fight on. Despite assurances from Darlan '… that whatever happened the French fleet should never fall into German hands.' Churchill had launched Operation CATAPULT and the fleet in Mers-el-Kébir was attacked by Force H under Vice Admiral James Somerville, resulting in the sinking and crippling of French ships and the death of 1,297 sailors.[4] The Germans were now very clear about Britain's intentions.

A key person for the SIS in Madrid, the Director of Naval Intelligence and the SOE, was Alan Hillgarth, the recently appointed Naval Attaché to the British Embassy in Madrid. Hillgarth, who was born George Hugh Jocelyn Evans, served as a junior naval officer in the Great War and also fought at Gallipoli, where he was shot in the head and in the leg. After the Great War he became an author of thriller books, a gold-hunter in Bolivia, a diplomat and spymaster. During the Spanish Civil War, he was the consul in Mallorca and, by acting as a mediator, saved countless lives on both sides.[5] In August 1939 Evans/Hillgarth took up the Naval Attaché post in Madrid and was recalled to the navy's active list. There had been no Naval Attaché in Madrid for 16 years, so he faced a number of daunting challenges but quickly got to work building up a British Intelligence gathering network across the Peninsula and mapping out the numerous espionage groups to be found in the capital. Key to this was probably the most important contact he had, Juan March Ordinas, one of the wealthiest men in Spain who had been dubbed 'The Pirate' by Colonel Charles Thoroton. Thoroton had run British Naval Intelligence in Spain during the Great War and had convinced March to join his network in May 1915. Hillgarth may have met March in Mallorca during his time as consul but was nonetheless formally introduced in September 1939. March had made his first fortune smuggling from North Africa into Spain in the 1920s. During the Second Republic, he had been imprisoned but then released (it is said, by paying off his jailors and taking them with him to Paris), and it was March who had financed the de Havilland Dragon

---

3 Richard Wigg, *Churchill and Spain. The Survival of the Franco Regime 1940–1945* (Brighton: Sussex Academic Press, 2008), p.11.
4 Colin Smith, *England's Last War Against France, Fighting Vichy 1940–1942* (London: Weidenfeld & Nicolson, 2009), pp.76–88.
5 Duff Hart-Harris, *Man of War: The Secret Life of Captain Alan Hillgarth. Officer, Adventurer, Agent* (London: The Random House Group, 2012), pp.148–182.

Rapide aircraft which had taken Franco from the Canaries to Morocco in July 1936 to begin the coup which led to the Spanish Civil War.

In September 1939, Hillgarth sent March to London where he met Admiral John Godfrey, Director of Naval Intelligence. Godfrey was impressed by March and Churchill was himself interested in meeting him and in a note said, 'This man is most important, and may be able to render the greatest service in bringing about friendly relations with Spain.'[6] Despite trust being initially an issue, it was clear that March had Spain's interests at heart and would be key to helping keep the country out of the war. A new plan was also hatched to bribe high-ranking Spanish officers to pressure Franco to not join the Axis in fighting in the war. Churchill agreed, and the money was laundered through Spanish banks and businesses by March. In 1940 alone, $10 million was made available from British funds held in US Banks. In all $200 million (in today's money) would be paid.[7]

In May 1939 Lieutenant Commander Ian Fleming had been taken on as the assistant for Admiral John Godfrey and had already proved himself as a '… skilled fixer and vigorous showman.'[8] By mid–1940 he had been charged with setting up GOLDEN EYE which was to be the overarching operation to monitor Spain, prevent it from entering the war and also undertake sabotage operations should Germany invade the Iberian Peninsula. By June 1940, after being in France when it fell to the Germans, Fleming travelled to Madrid via Lisbon and stayed with the Hillgarths in order to report on developments to Godfrey. He then went on to Gibraltar to establish an office there, principally linked in with Operation GOLDEN EYE. Hillgarth would be key to understanding the situation in Spain and Portugal and in setting up the necessary contacts and networks should the requirement for sabotage operations be activated. While in Gibraltar Fleming met Colonel William 'Wild Bill' Donovan, Roosevelt's Chief of Intelligence. Fleming then moved to Tangiers to set up a back-up facility should Gibraltar be taken by the Germans. Returning to Britain, it was clear that he would have to put his skills to the test to smooth over a number of frictions, especially those between the heads of the SOE and the SIS. The planning for GOLDEN EYE would now be high on his agenda.

It was not until 9 November 1940 that the OKW (*Oberkommando der Wehrmacht*) assigned the code name Operation FELIX for the operation to seize Gibraltar via the Iberian Peninsula. Planning had already started and by the end of August, Hitler had approved a general plan to seize 'The Rock'. A series of meetings had then taken place which led to the Hendaye railway station meeting. It was not until 4 November 1940 that the final draft of the protocol between Germany, Italy and Spain was completed, and it only mentioned Spain entering the war when ready 'at a time to be set by common agreement of the three powers.' This was far from ideal for Germany as Hitler knew the war would inevitably expand.

It was in the above context that the Spaniards from No.1 Spanish Company were recruited for the SOE. After visiting Plymouth, Quennell travelled to Madrid where he met up with Hillgarth, as well Sir Samuel Hoare, mostly to discuss the role of the SOE should the Germans invade the Iberian Peninsula. It was agreed that he was not to contact 'the lawless and anarchist elements conveniently labelled 'Reds' for fear of restarting the Spanish Civil War.'[9] Concerns now also grew about an impending German attack on Gibraltar, so Operation BLACKTHORN was conceived to plan the invasion of the Peninsula by the Allies. To support this, sabotage Operations MAD DOG and RELATOR were also planned. RELATOR involved the recruitment and training of 40

---

6 Duff Hart-Harris, *Man of War: The Secret Life of Captain Alan Hillgarth. Officer, Adventurer, Agent* (London: The Random House Group, 2012), p.191.
7 Richard Norton-Taylor, 'MI6 spent $200m bribing Spaniards in Second World War,' *The Guardian*, Thursday 23 May 2013.
8 Mark Simmons, *Ian Fleming and Operation GOLDEN EYE. Keeping Spain out of World War II* (Oxford: Casemate Publishers, 2018), p.7.
9 TNA, HS7/163, Iberian section history 1940–45 by Major Morris and Major Head.

Spanish-speaking British officers to be infiltrated as organisers, wireless operators, and saboteurs into Southern France, Spain and Spanish Morocco to attack certain targets and act as liaison with Spanish resistance units.[10] One of the officers recruited for this was Peter Kemp, an interesting character and ardent anti-communist, who had been studying for the bar in 1936 when the Civil War had begun. The coup by the nationalist side had presented an opportunity to Kemp and he was soon in Burgos in Northern Spain and joined the Navarrese *Requetés* in November. He then fought in the Battle of Jarama, then transferred to the Spanish *Legión*, fighting in Teruel and Caspe. At Caspe, before the Battle of Belchite, he was wounded in the throat and arm and in May 1938, after returning to the front, he was wounded at the Battle of the Ebro. He travelled to Britain to recuperate and in July 1939 returned to Spain to receive his discharge, having a private audience in Burgos with Franco himself.[11] Once the war had started, Kemp joined the SOE, was on the RELATOR list and afterwards participated as a member of the Small Scale Raiding Force crossing over the channel to France before being sent by the SOE to Albania, then Poland, and finally the Far East as an SOE operative. Luckily, Peter Kemp never got to meet the SCONCEs and it is probably a good job that he did not![12]

SCONCE Training

SCONCE I completed its initial SOE training at Brickendonbury (War Office Specialist Training Centre 17, or simply STS 17) south of Hertford, just before Christmas 1940.[13] One of the first reports on them (written by Kim Philby) says:

> The course ended on a very successful note indeed. Not only were the work results up to a very high standard, considering the inevitable sketchiness of a short preliminary course; but the morale of the men improved by something like one hundred percent.[14]

The SCONCEs were then given 24 hours leave for Christmas Day in London and stayed at the Rhodesia Hotel in South Kensington at the SOE's expense. The following day they took the train to Glasgow and after an overnight stay in the Transit Billet at 29 West George Street they travelled, again by train, to Fort William and then on another train to Arisaig, home to the HQ of SOE's paramilitary training schools in Invernessshire. Once there, they were moved by truck to Inverailort House (STS 25) for four weeks of training. David Niven would carry out his training at STS 25 before becoming commander of 'A' Squadron in *GHQ Liaison Regiment,* better known as *Phantom*, and reaching the rank of Lieutenant Colonel by the war's end. The Special Air Service used the facilities at STS 25 prior to D-Day. SCONCE I was also referred to as 23A (23 for Spain and A as it is the first group).

The SOE had established a four-week intensive course covering a wide variety of activities which included the need for students to show stamina in day and night forced marches, rope work and rock climbing, as well as theoretical and practical lessons in field craft, outdoor survival and explosives. They were also taught Morse code, advanced map reading, raiding tactics, unarmed combat and knife fighting.

---

10 TNA, HS7/163, Iberian section history 1940–45 by Major Morris and Major Head.
11 Peter Kemp, *Mine were of trouble* (London: Cassel and Company Ltd, 1957), p.200.
12 Judith Keene, *Fighting for Franco: International Volunteers in Nationalist Spain during the Spanish Civil War, 1936–39*, (London: Hambledon Continuum, 2001), pp.114–115.
13 For a full list of those Spaniards who carried out SCONCE training see Appendix II.
14 TNA, HS6/961, Training for SCONCE (Spanish Republican refugees in UK): to be re-infiltrated into Spain in event of German invasion.

No sooner had SCONCE I finished at Brickendonbury than SCONCE II arrived. The group was accompanied by Lieutenant Richard Hambro who had been a cattle rancher in Argentina as well as working in Uruguay before signing up, and becoming one of the SCONCE's interpreters and conducting officers. Linguistic difficulties were still an issue.[15] Philby's report on them was much shorter:

> SCONCE II is doing well. The new lot are quite different to the last. They are quieter, more modest, less conceited, and much more respectable. They lack the scallywag qualities of the last crowd. They possess no outstanding personalities and, with two possible exceptions, would have to be led.[16]

Parachute training was now planned, but as there was no accommodation available near Ringway (now Manchester Airport), it was decided that the first two SCONCEs would be moved to Lord Montagu's Beaulieu estate in the New Forest, south of Southampton. They were to be accommodated in the Specialist Training Schools at 'The House on the Shore' (known as STS 33) and 'The Drokes' (known as STS 34). Philby was responsible for the training programme set up there which consisted of: propaganda training, political training, security, secret service training, targets and sabotage, organisation and specialised training. The H Section Journal for early 1942 reported that there had been difficulties with one of the SCONCES and that morale may prove to be an issue, so they were given more leave, in batches of six, in London. More Spaniards were then requested to make up SCONCE III.[17] This third group seemed to be far worse with the initial report stating:

> … the new men are not up to the previous two squads and that we shall find it very difficult anything trustworthy or worthwhile after this lot … Certainly we have had the best men and just what can be done with the rest I don't know.[18]

SCONCE I & II were moved from Beaulieu to Thame House (STS 42), east of Oxford which was used as a holding station for agents until they were able to be transported into the field for their mission. By March 1941 Operation SPRINKLER had been planned which:

> Had as its object the landing in the North of Spain of these so-called 'Red' Spaniards with a few English officers in charge to contact their own 'Red' friends in Spain and assist in resistance to Germany. If there was no formal organised resistance to the Germans, then the alternative scheme SCONCE would be put into operation, and the Spanish 'Reds' would be infiltrated to make their own contacts without the supervision of British officers.[19]

The operation never took place, but the SCONCEs were stood by, nonetheless. By early March a SCONCE IV was established. The SCONCE report dated 13March 1941 said:

> The training of the SCONCES 1 & 2 is now complete and they have been sent to Thame Park. These two squads comprise of 30 men in all. Squad No.3 which consists of 22 men, has gone to Arisaig for the second part of their training. A fourth squad has been chosen consisting of

---

15 TNA, HS9/649/2, Richard Everard Hambro, born 29 December 1900.
16 TNA, HS6/961, Training for SCONCE.
17 Bernard O'Connor, *Blowing up Iberia: British, German and Italian Sabotage in Spain and Portugal during the Second World War* (Bedford: Bernard O'Connor, 2019), pp.104–105.
18 TNA, HS6/961.
19 TNA, HS7/163.

24 men, and they started their training at Brock Hall near Northampton yesterday 21st of March. There are thus, 70 SCONCE men at present trained or undergoing training.

Reports as to their morale is that it is good. The whole of the second SCONCE men are reported to be below the general standard of the first, and the third are below that of the second. The fourth squad may be rather better. Many of them are NCOs in the Spanish company and seemed to be on the whole rather better educated than the third squad.

Two more squads of 30 men each can, if accommodation is available through the courtesy of M (Training section) and D/ FIN (Finance section), be produced in the next 28 days. These squads are likely to make up in toughness what they lack in intellectual refinement.

On 20 March the report stated:

Squad No.3 has now joined the first two squads at the holding school at Thame. The fourth squad is at Inverie House. Four further black sheep [badly behaved personnel] have had to be eliminated so there are thus now 72 … men trained and undergoing training.

Earlier in February, accommodation had finally been organised for parachute training at Ringway and the SCONCES were to be housed in Dunham House, Bowdon along with other agents. The training at Ringway consisted of physical training, parachute instruction, parachute control and container drill. The course was to last a week.

Members of SCONCE IV pose for a group photo at Thame House (STS 42). The following are confirmed in the photo: Standing from left to right – second, Sergeant Manuel Espallargas; fourth, Miguel Bon; eighth Corporal Augusto Pérez Miranda; ninth Corporal Antonio Grande; tenth Esteban Molina; and twelfth Corporal Francisco Balagué. Front row from left to right: second, Major Tristam Grayson (CO of Thame House) and fourth, Major James Hamilton (as Assistant in H Section of the SOE).[20] (Augusto Pérez Miranda archive)

---

20 Other members of SCONCE IV were: Corporal Pedro Herreros, Corporal Juan Colomé, Lance Corporal José Bernard, Privates José Pardo, Benito Panchame, Juan Prades, José Sánchez, José Planella, Courado González, Armando Ortoz, Silvenia Marco, Modesto López, Alfonso Pujol, Sebastián Salvador, Juan Romea and Francisco Villa Fivor. The spelling of the names is based on SOE documents.

Initial reports on SCONCE IV soon came in. Lieutenant Colonel Ivor Evans, the Commandant of Arisaig, wrote on 7 April that 'the students were in every way a better lot than others of their nationality we have seen ... They will have reached a fairly high standard by the time they leave here on the 19th.' This SCONCE consisted mostly of NCOs. On the same day, Evans went on to add:

> They were found to be about one week in advance of most parties arriving here. They are about the best lot I have yet encountered, always cheerful and on the whole very keen. In field craft and guerrilla warfare they are excellent. Given a good leader, I feel sure that as a party they would do well, even without further training. They have great confidence in themselves and their weapons and have a hatred of Fascists and the greatest contempt for the Italians generally.[21]

Sergeant Manuel Espallargas.
(Manuel Espallargas collection)

With most of SCONCE IV being NCOs, it was perhaps obvious that they would excel. Amongst this group was Manuel Espallargas, who had done so well in Narvik.

The group contained 13803015 Augusto Pérez Miranda whose story was also remarkable. Augusto was born in Santander on the north coast of Spain and had served, prior to the Spanish Civil War, in the *Guardias de Asalto* in Morocco in a town called Alhucemas, made famous by the Rif War. It was here that he had been joined by his wife, Carmen, and they had five children. When the Civil War broke out, Augusto was able to get his family to safety in Barcelona and then joined the Republican Army. He fought in several battles and then crossed over into France leaving his family in Barcelona. In one of the French internment camps, he volunteered to join the *Légion Étrangère*. In No.1 Spanish Company he had been promoted to corporal and was one of the more mature members of the SCONCEs having been born in 1907.

While SCONCE IV trained, issues with discipline took place with a few individuals from SCONCES I and II; Del Rio and Montane were sent back to Plymouth to rejoin No.1 Spanish Company at Marsh Mills Camp in Plympton. By the second week of March 1941, there were 72 SCONCES awaiting a mission and 24 members of SCONCE III were carrying out their paramilitary training at Meoble Lodge in Invernessshire. Once SCONCE III had ended, all the Spaniards were transferred to Thame House as their main holding school. On 17 April a further 24 were released from No.1 Spanish Company to make up SCONCE V (also known as SCONCE E) and they were quickly at Brock Hall.

By the end of March 1941, Operation SPRINKLER was still potentially on the cards. Parachute training at Ringway started in early April, minus four Spaniards who had caused some problems,

---

21 TNA, HS6/961.

but they were quickly replaced. The six who carried out the parachute training at Ringway did well, but one did not do the night jump and two others were injured. Parachute training at Ringway had been established in the summer of 1940 as No.1 Parachute Training School. By June 1941 6,532 jumps had taken place during the parachute training as a whole. It was not surprising that some were injured due to hard landings and the types of aircraft they were to use which did make the training difficult and intense.[22]

RAF Ringway was set up as the parachute training school in May 1940 and the school remained there until 1947. Between June 1940 and August 1945 it trained hundreds of parachute jump instructors and assistant parachute jump instructors, and thousands of men and women from all services, some secret, from many nations. Pre-jump training took place near Ringway at the Specialist Training School No.51 which was divided into three locations – Altrincham, Wilmslow and Timperley. STS 51 trained 7,204 men and women during the war including 872 SIS/MI9 agents, 172 French SAS troops, 420 Jedburghs and 520 'Army personnel'. It must also be mentioned that the Polish carried out their own parachute training and awarded 6,252 sets of parachute wings. Many hundreds of these were to non-Poles and included Peter Kemp who was awarded a Polish Combat Wreath.

Corporal Augusto Pérez Miranda is easily recognisable in this photo at the back just below the flag. (Augusto Pérez Miranda archive)

H Section diary on 23 April stated:

> The first four Squads are now at Thame, and the fifth Squad is undergoing the first part of its training at Brock Hall. Six of the first two squads are undergoing parachute training. No detail has yet been worked out for SPRINKLER until further information as to reception facilities for the men in the North of Spain are received, in which district it is intended to use them. The possibilities of using SCONCES immediately if there should be a sudden invasion, is under consideration.[23]

At the end of April, Hillgarth had returned from Spain and reported that there had been progress in the organisation of forces in the Iberian Peninsula should there be a German invasion. The plan was that if there was no organised Spanish resistance as such the SCONCE operation would be enacted. At the same time as this, three RELATOR officers volunteered to join the SCONCES if

---

22 John Greenacre, *Churchill's Spearhead: The Development of Britain's Airborne Forces during World War II* (Barnsley: Pen and Sword Books Ltd, 2010), pp.103–109.
23 TNA, HS7/163.

this should take place. With the German occupation of Greece, and fears that things would escalate, further plans were devised using the SCONCES, especially now that Sir Samuel Hoare, the British Ambassador in Madrid, had refused to allow Quennell's RELATOR mission to proceed in Spain without Franco's agreement. The updated plan saw the SCONCES being dropped in the south-west of France and the north of Spain (the Basque Country and Santander) to disrupt the electrical system thus compelling the Germans to use slower steam locomotives which they had fewer of. It envisaged the insertion of agents along the north coast of Spain in parties of five or six in two waves of about 30 men who would target a series of locations from the Catalan Mediterranean coast across the Ebro Valley and as far as places such as Salamanca.[24] Shortly after this, Captain Kaplowitch, the wireless telegraphy instructor at Beaulieu took charge of four of the SCONCES to carry out the important wireless training. This took place at the Wireless Training School at Fawley Court. SCONCE IV carried out parachute training at Ringway which resulted in some more injuries – 13802604 Velasco and 13802524 Nadal – and then joined training at Beaulieu after 48 hours of leave in London. The decision was now made to split up the SCONCEs into 14 parties based on their geographical knowledge. But at the end of May it was difficult to keep many of the SCONCES motivated and it was thought that many might not volunteer for SPRINKLER.

By mid-June 1941 Hitler had decided to delay Operation FELIX (the invasion of the Iberian Peninsula and attack on Gibraltar). The Germans began Operation BARBAROSSA (the invasion of Russia) on 21 June 1941. Europe stood on the edge of the abyss and Franco went on his summer holidays in Galicia safe in the mind that internal issues in Spain must wait for outcomes elsewhere in the world.[25]

Earlier in 1941 a series of meetings and exchanges had taken place where Hitler urged Franco to enter the war. A message delivered by Franco's Foreign Minister, and brother-in-law, Ramón Serrano Suñer on 25 January stated:

> the date of our entry into the war is conditioned by very clear-cut and highly specific concrete requirements, which are not clumsy pretexts for delaying entry into the war until the moment when the fruits of victory won by others can be garnered … Spain wishes to contribute materially to the victory, to enter the war, and to emerge from it with honours.[26]

But this did not give the Germans a date and caused great annoyance to Hitler who replied in February with a further effort to get Spain to join the war. The same month, Baron Eberhard von Strohrer received a memorandum from the Spanish General Staff on the requirements to improve Spain's military situation, which was dire. This seemed to signal for many an expression of Spain's effort to avoid entering the war.[27] Franco met up with Mussolini in Bordighera on 12 February, where he reiterated the importance of the support he needed, and that Italy depended more on Germany than Spain herself. *Il Duce* was inclined not to push Franco further and as Hitler was now already giving more support than he had anticipated to the Italians (after their disastrous involvement in the Balkans), relations slowed a little. By the end of February Hitler had written to Mussolini telling him that Spain had effectively priced itself out of the war through its demands. Franco on the other hand, remained full of admiration for the Third Reich ideologically

---

24 Bernard O'Connor, *Blowing up Iberia: British, German and Italian Sabotage in Spain and Portugal during the Second World War* (Bedford: Bernard O'Connor, 2019), pp.143 – 145.
25 Richard Wigg, *Churchill and Spain. The Survival of the Franco Regime 1940–1945* (Brighton: Sussex Academic Press, 2008), pp.43–45.
26 Paul Preston, *Franco*, (London: Harper Collins, 1993), pp.419–420.
27 Paul Preston, *Franco*, (London: Harper Collins, 1993), p.422.

but he knew that the war would be a protracted one and that Spain would not be able to sustain a long conflict due to its economic and military position.[28]

In Britain, some of the SCONCES were carrying out wireless and telegraphy training at Grendon Hall and by 4 June SCONCE V had completed their training in Scotland. The total number at Thame was now 94 men, divided into 18 groups of five.[29] Later in the month, 13802853 Corporal Carlos Busquet, who had enlisted in the Pioneer Corps in Liverpool and was in SCONCE V, had come to the attention of the SOE and SIS staff as he had been suggesting that Britain should be concentrating on activities in South America and had offered his services. He was suspected of being a Vichy sympathiser and was seen as the odd man out in the SCONCE parties. Even though it was thought that the suspicion aroused was probably misplaced, he was still closely watched. The possibility of using him for activities in South America was interesting but nonetheless implausible at the time.[30] Numbers were also being pruned down as there were some who were behaving badly and failing some of the new 'hurdles' put in their way. A further test of observation skills was also introduced where SCONCES were tasked to visit the seedier places in Soho to find out information on some of the French and Italians operating from these locations. During this period, Privates 13802536 Francisco Alapont and 13802604 Jesús Velasco were both commended for their keenness and wit.

Photograph of Francisco Alapont who became a good friend of José García Flores, another SCONCE. (José García Flores collection)

Later, because of the suspicion that German U-boats were being resupplied in the Canaries, it was decided to invoke Operation WARDEN which was a plan to attack German and Italian ships in the port of Las Palmas. The operation was another one dreamt up by Ian Fleming and it was proposed that SCONCEs be involved. Of the 88 Spaniards now available at Thame, 34 were suitable for SCONCE and SPRINKLER, seven for ship sabotage, 42 for raiding parties and there were five washouts who were nonetheless retained. By 7 August a group of 11 had been selected for the maritime mission. But things started to slow down and because of transport issues the SCONCE operation was put on hold again. As their future was contemplated, an additional advanced special course was planned, and 16 SCONCES were selected for it. The lack of suitable means of inserting the SCONCEs into Spain (it was too risky for the Royal Navy and it would use too many aircraft for the RAF)[31] meant that the decision was taken to severely reduce the

---
28 Paul Preston, *Franco* (London: Harper Collins, 1993), p.425.
29 TNA, HS7/164, Iberian section history 1940–45 by Major Morris and Major Head.
30 Bernard O'Connor, *Blowing up Iberia: British, German and Italian Sabotage in Spain and Portugal during the Second World War* (Bedford: Bernard O'Connor, 2019),pp.173–174.
31 The level of risk for a littoral insertion with the Royal Navy was high, and for the RAF this would detract from

Three students at the Wireless Training School at Fawley Court take a break. Note that the man in the middle is wearing French Parachute wings on his right pocket. (José García Flores collection)

number of Spaniards to be used. Lieutenant Charles Scott RN, who had taken over from Hugh Quennell, now had to do some work to reduce the numbers. While an advanced course took place for a dozen or so Spaniards in August, others attended wireless training (13802496 José García Flores and 13802502 Lorenzo Montoursie) at STS 52. Those who had been on wireless training previously (13802494 Francisco Fernández, 13802500 José Luque, 13802480 Francisco Navarro and 13802382 Francisco Muñoz) were returned to No.1 Spanish Company.

With increasing numbers of people carrying out training, the SOE came up with a classification system to best describe students. The group that had been carrying out advanced training at Beaulieu (known as 23F) had a report written on them by Major Barcroft towards the end of September which read:[32]

- CASABAYO – An intelligent man and quick thinker. He has worked hard and done a good course. Category B.
- ALAPORT – Intelligent and confident. Hard working; inclined to be a little impetuous. Category B.
- ESPALLARGAS – An old soldier type. Slow thinker. Not very intelligent but interested and a hard worker. He has little inventive power and very little capacity for organising. He should be, however, an excellent N.C.O for raiding practice. Category I.
- BUSQUET – Intelligent and with some experience of this work as an ex-police agent in France and Spain. He has not paid much attention to lectures and suffers from a pronounced superiority complex. Not a very good influence over the other students and not recommended for use.
- DELGADO – Simple, pleasant, straightforward person, but gives an impression of reliability. Good personality. Category B.
- IZQUIERDO – Medium intelligence only, but very interested and hard working. Category G or I.
- BOSQUE – Intelligent and hard working. Keen, quick and interested. Fairly strong personality. Might make a grade of B.
- GOMEZ – Not very intelligent but reliable. Works hard in the schemes. Category I.
- PARDO – Medium Intelligence. Has worked hard. Category I.
- IOVINO – Young and keen. Fairly intelligent. Has worked well in schemes. Category G or I.
- RUIZ – Very mediocre intelligence. Lectures right above his head (unable to be understood). Category B.

---

the effect of Bomber Command. Following the Blitz, a shift to area bombardment had just begun.
32 Bernard O'Connor, *Blowing up Iberia: British, German and Italian Sabotage in Spain and Portugal during the Second World War* (Bedford: Bernard O'Connor, 2019),p.255. The classification system established by SOE by the autumn of 1941 was as follows:
A – First Class Operator capable of taking charge of a large area and of influencing important people or existing movements and operations.
B – Second Class Organisaer, who is not of the same grade as 'A' but capable of taking charge of a local area and influencing individuals or organisations therein.
C – Person able to act as a staff officer to 'A'.
D – Suitable for the leadership of a diverse band.
E – Person possessing special technical knowledge of any particular industry or trade and who could influence executives or other officials or operatives.
F – Person suitable as an instructor in tactics and techniques.
G – Courier.
H – Wireless operator.
I – Ordinary raiding party member.
J – Lone worker, possibly useful, but undisciplined and uncooperative.

- BELENGUER – Limited intelligence. It is doubtful how much he has taken in, but very interested and hard working. Not recommended.
- ÁLVAREZ – Quiet personality. Limited intelligence. No initiative and does not seem to have much guts. Not recommended.
- PUJOL – Quiet personality. Has worked hard on the course and displayed interest but rather a slow thinker. Category I.

Sadly, further obstacles were put in the way of SOE's and H Spanish Section's plans and were revealed in a memo from Lieutenant Colonel Robert Guinness who was the SOE officer at the War Office. This memo sent to Lieutenant Brian Clark, the head of SIS and Special Operations in the Mediterranean (based in Gibraltar), as well as William Mac at the Foreign Office said that General Dwight D. Eisenhower wished:

> That no contact be made with Republican elements in southern Spain in advance of an emergency, and that no arrangements be made now to store arms and explosives in Tangier with a view to expanding expediting distribution to the Spanish soon after the emergency. In view of these two restrictions, it will of course be impossible for the SOE to give any assistance to the force in these areas and you might like to inform General Eisenhower accordingly.[33]

At the end of October 1941, Hoare visited London and it was around this time that the morale of the Spaniards fell quite sharply. One of the thoughts was to see if some of the men could be returned to the Pioneer Corps where they could be better employed and carry out obviously more useful and productive work. It was considered that some 20 Spaniards could probably no longer continue, but in the end only nine were nominated and returned to No.1 Spanish Company.[34] A further report on activities and links in the Iberian Peninsula did not paint a pretty picture and conclusions were that SOE had not been able to make any substantial advances in preparing organised guerrilla warfare in Spain. This was mainly because of the lack of links they were able to establish with Republican and anti-Franco elements (without whose cooperation the SCONCE and RELATOR plans would be virtually impracticable). It was always going to be difficult to track these people down given the restrictions put in place by the Allies and in particular the limits on introducing key technical personnel into the country as well as the sending of any arms and equipment.

Training of the small groups of SCONCES continued for the rest of the year, but despite this, the boredom, lack of hard work and the increasing probability that they would not be sent to Spain caused unrest amongst some of the Spaniards. In particular, three were highlighted as being very problematic. These were privates 13802446 José Bosque, 13802471 Luís Álvarez and 13802498 Francisco Iovino and soon a plan was conceived to transfer them from Thame but not back to their unit. A letter written by one of the instructors in early December covered what should be done:

> I strongly wish to recommend that these three men be definitely removed from the 23s. As conducting officer, I have known these men since January 1941. They are continually a source of problem. They are definitely a very bad influence on the rest of the 23s, Bosque in particular. Bosque is the leading light. This man has a strong personality which he might

---

33 TNA, HS7/163.
34 Bernard O'Connor, *Blowing up Iberia: British, German and Italian Sabotage in Spain and Portugal during the Second World War* (Bedford: Bernard O'Connor, 2019), p.259. These were confirmed as: Sergeant J. Jurado, Corporal M. Delgado and Privates Laiseca, A. Fernández, Palomar, C. González, Iniesta, Gallego and Gutierrez. They were returned to Plymouth.

Members of No.1 Spanish Company take a rest during SCONCE training. (José García Flores collection)

have employed for good. He has, however, employed it to the detriment of general discipline and instruction … For reasons of security I do not think it advisable that they should be returned to their unit. Further, as they have been the root of much trouble we have experienced in the past, I consider they should be removed to a place where they will be not heard again. They are useless to us.[35]

It was agreed that these three would be sent to the 'cooler'. While some SCONCEs had returned to their units there was a security risk sending back people who knew details of the locations of the SOE schools. It was therefore decided that a requisition of two properties in Scotland and another in the south of England would be made to house these types of individuals. These were known as 'coolers'.

A further report also confirmed that Bosque, Iovino and Álvarez were a problem, Bosque especially. The report had been written by Lance Corporal Pickering, one of the long-term instructors of the SCONCEs and was sent on 13 December with a note that on no account was it to leave the Security Section. This report was quite telling and very clear that even though the Spaniards had been treated badly by the French, the British had failed to make the most of an opportunity. It stated that while the Spaniards needed discipline, a fair hand was also required. Interestingly enough, it then went on to cover the fact that a 'Negrín Committee' (Dr Juan Negrín López was the pro-Soviet Union Prime Minister of the Spanish Republicans who was in exile in Britain at the time) based in London had been seriously considering setting up some sort of communist secretariat to 'control' Spaniards in the Pioneer Corps and elsewhere. This group would be the kind of group that Bosque could use to sow anti-British sentiment. The report also went on to deal with issues amongst the other SCONCES, in particular that they had not really been fully educated because of the outbreak of the Spanish Civil War and therefore were quite unsuitable for some aspects of SOE work. Moreover, it went on to say that those instructing, while good at Spanish had little understanding of Spain due to either never having been there or to spending their time in South America instead. The report concluded by saying:

---

35 TNA, HS6/918, SOE Spanish Section, General correspondence, dated 10 December 1941

It is a pity, however, that junior officers would not have been picked from Spanish Republicans living in the UK, amongst who there are several ex-officers. By ex-officers, I do not mean officers created during the civil war, but regular officers, having received instruction at a Military Academy.

Were the SCONCEs to be officered by educated and experienced Spaniards, I believe they would lose the feeling that they are only mercenaries under the orders of foreign officers, who have nothing in common with them. This, I believe, is at the root of the problem.

Then, just before Christmas 1941, the SOE transferred all the SCONCEs to new accommodation in Comely Hall (STS 41) near Market Harborough, Leicestershire. A year that had begun so well with several groups being trained across the whole of the United Kingdom was now ending with frustration, boredom and negativity. For all of 1941, H Section knew that the SCONCEs had been kept in a state of perpetual preparedness. It now became increasingly difficult to justify the holding of large numbers of SCONCES and having them at high readiness. Many were given some local leave over Christmas.

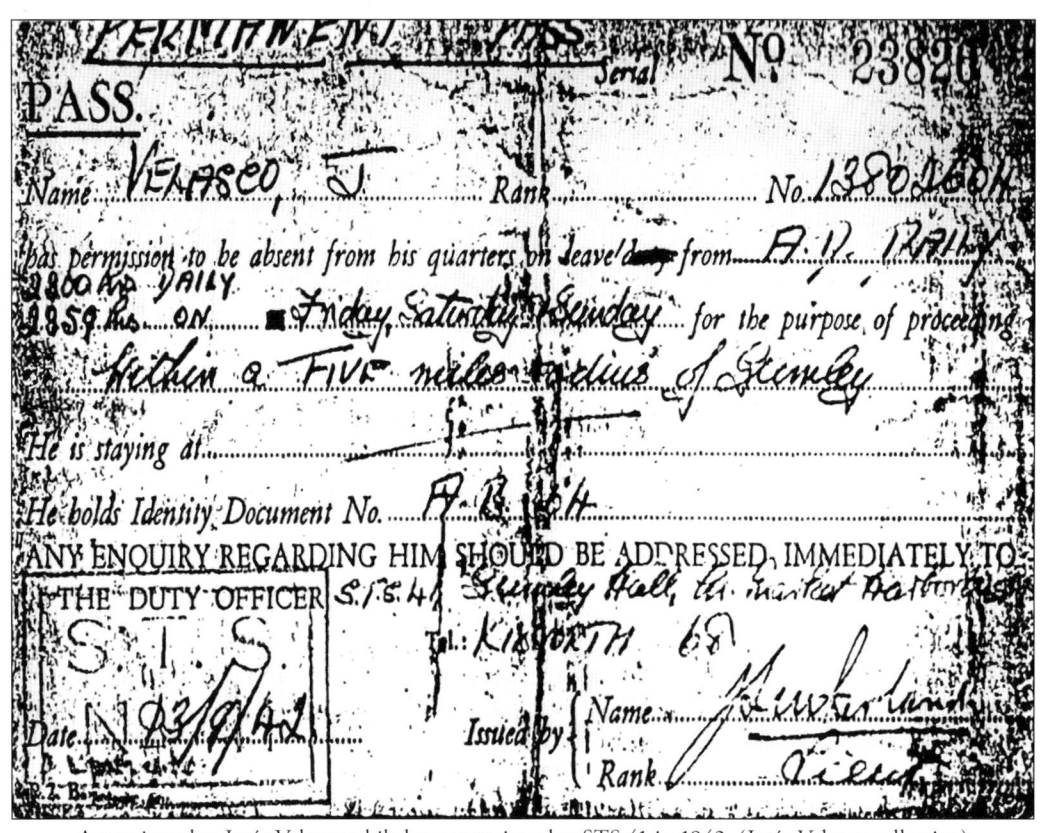

A pass issued to Jesús Velasco while he was stationed at STS 41 in 1942. (Jesús Velasco collection)

As well as the removal of Bosque and the other two, the following were also returned to No.1 Spanish Company: 13802523 José Muntane, 13802546 Cristobal Aguero, 13802596 Teodoro Fernández, 13802493 Ignacio Egea and Francisco Trujillo. But in the end Bosque and Casabayo were incarcerated at Camp 020 and put in solitary confinement.

José Bosque and Fernando Casabayo

13802446 José Bosque was born in Barcelona in 1912 and was an anti-fascist from a Catalan middle-class background and with a good education. He worked as an electrician, then served as a major commanding a battery of machine guns during the Spanish Civil War and was a specialist in the positioning of trench machine guns and mortars. Initially, through his SCONCE training, he was singled out as having good potential but by the summer of 1941 he was starting to have a negative influence on the other SCONCEs. Given his destructive attitude and his unwillingness to be involved in operations it was decided that he should be discharged from the service. At the end of January 1942, a detention order was issued, and he was sent to Camp 020. He was then transferred to the Field Security Headquarters in Norbiton and confined to barracks. At the end of January 1942, he wrote a series of letters of apology and some others which were to a Miss Dorothy Woodward, who it turned out Bosque was engaged to. She was visited by MI5 and there were no indications that he had discussed anything of security implication. MI5 then recommended that she be told that he had gone overseas and was not in a position to receive letters, which she accepted. Following a series of interviews and written reports it was decided that he would be kept under supervised employment. In March 1943 after a year of good behaviour, Bosque was released and then demobilised fully although his record says that he was demobilised 9 March 1942. He was found employment at Haig's Motor Limited in Birmingham and travel restrictions were placed on him prohibiting him from entering within a given radius of various locations so he was unable to make contact with SCONCEs or members of No.1 Spanish Company. At the end of the war Bosque was released and although little is then known about him, it would appear that, owing to his work in the Midlands, he settled down in Birmingham and married locally. Children followed and he died in 1984.

If Bosque had been a very bad influence on the other Spaniards and was seen as a risk for the SCONCES and the wider SOE by the chain of command, Fernando Casabayo went far further and sold his secrets to the Franco Regime. 13803004 Fernando Casabayo was born in St Raphael in France in 1910 before moving to Spain and although not seen as an outstanding SCONCE in many aspects, he had shown some potential when he started training. A cartographer in the Republican Army and prior to that a decorator in Barcelona, he had fought in the last two years of the Spanish Civil War before crossing over the Pyrenees and being interned at Argelès-sur-Mer camp. In May 1939 he volunteered to join the *Légion Étrangère* and like many other Spaniards was sent to Africa before eventually fighting in Narvik as a member of *13ᵉ DBMLE*. Unlike many of his compatriots he left Trentham Park with three others and travelled to Manchester before enlisting in the Pioneer Corps at Swanwick on 7 October 1940 and was then moved to Plymouth with No.1 Spanish Company. From there he took part in his SCONCE training as a member of SCONCE IV.

On 12 August 1941 he married Margaret Kathleen Hughes and the day after his daughter Dianne was born. They met in Plymouth where Margaret was a bus conductress and she eventually moved to near Oxford in search of work. That summer, his enthusiasm had started to wane and along with 13802850 Sebastián Salvador he had volunteered to be sent to a British unit in the Middle East.[36] At the beginning of January 1942 he was reported AWOL (Absent Without Leave), it was thought because he was heavily in debt with other SCONCEs. His home near Oxford was visited by the police and his wife informed them that he had told her he had a leave extension and had presumably left for Henley. She then visited London herself and found out some information about him, which she passed to the police. He did return home briefly but then disappeared

---

36 TNA, HS7/164, dated 12 June 1941.

again on 7 January 1942. He was tracked down a week later because he had been arrested and had appeared at Marylebone Police Court on a charge of larceny (theft). He was then handed over to the military authorities. Like Bosque, he was sent to Camp 020 but it was not until March 1942 that the full details of what Casabayo had got up to were made clear when all relevant reporting had been brought together. The written reports made grim reading. It turned out that a previous report which had stated that a Spaniard had betrayed highly secretive information to the Spanish Embassy was in fact Casabayo. The story of his betrayal is quite convoluted but worth telling.

On Tuesday 23 December 1941, Casabayo was given 48 hours leave which he had spent at his home near Oxford. When this period was over, he decided he did not want to return to his unit and came up with the idea of leaving the army and changing his identity, and on 29 December he left his home to try his luck at doing so. He borrowed some money from a friend and went by train to London, arriving at the house of José Río, with whom he had been with in Narvik. That evening Río showed Casabayo some identity papers which had been taken from a dead colleague called Basilio Beltrán who had been killed in Narvik. The following morning, Casabayo took some of Río's clothes and the Beltrán papers because he thought they would be useful and left Belsize Park Gardens, the location of Río's flat. That day he met with a girl called Carmen Luria whom he had met the previous summer, and they went to the cinema. As he could not go back to Río's flat, he spent the night in an air raid shelter at Paddington station. The following day he went to the Free French Recruitment Office introducing himself as Beltrán to try and see if he could get documents which would regularise his papers. The Free French called the police, and he was duly taken to a police station where he spent the night of 31 December. On 3 January he tried again at the Free French Recruitment Office but had to leave. Casabayo then made three visits to the Spanish Embassy between 3 and 7 January. The first time he met with the Ambassador himself, José Fernández Villaverde, who gave him £1 and told him to return on 6 January. He then stayed at Westminster House before returning on the agreed date and met the Press Attaché, José Brugada. During this second visit he continued to press his wish to return to Spain and revealed his true identity. He then went on to pass on a great deal of information about his training with the SOE and talked about the special company made up of Spaniards that would operate in Spain should they be deployed. After a series of further visits to the Embassy, where he was given money by Brugada, he returned to Oxford. Here he met up with his wife and on Tuesday 13 January Casabayo went to Oxford police station and gave himself up.[37]

Later that month it was reported by MI6, through contacts in Spain, that Casabayo's information about the SCONCEs had actually reached Madrid. A memo dated 1 February (probably from Hillgarth) stated:

> Our representative in Madrid, who has access to the private papers of a Spanish official whom we know to be passing information to both German and Japanese reports as follows:
>
> 1. A report from the UK dated the 17.1.42 contains the following information derived from a deserter from a Spanish commando.
> 2. Members of the commando were instructed that they would be dropped by parachute in various parts of Spain wearing appropriate uniforms.
> 3. They were then to form cells or find active sympathisers who could in turn form other cells and proceed to organise sabotage and transmit information.
> 4. Deserter attended 15-day course in the Isle of Wight where he was instructed in great detail on the various units of the Spanish army, names of commanders, locations, etc.
> 5. Other courses were connected with Spanish coastal geographical and military objectives.

---

37 TNA, HS9/276/2, Fernando Martínez Casabayo – born 07.08.1911 file, dated 31 March 1942.

The above is merely a cabled extract of the full report which is being photographed and sent here. If any further details of interest to you emerge from the full report, I will send them on immediately.

We have strong reasons for supposing that the focal point of the Spanish espionage system in the UK is an official in the Spanish Embassy. The significance of this, in view of the wanderings of Casabayo, will not be lost on you.[38]

Casabayo was not discharged from the Army on the behest of the SOE so as not to raise any alarms with the Spanish Embassy in London. When Mrs Casabayo wrote a letter to the War Office in April 1943 enquiring about her husband however, concern was raised about what was going on with him. MI5 was at pains to assure the War Office that there were good reasons for his continued incarceration, but it was discovered that he had received no pay for almost a year. Two officers visited Mrs Casabayo on 7 June 1943 and reassured her that her husband was well and in detention. She did not seem too upset but was obviously glad to know that her husband was well. She did however explain that she was having some difficulties in finding employment to best support her children. The report on the visit concluded:

I feel that so long as Mrs. CASABAYO continues to receive her army allowances and is permitted to communicate with her husband and vice versa and is given every facility in her search for employment that we will have no further trouble from her.

She has promised to write to me in the near future informing me as to her future plans and when she does so I will get in touch.[39]

The SOE arranged for Casabayo to be added to the nominal roll of 253 Pioneer Company and he was given an increase in pay. Mrs Casabayo then moved to Plymouth city centre with her two children. Her husband was not released until July 1945, after the end of the war, when he was allowed to join 361 Pioneer Company which contained mostly Spaniards. After the war, the Casabayos settled in the Plymouth area – Fernando died in 1973 and his wife in 1976.

Operations PANTHINO, POSTMASTER and PENNINE

At the end of 1942 a complementary operation to Operation TORCH was planned to distract and slow down the Germans should they decide to invade the Iberian Peninsula and cut off the Allied lines of operation into North Africa. The operation was to be called Operation PANTHINO and consisted of 20 personnel being sent to the south-west of France between Bordeaux and the Spanish frontier. A succession of misfortunes meant that members of the teams allocated were not able to deploy and the operation was eventually cancelled in mid–1943.[40] Prior to the planning of this operation, additional Spaniards who were not members of No.1 Spanish Company were also recruited. Some were Spaniards brought to Britain having been involved in Operation POSTMASTER.

Operation POSTMASTER was a successful British special operation conducted on the Spanish island of Fernando Po, off West Africa in the Gulf of Guinea. The mission was carried out by

---

38 TNA, HS9/276/2, dated 1 February 1942.
39 TNA, HS9/276/2, dated 11 June 1943.
40 Bernard O'Connor, *Blowing up Iberia: British, German and Italian Sabotage in Spain and Portugal during the Second World War* (Bedford: Bernard O'Connor, 2019), p.419.

the Small Scale Raiding Force and the SOE in January 1942. Their objective was to board the Italian and German ships in the harbour and sail them to Lagos. The British authorities in the area refused to support the raid, which they considered a breach of Spanish neutrality. Permission for the operation to go ahead came eventually from the Foreign Office in London. On 14 January 1942, while the ships' officers were attending a party arranged by an SOE agent, the commandos entered the port aboard two tugs, overpowered the ships' crews and sailed off the ships, including the Italian merchant vessel *Duchessa d'Aosta*. The raid boosted SOE's reputation at a critical time and demonstrated its ability to plan and conduct secret operations no matter the political consequences.[41] Hugh Dalton, the Minster of Economic Warfare who had been set the task of 'Set Europe ablaze' informed Winston Churchill of the outcome of the raid. He also stated that, 'other neutral governments would be impressed that Britain would if needed disregard the legal formalities of war in their efforts to succeed.'[42]

The Spanish Government was furious about the raid, which was seen as a breach of the country's neutrality. Ramón Serrano Suñer described the operation as an:

> … intolerable attack on our sovereignty, no Spaniard can fail to be roused by this act of piracy committed in defiance of every right and within water under our jurisdiction. Do not be surprised, if we return the answer which the case demands – that of arms.[43]

In an interesting turn, Spaniards who had supported POSTMASTER ended up moving to Britain and being trained as SCONCES. One of these was Alberto Lagara Morillez from Chirivel, Almería and had been a farmer before the Spanish Civil War. He may also have been someone who signed up for the Free French in 1940 and then ended up deploying to Douala in French Cameroon before either finishing his short enlistment or deserting and then getting involved in events in Fernando Po. He arrived in Britain in August 1942 and was soon attending SCONCE training. When Operation PANTHINO was called off in early 1943, he was returned to No.1 Spanish Company and then released to civilian life.[44]

In early January 1943 Operation PENNINE was conceived after authorisation from the Chiefs of Staff and was envisaged as a scheme to dispatch small combined British and Spanish teams to specified areas of Spain to establish contact with resistance groups and 'guerrilla bands'. In total there were to be 13 British, Spanish-speaking, officers, 34 Spanish demolition personnel, four British wireless operators and nine Spanish wireless operators. Great efforts were made to prepare the groups and they were put on standby to deploy at short notice from April 1943 onwards but were never utilised. By the summer of 1943 it was decided that the SCONCES were no longer required for operations.[45]

The End of the SCONCE Programme and Other Stories

Members of SCONCE IV were most definitely the more able members of the SCONCEs. Antonio Grande had been in SCONCE IV, and in his account *Number One Spanish Company Memorias de*

---

41 Marcus Binney, *Secret War Heroes* (London: Hodder and Stoughton, 2006), p.121.
42 Marcus Binney, *Secret War Heroes* (London: Hodder and Stoughton, 2006), p.147.
43 Marcus Binney, *Secret War Heroes* (London: Hodder and Stoughton, 2006), pp.148–149.
44 Jesús Ramirez Copeiro del Villar, *Objetivo Africa, Crónica de la Guinea Española en la II Guerra Mundial* (Huelva: Imprenta Jimenez S.L., 2004), pp.313–330.
45 TNA, HS7/164.

Antonio Grande[46] he goes into a lot of detail about the training he underwent and even talks about many who went to Ringway for parachute training getting stuck in trees upon their descent because of 40-kilometre-an-hour strong winds on a night drop. He also mentions the disappointment felt by the SCONCEs when they were eventually told they would be finally stood down. He concludes this part of his story by quoting what the Spaniards were told in 1943 by one of the SOE officers:

> Gentlemen, you will all know that the international situation regarding the world war is continuously changing all the time and with the Germans advance on Stalingrad, Montgomery's troops taking Tunisia, Mussolini being arrested ... Franco would be a madman if he thinks he can join Germany thinking that his friend Hitler still has a chance of winning the war. Today our government knows that Franco knowing this situation wants to get closer to the Allies, with the idea of avoiding the risk of what the future holds for his friends Hitler and Mussolini.[47]

Manuel Espallargas returned to the No.1 Spanish Company in July 1943 after his discharge from the SOE. For his hard work and determination along with his strong team spirit, he was awarded a Commander Home Forces Commendation for Good Service which was listed in the King's Birthday Honours List that summer. Manuel would return to being a sergeant in the company as it prepared for D-Day.

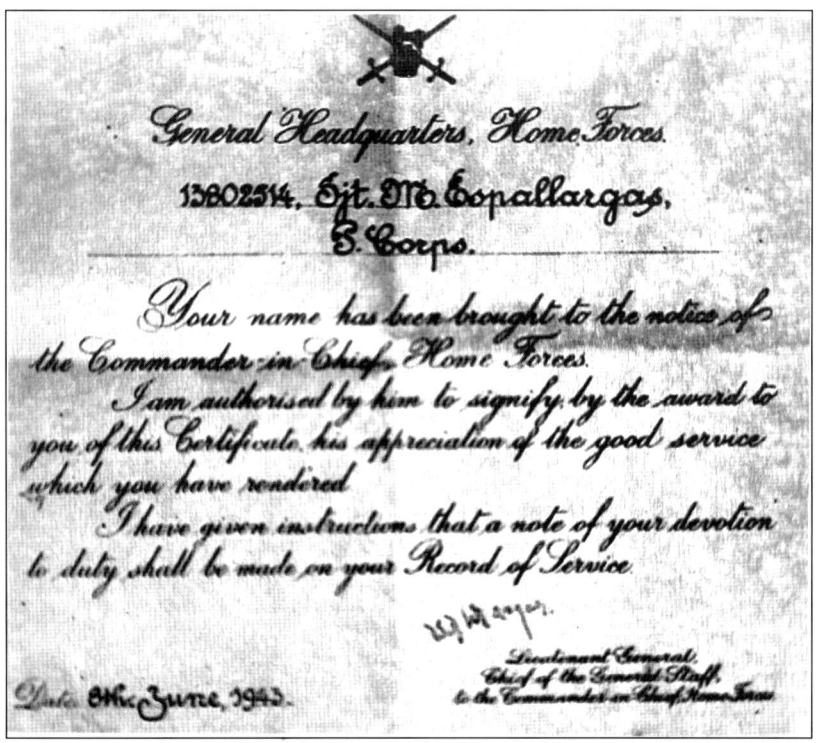

A copy of the Commander Home Forces Commendation for Good Service to Sergeant Manuel Espallargas. (Agustín Roa Ventura Collection)

---

46 Antonio Grande Catalán, *Number One Spanish Company. Memorias de Antonio Grande* (Alicante: Imprenta Gamma, 2002).
47 Antonio Grande Catalán, *Number One Spanish Company. Memorias de Antonio Grande* (Alicante: Imprenta Gamma, 2002), p.68.

Another SCONCE of interest is 13802415 Esteban Molina, who was born in 1921 in Valdepeñas near Ciudad Real, had been an apprentice electrician and later fought in the Spanish Civil War. Like the majority of men, he then enlisted in the *Légion Étrangère*. Molina was also part of SCONCE IV and one of those selected for extra radio training. He married an English girl from Aylesbury and they had two children. His file has him being 'Returned to Unit' at the end of July 1943, presumably similarly to the other Spaniards who had been retained until that point.[48] According to interviews with Daniel Arasa in the 1980s both Molina and Jesús Velasco were part of a group of eight Spaniards who did not return immediately to No.1 Spanish Company but were used in operations.[49] 13802604 Jesús Velasco from SCONCE II said:

> Eight Spaniards stayed and we thought we were still going to be used for potential operations in Spain. But we were posted to an Intelligence Unit and in 1944 when they were preparing for the landings in Normandy, we were parachuted into France to make contact with the Resistance.[50]

Velasco went on to say that the British were keen to stop France falling into communist resistance hands and that the group participated in various drops into enemy territory. The Spaniards were of particular use because of their anti-Franco background, something which was generally seen very positively by the French Resistance. Molina also said

> ... García, Tuset and I were together.[51] I was in France twice and my role was that of a wireless operator. We received and sent signals but as they were always in code, I never knew the contents of the information that passed through my hands.[52]

Molina would later settle in the UK and eventually remarry, having another son, the now well-known Hollywood actor Alfred Molina.

13802496 José García Flores, who had been in No.1 Spanish Company since its establishment in 1940, volunteered to carry out training with the SOE with the SCONCES. After initial training he was selected for wireless training and then moved on to join the Royal Signals in mid–1944. It is probable that he also carried out parachute training and was attached to the French for operations behind enemy lines during the summer of 1944. He spent the rest of the war in the Royal Signals.

Parachute wings of José García Flores (José García Flores collection)

---

48 TNA, HS9/1048/7, Esteban MOLINA – born 19.11.1921, file.
49 TNA, HS7/164. The summary report on the SCONCE operation states that four Spaniards were trained as wireless operators and six underwent parachute training at Ringway.
50 Daniel Arasa, *Los Españoles de Churchill* (Barcelona: Editorial Armonía Poética, 1991), p.312.
51 Here Molina is referring to 13802425 Juan Tuset and 13802496 José García Flores.
52 Daniel Arasa, *Los Españoles de Churchill* (Barcelona: Editorial Armonía Poética, 1991), p.312 where Molina states '*Estuve en Francia dos veces y tenía la misión de radiotelegrafista. Captábamos y emitíamos mensajes ...*' ('I was in France twice as a radio operator. We received and sent messages ...')

Other SCONCES had different experiences. 13802853 Carlos Busquet, who as already mentioned, was quite vocal about wanting to be used for any operations linked to South America, seems to have got his wish. His entry in the Pioneer Corps enlistment records says he was released to the reserve on 13 November 1942, and then rejoined on 2 October 1945 before being demobilised in September 1946.

Carles Busquet I Morant (as he was actually named), had been a government official in the *Generalitat* in Girona during the Spanish Civil War. He settled in Britain after the Second World War and applied in 1948, along with his wife Rosa Porta and daughter Maria Teresa, for naturalisation. What is interesting is that in the interview by Daniel Arasa in the 1980s, we gain insights into his time between 1942 and 1945. Initially at the end of 1941, he had been accepted for service with the French and there was a lot of discussion on the references and paperwork required.[53] But in his interview with Daniel Arasa he went into further detail and talked about how he was recruited for the SOE in 1942 after being interviewed by none other than a Briton who had been in the International Brigades and whom he had served with in the Spanish Civil War. He then carried out his training. According to what he said in the interview, he soon became a sailor and worked on fishing vessels in the Atlantic – passing messages, stopping acts of sabotage and above all passing on information about German submarine movements. Busquet's army record has him being released from service in November 1942. He worked in trawlers belonging to the Pair Fishing Company Ltd and soon changed to cargo ships travelling from Britain to the USA and he also ended up travelling to Brazil. Towards the end of the war, he carried out some shorter journeys to France and Belgium to contact the resistance and was even involved in some sabotage against German ships in Brest. He was never on a mission with the same people twice and got his orders via a coal company based in Trafalgar Square.[54]

Photograph of José García Flores one of the SCONCEs. (José García Flores collection)

Another member of SCONCE IV, 13802444 Francisco Balagué, according to his interviews with Daniel Arasa many years later, was selected for officer training but turned it down after being told he would go to Burma.[55] When questioned by a local newspaper years afterward, he would say this about his experience:

---

53 Bernard O'Connor, *Blowing up Iberia: British, German and Italian Sabotage in Spain and Portugal during the Second World War* (Bedford: Bernard O'Connor, 2019), p.271.
54 Daniel Arasa, *Los Españoles de Churchill* (Barcelona: Editorial Armonía Poética, 1991), pp.309–311.
55 Daniel Arasa, *Los Españoles de Churchill* (Barcelona: Editorial Armonía Poética, 1991), p.62.

You may ask why train Spanish men for the purpose mentioned? We were never told officially, but we knew at least two reasons why we would be used – remember, Britain was fighting for her life, alone – firstly if Franco declared war against Britain on Hitler's insistence, secondly if Hitler invaded Spain because Franco did not want to declare war against Britain. The main objective would have been to capture Gibraltar which would have been very easy once Germany had control of the Spanish airfields, and artillery bombardment from the mainland, thus closing the Strait. The British authorities knew that if Hitler had invaded Spain and Franco had put up a fight, we would have been willing and ready to fight the Germans once more, even if it meant helping a traitor.[56]

---

56 *Henley Standard*, 'Fought in Spanish Civil War, French Foreign Legion and for Britain,' 29 September 1989.

Chapter 4

'Vagabonds'

From Syria to Crete and Beyond – No.50 Middle East Commando

> How could I forget those Spaniards! … Considering language difficulties, the fact that they were strangers in a foreign army, etc, I think the Spaniards were as good as most British troops, especially at commando work.[1]

In the Middle East Republican Spaniards who served in the Middle East Commandos, based initially in Egypt, present an intriguing story. The 63 documented individuals that became commandos were Spaniards that had signed up for service in the French armed forces either in the *Régiments de Marche de Voluntaries Étrangers* or in the *Légion Étrangère* and had been posted to the Middle East. They subsequently joined the British, trained as commandos, fought in the Eastern Mediterranean and in the Battle for Crete in 1941 as part of Layforce – a commando force established in the Middle East after the arrival of commandos from Britain commanded by Colonel Bob Laycock. Many became prisoners of war and endured a great deal of hardship towards the end of the war. Those not taken prisoner would continue fighting in the British Army until the end of the war, some even as members of the Special Air Service.

The *1ᵉ* and *11ᵉ* BVE

How did these Spaniards get to Lebanon and Syria and eventually Egypt? Some came from units within the *Légion Étrangère* in the Middle East, but the majority had come from what became the *11ᵉ Bataillon de Volontaires Étrangers* (*11ᵉ BVE*), which was initially known as the *1ᵉ Bataillon de Marche de Volontaires Étrangers*. On 21 February 1940 the *1ᵉ BMVE* was formed at Le Bacarès (the *Dépôt Comun des Regiments de Marche de Volontaires Étrangers – DCRMVE*) in the Pyrénées-Orientales. It was made up of the best trained elements of the *21ᵉ* and *22ᵉ RMVE* and consisted of 750 all ranks. These *Étrangers Volontaires pour la Durée de la Guerre (EVDG)* would be linked to the *Légion* throughout their service for France. They wore the French Army uniform but were paid less than their contemporaries in the main *Légion* units because they were not graded as *Légionnaires*.

Training for those who volunteered to join *Bataillons de Volontaires Étrangers* at Le Bacarès Camp would last three months. Records show that it was carried out well overall by the Spaniards. In the first month they underwent individual training where they concentrated on weapon handling skills and the use of terrain. In the second month, they then moved on to more team related and

---
1 Testimony by Major Bob McGibbon, Middle East Commando Research Group Archive.

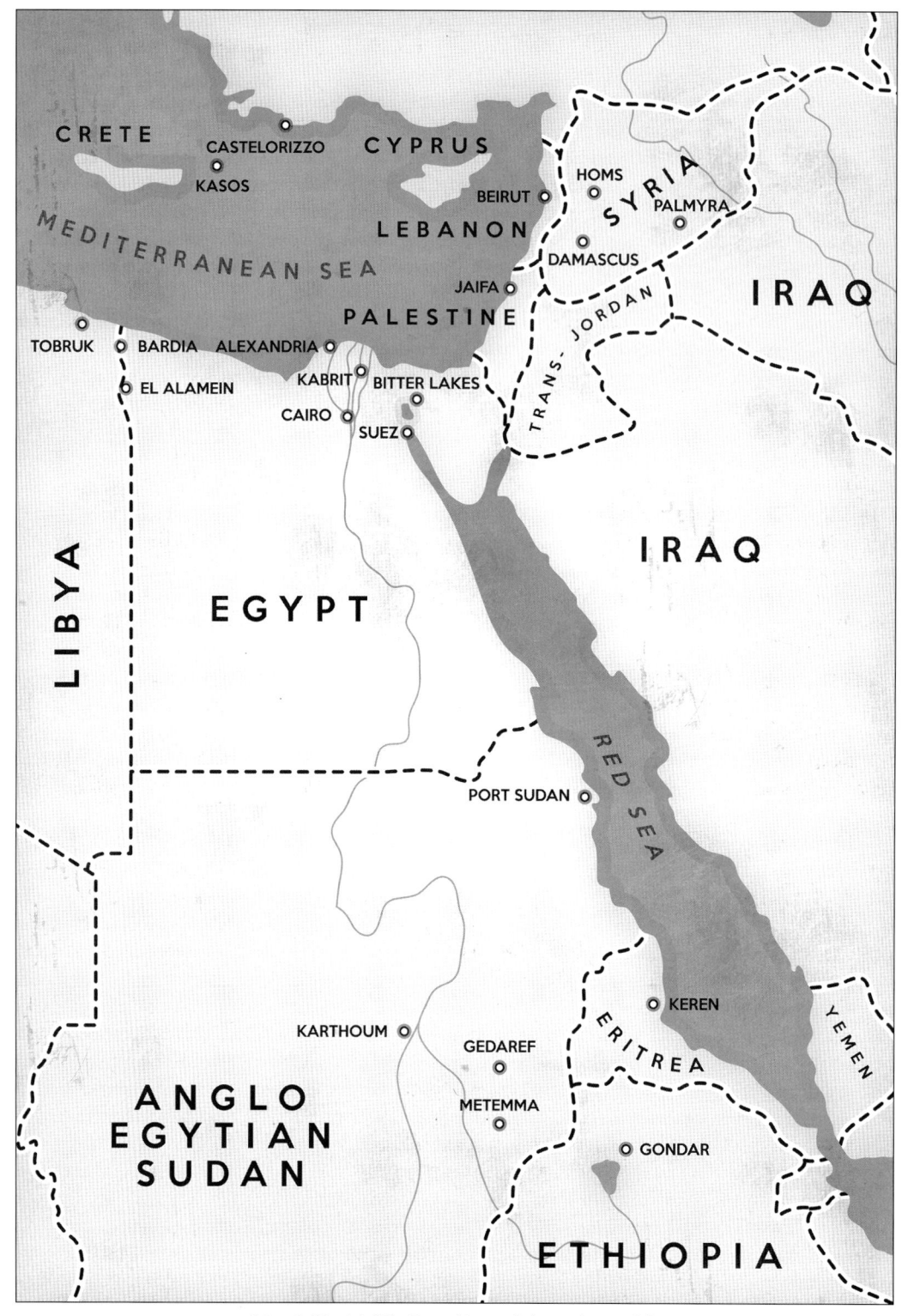

Map 5 The Middle East. (Artwork by Mike Heald)

specialist skills such as machine gun drills, communications, and pioneer work. On occasions, through a lack of equipment, it was not possible to carry out all training. The third month tended to be spent working as part of the battalion and regiment. Much of this consisted of marching long distances. After these three months of intense training, the volunteer regiments would deploy to Larzac for a period of live training, which consisted mainly of ranges, field craft, combat exercises and night exercises.[2]

Despite initially planning to send the battalion to Finland, *1ᵉ BMVE* arrived in Beirut on 15 April 1940 and was in Baalbeck by 16 April. On 28 April according to the orders issued (instructions N° 308/I, dated 22 April 1940) *Général* Massiet, who was General Officer Commanding *Groupe Forces Mobiles du Levant*, directed that the battalion be posted to the *6ᵉ REI (6ᵉ Régiment Étranger d'Infanterie)* based at Baalbeck, north of Beirut in the Beqaa Valley, and would be formally changed from *1ᵉ BMVE* to the *11ᵉ BVE*. The battalion was commanded by *Major* Knocker and the *6ᵉ REI* had *Colonel* Fernand Barre as its *Chef de Corps*.

Not all Spaniards with the French in Syria were members of *11ᵉ BVE*. 6100554 /13808262 Cleto Sánchez Monterrubio ended up in Syria because he had joined the *Légion Étrangère*. Like so many others, after being held in a series of camps across the border in France he made the decision to join the *Légion Étrangère* and after going to Marseilles and Orán he travelled to Syria:

> On our way to Syria while at sea, we were given orders to call into Tunis. Germany had invaded Poland, it was September 1939, soon we arrived in Malta which was still English and then Alexandria moving to Beirut in Lebanon. We finished the journey in a place called Palmeras a small town where the people were very nice and got on well with the Spaniards because they understood our language and used to invite us to have tea …[3]

It is probable that Sánchez was posted to the second battalion of the *6ᵉ REI* which *Colonel* Fernand Barre took command of in late December 1939. The battalion had troops based in Homs and Palmyra in the centre of Syria. Between January and March 1940, the *6ᵉ REI* was reorganised and by the time the *11ᵉ BVE* was renamed and based in Baalbeck, *6ᵉ REI* was a mountain unit based in Homs and remained under the command of *Colonel* Barre. It comprised a Headquarters, a 1st and a 2nd Battalion and then soon after, the recently arrived *11ᵉ BVE*.[4] By this point the *11ᵉ BVE* consisted of 19 officers, one Officer Cadet, 80 Warrant Officers and NCOs and 729 Other Ranks. Sánchez would go on to be part of a group of six Spanish *Légionnaires* who would escape to Palestine in the summer of 1940. One of these was Francisco Geronimo who later served in 2nd SAS.

Things came to a head though when France was invaded in May 1940 and those who were in command of the Levant had to make decisions. The whole of the *6ᵉ REI* had moved to Baalbeck on 3 June to take part in a training exercise near Katana in the desert to the southwest of Damas as part of the *192ᵉ Division d'Infanterie*. The exercise was cut short on 10 June because of Italy entering the war. According to Luís Bracero who served in the *11ᵉ BVE*:

---

2 Stéphane Leroy, 'Les Exilés Républicains Espagnols des Régiments de Marche des Volontaires Étrangers. Engagement, présence et formation militaire (janvier 1939-mai 1940),' *Cahiers de Civilisation Espagnole Contemporaine*, 6 (2010), DOI: <https://doi.org/10.4000/ccec.3285>. Accessed 10 November 2021.
3 Stéphane Leroy, 'Les Exilés Républicains Espagnols des Régiments de Marche des Volontaires Étrangers. Engagement, présence et formation militaire (janvier 1939-mai 1940),' *Cahiers de Civilisation Espagnole Contemporaine*, 6 (2010), DOI: <https://doi.org/10.4000/ccec.3285>. Accessed 10 November 2021.
4 Sixth Foreign Infantry Regiment <http://foreignlegion.info/units/6th-foreign-infantry-regiment/>. Accessed 10 November 2021.

A group of Spanish *Légionnaires* pose for a photo in Syria. In the middle, crouching down, is Francisco Geronimo, who would later escape to join 2nd SAS. Geronimo was a born survivor just like his namesake. (Francisco Geronimo collection)

> We were surprised when the armistice was signed between France and Germany and were on exercise marching from Baalbek to Katana some 70km away. When we returned, Major Knocker ... told us of the surrender of France. He did however tell us that it was his plan to continue the fight against Germany alongside the British.[5]

When *Général* Mittelhauser in Beirut announced on 24 June that he would not support a capitulating French Government he was applauded by all ranks. The armistice between France and Germany was signed soon after and on 27 June, *Général* Mittelhauser's Chief of Staff, *Colonel* de Larminat, sent out a note encouraging units in Lebanon and Syria to join the British forces stationed in Palestine. When he returned to Homs, *Major* Knocker was issued with this note, which, amongst other things, stated:

> All personnel, French and foreigners, who refused to obey orders and or accept the risks that are linked to a rebellion, are welcome in the ranks of the British Army or they will make up a group of French volunteers and will continue the fight against the enemy in Egypt. The aim of this memo is to organise the structure, the joining up and the deployment to Palestine of a core of volunteers who are well armed and equipped.[6]

---

5   Daniel Arasa, *Los Españoles de Churchill* (Barcelona: Editorial Armonía, 1991), p.145.
6   André-Paul Comor, *L'Epopée de la 13e Demi-Brigade de Légion Étrangère, 1940–1945* (Paris: Nouvelles Editions Latines, 1988), p.144.

Having read it and had a bit of time to reflect, Knocker immediately discussed the matter with his commanding officer who had also received the note. They were both in agreement that they should join the British. He then rejoined his battalion and discussed it with his men telling them to think about it overnight but that the battalion would leave for Palestine the next day all being well. The biggest issue was that as the *6ᵉ REI* travelled on foot and had no vehicles in the unit it would have to use the vehicle pool in Baalbeck. When asked if they would volunteer or not, all of the Spaniards in the battalion stepped forward. They were split into three groups to get the kit and equipment ready to set off the next day. The situation amongst officers and men across French units in Syria and Lebanon now became very similar to what had been happening in Trentham Park. While the rank and file and many junior officers were keen to join the British, many senior officers were not convinced. Once the conditions of the Armistice were clear, *Général* Dentz who was the Commander in Chief of the *Armée du Levant* (Army of the Levant) and High Commissioner of the Levant, decided that the French Army in the region would remain loyal to Vichy.

The next day back in Baalbek nothing happened, nor the next and eventually, following orders, *Colonel* Barre was forced to accept that the move to Palestine would not take place. *Colonel* de Larminat was placed under arrest as were many other officers, but he escaped after an audacious plan was hatched by some junior officers to free him and get him to Palestine. He duly left and became a leading officer in the Free French Army later in the war, commanding the *6ᵉ Division Française Libre*. Many Spaniards attempted to escape but were stopped and jailed. The first battalion in *6ᵉ REI* was forced to restore order in Baalbek and as a result, some 300 Spaniards were incarcerated and sentenced to two months hard labour. The largest group of around 110 was arrested and imprisoned in Homs. Despite arguing that they had only signed up *pour la durée de la guerre*, the Spaniards were disarmed and the third company from the *11ᵉ BVE* dissolved later in August. The Spaniards then made up a labour company and were soon occupied with infrastructure construction works in the Levant (building roads, rails, bridges, et cetera). The *11ᵉ BVE* was completely disbanded in October 1942 to form the *Groupement de Travailleurs Étrangers du Levant*. Nevertheless, several Spaniards would be allowed to join the *6ᵉ REI* as regular *Légionnaires*.[7] Those who stayed would eventually form part of the famous *13ᵉ DBLE* that fought as the Free French at Bir Hakeim within the 8th Army during the summer of 1942.

To the British, the Queen's Royal Regiment and No.50 Middle East Commando

Some Spaniards did get away and this is where the story of the Spaniards who served in the Middle East Commandos properly begins. Having studied various accounts and personal memoirs, it would seem that there were most likely three groups of Spaniards that were able to get across to join the British. The largest of these was just over 50 men who used two trucks to get across the border, the other two groups travelled on foot. One of the founding members of the Middle East Commandos, the first commanding officer of No.50 Middle East Commando and later D Battalion of LAYFORCE, the then Major George Young, would afterwards say:

> After Dunkirk the French in Syria had got into a terrible mess. Some wanted to continue others said 'Well if the government at home gives up we must do the same.' The Spaniards who were serving in Syria in a foreign service battalion said: 'It is no good us staying here because if we come under the Nazis we will be for it!' So they departed for Palestine, which

---

7 André-Paul Comor, *L'Epopée de la 13e Demi-Brigade de Légion Étrangère, 1940–1945* (Paris: Nouvelles Editions Latines, 1988), pp.145–50.

Spaniards of *6ᵉ REI* in Syria wearing their *Croix de Dauphiné* of the *13ᵉ DBLE* in 1941. (Manuel Surera collection)

was then a British mandate with a couple of lorries. I'm not sure if they had one of the company's safes too! They left under a slight cloud and then came down to the canal zone eventually where there was a camp of about 2,000 of what was going to be Free French … they were billeted there. [8]

It is certain that the Spaniards who travelled by lorry were members of the *11ᵉ BVE*, and there are several accounts that confirm this. Amongst these, four accounts stick out and give us a good feel for what happened. The first two are about the large group in the lorries.

Before his death in the 1990s, 6100540/13808256 Jaime Trill, with the help of his wife (who typed the transcripts) wrote a full account of his bizarre wartime experiences and had them sent to the Imperial War Museum.[9] In these, he talks about what happened as the large group made their way across to Jordan. This is further backed up by 6100530 /13808252 Francisco Navarrete who talks about coming across several patrols en route to the Jordanian border before arriving at the French frontier post.[10] The group in the trucks had a certain Basilio as their leader. It is not clear which Basilio this was as there were in fact two: 6100528/13808251 Basilio Marín and 6100536/13808231 Santiago Basilio. It is most likely that it was the latter as most were called

---

8 George Alan Dawson Young, IWM Interview, Catalogue Number 7328, 1983.
9 James Trill, 'Biography of a Spanish Soldier 1939 – 1946,' IWM Collection, private papers of J. Trill, document. 3705, p.12. This document is of interest but sadly contains a great deal of exaggeration and is factually incorrect in many places, especially after he joins the British Army. The key inaccuracy being that Jaime Trill was in fact taken POW at Crete in early June 1941 and remained imprisoned for the rest of the war. Military records have him in Stalag 383. Something he totally omits in his account.
10 Daniel Arasa, *Los Españoles de Churchill* (Barcelona: Editorial Armonía Poética, 1991), p.148.

by their surnames or a nickname. Santiago Basilio would go on to serve in the Pioneer Corps later in the war and be posted to Britain. What is also corroborated by several families is that at the French frontier post there was an altercation that was eventually resolved by 6100512/13808242 Joaquín Fajardo; his son, Tony, takes up the story:

> At the frontier, they were stopped by a French Colonial soldier who refused to let them through despite the many attempts in Spanish and French to negotiate their exit. At this point, my father jumped down from the back of one of the trucks and hit the soldier on the shin with his rifle butt sending him to the ground and raising the barrier to let the trucks through.[11]

According to Francisco Navarette, the Spaniards in this group passed into safety as they crossed the border and the River Jordan. Once across, they made it clear they were keen to join the British Army and serve under British officers as British soldiers.

Jaime Trill who joined the Middle East Commandos and fought in Crete in 1941. (Fernando Esteve collection)

The story of the two other groups is also quite remarkable. Cleto Sánchez Monterrubio who served in the *2e Bataillon* of the *6e REI* escaped to safety in a group of six. Here is his story:

> I marched with my Platoon towards the Iraqi border in the desert and it was there that we found out that the Germans had invaded France. Because we were Spanish Republicans, we were afraid that our lives would be in danger under the Germans ... so six Spanish *Légionnaires*, with me being one of them, deserted from the French Foreign Legion.
>
> During our escape we marched by night and during the day we remained hidden. On the first day we stayed in a small birdhouse out of fear of being arrested by the French police. This was the longest day. In the group we were: Geronimo, Carmona, Martínez 'El Barbero', Ramirez 'El Chato', Bravo and a servant. 'El Barbero', soon fell to the floor with thirst as we had not drunk since our escape. We were not sure if it was a good idea to leave there or wait and be discovered by the police. We decided to stick together. It was at that time that we now heard sound the sound of small bells that told us cattle was nearby. Four from the group went to ask the locals for water whereas I stayed with 'El Barbero'. Soon they came back with a litre of water which they had bought for 300 francs the others already drunk when they arrived. We then came across sheep and approached the shepherd and asked if he had water. He said no but he took us to his hut and gave us water and some food. In the meantime, he went down to the town and returned with the police. When we saw them enter in their uniforms, we knew we were in Jordan and as you can imagine we were really relieved. That night a lorry arrived with an English escort ... and that is how the story of serving in the French Foreign Legion ended.

---

11 Transcript of interview with Tony Fajardo, 10 June 2020. This information came from his discussions with his father's friend, Francisco Navarrete.

British troops gather as the Spaniards unload their truck on arrival from Syria in the summer of 1940. (Miguel Martínez collection)

Once safe, they entered Palestine:

> Escorted by British troops we arrived in a town in Palestine. I can't remember the name as it was night and we could hardly see where we were going. There they interrogated us or questioned us about our identity and where we came from. None of us had any documentation only that we were *Légionnaires*. When daylight came, we got moved to Jaifa in Palestine and we were sent directly to a camp of Polish soldiers who have been escaping their country. During the day we visited the town where we met a lot of people who could speak Spanish most of it learnt in Argentina and we were invited in to have tea.
>
> Then, later, they took us to a French camp on the Suez Canal. The French officers asked if we wanted to stay in the French Army and we said no, we wanted to be free. The British officers told us that we could not be part of the British Army because foreign elements or a Foreign Legion did not exist as such so we asked them if we could just be taken to another border because we could not return to Spain. Then they told us that they were setting up a new volunteer battalion and asked us if he wanted to be part of it. We said yes.
>
> I joined 50 Middle Eastern Commando in July 1940.[12]

---

12 Cleto Sánchez Monterrubio, *Memorias de Tres Banderas*, unpublished memoir. Translation by the author.

Another group of Spaniards that escaped on foot was led by 6100562 /13808271 Francisco Pereira Martínez. Originally from La Zarza, west of Badajoz in Extremadura, Martínez fought in Madrid during the early days of the Spanish Civil War and had served in the *Carabineros*. After being wounded at the Battle of Jarama in early 1937, he had then fought in the Guadarrama and at Brunete later that year. At the end of the year, he was sent to the Aragón front where he continued fighting until the end of the war. Like countless others, he crossed into France in early 1939 and was soon interned. He joined the *Légion Étrangère* that summer and was eventually posted to the *1ᵉ Bataillon* of the *6ᵉ REI* based at Belabaye in Syria. By the summer of 1940, following the news, he had decided to desert from the French Army. Having secured a weekend leave pass, he escaped along with another three Spaniards, one of them was 6100558/13808264 Julián Lillo, a tough young man from near Ciudad Real who had fought at the Battle of Teruel in 1938 and who would eventually settle down in Britain as an overhead crane operator. Lillo had also fought at the Madrid front and had joined the *Légion Étrangère*, an organisation he regarded as the strictest he had ever been in. In a daring nine-day escape into Palestine, the group endured many hardships and eventually gave themselves up to British Military Police. Following a week of questioning, they were moved to Haifa where they met other Spaniards. One of these was Cleto Sánchez.[13]

With the arrival of these three groups (that we know of) into Palestine and Jordan along with several other groups from different nationalities, the big dilemma for the British authorities was what to do with them. As these Spaniards did not want to remain members of the French armed forces (even the Free French) and dreaded being sent back to Spain for obvious reasons, they pushed hard to be able to serve in the British Army if at all possible. George Young went on to explain:

> Then the question arrived at my branch that they (the Spaniards) were quite prepared to continue fighting against Hitler but must have British officers not French. This is when the commandos were beginning to be formed up. I was told: 'Look here, if those chaps would be any good, go and have a look.' So I thought and I went down to see … and they were quite good. There were all sorts and types about 70 of them. Some were students, one or two were graduates and quite a lot were working-class chaps as well as a few members of ordinary agricultural labourers, chaps who had worked in vineyards and things like that. So, I had a look at them with Fox-Davies and we thought 'they will do, they've had quite a lot of military training and quite a lot of service training having been pushed out' … we enlisted them and got hold of a chap who had been their spokesman, who is a graduate of Cadiz university and we said 'Find good chaps who I will promote to acting Corporal and they will each command a quarter of your fellows and if they succeed I will confirm them after a month and anybody else who is eligible for full promotion I will consider for another rank' … they went off and came back with four names and it was a great success in a way because these chaps were elected by popular vote you see. The section they ruled over said 'if we do not back him up we should look pretty foolish.' So they did that and we never had any trouble on the internal discipline side at all with them cause all you had to do was say to one of the NCOs for example 'Gomez hasn't shaved today' (it was awfully difficult to get them to shave once a day) and the next day you would see Gomez walking about with his face looking like it had been rubbed with sandpaper![14]

---

13 Francisco Pereira, *Life Stories*. Unpublished memoirs, made available by the family.
14 George Alan Dawson Young, IWM Interview, Catalogue Number 7328, 1983.

At the end of June 1940, Colonel Adrian Simpson, head of the Military Intelligence (Research) (MI(R)) Branch at GHQ Middle East Forces (MEF), had been tasked with raising the Middle East Commando. Second in command of MI(R) Branch at GHQ MEF at the time was then Major George Young, a Sapper officer. He had been sent to the Middle East to be involved in various projects. The most noteworthy of these was a planned operation to destroy the Romanian oilfields. Young was able to get a Royal Engineer Field Company to Turkey to be ready to carry out the necessary demolitions but with the fall of France, the operation was aborted. On 6 July, Young was joined by Captain Harry Fox-Davies from the Durham Light Infantry who had been interested in the concept of commando style operations and was keen to instigate units of this kind. By the middle of July 1940, a provisional establishment had been hatched out for the soon to be established Number 50 Middle East Commando, and had been approved. This establishment consisted of: A HQ with three troops (companies), each troop consisting of four sections (platoons). The sections would be commanded by an officer and contain 25 men. There would also be a small medical team, an armourer and some interpreters. In total there would be 371 all ranks. The manpower for the Middle East Commandos would come from volunteers from units in the Middle East.[15]

When men joined, they were presented with the following letter:

ADDRESSED TO ALL RANKS JOINING MIDDLE EAST DEPOT COMMANDO

You have today joined Commandos.
Commandos are units of picked, highly trained fighting men designed to carry out the type of enterprise which should be dear to the heart of every soldier.

You are here to undergo instruction in the type of warfare you are going to wage and the weapons you will use for it. You will have to work hard with your brains and your bodies. Don't grumble if you are tired. Remember you are being toughened to be able to do the maximum amount of harm to the swine who are bombing your women at home. There is only one good Italian or German: that is a dead one, and you are going to be taught the most up-to-date methods of killing him.

The discipline here will be strict. You have come here to learn to be a kind of super soldier. You must behave like one. You belong to a crack corps. Be proud of it and remember that now you are in a unit formed from many different corps you represent the regiment you have left. Be a credit to it.

In your leisure hours we want to make your stay here as comfortable as possible. If you have a legitimate complaint, your officers are there to hear it and try to put things right. We have a lot of work to do. Let us pull together, work hard, tidy up these would-be world beaters and get home.
NOT TO BE TAKEN INTO ACTION

On 31 July, George Young and Harry Fox-Davies visited the Spaniards at Moascar and interviewed them all. The first intake was then taken onto the books of the Queen's Royal Regiment (West Surrey) to legalise their position. This was because members of No.50 Middle East Commando came from volunteers from units already in the region. With the British authorities' approval, the Spaniards were incorporated into No. 50 Middle East Commando as British soldiers for the

---

15 Charles Messenger, *The Middle East Commandos* (Wellingborough: William Kimber& Co Ltd, 1988), pp.13–17.

GENERAL HEADQUARTERS, 2nd ECHELON, M.E. FORCES

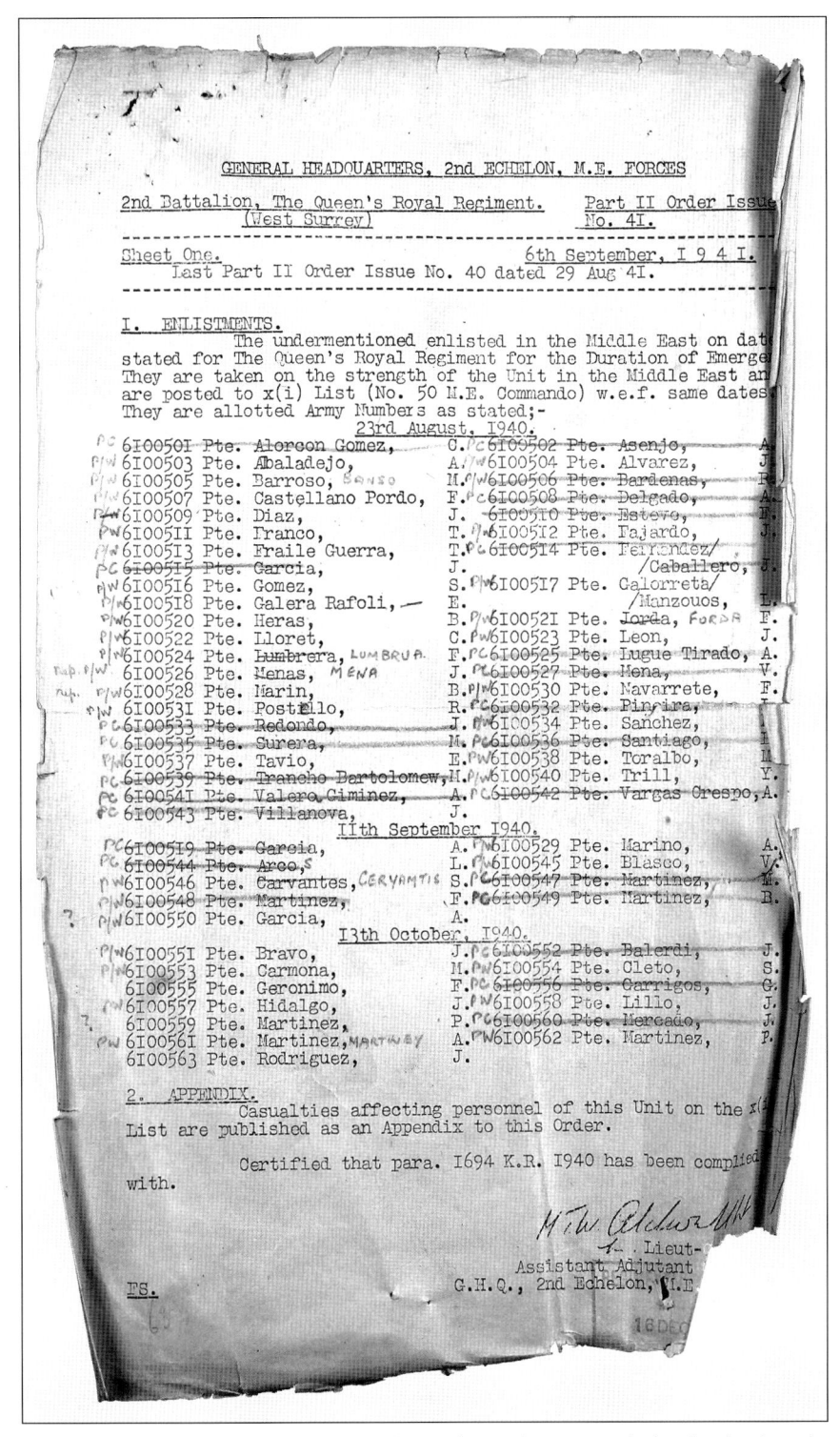

2nd Battalion, The Queen's Royal Regiment.　　Part II Order Issue
　　　　　(West Surrey)　　　　　　　　　　　　　No. 41.

Sheet One.　　　　　　　　　　　　　　6th September, 1 9 4 1.
　　Last Part II Order Issue No. 40 dated 29 Aug 41.
----

1. ENLISTMENTS.
　　　　The undermentioned enlisted in the Middle East on date
stated for The Queen's Royal Regiment for the Duration of Emerge
They are taken on the strength of the Unit in the Middle East an
are posted to x(i) List (No. 50 M.E. Commando) w.e.f. same dates
They are allotted Army Numbers as stated;-
　　　　23rd August, 1940.
PC 6100501 Pte. Alorcon Gomez,　　C. PC 6100502 Pte. Asenjo,　　　A.
P/W 6100503 Pte. Abaladejo,　　　　A. P/W 6100504 Pte. Alvarez,　　J.
P/W 6100505 Pte. Barroso, SANSO　　M. P/W 6100506 Pte. Bardenas,　R.
P/W 6100507 Pte. Castellano Pordo, F. PC 6100508 Pte. Delgado,　　A.
P/W 6100509 Pte. Diaz,　　　　　　J.　 6100510 Pte. Estevo,　　　N.
P/W 6100511 Pte. Franco,　　　　　T. P/W 6100512 Pte. Fajardo,　　J.
P/W 6100513 Pte. Fraile Guerra,　 T. PC 6100514 Pte. Ferrandez/
PC 6100515 Pte. Garcia,　　　　　J.　　　　　　　　　　/Caballero, J.
P/W 6100516 Pte. Gomez,　　　　　S. P/W 6100517 Pte. Galorreta/
P/W 6100518 Pte. Galera Rafoli,— E.　　　　　　　　　/Manzouos,　L.
P/W 6100520 Pte. Heras,　　　　　B. P/W 6100521 Pte. Jorda, FORDA F.
P/W 6100522 Pte. Lloret,　　　　 C. P/W 6100523 Pte. Leon,　　　 J.
P/W 6100524 Pte. Lumbrera, LUMBRUA F. PC 6100525 Pte. Lugue Tirado, A.
P/W 6100526 Pte. Menas, MENA　　 J. PC 6100527 Pte. Mena,　　　　V.
P/W 6100528 Pte. Marin,　　　　　B. P/W 6100530 Pte. Navarrete,　F.
P/W 6100531 Pte. Postello,　　　 R. PC 6100532 Pte. Pinira,　　　I.
PC 6100533 Pte. Redondo,　　　　 J. P/W 6100534 Pte. Sanchez,　　I.
PC 6100535 Pte. Surera,　　　　　M. PC 6100536 Pte. Santiago,　　I.
P/W 6100537 Pte. Tavio,　　　　　E. P/W 6100538 Pte. Toralbo,　　M.
PC 6100539 Pte. Trancho Bartolomew, M. P/W 6100540 Pte. Trill,　Y.
PC 6100541 Pte. Valero Giminez,　A. PC 6100542 Pte. Vargas Crespo, A.
PC 6100543 Pte. Villanova,　　　J.
　　　　11th September 1940.
PC 6100519 Pte. Garcia,　　　　　A. P/W 6100529 Pte. Marino,　　　A.
PC 6100544 Pte. Arcos,　　　　　 L. P/W 6100545 Pte. Blasco,　　　V.
P/W 6100546 Pte. Carvantes, CERVANTIS S. PC 6100547 Pte. Martinez, M.
P/W 6100548 Pte. Martinez,　　　 F. PC 6100549 Pte. Martinez,　　B.
P/W 6100550 Pte. Garcia,　　　　A.
　　　　13th October, 1940.
P/W 6100551 Pte. Bravo,　　　　　J. PC 6100552 Pte. Balerdi,　　　J.
P/W 6100553 Pte. Carmona,　　　　M. P/W 6100554 Pte. Cleto,　　　S.
　　6100555 Pte. Geronimo,　　　 F. PC 6100556 Pte. Garrigos,　　G.
　　6100557 Pte. Hidalgo,　　　　J. P/W 6100558 Pte. Lillo,　　　J.
　　6100559 Pte. Martinez,　　　 P. PC 6100560 Pte. Mercado,　　　J.
P/W 6100561 Pte. Martinez, MARTNEY A. P/W 6100562 Pte. Martinez, F.
　　6100563 Pte. Rodriguez,　　　J.

2. APPENDIX.
　　　　Casualties affecting personnel of this Unit on the x(i)
List are published as an Appendix to this Order.

　　　　Certified that para. 1694 K.R. 1940 has been complied
with.

　　　　　　　　　　　　　　　　　　　　　Lieut-
　　　　　　　　　　　　　　　　　　Assistant Adjutant
　　　　　　　　　　　　　　　　　G.H.Q., 2nd Echelon, M.E

FS.

Part II Orders for the 2nd Battalion Queen's Royal Regt (West Surrey), dated 1941, show the dates that the Spaniards were taken onto the books of the battalion before being transferred to No. 50 Middle East Commando. (Surrey History Centre)

duration of the war.[16] The unit then started to form in Genaifa in Egypt in the first week of August 1940. The other groups of Spaniards were then added as they were rounded up and the police finished their investigations. A full list of all the Spaniards that joined No.50 Middle East Commando forms Appendix III of this book.

Sadly, things did not start off well for the Spaniards. A few accounts tell of an altercation in a nightclub where there was a shootout. Captain Bob McGibbon, a Canadian who had volunteered to join the Middle East Commandos from the Leicestershire Regiment and who would command the Spanish Troop in Crete, described what happened:

> Two of the Spaniards were arrested before the group was fully incorporated into No.50 Commando and were sentenced by a Courts Martial in September-October 1940 for shooting at two sergeants from the French Foreign Legion. At a cabaret the French NCOs insisted that the Spaniards salute them, they refused, and a fight ensued. They were sentenced by the Courts Martial, but later on, their sentence was commuted and one of them was awarded the Military Medal in Italy.[17]

This was certainly 6100543/13080234 Private Josep Vilanova who, later, as a member of 1/5th Battalion of the Queen's Royal Regiment (West Surrey) was awarded the Military Medal when he 'showed great courage and daring' during the crossing of the Volturno River in October 1943.

Some of the Spaniards in No.50 Middle East Commando in Egypt. (Joaquín Fajardo collection)

---

16 TNA, NRA 44612. Further research from Enlistment Registers held at the Surrey Heritage Centre, show that the Spaniards signed up in three groups.
The first of 41, which included Francisco Navarrete & Joaquín Fajardo enlisted on 23 August 1940. This group is most probably the one that escaped by truck.
The second group of 9 were enlisted on 11 September 1940.
The final group of 13 includes Francisco Geronimo and Cleto Sánchez Monterrubio.
The above dates do not necessarily match with the timeline of the establishment of No.50 Middle East Commando, but it was normal for records to be done after the event.
17 Daniel Arasa, *Los Españoles de Churchill* (Barcelona: Editorial Armonía Poética, 1991), p.155.

Training and Initial Operations

The newly formed No.50 Middle East Commando in Genaifa underwent intensive training and, despite the language barrier, the Spaniards soon gained respect for their fitness and guile, especially during night exercises. The Spaniards were in two sections in B Troop headed up initially by Captain Brodie and later by Captain Bob McGibbon, who would command them in Crete in 1941. One of the first officers to join during training was Major (later Lieutenant Colonel) Stephen Rose, who became No.50 Middle East Commando's Second in Command. He later commented:

> They were good soldiers overall but not necessarily up to the same level as their British counterparts and depended greatly on their officers for orders, but they were nonetheless well disciplined.[18]

The role foreseen for Middle East Commando was mainly to carry out raids behind enemy lines, that is against the Italians. As there was an urgent operational requirement for them to be ready as soon as possible, a six-week programme was devised to get them up to the requisite level of readiness. The programme consisted of the following:

Week	Activity
1	Map reading and compass work Stalking and use of cover Knotting, lashing and demolitions (officers and section commanders only) 24-hours scheme (training exercise comprising load carrying over distance in a 24-hour period) Lectures on night work and stalking
2	Map reading and compass work Camel riding, rowing and swimming Knotting, lashing and demolitions 36 hours scheme – desert country Lectures – guerrilla tactics and First Aid
3	Weapon training – rifle and revolver Compass marching and stalking Camel riding and rowing (this was for ship to shore operations) 48 hours scheme – bush country Lectures – First Aid
4	Weapon training – rifle and revolver Bridging expedients Camel riding and rowing 48 hours scheme – crossing water obstacles
5	Weapon training – grenades and demolitions (night and day) Rowing and boat work 48 hours scheme – landing from ships' boats
6	Weapon training – Fanny [dagger/knuckleduster], bayonet, Tommy gun and machine pistol Method of attacking specific targets 48 hours scheme – night rowing, landing, crossing, obstacles

Physical training (PT) was carried out each day when in camp.[19]

One of the most important aspects of being a member of the Middle East Commando was fitness and endurance. The standard of being able to cover the distance of 30 miles on foot over

---

18 Daniel Arasa, *Los Españoles de Churchill* (Barcelona: Editorial Armonía Poética, 1991), p.156.
19 TNA, WO 169, PRO 57/1637, War Diary G(R) Branch GHQ, Middle East Forces.

three successive days, cross country, carrying all food, water and equipment was soon established. Rigorous restrictions were put in place to regulate the amount of food and water that could be consumed. The Spaniards, who had already been used to this in the *Légion* as well as being accustomed to the heat, coped well. A great deal of work was carried out at night, and this is where the Spaniards excelled. The standard plan for a three-day exercise was to be taken by ship to the Red Sea and march back, carrying out exercises en route. There was also experimentation regarding ration packs and vitamin tablets as well as water purification kits. As there were no specialised landing craft in the Middle East, the Middle East Commandos made do with ships' whalers and had to learn about improvised rafting. Much work was done on watermanship and amphibious training in the Great Bitter Lakes. Demolition training was also a key component of what the commandos were taught, and the idea was that all ranks would be able to prepare and use simple explosive charges.

Spaniards carrying out rowing training on the Bitter Lakes. Rowing hard here is Moisés Trancho Bartolomé one of the junior NCOs of the Spanish group. Note his missing little finger on his right hand which had been shot off during the Spanish Civil War. (Miguel Martínez collection)

When interviewed by Daniel Arasa, Stephen Rose spoke about the training:

> The training for No.50 Commando was the same for all ranks. Those in charge had to be tenacious, solve problems and be proud of being able to go that bit further as well as being able to lead men who had been selected for their physical endurance, vivacity and enthusiasm. We had to learn new skills … On many occasions I had to lead by example and I remember hand to hand combat with a very tough Spaniard … it was important to show that we were as prepared, strong and aggressive as the men we commanded.[20]

---

20 TNA, WO 169, PRO 57/1637, War Diary G(R) Branch GHQ, Middle East Forces, pp.157–158.

Spaniards carrying out training amongst reeds near the Bitter Lakes. Note the Australian slouch hats being worn as part of the uniform. (Miguel Martínez collection)

But according to Captain Bob McGibbon:

> How could I forget those Spaniards! … Considering language difficulties, the fact that they were strangers in a foreign army, etc, I think the Spaniards were as good as most British troops, especially at commando work. They were particularly good at night work and had no compunction about using a knife or dagger. They never complained about conditions, were keen to learn to use new weapons or tactics and were most anxious to be considered as real members of the British Army. Physically they were tough, even the older ones could march for miles without tiring. They stuck together and were genuinely concerned with a lot of their fellow Spaniards. They looked out for one another. They also knew they had no chance of returning to Spain and had no family ties to fall back on.[21]

In the newly formed unit, more stress was placed on the individual and many of the formalities of parades and saluting were dispensed with. This would be something that would continue into being as units such as the SAS were set up later in the war. The Spaniards were very amenable to this form of discipline but, as there was little time to properly train their NCOs, they were heavily reliant on their officers, something which would prove problematic later. With respect to the uniform, it was decided to dress in a slightly more unconventional manner using loose-fitting

---

21 TNA, WO 169, PRO 57/1637, War Diary G(R) Branch GHQ, Middle East Forces, p.153.

clothing, rubber soled boots, bush jacket and Australian slouch hat. The Middle East Commandos adopted their own form of specialised weapon and not the Commando dagger. This was a knife-cum-knuckleduster known as a 'Fanny', which had been found in Cairo and was mass produced for the Middle East Commandos. The 'Fanny' also made up the Commando's cap badge, although this was rather small so as not to stand out. Officers, warrant officers and sergeants were issued with pistols and Thompson submachine guns. Other Ranks used the standard Short Magazine Lee Enfield and Bren Guns as well as the Lanchester submachine gun. These smaller weapons allowed for better movement and were light and portable. As most of their work was done on foot, transport continued to be an issue as most Middle East Commando units did not have many vehicles on their establishment table. This would cause problems on many occasions in the future.

The Spaniards settled in and eventually impressed their British counterparts. Bob McGibbon added:

Manuel Sánchez proudly wearing his Middle East Commando Australian slouch hat. Note the 'Fanny' cap badge. Sánchez would later be one of over 30 Spaniards taken prisoner during the Battle of Crete in 1941. (Fernando Esteve collection)

> Our British troops initially did not like the Spaniards. They were nervous of them and always wanted to avoid night exercises involving the Spaniards in the dark, the Spaniards would keep awake and absolutely silent, whether moving about or lying still. British troops tend to be somewhat noisy and got themselves captured by a silent Spanish patrol time and time again.[22]

Captain Peter Selerie who had transferred from the Sherwood Rangers to become Adjutant of No.50 Middle East Commando would also comment:

> In the training and exercises it was clear straight away that the Spaniards were born fighters. We often used them to show the high level that the Commandos required in the dark.[23]

By 5 October 1940, the first troop and the Spaniards in No.50 Middle East Commando had completed their training. George Young was promoted to lieutenant colonel and became the commanding officer and Harry Fox-Davies was promoted to major and became the Second in Command. It was not long before they were stood to to deploy on their first operation. The Italians had gone on to the offensive in Somalia and Sudan and by mid-September 1940 had launched an invasion from Libya. Major General A.P. Wavell, Commander-in-Chief Middle East Land Forces, made the decision to enact a policy of harassment and the Middle East Commandos had a key role

---

22 Testimony by Major Bob McGibbon – Middle East Commando Archive.
23 Daniel Arasa, *Los Españoles de Churchill* (Barcelona: Editorial Armonía Poética, 1991), p.153.

to play in this. At a meeting at GHQ MEF on 12 September, the decision was made to expand the force to four British and three Indian Commandos. No.50 Middle East Commando was soon training and preparing for a raiding operation on the Italian base at Bomba. The planning was detailed and on the night of 27/28 October they were embarked on HMS *Decoy* and HMS *Hereward*. However the operation was aborted because of Italy's invasion of Greece and the threat to Crete. The unit was understandably not happy, and morale plummeted.[24]

In October, the Middle East Commandos expanded with the establishment of No.51 and No.52 Middle East Commandos. The remainder of No.50 was also being trained. No.52 was to be raised from units in the Middle East in the same way as No. 50. The situation was different with No.51 however, and it had some unusual origins. No.1 Palestinian Company of the Auxiliary Military Pioneer Corps (AMPC) had Major H.J. 'Kid' Cator of the Royal Scots Greys as its commanding officer. He had taken command on 31 January 1940 and in February the company had embarked to France as part of the BEF. When he first saw them on parade Cator sized up his men:

> A 'foreign legion' would be a more accurate way of describing them, than by calling then Palestinian Pioneers. Three-quarters of them were Jews and about a quarter Arab, Czechs, Russians, Bulgarians, Romanians, Austrians, Germans and Spanish, even Portuguese and Latvians, amongst the Arab section, Sudanese, Egyptians, Iraqis and Senaites and Palestinians.[25]

The mention of Spaniards above is interesting as so far there has been no information found of Spaniards who served under Cator. The company was to have a frustrating time in France and eventually made it back to England at the end of June. Although it is difficult to fully know, it is possible that Spanish members of Cator's company may at this point have become members of No.1 Spanish Company. On 15 September 1940, the company arrived in the Middle East and on the 15 October No.51 Middle East Commando officially came into being with Major H.J. Cator as its commanding officer. No.52 Middle East Commando was formed two weeks later with no less than 35 different cap badges being represented in it. The establishment of a further three Middle East Commandos from Indian units was aborted as the Indian Army was undergoing a huge expansion scheme and there was a severe lack of suitable officers. Soon after, in December 1940, a Middle East Commando depot was established under the command of Major D.W. Melville MC, which would be responsible for the training and supplying of individual reinforcements to the three Commandos.[26]

Before deploying to Bomba, some of the Spaniards worked for Bob McGibbon in discovering information from Vichy sailors who were trying to get the Spaniards to join them or, worse still, spy for them. He chose to work with two of his Spanish sergeants and pretend he was one of them. There were many incidents in bars and clubs in Cairo and Alexandria. On one occasion, an amusing incident took place involving the unit's chaplain:

> On one occasion we three 'Spaniards' were just getting into a cab together when we were joined by the camp padre. This was most unfortunate, for the padre said he was certain he'd met Middle East before. I just shrugged and said in Spanish that I didn't understand English. My two Spaniards explained in their broken English that I only talked Spanish and

---

24 Charles Messenger, *The Middle East Commandos* (Wellingborough: William Kimber & Co. Ltd, 1988), pp.20–21.
25 Charles Messenger, *The Middle East Commandos* (Wellingborough: William Kimber & Co. Ltd, 1988), p.23.
26 Charles Messenger, *The Middle East Commandos* (Wellingborough: William Kimber & Co. Ltd, 1988), p.27.

Spaniards rest below the Great Sphinx on a visit to the Pyramids of Giza. (Manuel Surera collection)

some French. The padre, who only spoke English, kept staring at me and I had a terrible time keeping a blank look as he chatted to my two sergeants. Fortunately, I didn't get detailed for church parade for a couple of weeks, by which time the padre had forgotten all about the incident.[27]

Given the recent invasion of Greece by Italy and the threat to Crete, it was decided to send No. 50 Middle East Commando to the island. By the middle of November 1940, the Commando was on its way and under the command of 14th Infantry Brigade on the island. At this time Harry Fox-Davies was replaced by Stephen Rose. George Young took over command of No.52 Middle East Commando and Lieutenant Colonel Peter Symons of the Royal Engineers took command of No.50. The bulk of No.50 Middle East Commando's troops arrived at Heraklion in Crete at the end of November. A lot of training now took place, including organising drills for embarkation and disembarkation.

In the meantime, No.51 and No.52 Middle East Commandos had also been busy training and preparing to deploy. No.51 was warned off to support Operation COMPASS and land at Sollum Bay by the border with Libya, in early December 1940. The operation was called off due to bad weather, but 'Kid' Cator and his men were soon returning to the west with the Coldstream Guards to land at Bardia. Further frustration took place and Cator and No.51 ended up in Sollum and on standby to capture Bardia, but the operation was cancelled and No.51 returned to Genaifa and then moved to fight the Italians in Abyssinia and Eritrea.

---

27 Testimony by Major Bob McGibbon – Middle East Commando Archive.

A small group photo while probably on range training in Crete in late 1940. Second from the left, crouching, is Joaquín Fajardo. (Miguel Martínez collection)

Left: Supporting the garrison in Crete, the Spaniards were also on standby for potential raids in the surrounding parts of the Mediterranean. Serafín Gómez is standing on the far left, Manuel Surera second from the right and Fernando Esteve far right. Note the two Spaniards sitting in the middle with Lanchester submachine guns. (Manuel Surera collection)
Right: Manuel Surera in the middle with two fellow members of No.50 Middle East Commando on Crete, early 1941. (Manuel Surera collection)

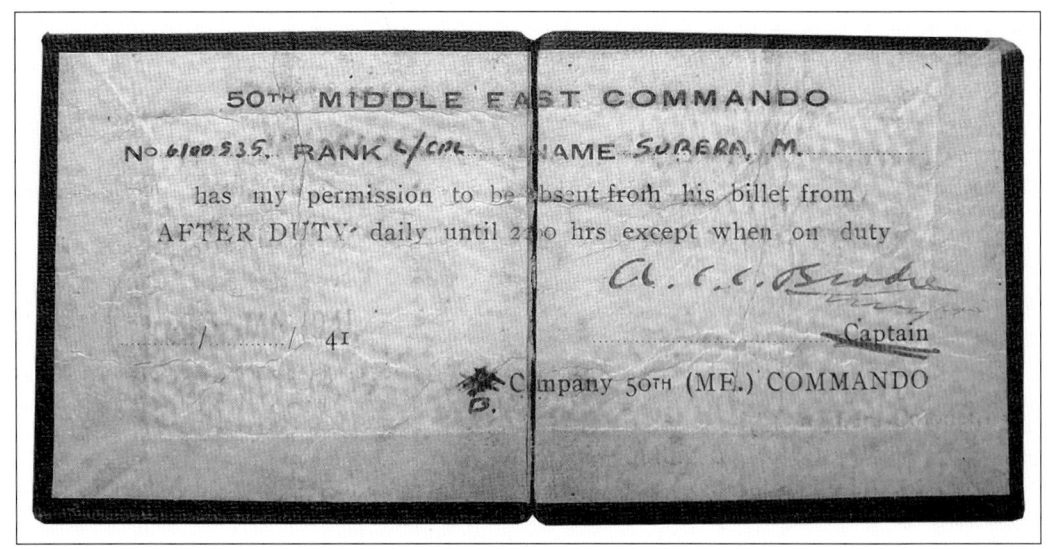

A No. 50 Middle East Commando pass issued in Crete for Manuel Surera. (Manual Surera collection)

Back on Crete, No.50 Middle East Commando was alerted for a raid on Kasos in early January 1941. Despite using an old ship, the landing was successful only to then be cancelled. The operation was resurrected in mid-February but was aborted at the last minute due to badly chosen beaches and well defended Italian positions. After this disappointment, the focus turned to the island of Castelorizzo and Operation ABSTENTION. It was decided however, not to use the Spaniards in this raid to avoid confusion as to the ears of the British soldiers, Italian and Spanish sounded too similar.[28] Operation ABSTENTION took place but was not a great success and resulted in some members of the Commando being killed and captured, a very negative result. A Joint Services Board of Enquiry was convened whose findings proved to be rather sobering as the Middle East Commandos were seen as the main reason for the operation's failure. No.50 Middle East Commando had returned to Egypt by the end of March 1941 where they were joined by No.52 Middle East Commando which had just returned from being in the midst of the fighting further south.

On 16 December 1940, No.52 Middle East Commando left Geneifa by train for Port Said and sailed to Port Sudan on the Red Sea, over 900 miles to the south; from there they travelled to Gedaref by train. The commandos were briefed on the disposition and strength of the Italians. The overall strength of the enemy was numerically greater, but their number included many native troops. The Italians also had command of the air since Allied air cover was almost nonexistent. No.52 Middle East Commando was tasked to patrol the front line area to gather information and engage with the enemy where prudent to do so. On 8 January, the Commandos carried out a long-distance raid on the enemy's lines of communication between Khor Kumar and Khor Abd-er Razzag.

The next target was an important crossing on the Atbara River (now known as the Red Nile) near Gondar, Ethiopia – about two day's march away. The operation was unsuccessful and a further raid into this area began on 17 January, essentially a carbon copy of the previous one although with a few modifications. The attack was postponed but a series of ambushes were able to take place. A third and final attempt to attack the enemy on the Metemma-Gondar Road (linking

---

28 Daniel Arasa, *Los Españoles de Churchill* (Barcelona: Editorial Armonía Poética, 1991), p.159.

Spaniards await embarkation for an operation in Crete, possibly for the raid of Kasos. Standing, from left to right, are Manuel Barroso, unknown, Vicente Blasco, José Álvarez, Cleto Sánchez, Francisco Geronimo, Garrigos and crouching is Enrique Galera. (Courtesy of Francisco Geronimo collection)

Sudan and Ethiopia) was foiled when the commandos faced a strong enemy force. After engaging with the enemy, they were forced to withdraw due to the enemy's superior numbers and firepower. The Commando suffered a few light injuries. On 31 January, a commando patrol discovered that the enemy had withdrawn from Djebel Dufeir and Djebel Negus. This withdrawal, together with that in Abyssinia, brought an end to the Italians brief period in East Africa. The commandos had served their purpose and were, effectively, stood down. They then travelled on foot to Gedaref in south-east Sudan where men of No.51 Middle East Commando were billeted. On 24 February they boarded a train for Kassala and eventually arrived at Abassia in Egypt on 9 March reaching their camp at Geneifa on 23 March 1941.[29]

On 24 January 1941, No.51 Middle East Commando sailed from Suez for Port Sudan and moved to Gedaref in Eritrea. Cator's orders from the divisional commander were to institute a programme of patrolling and ambushes to support the manoeuvres of the brigades in the division. There followed a series of operations which were largely a success, and the Commando was able to keep the enemy battalions away from the British main effort on several occasions. Cator was injured and the Second in Command Major C.D.O. Miller, 10th Hussars, took over and received a promotion. No.51 Middle East Commando was thrown into the thick of it almost immediately after it was decided that they would carry out a series of attacks into the Italian flank. There were

---

29 Charles Messenger,, *The Middle East Commandos* (Wellingborough: William Kimber & Co. Ltd, 1988), pp.20–21.

Spaniards in No.51 Middle East Commando and scenes reminiscent of the fighting in Narvik by Spaniards in the *Légion* now occurred, with them showing their worth:

> Toni Garcia who hails from Toledo rushes at an Italian officer and with a curse what makes the blood freeze in one's veins plunges his bayonet into him. This is not an ordinary fight between soldiers of opposing powers. This is a fight full of hatred, nursed for many years in exile and made worse through the feeling of being unwanted, or living without aim and homesickness.
>
> It was a ghastly scene of dead, twisted bodies laying amongst arms and equipment. Empty cartridges and boxes of ammunition were strewn all over the place. We went through the pockets of the dead and found that they belonged to the crack Savoy Grenadiers. Fifty yards ahead were the three waterholes we were supposed to find, but which we certainly would have missed, had the enemy not put up the fight, for they were as vital to him as they were to us. As we filled our water bottles with the deliciously fresh water, Garcia, the former Republican captain and corporal in the Pioneers sighed: 'I have been looking forward to this meeting for three years'.[30]

On 25 March the final big battle in Eritrea took place and the Commando successfully supported the 9th and 10th Brigades of the Fifth Indian Division when they seized the Keren battlefield; two weeks later all of Eritrea had surrendered to the Allies. After a period of recovery, the Commando was moved to Abyssinia. Here it successfully took Commando Hill and had further skirmishes at the Flaga Pass and Wireless Hill. Then in mid-June, after a recuperation period at Adi Ugri, the Commando was moved to the Gondar area of Abyssinia where Italian resistance remained strong. During this period the Commando patrolled aggressively and incessantly against enemy outposts until it was moved to Adowa in mid-August, remaining there throughout September. Leslie Wright, a sergeant in the Middle East Commandos remembered there being Spaniards in the unit:

> We blew up an Italian ordnance depot with supplies and an airfield … we had these Spaniards in our battalion. About fifteen or sixteen Spaniards who were very good with the knife. They were excellent people to dispose of sentries … They used to go out on these raids and kill sheep and bring them back to camp and skin them and cook them over a fire …[31]

Gondar was surrendered to the Allies in November and the campaign in East Africa ended. No.51 Middle East Commando had played a significant role in the Allied successes in Eritrea and Abyssinia, and returned to Egypt in November 1941.[32]

Following the cancellation of Operation WORKSHOP (the capture of the island of Pantelleria between Sicily and Tunisia) in early January 1941, the recently formed Numbers 7, 8 and 11 Commandos were sent out from the United Kingdom as part of what became Layforce. In June 1940, Bob Laycock was a 33 year old captain bound for a staff job out in the Middle East, but by the end of the year was commanding 8 Commando back in Britain. He was promoted to colonel and placed in command of Force Z which left Britain on 1 February 1941. Amongst

---

30 Captain C. Hilliman MC MM RPC, 'Looking Back at 51 Commando,' *The Pioneer Magazine*, No 132, September 1977, pp.22–23. Hilliman served as a soldier from the Pioneer Corps in No.51 Middle East Commando in 1940 and 1941.
31 Leslie Wright, IWM Interview, Catalogue Number 7311, Reel 2, 1983.
32 Charles Messenger, *The Middle East Commandos* (Wellingborough: William Kimber & Co. Ltd, 1988), pp.56–71.

Spaniards were far more used to living off the land than their British counterparts. Here, three are plucking a duck. The soldier on the far left in a white vest is possibly Moisés Trancho Bartolomé. (Manuel Surera collection)

the officers under his command was Evelyn Waugh who ended up being Laycock's Intelligence Officer. Another was David Stirling who during the journey by ship gained the nickname 'the giant sloth' due to spending so much time in his cabin sleeping. The convoy arrived at Suez on 7 March and the following day Laycock reported to his General Officer Commanding, Major General John Evetts, who informed him that there was an operation in the making; capturing the island of Rhodes. In the meantime, the commandos disembarked at Kabrit and moved to Genaifa on the Great Bitter Lake.[33]

According to some personal accounts by the Spaniards, upon their return at Genaifa, No.50 Middle East Commando were granted some local leave and visited Cairo and Alexandria for a few days. Here they struck up an interesting relationship with a Spanish Sefardic Jew who had fled Spain and had set up a series of businesses in the city. Whether this was shortly after returning from Operation ABSTENTION or after their time in Crete earlier on in the year is not certain. But it is nonetheless an interesting story. Several photos passed on by the family show the Spaniards with Mr Carreno who treated them all well. Later after his death, his family kept in contact with many of them.[34]

Shortly after, Layforce was formally established as:

    A Battalion (Lieutenant Colonel J.B. Covin) formerly No.7 Commando
    B Battalion (Lieutenant Colonel D.R. Daly) formerly No.8 Commando
    C Battalion (Lieutenant Colonel R.R. Pedder) formerly No.11 Commando
    A fourth battalion, to be D Battalion, was to be established from Middle East Commando units

---

33 Richard Mead, *Commando General: The Life of Major General Sir Robert Laycock KCMG CB DSO* (Barnsley: Pen & Sword Books Ltd, 2016), pp.66–70.
34 Cleto Sánchez Monterrubio, *Memorias de Tres Banderas and Francisco Pereira, Life Stories.* Unpublished memoirs.

Spaniards pose with Mr and Mrs Carreno in Egypt. (Miguel Martínez collection)

It was decided to amalgamate Nos.50 and 52 Middle East Commandos to make up this fourth battalion, combining as five companies, each company having two troops of 50 men each. This restructuring brought consistency with the United Kingdom formed Commandos which formed the other Battalions of Layforce. Lieutenant Colonel George Young was now in overall command of No.50/52 Middle East Commando (D Battalion Layforce). D Battalion was formally formed at Geneifa on 28 March with all ranks being posted to the battalion on the 24 March. The Company Commanders were:

    A Company – Captain K.E. Hermon, Durham Light Infantry.
    B Company – Captain C. Parish, Royal Sussex Regiment
    C Company – Captain W.J. Burton, York and Lancaster Regiment
    D Company – Captain R. Boyle, Black Watch.
    E Company – Captain L.N.R. Wilson, Royal Sussex Regiment[35]

The Spaniards made up a full troop of 50 men in B Company which would be commanded by the then Captain Bob L. McGibbon with Lieutenants Sandbach and Russo. The situation with this last officer was interesting; the Spaniards did not trust Russo who came from Gibraltar and had supposedly been involved in the Spanish Civil War on the Nationalist side. Russo had been at university during the Civil War and so it is unlikely that this was actually the case. He transferred from 3rd Hussars into D Battalion on 28 March 1941.

Further intensive training, especially in minor tactics at platoon and company level, was carried out by the battalion until the end of May. During this period, Layforce was busy with planned operations for Rhodes and the Libyan coast. Another period of intense frustration followed with B and C battalions being deployed. D Battalion in the meantime continued its training and was

---

35 Charles Messenger, *The Middle East Commandos* (Wellingborough: William Kimber & Co. Ltd, 1988), p.73.

even used to guard Alexandria docks. However, before long, the battalion found itself embarked, and on its way back to Crete subsequent to the German airborne invasion of the island. Despite returning to Egypt once, they were eventually on their way again late on 26 May. The total force consisted of A and D Battalions plus a small HQ.

The Battle for Crete, 1941

The battalion arrived in Suda Bay and started disembarking at 2300 hours on 26 May and were soon in the thick of it as General Freyberg, of the 2nd New Zealand Expeditionary Force and who commanded the British forces defending the island, had by this time decided that the island should be evacuated. This was confirmed when D Battalion's C company commander, Bill Burton, bumped into Freyberg himself, who confirmed the intentions. Laycock received his orders from General Weston and Layforce was to be used as the rearguard as troops withdrew south to Sphakia. Later that morning Laycock and Evelyn Waugh were able to travel by truck to Freyberg's HQ. As Laycock later wrote:

> Later in the morning I found General Freyberg. He confirmed that the battle of Crete was lost, that our forces in the island were utterly exhausted and that it now only remained to evacuate as many of them as possible. Since Layforce was composed of comparatively fresh troops it was to be used to take the brunt of the rear-guard fighting, necessary to cover the withdrawal.[36]

D Battalion was given orders to take up a position in depth on a ridge some six miles from Suda Bay which was next to where the road to Sphakia turned south, not far from Beritiana. By 0515 the Battalion had arrived and spent the rest of the day under cover and coming under air attack. That afternoon, George Young received orders from Laycock to withdraw D Battalion to a defensive position at Babali Hani further south. However there was a catch, Young was ordered to leave a company behind where the main road went left and turned south. Despite protestations from Young, the order was confirmed by General Weston. After a recce, Young withdrew the battalion to its new location leaving behind B Company holding the forward position. In order to get into position properly, B Company had to move west into as good a position as possible. Bob McGibbon, with many years of experience later explained:

> This meant marching headlong into fleeing British troops – most of them had not an officer to be seen anywhere and damn few SNCOs. It wasn't a retreat but a rout. I remember Lt Russo saying 'Christ Bob, we'll never get out of this mess', and I silently agreed. It was hard to explain to the Spaniards why British troops did not stand and fight – or it would have been hard – had they asked the question. In any case, we took up our position … Young had explained the slim chances of us ever getting out, but he was very fair about it. Shortly afterwards a platoon of New Zealand Maoris came through us – commanded by a 2nd Lieutenant. All were carrying not only their own weapons but also German weapons. They asked if they could join us – for a chance to fight the Germans! They stayed and later I sent them on a bayonet attack.[37]

---

[36] Richard Mead, *Commando General: The Life of Major General Sir Robert Laycock KCMG CB DSO* (Pen & Sword Books Ltd, Barnsley, 2016), p.84.
[37] Charles Messenger, *The Middle East Commandos* (Wellingborough: William Kimber & Co. Ltd, 1988), p.84.

B Company was later reinforced by two further Maori companies and by 0800 the next day were in contact with the enemy. What happened next remains unclear with different stories that ultimately end up with the same outcome. Not for debate is that 37 Spaniards were captured in Crete and became prisoners of war; the contention is exactly at what point and precisely where they were captured. Prior to the German troops attacking from the north and south, during the night orders for a limited withdrawal (if they could) had been given to some of the officers by George Young, amongst whom was Parish to the rear of the Spaniards. Bob McGibbon takes up the story:

> Sometime during the night, Parish received word from George Young that we could pull back, if such a move was thought feasible. I went back to discuss the situation with Parish. Evidently his situation was better than ours and his troops were already on their way back. Word got around to some of our men who assumed we could also pull out and some sections started to do so before we could hold them. In the dark and in awkward rocky country confusion arose. After discussion with Sandbach and Russo we decided our positions would be held. To have done otherwise in the circumstances would have been pretty grim. We sent back all those men we could contact and who had mistakenly thought our orders were to pull back. We missed some of them and these headed back to the rear. How many there were I don't know but they represented both British and Spanish.[38]

A view of the ground looking south where members of B Company, D Battalion of Layforce fought on the bend of the road near Beritiana. The commandos under Captain Bob McGibbon were positioned next to the road in the centre. The two Maori companies were on the hills above on either side. (Philip Brazier)

---

38 Testimony by Major Bob McGibbon – Middle East Commando Research Group Archive.

How many of the Spaniards withdrew at this stage is not fully known but what is certain is that Bob McGibbon was injured in the ensuing firefight and taken prisoner soon after. In his diaries, Evelyn Waugh talks of the company from D Battalion being cut off and that 'I do not know if this company surrendered or fought it out'.[39] Judging from some accounts, it would seem that there were Spaniards who surrendered and some who fought. Other accounts also talk about many of the Spaniards withdrawing because they believed that the position was untenable. McGibbon states:

> By dawn the Germans attacked, beginning with mortar fire and followed by glider troops acting as infantry. The distance between the two forces was a matter of perhaps 50 to 100 yards at maximum. Eventually, it became clear that we had done all we could in holding the Germans up and they were very numerous. Just before we decided to pull back, I was badly injured. I instructed Sandbach and Russo to move out leaving me behind as I could not move. They did so with the remaining Spaniards and British commandos and the Maoris.[40]

All of those who were not captured at this stage did now fall back to Babali Hani where the Battalion had set up in preparation for another confrontation with the advancing German troops. A firefight soon followed during 28 May and by the end of it, Layforce was withdrawing further south to Sphakia near Vrysos. The following day it moved to Askyphos and remained there for the next 24 hours or so before moving down to the Sphakia area itself on 31 May. The order was now given that Layforce provide further cover in Sphakia and after disengaging with the enemy, it would embark last. Laycock and Waugh visited General Weston's Creforce HQ where they discovered that there was to be a surrender. Laycock and two of his HQ staff (this included his Intelligence Officer Evelyn Waugh) were able to be evacuated that night and it was clear that he still had half of Layforce elsewhere. George Young ended up being the senior officer to negotiate the surrender, which he did. Beforehand, he told the men of A and D Battalions that those who wished to break the German cordon and go into the mountains or escape by boat could do so. Many did, one of these was Francisco Geronimo who would escape and evade in Crete for the next 11 months. It is probable that he was initially captured and then escaped within a few days. It is said that some 15 to 17 Spaniards made it back from Crete after the battle.[41] Coupled with those who did not even manage to get to Crete due to injury or sickness, by July 1941 there were now only 26 Spaniards left in the Middle East Commandos. The stories of what happened to those captured and those who continued serving are worth recounting.

Capture and POW Life

For those that became POWs, most would remain in captivity for four years. The majority were placed on the 'missing' list on 2 June 1941.[42] Initially they were forced to march back to the north of Crete pretty much walking the route they had initially followed in reverse. Once further north they were used to clear the airfield at Maleme before being moved to Suda. From here they were

---

39 Michael Davie (ed.), *The Diaries of Evelyn Waugh* (London: Weidenfeld & Nicholson, 1976), p.501.
40 Testimony by Major Bob McGibbon – Middle East Commando Research Group Archive.
41 Daniel Arasa, *Los Españoles de Churchill* (Barcelona: Editorial Armonía Poética, 1991), quotes 17 Spaniards escaping from Crete whereas Messenger says 15. For a full breakdown of information on the 63 Spaniards in the Middle East Commando see Appendix III.
42 NRA 44612. Surrey Heritage Centre Archive, 'Queen's Royal Regiment, Enlistment Book, Allotted to 2nd Battalion, 1940, Egypt,' pp.19–26.

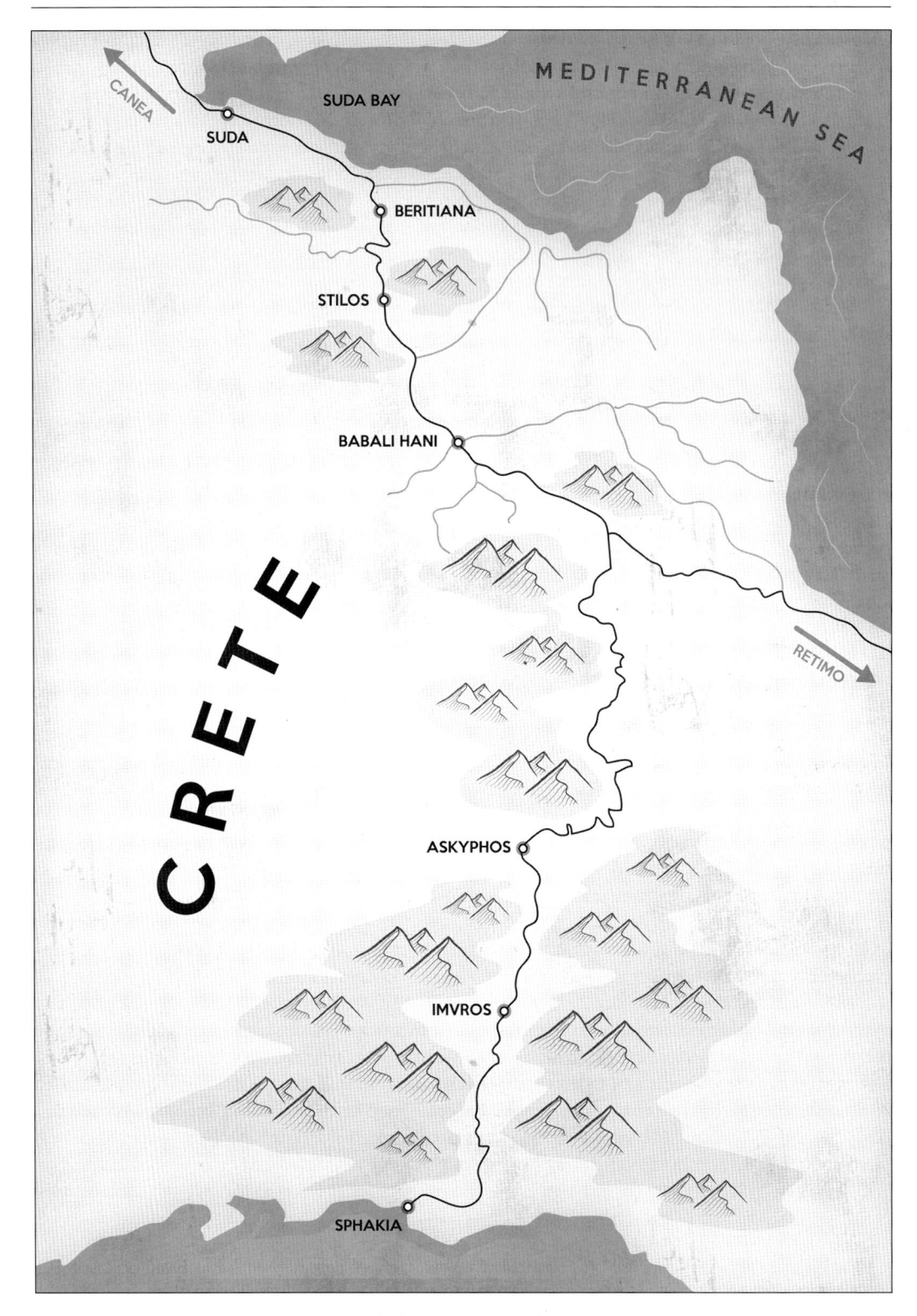

Map 6 The Battle for Crete. (Artwork by Mike Heald)

shipped to Corinth and then to a POW camp in Thessaloniki. Cleto Sánchez recalled the camps they were held in:

> After about a month we embarked for Thessaloniki which is there where we were put in an abandoned Greek Barracks where there were lots of bedbugs, more than hairs on my head. We ended up staying outside because indoors was too risky. We were then moved to another camp in Thessaloniki which was a bit better but after about 20 days we started to get very hungry. We only had biscuits and olive oil to eat …[43]

The commando POWs had two further issues. Firstly, the Germans were starting to be greatly interested in the Middle East Commando dagger and many were interviewed about it. It is said that there was a well in Sphakia which contained an unhealthy number of discarded blades, great for souvenir hunters. A second issue was that the Spanish POWs were now greatly concerned that they would face real consequences should the Germans find out that they had fought on the Republican side in the Spanish Civil War. But luck was on their side when Captain Archie Cochrane of the Royal Army Medical Corps, D Battalion's Medical Officer, came up with an ingenious plan. Cochrane had studied at King's College, Cambridge and then University College, London but interrupted his studies in 1936 to provide medical support to Republican troops in the Spanish Civil War. He had first served in a field ambulance unit of the Spanish Medical Aid Committee and then joined a medical unit of the International Brigade. He returned to Great Britain in 1937 and finished his medical degree the following year. At the beginning of the war, he enlisted and joined the Royal Army Medical Corps. Back in Crete, Cochrane suggested that they all pretend to be Gibraltarians, a ruse which seemed to work. Archie Cochrane later remarked:

> As we began to march up to get registered, I was suddenly inspired. I decided that all the Spaniards had been born in Gibraltar! I held a hurried discussion with them and the whole registration went off without the Germans raising one eyebrow. The Spaniards were delighted and I felt a mild glow …[44]

George Young commented:

> I protested [to Laycock] against sending them [B Coy including the Spaniards] as the rear guard in Crete and eventually they were captured. Then it was all difficult because they were particularly anxious not to be known to the Germans you see. Their one remaining officer, who spoke Spanish as it happens, said 'Well look here there's only one thing left for you to do and that is to say that you are British subjects and Gibraltarians!' This is something I thought was pretty ingenious solution. It worked and they survived the war and at least one of them I met in London after.[45]

After some months the prisoners were taken from Greece to Germany by train. Cleto Sánchez takes up the story:

> We were put into trains and travelled to Germany, roughly 40 people in a wagon. These wagons were locked and we were only allowed to get out when we needed to go to the toilet.

---

43 Charles Messenger, *The Middle East Commandos* (Wellingborough: William Kimber & Co. Ltd, 1988), p.98.
44 Archibald L. Cochrane, 'One Man's Medicine,' *The British Medical Journal*, 1989, p.63.
45 George Alan Dawson Young, IWM Interview, Catalogue Number 7328, 1983.

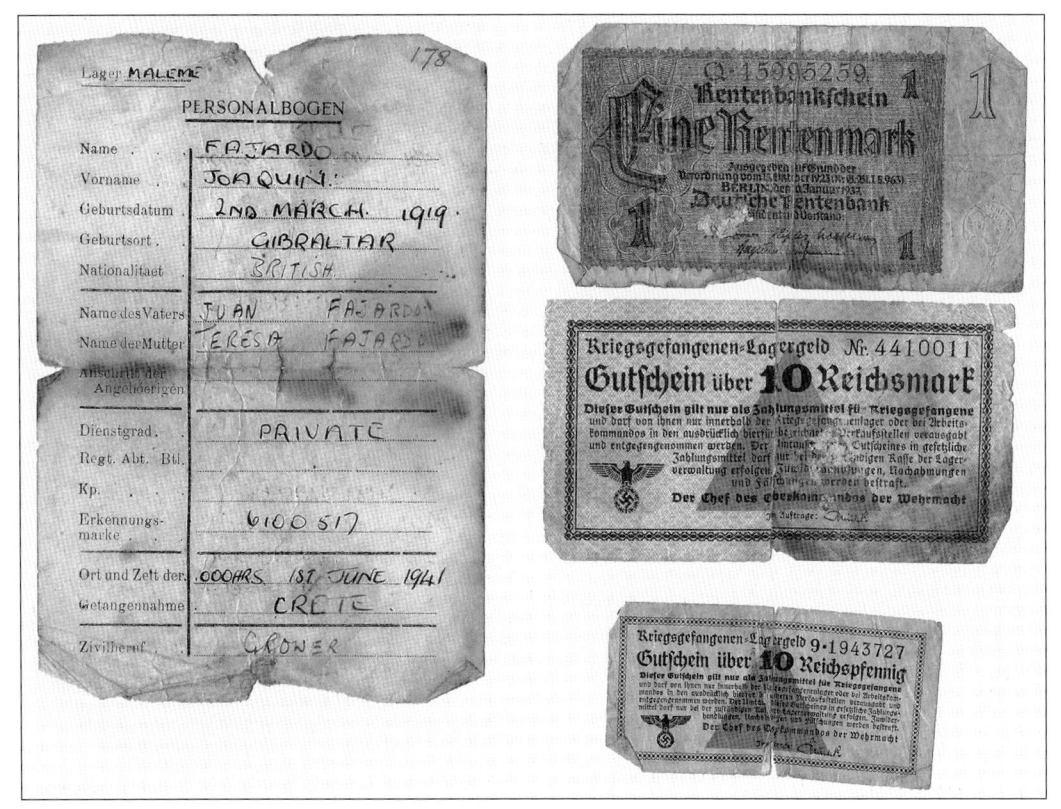

POW documents for Joaquín Fajardo. Note the place of origin is down as Gibraltar. (Joaquín Fajardo collection)

> I do not know which countries we crossed but I do remember passing through Austria, especially Vienna because there we were given one loaf of bread for 5 or 6 people.[46]

Upon arrival in Germany many of the prisoners were split up and sent to camps in Poland, eastern Germany and elsewhere. The Spaniards were spread out across many camps too in small groups.

A curious tale is that told by George Beeson in *Five Roads to Freedom*. In it, he talks of the Spaniards he came across who helped in his escapes. In one camp, Spaniards helped in calculating the trajectory of tunnels to help get them on the right track and avoid obstacles such as stones and buildings. He also mentions a Spaniard was a specialist in dying uniforms for escapees.[47] Beeson went on to be interviewed by the Imperial War Museum in the early 1980s. In this interview he mentions the Spaniards:

> We had a prismatic compass and I used to give the readings of our workings to a Spaniard who had been a Master Sailor … who fought against Franco in the Spanish Civil War … who had to come out of Spain in a hurry and joined the Palestinian Army and he and his other five mates were captured in Crete. So they did all the hours and they kept us on the straight path.[48]

---

46 Cleto Sánchez Monterrubio, *Memorias de Tres Banderas* and Francisco Pereira, *Life Stories*. Unpublished memoirs.
47 George Beeson, *Five Roads to Freedom* (London: Corgi Books, Transworld Publishers, 1977), pp.52–62.
48 Wilfred George Beeson, IWM Interview, recorded 13April 1981, IWM 4802.

Joaquín Fajardo (centre crouching) and Basilio Marín (centre standing) pose with other POWs. (Joaquín Fajardo collection)

As no names are mentioned, there is no way of knowing fully if any of these Spaniards were from No.50 Middle East Commando or not, because there were several Spanish POWs who were in camps after serving with the French. However, further investigation of POW lists for those in Queen's Royal Regiment place six Spaniards in Stalag 383 (in Hoenfels, Bavaria), which is where Beeson was.[49] He also talked about an escape by Spaniards from the same camp:

> All the camp fused. This came about because these six Spaniards that I mentioned before … they were going to escape. They had asked Middle East to tell them about a form of escape where the six of them could get away. Would I get them some things to get away with. The only two things I could get them were two trilbies. Now, their means of escape was quite interesting. There had to be some from the hut that did not want to escape. So they had to be odd men … and that meant they would collect a plank of wood … to act as a kind of ladder. So one would place that against the wire … the next one who was going to escape, he would go up the ladder and with a plank he would lay across the two strands of wire and rolls of barbed wire … so they had four feet of planking and walked across and then dropped down to the ground. This had to be repeated until the fourth man was over … in the dark … and they had to make a sling of wire to fuse the perimeter.[50]

---

49 Spaniards from No.50 ME Commando (Queens' Royal Regiment) recorded as being at Stalag 383 were Álvarez, Barroso, Díaz, Marín, Trill and Postello.
50 Wilfred George Beeson, IWM Interview.

A group of Allied POWs that include some Spaniards. Far right is Joaquín Fajardo, second from right, with a hat on, is Manuel Barroso and in the centre in a shirt is Braulio Heras who sadly would be killed shortly before the end of the war. (Joaquín Fajardo collection)

A Spaniard who escaped and evaded capture for 10 months was 6100529/13808272 Ángel Marino. Originally from Bilbao, Marino had been a waiter before the outbreak of the Spanish Civil War. In Crete he was able to get away soon after the surrender in Sphakia and hid in the hills with many other escapees. It is not known if he was with other Spaniards at any point but what is certain is that in April 1942 he was arrested by two Greek policemen and handed over to the Germans. He remained in Stalag 344 in Lamsdorf, Upper Silesia for the remainder of the war.[51]

6100545/13808257 Vicente Blasco was moved around quite a bit upon his arrival in Germany. Between the end of 1941 and late 1943 he spent time in Stalag 3D in Berlin before being moved to other camps nearby. Towards the end of the war he was moved to Stalag 4C located in Bystřice (now part of the town of Dubí) in German-occupied Czechoslovakia (now Czechia) until the end of the war. Here he came across many other Spaniards from Crete. It was also here that he struck up a friendship with a light infantry soldier named Sykes. Blasco hardly spoke any English and Sykes no Spanish, but they soon became inseparable. Sykes loved badges and had many extra ones sewed onto his sleeves. They were often seen wandering together around the perimeter. The Germans were so fascinated by Sykes that they nicknamed him 'Feldmarschall'.[52]

Another who talked about some of the things that happened while in captivity was Francisco Navarrete. Unlike the previously mentioned group, Navarrete was in Stalag 8C (near Sagan in Lower Silesia – now Żagań in Poland) along with three others, one of whom was Cleto Sánchez. Navarrete gave the testimony below to Daniel Arasa, which is corroborated by Cleto Sánchez's account:

---

51 TNA, WO 416/246/118, Angel Marino POW file.
52 Sidney Litherland, *The Junak King, Life as a British POW 1941–45* (Stroud: Spellmount, 2014), p.184.

Joaquín Fajardo with the guitar on the left and Manuel Barroso in a hat on the right during their time in a POW camp. (Joaquín Fajardo collection)

> During our years imprisoned we were very cold and hungry and we were made to work. Five of us worked in a quarry outside the camp and this was better that being inside. The worst period was the last two months of the war, where they moved us from East to West, marching on foot, sleeping anywhere and many times with no food at all. In the space of five weeks, we marched from Breslau to Hannover.[53]

Overall, the largest group of Spanish POWs seems to have been in Stalag 4C.[54] After arriving at the camp they were photographed with some Belgians and were later split into two work camps. Apart from Fajardo, Heras, Lumbrera and Mena there was one more Spaniard by the name of Hidalgo but who was not particularly friendly with the others.[55] After his father's death, Tony Fajardo through the Commando Veterans Association was able to track down Peter Mowlem who was also at 4C and knew the Spaniards.[56] One incident during their meeting in 2002 stuck out which gives another example of where old enemies from the Spanish Civil War met:

> One day as part of a work detail, Peter Mowlem, my father and many others were working at a railway station when a train pulled in full of soldiers. The next thing he noticed was my father angrily waving his arms and shouting at the soldiers looking out of the windows, then picking up stones and throwing them at the soldiers. Peter Mowlem said a number of POWs ran over to my father and quickly pulled him away before the German guards noticed what had happened. When they got back to the camp, one of the other prisoners who spoke Spanish was able to ask my father why he had reacted in that way. The reply was that the train was full of General Franco's fascist Spaniards. In fact, they were volunteers in the Blue Division on their way to fight for Germany on the Russian front.[57]

One of the supposedly lucky ones amongst the Spanish POWs was 6100526/13808269 Juan Mena. Lucky because he was repatriated, albeit under rather sad circumstances. Little is known about his background, but along with the other Spaniards he was declared missing and then as a POW shortly after Crete. In January 1942 he was listed as being in the Pioneer Corps but still as a POW. The enlistment record book for 1/5th Battalion of the Queen's Royal Regiment (West Surrey) from 1940 has follow up notes saying he was taken prisoner on 2 June 1941 and was repatriated on 3 November 1943. This is interesting, as it is probable that he was repatriated as an injured soldier and exchanged via Barcelona. It is not clear what his injuries were and there seem to be two theories: firstly, that he was suffering from turberculosis and, as a consequence, was sent to Berlin from where he was repatriated;[58] secondly, that he may had tried to commit suicide while in the camp and was subsequently saved by a fellow POW 408910 Arthur 'Tim' Claude Darby after which he was sent to Berlin for treatment. This is backed up by Peter Mowlem, who confirmed that Mena was sent to Berlin in September 1942.[59]

---

53 Daniel Arasa, *Los Españoles de Churchill* (Barcelona: Editorial Armonía Poética, 1991), pp.171–172. Breslau, now Wroclaw in Poland, to Hanover is around 525km – an impressive feat of marching!
54 POW records name the Spaniards as being: Fajardo, Fraile, Franco, Galoretta, Heras, Hidalgo, Lumbrera& Castellano. However, this does not seem to tally with personal accounts.
55 Transcript from interview with Tony Fajardo, 10 June 2020. The information came from Peter Mowlem from diaries he had kept while a POW.
56 Transcript from interview with Tony Fajardo, 10 June 2020. Tony also received a letter from William (Bill) Regan, 7 Commando, dated 7 April 1995 in which he mentions being in Stalag 4A with four Spaniards. We know that they were Cervantes, Martinez A, Martinez F and Torralbo.
57 Transcript from interview with Tony Fajardo, 10 June 2020.
58 Testimony by Archibald L. Cochrane, Middle East Commando Archive.
59 Transcript from interview with Tony Fajardo, 10 June 2020. The information came from Peter Mowlem from

'VAGABONDS' 149

Fajardo and his good friend Francisco Lumbrera. Both became POWs after Crete. Lumbrera would sadly be killed in early May 1945. (Joaquín Fajardo collection)

Braulio Heras stopping for a cigarette. (Manuel Surera collection)

As far as these repatriations were concerned, Germans held from the Middle East were exchanged for British and Commonwealth POWs. The Germans were transported aboard two ships: the *Tairea* and the *Cuba*; the British and Commonwealth POWs sailed to Barcelona aboard the *Aquilea* and the *Djenné* and arrived 27 October.[60] Something which must have been particularly painful for Juan Mena.[61]

Sadly tragedy struck those in Stalag 4C at the end of the war as the Russians advanced. Following artillery fire or aerial bombardment upon the camp, 6100520/13808248 Braulio Heras and 6100524/13808250 Francisco Lumbrera were killed. Shortly after the war's end in Europe those Spaniards who had been in captivity were sent to the United Kingdom, the majority settled in the country, many taking British nationality.[62]

Continuing the Fight

A far more complicated story is that of those Spaniards who were able to either escape Crete or who were not able to be there for one reason or another, for example injury or sickness. The journey of these 26 Spaniards and their continued service for the rest of the war is rather convoluted and it is not fully known what everyone did and where they went. A period of limbo certainly followed the return from Crete. In mid-June it was decided to disband Layforce. C Battalion was to remain on its present organisation which left 47 officers and 692 other ranks from the remainder.[63] Many would return to their original units and all of the remaining Spaniards were initially posted to the Depot Commando Training and Holding Unit and placed on 'Special Duties'.[64]

When it comes to what paths they took, we can essentially divide these men into three groups: those that ended up in the Special Forces, those that eventually transferred to the Pioneer Corps and a final group of those who rejoined the Queen's Royal Regiment. But initially it would seem that the Spaniards were held at the Commando depot and then placed on the books of the Pioneer Corps in January 1942 only to be returned to the Middle East Commando depot and become members of 1 Special Service Regiment later in 1942. They went through a great deal of training and were probably involved in operations which are discussed in later chapters. Also, by this stage David Stirling had set up a new Special Forces unit, L Detachment Special Air Service Brigade, and in October 1941 this became part of the reconstituted Middle East Commando. According to Daniel Arasa, Spaniards were placed onto the books of D Squadron, 1st Special Service Regiment which worked with the Long Range Desert Group amongst many others.[65]

In Crete, 6100555/13808268/ME138041867 Francisco Geronimo managed to escape and evade capture for a period of 11 months. After many adventures, he was taken off the island by the

---

diaries he had kept while a POW.
60 David Miller, *Mercy Ships, The Untold Story of Prisoner-of-War Exchanges in World War II* (London: Continuum UK, 2008), pp.16–19.
61 Hansard Archive, *Disabled Prisoners Of War (Exchange With Germany (HC Deb 19 October 1943)*, Vol.392 cc1217-20. <https://api.parliament.uk/historic-hansard/commons/1943/oct/19/disabled-prisoners-of-war-exchange-with>. Accessed 6 August 2021.
62 Daniel Arasa, *Los Españoles de Churchill* (Barcelona: Editorial Armonía Poética, 1991), pp.172–173.
63 Richard Mead, *Commando General: The Life of Major General Sir Robert Laycock KCMG CB DSO* (Pen & Sword Books Ltd, Barnsley, 2016), p.97.
64 A euphemism for being part of the fledgling Special Forces.
65 Daniel Arasa, *Los Españoles de Churchill* (Barcelona: Editorial Armonía Poética, 1991), p.177. The Spanish names are: Alarcón C., Arco L., Asenjo J., Balerdi J., Fernández J., García A., García A., García J., García E., Garrigós A., Jeronimo F., Martínez F., Martínez B. Martínez J., Martínez M., Mercado J., Morales G., Piñeira L., Soriano A., Santiago B., Surera J., Trancho M., Valero A., Villanova J.

'VAGABONDS' 151

Spaniards gather back in their camp in Egypt after their return from Crete in 1941. Crouching, second from the left is Manuel Surera, standing third from the left is Fernando Esteve and crouched with the tam o'shanter hat is Francisco García Garrigos. (Miguel Martínez and Francisco García Garrigos collection)

Manuel Surera in Middle East Commando uniform. Note the tam o'shanter hat he is wearing along with the 'Fanny' cap badge and Middle East Commando shoulder flash. This photo dates to his time in 1st Special Service Regiment. (Manuel Surera collection)

Francisco Geronimo on the right with an unknown soldier wearing a tam o'shanter. Because of his time spent escaping and evading in Crete for 11 months, Geronimo did not serve in the 1st Special Service Regiment as long as the other Spaniards. (Francisco Geronimo collection)

SOE in May 1942 as part of the Cumberledge/Saunders group under the overall direction of Force 133 (SOE). From here, Geronimo served in the 1st Special Service Regiment and was soon back on operations. By the end of 1943, he and 6100552/13808212/13041866 Justo Balerdi, a proud Basque, were members of the newly formed elite 2nd SAS Regiment.

The largest group of Spaniards who were able to escape from Crete or who had been injured or hospitalised beforehand ended at the end of 1942 serving in the Pioneer Corps.[66] If you look at the army service records of a few individuals, you can see that they were posted to the Pioneer Corps Base Depot in November 1942. As stated above, most of the Spaniards were placed on the books of 1st Special Service Regiment before this and at the Depot Commando Training and Holding Unit prior to that.[67] By the end of 1943 a large number of these men were on the nominal roll of 361 (Alien) Company and by October 1944 some of these men were also in 362 (Alien) Company. Ironically, these two companies were sent to the United Kingdom in October 1944.

---

66 It is worth noting that all of the POWs were given Pioneer Corps numbers almost immediately after their capture in 1941, all others received similar Pioneer Corps numbers on 5 January 1942.
67 The Service Record of 6100535/13808232 Manuel Surera who ended up serving in the Pioneer Corps fully from early 1943 to the end of the war, has the following key entries from the summer of 1941 to late 1943: Disembarked Egypt 31 May 1941 / Attached Depot Commando 17 Jul 1941 / Attached ME Depot Commando 6 Sep 1941 / Posted to ME Commando from G(R)B Pool 20 Jan 1942 / Posted to 1 SS Regt 12 Jul 1942 / Posted to Pioneer Corps Base Depot 8 Nov 1942 / Embarked for N Africa 9 Aug 1943 / Posted to 361 (Alien) Coy 3 Oct 1941.

Another captivating, if sad, story is that of 6100539/13808214 Corporal Moisés Trancho Bartolomé. Moisés was a Basque from Barakaldo, born in November 1916, who volunteered to join *1ᵉ BMVE* in Le Bacarès Camp. Le Bacarès had been opened as a temporary camp on 18 February 1939 to house Spanish refugees just like the nearby camps in Argelès-sur-Mer and Saint-Cyprien. The camp remained open until 1942 and as mentioned above was a training depot for those who joined the *RMVE*s. During the Spanish Civil War, Moisés had been a *gudari* (a soldier in the Basque Army) and served in the *UGT 1 Batallón Fulgencio Mateos*. He joined the battalion in October 1936 and was soon in the action in the north. On 5 May 1937 he was hospitalised after being wounded in action and not long after he had his little finger on his right hand amputated. He was medically discharged from the army as a result of his injuries, and on 16 June he was married to Consuelo Gallego Santines in Barakaldo. Soon after, they were forced to flee to Santander as refugees. Bilbao fell on 19 June. In Santander, Moisés volunteered to rejoin his old battalion and was soon in the thick of it again. Consuelo, in the meantime, was able to get on the ship *Marvia* and escape to Normandy that August. Santander fell on 26 August, but Moisés and a few others were able to escape and join a mixed battalion fighting further west. Gijón was taken by Franco's Nationalist Rebel forces on 21 October 1937, bringing an end to the campaign in the north. By the middle of 1938 Moisés was a prisoner in the north and placed into the 122nd Labour Battalion. He escaped to France with another 10 Spaniards on 25 September 1939, was interned initially in Septfond and volunteered to join *122ᵉ CTE* at Toulouse. He then escaped again on 22 October and volunteered to join *1ᵉ BMVE* at Le Bacarès.[68] His brother Juan Trancho Bartolomé also escaped to France and ended up fighting in the French Resistance.[69] The two would never meet again as Moisés died on 29 July 1943, having escaped from Crete in the summer of 1941. Little is known of the circumstances of his death and what exactly he went through after the Crete evacuation except for his being in D Squadron 1 SSR. In Daniel Arasa's book he was recognised as an amazing singer (a typical Basque trait) and a great sportsman. It is said that when in Le Bacarès he was released frequently to play football for a local club. It would seem that prior to the Spanish Civil War he was a semi-professional player for Barakaldo Football Club, but his surviving relatives are not completely sure.[70]

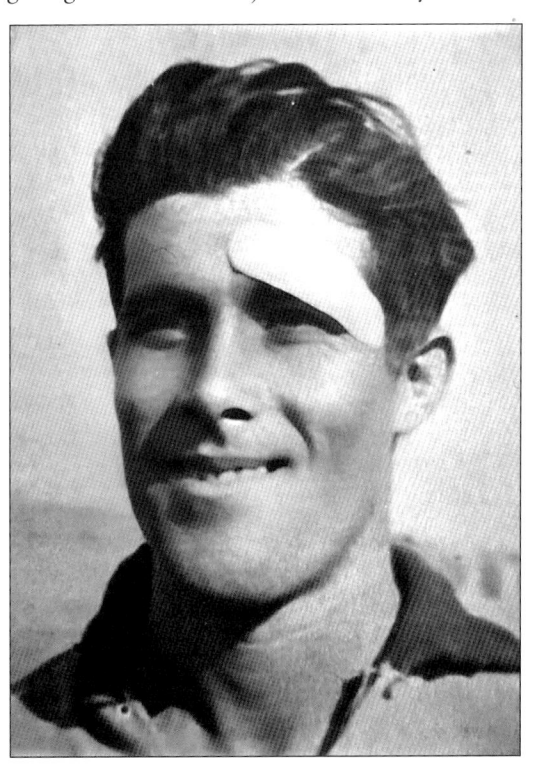

The athletic and highly respected Moisés Trancho Bartolomé who died in July 1943 and is buried in the Ramleh Commonwealth War Graves Cemetery in the Middle East. (Joaquín Fajardo collection)

---

68 Information provided by Moisés Trancho Bartolomé's nephew Joseba Trancho from Spanish Archives. Interview 20 December 2023.
69 Basque files of personnel held at Gurs Camp. <https://www.euskadi.eus/gobierno-vasco/-/noticia/2017/acceso-al-listado-de-las-personas-confinadas-en-el-campo-de-gurs/>. Accessed 10 August 2021.
70 Daniel Arasa, *Los Españoles de Churchill* (Barcelona: Editorial Armonía Poética, 1991), p.152. When interviewed

Amongst the final group of surviving Spaniards from Crete were three who rejoined the Queen's Royal Regiment (West Surrey) and served in the 1/5th Battalion in July 1943. One was injured in the crossing of the Volturno in October 1942 in the early stages of the Italian Campaign, another shortly after D-Day in Normandy and the last one would stay with the battalion from Normandy all the way to the capture of Hamburg in the second half of April 1945.[71]

The 63 men who served in the Middle East Commandos came from disparate backgrounds from the Spanish Civil War and had undergone so much together: internment camps in France, *Légion Étrangère* training and service in Syria and Lebanon, escaping to the British, becoming part of the Middle East Commandos and fighting against the Italians and Germans. Just over half spent the rest of the war after Crete in captivity while the others were continuing their fight against fascism. Despite being vagabonds as the Second World War progressed, pretty much all of the 63 Republican Spaniards who served in the Middle East Commandos would end up in Britain at the end of the war and settle there. As Bob McGibbon said to Daniel Arasa:

> They were all very proud of being members of the Queens Royal Regiment and all of them hoped (and believed) that they would become British citizens. I believe they did eventually.[72]

---

    by Daniel Arasa, Peter Selerie, who had served as a captain in the Sherwood Rangers before becoming adjutant of No.52 Middle East Commando said: 'The best of the Spanish NCOs was Sergeant Trancho. He was Catalan, a brilliant football player, who it was said had played for one of the top teams. Trancho also had a very good voice and when we were together in the desert around the campfire he sang 'La Paloma' and other Spanish songs. British soldiers were left spellbound despite not understanding a single word.'

71 NRA 44612. Surrey Heritage Centre Archive, Queen's Royal Regiment, Register of Soldiers, Transfer in 1943, p.102.

72 Daniel Arasa, *Los Españoles de Churchill* (Barcelona: Editorial Armonía Poética, 1991), p.153.

Chapter 5

'See You In Hell'

Spaniards Enlist into the British Army in North Africa

Yo tuve que morir un par de veces para aprender a valorar la vida, y cuando hablo de morir, no hablo de dejar de existir. Hay situaciones que matan tu espíritu y mueres, aunque estés respirando.[1]

Mario Benedetti

North Africa is where the largest groups of Spaniards would volunteer to join the British Army after Operation TORCH in 1942, primarily into the Pioneer Corps. Most of these men had been interned in camps across the region ranging from Morocco to Tunisia. They had arrived in the latter stages of the Spanish Civil War, but countless others were those who had either been serving in the French Army or *Légion Étrangère*, or who had been interned in mainland France in 1939, or were members of *GTE*s and had been moved to other camps in North Africa. The defeat of France in 1940 and the subsequent setting up of the Vichy Regime, meant that many exiled Spanish Republicans were *persona non grata* in the French *Metropole* or in French Africa. By 1942, groups would be heavily involved in operations with the SOE, and the US equivalent the OSS, as Operation TORCH took place and beyond. Once they had enlisted, Spaniards were working in the rear areas as the war progressed across the region. A few would end up joining elite units such as the SAS, while many would remain in North Africa until the end of the war. Several hundred finished the war in Britain where they would eventually be allowed to settle.

The Final Exodus

As described previously, throughout – and more specifically at the end of – the Spanish Civil War, there were several large movements of Republican refugees leaving Spain. The final wave of up to 12,000 Republican refugees got away by ship from the east coast, from places such as Alicante and Cartagena, and escaped to North Africa. This last move is regarded as the fifth and final large exodus of Spanish Republicans at the end of the Spanish Civil War. The three key locations that they moved to were Orán, Algiers and Tunis. It was to be largely those Spanish Republicans who were either from the Republican military or more politically involved that would get to North Africa. Just as in France, their arrival was greeted with some unpreparedness by the French authorities who reacted rather haphazardly to the arrival. Initially, most were kept on their ships

---

1 I had to die a couple of times to appreciate life. And when I speak of dying, I don't mean ceasing to exist. There are occasions that kill your spirit and you die, even though you are still breathing.

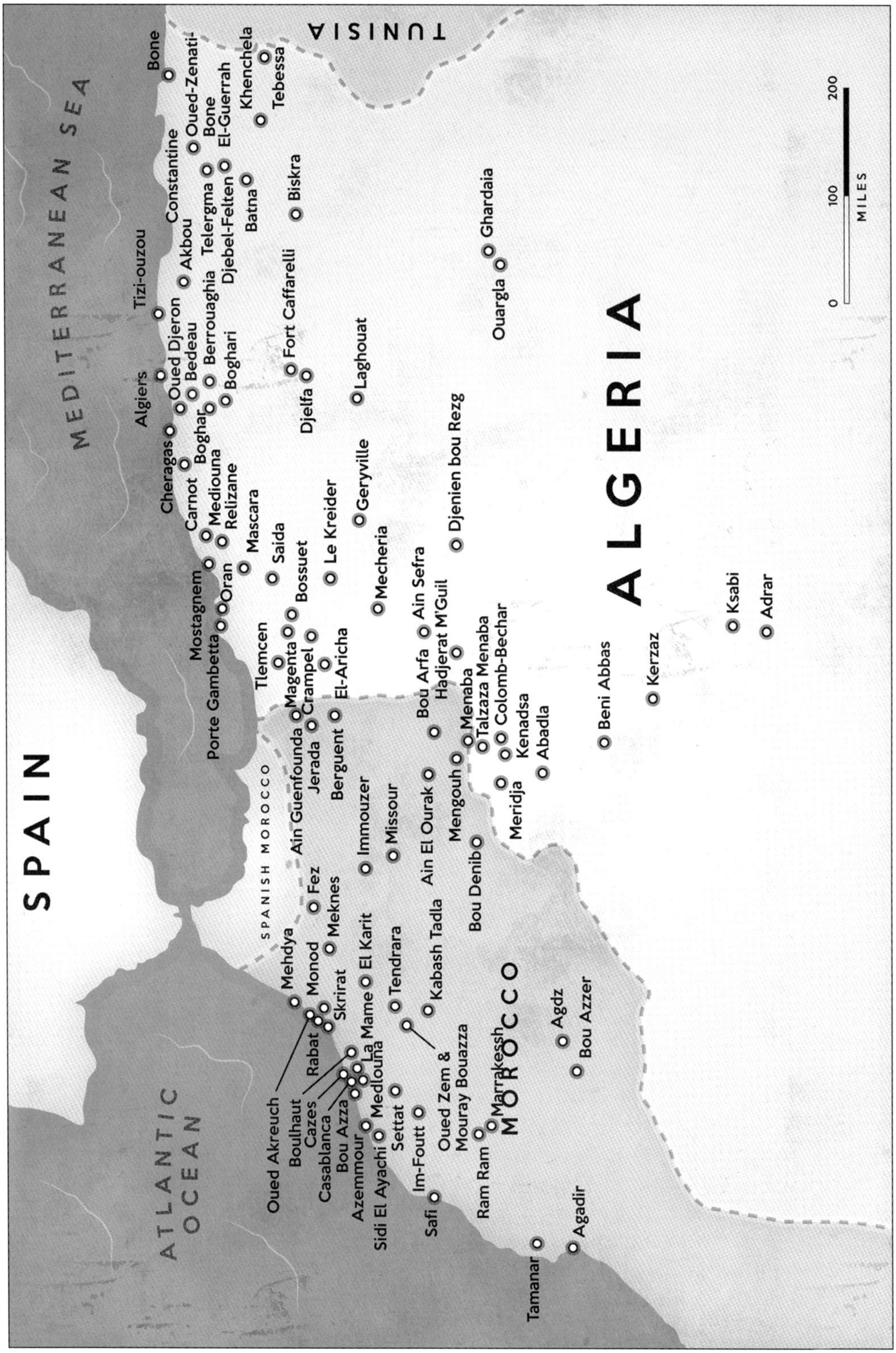

Map 7 Camps and locations in North Africa. (Artwork by Mike Heald)

before the authorities were able to deal with them. Once off their ships, again as in France, these individuals were classified and then held in camps. Initially, the authorities had wanted to turn the refugees away, but were forced to come up with a plan. In Algeria, during February and March 1939, telegrams were sent from the *Gouverneur Général de l'Algérie* (Governor General of Algeria) to the commander of the *Division d'Algérie*, as well as to prefects and sub-prefects, warning them of the waves of Spanish refugees who were on their way.[2] All sorts of vessels had been used to get to North Africa from fishing boats to cruise ships and cargo ships.

Amongst the first to escape in this last wave were many from the Republican Navy, particularly those led by *Almirante* Miguel Buiza Fernández-Palacios who left Cartagena on 5 March 1939 along with the majority of the Republican Fleet. This was to prevent these elements falling into Franco's hands and he had been warning the Republican Government that he would do so from February. Buiza was a career sailor who had risen quickly up the ranks of the Republican Navy. He had refused to join the coup in 1936 and commanded elements of the fleet before being relieved from command after the Battle of Cape Cherchell. Buiza was reinstated as *capitán general* of the Republican Navy in February 1939. The fleet took an eastward course, led by Buiza aboard the cruiser *Miguel de Cervantes* and reached Algerian waters. Off Orán, Buiza asked for permission to anchor, but the naval authorities of French Algeria would not allow him to lead the Spanish Republican ships into their main port. They directed him to Bizerte in the French protectorate of Tunisia, where the fleet arrived on 7 March. Not long after anchoring, the fleet was interned by the French authorities.

They arrived at the naval base in Tunis on three cruisers, eight destroyers and a submarine. Some 4,000 military and civilian personnel handed themselves over to the French authorities at the Bizerta naval base in Tunis two days later.[3] Except for a few crewmen who were put on guard duty on the ships, the Spanish Republican seamen and their officers were interned in a concentration camp at Meheri Zabbens, near Meknassy, in an abandoned phosphate mine. Miguel Buiza refused any special treatment and asked to be interned together with the other sailors. Due to the inhumane conditions in the camp, half of the Republican sailors (around 2,357), opted to return to Spain preferring to suffer jail or even death than stay in Africa.[4] Those who remained loyal to the Republic stayed rather than return to Spain. Among them was a radio officer Alfonso Vázquez. His daughter, Alicia, said that her father stayed on because 'he didn't trust them [the French]' and he hoped to reach Mexico. 'Later we found out that those who went back were put in concentration camps in Spain and some of them were shot.' Alfonso was interned in the Tunisian camp at Meheri Zebbens together with Paco Díaz his kindred spirit. He wrote in his memoirs about how they escaped from the camp at the second attempt. 'The first time they got out of the camp with two suitcases, one of clothes and the other full of books. They made an escape from a concentration camp with a suitcase full of books! It's mind-blowing.' said Alicia. The two fugitives crossed over into Algeria and reached Orán, where they settled and sought a living among the Spanish community.[5]

---

2   Kamel Kateb, 'Les Immigrés Espagnols Dans Les Camps En Algérie (1939–1941),' Belin, *Annales de Démographie Historique* 2007/1 n° 113 | pp.155 – 175. ISSN 0066-2062, ISBN 2701147086, <www.cairn.info/revue-annales-de-demographiehistorique-2007-1-page-155.htm>. Accessed 1 August 2019.
3   Diego Gaspar Celaya, *La Guerra Continua. Voluntarios Españoles al Servicio de la Francia Libre (1940-1945)* (Madrid: Marcial Pons Historia, 2015), pp.92–94.
4   Juan Ramón Roca and Ariane Reyes, *Españoles en Argelia: Emigración y Exilio, Memoria Gráfica*, segunda edición (Privately published, 2022).
5   Tomás Andújar, '*The Wound Covered in Sand*,' Auntament de Barcelona Archive, 2006. <ajuntament.barcelona.cat/lavirreina/sites/default/files/2020-06/La%20herida%20cubierta%20de%20arena-en-tau%20maquetat.pdf>. Accessed 12 June 2022.

Enrique Bernárdez's pass on the Republican cruiser, *Miguel de Cervantes*. (Enrique Bernárdez collection)

Another sailor of the Republican Navy who ended up in North Africa and joined the British Army later was Enrique Bernárdez. Originally from Vigo, he joined the Spanish Navy and by the time the Spanish Civil War began, he was serving on the cruiser *Miguel de Cervantes*. In 1939 he elected to stay in Tunisia and was sent to the Meheri Zebbens camp. Soon after he was part of a group that was released to work on forestry on Chambi Mountain (Jebel ech Chambi) a peak which sits above the Kesserine Pass. By 1943 he was in Algeria and had joined the British Army at Boufarik in early April.

Probably the most famous ship involved in the evacuation of Spaniards was the SS *Stanbrook* captained by Archibald Dickson, a Welshman from the district of Roath in Cardiff. The ship sailed into Alicante on 19 March. After the evacuation, Captain Dickson wrote a letter to the *Sunday Dispatch* newspaper in London:

> Owing to the large number of refugees, I was in a quandary as to my own position, as my instructions were not to take on refugees unless they were in real need … Amongst the refugees were a large number of women and young girls and children of all ages, even including some in arms … However, from seeing the condition of the refugees, I decided from a humanitarian point of view to take them aboard as I anticipated they would soon be landed at Orán in Algeria.[6]

The journey to North Africa took 20 hours, and the conditions were atrocious; there were just two toilets on board and there was a shortage of both food and water. When the ship arrived in

---

6 Archibald Dickson, letter to the *Sunday Dispatch* newspaper, dated 2/3 April 1939. <https://viewfromlavila.com/2018/03/28/the-stanbrook-story-the-unlikely-british-heroes-of-alicantes-darkest-hour/>.

Orán on 29 March 1939, the French colonial authorities at first refused to allow her to dock. An angry Captain Dickson first negotiated the landing of women, children and the elderly, but the men remained on board for days and were only allowed onto dry land when Dickson underlined the threat of a typhus outbreak. Sadly, six months later, just after the start of the Second World War, the *Stanbrook* was lost, torpedoed by a German submarine as she headed to Tyneside from Antwerp. The 47 year old captain and 22 officers and men perished after the ship broke in two. Dickson and his crew have gone down in legend and there is now a statue of him in Alicante.[7]

The arrival of thousands of exiled Spaniards in North Africa in the spring of 1939 was not met with the freedom that the Spanish exiles expected, except for those who had a passport with a visa enabling them to travel to Mexico (the dream destination for most). What was to follow, particularly for the men of a fighting age who had already suffered almost three years of war and hardships, was internment centres as well as concentration and work camps. According to Eliane Ortega, whose grandfather travelled to North Africa on the *Stanbrook*, some 70 detention centres of various categories were counted in Algeria alone and if those in the other Maghreb countries where the Spanish Republicans sought refuge are added the figure reaches 110.[8] The largest of the Algerian camps was the one in which her grandfather was held, Camp Moránd at Boghari. This was approximately 150 kilometres south of Algiers, where at its peak thousands of Spaniards worked and lived in confinement without the most basic conditions and having to withstand the extreme temperatures of the desert climate. They were guarded and punished as if they were the enemy. Opened in April 1939, the camp was intended to hold Spanish Republican militiamen. Located close to the Ouarsenis Mountains, conditions were harsh and were worsened by the lack of food and water as well as there being no infirmary. By May 1939, it housed 3,000 internees. Despite international protestations it still contained some 2,000 at the end of the year. In June 1940, Hitler's Germany took control of France. With the Nazification of the colonies, Spanish Republicans confined in the camps became likely enemies. Their separation by political affiliation was accelerated and those considered to be the greatest threat were interned in prison work camps in the Sahara.

In Algeria, by May 1939 new camps were established that allowed many of the refugees in the Algiers area to be housed. The *Préfecture d'Alger* reported on 20 June 1939 a total of 3,109 Spaniards housed in various camps in the area (Boghari: 2,446, Suzzoni: 238, Carnot: 262, Orléansville: 68). The *8ᵉ Régiment de Travailleurs Étrangers* was established in the summer of 1939. It contained a total of 12 *CTE*s that were mostly Republican Navy from Bizerta. It was formed at Moránd Camp and had companies spread widely from Morocco in the west to Tunisia in the east. Despite being numbered as the *8ᵉ* it was in fact the only *régiment* of its kind. When war was declared in September 1939, the majority of Spaniards who had been interned in Cherchell, Suzzoni and Moránd, were sent to Colomb-Béchar to be integrated into the *8ᵉ Régiment de Travailleurs Étrangers* to make up part of the 12 companies in the regiment. They were put to work renovating military facilities, repairing roads and more especially in the construction of a railway between Colomb-Béchar and Bou Afra.[9] The work on the railway started in February 1940 and Spaniards were employed in

---

7   Ted Richards, *Archibald Dickson – An Unsung Roath Hero* (Cardiff: Roath Local History Society, 2021), <https://roathlocalhistorysociety.org/2021/08/20/archibald-dickson-an-unsung-roath-hero>. Accessed 23 July 2022. For more information about the evacuation of exiled Spaniards using the Stanbook from Alicante to Orán, see: Juan B. Vilar, 'El Exilio Español de 1939 en el Norte de África', *¡Ay de losvencidos! El exilio y los países de acogida* (Madrid: Ed. Eneida, 2009), p.74 and Juan B. Vilar, 'La Última Gran Emigración Política Española. Relación Nominal de los Militantes Republicanos Evacuados de Alicante en el Buque Inglés Stanbrook con Destino a Orán en 28 de Marzo de 1939', in *Anales de Historia Contemporánea*, Univ. de Murcia, No.2, 1983.
8   Eliane Ortega Bernabeu has spent many years researching Spanish Republican exiles in North Africa and has written and spoken about the topic extensively.
9   Anne Dulphy, 'Sables d'Exil. Les Républicains Espagnols Dans les Camps d'Internement au Maghreb

its construction as part of the *Mediterranée-Niger* (*Mer-Niger*) *Compagnie*. The railway had been a French project for some time but was delayed on several occasions, but once the Second World War had broken out it took on new significance. German administrators endorsed the project as it was a useful way of moving Senegalese soldiers through the Sahara Desert. It was also a great way of exploiting the large quantity and variety of mineral and natural resources (including coal) found in the region.

Following the Vichy Regime's law on foreign workers, passed on 27 September 1940, in March 1941 *CTEs* were reconstituted as *Groupements de Travailleurs Étrangers* (*GTEs*).[10] By the last quarter of 1940, Vichy authorities had established a network of different types of camps in Algeria, Morocco and Tunisia. These ranged from penal colonies to labour camps, to internment camps. The camps had a wide variety of residents: Jews, other non-Jewish European refugees, those already residing in French colonial North Africa before 1940 (such as Spaniards), those deported for forced labour in the Sahara, Allied POWs and other civilians. The Ministry of Industrial Production and Labour managed the camps as well as the oversight of the internees. Internees were moved from camp to camp regularly to prevent unrest. Day-to-day administration of the camps in Morocco and Algeria was carried out by Senegalese troops (*tirailleurs*), Muslim conscripts or those paid to join the auxiliary service, by local Moroccan military auxiliary representatives (*goumiers*) and also by members of the French indigenous cavalry regiments (*spahis*). Residents of the camps tended to be made up of distinct classes of prisoners. For example, the camps of Djelfa, Djenien Bou Rezg, and Hadjerat M'Guil held mainly political dissidents, while Bou Arfa and Colomb-Béchar were reserved for *GTEs*. Other types of prisoners were confined in Vichy labour camps in French West Africa.[11]

In the forced-labour camps of southern Morocco and Algeria, internees faced harsh retribution. Food was limited to water and 100 grams of bread per day. Many internees died from scorpion stings, snake bites, typhoid and malaria. Heat and cold were suffered with scant clothing, blankets, or shoes. In Tunisia, circumstances diverged from those in Morocco and Algeria. Camps in Tunisia were supervised by French, German, and Italian overseers, depending on the period of the war. Libya was a key battleground of the Second World War and territory here passed back and forth between Italian and British hands. Camps were set up at Giado, Buqbuq and Sidi Azaz. Inmates were subjected to forced labour in all three camps, with conditions in Giado camp proving particularly harsh.

At this point it is worth giving some background to the Spaniards who were already resident in North Africa during the period leading up to 1939 and beyond, as well as how complex the situation became in northern Africa, especially after the summer of 1940. Spain had for centuries had a great impact across the north-west of Africa with its territories well-established across the region. Because of centuries of influence, there were well-established colonies from Tunis in the east to Morocco in the west. For example, in 1936 65 percent of around 206,000 Europeans in the city of Orán were Spanish, 41 percent of them being naturalised. Spaniards certainly became very prominent in the city, and their influence included bullfighting, Spanish food and religious processions. In the 1930s, Orán was also a hotbed of pro-Franco right-wing groups and from 1941 right-wing

---

(1939–1945),' *Exils et Migrations Ibériques au XXe Siècle*, 2009, pp.99–117.
10 By this stage, political prisoners and internees were organised into groups of foreign workers: the *Groupements de Travailleurs Étrangers* (*GTEs*, Groups of Foreign Workers), *Groupements de Travailleurs Étrangers Autonomes* (*GTEAs*, Autonomous Groups of Foreign Workers) and *Groupements de Travailleurs Démobilisés* (*GTDs*, Groups of Demobilised Foreign Workers).
11 United States Holocaust Memorial Museum. *Holocaust Encyclopaedia. Labor and Internment Camps in North Africa*. <encyclopedia.ushmm.org/content/en/article/labor-and-internment-camps-in-north-africa#:~:text=In%20Morocco%20and%20Algeria%2C%20many,the%20coastal%20cities%20of%20Algeria>. Accessed 12 June 2022.

The harsh conditions for internees in camps in North Africa are clearly shown in this picture of five Spaniards. (Agustín Roa Ventura collection)

political organisations and malicious Vichy Regime fed anti-Semitism in the region. But there were still many left-wing leaning groups that would provide support to the Allies in the future. Orán sent a significant contingent to fight in the International Brigades during the Spanish Civil War and from the spring of 1939 ships from Spain began to arrive with thousands of refugees aboard. Across the region there were several other nationalities that had settled in North Africa. Further east in Tunisia were over 200,000 Europeans who mainly lived around Tunis. Many were French although Italian remained a common language. Algiers was a large city with over a quarter of a million inhabitants; around 120,000 of them were classed as stateless and these consisted mainly of Spanish Republicans, Eastern European Jews and fugitives from Alsace-Moselle – all of whom had arrived in the late 1930s. In the west, and particularly in Morocco, there were over 20,000 Spaniards who had settled down along with large groups of Italians and of other nationalities.[12]

A typical example of someone who was able to settle within the Spanish community in Orán was that of Fausto Miguel García. Originally from Ávila in central Spain and later known as 13809717 Private Fausto Miguel, García had moved to Sestao in the Basque Country with his wife before the Spanish Civil War to work at Altos Hornos in Bilbao. In May 1937 he had evacuated his two sons from Bilbao as Basque refugee children to Great Britain and during March 1939 he escaped with his wife Teodosia from Cartagena to Orán. By this time, Fausto and Teodosia were already quite old parents compared to some others. Like many, they were keen to settle into a routine and one day hoped to have their children rejoin them. A series of letters written to their

---

12 Douglas Porch, *Defeat and Division, France at War 1939–1942* (Cambridge: Cambridge University Press, 2022), pp.438–440.

sons' guardian, a Mr Harry Livingston in Glasgow, via the *Centro Democratico Español*, allow us a rare insight into life for many of the Spaniards who had escaped to North Africa. Fausto and Teodosia seem to have been able to settle down to fairly normal living in Orán. Teodoro found work as an electrician and was paid around six francs a day for it. It was still impossible for the family to be reunited at this stage and this became even more unlikely with the fall of France in the summer of 1940. In July 1940, Fausto and Teodosia were interned and separated. Fausto ended up in the notorious concentration camp at Djelfa, until his liberation in early 1943. Because of his incarceration, he was not able to get any news of his children for nine months until a letter arrived from Glasgow in March 1941. He would not be able to write to his family again until May 1943 by which time he was a member of 361 (Alien) Company of the Pioneer Corps based in Algiers.[13]

Following the defeat of France in the summer of 1940, the British realised early on that de Gaulle was key for them and a geographical necessity for British security after the war. The Free French were soon accepted by the UK despite the difficulties of working with its leader. De Gaulle was recognised as the 'Leader of all Free Frenchmen, wherever they may be, who rallied to him in support of the Allied cause.'[14] Further afield, after the summer of 1940, the cult of *Pétainism* had struck a vein within the government of the French Maghreb and there were few Gaullist supporters in the major cities, or amongst the indigenous Arab and Berber population. *Général* Charles-Auguste Nogues in Morocco and *Amirals* Jean Abrial in Algeria and Jean-Pierre Esteva in Tunisia were determined to maintain French sovereignty and national honour, and the *Armée d'Afrique* was determined to fend off any invader. Things became strained as the Americans decided they would support the Vichy led North African Government. Soon after the Mers-el-Kébir attack early in the war, it was clear that the American disliked and mistrusted de Gaulle and had maintained diplomatic relations with Vichy while rejecting de Gaulle and the Free French. To the British this reinforced how little the Americans understood security in Europe.

In November 1940, *Général* Maxime Weygand became *Délégué Général* in North Africa. As Commander-in-Chief, Weygand had rallied to Pétain in June, but he was no collaborator. A Nationalist and anti-Semite, he was against the Vichy collaboration with Germany but backed many of its extreme policies. American diplomat, Robert Murphy was convinced early on that Weygand could be a person to deal with to enable better progress in the war with France. But due to his strong opposition to the Paris Protocols signed by the ardent Anglophobe *Amiral* François Darlan, Weygand was sacked in November 1941 and replaced by *Général* Alphonse Juin. To the SOE, and the fledgling American OSS, Tunisia was becoming a key focus for concern as it held the key to access east and west and was well linked to Europe via Sicily.[15] Murphy made approaches to Darlan who said he would be willing to negotiate if the USA was willing to intervene massively in North Africa. The shift in attitude to reinforce links with the British was typified by US Vice Consuls such as Robert Solborg, who had worked with Hoare and Hillgarth in Madrid (see above). This in turn meant that there was a softening in approach by the Americans around collaborating with British Intelligence agencies, especially as the SIS and SOE were well established in the region. Solborg then suggested that OSS and SOE in French North Africa coordinate an approach towards French oppositional groups in Morocco and Algeria. The British were gathering intelligence from French and Spanish sources in their major hubs in Tangiers and Gibraltar. The British had more established networks, transmitting stations and contacts amongst the Moroccans, French and Spanish, but the OSS had more pulling power.

---

13 Fausto García family archive.
14 Michael S. Neiberg, *When France Fell, The Vichy Crisis and the Fate of the Anglo-American Alliance* (Cambridge Massachusetts: Harvard Press, 2021), p.76.
15 Robert L. Melka, 'Darlan Between Britain and Germany 1940-41,' *Journal of Contemporary History*, Vol.8, No.2, April 1973, pp.57–80.

Fausto and Teodosia García in Orán shortly after their arrival. (Fausto Miguel García collection)

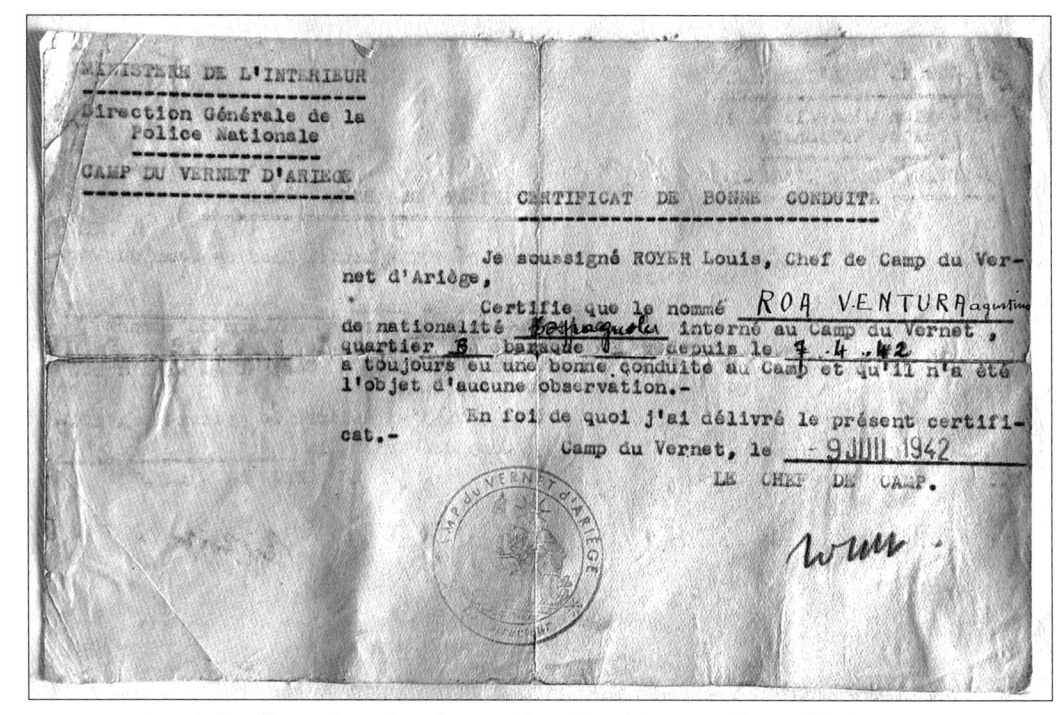

Agustín Roa Ventura's good conduct certificate from his time at Vernet d'Ariège camp. (Agustín Roa Ventura collection)

The Americans started to make contact with resistance groups in North Africa and made approaches to *Général* Henri Giraud who had recently escaped from German captivity on 17 April 1942 when he had escaped from Königstein castle near Dresden. From here he moved into Switzerland and secreted himself into Vichy France. For many at the time, Giraud was seen as a great leader, not involved with Vichy and very anti-German. He was, however, strongly anti-British.

The lead for the Allied invasion of North Africa – Operation TORCH – was to be taken by the Americans. Colonel William Eddy, US Naval Attaché in Tangier and senior OSS operative in North-West Africa, had established a far-reaching network in Morocco and was fully aware of the potential support available from Spaniards in the region. The Americans were also able to offer more for collaboration that the SOE could even begin to match.

Djelfa Camp

Augustín Roa Ventura left the camp of Vernet d'Ariège in France on 9 July 1942, and from there he travelled by train to Port Vendres. He was not alone; in total, 45 Spanish political prisoners were being taken to the coast close to the Spanish border. All were ready to resist should they be taken into Spain itself, a thing they all dreaded. It had been three and a half years since they had left Spain; they witnessed the defeat of the Popular Army of the Spanish Republic, the end of the Spanish Civil War, persecution, judgement, imprisonment and at worst death. Sitting on the train they were worried about where they were going, but soon realised that, as they arrived at the coast, they were still in France. At the port, the prisoners were loaded onto the ship *Djavel Jaures* and lowered into the depths of it. By 14 July they had arrived in Algiers. Once up on deck they were put in handcuffs and handed over to a local guard which took them across the city to where

Spaniards shortly after their arrival in Djelfa. Note the figure standing on the far right. This is almost certainly Daniel Fineboy, who joined the British Army in Algeria and was a member of 361 (Alien) Pioneer Company. He eventually settled in the Midlands after the war and was a good friend of Antonio Obis. (Antonio Obis collection)

they were held in a camp overnight. Agustín recalled that they were told that this was to be their last night of freedom and they were treated to a good meal, slept in a bed with sheets, and were allowed to write to their loved ones. The next day they were put on a train and were on their way into the interior to Djelfa. As they travelled towards the Sahara, the heat intensified, and soon they felt that they were leaving the real world. It was clear that they were actually 'entering hell', and it would be impossible to escape. At eight o'clock in the morning of 17 July the train stopped – they had arrived at Djelfa. A roll call was quickly taken, and they were marched into the camp carrying their belongings to meet the commandant, a tall corpulent Pole called Caboche. He greeted them with, 'I have good references on you all, but don't forget I am your worst enemy. If you respect the discipline of this camp, I will be just, but if you don't you will get to know me better.'[16]

Life in the camp was hell. The men lived in tents and were dressed in the clothes they had arrived in. It was freezing at night and when it rained the water swept through the camp. All were put to hard labour, whether it was working in a nearby quarry or carrying out other hard physical work. The men of the camp also set up cottage industries such as brick making and leather work that helped the local village and lined the pockets of those running the camp.

Those interned at Djelfa came from a huge mix of backgrounds. Most of the Spaniards were political prisoners and many were men who had been rounded up and sent there so they could not agitate any longer. An interesting addition to the list of Spaniards in the camp was Salvador Hernández Jiménez. Originally from Tenerife, at the outbreak of the Spanish Civil War, Hernández was conscripted into Franco's Nationalist Army and sent to Morocco. Here he was able to escape but was subsequently captured and interned and was probably forced to work on the railway between Colomb-Béchar and Bou Afra. From here, he was able to escape with a fellow

---
16 Agustín Roa Ventura, *Los Años de mi Vida, Personal Papers*, 1942–1950. Unpublished.

A group of Spaniards interned at Djelfa pose for a photo with their camp guards. The man second from the right of the pith helmet in the centre is Salvador Hernández Giménez who later joined the British Army. Note the accommodation tents in the background on the right. (Family archives of Joaquín Chamero Serena & Eliane Ortega Bernabeu)

Spanish prisoner. After crossing a stretch of desert, the two were saved by Bedouin tribesmen who assisted them. They then decided to sneak onto a train, where they hid amongst the coal trucks and eventually got to Orán. Once there Hernández managed to pass himself off as an Arab but during a routine stop to check documents he was arrested as he had none, he was beaten up by the police and eventually sent to Djelfa. Hernández would later become 13809792 Private Salvador Hernández and served in 361 (Alien) Pioneer Company until the end of the war.

As well as Spaniards, who were the largest group in the camp, there were German Jews, Poles and some Italians – many of whom had been fighting against fascism for some time. The camp also had a post office, but it rarely allowed post to get to its destination. Other buildings included the infirmary which was only for urgent cases and was headed up by Doctor Koffler, an ex-International Brigadier from the Spanish Civil War. He was supported by a dentist and other men who worked as nurses. Dates were the staple diet of most of the inmates which they would learn to loath. At night when it was hot, the sound of hyenas could be heard in the distance and flies were everywhere. All inmates had a daily parade at six o'clock in the morning when a nominal roll was taken. By half past seven work details set off to their work assignments (whether it was cleaning the camp or working outside the wire on tasks in the searing heat). Tobacco was a luxury but there was a sense of camaraderie and there were few thefts or violence amongst the internees. Torture and beatings were an everyday occurrence, and many suffered Caboche's whip. The youngest man amongst the Spaniards was 20 years old and had fought in the Spanish Civil War at the age of 14. The eldest was 56. One of the older members of the camp was Fausto García. Another internee at Djelfa was Antonio Obis who had been in *159ᵉ Compagnie de Travailleurs Espagnols* in Castres, France before being sent to North Africa. Eduardo Tamarit was 24 and had been sent from France having worked on the Maginot Line with the *105ᵉ CTE* earlier in the war.

Following a storm in early October 1942 which swept through the camp, Augustín was left paralysed. Everything that had happened over the previous five years had caught up with him and he was bedridden, unable to move due to his paralysis. Doctor Koffler soon got to work but it was not that easy to get hold of the necessary drugs. Across from his bed lay Miguel who cried

A group of Spaniards held at Djelfa stand outside their accommodation tent. Note the clothes they are wearing are what they had when they had been in France or elsewhere. No uniforms were ever issued. Sitting down, second from the left is Antono Obis who would later join 361 (Alien) Pioneer Company. (Antonio Obis collection)

with pain. Augustín could sense that he had now given up as it seemed that the life he had looked forward to had been destroyed by the Spanish Civil War and his exile. Miguel felt excluded from everything and everyone. The biggest thing Augustín told him was not to lose faith in oneself, but sadly a few mornings later when he awoke, he knew Miguel was dead. This was another pointless death that sent Augustín into a deep depression. By the autumn of 1942 the numbers of prisoners at the camp had reached almost 800, of whom 386 were Spaniards.[17] The tents were eventually replaced by huts but for many it was too late.

Meanwhile, the Americans had been working on *Général* Giraud to get him to agree to support the Allied invasion of North Africa. But he had a set of conditions. These consisted of deciding the date of the operation, becoming Supreme Commander of Allied Troops in North Africa and banning British troops from any of the landings. Eisenhower was having none of it. Planning for Operation TORCH was already in full swing. The contacts made with underground Spanish groups by Colonel William Eddy were starting to pay off.[18] While the Eighth Army was pushing westwards across North Africa the landings took place on 8 November 1942. The French (amongst them Giraud himself) were caught off guard and some stood and fought. *Amiral* Darlan had been visiting his ill son the day before and was captured. He soon struck a controversial bargain with the Allies but was assassinated on 24 December, thus freeing up Giraud to take over.

13301854 Juan Torrents Abadía (later known as John Colman and a member of 2nd SAS) had joined the *Légion Étrangère* and was sent to North Africa as a labourer attached to one of the *GTEs*:

---

17 TNA, HS3-50, SOE Africa and Middle East Group, Massingham, Prisons, internment and concentration camps, 1943.
18 Standard Operation Instructions – Lieutenant Colonel W. A. Eddy USMC, 14 October 1942. <https://www.cia.gov/readingroom/document/cia-rdp13x00001r000100330006-2>, accessed July 2024.

Internees pause during the building of accommodation huts in Djelfa. On the far right is Antonio Obis. (Antonio Obis collection)

Eduardo Tamarit stands amongst some of the tomato plants at Djelfa. A rare delicacy. (Eduardo Tamarit collection)

> We were put to work on roads and dams and works like that. The French had to give up their weapons. We were working in Morocco, Casablanca and Rabat and we were quite familiar with those places. For a spell, we were working on turbines to make electricity and smashing rocks. Then we were moved from one place to another and eventually to Rabat close to the sea and we used to listen … there was a chum who managed to put one of those radio things together. One of the fellows in our room could speak English and we were able to listen to Churchill. We had the feeling that Churchill was on our side when he decided it wasn't going to be peace in our times but decided to carry on with the war. That's when we knew … the Germans at the time … Churchill saw through that. We loved Churchill although he was right wing. We were all left wingers and I used to love listening to him on the radio.
>
> That was the biggest sensation, the moment that we thought would never arrive. As I said we were in Rabat and near the sea. We heard firing and shooting, the aeroplanes coming in. There were cries 'They're here!' and they were here! That sector it was the Americans that landed there. We saw the French retreating and the Americans started coming. But the thing is we were still kept in camps for a long time.[19]

Two months after the Allied landings in Algiers two jeeps arrived at Djelfa. In them were various Allied officers. As they entered the guard presented arms. The group was made up of American, British and French officers who immediately questioned Caboche. Straight after, they visited the prisoners and met up with their representatives. Caboche was not present. One of the British officers was Kenneth Younger an officer in the Intelligence Corps and a man who would later be heavily involved in the Labour Government of Clement Attlee. Amongst the Spanish representatives were men who had travelled with Augustín Roa from Vernet d'Arriège camp. A few days later the first small group of Spaniards were whisked away from the camp. It was a strange thing, according to Augustín these men were used in special operations by the British.

Along with the recruitment of underground Spanish groups to be found across Tunisia, Algeria and Morocco, the MASSINGHAM mission, a project of the SOE based at Club des Pins in Algiers to work with the OSS, became the main command hub and training centre for special operations across north-west Africa and later south-west Europe.[20] With a foothold in the region, the SOE and OSS turned their gaze to operations into Southern Europe and in particular southern France, Corsica and mainland Italy, Sicily and Sardinia.[21] Spain was not included because of the success Hoare and his team had had in ensuring Franco did not enter the war. But the immediate priority was the engagement of agents in Tunisia. This can be backed up by the account of 'Dumbo' Newman where he gives a great deal of information on the kind of things Spaniards were involved with on the BRANDON mission for the SOE. This came under the MASSINGHAM umbrella and operated behind enemy lines in Northern Tunisia from December 1942 to February 1943 carrying out sabotage, and to find Germans and kill them.

> We were to report to the Massingham mission at Guelma in Algiers. I set up a training school in Tunisia and reported there and the Brandon mission with a small group of Spaniards was invited to help the American army who had just had a setback when they were attacked by the

---

19 Interview with John Colman (Juan Torrents Abadía), recorded 27 December 1997, IWM 17730.
20 Standard Operation Instructions – Lieutenant Colonel W.A. Eddy USMC, 14 October 1942. J. Marco, 'Transnational Soldiers and Guerrilla Warfare from the Spanish Civil War to the Second World War', *War in History*, Vol.27, no. 3, pp.387–407. See <https://doi.org/10.1177/0968344518761212>. Accessed 12 June 2022.
21 Martin Thomas, 'The Massingham Mission: SOE in French North Africa, 1941–1944', *Intelligence and National Security*, 1996, 11:4, pp.696–721, <https://doi.org/10.1080/02684529608432387>.

Germans of Kesserine. I think the Spaniards had been able to get away out of Spain and had been in jail near Algiers. I didn't have anything to do with their release. We were invited to try and use them in ground operations. They were very keen ... and yes there was a language problem![22]

This must have been in February 1943 and fits well with the testimonies of many who were released. The SOE also managed to work well with anarchists, and it was not long before some who had been released would be guarding some of the SOE training centres. The OSS somewhat ironically approached the communists. The presence of the Spaniards was a deliberate policy, and despite Hoare's efforts, in early 1943 the need to resist and subvert a German advance through Spain still seemed a prospect. In concentration camps set up by Vichy France, the SOE found plenty, and brought them to the *Club des Pins*.[23] There were even plans made by the OSS to use some Spaniards in potential landings in Spain. In fact, this is something which came to fruition when a team of OSS trained communists made two landings near Málaga![24] The SOE on the other hand was keen to get able Spaniards to work for them further afield in France and Yugoslavia.[25] Nevertheless, in Tunisia Spaniards also fought with the OSS. In a report, American Carleton Coon, an anthropologist who was affiliated to the OSS reported that a staff officer in the HQ there wanted them to:

Go out behind the Germans, sit in foxholes and throw grenades at the Mark VIs [the Mk IV German heavy tank is probably what was meant] as they rolled over us. He thought we were some kind of special suicide shock troops. He did not know that we included three of the finest guerrilla commanders of the Spanish Civil War, one university professor, a Major of paratroops and other specialists who, could not easily be replaced; [and] that we were all at least bilingual.[26]

Liberation, Volunteers and 361 (Alien) Pioneer Company

Not taking into account those in the *Légion Étrangère*, there were some 14,000 exiled Spaniards in Orán alone. Many were politically active and a report by the Spanish Consul in the city reported that these could be broken down as: 7,000 in the *Partido Socialist Obrero Espanol* and *UGT*, 4,000 communists, 2,400 anarchists and also from the *CNT* (Spanish Anarchist Party) and some 400 republicans. A report by *Général* Jean Bergeret, *Général* Giraud's secretary, stated that over 3,000 Spaniards from the Republican Army were transferred to North Africa from France as they constituted a 'threat to the French State' and that it was 'willing to be generous enough to let them join the Foreign Legion where they could offer their lives to save France'. The Inter-Allied Commission which had been established in Algiers, soon got to work to investigate those interned to establish the truth and look at ways they could be employed. By early April 1943, the Commission offered the following five options to the Spaniards. They could:

---

22 Imperial War Museum interview with Eveleigh Earle Dennis 'Dumbo' Newman, IWM 27463, 13 December 2004,
23 TNA, HS 7/169, SOE Histories and War Diaries, MASSINGHAM: Special Projects Operational centre; operation in Corsica; BALACLAVA naval section; para-naval work.
24 J. Marco, 'Transnational Soldiers and Guerrilla Warfare from the Spanish Civil War to the Second World War',
25 Ramón Liarte, *¡Ay, de los vencedores!* (Barcelona: Ediciones Picazo, 1986), pp.92–94.
26 Carleton Stevens Coon, *A North Africa Story: The Anthropologist as OSS Agent, 1941–1943* (University of Michigan: Gambit Press, 1980).

A group of Spaniards with villagers in Djelfa. Taken shortly after the Allied landings in North Africa. (Antonio Obis collection)

1. Join the French forces, especially the *Légion Étrangère*.
2. Be allowed to emigrate to Mexico but costs for the journey would be borne by the exiled Republican organisations such as *CAFRE* (*Comisión Administrativa de Fondo de Ayuda a los Refugiados Españoles*).
3. Accept a contract to work in North Africa for the French authorities, which would produce residency at the end of the war.
4. Join the British Army and enlist into the Pioneer Corps for the duration of the war. This could not guarantee residency in the United Kingdom however.
5. Join the American Armed Forces. This would need those interested to travel to the USA and give up their own nationality. Costs for travel were not covered.[27]

On the whole, Spaniards opted for the first and fourth options unless they already had roots in North Africa. With the French, they would join the *Corps Francs* serving under *Général* Leclerc. Probably the most famous of these would be Spaniards from La Nueve, the *9e Compagnie* of the *Régiment de Marche du Tchad*, part of Leclerc's French 2nd Armoured Division. Some Spaniards who joined the French at this stage even ended up in the French regiments in the SAS Brigade (3rd or 4th SAS).

Back in Djelfa, at eight o'clock on the morning of 28 April 1943 (pretty much the same time of the day that he had arrived and some eight and a half months later) Augustín Roa Ventura left the camp for good. Despite having a stick, Augustín was determined now to walk by himself. A train had been organised and left the desert travelling towards the coast. Many hours later they arrived in Boufarik village near Algiers, where 361 (Alien) Company was established the following day.

---

27 Daniel Arasa, *Los Españoles de Churchill* (Barcelona: Editorial Armonía Poética, 1991), pp.200–203.

According to his memoirs, by 1 May 794 Spaniards had enlisted to join the British Army. It is not known if this is true or whether it was a mixture of nationalities by that date. In a statement to the House of Commons on 12 May 1943, the Foreign Secretary, Anthony Eden said of those who had been released that:

> No exact figures are available, but my latest information indicates that between 3,000 and 4,000 have been released during the past two months. I understand that there remain two to three hundred Frenchmen and probably rather less than 2,000 internees of all other nationalities. The majority of these are Spaniards, and a large number of these Spaniards are waiting until transport can be provided to take them to Mexico. Others are waiting for definite jobs and accommodation to be made available to them. There are likely to be a hundred or two who are medically unfit or incapable of employment for one reason or another. The medically unfit are to be admitted into a special rest centre organised with the assistance of the Red Cross. Up to 1st May, 794 internees had joined the British Pioneer Corps and a further 106 have been accepted for enrolment. [28]

Not only had Spaniards come from camps, but many were men who had signed up for the *Légion Étrangère* only to be put into hard labour or *GTE*s or who had managed to melt into the background reappearing after TORCH. Once 361 (Alien) Company was established in Boufarik they were issued uniforms, their army pay book and dog tags and training began. One of the biggest difficulties was the language barrier as orders were given in English and pretty much none of the Spaniards could understand it.

This was most certainly the case with Captain Edward Rose who commanded a civil labour unit in North Africa and was warned off to prepare for the invasion of Southern Europe. He was told that a group of sergeants would be given to him to act as interpreters. His account is typical of the situation at the time and rather amusing:

> My Sergeants reported for duty, and I had all six paraded before me in my office for interview. Quickly I glanced down the nominal roll and posting order which one of them had silently handed me – Serjeants Bodnaras, Ardines [recruited in Algiers 16 May 43 real name 13809823 Hoyos Abilio Ruiz alias Julio Bardenas Ardines], Swatkiwski, Dahler, Orchudesch and Badanelli, I read. Not much of a clue here as to where our secret destination was to be. Could be any place in Europe.
>
> 'Good morning, Sgts,' I said. 'I understand we are all to go on a little picnic together so we might as well get to know one another straight away. You have been travelling together for the last two days so will have teamed up by this. I am your commanding officer for this new show and I've little doubt you will soon learn my peculiarities, what I like and don't like in my NCOs and what I expect from you. To start off with I'd like to know which of you is which, and I'll just take down some particulars got my own records. Which of you is Sgt Bodnaras?'
>
> One man stepped forward and gave me an untidy salute, which coming from a senior NCO annoyed me. 'Sgt Bardenas, Sir,' he said. There was something strange about them all which puzzled me. When I had addressed them, their eyes had the attentive but non-understanding look one sometimes notices when talking in a subdued voice to those very hard of hearing. But my immediate attention was in Sgt Bardenas. His unsoldierly salute had irritated me I knew that I was frowning at him.

---

28 Hansard Volume 389: North Africa (Internees), debated on Wednesday 12 May 1943. <https://hansard.parliament.uk/Commons/1943-05-12/debates/c65a59d3-8ff7-4853-acd5-6b6089490acf/NorthAfrica(Internees)?highlight=spaniards#contribution-e218df29-1357-45fe-a13b-7c36ab2cd051>. Accessed 12 June 2022.

Eduardo Tamarit's pay book. Note his enlistment location and date. (Eduardo Tamarit collection)

'How long have you been in the army, Sergeant?' I asked.
'Sir?'
'I asked you how long you had been in the army, Sgt,' I repeated sternly.
'Oh, yes, sir.'
'What is wrong with you man? Don't you understand plain English?'
'H'English! Yes, I spik. Goof.' He smiled engagingly.
My God, I thought. The man hasn't understood one word I've said. I wonder if any of them have? I let my eyes travel along the line from one end to the other.
'Has any one of you the foggiest notion what I've been saying in the last few minutes?' I asked.
They looked at me uncomprehendingly, silent.[29]

361 (Alien) Company was not the first company to be established. Some released Spaniards were already living in Algiers and approached the British authorities soon after the Allied landings with a view to enlistment. At first the French raised objections, but on 11 December 1942, 337 Company, Pioneer Corps, was formed in Algiers with Major A.J. Ferris in command. Two-thirds of the Company had served in the *Légion Étrangère*; some had fought in the Spanish Civil War. Eighty percent of the unit had seen active military service. There were also many who had served under the BEF and who were keen to rejoin the British. It was to be a fruitful recruiting ground

---

29 Edward Rose, *A Gift of Tongues*, a personal unpublished memoir. Extract provided by the Royal Pioneer Corps Archive.

for the Allies as operations expanded further east. The Company in fact provided some excellent soldiers who would go on to serve in other parts of the British Army and in the SOE. One of these would be 13300008 Sergeant Alfonso Canovas who would later distinguish himself in France in August 1944. Following the liberation of camps into early 1943 the following Pioneer companies were formed: 338 Company (Major L.H. Fairtlough) on 1 April, 1943; as already discussed, 361 Company (Major W.T. Hubbard) on 29 April; 362 Company (Major J.G. Craster) on 16 May; 363 Company (Major J. Hepburn) on 1 August, and 364 Company (Major D.W. Jones) on 31 July. Two new Pioneer Group Headquarters were formed in Algeria in April 1943 to assist in the administration of the ever-growing labour force with First Army. These were 91 Group (under Lieutenant Colonel J.S. Pope-Smith) and 92 Group (under Lieutenant Colonel A.F. Mills MC). The majority of the companies that contained Spaniards fell under 91 Group.

Members of these companies formed a very cosmopolitan group: Austrians, Germans, Spaniards, Poles, Hungarians, Romanians, Italians and Russians predominating. In 362 Company alone there were 28 nationalities. Interestingly, the men of 338 (Alien) Company which contained many Spaniards, constructed the buildings in which the German emissaries who signed the final surrender of the German Army in Italy were housed, a task which must have given them a measure of satisfaction. Later in 1943 and into 1944 further Pioneer companies were established in Morocco. One of these was 406 (Alien) Pioneer Company which was established in Rabat in August 1944. This company ended up in Italy supporting the rear areas until the summer of 1945, the company had a strong Spanish contingent.

In 361 (Alien) Company, things were busy as it was sent to Hussein Dey only two weeks after formation. It was shortly after this that Augustín Roa Ventura was promoted to corporal. A few weeks later 362 and 363 Companies (which had a large number of Spaniards in them) joined Augustín and his comrades, as well as a group of Spaniards who had previously served in the Middle East Commandos who arrived in September 1943.[30]

In Hussein Dey the Company was working with the Royal Army Service Corps as well as the Docks Company of the Royal Engineers. Agustín Roa described the work they did:

> We worked on loading and unloading a lot of the ships in the harbour when things were being prepared for Sicily. They were really hard weeks, not just due to the intense work but also because of the many 'visits' we received from the German Airforce. As well as the danger of bombing, things were worsened by the cargo we loaded which was mainly explosives. The ships would set off straight after loading and drop anchor out beyond the harbour entrance, not just to free up dock space for others but also due to the danger their loads presented.[31]

The British authorities were pleased with the hard work of the Spaniards as they got to work and finished task after task in record time. The Spaniards were not really bothered about tea breaks and worked long hours to ensure they were given good rest time. Rest and time off were things that many of them had not had since fighting in the Spanish Civil War. Many also remembered when a ship blew up full of explosives and they were used to put out the fire. Luckily nobody was killed. For the Spaniards it was clear that many were not happy with an occupying force. An

---

30 ME 13808232 Manuel Surera's Army Record records him moving from the Middle East to North Africa by ship in August 1943. He was then taken on the strength of British North African Forces from Middle East Forces (MEF) on 1 September 1943 and was then posted to 361 (Alien) Company on 3 October 1943. It is presumed that the 15 or so other Spaniards who had served in the Middle East Commando joined the Pioneer Corps in North Africa around these dates.

31 Daniel Arasa, *Los Españoles de Churchill* (Barcelona: Editorial Armonía Poética, 1991), p.214. Interview with Agustín Roa Ventura.

Officers of 91 Pioneer Group serving in Algeria. In the centre sat down wearing gloves is its commander Lieutenant Colonel J.S. Pope-Smith. Major Hubert Cole who would command 361 (Alien) Company is standing top left wearing a belt. (Hubert Cole collection)

irony was that many of the Spaniards had been brought to Africa as prisoners and were now on the other side of the fence in British uniform. War certainly produced many changes and contradictions, something that was not lost on them.

In September 1943, there were six British Non-Commissioned Officers and 238 Alien Other Ranks in the Company, these were all Spanish. By the end of 1943 the Company had undergone quite a few changes in British personnel. A soon to be respected figure was Hubert Cole. He arrived as the Second in Command of the Company and took over command of it for a short period later on. A writer, he ended up working at *John Bull Magazine* after the war and kept in contact with many Spaniards, especially those who moved to Mexico. In his diaries, he remembered:

> I was officially posted to 361 (A) Company on 3 November 1943. I had actually been there some time before that.
>
> The Company was composed almost entirely of Spaniards, ninety percent of them having fought with the Republican Army in the Spanish Civil War and been interned by the French afterwards. They had been recruited direct out of North African internment camps by us in March and April of 1943 – several of them have been witnesses at the recent trials of officials in Algiers – the officials had been shot for various tortures and so on, though the men do not seem to be entirely convinced that the authorities have shot the right people.[32]

Corporal Agustín Roa Ventura shortly after his promotion in Hussein Dey. (Agustín Roa Ventura collection)

CSM J. Butler from near Stratford-Upon-Avon, who seemed to have been born to be a soldier despite his rounded appearance, freckles and red hair, created a real impression. It was not long, however, before he was given the nickname '*El polvorilla*' (Tinderbox) due to his hot and cold temperament. Not only did he maintain the discipline of the Company, but he also acted as a surrogate father. He could as easily shout at the soldiers and bark orders with some authority as he could turn to them in a paternal manner when something went wrong.

In January 1944 the Company was moved to Maison Carrée and it was here that they began to work and prepare themselves for train guarding duties. Major Cole takes up the story:

> We went into training at Maison Carrée, where I had to work out all the training programme as well as supervising it. I didn't mind – it was at least interesting … We concentrated on

---

32 Extracts from the 'Diary of Captain H.A.N. Cole, Pioneer Corps'. Unpublished and provided by his grandson Richard Normington.

teaching our Spaniards enough English to fill in the train guard and static guard report forms, and ended with an all too brief little exercise that I thought up mainly for my own amusement, in which squads of fatigue men marched in and out of 'sidings' on the roads through the camp, accompanied by train guards with the necessary forms, and halted at stations marked 'Madrid', 'Corruna' and so on, for more human wagons to be picked up or others dropped off. It turned out to be a very useful practical exercise, but we got orders to move after only two days at it.[33]

Based at Constantine, the Company now carried out its train guarding duties with great success, resulting in a large reduction in thefts of goods from them. Trains were guarded by a team headed up by a Spanish sergeant or corporal which would be relieved at various points along the line for example Orán – Algiers – Constantine – Tunis. Despite success in their tasks, the Spaniards were not immune to controversy. Cole commented in his diary:

After that, the fun started. In less than a month we have had everything except a case of rape. A man killed in a crash when a train ran into a tank at a level crossing at El Guerrah. A Corporal and Lance Corporal awaiting summary of evidence for threatening a French Maj on the Duvivier-Bône line and discharging a rifle. An absentee being looked out for who cut a CSM of REME on the face and hands with a knife after having been refused admission to a Sgt's dance at Le Khroub. A man dead yesterday through having been riding on top of a tank when a train passed under a bridge. And now last night's to-do.[34]

But what was this 'to-do'? Probably the saddest incident for the Company while in Africa was when one of the Spaniards on static guard at Constantine station had shot a French officer. Following an altercation in the French military canteen Private López shot a French officer several times. López then handed himself over to a British officer shortly after and made a full confession. The Frenchman died a few hours later. The French military authorities pressed for the Company to be taken off train guard duties. Cole was irritated by the French attitude:

I shall be annoyed if we are taken off (train guard), because the men have done an excellent job as guards and put down nearly all pilferage. The reason being that most of the pilferage is being done by Arabs inspired by the French, who control the real black market, and our fellows hate the French (their former captors) like poison. The French return the hatred with interest.

The continuing political pressure and other incidents over the following weeks (including the shooting of a Spaniard by the French in Phillippeville) meant that by 13 May 1944 the General Officer Commanding 57th Division decided that the Company should be relieved of train guarding duties because of the bad feeling between the Spaniards and the French. This was formally done by early June. Such events certainly had a detrimental effect on morale in the Company. On 13 June Cole wrote:

---

33 Extracts from the 'Diary of Captain H.A.N. Cole, Pioneer Corps'. Unpublished and provided by his grandson Richard Normington.
34 Extracts from the 'Diary of Captain H.A.N. Cole, Pioneer Corps'. Unpublished and provided by his grandson Richard Normington.

Eduardo Tamarit on the left poses with two of his comrades in 361 (Alien) Pioneer Company. (Eduardo Tamarit collection)

> López was shot yesterday in the quarry on the Bône road. They say he was completely unperturbed – I must write a story about that affair.[35]

Even though by the summer of 1943 the war in Africa had finished, a new wave of Spaniards entered British service in the spring and summer of 1944. These were Spaniards who had served in the *Légion Étrangère* and had just finished their five-year contract. One of these was Pere Esteve who explained that:

> The French wanted us to re-engage in the legion until the end of the war. Some accepted but others decided that we wanted to be demobbed. The British, on their side, were keen to take on those who had served with the legion. NCOs who had some Spanish were able to do a little bit of propaganda talking about why not join the Commandos or Parachute Regiments or other groups in the British Army. They were promised good pay and even British nationality at the end of the war. I remember that many Spaniards signed up.[36]

Francisco Merino, who was another Spaniard who had recently left the *Légion Étrangère*, said that the French:

> … issued us a certificate giving us fifteen days of leave in order to find work. If we were not able to we were to be interned in camps. That is what we got for having fought with them. Some people ended up going to Algiers and many of us ended up joining the British Navy. I joined HMS Daring.[37]

---

35 Extracts from the 'Diary of Captain H.A.N. Cole, Pioneer Corps'. Unpublished and provided by his grandson Richard Normington.
36 Daniel Arasa, *Los Españoles de Churchill* (Barcelona: Editorial Armonía Poética, 1991), p.214. Interview with Pere Esteve.
37 Daniel Arasa, *Los Españoles de Churchill* (Barcelona: Editorial Armonía Poética, 1991), p.216.

Marino was also one of the many who had also signed up to work with the OSS. Many of these men ended up in Italy and the Balkans. Other Spaniards worked as civilians in North Africa and supported British and Commonwealth troops across a variety of camps and locations. They were treated well and enjoyed their work. In June 1943 King George VI visited North Africa, upon meeting some of the staff working at one of the barracks he met Spanish workers who, despite the language barrier, were extremely enthused to meet him commenting that they wished Spain had a monarch such as him![38]

Hubert Cole was posted out of the Company on 5 August 1944. Following some further training and an influx of more Spanish recruits, the Company embarked at Algiers for the United Kingdom on 14 October. Three companies containing Spaniards were sent, these being 361, 362 and 363. In 361 were seven Spaniards who had served in No.50 Middle East Commando. 13809805 Antonio Vargas Rivas remembered the journey by sea well:

Antonio Obis pictured in North Africa in August 1944 not long before his company set sail for Britain. (Antonio Obis collection)

> We sailed to the Straits of Gibraltar. A few times by sight and other times using my imagination, I could see parts of our coast and know, pretty precisely, where we were passing … so close to my land and my family without any of them having a clue as to where I was.[39]

Originally from Adra in Almería, Antonio had been a rebel from an early age and was a member of the Anarchist *CNT*. At the end of the Spanish Civil War he had managed to escape Spain on a fishing boat, sadly leaving his wife and two daughters behind. While incarcerated in Djelfa, he would find out that his youngest daughter had died back in Spain. Antonio joined the Pioneer Corps and served until the war's end settling in the United Kingdom but also remaining a lifelong *CNT* member and one of the founders of the Spanish Ex-Servicemen's Association. He and Agustín Roa became lifelong friends.

The three companies landed in Glasgow to a great fanfare on 24 October, and 361 was taken by train to Kineton in Warwickshire where it immediately got to work on camp construction. At Christmas some leave was granted and this was the first time that these Spaniards were able to meet up in London with other exiled Spaniards. Later, 60 members of 361 were detached to be part on No.1 Spanish Company in Belgium. One of these was Antonio Vargas who remembered

---

38 Sir Douglas Dodds-Parker, *Setting Europe Ablaze: Some Account of Ungentlemanly Warfare* (Chichester: Springwood Books, 1983).
39 Antonio Vargas Rivas, *Guerra, Revolución y Exilio de un Anarcosindicalista* (Almería: privately published, October 2007 second edition), Part 2, Chapter 3.

well the forestry work the company was carrying out. Shortly after his arrival with the Company, Antonio was attached to a local bakery. With many of its members being old members of the *CNT*, Antonio joined part of a group in the Company that became politically active again, something which would help many after the war's end. Back in Britain, 361 was moved to the small arms ammunition factory at Radway Green in February 1945. A few months later it carried out camp maintenance in the area. After being moved to the Central Armaments Depot at Nesscliffe, the Company ended the war in Sudbury near Derby to work at the Central Ordnance Depot at Branston. Its last War Diary entry was on 31 December 1945.

Four members of 361 (Alien) Pioneer Company at Sudbury. On the far right is Miguel Martínez who had served in No.50 Middle East Commando before joining 361. Next to him is Antonio Obis. (Miguel Martínez collection)

'SEE YOU IN HELL' 181

Members of 361 (Alien) Pioneer Company rest between shifts at Branston (Antonio Obis collection)

Left: Antonio Obis on the left with two of his fellow Spanish comrades shortly after arriving in Britain. Note the North Africa Star medal ribbon on their temperate climate battle dress. (Antonio Obis collection)
Right: Two Spaniards (names unknown) from 361 (Alien) Pioneer Company while serving in Britain. (Antonio Obis collection)

362 Company which had 15 Spaniards, seven of whom had served in No.50 Middle East Commando, was sent to Middlewich, Cheshire before being moved to Longtown near Carlisle where it worked in storage and the construction of prisoner of war camps. Interestingly, at the end of May 1945, 23 other ranks volunteered for parachute training presumably for service in the Far East. By September, the company was based in Carlisle and at the end of the year was based in Carnforth where its last War Diary entry was on 31 December 1945. One hundred twenty-five Spaniards served in 363 Company which was based at Lowestoft until the end of the war. Although all three companies were disbanded by early 1946 and the majority were demobilised, some individuals did not leave the service until 1947.

A group of Spaniards from 361 (Alien) Pioneer Company pose for a photograph. Probably taken in the Midlands at the end of the war as many are wearing medal ribbons. Eduardo Tamarit is crouching at the front second from the left, and Antonio Obis is couching front row second from the right. (Eduardo Tamarit collection)

At the end of the war the fate of most of the Spaniards who had enlisted in North Africa still hung in the balance when it came to where they would be allowed to settle. Those who stayed in North Africa remained there and many would not return to Spain until after the death of Franco in 1975, or would be forced to leave places like Algiers due to the war that later raged with the French. But those who had been posted to the United Kingdom would have to wait to see what their future would hold. Agustín Roa remembered his demobilisation at Packington Park Camp near Meriden, Warwickshire well:

> No sooner had I arrived than they were calling folk forward to be demobilised. Those called were told to report to an office where they were given their passes and a train ticket that would take them to the main demobilisation depot in York. There they were given a cardboard box containing civilian clothing, a sum of money according to length of service and rank. Once

done, they were given another rail ticket to the location of their choice where they had decided to settle down … most of my friends decided to settle down in London, the capital, which I also chose …[40]

Spaniards enlisted into the British Army in North Africa in their hundreds from late 1942 onwards and constituted the largest group to join during the war. After suffering horrendous treatment in internment camps, their service in pioneer companies proved important to operations in the region, in Italy and eventually in the United Kingdom. Some would distinguish themselves fighting behind enemy lines in the SOE and SAS. Many would settle in the United Kingdom and become key members in continuing the fight against the Franco Regime from exile.

Corporal Agustín Roa Ventura towards the end of the war. Agustín chronicled a great deal of the service of Spaniards in the British Army and would go on to be a leading light amongst the post-war exiled Republican Spanish community in Britain along with his friend Antonio Vargas. (Agustín Roa Ventura collection)

---

40 Agustín Roa Ventura, *Los años de mi vida, Personal Papers*, 1942–1950. Unpublished.

Chapter 6

'Wonderful Way to Go'

Spaniards in the SAS

> Red light on! Green light on!
> Out through the door we go.
> Fighting for breath, battered near to death,
> Drifting down to earth below.
> The Boys Who Ride the Slipstream.[1]

It has been quite surprising to discover over a dozen Spaniards serving in the Special Air Service (SAS) from late 1943 onwards. While most of these men did not join the British Army until mid-1943, two had continued their service from the Middle East Commandos, and others served with the Free French beforehand. All have intriguing stories full of adventure, daring and true fighting spirit. The Spaniards who were motivated to join the SAS were involved in operations in France in 1944, then in Italy, Germany and Norway in 1945. Selection and training was extreme, their integration important and their service intense as they became known as the 'Funnies' along with other nationalities who wore the coveted SAS cap badge. One of them would lose his life only two weeks before the end of the war and another was awarded the Military Medal for 'showing remarkable courage'. Spaniards not only fought as members of 2nd SAS but also served in the French 3rd and 4th SAS from 1943 to 1945. Those who served with 2nd SAS would eventually settle in Britain at the end of the war and maintain a special bond of comradeship late into their lives.

New Beginnings – The Middle East Commandos and 1st Special Service Regiment

Getting involved in the Special Forces was not new to the many Spaniards who served in the British Army from 1940 to 1946. In Chapter 4, we saw how the remaining Spaniards serving in the Middle East Commandos were involved in training and deployed on raids and other operations. After the fall of Crete in the summer of 1941, the troubled existence of Layforce had finally come to an end for the men of 7, 8 (Guards), 11 (Scottish) and No.50/52 Commandos. Some went on to join the soon to be set up L Detachment, the Long Range Desert Group (LRDG), the Special Boat Service (SBS) or Mission 204 and many returned to their various parent regiments. Those who did not

---

[1] Malcolm Tudor, *SAS in Italy 1943–1945, Raiders in Enemy Territory* (London: Fonthill Media, 2018). Song of the 2nd SAS Regiment written by men of the regiment on duty on the Cisa Pass, sung to the tune of a famous German marching song.

Spaniards form up on parade after they the escape from Crete in 1941. (Manuel Surera Collection)

have a unit to return to (like the Spaniards) were left kicking their heels at their depot at Geneifa, engaged in training for operations or performing guard duties at Suez docks. These men were discussed in a conference on 11 October 1941 held at GHQ in Cairo. The upshot of this meeting was that a new Middle East Commando should be formed. It would be based around six troops: Depot Troop would be 1 Troop, L Detachment and Special Air Service Brigade would become 2 Troop, 11 (Scottish) Commando would form 3 Troop, 4 and 5 Troops would be from No.51 Middle East Commando and the SBS would become 6 Troop. L Detachment would not be part of the new Commando and they would operate independently. It would take some time to get all the arrangements together; training and guard duties would continue. Where the Spaniards were in this new set up is uncertain, but it seems likely that they were in Depot Troop.

Shortly after this, 3 Troop were in training for an ambitious project – the capture or assassination of Erwin Rommel – called Operation FLIPPER. The operation was executed in mid-November 1941.

Officers and men were landed from submarines in rubber boats in the vicinity of Cheschem-el-Chelb. One of those who got ashore was Robert Laycock. Owing, however, to the fact that some of the force (two Officers and 28 Other Ranks) were prevented from getting ashore from the submarine HMS *Talisman* by bad weather, the plan had to be modified and a great deal less was achieved than had been originally hoped. Ultimately, the mission failed and only four men from FLIPPER returned (including Robert Laycock), leaving their CO dead. Geoffrey Keyes was awarded a posthumous Victoria Cross for his role in the affair.[2] It is also possible that some Spaniards were involved in this operation. Family testimonies for 6100533/13808230 José Redondo and 6100535/13808232 Manuel Surera say the two were on the operation along with other Spaniards and were among those who failed to get ashore from the *Talisman*. Although we cannot currently verify this, it is known that both had been posted back to the Middle East Commandos in early September 1941.[3] This is further supported by the testimony of Luís Bracero,

---

2 TNA, WO 201/720, Operation FLIPPER: Lt. Colonel Laycock's report, 5 January 1942.
3 TNA, WO 201/720. Family accounts of 6100535 /13808232 Manuel Surera and 6100533/13808230 José Redondo both mention that they were involved in this operation. Their military records however do not record anything.

A group of Spaniards after carrying out some training or possibly about to deploy on a mission. Crouching down on the right in a white vest is Manuel Surera. On the far left standing with the mallet is Fernando Esteve. Note the German MG 34 machine gun being held overhead. (Fernando Esteve collection)

a Spaniard who served in the newly formed *13ᵉ DBLE* in the Middle East and who had served in Syria previously. When interviewed by Daniel Arasa in the 1980s he stated:

> Font, Julián Bruguera and I, the three of us being members of the Free French, met up one day in Cairo with various Spaniards who were part of the British Commandos; amongst them were García and Trancho. I perfectly remember our encounter, because García was from Montilla, Córdoba a town near mine. They told us that fifteen or sixteen Spaniards were in these British Commandos who had been in Crete where many other Spaniards had died or fallen prisoner … We were told later by our officers that those Spaniards were amongst those selected for a raid on the HQ of the Africa Corps and the killing of Rommel.[4]

Further discussions concerning the use and the future of the Middle East Commandos took place, and on 29 December 1941 its future was finally decided. Lieutenant Colonel J.M. Graham of the Royal Scots Greys would be the new commanding officer and they would be based at the already established Middle East Commando Depot at Geneifa. The bulk of the men that made up this Commando would be drawn from the defunct Layforce and from No.51 Middle East Commando. They would remain under direct control of the MEW Mission (Ministry of

---

4　Daniel Arasa, *Los Españoles de Churchill* (Barcelona: Editorial Armonía Poética, 1991), p.179.

A group of Middle East Commandos in 1st Special Service Regiment gather in a park, probably in Cairo. Crouched on the far right is Manuel Surera and third from the left with a small moustache and between two commandos with missing teeth is Francisco García Garrigos. (Manuel Surera and Francisco García Garrigos collection)

Economic Warfare) in Cairo and would be influenced by the SOE. With fears that the Germans would attack through Turkey, their attentions were orientated in this direction for the time being. While this was happening, during November 1941, men had been detached from the remnants of Layforce now at the Commando Depot at Geneifa and formed into the Commando Security Section, which patrolled the Suez docks area that included Port Tewfik (Taufiq), Port Ibrahim and the Petroleum Dock including its rail arteries to Cairo, Alexandria and Ismailia along with the causeway and Ataka port. They continued these patrols until the end of January 1942 when they returned to Geneifa.

The Commando was then reorganised into four squadrons. The squadrons were split into an HQ troop and three troops, each of which consisted of two officers and 26 other ranks. The troops could also be further broken down so that they could operate when required as three sections of seven men each. The full strength of a squadron was 90, comprising eight officers and 82 other ranks. The first three squadrons would be British and named A, B, and C while D Squadron would be drawn from No.51 Middle East Commando along with the Spaniards. By May 1942 the unit had been renamed 1st Special Service Regiment (1 SSR). The presence of Spaniards in D Squadron of the Regiment can be confirmed from that summer from the individuals' records. 6100552/13808212/13041866 Justo Balerdi became a member of the regiment on 31 March 1942, following a spell in hospital. 6100555/13808268/138041867 Francisco Geronimo was transferred to 1 SSR on 11 June after escaping and evading in Crete until May 1942. Redondo and Surera continued to be in the Middle East Commandos and were officially transferred to 1 SSR in mid-July. A nominal roll for D Squadron from that summer further expands on the Spaniards in the squadron. In total, there are 26 Spanish names (see Appendix IV for a full list).[5] Interestingly, five

---

5   The Middle East Commando Research Group Archive.

188 CHURCHILL'S SPANIARDS

of the men on this list were not in No.50 Middle East Commando and are probably Spaniards who escaped from Syria but subsequently joined No.51 Middle East Commando and served in Sudan and Eritrea. There are testimonies of other personnel in No.51 Middle East Commando that tell of the Spaniards that served in the unit and fought bravely against the Italians. Spaniards in this unit, including one named García,[6] have already been noted previously. The training records for the Combined Training Centre: Middle East based at Kabrit (which had opened on 3 May 1942) show that members of 1 SSR also went through parachute training from the end of May onwards.[7] The Parachute Training School then moved, in February, 1943, to Ramat David in Northern Palestine in February 1943.

Left: Manuel Surera in early 1942. Note the parachute wings on his shirt. (Manuel Surera collection)
Right: Basilio Santiago who served in 1st Special Service Regiment. Note the parachute wings on his right shirt sleeve. (Manuel Surera collection)

By August 1942, Tobruk once again became the centre of Allied planning as they had to deny the port and its facilities to the enemy. An ambitious plan was raised to put it out of action – Operation AGREEMENT. Men of 1 SSR would play a prominent role in this costly operation, enough to bring about the regiment's final demise. D Squadron would provide the bulk of the other ranks and work with the LRDG. This is also mentioned by Daniel Arasa.[8] It is not known, however, if the Spaniards took part in the operation. But another interview that Arasa carried

---

6 Captain C. Hillmann MC MM, *The Pioneer Magazine*, No. 132, September 1977. <http://www.royalpioneer-corps.co.uk/rpc/newsletters/2014_April_Newsletter.pdf>. Accessed 5 July 2021.
7 TNA, WO 201/2597, Combined Training Centre: Middle East, 1940–44.
8 Daniel Arasa, *Los Españoles de Churchill* (Barcelona: Editorial Armonía Poética, 1991), p.178.

Spaniards potentially waiting to be collected for a patrol with the LRDG. The man in the middle is Fernando Esteve. (Manuel Surera collection)

out with Marco Vidal, who was injured at Bir Hakeim as part of *13ᵉ DBLE* and before he had met 6100563 José Rodriguez in the military hospital in Cairo, sheds some light. He claims that Rodriguez had been injured on an operation behind enemy lines.[9] What seems to have happened is that members of 1 SSR were also used to carry out deep reconnaissance patrols behind enemy lines and were transported to their locations by the LRDG, then left in situ to be collected later. This may have been when the LRDG was carrying out what they aptly called the 'Road Watch' in 1942, which consisted of patrols sent to the coast road to monitor traffic. This had been done with some success during 1941.[10]

As mentioned above, we know that the majority of the Spaniards in 1 SSR were transferred onto the books of the Pioneer Corps early in 1943. By the summer of 1943 they had either decided to continue in the Pioneer Corps, become members of the 2nd SAS or transferred back to the Queen's Royal Regiment (West Surrey).

2nd SAS Recruitment and Initial Training

In May 1943, Lieutenant Colonel Bill Stirling had been given the task of recruiting and training a new SAS regiment, to build on the success of the old one, and to have them ready in time for operations in Southern Europe.[11] His younger brother, David, had been captured by German

---

9 Daniel Arasa, *Los Españoles de Churchill* (Barcelona: Editorial Armonía Poética, 1991), pp.181–182.
10 W. B. Kennedy Shaw, *Long Range Desert Group, The Story of its Work in Libya 1940–1943* (London: Wm Collins Son & Co Ltd, 1945), pp.207–220.
11 Francis Mackay, *Overture to Overlord, Special Operations in Preparation for Overlord* (Barnsley: Pen & Sword Ltd, 2005).

soldiers that January while on a raid in Tunisia. The depleted 1st SAS Regiment was reorganised into the 'Special Raiding Squadron' under Major R.B. (Paddy) Mayne and the 'Special Boat Squadron' under Major, the Earl Jellicoe. David Stirling ultimately ended up as a prisoner in Colditz Castle joining George Young who had commanded No.50 Middle East Commando and had been captured on Crete. For his distinguished actions as a prisoner, Stirling was awarded an OBE. 2nd SAS was raised at Philippeville, Algeria on 13 May 1943. Roy Farran (who is discussed below) was one of its first recruits.

Philippeville (today Skikda) on the coast some 300 miles east of Algiers was an unfortunate location to set up the regiment as it was located near a mosquito-ridden swamp teeming with malaria. By the time 2nd SAS was ready for deployment, more than half of its members had been in hospital with the disease and were unable to carry out missions. Many would carry malaria with them for the rest of the war. With a wealth of operational experience to rely on, the regiment functioned with specific and measurable standards from its conception. It also benefitted from the experiences of L Detachment, the SBS, as well as the LRDG and, of course, the commandos. This all meant that recruitment and training was a lot more stringent. But the biggest issue it had was the lack of quality soldiers fit for SAS duty. As with the Special Forces today, it was important to have officers and men who were self-motivated, mentally and physically tough, and who could make the most of situational opportunities to come up with solutions where others might not. By the time 1st SAS was being re-established towards the end of 1943 and early into 1944 it was able to draw on recruits and volunteers back in the United Kingdom. With 2nd SAS still being based in North Africa, few commanding officers in combat units were willing to let their best soldiers be transferred to the SAS.

Despite the recruiting difficulties which would endure in 2nd SAS beyond its arrival in Britain in March 1944, recruitment continued in North Africa at the end of 1943, and this is where the Spaniards start came into the picture. Operation TORCH, as discussed, led to the largest recruitment of Spaniards into the British Army during the war. By the early autumn of 1943 hundreds of Spaniards were serving in an array of 'Alien' Pioneer Corps units. Two who enlisted into the British Army together were 13301853 Rafael Ramos Masens and 13301854 Juan Torrents Abadía. Both were Catalan by birth, although Ramos spent most of his school years in Madrid.

Born in Barcelona in May 1919, Ralph (as he was later known) Ramos was educated at a Jesuit boarding school in Madrid. His father ran a successful printing and publishing business in Barcelona. Ralph had a large family but sadly did not get on at all well with his father; he often said that he had a better relationship with, and learnt more from, his 'adopted' father (the family that ran the Ramos household). Little is known about what 'Ralph' did during the Spanish Civil War; he would have been 17 when it broke out in 1936 and was certainly wounded at some point as he later talked about the leg wounds that he received. What is known, is that he fought at the Battle of the Ebro in 1938/39 and was taken prisoner. Ralph eventually escaped by simply, and boldly, walking out of the camp along with some of his comrades in arms, and was subsequently able to cross the border into France. Once across, he volunteered to join the *Légion Étrangère* and was sent to the *DCRE* in Nancy, joining the *3ᵉ REI* soon after.[12] This was a regiment that had various battalions at the beginning of the Second World War and was based in North Africa. When the Armistice was signed in June 1940 it seems that he was sent to Morocco, placed in a labour camp and worked on roads and perhaps the Trans-Saharan railway as Torrents did. The Allied landings at the end of 1942 meant that the Spaniards were going to be freed. Juan Torrents relates the story:

---

12 'Mémoires des Hommes, Portail Culturelle du Ministère des Armées, Engagés Volontaires Étrangers en 1939–1940.' <https://www.memoiredeshommes.sga.defense.gouv.fr/fr/arkotheque/client/mdh/engages_volontaires_etrangers/resus_rech.php>. Accessed 10 April 2021.

We were close to Rabat (Morocco) by the sea. The French told the Americans we were undesirables and so we stayed in the camp longer. I then got a job in a workshop turning pistons for car engines. That is when we decided to carry on fighting and join the Americans (in Casablanca). This was not possible. I think it was Ramos that said it. 'Let's do the next best thing. Let's go to the British Consulate.' Next thing you know we joined the British Army![13]

After visiting the consulate in Casablanca, both moved to Algeria where they enlisted in the Pioneer Corps at Hussein Dey on 16 October 1943. They were soon on the nominal roll of 363 (Alien) Pioneer Company. Torrents continues:

> Later they asked for volunteers for parachute training for the Second SAS Regiment. And that's the regiment I finished the war with.[14]

Also joining the Pioneer Corps after many trials and tribulations and then volunteering to join 2nd SAS were another five Spaniards who entered the British Army at other times and in different locations. These were in addition to Francisco Geronimo and Justo Balerdi who were in 2nd SAS by 16 December after some time in 337 (Alien) Pioneer Company. 13301810 Ángel Camarena, and 13301811 Francisco Revuelta enlisted on 12 October at Hussein Dey, Algiers and joined 361 Company before volunteering to join the SAS in December. 13301792 Francisco López Martín enlisted into 361 Company on 20 September, 13301469 Enric Boganim enlisted on 1 July 1943 at Maison Carrée and 13301840 Carlo(s) Bovio who joined Ramos and Torrents in 363 Company, having enlisting at Maison Carrée on 3 October.[15]

2nd SAS contained a lot of 'funnies' as they were called, but who were they? In his memoirs, Captain Joseph Patterson of the Royal Army Medical Corps, who became the Medical Officer for the regiment, went on to explain:

> The 'Funnies' were a wonderful collection of foreigners, many from the French Foreign Legion, and there were some Spaniards among them, survivors and fugitives from the Spanish Civil War. Swiss, French, Italians, some Germans and even Russians found their haven in

Francisco Revuelta at the end of the war. Note his SAS parachute wings on his right sleeve just visible at the far left of the photo. (Francisco Revuelta collection)

---
13 Interview with John Colman (Juan Torrents Abadía), recorded 27 December 1997, IWM 17730.
14 Interview with John Colman (Juan Torrents Abadía), recorded 27 December 1997, IWM 17730.
15 Both are listed in Appendix V, but their nationality is not confirmed.

the SAS. There were no doubt plenty of fugitives from justice amongst them and they were tough and rough. They mostly had pseudonyms, Irish, Welsh or Scottish names, as they were well known to the Germans and liable to summary execution if captured. Their odd English could possibly be explained to a dumb German by saying that they came from those wild and woolly territories of the British Isles. Some had a price on their heads.[16]

Once transferred to the SAS, training began almost immediately. Much of the already serving elements of 2nd SAS returned to North Africa from Italy in January 1944. A period of regeneration now followed as soldiers underwent parachute training and vigorous exercises.[17] The Spaniards were soon getting used to travelling long distances with heavy weights (up to 45 kilos in some cases) in rough terrain, as well as swimming and some parachute training. A fellow member of 2nd SAS, Elisha Roberts, remembered:

That's when we went to Philippeville in North Africa. We did the training there … it was … it was hectic. We did a lot of running you know, with full pack and swimming with full packs on. And you were told to get into a Jeep whether you had driven or not and drive over the sand dunes and wheel around the dunes like the Long Range Desert Patrol Group …[18]

The SAS Brigade and Preparations for D-Day

By the beginning of 1944 the decision had been taken to establish the SAS Brigade in Britain. The brigade was part of the 1st Airborne Corps but would answer directly to 21st Army Group. It formally came into being on 8 February 1944 and was established at Sorn Castle near Mauchline in southern Ayrshire, Scotland. The Brigade Tactical HQ was co-located with airborne forces headquarters at Moor Park in Hertfordshire. Recruiting, resulting in increasing numbers, for 1st SAS was working well. Although the official history of airborne forces talks of nearly 300 recruits arriving in the SAS Brigade coming from the Special Auxiliary Force that had been disbanded, that figure was probably higher. Even when it had arrived in England in March 1944, 2nd SAS still found it difficult to recruit and had problems bringing itself up to strength. Something that was not possible until well into the summer of 1944. All SAS personnel were transferred to the Army Air Corps on 1 April 1944 and subsequently had to wear the maroon beret.

By early 1944, the brigade also contained two battalions of French paratroopers and a company of Belgians. The *1ᵉ Compagnie de Chasseurs Parachutistes* from the Free French operated alongside David Stirling's men under the command of Captain George Bergie, whom Stirling later described as a co-founder of the SAS itself. It had returned to the Free French in March 1943 and was originally called the *1ᵉ Compagnie d'Infanterie de l'Air* (or *1ᵉ CIA*) and along with *2ᵉ CIA* formed the *1ᵉ Bataillon d'Infanterie de l'Air* (*1ᵉ BIA*). The unit was renamed the *4ᵉ BIA* on 1 November 1943. The *4ᵉ BIA* was joined by *3ᵉ Régiment de Chasseurs Parachutistes* (*3ᵉ RCP* and now called *3ᵉ BIA*), consisting of French volunteers from Egypt & Algeria. Together they establish a French Parachute *Demi-Brigade*. Many were able to carry out parachute training at the Polish Parachute Centre at Largo in Fife. The two battalions were incorporated into the SAS Brigade in December 1943 and started moving to the area of Auchinleck or Alloway in Ayrshire. There was always some antagonism between the two battalions as they were renowned for fighting over who had seniority. On 1

---
16 Joseph Henry Patterson, IWM Private Papers, Catalogue Number IWM 13225.
17 Roy Farran, *Winged Dagger: Adventures on Special Service* (Glasgow: Grafton Books, 1948), p.220.
18 Elisha Roberts, IWM Interview, Catalogue Number IWM 11942, 1989.

April *3ᵉ* and *4ᵉ BIA* were officially attached to the SAS Brigade as the 3rd and 4th SAS Regiments. In March 1944, the Independent Belgian Air Service Company became part of the Brigade – it became the Belgian Independent Special Air Service Squadron in June 1944 and by the end of the war was 5th (Belgian) Special Air Service Regiment.[19]

Something that probably deserves a book in itself is that, unbeknownst to most, 10 Spaniards (confirmed so far) served across 3rd and 4th SAS. Their enlistment into the French SAS was generally through two routes. Firstly, there were those Spaniards who had joined the French forces as either Free French or as *Légionnaires* earlier on in the war. Then there were those who joined the French Army after Operation TORCH and who ended up transferring to the French Special Forces in due course.[20] There is a summary list of Spaniards in the SAS in Appendix V.

In early 1944, the SAS Brigade HQ comprised three officers and 154 other ranks in addition to one officer and 23 other ranks from the Pioneer Corps. On 7 February 1944 Brigadier Roderick MacLeod was formally appointed to command the Brigade, with Desmond Berry as the Brigade Major. The new brigade staff then began to arrive. In February 1st SAS assembled at Darvel, east Ayrshire after returning from leave. Parachute training began at Ringway near Manchester as well as at Prestwick. Lieutenant Colonel Bill Stirling's 2nd SAS finally arrived at the end of March 1944 and established itself at Monckton near Prestwick.[21]

While 2nd SAS were enjoying a short period of leave after their arrival, the Brigade's role in the invasion of France was being formulated by Supreme Headquarters Allied Expeditionary Force (SHAEF). From early 1944 it was obvious that the role the SAS was intended to carry out was somewhat unclear. The initial plan had been to use the brigade very close to the landings in Normandy thus leading many to regard it as a suicide mission. This led to Bill Stirling taking a stand and being replaced by Brian Franks as Commanding Officer of 2nd SAS. Despite this being a huge loss, his action saved the SAS and meant that 21st Army Group changed the deployment of the Brigade. It would now be used in a more strategic role and the stage was set for it to operate deep in enemy territory.[22]

On 9 April, all the Spaniards in 2nd SAS were among the personnel carrying out parachute training at Ringway on the 111a Course. They all managed their allotted drops with a mix of 'pretty good' to 'excellent' ratings, some were even cast as 'enthusiastic' in their ability to fling themselves out of perfectly serviceable aircraft. The end of this course came a week later, on 18 April. On the following day Justo Balerdi's personnel file records him undergoing a name change and now going under the name Robert Bruce! So how does a Basque commando in the SAS end up with the given name of the King of the Scots?

A bizarre tale about name changes now enters the story of the Spaniards in the SAS. There are mixed versions of the exact location where this event took place. Was it in Phillippeville before 2nd SAS departed for Britain? Or was it after the course at Ringway? We cannot be certain, but the likelihood is that it occurred around the time of the course at Ringway, suggested by an entry in Balerdi's record and by a document sent by the Pioneer Corps Records Office to the Home Office (Aliens Department) dated 16 June 1944 in which a list of name changes is provided.[23] The reason for changing the names seems to have been due to the Commando Order issued by

---

19 Francis Mackay, *Overture to Overlord*, pp.188–194.
20 Thanks to the Association des Familles des Parachutistes de la France Libre it has been possible to ascertain information on these 10 men. More details are in Appendix V.
21 The Army Record of 6100552/13808212/13041866 Justo Balerdi records him arriving in Britain on 16 March 1944.
22 Gavin Mortimer, *The SAS in Occupied France: 2 SAS Operations, June to October 1944* (Yorkshire: Pen & Sword Military, 2023), pp.4–7.
23 TNA, HO 405/61458, Alien and Immigration, Applications for Naturalisation.

Hitler and the fact that they were Spanish 'Aliens' in the British Armed Forces who would probably end up being sent back to Spain if captured.[24] However, having said this, many of the operational reports in 1944 and 1945 still contained the original Spanish names. Phil Williams, grandson of Francisco Geronimo relates:

> The story is that one evening in a bar with the rest of the unit it was decided that the Spaniards' names be changed to British ones.
>
> The first one to have his name changed was Juan Torrents. His name was changed to John Colman, the reason being that Juan and John sound almost identical and Colman because he had an uncanny resemblance to the well-known actor Ronald Colman according to fellow members of 2 SAS in this bar. He had been in the famous film Beau Geste about *Légionnaires* which of course Torrents used to be.
>
> So, John Colman done, they turned to the others and ask what you want to be called? Three of them: my grandad Francisco Geronimo, Rafael Ramos and Justo Balerdi looked at each other and disappeared to the other side of the room to mull over the request. Coming back less than a minute later requesting the names Francis Drake, Walter Raleigh and Robert the Bruce, three very famous figures from British history. I can only imagine the laughter this elicited from the crowd. However, we know only Bruce's request was accepted and the reason why was confirmed in a phone conversation with Arthur Huntbach, who said all the other ranks loved the idea and were laughing. But as soon as the officers got wind of this, they thought things were going a bit too far in general silliness, so Francisco Geronimo became Frank Williams and not Francis Drake. Rafael Ramos did not change his name but regarded himself as Ralph. We assume the others also changed their names this way.

Justo Balerdi became a radio operator in 2nd SAS and was sadly killed in action on Operation TOMBOLA. (The SAS and LRDG Roll of Honour 1941-47)

Camarena and Revuelta changed their names to Alan Cooper and Robert Shaw respectably. Some other potential Spaniards who joined 2nd SAS were 13301469 Enric Boganim who changed his name to Henry Hall the famous band leader and 13301840 Carlo Bovio who changed his name to James Benson. 13301792 Francisco López Martín changed his name to Henry Martin.

Before deploying to the European mainland, the Spaniards and others in the SAS underwent a hard training regime mostly based in Scotland. It was all about improving physical fitness by simply loading the men with heavy weights and working them hard daily as well as regular visits to the assault course. Other elements included sabotage training on roads, railways, telecommunications

---

24 The Commando Order (*Kommandobefehl*) was issued on 18 October 1942 by the OKW. It stated that all Allied commandos captured in Europe and Africa should be summarily executed without trial, even if wearing uniforms or attempting to surrender.

facilities, power stations, factories and even places like dockyards. This included instruction in the use of weaponry as well as plastic explosives and all the devices required to set it off. All of this was combined with an understanding of how they would approach and train local partisans to carry out attacks behind enemy lines. A great deal of this training was taken from one of the founding members of the SAS – Jock Lewes, who had been killed in action in December 1941 but had left an enduring legacy. His strict training regime of water and ration discipline, improving individuals' attitude to, and powers of, endurance, learning day and night navigation and careful concealment in daytime hides, along with inventions like the Lewes Bomb for sabotage attacks, all helped to refine the necessary training. Accounts of SAS veterans at the time cover the training in detail but mentioned that, for some, the training was still not enough to train them to carry out combat operations behind enemy lines. Ambush and sabotage were also practised and drilled. In reality, these were the most effective techniques employed by the SAS in combat parties in France. Even though much has been spoken about the armed jeeps they used, well placed plastic explosives caused far more damage than mounted Vickers machine guns. Several exercises to escape and evade as well as long range navigation exercises carrying weight also took place.[25]

Ángel Camarena on the left and Francisco Geronimo on the right shortly after joining the SAS and arriving in Britain. (Francisco Geronimo collection)

During one exercise, Geronimo is said to have burst into the Operations Room at Prestwick Airport, which caused absolute havoc as personnel thought it was a German raid. Given his heavy accent and his foreign looks, it took some time for people to calm down! In Scotland, after a long range patrol exercise including some live firing, it is said that Ramos enjoyed a few whiskies late one evening and then decided to shoot up a solitary outside toilet so nobody else could use it after him!

The Spaniards were armed with a pistol and either a submachine gun or a .30 calibre American carbine. The carbine was not only lightweight but could also be folded and was therefore a widely distributed weapon. For pistols the .45 calibre Colt M191 semi-automatic pistol had replaced the Enfield, Webley and Smith and Wesson revolvers. The Bren light machine gun, the Thompson submachine gun, the PIAT, the American bazooka and even some German captured weapons such as the MP38 or MP40 were also used since they could use standard 9mm ammunition. Clothing wise, the new Denison smocks were to be worn with other items of clothing and boots. They were also issued with the Fairburn-Sykes fighting knife and a US Army issue one, which most found more useful. The biggest development was the introduction of the Bergan rucksack,

---

25 Roger Ford, *Fire from the Forest: The S.A.S. Brigade in France, 1944* (London: Cassell, 2003), p.284.

which became an SAS hallmark. It could carry a whole range of items including a down filled sleeping bag with a zip![26]

By the summer of 1944, the SAS Tactical HQ shifted to near Pewsey in Wiltshire and then later moved again to near Chelmsford in Essex. Soon after 1st SAS HQ moved to Nettlebed in Oxfordshire and 2nd SAS HQ moved to Shipton Bellinger near Tidworth, and would eventually be located at Wivenhoe near Colchester. The reason the SAS Brigade moved eastwards in 1944 was because operational areas moved east in France as the Allies advanced. This meant that 38 Group of the RAF had further to fly and drop or resupply during summer hours, hence the further east the airfield the better. The French battalions were transferred to Fairford (4th and 3rd SAS) and the Independent Belgian Squadron went first to Fairford, and then to Brussels.

It is also worth noting the very efficient and well organised logistic support the SAS was provided with while they were deployed. A great deal of this was delegated to the Royal Air Force and, in particular, to number 38 Group, Transport Command based in Netheravon on Salisbury Plain in 1944. When deploying, SAS parachutists left from Fairford but heavier parachute drops such as jeeps were normally launched from Tarrant Rushton. Two man reconnaissance teams, which often travelled with Jedburgh teams, used RAF Tempsford in Bedfordshire. Many other Jedburgh teams were also launched from Fairford, or from the US Air Army Force Base at Harrington in Northamptonshire.[27]

Operations in France, 1944

SAS operations in France, Belgium and the Netherlands can be divided into eight main phases. Firstly, operations around Brittany, and the establishment of a cordon of SAS bases from which attacks were able to be carried out on lines of communication to the Normandy bridgehead. Phase two was a series of short operations to harass the retreating enemy during the breakout from the bridgehead. Phase three consisted of the setting up of bases in central France to harass the Germans withdrawing to the south of the Loire. Due to delays, these operations were not as successful as they could have been. The fourth phase was the placing of bases designed to harass the withdrawal from the south of France. Phase five was a series of operations to attack lines of communication between Germany and France. Operations to attack German columns retreating through central France became the sixth phase and operations in Belgium became the seventh phase. The final phase was a series of operations in the Netherlands.[28]

2nd SAS did not launch straight into operations around the time of D-Day. This was not just because it was not fully at establishment yet but also because the French SAS regiments were used first, along with 1st SAS. Still, it must have been a frustrating time for those who wished to get into the action. By July, however, the situation had progressed, and it was not long before Corporal Bovio was deployed on Operation DEFOE, a reconnaissance of the Argentan area of Normandy. Balerdi, who by now had trained as a signaller (wireless operator) in 2nd SAS, was soon in action on Operation RUPERT. Justo Balerdi was a Basque born in Sestao, Bilbao in 1920 and had been

---

26 Charlie Radford, Francis McKay (ed.), *SAS Trooper: Charlie Radford's Operations in Enemy Occupied France and Italy* (Barnsley: Pen and Sword Military, 2010), pp.60–68.
27 Roger Ford, *Fire from the Forest*, pp.291–293. Jedburgh teams consisted of three personnel, usually two officers (one being French) and an NCO who was a wireless operator. The men were normally from the SOE and/or the OSS.
28 Lieutenant Colonel T.B H. Otway DSO, *Official History of the Second World War, Army, Airborne Forces* (The War Office, 1951, reprinted by The Naval & Military Press), pp.240–253.

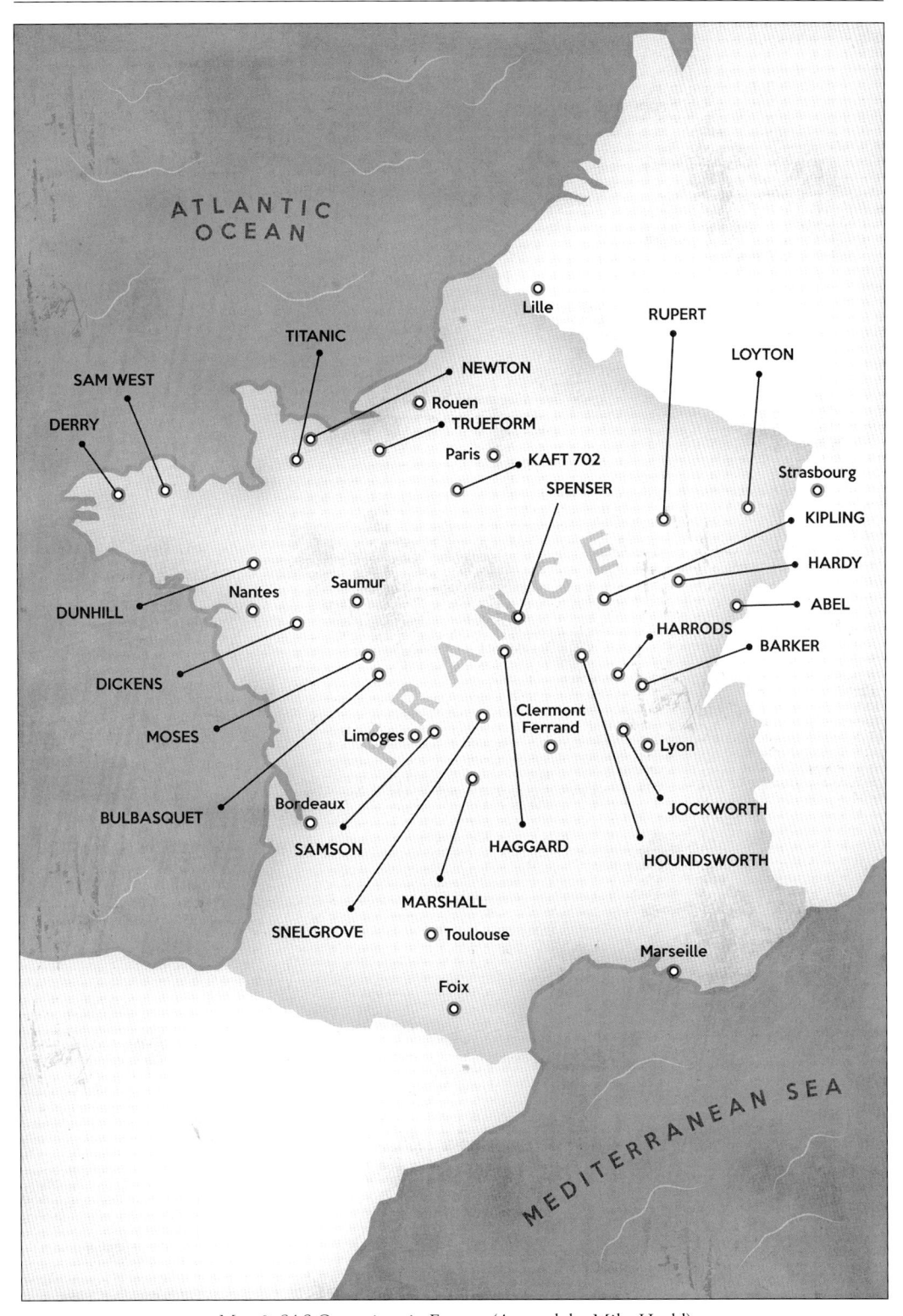

Map 8 SAS Operations in France. (Artwork by Mike Heald)

a telephonist. He would have been too young to fight in the Spanish Civil War straight away but by the end of it he was in France, had joined the *Légion Étrangère* and was then posted to Syria. Balerdi was one of 63 Spaniards who had joined the British Army and become members of the newly established No.50 Middle East Commando. Due to hospitalisation, he did not participate in the Battle for Crete. After being a member of 1 SSR and moving to Algeria in the summer of 1943, along with his good friend Francisco Geronimo, he volunteered and joined 2nd SAS that December as a signaller. Operation RUPERT took place from July to late August 1944 and consisted of 58 men from the regiments tasked with conducting sabotage and reconnaissance operations east of Paris. Balerdi was a member of the second reconnaissance party of eight under the command of Lieutenant D.V. Laws, which made as good a parachute landing as it could on 5 August near Bailly-le-Franc. On this operation, Balerdi served as a signaller for Major Oswald Basil 'Mickey' Rooney. Not long after a bad set of landings where Rooney damaged his back on an electric wire, things took a turn for the worse when a *maquisard* sat on the only available radio set. Balerdi frantically got to work to make a repair but eventually a replacement was found. Further groups had difficult landings and Laws was forced to limit his activities as the Germans in the area could clearly be seen withdrawing. On 31 August he and his party made contact with forward elements of the US 3rd Army, which had liberated the French city of Nancy a few days earlier.

From 4 to 14 August, five Spaniards were members of Operation DUNHILL V under the command of Lieutenant Denison. These were Corporal Bovio and parachutists Torrents, Geronimo, Ramos and Revuelta. The operation was made up of five teams, totalling 59 men, and they were tasked to disrupt German activity in advance of Operation COBRA, the American breakout from Normandy. In the event, four of the teams for DUNHILL were relieved by the advancing Americans within 24 hours. The fifth team (DUNHILL V), headed up by Denison, did come across some issues upon landing but soon got to work. Over the night of 5/6 August, the total of 13 members of this group were parachuted into the area south of the Bois du Creux, near St Denis d'Orques in the Loire region. During the operation Corporal Bovio was briefly captured but escaped. Unfortunately, Revuelta was not so lucky and was taken prisoner. 13301811 Francisco Revuelta was born in Santander and had fought in the Spanish Civil War at the end of which he had been taken prisoner and had been held in a Nationalist POW camp until 1940. A Military Tribunal in Bilbao then pardoned him and he was released in February 1940. Fast forward three years and Revuelta enlisted on 12 October at Hussein Dey, Algiers on the same day as Ángel Camarena and joined 361 Company before volunteering to join the SAS in December 1943. Upon being captured by the Germans, Revuelta was able to escape execution by claiming he was in the RAF and from Gibraltar. Just like the Spaniards in No.50 Middle East Commando in Crete in 1941, this ruse seems to have worked and saved his life. Revuelta spent most of his time in captivity in Stalag 9C.[29] On DUNHILL V, Denison's group had much greater success than the other four groups and was able to rescue 200 downed Allied airmen before it linked up with US ground forces on 24 August.

Operation BARKER, also in August 1944, was a greater success. Members of 3rd SAS were parachuted into the region of Salornaye to protect the right flank of General George C. Patton's 3rd Army as it advanced to the Rhine. Twenty-seven men were dropped into the Saône et Loire region of Burgundy and from mid-August to mid-September they operated in the German rear inflicting around 3,000 casualties including taking almost 500 prisoners. On this operation were two Spaniards. One was José García, who was born in Alicante in 1923 and had joined the Free French in Rouiba in September 1943. He soon embarked for the UK after joining the *3ᵉ BIA*. With him on BARKER was Gabriel García of Spanish parents who was brought up in Casablanca and

---

29 TNA, WO 416/304/136, German POW Record Card for Francis Revuelta.

also joined the Free French in Roubia in 1943. Both would also be on the hard-fought Operation AMHERST in the Netherlands in April 1945.

Francisco Geronimo was one of three Spaniards on Operation TRUEFORM in August 1944 where 102 personnel from 1st and 2nd SAS, as well as the Belgian Independent Parachute Squadron, jumped into 12 separate landing zones north-west of Paris towards Rouen, with orders to inflict maximum damage to the retreating German forces. As part of the second team on this operation under Lieutenant Samarine, Geronimo was immediately thrown into action upon arrival. The TRUEFORM II group operated south of the area of Le Neubourg from 17 to 25 August. During this period, it was able to inflict significant damage and wreak havoc on the retreating Germans.[30]

But 6100555/13808268/ME138041867 Francisco Geronimo was quite used to being a shadow and disappear when needed. Born in Málaga, Geronimo was from a working-class family and had been an apprentice electrician when the Spanish Civil War broke out in 1936. Having fought in the Battle of the Ebro and crossed into France, he joined the *Légion Étrangère* and was in Syria by 1940. His powers of endurance were truly incredible. Not only had he been on a six-day trek across the desert to join the British Army in Palestine in 1940, but in Crete in 1941 he was able to escape and evade capture during a period of 11 months. Escaping after initial capture, he got away into the White Mountains. Long periods of hunger and hiding followed.

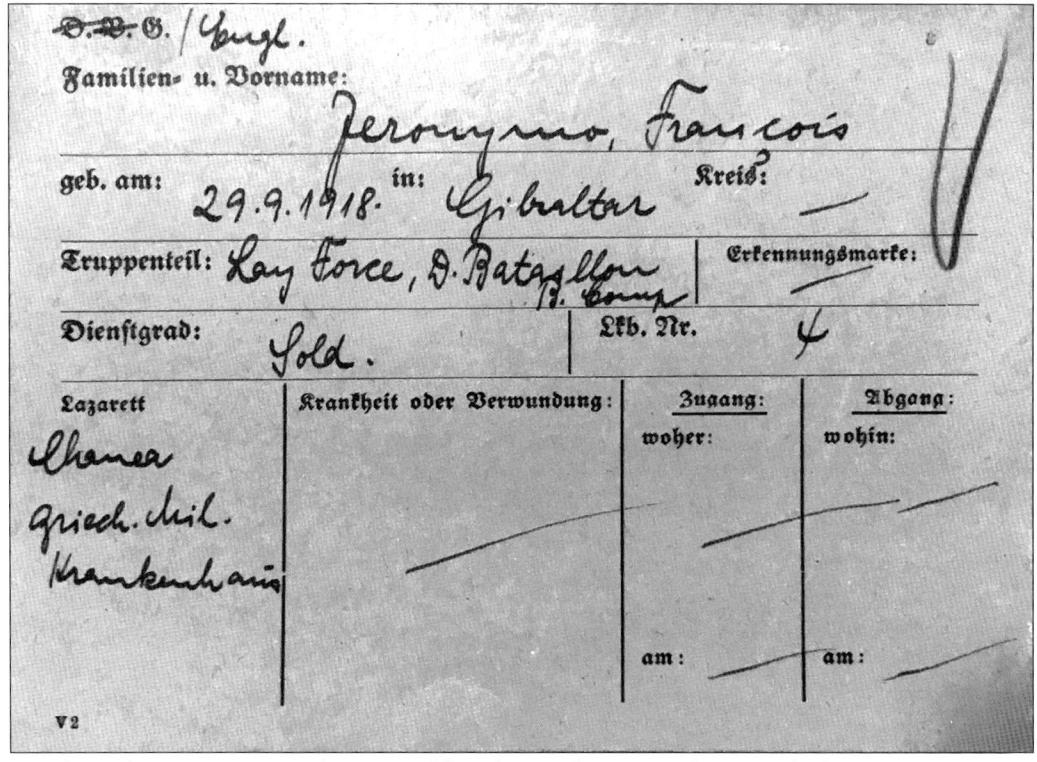

A photo of Francisco Geronimo's POW card from his initial capture in Crete in 1941. (Francisco Geronimo collection)

---

30 TNA, WO 361/719, France: special operations by the SAS (Special Air Service); Operation Trueform.

On many occasions later in his life, Geronimo told his family that he would awake with the sound of running water and laughing children in his ears. This was certainly the case when he took shelter in a village on one occasion where the locals were reticent about housing him due to the likely reprisals that would be taken by the Germans if he was found being sheltered there. However, one household took him in and let him sleep in a room at the rear of their house after feeding him. A few hours later he was awoken by the owner bursting in the room warning a half-awake Francisco that the Germans were in the village. In a drowsy but scared state he made a run for the open window and jumped at full speed to try and escape. However, he misjudged the height of his jump and the placement of the window frame and his forehead connected with it knocking him out. The momentum of his jump sent his unconscious body through the window and he hit the ground in a lane at the rear. A while later he came round and realised the Germans had left without finding him. Geronimo apparently picked up the language quite easily and was no longer dressed in military clothing, making himself look like one of the locals (his dark complexion probably aiding with the deception). Another story is that he helped a German remove his cart from a rut in the road for which he was rewarded with a cigarette by the soldier. Kosta Spirachi was the name he adopted during his time on Crete. He also had to forage for himself and find enough to feed two British officers he was looking after in a cave that he spent a great deal of time in. Allegedly the senior of the two officers made an offer to Geronimo when they returned to Egypt for him to become his batman. He turned the offer down due to being unwilling to 'clean the boots of another man'.[31]

One of these two officers was Lieutenant J.R. Snowden who went on to write his memoirs. Of Geronimo he says many things, much of which is reminiscent of the language issues faced by all parties in North Africa when Spaniards and other nationalities enlisted in join the British Army:

> About two hours later we were passing through a village when we saw a crowd of English, Cypriots and a lot of odds and ends in a café. They seemed to be having a good time, so we stopped and joined them; the village offered to accommodate twelve of us, so we decided to stop the night. It was in this café that Pat [another British officer] met Kosta, a Spaniard whose real name is Francisco Geronimo … in the holocaust of the Battle of Crete he found himself fighting a rear-guard action which ended with the capitulation at Sphakia.
>
> Now Kosta was under the impression that the Hun would have a good reception for him if he gave himself up, so he departed for the hills in company with a number of others and watched the Hun collect what was left. Eventually he made his way back to Cannea where he was taken ill, spent some time in hospital as a Greek and when visited by an American who tried to talk to him in English, a language Kosta … was unable to speak, he told the American to speak in French as 'your English is so bad, I can't understand it'.
>
> As soon as he recovered, he went back to the hills to live; he had a gift for languages and soon learned to speak a passable amount of Greek, certainly far more than the average German on the island at that time.
>
> At one period he was living in a small stone hut in a vineyard, the owner supplying him with food and clothing, when one morning a party of Germans arrived and wanted to buy some grapes. Kosta had not the slightest idea how much he should charge, he just stated a nominal sum of a few Drachmas and let the Germans have what they wanted; the Huns went away very pleased with themselves and the next day Kosta also decided to go as he felt that a second visit might not turn out so successfully.
>
> One of his more amusing stories was of the Australian he was with [during] part of his wanderings. The cretin has an insane desire for news – one of the first things he will ask for is

---

31 Transcript from interview with Phil Williams, the grandson of Francisco Geronimo, 19 August 2020.

news – and it was the experience of most of us that, if the news was good we lived well but, if it was bad the standard of living was also bad. Well Kosta noticed that the Aussie always had plenty of news for the villagers wherever they stopped for a chat, so he watched him carefully and listened to all the news items for a time, then one day he said 'how is it that you are able to supply all this fresh news, I have not left you for a week, nobody has given you any news, yet you have had a fresh lot every day.l To this the Aussie replied "Well one must live so I make it up as I go along!" And I think that is how most of the news on the island originated; there were a few hidden receiving sets which picked up the Greek news from various foreign stations – this source was notoriously inaccurate and rather like the Aussies, all good. And to confound the issue further there were the official British propagandists to tell them the truth but only half the truth.

When anything came under discussion between our party and the Greeks the following procedure was adopted; Kosta spoke to the Greeks in Greek, told Pat in French what had been said and Pat translated into English. This system was not entirely satisfactory and was eventually the cause of a lot of ill feeling, Kosta would talk for half an hour, would take fifteen minutes to tell Pat, and Pat would tell us in five; normally we didn't care, but when it was something that affected us all we considered that we had a right to know all the facts. After quite a short time I found I could understand at least 75% of the French and eventually 50% of the Greek, Bunny never learned very much Greek while we were together, but neither of us ever admitted how much Greek or French we knew, so were able to discover a fair amount of what was going on behind the scenes.[32]

Research would suggest that Geronimo was able to get away as part of a group taken off the island by the SOE in May 1942 and called the Cumberledge/Saunders Group. Under the overall direction of Force 133 (SOE) operations in conjunction with MI9, the group was taken from a small beach at Trofalas below the village of Krotos on 22 May 1942 and they reached Alexandria three days later.[33] From here, Geronimo was soon on the books of 1 SSR and back in the thick of things before joining 2nd SAS in December 1943.

Also on TRUEFORM, but in the fourth team, were Torrents and Ramos. 13301854 Juan Torrents Abadía was a proud Catalan and a good friend of Ramos. As a young man he had undertaken an apprenticeship in the Hispano-Suiza car factory in Barcelona and had become heavily politicised joining *Esquerra Republicana* and the *Union General de Trabajadores*, a well-established trade union throughout all of Spain. During the Spanish Civil War, he had served as a policeman and had operated in the Barcelona equivalent of the CID. At the end of the Civil War, he travelled across into France and volunteered to join the *Légion Étrangère*. Under the command of Captain Baillie, Torrents ended up being a team leader on TRUEFORM IV which was dropped into the area south of Elboeuf and operated in that area over the period of 17 to 24 August. In a controversial part of the operation, Torrents was forced to open fire and kill a German soldier as a German foraging party got too close to the SAS group. The group escaped but Baillie was left behind. Other members of the group felt haunted for years afterwards wondering if they had done the right thing or not.[34] Torrents would later say:

---

32 J.R. Snowden, Private Papers, IWM Archive, Catalogue number 12555.
33 <http://www.anzacpow.com/Part-5-Other-European-Free-Men/chapter_5__crete>. Accessed 18 June 2022. On the nominal roll of personnel, the following detail is included: Private F. Jaronemo, Regiment No. 6100555, Unit: Layforce (52 Cmdo) (name and unit incorrect). Two other members of Layforce landed with that group: Private T. Moan and Lance Corporal G. Moon.
34 Gavin Mortimer, *Stirling's Men: The Inside Story of the SAS in World War 2* (London: Weidenfeld & Nicolson, 2004), pp.244–246.

> I had five blokes with me. All of a sudden, a bloke appears out of the trees and a gun. As soon as I saw the uniform, I had my thing already cocked in my hand and I let him have it. We had to run then because we knew they were going to attack and luckily for us we ran in the right direction away from the Germans.[35]

Arthur Huntbach was on the same operation and had been due to go on LOYTON:

> I asked to join the French Squadron of the 2nd SAS as I was a fluent [French] speaker. They were a tough lot, mostly ex-Foreign Legion, and Free Russians and Spaniards, many of whom had fought against Franco in the Spanish Civil War. One of the finest was Corporal Torrance, who after the war took British citizenship as 'John Coleman'

He was with Torrents when during the encounter:

> The Germans were combing the woods looking for us when one of their troops spotted one of our haversacks. Corporal Torrance shot the German soldier and all hell broke loose. There were four of us on the run – myself, Corporal Torrance, Taffy Rogers and Jack Sinclair. We hid up that afternoon and tried to make our way to the Allied lines which were a few miles away …[36]

Probably one of the most ill-fated SAS operations of 1944 was Operation LOYTON in September. Two Spaniards were involved in it and deployed as part of the Northern Team. Very little is known about how 13301792 Francisco López Martín came to be in North Africa in 1943. What we do know is that he enlisted on 20 September into 361 Company at Maison Carrée in Algeria. For LOYTON, however, the SAS had the misfortune to be parachuted into the Vosges Mountains at a time when the Germans were reinforcing the area against the advance of Lieutenant General George S. Patton's 3rd Army. Consequently, the Germans quickly became aware of the SAS team's presence and conducted operations to destroy them. With their supplies almost exhausted and under pressure from the Germans, the teams were ordered to divide into smaller groups and try to return to the Allied lines. During the fighting and breakout operations 31 men were captured and later executed by the Germans. Both Francisco López Martín and Ángel Camarena were able to survive LOYTON. Sadly, the commander of the Northern Team, Lieutenant Joseph Maurice Rousseau, a French Canadian, was captured and died although it is still uncertain if he was murdered or died of wounds.[37]

13301810 Ángel (Higinio) Camarena Espinosa was born in Madrid and was an athletic man and natural survivor. His mother died very young; his father re-married and with his new wife had a daughter. Ángel was a free spirit and left home as a youth to travel. We know that he went to Huelva among other places, that he wrote home to his sister Isabel, and that he composed poems which he sent to her. Like many of his generation, he was a supporter of the democratically elected Republican Government in the early 1930s. Before the Nationalist uprising took place in July 1936, Ángel (or Higinio as he had originally been called) had joined the Corps of Engineers in the Republican Army in 1935. He was soon posted to the Canary Islands as a driver in the chauffeur pool. In fact, he was Franco's driver. Later in life, he recalled being physically very close on many occasions to 'El Caudillo' (The Dictator) and having to suppress a very strong desire to kill him.

---

35 Interview with John Colman (Juan Torrents Abadía), recorded 27 December 1997, IWM 17730
36 Mike Morgan, *Daggers Drawn: Real Heroes of the SAS & SBS* (Staplehurst: Spellmount, 2012), pp.233–235.
37 Philippe Get, *L'Equipe du Nord, Igney 09–18 septembre 1944* (Toulouse: CoolLibri, 2021).

He also recalled that he would often push Franco's daughter, Carmen, on her swing in the garden as he waited for Franco.

Camarena was a very forthright person and would have spoken his mind. This was to be to his detriment, as soon after the rebel uprising, he was arrested and condemned to death by firing squad. It may be that, due to his proximity, he may have been implicated in a plot to kidnap Franco's daughter. What is confirmed is a published judgement at the time where he was placed on a list of 61 arrested people and was one of 21 condemned to death.[38] He was incarcerated and placed on an improvised prison boat before the fateful day. Improvised floating prisons were used by the Nationalists in the Canaries to incarcerate those captured as they were not able to hold the large number of prisoners arrested after July 1936. Prisons were filling with men and women so fast that the machinery of repression had to 'commandeer' new ones such as the Fyffes vessels belonging to the fruit company in Santa Cruz de Tenerife. Prison ships, like the four ramshackle vessels the *Santa Rosa de Lima*, the *Santa Elena*, the *Gomera* and the *Adeje*, were soon crammed with republicans, communists, socialists, anarchists or anyone thought to be hostile towards the Nationalist uprising. The ominous day came and as Camarena and others were lined up on the deck to be shot they jumped overboard. One of them could not swim and drowned, but the others were picked up by a passing British ship; they were handed back to the Spaniards on the understanding that the death sentence was commuted, and this was agreed. Camarena then spent the next five years imprisoned in Spanish Morocco and was released in 1941 when Franco announced one of his first large amnesties for prisoners from the Spanish Civil War. Camarena returned home to Madrid. His sister later recalled that he felt he had no option but to leave the country soon after as he was convinced that Franco would in due course come after all those who had been released whom he continued to consider his enemies. As narrated above, he made his way to North Africa after Operation TORCH and joined the British Army in October 1943.

There were also Spaniards who deployed on other operations as members of 3rd SAS. The aim of Operation DICKENS was to cut German controlled rail networks, gather intelligence and organise the local resistance groups around the Forêt de l'Absie in western France. The operation took place between 16 July and early October 1944 and was a great success. Commanded by Captain Fournier, 65 men were parachuted into the area, totally disrupting German rail communications and in the process killing more than 500 Germans and destroying 200 vehicles. One of the SAS troopers was Spaniard Benitez García who had rallied to the Free French flag in 1943 and eventually joined 3rd SAS, serving in the 3rd Squadron.

Operations in Italy

Although 2nd SAS had featured heavily in operations in Italy in 1943, it was not until the end of 1944 that it returned to that country. No.3 Squadron, under the command of Major Roy Farran, arrived in southern Italy on 15 December. Four Spaniards would take part in the operations that followed. Unlike the operations in France and further east, the SAS troops were in close liaison with the SOE in the Italian theatre, which in this theatre was known as Special Force. Its forward Tactical HQ was set up in a villa on the Via delle Forbici, the road between Florence and Fiesole. Overall, it coordinated six British and Italian missions, which, in turn, operated forward carrying out sabotage operations, reconnaissance and working with partisans. The Tactical HQ answered

---

38 Documento de Sentencia de la Causa 246-1936, Recogida en: AHPSCT. Expedientes de Reclusas de La Prisión Provincial de Santa Cruz de Tenerife, Expediente no 3798. <https://pellagofio.es/islenos/yo-fui-en-el-correillo/prisiones-flotantes-en-el-puerto-de-santa-cruz>. Accessed 9 November 2021.

A group picture of 2nd SAS members who made up the Italian Detachment. This picture was taken in Wivenhoe at the end of the war in October 1945 not long before the SAS was disbanded. Major Roy Farran can be seen sitting in the middle on the front row. Note the 75mm Pack Howitzer named *Molto Stanco* at the front, which had been used during Operation TOMBOLA. Two Spaniards are in this photo: Ralph Ramos is standing in the third row, fourth from the right with his head slightly tilted to the left. Francisco Geronimo is immediately behind him third from the right with a big grin on his face. (Francisco Geronimo collection)

to Colonel Riepe, a US officer at 15th Army Group Headquarters in Florence. Farran soon built his relationship with the SOE lead, Major Charles Macintosh, a New Zealander who had been brought up in Venezuela. Between December 1944 and the end of the war, the 2nd SAS Italy Detachment carried out six operations in country. Three of them had Spaniards on them, these being BRAKE II, GALIA and TOMBOLA.[39]

The first of these operations was GALIA. Following the initial success of the German Ardennes offensive, it was feared that something similar could occur in northern Italy, especially as the US 5th Army was severely stretched across Italy and France. A British SOE operative known as Blundell Violett (whose real name was Major Gordon Lett), had come up with a plan to carry out a series of attacks against the Germans. His plan required support, as even though he was preparing his partisans well they would need reinforcement and further training. This is where the recently arrived SAS troops were ideal. The plan for Operation GALIA was conceived and put into practice in only two weeks. The SAS team consisted of 33 personnel, and it began on 27 December 1944. One of these was Corporal Benson (Carlos Bovio).

Dropped in by day into the area of Chiesa Di Rossano in the hills north of La Spezia to make it look like a whole brigade was landing, the teams, commanded by Captain Bob Walker-Brown, soon got to work.[40] Walker-Brown was a Scotsman who had originally been commissioned into the Royal Engineers at the beginning of the war. He had transferred to the Highland Light Infantry and been wounded and captured in North Africa and then sent to the notorious Chieti POW Camp in the Abruzzo region, not far from the Italian east coast. When Italy had declared an armistice in September 1943, he was able to escape and ended up joining the SAS back in Britain. He had commanded in France in 1944 and was a gritty officer who would not let his men do anything unless he could do it himself. Like many in the SOE, he had some misgivings about the partisan groups, but they soon got to work. A few days into their deployment they attacked a convoy as well as the garrison in Borghetto di Vara. In this attack they used a three-inch mortar to devastating effect. A small patrol was captured in early January and luckily they remained safe as POWs and were not murdered. With it being a very harsh winter, conditions were remarkably hard with deep snow and very low temperatures. GALIA was able to be replenished by air but, due to the ground they were operating across, everything they did was very difficult. Even when there was a resupply by the very able Dakotas some of the communist partisan groups continued to take a large percentage of what was dropped. This resulted in the SAS avoiding operating with the communists as they felt they could not trust them.[41]

By mid-January 1945 it was clear that the Germans were looking to expand their operations in the area to clear out resistance. A further resupply provided the team with some Vickers machine guns which would be used immediately in an ambush on the Pontremolli-Aulla road. The SAS had also met up with Major Lett's partisans to carry on fighting in the area. A pursuit now followed as German mountain troops arrived in the area and started clearing it of their enemy. Luckily, the SAS men were able to get back to their forming up point before the Germans. To travel light and at speed it was decided that they would need to leave some equipment behind and bury it, and this included one of the radio sets.

At the end of January 1945, the whole of 3 Squadron, 2nd SAS was in Italy. On 31 January Operation BRAKE II was launched. This was a small team of four led by Sergeant Guscott, Parachutist Rafael Ramos, Private Simpson and an Italian partisan. It had been tasked to carry out

---

39 Malcolm Tudor, *SAS in Italy 1943–1945, Raiders in Enemy Territory* (London: Fonthill Media, 2018), pp.129–131.
40 Interview with Edward Lyster 'Tinker' Gibbon, 2000, IWM 20119.
41 Robert Hann, *SAS Operation GALIA, Bravery Behind Enemy Lines in the Second World War* (Peterborough: Fast Print Publishing, 2013), pp.35–41.

Map 9 SAS Operations in North Italy. Operations GALIA, BRAKE II and TOMBOLA. (Artwork by Mike Heald)

From left to right, Private Simpson, Private Ramos and Sergeant Guscott pause in the snow on Operation BRAKE II. This photo was taken shortly after it joined GALIA. Note Ralph Ramos sitting on his 'Bergan', a pack synonymous with the SAS. (Robert Hann collection)

some reconnaissance and meet up with the GALIA team. On 11 February BRAKE II arrived in the Rossano Valley and met with Captain Bob Walker-Brown. On the same day GALIA decided that it would withdraw back to the Allied lines. The operation had been a spectacularly successful one, both in the results achieved and the determination of the SAS when faced with the difficulties of the terrain and the winter weather. It inflicted many losses on the enemy and had shown that the skilful use of the three-inch mortar and Bren guns could be deadly. Additionally, a 59 hour march without rest or rations had stretched the GALIA team hard but given them enough breathing space to get away from the German pursuit. By the early hours of 15 February, GALIA had reached the Allied lines via Seravezza.[42]

The plan for BRAKE II had been to get the team to stay in the area and be reinforced to carry out further operations but it was decided that they would not remain in the Rossano Valley but join another operation further to the east – TOMBOLA. The team had already spent 11 days slipping through the enemy lines undetected and had trekked across arduous terrain and winter conditions to meet up with GALIA. It now spent the next month winding its way northeast to link up with TOMBOLA by 17 March. That was effectively six weeks of trekking with heavy Bergans, deep in enemy territory, and covering a total of some 200 miles. Reminiscent of the long patrols in the deserts of North Africa, these types of operations were the hallmark of the SAS. Rafael Ramos certainly fitted the bill!

Operation TOMBOLA was organised to harass the enemy to the south-west of Modena and took place between 4 March and 24 April 1945. This operation was led by Major Roy Farran and

---

42 TNA, WO 219/2403, Special Air Service reports: operation Galia.

Ralph Ramos and Sergeant Guscott on the left rest with partisans. (Rafael Ramos collection)

was probably the most successful operation the SAS conducted in Italy.[43] In his post operational report he would summarise the operation as being one where:

> The details of the story might be from a book by Forrester. The artillery piece called 'Molto Stanco', the two women Staffetas sent ahead to reconnoitre, Barba Nero surrounded by his Q staff of swindlers, Victor Modena the swashbuckling Russian, and finally Major McGinty who by threats and persuasion was able to achieve cohesion and efficiency from so heterogeneous a force.[44]

Three Spaniards would take part in the operation: Balerdi, his close friend Geronimo, and Ramos who as we know would join them in mid-March. The TOMBOLA team was inserted into the mountains near to Reggio Emilia from 4 March onwards. Farran (who went under the name of Major McGinty during the operation because he had a price on his head) and his advance party of seven including Balerdi and Geronimo parachuted in first. Despite being ordered not to, Farran jumped in with his team. The rest of the SAS team then regrouped in the small town of Secchio, not far from Monte Cusna, where Farran met up with SOE to plan the activities. The plan agreed was to bring together a force of 140 Italian partisans of 'mixed political affinities', 100 Russian deserters and the 40 or so SAS soldiers into a fighting force named the *Alleato Battalion*. Farran would go on to say that the first parade resembled more of a scene from Wat Tyler's rebellion from the period of Henry II![45] A great deal of training of the partisans by the SAS to ensure all were as ready as possible now took place.

---

43 TNA, WO 218/215, Operation Tombola: report. These Staffetas were Italian young partisan women who had 'novel' means of gaining information from the Germans.
44 TNA, WO 218/215, Operation Tombola: report.
45 Farran's memory of history is in error – Wat Tyler's rebellion took place under Richard II.

The Spanish Ex-Servicemen's Association Badge. (Courtesy of Mike Heald)

The standard of No.1 Spanish Company embroidered with the words '1940 until Victory'. Note the red and green diamond with a yellow 'S' in the middle which is the badge the company wore on its arm. Also note the Spanish Republican flag colours in the lace on the left. (Courtesy of Royal Logistics Corps Museum collection)

Commando service certificate of Joaquín Fajardo. All commando trained personnel were issued with a certificate for their loyal service, signed by Bob Laycock. (Courtesy of the Joaquín Fajardo collection)

Front cover of one of the Spanish Ex-Servicemen's Association Newsletters. It was produced in London and issued to all members. (Courtesy of the Agustín Roa Ventura collection)

Front cover of the booklet *Franco's Prisoners Speak* published in December 1960 by the Spanish Ex-Servicemen's Association. (Author's collection)

Miguel Bon's (Michael Montgomery) Alien registration card. Bon served in No.1 Spanish Company, was trained as a SCONCE and settled on the south coast of England. (Courtesy of the Miguel Bon collection)

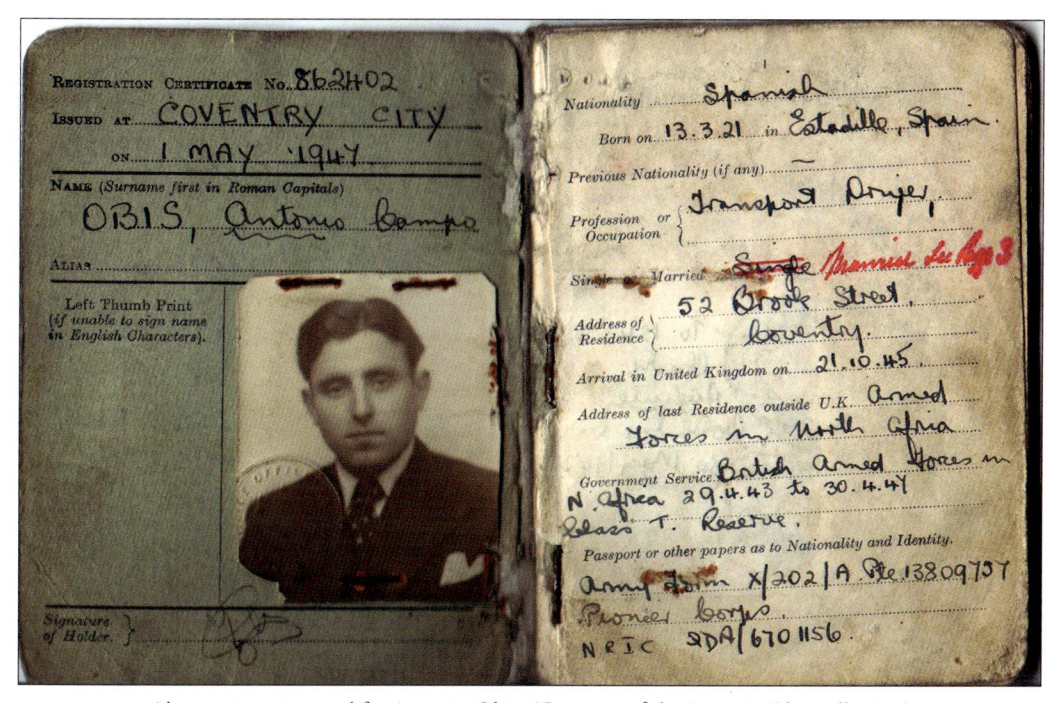

Alien registration card for Antonio Obis. (Courtesy of the Antonio Obis collection)

Certificate No. **AZ 43562**　　　　Home Office No. **G. 36667**

BRITISH NATIONALITY AND STATUS OF ALIENS ACT, 1914

CERTIFICATE OF NATURALIZATION

Whereas　　　Jose Garcia

has applied to one of His Majesty's Principal Secretaries of State for a Certificate of Naturalization, alleging with respect to　him　self the particulars set out below, and has satisfied him that the conditions laid down in the above-mentioned Act for the grant of a Certificate of Naturalization are fulfilled in　his　case:

Now, therefore, in pursuance of the powers conferred on him by the said Act, the Secretary of State grants to the said

Jose Garcia

this Certificate of Naturalization, and declares that upon taking the Oath of Allegiance within the time and in the manner required by the regulations made in that behalf he shall, subject to the provisions of the said Act, be entitled to all political and other rights, powers and privileges, and be subject to all obligations, duties and liabilities, to which a natural-born British subject is entitled or subject, and have to all intents and purposes the status of a natural-born British subject.

In witness whereof I have hereto subscribed my name this 11th day of June, 1948.

H. Maxwell

HOME OFFICE,　　　　　　　　　　　　　　　　　Under Secretary of State.
LONDON.

PARTICULARS RELATING TO APPLICANT

Full Name	Jose GARCIA.
Address	67, Windsor Road, Ealing, London, W.5.
Trade or Occupation	French Polisher Improver.
Place and date of birth	Madrid, Spain,　9th February, 1923.
Nationality	Spanish.
Single, married, etc.	Married.
Name of wife or husband	Juliet Constance.
Names and nationality of parents	Emilio and Romana GARCIA. (Spanish)

(For Oath see overleaf)

José García Flores who served in No.1 Spanish Company and Royal Signals became naturalised in 1948. (José García Flores collection)

A protest in London showing solidarity with the miners of Asturias. (Agustín Roa Ventura collection)

Frank Williams (Francisco Geronimo) on the left and Alan Cooper (Ángel Camarena) relaxing at home in Cardiff in the 1970s. (Francisco Geronimo collection)

Agustín Roa Ventura and his wife Matilde Díaz with his lifelong friend Antonio Vargas in the 1980s. (Agustín Roa Ventura collection)

Left: Members of the *Alleato* Battalion travel through the deep snow. (Dr Grizi Collection)
Right: An iconic photo of Ralph Ramos helping to train the partisans prior to the attack on the HQ of the LI German Mountain Corps. Note that he is wearing a Denison smock and his .45 calibre Colt in its holster is clearly visible. The partisan is firing a .30 calibre American carbine. (Dr Grizi Collection)

Captain Mike Lees of the SOE had already identified the HQ of the German LI Mountain Corps which would be the first target. It was located in two villas (Villa Rossi and Villa Calvi) at Botteghe, in the Albinea Commune very close to Reggia Emilia. Lees had an excellent network of people gathering information. Amongst them were two Italian *Staffeta* women spies who were able to supply a great deal of information about the HQ. This in turn gave the *Alleato Battalion* the chance to prepare accordingly. Farran initially received orders to delay an attack; orders which reinforced the need for training as well as much-needed time for preparing defences for any post attack activities, should there be a requirement.

A few days later, a decision was made to launch the attack and things began on 23 March with the battalion moving out. Travelling by night, they arrived at Casa del Lupo early on 26 March and waited there until the attack started at 2300 hours. Ironically, a signal had been sent by radio to Farran ordering him to not carry out the attack because it was not the right time due to the imminent Po Valley offensive, but he did not receive it. The *Staffetas* were used to carry out a final reconnaissance of the area and confirmed the sentries at the two villas to be attacked. The Corps Commander was due to be in Villa Rossi so the first group set off for the Villa. Then the group of Russians under the command of Victor Modena set up a protective screen, before the final group moved to Villa Calvi. The attack went in at 0200 hours with firing starting on the Villa Calvi from the unit under the command of Lieutenant Ken Harvey, a Rhodesian. Unable to fire the bazooka to start the attack due to two misfires and with approaching German sentries, Harvey opened fire and all hell broke loose. This did not help as the key attack was supposed to be on Villa Rossi. In the meantime, Farran had Piper David Kirkpatrick from the Highland Light Infantry play 'Highland Laddie'. Farran had called for a piper to be parachuted in because he knew that its playing would signal that the attack was a British one and thus hopefully prevent any reprisals on the local community. The psychological effect on the Germans was also very apparent.

Villa Rossi today. (Author's collection)

The attack on Villa Calvi was fierce. In Villa Rossi Lieutenant Riccomini who led the team and Sergeant Guscott were, sadly, killed on the staircase. Significantly, both had volunteered to carry on fighting after being involved with GALIA and BRAKE II; they were a major loss to the unit. Mike Lees was severely wounded in the leg by a grenade but was rescued and evacuated out of the building to safety. It was here that Rafael Ramos came into his own as the SAS battled away. His Military Medal citation reads:

> On the night of 26–27 March 1945, parachutist Ramos was a member of a party of mixed British parachutists and Italian partisans which attacked the Corps Commander's Villa in the headquarters of the German 51 Corps at Albinea, ten miles south of Reggio nel' Emilia.
>
> During the very fierce fighting which ensued in the house, Ramos was always in the forefront, killing at least six German officers on the spiral staircase. In an attempt to ascend the staircase in the face of intense fire, a British officer was seriously wounded. Ramos picked him up and carried him to the door, returning afterwards to the fight.
>
> When the party was ordered to withdraw and the villa had been set on fire, Ramos, with one other British parachutist, carried this officer, who weighed thirteen stone, through heavy machine-gun fire and an area alive with angry Germans, six miles to a cottage.
>
> For the next two days they carried this wounded officer on a ladder through the plain to a safe house near Reggio, despite the searching German troops who knew they were in the area. Having ensured that this officer was safe and well looked after Ramos returned to his base in the mountains.

A group photo of members of Operation TOMBOLA. In the middle with a cigarette in his mouth is Justo Balerdi who was tragically killed on 21 April 1945. (Francisco Geronimo collection)

It is considered that RAMOS showed remarkable courage both during and after the attack. His intelligence and initiative in a strange country thirty miles behind the enemy lines showed a devotion to duty worthy of the highest praise and resulted in preserving the life of a valuable British officer.[46]

Rafael Ramos had not only trekked across the mountains over a six-week period to get to TOMBOLA but had also been heavily involved in training the partisans upon arrival. Now, he was in the thick of the action along with Geronimo and Balerdi. It took Ramos a few days to escape and evade with Parachutist Burke, a red-headed Irishman, along with Lees on the ladder. Lees was eventually evacuated by air to safety. The attack was a big blow to the Germans with heavy casualties and the death of the headquarters' Chief of Staff.

The established SAS defences in the hills were soon put to good use as the Germans carried out large sweeps to track down the attackers. A major attack was repelled on 10 April. On 5 April the team had been reinforced with two jeeps and a 75mm Pack Howitzer nicknamed *Molto Stanco* which caused havoc over the coming few weeks. Up to 300 German casualties and some 15 trucks were destroyed as a result. Attacks between 20 and 24 April continued to cause panic but there was a cost. Balerdi was killed by a bullet to the head and died instantly during an attack in Torre Maina, south of Modena on 21 April. His best friend Francisco Geronimo, who had gone through so much with him, would bury him.[47] Balerdi would be disinterred twice and eventually laid to rest in the Commonwealth War Graves Commission Cemetery in Milan. His grave is marked R. BRUCE.[48]

---

46 TNA, WO 373/13/478, Recommendation for Award for Ramos, Raphael.
47 Roy Farran, *Operation Tombola* (London: Arms & Armour Press, 1960), pp.231–232.
48 Guillermo Tabernilla and Ander González, *Combatientes Vascos en la Segunda Guerra Mundial, Fighting Basques Project* (Madrid: Desperta Ferro Ediciones SLNE, 2018), pp.76–77.

The grave of Justo Balerdi in the Commonwealth War Graves Commission Cemetery in Milan. He is named as R. BRUCE. (Author's collection)

'WONDERFUL WAY TO GO' 213

Ralph Ramos on the left and Francisco Geronimo on the right whilst on leave in Rome at the end of the war. (Francisco Geronimo collection)

A group photo of some of the members of 2nd SAS who took part in Operation TOMBOLA. The photo was taken in Wivenhoe in October 1945. Ralph Ramos is second from the right standing in the second row and Francisco Geronimo is in the back row third from the left. (Francisco Geronimo collection)

An iconic photo of Francisco Geronimo taken in Rome on the left with the author on the right in the same location. The location has been tracked down to Via Attilio Regolo, north of Castel Sant'Angelo and to the east of the Vatican. (Francisco Geronimo collection and Author's collection)

Northwest Europe and the End of the War

In north-western Europe, operations were continuing on Operation AMHERST between 8 and 16 April. Amongst those deployed in 3rd and 4th SAS was Francisco Golf Roma. Born in Alicante in 1925, Francisco joined the Free French cause in Tunisia in June 1943. He joined *3ᵉ BIA* and, once in Britain, carried out his parachute training at Ringway in January 1944 as a soldier in 3rd SAS. AMHERST aimed to disrupt German rear-area communications in the region of Apeldoorn in the north-east Netherlands and was planned in concert with Operation KEYSTONE. The French enjoyed a great deal of success on this operation but lost 34 dead, 60 wounded and 69 missing, in exchange for German losses of 270 killed, 220 wounded and 187 taken prisoner.

With the final stages of the war approaching, the Allies were pushing into Germany. The mission the SAS now had was to press into German territory harassing the German retreat, the operation was called ARCHWAY. In tandem with Operation VARSITY, elements of 1st and 2nd SAS crossed the Rhine on 25 March in a fleet of jeeps. Some were even carried across in Buffalo LVT (Landing Vehicle Tracked) 2s. On the operation were Torrents and Camarena. Travelling along back roads, the SAS teams often ran into determined German resistance. On many occasions, the SAS would drive up, rip through the buildings with their jeep-mounted twin machine guns, then finish off the survivors inside with gunfire and grenades. By 12 April 2nd SAS had pushed towards Celle, in north-central Germany. Three days later, Lieutenant John Randall from 1st SAS entered Bergen-Belsen. A week or so later and they were not far from Hamburg. Here is where another curious meeting of old enemies from the Spanish Civil War took place. This time, the roles were certainly reversed. John Colman described it:

> I tell you something that happened ... We stopped at a hospital very near Hamburg. A civilian bloke who must have been wounded in the leg came over and he was listening to us. I was talking to Camarena, a Spaniard you know, a soldier like me. He approached us and he said in French 'You are Spaniards?' We said yes. I could speak French, Camarena could speak French. So he says 'There's a nurse ... a Franco woman here' ... Camarena who was the Spaniard with me like Ramos says 'That blinking woman'. I said let her be. But the woman comes along and Camarena places himself in front and he said 'You're a Spanish woman aren't you?' She said 'Yes, what?' Camarena starts insulting her you know. That I would not have done. The lady said 'You never let us in peace, let us die in peace now'. That's what that Spanish nurse said to Camarena. Then she went ... I would not have insulted her like that.[49]

By the time the war in Europe was over in May, the SAS Brigade had suffered many casualties but had inflicted heavy losses on their enemies. When the end of the war was declared, members of ARCHWAY returned to the UK and their base in Wivenhoe near Colchester only to be deployed to Norway shortly after. Around 300,000 Germans were stationed in Norway and had surrendered. 1st and 2nd SAS were deployed to disarm and process German soldiers stationed across the country. Troops were flown in and rounded up all kinds of German personnel including U-boat crews. On the whole, they were able to enjoy some good days with locals who were, by and large, very

Angle Camarena on Operation ARCHWAY. He is standing in front of his jeep and is next to Parachutist Taff Tate. (Martin Tate)

---

49 Interview with John Colman (Juan Torrents Abadía), recorded 27 December 1997, IWM 17730.

grateful. At the same time 5th SAS were in Denmark and Germany carrying out counter-intelligence operations.

During September, 5th SAS was disbanded and handed over to the recently reformed Belgian Army. On 1 September, 3rd and 4th SAS were handed over to the French Army. The formalities took place in Tarbes on 2 October and commander of the SAS Brigade, Brigadier Mike Calvert, handed over command to *Général* Auguste-Leon Bonjour. Calvert bestowed upon the two regiments their respective *fanions* (a small standard used by the French Army) and hats of Napoleon and the Duke of Wellington, a sign of friendship and fraternity in arms.[50]

2nd SAS held an inter-squadron sports day on 29 September and Thanksgiving Service the day after in St Peter's Church, Colchester. By the end of 1945 1st and 2nd SAS regiments had been disbanded. For the Spaniards this meant that they were now on the books of the Army Air Corps and they would spend the next few months going through the process of demobilisation. Their path to civilian life took them to the Depot Company of the Army Air Corps in Chesterfield before then being moved to its Holding Battery in Boroughbridge (today Dishforth Airfield) and then being handed back to the Pioneer Corps and held in Delamere Camp in Cheshire before being demobilised in the summer and autumn of 1946.

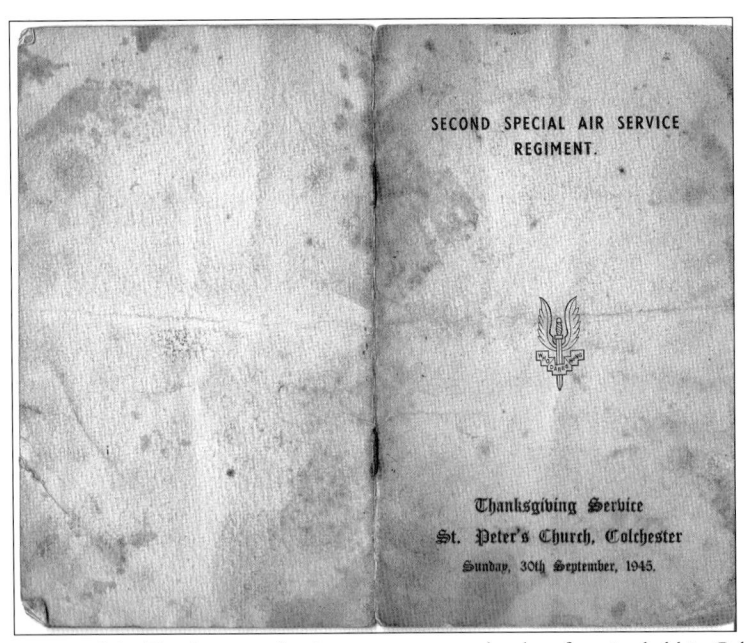

The front cover of the Thanksgiving Service programme and order of service held in Colchester for 2nd SAS prior to its disbandment. (Francisco Geronimo collection)

Spaniards in the SAS were a close-knit group by the end of the war and had been through a great deal. Serving across three regiments of the SAS Brigade, their experiences were unique amongst those Spaniards continuing the fight beyond the Spanish Civil War. The majority of those who served in 2nd SAS would initially settle in South Wales and remain in Britain.

---

50 Photograph: Command of French Units handed to *Général* Bonjour, 2 October 1945, IWM B 15793.

Chapter 7

'Flying Through The Smoke'

The Brave Few

> I still remember him today, as a wonderful soldier – highly intelligent, immensely brave, and with a capacity, which the average Englishman doesn't have, for giving enormous personal loyalty.
>
> John Marshall[1]

Moving on from the larger groups of Spaniards who volunteered to join the British Army as the war progressed, we now turn to smaller groups and individuals whose stories remain utterly compelling. These young men would fight in a hugely wide-ranging array of battles and theatres, stretching from the beaches at Salerno to those of Normandy, and included Spaniards fighting in the airborne forces in Normandy and at Arnhem in 1944. Additionally, there were incredible acts of bravery by Spaniards serving in the SOE and fighting alongside their comrades in arms in the *maquis* in Southern France.

With the Queen's Royal Regiment in Italy, France and Germany

As covered above some of the Spaniards of No.50 Middle East Commando who had fought in Crete in 1941 and were not taken prisoner decided to transfer to the 1/5th Battalion of the Queen's Royal Regiment (West Surrey) (QRR). This transfer took place on 21 July 1943 before most Spaniards, who had been in 1 SSR, and subsequently the Pioneer Corps, were transferred to North Africa.[2] Three names appear in the Queen's Royal Regiment (West Surrey) transfer book for 1943 of men who had enlisted three years previously.

Although it is not possible to get the full records of these men because these were damaged when they were sent to Jerusalem at the end of the war, the transfer book for 1943 gives a good amount of detail about their actions over the following three years.[3] 1/5th Battalion of the Queen's Royal Regiment (West Surrey) was part of 131st (Queen's) Infantry Brigade. In April 1940 the Brigade went to France and withdrew through Dunkirk. Following a period in Britain, it was reorganised and sent to join the 8th Army in North Africa. After the Battle of El Alamein, it became the Lorried Infantry Brigade of the 7th Armoured Division, 'The Desert Rats'. The Brigade would remain part

---

1 John Fairey, *Remember Arnhem: Story of the First Airborne Reconnaissance Squadron at Arnhem* (Bearsden: Peaton Press, 1990), p.119.
2 For more information on 1 SSR see Chapters 4 and 6.
3 NRA 44612, Surrey Heritage Centre Archive, 'Queen's Royal Regiment, Register of Soldiers, Transfer in 1943,' p.102.

Extract from Queen's Royal Regiment (West Surrey) transfer book from the summer of 1943.
(Surrey Heritage Centre Archive)

of the 7th Armoured Division until the end of the war. Under XXX Corps, commanded by Oliver Leese, 1/5th Battalion fought through to the end of the Tunisian Campaign in mid-May 1943 when the Germans and Italians fighting in North Africa finally surrendered. Instead of being used in Sicily for Operation HUSKY, the whole of 7th Armoured Division was rested at Homs as it carried out regeneration and amphibious training. It was during this period of recovery that Esteve, Vilanova and Mena transferred to the battalion.

1/5th Battalion saw action again in the Allied landings at Salerno in Operation AVALANCHE and the Brigade landed on 16 September. After heavy fighting against intense German counterattacks, a breakout from the initial landing area was made. 131 Brigade led the advance across the Naples plain and towards the mountains of central Italy. The US 5th Army soon began its attack northwest towards Naples with the 7th Armoured Division passing through the 46th Division to take the city, where the Allied troops arrived on 1 October following an uprising there. The 1/5th Battalion's diary records that, by this date, it had moved to Passanti and that by 4 October it was in the area of Aversa having crossed the Regni Lagni canal. The following day, the battalion advanced northwards to Capua and San Maria Capua Vetere. Two nights later Lance Corporal Fernando Esteve and Private Josep Vilanova distinguished themselves as the build-up to the crossing of the Volturno River began.[4]

The first two men of the Allied armies to cross the Volturno, which coiled through no man's land between the US 5th Army and the Germans north of Naples, turned out to be the two young Spaniards who had fought for the Republican cause in the Spanish Civil War and were now in their *seventh* successive year of war and under their *third* flag. The Volturno meandered through tough country between the German held mountains in the north and Naples to the south. Beyond the river, the plain was low, rather swampy and thick with vegetation. Banks around 10 feet high

---

4 Surrey Heritage Centre Archive QRWS/8/2/14, Reports of the campaigns in the Western Desert and Italy, War Diary for 1/5 Battalion, October 1943.

with a distance between them of 300 to 400 feet in places separated each side. Both men volunteered to carry out a reconnaissance and, after swimming across on 7 October, Vilanova and Esteve threaded their way between German machine gun nests, studying the lay of the land until they were challenged for the password by a German sentry. They withdrew silently. Upon their return they reported all they had seen and a fighting patrol was organised to take place a few nights later commanded by a Lieutenant Eve.

Shortly after midnight on 11 October the fighting patrol crossed the river by boat reaching the shore that had been popping with German fire throughout the previous day. The current was swift and powerful enough to make it difficult at night, but Esteve and Vilanova found the land they knew on the opposite bank and began to stalk the Germans through the damp darkness. Corporal George Corey, a Liverpudlian, went with them as the third man of the reconnaissance team. They were almost at the edge of the German listening post when a German standing by a tree shouted halt! It was to be his final word as Private Vilanova's 'Tommy gun' silenced him with a burst. Vilanova was wounded in the shooting that ensued, Corey and Esteve, closing in, found the two remaining Germans at this post in a ditch and killed them. Hearing the fire, German machine gunners soon got to work. Vilanova was able to go about 200 yards on his own and Esteve carried him the remaining 600 yards to the river. It seemed as though every enemy machine gun south of Rome was engaged by now but in the darkness no one was hit. Esteve, swimming, guided Vilanova in the boat and Cory swam back with the rest of the party. Members of A Company, 1/5th Battalion Queen's Royal Regiment (West Surrey) had now gained an advantage and secured a way of crossing the Volturno, which, would be crossed a week or so later.[5]

For his prompt actions in saving his patrol, 13808234 Josep Vilanova was awarded an immediate Military Medal. The citation reads:

> On the night of Oct 7, the Coy to which Pte. VILANOVA belonged was engaged in constructing slipways on the bank of the Volturno River.
>
> It was necessary for a recce to be made of the further bank, and this soldier volunteered to cross to the enemy side and carry the recce. In company with another man, he waded and swam to the other side in spite of the strong current which swept them both away on two occasions. They reached the enemy bank successfully, but after 30 minutes they were in danger of discovery by a German patrol of about 25 men, who had heard the crossing, and as the only weapons they had was a grenade apiece, they returned across the river, bringing back valuable information. Although frozen and wet through, Pte VILANOVA asked to be allowed to return and deal with the enemy patrol, until persuaded against it.
>
> On the night of 10/11 Oct at 02.00 hrs, a small fighting patrol of 'A' Coy was sent over the river in company with the battle patrol. Pte VILANOVA was the leading scout, and after proceeding for about 800 yds along the opposite bank, he was challenged by the enemy. He replied in Italian and with the help of another tommy-gunner, shot and killed three German, although he was himself seriously wounded in doing so.
>
> Pte VILANOVA in these two incidents showed great courage and daring and by his prompt action on this second occasion undoubtedly saved the patrol from being wiped out.[6]

13808234 Josep Vilanova was a Catalan from a town on the Costa Brava and had fought in the Spanish Civil War from the age of 17. By the time he crossed the Volturno, this was his eighth year

---

5 John Lardner, 'Two Spaniards First of Troops to cross Volturno in Italy,' *North American Newspaper Alliance*, October 1944.
6 TNA, WO 373/4/392, Military Medal citation for Pte Vilanova.

Private Josep Vilanova MM. This photograph was taken while he was serving with No.50 Middle East Commando in Crete in early 1941. (Fernando Esteve collection)

of fighting. He suffered three gunshot wounds to his left arm, which meant that he had to be evacuated back to Britain for treatment, where he was treated by Dr Josep Trueta Raspall. Trueta was a Catalan nationalist who had fled into exile in England in 1939. During the Spanish Civil War he had been chief of trauma services at the main hospital in Barcelona, where he led the management of air raid and battlefield casualties, developing a special interest in severe soft tissue and bone injuries. His booklet entitled *Treatment of War Wounds and Fractures, with special reference to the Closed Method as used in the war in Spain* was acclaimed in Britain and consequently accepted by the Royal Army Medical Corps.[7] He helped organise medical emergency services where his use of a new plaster cast method for the treatment of open wounds and fractures helped save a great number of lives and even more limbs. Such was the case with Vilanova, whom he treated for the rest of the war. Trueta also joined the team run by Florey and Chain that developed Penicillin F in Oxford, and part of the team that injected the first ever animal with the ground-breaking antibiotic. Later, from 1949 to 1966 he was the third Nuffield Professor of Orthopaedic Surgery at the University of Oxford and directed the Nuffield Orthopaedic Centre (the Wingfield-Morris Hospital) in the city.[8]

Due to the severity of his injuries, Vilanova was unable to continue serving and was eventually medically discharged from the British Army in England on 20 June 1944. Fernando Esteve and Vicente Mena continued in the battalion. 6100510/13808218 Private Fernando Esteve had been a smithy before 1936 and had even worked in a department store – a very far cry from fighting the Germans in Italy. He was a native of Vilanova, a small town just south of Sitges, which is itself along the coast south of Barcelona in Catalunya. Like his Spanish compatriots, he had been one of the 63 Spaniards who became members of No.50 Middle East Commando and attained the rank of lance corporal.

In Italy, the 7th Armoured Division was withdrawn in November 1943 and transferred to Britain to be part of the landings planned for the summer of 1944 in Normandy. 131 Brigade was brought back up to strength and began training for the forthcoming fighting on the second front. 1/5th Battalion landed in Scotland on 5 January 1944 and was then based in the Hunstanton area of Norfolk, between January and May 1944, and as the training progressed and the Battalion prepared the date for D-Day got closer. The Battalion landed in Normandy on 8 June and by the early hours of 12 June had established itself at Le Pont de la Guillette, 12 miles west of Caen, and was pushing southwest towards Tilly-sur-Seulles. Two days later, the Battalion faced a strongly emplaced enemy across the whole of its front and towards the end of the day had to deal with an enemy infiltration between A Company and B Company. It was to suffer a total of two officers wounded, six other ranks killed and a further 36 other ranks wounded. One of the wounded was 13808227 Private Vicente Mena who was sufficiently badly wounded to be evacuated to Britain and medically discharged on 4 October that year.[9]

There were other Spaniards who landed in Normandy on D-Day and after. Sergeant Antonio García was in 295 Field Company Royal Engineers, part of 231 Infantry Brigade, 50th (Northumbrian) Division and landed on JIG sector of GOLD Beach. A War Diary states:

> The night of 5–6 June was quiet and all craft in the convoy passed through the minefield without damage. We arrived at the lowering position at 0430 hours. The coast of Normandy was visible faintly; there was spasmodic bombing from the shore batteries. Breakfast was given to troops on board L.S.I. before lowering. There was a fresh wind and the sea choppy. H-Hr

---

7   Originally published in Catalan it was republished in London by Hamish Hamilton in 1939.
8   Daniel Arasa, *Los Españoles de Churchill* (Barcelona: Editorial Armonía Poética, 1991), p.190.
9   Surrey Heritage Centre Archive, QRWS/8/2/14.

was at 0725. The air & other types of support which would have been put on the defences at Le Hamel failed completely … heavy opposition was met from strong points on the sea wall, which fired LMGs onto the beach. These were not finally cleared until H+6 … Snipers were very troublesome, both on the beach and inland. Very few underwater obstacles were cleared with the result that many landing craft were damaged and beached far out, causing heavy loss of vehicles. The Assault Platoons managed to open exits from the beach by H+2 … Movement inland was slow as enemy opposition was stiff and continued to a depth of some miles.[10]

This was stiff opposition and 50th Division suffered casualties of 413 killed, wounded or missing by the close of D-Day, 6 June. Sergeant García was wounded in action but eventually returned to his company, fighting on until the end of the war.

The only Spaniard remaining in 1/5th Battalion in Normandy (that we currently know of) was Fernando Esteve. The Battalion would fight now pretty much non-stop until the end of the war and was initially involved in a series of battles for Normandy. Throughout the rest of June, it fought battles in the *bocage* and in July was involved in Operation GOODWOOD around Caen. In August it was in Caumont and Operation BLUECOAT before fighting at Mont Pinçon and as part of the breakout to the Seine. September saw the Battalion advancing from the Somme near Amiens to Ghent and then carrying out operations in the Low Countries. By mid-December 1/6th and 1/7th Battalions had taken heavy casualties and were transferred out of the brigade. Some ended up strengthening 1/5th. Between 13 and 26 January 1945 the Battalion was part of Operation BLACKCOCK, which involved driving the German 15th Army back across the Roer and Wurm rivers and moving the front line further into Germany. By the end of the month the Germans had been cleared from the area and the operation was a success for the Allies with all its objectives met. The German divisions were thrown out of the Roer Triangle except for the area immediately south of Roermond. It was now time for the Battalion to be part of operations to cross the Rhine. Detailed preparations began in early March 1945 with practice river crossings across the Maas, in Buffalos,[11] in the area of Papenhoven. The Battalion was visited by Field Marshal Sir Bernard Montgomery on 5 March and then carried out a series of Tactical Exercises Without Troops to consider the issues it would face. A series of study days, cloth map model exercises and briefings followed, with the Operational Instruction for Operation PLUNDER (the crossing of the Rhine) being issued on 25 March.

The Battalion crossed the Rhine around Xanten and was in its concentration area on the east bank by 0300 hours on 28 March. A spectacular operation to take Ahaus a few days later meant that it was soon quickly advancing deep into Germany.[12] Within a week it was approaching the River Weser at Sulingen, between Minden and Bremen, in support of 22nd Armoured Brigade which had 8th Hussars under command. Over the next few days, the Battalion pushed to the West of Bremen with Fernando Esteve's A Company in the lead. The Battalion crossed the Weser at Nienburg on the morning of 13 April. On 15 April it managed to cross the River Aller at Fallinbostel further north-west, after some hard resistance. It then moved further east towards Soltau but avoided it by moving northwest to Schneverdingen and swung north to Tosdedt en route to Hamburg. By 20 April the Battalion was ordered to capture Hollensted, which it did and a few days later it cleared the Harburg Forest. The Battalion had by now returned to 131 Brigade and after a few days' heavy fighting entered Hamburg on 3 May 1945 after Germany's unconditional surrender had been announced. Upon arrival at the town hall, the adjutant of the battalion hoisted

---

10 Royal Engineers Museum Archive, Extracts from 295 Field Company RE (TA), 3 Sep 1939 to 2 Mar 1946.
11 American designed and manufactured, an armed and armoured amphibious tracked personnel or cargo transporter.
12 Surrey Heritage Centre Archive, QRWS/8/2/14. Report by CO dated 1 Apr 1945.

Members of 1/5th Battalion move along congested roads in Germany. (Fernando Esteve collection)

Part of the Victory Parade in Berlin that 1/5th Battalion was involved with in July 1945. (Fernando Esteve collection)

the regimental flag bringing a fitting end to its fight against Germany.[13] On 11 June it was moved to Bad Segeburg and then ended up travelling to Berlin.

On 21 July, the British held a Victory Parade through the ruined streets of Berlin to commemorate and celebrate the end of the war. Around 10,000 troops of the British 7th Armoured Division paraded under review by British Prime Minister Winston Churchill and Field Marshal Bernard Montgomery. Fernando Esteve was now a corporal and was mentioned 'in recognition of gallant and distinguished service' in the King's Honours List of April 1946.[14]

---

13 Surrey Heritage Centre Archive, QRWS/8/2/14. Report by CO dated 17 May 1945.
14 Supplement to the *London Gazette*, 2 April 1946.

Corporal Fernando Esteve stands next to a colleague. Photograph taken at the end of the war in Germany. (Fernando Esteve collection)

Corporal Fernando Esteve. He fought in British Army uniform from August 1940 until mid-1946. (Fernando Esteve collection)

Flying Through the Smoke

Two other individuals were to pay the ultimate sacrifice as members of the airborne fraternity. Lucío Sauquillo Echevarría and José 'Joe' María Irala were Basque refugee children who had remained in Britain at the beginning of the war. Both volunteered to join the British Army in 1943 and transferred to airborne forces. Lucío Sauquillo Echevarría was killed a few days after D-Day as a member of 12th Parachute Battalion in the area of Breville. He had already lost two brothers in the Spanish Civil War. 'Joe' María Irala died of his wounds during fighting at Arnhem in September 1944.

In 1937 public opinion was outraged by the bombing of Guernica in Spain. It had been the first ever use of saturation bombing on a civilian population and drew worldwide indignation and shock. Shortly after, the Basque Government made a plea to nations to give temporary asylum to Basque children. The British Government adhered to its policy of non-intervention in the Spanish Civil War. However, the Duchess of Atholl, President of the National Joint Committee (NJC) for Spanish Relief, took up the campaign to urge the government to accept the Basque children and finally, permission was grudgingly given.[15] There was a catch, however, the Government refused to be responsible financially for the children, saying that it would violate the non-intervention pact. By the end of April 1937, the NJC had raised over £20,000. In Spain, Mrs Leah Manning had gathered over 4,000 children to evacuate to France and Britain. The plan was to shelter them in the country for six months before they were to be repatriated. A reception camp began to be constructed in Southampton. By mid-May the British Government had agreed to allow 2,000 children, 100 teachers and 15 priests to enter the country. On 31 May, various groups met in the House of Commons and it was agreed to set up a new organisation called the Basque Children's Committee. It would be headed up by the Duchess of Atholl with Miss Eleanor Rathbone and Mr H. Tewson (from the Trades Union Congress – the TUC) as vice presidents.[16] This new committee would have to guarantee funding for the care of the Basque refugee children during their stay in the country.

Meanwhile, in Spain, the children left for Britain on the steamship SS *Habana* on 21 May 1937. The ship was supposed to carry around 800 passengers and now carried 3,840 children, 80 teachers, 120 helpers, 15 catholic priests and two doctors. The crossing was cramped and very rough, but by 23 May *Habana* had arrived in Southampton.[17] A camp had now been established at North Stoneham in Eastleigh. It was soon realised, however, that the children would need to be distributed across Britain to separate sanctuaries. This started with immediate effect and by the end of June 2,529 children had left the camp.[18] A total of 45 'colonies' were established by the end of the year across the country. Huge debates now raged across society, including in the Houses of Parliament, about repatriating the children.[19] This even included false rumours going round from Spanish Nationalists that the children were being used for propaganda. The first groups of children to be repatriated started in early 1938 but by February 1938 there were still some 2,500 children remaining in Britain. This was reduced to just some 1,600 by the end of the year. The NJC also now organised for many of the children to be

---

15 TNA, HO 213/287, letter from Mr W. Roberts to the Home Office, 27 April 1937.
16 Luís Monferer Catalán, *Odisea en Albion* (Madrid: Ediciones de la Torre, 2007), pp.37–39.
17 <www.basquechildren.org/colonies/history>. Accessed 1 March 2021.
18 Luís Monferer Catalán, *Odisea en Albion*, p.43.
19 Volume 107: Hansard, *Refugee Children From Spain*, debated Tuesday 2 November 1937, <https://hansard.parliament.uk/Lords/1937-11-02/debates/0f5c2cde-a65d-4f2b-9915-64628ebdbd84/RefugeeChildrenFromSpain?highlight=refugee%20children%20from%20spain#contribution-f0e47155-ffeb-41cd-88aa-a50907c7a13c>. Accessed 15 August 2023.

housed and 'adopted' by individual families.[20] Various fund-raising activities continued to take place to support the children. By April 1939, when the Spanish Civil War ended, there were still 1,500 children who had not been repatriated. This figure fell to just under 600 by the end of the year. In July 1942, the British Government no longer considered the Basque refugee children as 'enemy aliens' and so they were able to get full support from the state – there remained 416 children in the country.[21]

In the summer of 1945, Luís Sauquillo Ereñaga, a Basque politician from *Acción Nacionalista Vasca* (Basque Nationalist Action), arrived in Paris from Cordes-sur-Ciel to visit the Basque Government delegation. He was from Aretxabaleta, a town northwest of Vitoria, nestled in the Basque hills that resembled a Swiss scene. While he was in Paris he found out that his son Lucío had been killed in action in June 1944. His other son, Gabriel, was alive. But the blow was even harder to take because Luís had lost two other sons fighting in the Spanish Civil War. One had been killed in action and the other shot by the Nationalists. What was worse, was that he found out that Lucío had enlisted to join the British Army without his consent, something which had been impossible for him to prevent. Lucío was born in 1923 and so when he signed up for the British Army he was 19, which was possible at the time since the age bracket for recruiting was 18 to 41. He and his brother Gabriel had arrived on the *Habana* in 1937 and, by the time the war broke out, were based in the Midlands and remained in Britain due to their parents being exiled in France. It seems that Gabriel stayed in the Midlands and Lucío moved to Scarborough where he began his apprenticeship as an electrician. He started a relationship with a local girl named Olive Annie Agar and she gave birth to a son called Harry in Carlin How on 6 December 1941. The couple did not marry.[22]

According to his army record, 14411756 Private Lucío Sauquillo Echevarría enlisted on 16 November 1942 and started his training at 99 Primary Training Corps where he carried out his basic training before joining the Royal Electrical Mechanical Engineers (REME) as a craftsman in 100 Company REME on 17 February 1943. The REME had only been established in October of that year and, given his electrical skills, he seems to have been an ideal fit. On 14 September he transferred to the Army Air Corps and subsequently joined the 12th (Yorkshire) Parachute Battalion which had been established in May of that year. The battalion was part of the 5th Parachute Brigade, 6th Airborne Division, formed in direct anticipation of the much anticipated Normandy landings. Originally, the Battalion had been 10th Battalion Green Howards. Intensive training soon followed, including parachute training itself at Ringway. It was then based at Larkhill in Wiltshire, north of the iconic Stonehenge. In October 1943, the Battalion carried out a tour of Yorkshire and had a spot of leave which was very well received.

On the return to Larkhill, hard work began again in early 1944 as time was getting short before D-Day. The general plan for the part to be played in Normandy by the 6th Airborne Division was revealed to senior officers many days in advance of the actual operation. The following primary tasks were given to it:

a. The capture of the bridges at Ranville and Benouville.
b. The destruction or neutralisation of the coastal battery at Franceville Plage (later known as Merville Battery).
c. The destruction of the bridges over the River Dives at Varaville, Robehomme, Bures and Troan to delay the enemy.

---

20 TNA, HO 213/289, letters updating on the Situation Regarding the Basque Refugee Children.
21 Luís Monferer Catalán, *Odisea en Albion*, p.76.
22 Guillermo Tabernilla and Ander González, *Combatientes Vascos en la Segunda Guerra Mundial, Fighting Basques Project* (Madrid: Desperta Ferro Ediciones SLNE, 2018), pp.78–79.

d. Subsequently, carry out a mop-up operation between the Rivers Orne and Dives and then operate offensively against any enemy reserves moving from the east and south-east.[23]

At the end of May, and 10 days before the eventual invasion date, the Battalion moved to Keevil aerodrome. Parachuting into Normandy at 0100 on 6 June 1944, 12th (Yorkshire) Parachute Battalion dropped into its drop zone and was soon assembling at its rendezvous in a stone quarry near a road running parallel to the River Orne and the canal. The battalion were to guard the east bank, facing south towards Caen and by 0315 it was moving off towards Ranville. The village was reached without the enemy being encountered, and the Battalion's companies deployed to their allotted positions, digging in. The first German counter-attack came in C Company's area at around 1130 and consisted of some 100 infantry and a few tanks. It was repelled but at a cost to the company. Two tanks were knocked out by anti-tank guns in B Company's positions. A Company pushed forward beyond C Company. A visit by Major General R.N. Gale passed on the information that the bridges had been captured intact, though the 7th Battalion on the opposite bank were meeting tough opposition. Early the next day a company from the 1st Battalion Royal Ulster Regiment (1 RUR) moved forward of A Company but was driven back. Three German tanks were then destroyed. 1 RUR advanced and attacked, capturing Longueval one and a half miles south towards Caen. Just before dusk, 12th (Yorkshire) Parachute Battalion was relieved in place and withdrew to a rest area close to the Chateau de Guernon in Ranville, where it remained until later the following day. On 9 June the Battalion received orders to relieve 1st RUR at Longueval but, due to continued heavy mortar fire, it was decided to withdraw the Battalion back to near Ranville and try to retrieve the casualties. They rested and reorganised over the day and were then placed under the command of 1 Special Service Brigade moving to Hauger and then taking up positions north to Amfreville. An attack on Breville was needed and at 2215 on 12 June the battalion attacked with B Company in the lead. A series of friendly fire and counter barrages caused a great deal of casualties and took their toll. Amongst the three officers and 28 others ranks killed that day was the commanding officer, Lieutenant Colonel A.P. Johnson who was posthumously awarded the Distinguished Service Order. A further five officers and some 100 other ranks were wounded in action. Although depleted in numbers, reinforcements were received from within the brigade and the battalion continued to fight on as a unit.[24] Sadly, Lucío was amongst those severely injured on 12 June and died of his wounds the following day. He is buried at the Commonwealth War Graves Cemetery at Hermanville.

14428239 Trooper José 'Joe' María Irala y Vara was born in Bilbao on 15 October 1923 and lived in the town of Getxo before he was evacuated to England, with his brother Rafael, in 1937. By the end of the Spanish Civil War, they were not claimed by his parents, because they had gone into exile in Bayonne and felt that it would be safer for the brothers to remain in Britain.[25] Between 1941 and 1943 Joe lived in the Midlands and was residing with a Mrs Woodbine in Dudley. At this

---

23 Lieutenant Colonel T. B. H. Otway DSO, *Official History of the Second World War, Army, Airborne Forces*, (London: The War Office, 1951. reprinted by The Naval & Military Press), pp.173–173.
24 TNA, WO 171/1245, Allied Expeditionary Force, North-West Europe (British Element): War Diaries, Second World War, Army Air Corps, Parachute Regiments, War Diary for 12 Battalion, June 1944.
25 Guillermo Tabernilla and Ander González, *Combatientes Vascos en la Segunda Guerra Mundial,* pp.79–82. Towards the end of the Spanish Civil War, the Franco Regime had already begun to put pressure on the British authorities to release the Basque refugee children. Joe's father had written to the Basque Evacuation Committee: 'I authorize nobody under any motive of pretext to take neither of my sons José María Irala y Vara and Rafael Irala y Vara out of England. They are being cared for delicately and exquisitely by the amazing Miss Leah Manning and respectable English authorities to whom I am very grateful. The colony where my sons are at is: The old hospital – Park Lodge Lane – Wakefield'.

The grave of 14411756 Private Lucío Sauquillo Echevarría at Hermanville Cemetery. (Paul Woodadge)

stage, his parents had returned to Spain and were living in Madrid. Joe enlisted into the British Army on 6 April 1943 in Birmingham and was sent to initial training, and then on to 52 Training Regiment, becoming a member of the Royal Armoured Corps. His training continued all of that year until he joined the 1st Airborne Reconnaissance Squadron on 3 April 1944.

The 1st Airborne Reconnaissance Squadron was a Reconnaissance Corps unit formed as part of the 1st Airborne Division and which saw service in North Africa, Italy, Arnhem and finally in Norway. The Reconnaissance Corps was established in 1941 and was intended to be an elite part of the British Army which could man fast vehicles while delivering fire power. It was put on a par with the commandos and paratroopers. Initially known as the 1 Airlanding Reconnaissance Squadron, its main role was to obtain and pass back information on the battlefield but, due to its fire power and mobility, it was often used as an attack force or emergency defence force as circumstances required. Because of the available air transport capacity, the Reconnaissance Squadron was restricted to airborne jeeps which were landed in Horsa gliders. Commanded by Major Freddie Gough, a strict disciplinarian, the squadron was soon licked into shape to become 'the best of the best' and was busy in North Africa and Italy. Once back in Britain at the end of 1943 it was housed in Spalding in Lincolnshire before eventually moving to Ruskington in early 1944. It soon became clear that because of the scarcity of glider resources, a contingent from the squadron would be required to jump into operations. On parade, every man in the squadron volunteered to carry out parachute training and thus the 1st Airborne Reconnaissance Squadron was born. Joe attended parachute training course number 109 at Ringway from 27 March to 7 April. Intensive training was now carried out and the squadron members underwent a very frustrating period as 16 consecutive operations were aborted in the spring and summer of 1944. But in the end, preparations for Operation MARKET GARDEN meant that the squadron would be put to use.

Joe Irala, D Troop, 1st Airborne Reconnaissance Squadron. (www.paradata.org.uk)

Operation MARKET GARDEN was the ambitious plan of Field Marshal Bernard Montgomery and was expected to result in the capture of a series of bridges in Holland over the Maas, Waal and Rhine rivers. It would involve American, British and Polish airborne forces who would wait for the arrival of their own armoured columns. The plan was to then launch an offensive to compromise the German Fifteenth Army which would consequently bring a quick end to the war at the end of 1944, after a push across the Ruhr basin and finally the arrival in Berlin. It would be up to British paratroopers to capture and secure the Arnhem Bridge on the Rhine, the furthest distant of all of the bridges. This was the biggest airborne operation of the whole of the Second World War up to that point.

After several postponements, the squadron was eventually ordered to deploy and on 16 September it carried out its final preparations and briefings. The following day, the first glider elements consisting of 45 men and 22 Horsa gliders containing the squadron's jeeps and heavier equipment, took off at 1020 from Tarrant Rushton Aerodrome. The parachute element of 160 men and eight Dakotas took off from Barkston Heath near Grantham at 1100.[26] Joe was a member of

---

26 TNA, WO 171/406, 1 Airborne Reconnaissance Squadron, September 1944.

'FLYING THROUGH THE SMOKE' 231

Site of the main Drop Zone X-ray today. (Author's collection)

The Hartenstein Hotel today. (Author's collection)

10 Section in D Troop and he parachuted into Drop Zone X-ray (DZ X) later that day whereupon he met up with his section officer, Lieutenant John Marshall. The DZ was to the west of Arnhem, a city situated on both banks of the rivers Nederrijn and Sint-Jansbeek. They set off north and made their way to the rendezvous point near the corner of a wood and south of the railway line but somehow took a wrong turn when the squadron set off and were heading off towards Renkun, which sits on the banks of the Nederrijn. An encounter with a German armoured vehicle made them retrace their route, but they then headed towards Arnhem. Marshall would later recall 'I saw this German armoured car somewhere up on the horizon and, as I didn't think that jeeps and armoured cars really went together, I said to Irala, 'Let's get the hell out of it.' By then, they were shooting down the road at us, so we backed out, skedaddled away and found another road for ourselves.' They eventually managed to link back up with the squadron, back near the landing zone, before the end of the day. [27]

---

27 John Fairey, *Remember Arnhem: Story of the First Airborne Reconnaissance Squadron at Arnhem* (Bearsden: Peaton Press, 1990), p.53.

Between 1240 and 1430 on that day, Freddy Gough's men had parachuted into the DZ and mounted their jeeps. Although they were forced to make do with fewer than three-quarters of their vehicles, they sped towards neighbouring Oosterbeek with the aim of reaching the Arnhem Bridge before the infantry relying on the firepower of their Vickers K machine guns and towed 20mm Polsten guns. But their lack of armour soon became strikingly clear as the vanguard jeeps fell into an ambush set up by German armoured vehicles. It was immediately apparent that Allied intelligence had made the serious mistake of not detecting the presence of two SS Panzer divisions, even though they were quite far from their assembly areas. In the end, Gough's men could not advance to Arnhem as the vanguard as planned. The following days were extremely frustrating for the Squadron as it constantly tried to see if they could find a way round the German opposition and blocking positions, until it was realised that it was hopeless. Squadron vehicles also increased their efforts to maintain communication between Arnhem and Oosterbeek, where General Urquhart, commander of the 1st Airborne Division, had set up his command post. The troops in Arnhem also had to prepare the way for the arrival of Polish Airborne troops and so the Squadron was also designated as a mobile reserve to open a route in for the Poles. On Wednesday 20 September, the main body of the Squadron was gathered opposite the Hartenstein Hotel, when it was reported that a German self-propelled gun was heading their way from the Oosterbeek crossroads. It was also the day that the German armoured vehicles finally made their way to the Arnhem Bridge, thus sealing the fate of the British soldiers in the area as house-to-house fighting began in earnest. In the scramble to get the jeeps clear, Joe Irala was caught by a burst of machine gun fire. *Remember Arnhem* sums up what happened next:

> On a signal, there was a simultaneous mounting of the vehicles and the Squadron moved off at speed. As the jeeps revved away, a burst of machine-gun fire from the armoured vehicle suddenly raked across the last one. The jeep had already begun to move, but Trooper 'Joe' Irala, who was in the act of jumping on, was hit. John Marshall remembers that, as they pulled him aboard, he complained about having been shot in the leg, although it was obvious to the others that it was much more serious. 'When I saw what had happened to him,' said Marshall, 'I drove straight across to the first-aid post at the Hartenstein. We were shot at continuously on the way, but I didn't pay any attention to it. By the time we'd arrived, "Joe" was unconscious.' In fact, Irala, the boy who had come from Spain to fight for the British, had taken a machine-gun burst full in the stomach, and he died just thirty minutes later. [Note: This is probably a statement meant for the family, as he actually died at the St Elizabeth's Hospital two days later and was buried there.] For Marshall personally, it was a particularly tragic episode, as there was a strong bond of friendship between the two men which transcended the difference in rank. 'I still remember him today,' said John Marshall, 'as a wonderful soldier – highly intelligent, immensely brave, and with a capacity, which the average Englishman doesn't have, for giving enormous personal loyalty.'[28]

Joe was taken to the Hartenstein RAP (Regimental Aid Post), where he became unconscious and was then transported to the St Elizabeth's Hospital in Arnhem, where he died two days later on 22 September and was buried. He was just 20 years old. The Squadron lost 29 men during the operation, most of who are now buried at Oosterbeek War Cemetery, Arnhem, where Joe now lies at rest.

---

28 John Fairey, *Remember Arnhem: Story of the First Airborne Reconnaissance Squadron at Arnhem* (Bearsden: Peaton Press, 1990), p.119.

The grave of Trooper 'Joe' Irala who died of his wounds on 22 September 1945. (Author's collection)

The grave of 2719596 Guardsman Marcial Fernández, 2nd Irish Guards. (Author's collection)

Close to where Joe is buried lies the grave of 2719596 Guardsman Marcial Fernández, 2nd Irish Guards who was 26 years old when he was killed near Arnhem on 21 September. In the attack from the south to link up with airborne forces in the Arnhem areas, the Irish Guards were the spearhead of XXX Corps' advance to Eindhoven. By 18 September the Irish Guards had reached their objective and were outside Son while 14 Field Company Royal Engineers built a 110 feet standard build Bailey Bridge to aid the advance. This bridge was completed the following day, and XXX Corps continued their advance with 2nd Irish Guards leading and soon began to link up with the US 82nd Airborne Division which was at Nijmegen. The advance had to be halted, however, because the 82nd was not able to take the bridge. By the evening of 20 September, the bridge was finally taken but the Guards Division was having to defend its rear from continuous German attacks as well as trying to secure Nijmegen. It was to be during one of these attacks that Marcial was killed in action on 21 September. Additionally, the Germans had begun to launch major counterattacks on both sides of the corridor held by the Allies, known as 'Hell's Highway', between Eindhoven and Nijmegen. 43rd (Wessex) Infantry Division was able to establish a link with 1st Airborne Division which was still holding out despite countless attacks on its perimeter but XXX Corps was unable to get troops across to reinforce. The evacuation of the survivors across the Lower Rhine began on the night of 25 September. This costly defeat meant that Operation MARKET GARDEN was a failure, but at least the Allies had managed to establish a lodgement area from which they could launch an offensive into the German Rhineland. Which they did in March 1945.[29]

Fighting with the Spanish Maquisards

In January 2019 the people of Foix and Pamiers in the Ariège region of the French Pyrenees, were saddened to hear of the death of Alfonso Canovas García. Known as the 'French Sergeant' and part of the Allied AUBE mission parachuted into Ariège in 1944, he would be sorely missed by many. But Alfonso was not just someone who fought in British Army uniform in France, it would be remiss to not mention his entire family as well; they were well-known figures in the region and have a remarkable story.

Alfonso's parents, Antonia García Navarro and Antonio Canovas Alonso moved the family to the region in 1928 as economic immigrants from Almería in southeast Spain. They had struggled to make ends meet in Almería and so found work in France to live a better life. With the outbreak of the Civil War back in Spain, Antonio decided to return with the family but left his mother in France. They settled in Manresa, Catalunya. Alfonso had a sister, Ángeles, but his older brother, also named Antonio after his father, was 14 and decided to leave Manresa to fight on the Aragón Front. This was to be a baptism of fire for him. Due to his age, his commander used him as a courier and also involved him in supplying his unit at the front, something which generally kept Antonio out of danger. After a few months, he left the front and instead took up work in a munitions factory. At the end of the war the whole family returned to France to rejoin the grandmother who had continued to live in Pamiers. Alfonso's father was interned at Vernet d'Arriège for some months in 1939 but soon released. Ironically, he decided to return to Spain in 1943, was immediately imprisoned by the Franco Regime, and only released once the Second World War was over. In 1942, Alfonso's older brother was denounced to the Vichy authorities and arrested. This was due to the discovery that he was a member of *Reconquista De España*, a Spanish organisation with communist sympathies. Incarcerated initially in Foix, then Toulouse (in Furgole military

---

29 TNA, WO 171/1256, 2 Irish Guards (Armoured Battalion) War Diary, Jan to Dec 1944.

prison), Antonio was sent to a concentration camp in Noé and then to Vernet d'Ariège. Sentenced to one year in prison, he served the rest of this sentence in prison in Foix, and was then sent back to Vernet. On 27 May 1942, he was part of a deportation convoy of about 350 men, two-thirds of whom were sent to Alderney concentration camp in the German-occupied Channel Islands. A few prisoners, including Antonio, were held for a few days in a Parisian barracks, then taken to Willemzagen labour camp near Berlin as political prisoners. He managed to escape with some Spanish friends but was re-arrested in Munich. He was able to escape a second time and get to Switzerland where he was able to seek refuge. He had lost so much weight by this stage he only weighed 40 kilos. In 1945 Antonio was told by the Swiss authorities that he had to be repatriated – to Spain! Not wanting to be incarcerated by the Franco Regime, he managed to escape into France and get back to his family. A Spanish Civil War veteran, prisoner of war and escapee, Antonio was not able to get his French citizenship until 1981 after a lifetime of work in Pamiers.

Meanwhile, Alfonso had been lucky and managed to go back to work following his return from Spain in 1939. In 1943 he was working in Lourdes but decided that he needed to go back to Spain. Not long after, he was in Barcelona living in an uncle's house. His idea was to enlist and join the Allies in North Africa. When he found out that the British and Americans were allowing Frenchmen into their ranks he jumped at the chance and made his way to the British Consulate in the city where he declared he was French. A few weeks later, and armed with the necessary documentation, he travelled to the south of Spain with three other Spaniards intending to reach Gibraltar. From there he crossed over the Mediterranean to Casablanca. Initially, it seems that Alfonso joined the French and enlisted as a soldier in Leclerc's French 2nd Armoured Division before deciding to join the British.

1330008 Private Alfonso Canovas enlisted in Algiers on 16 January 1944 and was soon listed as a member of 357 (Alien) Company in the Pioneer Corps. Shortly after enlisting, Alfonso volunteered for special training along with another 10 Spaniards. This was in order to train as a member of the SOE in support of the resistance in southern France as part of the MASSINGHAM Mission in North Africa, which was based at Club des Pins. It was during this training that he met Lieutenant Marcel Bigeard who asked him if he knew the Ariège!

Born in 1916 into a staunchly patriotic working-class family, Marcel Bigeard was the son of a railway worker. He had served as a warrant officer on the Maginot Line, in the fortified sector of Hoffen in Alsace, during the invasion of France. After internment, he escaped to Africa where he was eventually commissioned into de Gaulle's Free French forces. After the war, Bigeard became one of France's most adored and decorated military commanders and was a veteran of a further two wars. As well as fighting in the Second World War, he was also in France's colonial wars in Indochina and Algeria. He commanded the *6ᵉ Bataillon de Parachutistes Coloniaux* at Diện Biên Phù in 1954 and a parachute battalion in the Battle for Algiers in 1957. In a thirty-year career, he rose from the lowest rank to become a French four-star general.[30]

The AUBE mission was launched on 8 August 1944. The team for the operation consisted of its commander, Bigeard (*nom de guerre* Aube), the Englishman Major Bill Probert (*nom de guerre* Krypte), the Canadian Lieutenant John Deller (*nom de guerre* Hibou), the Frenchman 2nd Lieutenant Grangeaud (*nom de guerre* Rale) and the Spaniard Sergeant Alfonso Canovas (*nom de guerre* Sergeant Wilson). The flight in was a long one. Departing from the North African coast, Alfonso reported that they were able to see the Balearic Islands en route and the flight was smooth

---

[30] Martin Childs, 'General Marcel Bigeard: Soldier who Served in Three Conflicts and Became an Expert on Counter-Insurgency,' *The Independent*, Thursday 1 July 2010, <www.independent.co.uk/news/obituaries/general-marcel-bigeard-soldier-who-served-in-three-conflicts-and-became-an-expert-on-counterinsurgency-2015150.html>. Accessed 12 June 2023.

A photo of three of the key officers of the AUBE Mission. On the left is Major Bill Probert, in the centre is Pascual Gimeno who led the local brigade of the *Agrupación de Guerrilleros Españoles* and on the right is *Commandant* Marcel Bigeard. (Alfonso Canovas collection)

and they were well treated by the crew.[31] The team was dropped by RAF Halifax number 896 from 624 Squadron flown by Flight Sergeant Kirk, on the night of 7 August. As well as the five agents, a further 15 containers and five packages were also parachuted in. These contained an array of equipment for the team as they knew they would be staying for some time.[32]

Five months earlier, on the night of 9/10 April, Captain Peter Lake had parachuted into the Dordogne as a member of the SOE to train and assist the *maquis* and French Resistance. The first two *maquis* groups he instructed were:

> ... composed mostly of Spaniards, led by a Spanish ex-artillery captain (Carlos). Many of them were tough, experienced veterans of the Civil War in Spain, well-disciplined and often well versed in modern explosives. Some of the best work in that area was done by Carlos following the June 6th landings ... blowing of bridges and successful guerrilla tactics against German columns ...[33]

Many Spanish *maquis* groups had been fully operational in southern France for some time. For the AUBE mission the SOE would carry out operations with other Spaniards, namely the local brigade of the *Agrupación de Guerrilleros Españoles*, an all-Spanish component of France's communist-led FTP. It was commanded by 28-year-old Pascual Gimeno, known locally by his *nom de guerre*, Royo. His brigade was about 225 strong and provided the nucleus of resistance in the Ariège. Major Bill Probert was an experienced British officer who had seen prior service in Madagascar and North Africa and immediately noticed how badly armed the Spaniards were, having only

---

31 TNA, GR 28P4 3277, Report by Alfonso Canovas, dated 7 October 1944.
32 TNA, HS9-150-6, Report by Commandant Bigeard, dated 15 September 1944.
33 TNA, HS9-877-5, Report by Captain Peter Lake on activities in France in 1944, dated 11 October 1944.

A newspaper article cutting from the 1980s about the liberation of the Ariège in 1944. The photo with the parachute shows Alfonso Canovas on the left with Lieutenant Marcel Bigeard. (Alfonso Canovas collection)

a few weapons and little ammunition. As a consequence of *Commandant* Bigeard's request to send more arms and ammunition, four different drops took place between 8 and 16 August. These drops included a Hotchkiss machine gun, Bren and Browning machine guns and also Mills grenades and a great deal of ammunition. The containers' contents were then split evenly between the Spaniards and the other French Resistance groups in the area. But the reality was that, given the increase in German activity in the area, the arms were taken from the containers, the *maquisards* were given a ten-minute course of instruction on the weapons' use and then immediately dispatched to ambush convoys.[34]

Such tactics bore immediate results with an initial attack resulting in 30 German casualties where, even though the Hotchkiss had a stoppage, the Spaniards were able to continue their attack with Mills grenades. The biggest part of the joint SOE/*maquis* activities soon followed with an attack on Foix, the Ariège's principal town. The German garrison in the town had fortified areas with machine gun nests in prominent places and was, in fact, larger than expected, being some 150 strong. They had also been expecting the attack to take place. Nevertheless, Royo led his men into the attack. Pinned down by machine gun fire from the main bridge in the town, Alfonso now led a small team in a daring push to ensure the attack was successful. The story of this daring action is summed up in Alfonso's Military Medal citation:

> This N.C.O. volunteered for a mission to work with the resistance and was parachuted into the Aude on the 6th of August 1944. He was of great assistance in organising local groups and in leading operations against the enemy.
>
> During the attack on Foix on the 19th of August, the Spanish *maquis* groups were held up by two German Machine Guns situated on the bridge covering the main entries into the town. Sjt CANOVAS and the Spanish Maquisards armed with one Bren and Stens, forded the Ariège below and into the rear of the town where they engaged the German Garrison in fierce street fighting. Sjt CANOVAS received a bullet in the leg but continued to fight with exemplary courage. This attack forced the Germans to withdraw the machine guns from the bridge, then permitting the main maquis forces to enter the town.
>
> In subsequent operations on the 20th, 21st and 22nd August, Sjt CANOVAS continued to show great coolness and courage and his devotion to duty was a source of inspiration.[35]

The impact of the small SOE team continued over the following days. On 20 August, an 18-truck convoy at Prayols, south of Foix, was intercepted and after a two and a half hour battle, 50 Germans were killed, 40 wounded and another 40 captured for the loss of one Spanish officer killed. The next day, another large German force was attacked on the road between Foix and St-Girons by some 60 Spaniards. A 36 hour stop-start battle continued until the Germans gave themselves up resulting in 220 men killed, 120 wounded, 1,250 taken prisoner and dozens of trucks, 43 anti-tank guns and large quantities of arms and ammunition captured, against 15 killed and 40 wounded on the French-Spanish-British side. Despite his injuries a few days previously, Alfonso continued to be in the thick of things. Major Probert both liked and admired Royo and his men, while he suspected that they could be ruthless, too. The alleged killing of 25 German officers captured at Foix, apparently at the end of SOE-delivered submachine guns and grenades, was a sad end to operations in the area. It was reported that while these prisoners were held in a stable, their Spanish

---

34 TNA, HS9-150-6.
35 TNA, WO 373/98/802, Military Medal citation for Sjt Canovas.

Alfonso Canovas later in life back in Saverdun in 2004. He is wearing his parachute Regiment beret and badge, and his Military Medal. (Alfonso Canovas collection)

guards 'tossed a dozen or so Mills grenades among the sleeping officers and completed their work with Stens and revolvers.'[36]

A few weeks after the operations in the Ariège, *Commandant* Bigeard ordered Alfonso to Avignon, where MASSINGHAM's HQ now was (known as the Special Projects Operations Centre/Center) to be stood by for operations elsewhere. It is believed that he also travelled to Paris where he was stationed for some time. By early 1945 he was in Great Britain where he carried out further parachute and special forces training as part of a team to be used in the Far East against Japan. He was discharged from the army in October 1945, married and settled in Blackpool.

Despite not being part of large groups of Spaniards serving together in the British Army, it is important to highlight the brave few who were also continuing the fight against fascism far and wide. Most of these men would settle in Britain but some, as we have seen, paid the ultimate sacrifice.

---

36 TNA, HS9-150-6.

Chapter 8

'Did You Make It Safe?'

The End of the War And New Beginnings

> Españolito que vienes
> al mundo te guarde Dios.
> una de las dos Españas
> ha de helarte el corazón.
>   Antonio Machado, *Poesías completas*

The end of the Second World War brought a great deal of uncertainty to the Spaniards who had ended up in Great Britain. While the 300 or so members of No.1 Spanish Company, SAS and No.50 Middle East Commando were given the immediate opportunity to stay in the United Kingdom, others were not so lucky. This is where 13809776 Agustín Roa Ventura and others played an important role. As one of the representatives of the three companies that had been sent from North Africa, he and a few others visited London shortly after the war to petition Labour MPs regarding the Spanish veterans' plight.[1] By mid-1946 it was agreed that the Spaniards who had been recruited in North Africa and were now stationed in Britain would not need to go back and would be given the opportunity to stay in Britain. Many Spaniards did, but many decided to go elsewhere, such as Mexico where a large exiled Spanish Republican community was now based. What was evident, though, was that many of these veterans felt that Britain had let them down by not going after Franco next. However, many stayed and settled across the United Kingdom and applied for naturalisation. Some remained politically active during the period of the Franco Regime and in London a Spanish Ex-Servicemen's Association was set up in 1960, which was involved in the organisation of protests and campaigns, building awareness of the Franco Regime in Britain.[2] By the time of Franco's death in 1975, many of the exiled groups in Britain were fully established with strong ties across society. While many Spaniards had taken up British nationality, many others did not, although they remained in the country. Once Spain entered its *Transición* to democracy, many returned to Spain to visit, and a large number would retire in their homeland.

---

1 Hansard, Volume 420: Debate on Pioneer Corps (Release of Aliens), 5 March 1946, <https://hansard.parliament.uk/Commons/1946-03-18/debates/5f3727f5-638a-4cb0-b5a7-132a370f3043/StraitsSettlements(Repeal)BillLords?highlight=release%20aliens#contribution-20dd2598-4f1e-41ae-95a7-72d568159be1>. Accessed 12 December 2022. Hansard, Volume 423: Debate on Aliens (Place of Release), 4 June 1946, <https://hansard.parliament.uk/Commons/1946-06-04/debates/59c92b60-2336-41f9-a028-26810bc579cf/Aliens(PlaceOfRelease)>. Accessed 12 December 2022.
2 Luís Monferrer Catalán, *Odisea en Albión: Los Republicanos Españoles Exiliados En Gran Bretaña (1936 – 1977)* (Madrid: Ediciones de la Torre, 2007), p.393.

Exiled Republicans and the War

In order to better understand how things progressed for Spaniards who served in the British Army once the war finished, it is probably worth explaining a little about the exiled Spanish Republican groups that had been set up in Britain during the war, and what support mechanisms they established for Spaniards. By the autumn of 1940, Britain's official political take on Franco's Spain was that it wanted to appease him while at the same time ensure he remained neutral. In fact Britain had dispatched Hoare to Spain because it wanted to 'keep Spain neutral, to support and strengthen the elements in Spain desiring to maintain neutrality, to counter and reduce German and Italian influence and to obtain greater facilities for our own propaganda.'[3] As such, this explained the unwillingness of the British Government (at least in an overt way) to fully support the arrival of refugees from Spain early on in the war. This had also been the case in the summer of 1939, but many exiled Spanish Republicans had been allowed to move to Britain as 'political' or 'war refugees' because the Government had not wished to discriminate against different refugee groups. As such, many of the exiled Spanish elites, who had arrived in Britain at the end of the Spanish Civil War in the summer of 1939, were able to find work in the country.

It must be emphasised though that Britain had, in fact, only accepted a few hundred refugees out of the tens of thousands of Republicans in the camps across southern France after the end of the Spanish Civil War, which increased by late 1940.[4] However, this did not stop Scotland Yard from interviewing all key Spanish Republican political refugees since they were very concerned about the influence the more communist elements might have. In particular, they were concerned about Dr Negrín's influence in Britain while he was in exile in the country. Dr Juan Negrín López was the leader of the *Partido Socialist Obrero Espanol* (*POSE* – the Spanish Socialist Workers' Party) and the last Prime Minister of the Spanish Second Republic during the Spanish Civil War. Between 1939 and 1945 he was also the President of the Council of Ministers of the Second Spanish Republic and the Spanish Republican Government in exile. At the beginning of the war, Negrín decided to openly support the Franco-British alliance against Germany and Italy. He remained in Paris until the fall of France and then moved to London where he resided throughout the war. Negrín was also responsible for the establishment of the *Servicio de Evacuación de Refugiados Españoles* (*SERE* – the Spanish Refugee Evacuation Service) to help Republican exiles. *SERE* had been the main force behind getting exiled Spanish Republicans to Mexico.[5] Elsewhere in exile, other groups were also formed such as the *Junta de Ayuda a los Refugiados Españoles* (*JARE* – Spanish Help to Refugee Group). This organisation was presided over by Indalecio Prieto, a rival in exile to Negrín.

When it comes to understanding the numbers of Spanish exiles in Britain from the early 1930s to the early 1950s, it is only necessary to look at the census figures. The 1951 census gives an indication of the size of the exiled Spanish community at that time. It showed that 6,558 Spanish-born individuals were resident in England and Wales, compared with 4,315 in the previous census of 1931. More than half of these people, 3,309, were living in London.[6] If you delve more deeply into

---

3   Richard Wigg, *Churchill and Spain. The Survival of the Franco Regime 1940–1945* (Brighton: Sussex Academic Press, 2008), p.9.
4   Lala Isla (ed.), *Aventuras en la Nostalgia: Exiliados y Emigrantes Españoles en Londres* (Madrid: Ministerio de Trabajo e Inmigración, 2008), p.14.
5   Lala Isla (ed.), *Aventuras en la Nostalgia: Exiliados y Emigrantes Españoles en Londres,* (Madrid: Ministerio de Trabajo e Inmigración, 2008), pp.121–131.
6   Census 1951, England and Wales: general tables comprising population, ages and marital condition, non-private households, birthplace and nationality, education. General Tables for England and Wales, HMSO, 1956, tables 30 and 33. Jim Jump, 'Spanish Republican Exile Activism, Anguish and Assimilation,' *Theory & Struggle*, Volume 121, <https://doi.org/10.3828/ts.2020.17, pp.134–143>.

the figures during the war and up until the late 1940s, the influx of Spaniards into Britain who had served in the British Army increased the overall community by a great margin with figures for London increasing from 1,777 in 1942 to 2,308 in 1948. This does not, however, take into consideration the many that applied for naturalisation from 1947 onwards which means that these numbers were most likely higher.[7]

On 17 October 1941 a Spanish Exiles Community Centre called *El Hogar Español* (the Spanish Home) was established. It was based at 22 Inverness Terrace, Bayswater in London and opened its doors after a lease had been signed. The opening ceremony was attended by Dr Negrín and had H.G. Wells as its principal English guest speaker. The centre would become a key point of focus over the coming decades as exiled Spanish Republicans settled down and the community expanded. Although London-centric, it remained a very important aspect of Spanish culture, it had a library and held regular events which were widely advertised. Initial funding had been provided by Dr Negrín using exiled Government funds. By the end of the war, it was publishing a regular newsletter (*Spanish Republican News*) which had a wide readership. Herminio Martínez, who was one of the Basque refugee children that had remained in Britain after 1939, later recalled:

> Suddenly, all the pent-up energies of the diverse groups of *Republicanos* were released … Gradually, many of the exiles and refugees tended to move to London. They now had a 'home'. Deep friendships and comradeship were forged. Apart from the socialising and political campaigning, there were some wonderful cultural activities. A mixed choir was formed under the direction of Manolo Lazareno, who had been a professional musicologist in Spain. It was wonderful to see such a diverse set of young exiles taking so well to this work. A theatre group was set up under the direction of Pepe Estruch and a folk-dancing group was run by several other individuals. Also, an excellent football team was established … For many of us who had missed out on living our early life in Spain, it was a priceless opportunity to encounter the richness of Spanish culture.

The Basques and Catalans also set up their own centres in the UK. The *Eusko Etxea* (the Basque Centre) was established in South Kensington before *El Hogar Español* and was funded mostly by the *Partido Nacionalista Vasco* (the Nationalist Basque Party). In the last two years of the war, the centre was particularly active and held many events. One of these was a launch event it organised in December 1944 with Armando Cortesano, a Portuguese exile, as its main speaker. The event called for the establishment of an Iberian Confederation of Nations to be set up post-Franco. As it was attended by a large number of both Spaniards and Portuguese, it is very possible that this is where Francisco Geronimo met his future wife Laura Bravo for the first time. Laura was one of the Basque refugee children who had arrived in Britain in 1937. By 1944 she was an auxiliary nurse and a big supporter of the *Eusko Etxea*, attending many events in London. The centre closed in the late 1940s.

The *Casal Català* (the Catalan House) was established on 25 January 1942 in Hamilton Terrace, London. Key personalities in its establishment were Carles Pi I Sunyer and Dr Trueta. Most of the Catalans who were exiled in Britain became members (some 200). Despite a lot of activity taking place in the centre, *Casal Català* did not attract many more members. However, they continued to commemorate the tragic death of Lluís Companys i Jover. Companys had remained the Head of

---

[7] TNA, HO 213/828, Return of aliens registered as residing within Metropolitan Police District: 1942. For further work carried out on exiled Spaniards in Britain see Luís Monferrer Catalán, *Odisea en Albión: Los Republicanos Españoles Exiliados En Gran Bretaña (1936 – 1977)* (Madrid: Ediciones de la Torre, 2007), pp.64–67.

the Catalan Government during the Spanish Civil War, remaining loyal to the Second Republic. He crossed over to France after the war and was captured by the Gestapo, who then handed him over to Franco. He was executed on 15 October 1940. A few days later, Himmler was hosted by Franco's Foreign Secretary, and brother-in-law, Ramón Serrano Suñer for a tour around Spain. For the fifth commemorations of the death of Companys at *Casal Català* in 1945, two groups of Spaniards serving in the British Army sent their condolences and were added to the list of those sending their sympathies. The first group was of 18 Catalans serving in 361 (Alien) Pioneer Company and the second of 15 Catalans serving in No.1 Spanish Company.[8]

Should I Stay of Should I Go?

When Agustín Roa Ventura first visited London on leave at the end of 1944, he and his Spanish compatriots from 361 Company enjoyed visiting the iconic capital. Initially based in the NAAFI (Navy Army and Air Force Institute) near Victoria Station they soon visited other parts of the city and caught up with exiled Spaniards based in the capital. They even had to take cover when some V1 rockets exploded in the city! Little did they know that by the end of the war, many of them would be settling in the capital.

During 1940 and 1941, Britain was highly interested in the continued neutrality of Spain. Franco's regime also clung to remaining a non-belligerent as domestic crises continued in the country after the Civil War, especially within the economy and in severe food shortages. Mutual existence and survival had been key for both countries in the first few years of the war. Ultimately, Churchill's appeals to the US to support him in helping the Franco Regime on strategic grounds would have long-term consequences for Britain. In the summer of 1941, with everything in the balance for Britain, Franco had even said that the Allies had lost the war, and decided to send the Blue Division to the Eastern Front to support Hitler. This division of mostly falangist volunteers (known as the *División Española de Voluntarios*), fought on the Nazi side from 1941 to 1944. The return of the monarchy in Spain had also been seen as a possibility and was supported by Churchill but Juan Borbón did not prove to be a worthy enough alternative for the time being. Even though 1942 began as badly as 1940 for Britain, it ended with the landings in North Africa and the victory at El Alamein. The tide was turning in the Allies' favour and Franco began to see an opportunity to bargain for crucial economic support whilst also guaranteeing his and Spain's sovereignty, as he turned a blind eye to the TORCH landings. When TORCH took place, the Franco Regime was relieved to an extent, but things remained tense. Reassurances made by both Churchill and the US calmed the waters.[9]

By mid-1943, Franco had secured his position in Spain against internal threats by putting Spain's armed forces under his direct command. He was therefore not troubled when some of his leading generals suggested he give way to the monarchy, and he summarily dismissed many of his senior

---

8   Catalan members of 361 (Alien) Company listed were:
    Joan BERNADES, Josep BERNADES, Rafael BORÍ, Josep CANADELL, Joan GASCÓ, Anton GRAU, Joan GIRONA, Anton MANSOT, Josep MAYDEU, Josep MARTÍ, Joan PALLEJÀ, Josep PEIRÓ, Miquel PEIRÓ, Joaquim PORCAR, Jaume PADRÓ, Óscar ROBERT, Samuel SARRIÓ, Lluís VILÀ
    Catalan members of No.1 Spanish Company were:
    Josep AMILS, Emili BORRÁS, Joan COLOMÉ, Manuel CORTIELLA, Pere DELATORRE, Francesc DALMAU, Josep FERNÁNDEZ, Conrad GONZÁLEZ, Llorenç MONTOURSI, Francesc MUNYOZ, Josep MUNYOZ, Agustí NEGUEROLES, Josep NICOLAU, Miquel ORTÍ, Jaume VAQUER
9   Richard Wigg, *Churchill and Spain: The Survival of the Franco Regime 1940–1945* (Eastbourne: Sussex Academic Press, 2008), pp.52–76.

generals thus making things even harder for the Spanish monarch in exile. Even though the Allies had a powerful stranglehold over the Spanish economy, Franco had a secure enough base in Spain to hold on. With a rivalry building between Britain and the US about what to do regarding Spain, especially over the issue of how to stop Germany from getting its essential wolfram supplies from the country, Franco knew he had a good bargaining position. This became especially apparent when Franco stopped (or severely reduced the amount) supplying Germany with wolfram because of the ceasing of US petrol supplies in January 1944. Churchill's intervention in allowing Spain to have a new supply of oil because it would be serving British strategic interests meant that there was '… no doubt at all the arrangement consolidates Franco' as Anthony Eden said in his diary.[10] As a consequence, Anglo-American relations were damaged, and Franco could see a future opening. Churchill's appeasement of the Franco Regime rankled in Washington political circles, and it was not long before Churchill and Eden were also disagreeing over it. The appointment of José Félix Lequerica as Franco's Foreign Minister in 1944 also showed that Franco wanted to strengthen his links with the US.

As Germany succumbed to the Anglo-American and Soviet forces, Franco attempted a rapprochement with a view to building an alliance against communist Russia. Churchill was not having any of it, stating that 'His majesty's Government [was not] prepared to consider any groupings of powers in Western Europe … on a basis of hostility towards or of the alleged necessity of defence against our Russian allies.'[11] This view was endorsed by the British War Cabinet on 27 November 1944. Key to all of this, from a British perspective, was to ensure that the Spanish left either in exile or underground in Spain were not given the opportunity to undertake unwise and precipitate action that could lead to another civil war in the country. An example of this action had been the failed attack on the Val d'Aran by around 2,500 members of the *Agrupación de los Guerrilleros Españoles* led by Colonel López Tovar. The attack was beaten off quite easily by Franco's forces and many of those who survived were persecuted for years by the regime.[12] By the end of 1944, Churchill had taken on full responsibility regarding Britain's policy over what to do about the 'Spanish anomaly'. Despite being urged to be hard over Franco and state that it would be what Franco did internally in Spain that would affect its position after the war and potential membership of the United Nations, Churchill did not give Franco this final warning. By not being specific enough in his letter to Franco in January 1945 about the barriers preventing him having more friendly relations, he had given Franco another chance to survive.[13] Given the quarantine imposed upon Spain by the soon to be victorious Allies from the end of 1944 onwards, Franco was not overly dismayed and would now have a stronger grip internally while he played the long game.[14]

Back in Britain in April 1945 the first Spanish POWs who had been serving in the British Army arrived in Britain. These were members of the Middle East Commando captured in Crete in 1941. None of them had ever been to Britain and were surprised how intact the country was. Much of the German propaganda in the POW camps had led them to believe that Britain was

---

10 Richard Wigg, *Churchill and Spain: The Survival of the Franco Regime 1940–1945* (Eastbourne: Sussex Academic Press, 2008), p.150.
11 TNA, CAB 66/59/35, Anthony Eden, *Policy Towards Spain*, Cabinet War Office Memorandum, dated 12 December 1944.
12 Robert Gildea and Ismee Tames (eds), *Fighters Across Frontiers: Transnational Resistance in Europe, 1936–48* (Manchester: Manchester University Press, 2020), pp.428–429.
13 Richard Wigg, *Churchill and Spain. The Survival of the Franco Regime 1940–1945* (Eastbourne: Sussex Academic Press, 2008), pp.169–199.
14 Denis Smyth, *Diplomacy and Strategy of Survival, British Policy and Franco's Spain 1940–41* (Cambridge: Cambridge University Press, 1986), pp.242–251.

a wasteland and its population still on their knees. Upon arrival they were housed in a camp somewhere on the South Coast where they were issued clean uniforms, cleaned up and given haircuts. During their incarceration they had been transferred fully to the Pioneer Corps. Most were placed on the nominal roll of 361 Company and were given slightly different tasks, mainly the escorting of soldiers who had gone AWOL back to base. As the Spaniards were regarded as Gibraltarian, they were free to leave but were unable to, due to not having anywhere to actually go! The Joint Committee soon took care of moving them to Brighton after inviting them to some events in the centre of London at the *Eusko Etxea* and elsewhere. They were looked after by the Red Cross and some ladies who lodged them in Hove, Lancing and Worthing. For the majority, arriving in England for the first time after a long period of captivity and war came as a real shock. Of particular interest are the prisoner of war de-briefing notes from the interviews they were given upon arrival in Britain. 6100511/13808241 Tomás Franco García, a native of Zaragoza, had been in Stalags 4b and 4c and been forced to work in factories and quarries. He had little time for the Germans, calling them '100% criminals' and described the Russians who liberated him as having 'No culture. No help given. Plenty of looting.' He was housed by a family in Worthing and was soon escorting AWOL soldiers back to their units. A mundane task, but at least he was able to travel the country and see it for himself. Joaquín Fajardo, who was liberated from a German POW Camp in the spring of 1945, often told his son about some of the places he visited while on POW escort duties. These places included Glasgow, Newcastle, Hereford, Aldershot, Oxford and London. Consequently, he had been able to go to football matches and was even at the famous Chelsea v Moscow Dynamo game in November 1945 which attracted a huge crowd and subsequently Chelsea FC became his passion.[15] Demobilisation came for most of these soldiers in the summer of 1946.

On 1 May 1945, the Red Flag was flying over the Reichstag. The next day Berlin capitulated. *Generaloberst* Alfred Jodl then signed the unconditional surrender of Germany on 7 May – the war in Europe was over. In the wake of Germany's surrender, gates, doors and barriers were opened and the horrors of the concentration camps were uncovered. At Mauthausen, several thousand Spaniards were freed when the Americans arrived on 5 May but nearly 5,000 had perished. Many of the anti-Franco exiles soon thought that his days were numbered, especially after the founding conference of the United Nations in San Francisco between 25 April and 26 June. The Mexican delegation had proposed the exclusion of any country that had been established by any of the states that had fought against the United Nations – this obviously included Spain and was approved. Several people in Spain and elsewhere now believed that the restoration of the monarchy in the country was inevitable.[16]

Back in Britain, the soldiers who had arrived from North Africa and were now based in Radway, near Warwick, were waiting to find out if they would either go to the Far East or be demobilised. With the detonation of an atomic bomb over Hiroshima on 6 August and then over Nagasaki on 9 August and the subsequent surrender of Japan, it was clear that the Far East was now no longer likely. Concern soon grew amongst the Spaniards as rumours spread of their potential return to North Africa.

A few weeks later, Agustín Roa Ventura asked to meet with his commanding officer, Major Muirhead. The meeting was a fruitful one as he was able to surmise that they would most certainly be returned to North Africa as it was there that they had volunteered to join the British Army. This was standard practice but of course seen as a bit mad, as the majority of the Spaniards had nowhere to go because they had been interned. Agustín was able to gain permission to visit London to

---

15 Transcript of interview with Tony Fajardo, 10 June 2020.
16 Paul Preston, *Franco* (London: Harper Collins, 1993), pp.534–537.

Joaquín Fajardo at the end of the war shortly after being liberated and sent to Britain. Note he is wearing his Queen's Royal Regiment (West Surrey) cap badge rather than his Pioneer Corps one. (Joaquín Fajardo collection)

lobby for support to be able to stay in Britain. After talking to all the members of 361 Company as well as Spaniards from 362 and 363 Companies, it was decided that Agustín would depart for London along with two others. They travelled by train and stayed the night in the NAAFI before setting off the next morning to different parts of the capital. Between them they visited the *Hogar Español* and *Casal Català* and Spanish Republican representatives in London. After a day of making contacts, a visit to the Palace of Westminster was organised to meet up with various Labour MPs. In the end, Agustín and his compatriots entered in uniform and were met by Mr Philip Noel-Baker, MP for Derby South, Miss Ellen Wilkinson, MP for Jarrow, Commander Harry Pursey, MP for Kingston upon Hull East, Mr John Dugdale, MP for West Bromwich, and Mr George Jeger, MP for Goole. The Spaniards pushed their strong argument and were reassured by the MPs that the order for them to be sent to Africa would be rescinded. They returned the next day to tell their colleagues about the outcome. A few months later this was confirmed, and the company was moved to Nesscliffe at the end of October. Soon after, the company was granted two weeks leave. Agustín decided to travel to France to catch up with his family in Montauban. It was an emotional time for him, but he was able to put many ghosts to rest.[17]

Members of 361 (Alien) Company pose for a photo in 1945. Pictured are Spaniards who had served in No.50 Middle East Commando beforehand. From left to right on the back row are Miguel Martínez, Manuel Surera and Andrés Delgado. Front and second from the right seated is José Redondo. Note that Redondo is wearing parachute wings on his right arm and the Spaniard to his right has them above his left pocket. (Manuel Surera collection)

Upon Agustín's return to 361 Company, the Company moved to Sudbury in Suffolk where it worked in a textile factory. By the end of the year, No.1 Spanish Company had been disbanded and many of its members were demobilised at the beginning of 1946. Then shortly after, the strange order came in that the Company was to be moved to Italy and the soldiers demobilised

---

17 Agustín Roa Ventura, *Los años de mi vida, Personal Papers*, Vol.IV, 1942–1950, unpublished, pp.63–89.

there. Members of the Company also found out that the same fate had been decided for 362 and 363 Companies. This caused a great deal of consternation amongst all concerned and a plan was quickly hatched to organise a sit-down protest. This was carried out a few weeks later and soon had the desired effect. It turned out that this, along with several other heavily publicised press events, made a difference. One of these was the plight of 6100533/13808230 José Redondo. Redondo was from a small town called Montilla, which sits in the hills between Sevilla and Granada, to the south of Córdoba. He had fought in No.50 Middle East Commando, escaped from Crete and continued to fight in the British Army. By the end of 1944 he was in 361 Company and was in Britain. Here he met his soon to be wife, Marjorie, a Lancashire mill girl. By the end of the war, they were married and when word of him being sent to Italy was announced, she wrote to Clement Atlee to plead for José to be allowed to stay. His case was also highlighted in the Houses of Parliament when Anthony Greenwood MP asked the Secretary of State for War if he could:

> … reconsider as a matter of urgency the case of 13808230 Private J. Redondo, a Spanish citizen who volunteered for service in the British Forces in 1940, and who, although he has a wife and child in this country, has been told that he is being sent to Italy this month for demobilisation.[18]

Redondo's case was further supported by the cartoonist Vicky in the *News Chronicle*. In the cartoon José Redondo was hugging his English wife and saying goodbye to embark for Italy. In the background of the cartoon was a boat with Poles in it and the figure of 100,000 and their Italian wives who were about to be demobilised in Britain instead of Italy! Redondo would settle down in the north-west and have his close friend 6100535/13808232 Manuel Surera, also from Córdoba, living nearby. By the middle of summer 1946, the order to send the Spaniards and other nationalities to Italy or even still North Africa was cancelled. Over the following months, Spaniards were demobilised and started to look at places to settle down. Many would eventually decide to go to Mexico instead, where the largest exiled Spanish Republican grouping outside of Europe was based.[19]

For those who decided to remain in Britain, it was now a question of finding work and places to live. Many members of No.1 Spanish Company who were demobilised in the south-west decided to stay in that region too and married local girls. One of these was 13802470 Rafael Tresserras. A native from the village of Labrador in the high Pyrenees, he met his English wife in Sidmouth after being based in Chard in the autumn of 1945. This was after his company had returned from mainland Europe. Rafael was 'demobbed' on 3 March 1946 in Chard and was married to Margery Seward in 1947 in Honnington. After working in Exeter and Sidbury in Devon they moved to Marshwood, where they settled and started a family.

A large contingent of Spaniards settled in the Midlands. As many had been demobilised in that region, they gravitated to cities like Birmingham and Coventry. Birmingham had the largest group of Basque refugee children, so it was well established. Also, some who had served in the *13e DMBLE* and who did not join No.1 Spanish Company, had elected to work in munitions factories in the Midlands. Some of those who were demobilised in 1946 found work in factories. One such was 6100540/13808256 Jaime Trill. On arrival in Britain after being a POW in Crete and after his demobilisation, he married a local Catshill girl (near Bromsgrove and some 10 miles south of Birmingham) and found employment at the then Austin Motor Company at Longbridge, where he worked for many years. He finally 'went out on his own' and developed a local French-polishing and joinery business. Sadly, he died from a heart attack at the age of 63 years and his widow died a

---

18 Hansard, Volume 423: Debate on Aliens (Place of Release), 4 June 1946.
19 Agustín Roa Ventura, *Los años de mi vida, Personal Papers*, Vol.IV, pp.87–90.

few years later. The name Trill is still plainly seen on the touchline advertisements at Bromsgrove Rovers Football Club at the time of writing. Another Spaniard who settled in the Midlands was Antonio Obis, who finished his time in the army in 361 Company and had transferred to the commandos when he arrived in Britain at the end of 1944. He eventually moved to Coventry where he was demobilised in April 1947. It was here that he would settle down and start a family as well.

Another small group settled in the North-East of England. Juan Francisco Fernández Caballero had served in the *Guardias de Asalto* during the Spanish Civil War and later served with the French after which he then became a member of No. 50 Middle East Commando, survived Crete, transferred to the Pioneer Corps and moved to Britain as part of 361 Company in 1944. Soon after, he had transferred to the Parachute Regiment. By the time he was demobbed, he had decided to move to the North-East to work in the steel industry. He was joined by 6100545/13808257 Vicente Blasco, a Catalan from Barcelona and 6100509/13808240 Juan Díaz from Córdoba. Both had been POWs after Crete. All three became good friends, settled in Stockton-on-Tees and would work in the Cochrane Iron Works in Middlesbrough. They were also joined by 6100503/13808266 Alejandro Abadalejo and 6100515/13808244 Juan García Carrión who had been POWs after Crete.

Antonio Obis at the end of the war. Note he is wearing a Commando flash on his shoulder and has the Bren Gunner patch on his left sleeve.
(Antonio Obis collection)

Juan Francisco Fernández Caballero decided to apply to be granted British citizenship after the war in July 1949 and changed his name to Morgan. He married a Basque girl from Bilbao called Vicenta Bartolomé Guzmán, who he met in England and they were married in St Patrick's Church in Middlesbrough. After being granted their British passports they applied to visit Spain in 1958. They travelled through France to Hendaye and crossed the border to visit Vicenta's family in the Basque Country initially and then to Almería. Fanning themselves with their British passports as they queued in the foreigners' line at the border, they certainly felt safe and secure in their minds that nothing would happen to them. Their son Ricardo is still the Roman Catholic priest for Saltburn at the time of writing in 2024.

Most, of course, gravitated to London which was the obvious place to find work and be amongst many of the already established Spanish exile networks. Agustín Roa Ventura, for example, chose to live in London and initially lived in a shared house with Manuel Espallargas in Ladgrove Road after demobilisation. House sharing was an important way for many to be able to afford to live in the capital as they started to find work and start a new life. Agustín was fortunate to get into the printing industry a few years after the end of the war because of his qualifications as a typographer. He soon gained a post at Chatto & Windus on William IV Street, near Trafalgar Square. After some months he moved to another house, in Swiss Cottage, which he shared with 13802851 José Pardo García who had been in No.1 Spanish Company and trained as a SCONCE.

Juan Francisco Fernández Caballero (front row, second from the left) during his parachute training in early 1945 as a member of the Parachute Regiment. (Juan Francisco Fernández Caballero collection)

Many others found work in London in catering or service industries. A few even turned to a life of crime. One of these was 6100505/13808239 Manuel Barrosso. Having already been involved in prostitution, or being a 'white slaver' as his commander in Crete called it, he turned to crime in Paris after the Spanish Civil War. Barrosso had elected to join the *Légion Étrangère* rather than be interred.[20] He was captured in Crete in 1941 and was in Stalag 383 for most of the rest of the war. Upon arrival in Britain after the war, he became a 'heavy' in one of the Maltese gangs in London and did a few stints in prison!

Those who worked in catering were typically waiters and chefs. Antonio Vargas, who had been in Djelfa and served in 361 Company, got a job in the Martínez Restaurant on Swallow Street, off Regent Street. This restaurant would play an important role for the Spanish community in London. Fernando Esteve did something similar, and after finding a place to live in Paddington, eventually became one of the principal chefs at Le Caprice in St James. Jesús Velasco from No.1 Spanish Company, and a SCONCE, got a job with Clark Blanch & Co Ltd in Leadenhall Street. In May 1947 he married a Belgian girl called Esther who he had met while in Belgium towards the end of the war. Velasco would become an accomplished businessman in fruit and vegetable imports and a leading light in the reunions that the Spaniards from No.1 Spanish Company would have. Antonio and Esther settled initially in Brixton and then moved to Petts Wood.

---

20 Middle East Commando Archive, Captain Bob McGibbon testimony, in it he states: 'one Spaniard, a corporal with me, was a white slaver in France, another a sergeant had served two or three years for knifing a Frenchman who had insulted his girlfriend.'

Fernando Esteve while he was a chef at Le Caprice in St James, London. (Fernando Esteve collection)

13802496 José García Flores had been a member of No. 1 Spanish Company, trained to be a SCONCE and transferred to the Royal Signals in 1944. In England he had met Juliet Constance at a dance. He was immediately struck by her naturally wavy auburn hair and freckles. Despite the language barrier, he plucked up the courage to ask her to dance. They were married in Brentford in 1947. The Spanish community helped each other secure work. José initially worked as a French Polisher, but work dried up as furniture fashion changed. He then began his career in fruit importing at a time when the importation of fruit and vegetables from the Continent was really taking off. He had very little English to begin with, so he was employed by Jesús Velasco as a sort of runner/junior and tasked with helping the Spanish lorry drivers get from Dover to Covent Garden – they often got lost and called him in the middle of the night. Over time he, like Velasco, developed his own fruit importing business.

For the Spaniards who had served in the SAS, most were demobilised in mid-1946. After the disbanding of the SAS in October and their movement to different units, most then initially gravitated to London. While on leave in London in late 1945, Ralph Ramos met his future wife

José García Flores and Juliet Constance on their wedding day in 1947. (José García Flores collection)

Libode Kodešová, who had escaped the grips of Soviet-occupied Czechoslovakia with the assistance of a Russian ballerina. They married three weeks after first meeting, on 31 October in Paddington Registry office. Fellow SAS veteran, Francisco Geronimo (Frank Williams) was one of the witnesses. They had a daughter, Christine, not long after. Ramos attended an SAS reunion in 1947, where he met Ernest Bevin. Through this encounter he was able to obtain a union card, thereby permitting him to find employment in the stereotyping department of *The Express & Echo* newspaper in Exeter. In the early 1950s, he transferred to the *Birmingham Post & Mail*. A kind man, fortunate to have a wide-ranging sense of humour, Ralph Ramos sadly died after a short illness in 1961, aged 42.

The remaining SAS veterans headed to South Wales apart from Juan Torrents (John Colman) who settled initially in Scotland. Francisco Geronimo (Frank Williams) married Laura Bravo in Surrey in early 1946. They decided to move to South Wales and settled in Cardiff. They were joined by Ángel Camarena (Alan Cooper) and Francisco Revuelta (Alan Shaw), who eventually moved to Australia in the 1950s. Francisco Martín (Henry Martin) was first based in London where he met Hilaria Alonso. Hilaria had been one of the teachers of the Basque refugee children who had travelled with them in 1937, subsequently stayed after 1939 and worked in sewing and cooking in England, moving to London towards the end of the war. They were married in London in 1947 and settled in Huddersfield a year later, which is where Hilaria had been based while teaching Basque refugee children previously. The two of them were naturalised in 1954.

For most of the Spaniards though, it was a difficult time as the war came to an end because the majority had no family of any sort by their side. This meant that many had to learn to start afresh. Some were lucky enough to have their families join them after 1947 when the British Government granted them the right to have wives and children come to the UK. This was the case with Antonio

Ralph Ramos and Libuše Kodešová on their wedding day on 31 October 1945. (Rafael Ramos collection)

Frank Williams and Laura Bravo on their wedding day in Surrey in 1946. (Francisco Geronimo collection)

Augusto Pérez Miranda and his wife Carmen in Trafalgar Square not long after her arrival with their children in 1947. Upon arrival Carmen had to be treated for malnourishment. (Augusto Pérez Miranda collection)

Vargas Rivas who was joined by his wife and daughter in October 1947. Sadly, his other daughter had perished in Spain.[21] Others would have family members who continued fighting against Franco as part of guerrilla groups in Spain. Joaquín Fajardo had two brothers who joined guerrilla fighters back in his home village of Otivar near Granada. Manuel and Antonio Fajardo were killed in 1951 and 1952 respectively in skirmishes with the Franco authorities. Joaquín established himself in London and married a Portuguese girl, settling down near Stamford Bridge.

Another Spaniard who was able to bring his family over from Spain was 13803015 Augusto Pérez Miranda. At the end of the Civil War, Carmen and his five children had managed to stay safely in Barcelona during the war. Once he had carried out all necessary procedures, the family was able to travel to England, thanks also to Carmen's brother who paid for their flights to Britain.

---

21 TNA, 13/GEN/1954 (Demob. 5A). A War Office Memorandum dated 21 January 1947 stated that wives, and children under 21 of Spaniards who had served in HM Forces were allowed to enter the country and that their passage would be paid for by the public purse. Most of this was facilitated by the British Embassy in Madrid and its Military Attaché office through O.C. Smith Brigham.

From 1947 onwards, as the institutions set up by the Republican Government in exile either closed or were reduced, and as Dr Negrín and others moved away, less formal associations and networks became more important to the Spaniards. In cities such as London, these centred around restaurants such as Martínez or Fox Primary School in Kensington Place in Notting Hill. Martínez Restaurant, even though mostly out of many Spaniards' price range, was used as a venue for gatherings, mostly reunions from the 1950s onwards.

Meanwhile, back in Spain immediately after 1945, forever the grand opportunist, Franco had made the decision to sit out the international siege placed upon him by the Allies and wait until the natural antagonism between the communist and capitalist blocs crystallised. This would in turn permit him to gain admittance to the Western Alliance due to his plan of providing strategic support in the Western Mediterranean and beyond. In December 1946, the General Assembly of the United Nations adopted Resolution 39, which excluded the Spanish Government from international organisations and conferences established by the United Nations. In the same month Bevin had stated to the recently arrived Spanish Ambassador in London, Domingo de la Barcenas, his 'very great regret that the Franco Regime was still being maintained' and requested that Franco be informed that British patience was 'becoming exhausted'.[22]

The 'Spanish Question' was one that nations grappled with continuously for the years ahead. Franco could see that the best policy was to court the United States rather than Britain. On 22 November 1948, in an issue of *Newsweek*, Franco made his intentions clear by stating that Britain was blocking a way forward for Spain's incorporation into the fold. This was mainly a jibe against the Labour Government but was not helped when Churchill himself, who echoed some of the calls made by American politicians, went on to exaggerate Franco's support for the Allies by stating in the Houses of Parliament that 'No British or Americans were killed by Spaniards and the indirect aid we received from Spain during the war was of immense service.' Churchill then went on to say:

> I say there is certainly far more liberty in Spain under General Franco than in any of the countries behind the Iron Curtain. I do not wish to live in either set of countries and I expect I should get into trouble in both cases, but, at any rate; we must look at these facts. The great mistake is to allow legitimate objections to Franco and his form of Government to be a barrier between the Spanish people and the Western Powers with whom they have many natural ties, especially with Great Britain … There is the folly which, so far from leading to the downfall of Franco, has in fact, consolidated his position at every stage. I was sure it would be so.[23]

Christopher Mayhew, Labour Parliamentary Under-Secretary of State for Foreign affairs replied 'the record of Franco's Spain during the war is a serious reason why we cannot consider the welcoming of Franco's Spain into the community of Western Europe.' Franco continued to try to drive a wedge between Britain and America when it came to supporting his regime.[24]

Moreover, Spain was not to receive any Marshal Aid. By the early 1950s Britain had certainly realised the important role Spain had in the Cold War in the Collective Defence Plan that was being hatched. This is shown in that the Cabinet sat in the summer of 1951 to discuss the subject. In a report for the British Chiefs of Staff to the Cabinet it was said that:

---

22 Paul Preston, *Franco*, (London: Harper Collins, 1993), p 548.
23 Hansard, Volume 449: Debate on Foreign Affairs, 10 December 1948, <https://hansard.parliament.uk/Commons/1948-12-10/debates/2a8b1ed1-d7e8-4922-b5d6-14e7d4c7c90c/ForeignAffairs?highlight=debate%20foreign%20affairs#contribution-b6bd55f7-b5be-4812-a717-a6c9e3bb1ff7>. Accessed 29 December 2023.
24 Paul Preston, *Franco*, (London: Harper Collins, 1993), p.585.

> Spain occupies an important geographical position particularly in relation to Allied sea communications in the Western Mediterranean and Eastern Atlantic areas. The availability of Spanish ports and airfields would be of assistance in the control of sea communications in these areas. If the French Atlantic Coast fell into enemy hands, use of Spanish bases would be of considerable value in meeting the increased submarine and air threat to Allied convoys. If Russia were to occupy Spain, she would gain valuable naval and air bases from which to intensify her operations against Allied sea communications in the Atlantic and, by closing the straits of Gibraltar, she would deny the Western Mediterranean to Allied shipping.

But the report also said:

> The Chiefs of Staff considered the question of the inclusion of Spain in the North Atlantic Treaty Organisation. They concluded that in the long-term the advantages of including Spain in NATO would outweigh the disadvantages. In the short-term however, they recognised that there might be serious political reactions on the morale of western European countries if Spain were awarded membership prematurely, and her inclusion might also involve a diversion of equipment to her at the expense of other countries. They suggested that the ultimate desirability of including Spain in NATO should be borne in mind when framing future policy towards her … It has now become necessary, in the light of the recent American approach to Spain and the present world situation, to re-examine the question of associating Spain with Western defence.[25]

In the USA, the Chairman of the United States Joint Chiefs of Staff, General Omar Bradley, communicated to his political superiors the Pentagon's view that Spain's geographical position made it the definitive defensive stronghold against any Soviet invasion in Western Europe. Furthermore, he argued that Spain should be fortified by American military aid otherwise the USA would not retain a European springboard from which to reconquer the Continent should the Russians attack, something which was greatly feared at this stage. However, Britain's Labour Cabinet resolved in July 1951 to inform the United States Government to abandon their policy of promoting the association of Spain with the Western democracies. By this stage, this advice ran against the tide of opinion in the American capital. Some clever lobbying from strong catholic and anti-communist groups did swing things and in July 1951, the American Ambassador, Admiral Sherman conferred with *General* Franco on the terms of an agreement of collaboration between Spain and the USA in helping to defend the West to counter the threats of aggression from communist Russia.[26]

The way was now clear for negotiations that brought about a great many new developments for Franco's Spain. Spain was admitted into UNESCO on 17 November 1952. She signed a Concordat with the Vatican on 27 August 1953 and then the Pacts of Madrid, the United States-Spanish Defence, Economic Aid and Mutual Defence Assistance Agreements, came in September 1953. These agreements consisted of a package in which Spain granted strategic facilities to the USA in return for military and economic aid. Britain had concluded that the only way that Spain could be incorporated was via an agreement with the USA rather than NATO. Franco had escaped to fight again another day. Exiled Spanish Republicans across the world felt betrayed but realised that the fight against the Franco Regime still had to continue. Franco's Spain was eventually able to join the United Nations on 14 December 1955.

---

25 TNA, CAB 129/46/34, Cabinet Office Memorandum, Title: Spain, Author: Herbert Morrison, 29 June 1951.
26 Denis Smyth, *Diplomacy and Strategy of Survival, British Policy and Franco's Spain 1940–41* (Cambridge: Cambridge University Press, 1986), pp.250–251.

The Spanish Ex-Servicemen's Association and Defying Franco to the End

Despite the frustrations of being in Britain and having little influence over politics in Spain, many Spaniards who had served in the British Army remained politically active after the war and turned their energies to keeping the fight alive. However, it was decided from an early stage that protests and anti-Franco demonstrations in Britain would be peaceful ones. The first of these was a protest at the Stoll Theatre when the Franco Regime had sent dance and choir groups to give a concert. The Spanish Ambassador at this time was Miguel Primo de Rivera and he was hugely surprised when the curtain went up and leaflets protesting against the Franco Regime filled the air. There were also many smaller protests in London attended by Spanish ex-servicemen.

A small protest in Trafalgar Square, attended by Fernando Esteve, shortly after the war. (Fernando Esteve collection)

By the late 1950s the British Labour movement was starting to become more vocal about Spain and had established the Committee for Help to Spanish Democrats, set up by Clement Attlee with other figures including Anthony Wedgwood-Benn; one of its funding sources was the Labour Party. Another member of the Committee for Help to Spanish Democrats was Peter Benenson, a magistrate and later founder of Amnesty International. Exiled Spaniards would have a strong link with him a few years later.

Following the attempt to place the well-known Nazi sympathiser and Blue Division member, Fernando María Castiella as Ambassador, further protests took place in 1958. This sparked an idea, and soon Agustín Roa Ventura had organised a letter of protest to hand in to No.10 Downing Street along with the laying of a wreath for the fallen of the Second World War. This was to take place at the Cenotaph and was accompanied by a separate protest that started at Marble Arch protesting against the potential inclusion of Spain in NATO. Large banners were seen displaying 'Freedom for Spain' or 'Freedom for Prisoners' on them.

Agustín Roa Ventura and Antonio Vargas laying a wreath in Whitehall in 1958. (Agustín Roa Ventura collection)

Such protests in the late 1950s sparked interest amongst the Spaniards in Britain who had served during the war. The majority were working in London and a few were involved in the British Trade Unions. One of these was Agustín Roa Ventura, who had become a Father of the Chapel for the Trades Union of the graphic industry in London, by this time he was working for W.H. Smith. A second laying of a wreath at the Cenotaph was organised for 30 December 1959. This time, it was laid by Lady Violet Bonham-Carter, grandmother of the actress Helena Bonham-Carter, accompanied by a group of Spanish veterans. The event resulted in further interest and Labour politicians urged Spaniards to set up an association to take things further. This led to the establishment of the Spanish Ex-Servicemen's Association, an organisation that would be active in continuing the fight beyond the death of Franco in 1975.

By early 1960, most of the Spanish veterans in Britain were approached for subscriptions and as a result a committee was established to get the Association launched. The first members of this committee were: President – Manuel Espallargas from No.1 Spanish Company, Secretary – Agustín Roa Ventura from 361 Company, and Committee Members – Manuel Borí from 361 Company, Juan Fajardo from No.1 Spanish Company, Martín Baldo from 361 Company, Antonio Vargas from 361 Company and Miguel Pino from No.1 Spanish Company.[27] The Association was registered at 178 Kensal Road in London. A few months later, in June, the Spanish Ex-Servicemen's Association issued its first newsletter which was well received. In it, members were reminded of the situation in their homeland

---

27 Agustín Roa Ventura, *Los años de mi vida, Personal Papers*, Vol.IV, 1942–1950, *En las Trade Unions*, unpublished, pp.21–77.

and that they needed not to look back to the Civil War necessarily but at the Spain of today and what they could do to help.[28]

The year would indeed be a busy one for Spaniards in Britain protesting against the tyranny of Franco's Regime. New members of the Association would get a huge chance to showcase the plight of Spaniards in Franco's Spain to the wider world as, in conjunction with other groups as well as individuals such as Peter Benenson, it organised a well-publicised and very well attended protest on 10 July 1960 in London. The protest was the result of a visit by Franco's Foreign Minister, Fernando María Castiella who was regarded by many as a hardened fascist. Several thousand people took part in the day's events which began at Marble Arch and ended with a large rally in Trafalgar Square. The Labour MP Bob Edwards ensured that backing for the day was not only linked to Spaniards in exile and that there were several other groups in support. The Labour Party was also willing to participate and had also organised a protest outside Victoria Station on the day, which is where Castiella was due to arrive. The British press became agitated by the visit and several articles were published during the days and weeks before Castiella's visit. In general, there we three main reasons to protest:

> Firstly, that Castiella was in fact a self-confessed fascist who had fought on the Eastern Front as a member of the Blue Division and had written extensively in the past against Britain and democracy.
> Secondly, that Human Rights were still being violated daily in Spain and that an amnesty was now needed for political prisoners under the Franco Regime.
> Finally, that Castiella's main reason for visiting Britain was to discuss the admittance of Spain into NATO and that this could not happen given the present circumstances in the country.

The day of the protest turned out to be grey and rainy. Castiella was collected from Gatwick Airport by car and whisked off to the Spanish Embassy, thus avoiding the protests at Victoria Station where many thought he would arrive. At 11 o'clock the Spanish Ex-Servicemen's Association, accompanied by MPs and other Spaniards, laid a wreath at the Cenotaph to commemorate the dead. Groups then moved up to Marble Arch and assembled in readiness. The weather improved somewhat so that by the time the protest march started, all manner of banners could be seen. What surprised many was the diversity of the large crowd. Not only did the march contain British MPs but also a huge variety of political groups ranging from anarchists to Catalans and Basques. As the protest march moved south it was joined by many others. The route followed a part of Oxford Street, Regent Street, then Haymarket before arriving in Trafalgar Square. Here all were greeted by a stage set up by Nelson's Column and a huge banner with 'FREEDOM FOR SPAIN' on it.

Agustín Roa Ventura opened proceedings with a speech thanking all for being there and explaining the importance of what they were doing. This was followed by other speakers and the reading of several letters of support. Proceedings were brought to a close with the reading of the letter that had been sent to the Prime Minister at Number 10 Downing Street. This was signed by the Spanish Ex-Servicemen's Association Committee as well as James Griffiths, Elwyn Nones, Manuela Sykes, John Clark, Robert Edwards, George Jeger, Ernest Davies, F. Noel-Baker, Dr Donald Soper and Davis Emnals. The day's proceedings for Sunday 10 July 1960 had been a success.[29]

---

28 Antonio Vargas Rivas, *Guerra, Revolución y Exilio de un Anarcosindicalista* (Almería: privately published, October 2007 second edition), part 2, chapter 9.
29 Agustín Roa Ventura, *Los años de mi vida, Personal Papers*, Vol.IV, 1942–1950, *En las Trade Unions*, unpublished, pp.21–77.

Protestors gather in Trafalgar Square on 10 July 1960. (Agustín Roa Ventura collection)

Agustín Roa Ventura opens proceedings in Trafalgar Square on 10 July 1960.
(Picture: Agustín Roa Ventura collection)

Not long after, the committee met with Peter Benenson, who had already set up the movement called Justice. The Communist Party of Great Britain had launched a campaign in 1959 demanding an amnesty for Spanish political prisoners, which coincided with the twentieth anniversary of the end of the Spanish Civil War. The 'Appeal for Amnesty in Spain' was sponsored by a wide range of public figures, including John Arlott, the journalist, the historian Hugh Trevor-Roper and the sculptor Henry Moore. Amongst those more actively involved were the artist Michael Ayrton and the recently elected Liberal MP Jeremy Thorpe, who amongst other things, would later be involved with the work of Amnesty International.[30] This campaign developed momentum, and in March 1961, a major international conference in Paris was organised, attended by over 60 British delegates, which in turn launched a worldwide campaign. Even though this campaign was separate to that of Benenson's, it is clear that the plight of Spanish prisoners and the whole idea of Amnesty struck a chord with him. The Spanish Ex-Servicemen's Association followed up the July 1960 demonstrations with a booklet published in December 1960 called *Franco's Prisoners Speak*. The information had been gained via 'Appeal for Amnesty in Spain' and told of the horrendous situation of hundreds of political prisoners held in Burgos Prison. In a letter to the committee, Benenson had written 'I hope your excellent work can help your compatriots, people I will not cease to work for.' Benenson then wrote a piece in the *Observer* in May 1961 entitled 'The Forgotten Prisoners' which in turn sparked the Appeal for Amnesty in 1961. Many members of the 'Appeal for Amnesty in Spain' movement joined them. Benenson contacted the Spanish Ex-Servicemen's Association Committee to request an article for his new magazine entitled 'Evidence' which soon after was renamed 'Amnesty'.[31]

Repression continued in Spain, however. In 1963, massive strikes took place in Asturias, but there were significant consequences with many arrests and some deaths. The Spanish Ex-Servicemen's Association launched a series of demonstrations and continued to push hard for recognition for those imprisoned in Spain. This included an exhibition at the St George Gallery near Piccadilly Circus of work by one of the better-known prisoners in Burgos, Agustín Ibarrola. This was done to coincide with a Goya Exhibition at the Royal Academy. Over the following years, 'Appeal for Amnesty in Spain' continued to work tirelessly organising many other events across Europe.[32]

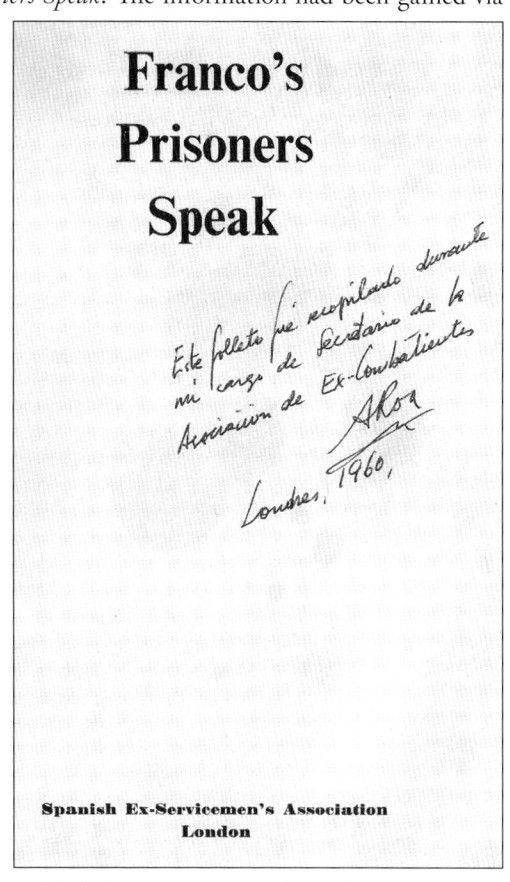

The inside cover of the booklet published by the Spanish Ex-Servicemen's Association in July 1960 with a note from Agustín Roa Ventura. (Agustín Roa Ventura collection)

---

30 Tom Buchanan, 'The Truth Will Set You Free: The Making of Amnesty International,' *Journal of Contemporary History*, Vol.37, No.4, October 2002 (London: Sage Publications, 2002), pp.575–597.
31 Agustín Roa Ventura, *Los Años de mi Vida, Personal Papers*, Vol.IV, 1942–1950, *Causas y Orígen de la Amnistía Internacional – La Contribución Española*. Unpublished
32 Agustín Roa Ventura, *Causas y Origen de Amnistía Internacional, La Contribución Española*, pp.14–26.

One of the protests in 1963 to bring to attention the plight of many prisoners held by the Franco Regime. Antonio Vargas holds up a placard calling for *LIBERTAD PARA LOS PRESOS* (Set the Prisoners Free).
(Agustín Roa Ventura collection)

As well as being heavily involved in many political aspects of their exile in Britain, Spanish veterans also had to make a living and bring up their families. Now that so many had settled in Britain, they had been augmented by new waves of economic Spaniards who had been allowed to leave Spain in the early 1960s. Having had a unique experience in the British Army compared to most exiled Spaniards, reunions and get togethers were important, especially once many were fully established. Many of the larger gatherings took place in the London area.

One of the organisers of gatherings of Spaniards was Jesús Velasco who had served in No.1 Spanish Company and been a SCONCE. After buying a house in Petts Wood (and with his import/export fruit and vegetable business doing so well) he bought a property and land outside of London, near Sevenoaks in Kent. With this began a tradition of regular gatherings at his house. As many of the Spaniards were working in the catering industry, it was not a surprise that the food and drink at these occasions was excellent. Usually starting at 10 o'clock in the morning, whole families would descend for the day. *Los Reclutas* (as the members of No.1 Spanish Company were affectionately called) ate, danced, sang and had a wonderful time catching up with old brothers in arms. However, many of the Spaniards who attended still did not have families of their own and were struggling financially.[33]

Other events were organised in the Martínez Restaurant where an annual get together took place. Sara García (daughter of José García Flores) recalled attending the events as a child and remembered much hugging and crying. Tickets were sold but those who could not afford it were subsidised. A lot of money was raised for widows and children of the company through crazy auctions:

---

33 Jesús Velasco Zapico, *Una Vida Española, a Personal Family Memoir, 1915–1995*. Unpublished memoir. Author's collection and copyright.

They'd auction an item, it would be won and paid for then the person who won it just put it back to be auctioned again. It didn't matter much what the item was. One time I remember someone running to the kitchen and retrieving a cabbage and they auctioned that for a large sum of money. That was typical of the enormous fun and camaraderie there was. They must have relived a fare few traumatic experiences. I remember a man called Vargas, who was also, coincidentally, a waiter at the Martínez on other days, always ending up crying onto my dad's shoulder.[34]

A reunion of *Los Reclutas* at the Martínez Restaurant. At the back standing tall with a big grin in front of the picture frame is José García Flores. Second from the right, seated, is Jesús Velasco and to his right (our left) is Manuel Espallargas. (José García Flores collection)

The Martínez Restaurant would also be a frequently visited venue for key Spanish personalities and figureheads. One of these was the chameleon-like character Manuel Fraga Iribarne, who was forced out of office in 1969 by his *Opus Dei* opponents within the Franco Regime. Out of politics, he turned towards building an image as a reformer to position himself for post-Franco times. In 1973 he became Spanish Ambassador in London. Fraga would often be found in Martínez with other Spanish leading lights. According to Antonio Vargas, who worked there, it was obvious he was up to something.[35]

By the early 1970s, it was clear that Franco's ailing health was leading to the inevitable conclusion – the end to his regime. He had already made arrangements, and lined up a successor in Juan Carlos who would take over on his death. Different groups agitated. Franco handpicked *Almirante* Luís Carrero Blanco as his successor in the role of Head of Government, with Carrero

---

34 Interview with Sara García, 28 December 2022.
35 Antonio Vargas Rivas, *Guerra, Revolución y Exilio de un Anarcosindicalista* (Almería: privately published, October 2007 second edition), part 2, chapter 9.

266　CHURCHILL'S SPANIARDS

taking office in June 1973. Not long after he became Prime Minister, Carrero Blanco was assassinated in a streetside bombing on 20 December 1973 when his car was blown up in Madrid by the Basque nationalist group *Euskadi Ta Askatasuna* (ETA). Despite these events, the Franco Regime remained hard on many and there were still regular arrests and detentions.

As Big Ben sounded 11 o'clock on Sunday 19 October 1975, a group from the Spanish Ex-Servicemen's Association led by 13802478 Jaume Más and Agustín Roa Ventura laid a wreath at the Cenotaph in Whitehall. They bowed their heads and reflected on the many who had suffered for so long as well as their brothers in arms from their service during the Second World War. After a minute's silence, Agustín's daughter, Vida, laid five carnations on the monument. Each of the carnations represented a prisoner who had been recently executed by the Franco Regime. The group was then escorted by the police down Whitehall to No.10 Downing Street where a letter of protest was handed in. They were smartly dressed, represented practically all parts of the Army that Spaniards had served in and were each wearing the medals they had been awarded for service in the British Army. Among them was Luís Gabriel Portillo, a Republican academic, who had been in exile in Britain since the end of the Spanish Civil War – he is the father of British politician and broadcaster Michael Portillo.[36]

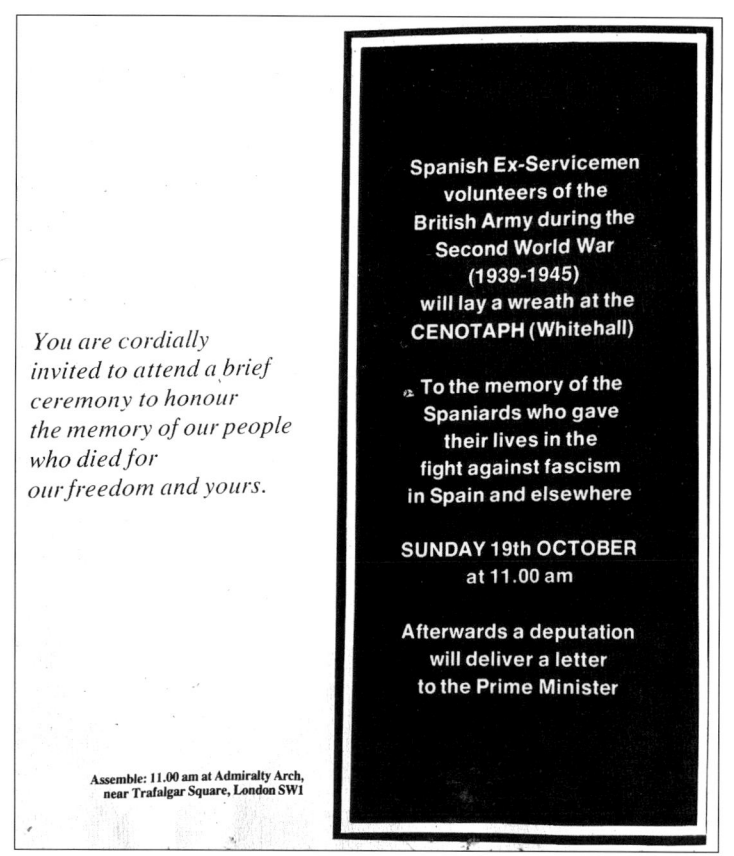

A leaflet issued by the Spanish Ex-Servicemen's Association on their peaceful protest on Sunday 19 October 1975. (Agustín Roa Ventura collection)

36　Agustín Roa Ventura, *Agonía y Muerte del Franquismo (Una Memoria)* (Barcelona: Barral Editores, 1977), pp.359–362.

Members of the Spanish Ex-Servicemen's Association gather on Whitehall before moving to the Cenotaph to lay a wreath. In the picture are: Front row from left to right: Agustín Nogueroles (No.1 Spanish Company), Jaume Más (No.1 Spanish Company), Agustín Roa Ventura (361 (Alien) Company) and furthest to the right Antonio Vargas (361 (Alien) Company). Second row from left to right: Miguel Pino (No.1 Spanish Company), Luís Portillo, Carles Busquets (No.1 Spanish Company). Third row from left to right: Miguel Ramira (No.1 Spanish Company). Behind Ramira is Francisco Navarrete (No. 50 Middle East Commando). (Agustín Roa Ventura collection)

The Spanish Ex-Servicemen's Association hands in a letter at No.10 Downing Street on Sunday 19 October 1975. From left to right are: Agustín Roa Ventura, Jaume Más, Carles Busquets, Agustín Nogueroles, and Antonio Vargas. (Picture: Agustín Roa Ventura collection)

Franco died just a month later, on 20 November 1975. Despite there being some order in the actual transition, chaos ensued in Spain with several protests and groups agitating for a voice as the country moved into a period of uncertainty. With the end now coming, it was somewhat ironic that Spaniards who had fought in the British Army were witnesses to elements of the beginning and end of Franco and his regime. 13301810 Ángel Camarena Espinosa, who ended up serving in the SAS, had been in Tenerife when *General* Franco was Governor and had driven him as a military chauffeur shortly before he had been whisked away to join his Army of Africa in Morocco, as narrated above. At the Martínez Restaurant in London, 13809805 Antonio Vargas Rivashad witnessed the preparations and behind the scenes work carried out by Manuel Fraga Iribarne to return to politics in Spain after Franco (he became Home Secretary and Deputy Prime Minister in Carlos Arias Navarro's caretaker Government). Fitting 'book ends' to a nearly 40-year period of turmoil for millions.

Many, probably most, people in Britain are completely unaware that proud Spanish Republicans served in the British Army throughout Churchill's premiership during the Second World War. Several have said that the Country owes them a debt of gratitude for the freedoms we all enjoy today. Yes, it was a small contribution but, nonetheless, one that has become part of the history and heritage of the multicultural British Armed Forces we have today. This book hopes to repay at least some the debt we owe these men by telling their story.

I will let Agustín Roa Ventura have the final words as he pays a fitting tribute to these Spaniards 'Continuing the Fight'…

> *A los españoles caídos defendiendo la libertad; en los campos de concentración; en el desierto africano; sepultados en la nieve en los picos de Noruega; en los océanos tripulantes de la marina mercante aliada; en los caminos de la evasión; a los fusilados; a los abandonados en los trópicos; a los calcinados en los hornos nazis; a los que murieron en los hospitales de exilio; y a los que se consumieron en las celdas de castigo. Ellos hicieron la historia, y ellos se merecen el tributo del autor.*[37]

---

37 'To the Spaniards who fell defending liberty: in the concentrations camps; in the African desert; buried on the snow-capped peaks in Norway; in the oceans as crew of Allied merchant ships; on the escape lines; those who were shot; those abandoned in the Tropics; those exterminated in the Nazi ovens; those who died in exile in hospitals; and those who were consumed in punishment cells. They all made history, and they deserve a tribute from the author.' Agustín Roa Ventura, *El Fracaso de la Victoria*, unpublished.

Appendix I

No. 1 Spanish Company, Nominal Roll Dated 5 December 1942

Regimental Number: 1380–	Rank	Name	Initials	Age	Province of origin	Trade	Remarks
2391	Sgt	Delgado	M M	23	Jaen	Labourer	
2598	Sgt	Izquierdo	C P	26	Madrid	OTC	W/T, Married in England, Good NCO
2703	Sgt	Colomo	J	30	Barcelona	Mechanic	
2518	Sgt	Jurado	J	21	Malaga	Tailor	
3895	Cpl	Bessudo	E	32	Constantinople	Cameraman	
2392	Cpl	Garcia	J	30	Cartagena	Hairdresser	Dems, Speaks French & Italian
2423	Cpl	Haro	R	30	Almeria	Labourer	
2482	Cpl	Perez	G	33	Madrid	Chauffeur	
2468	Cpl	Rojano	A	23	Cordoba	Labourer	Dems, Married in England
3020	Cpl	Roig	A	26	Barcelona	Dyer	Dems
3021	Cpl	Rubio	A	25	Badajoz	Bootmaker	
2484	Cpl	Sanfelix	J	25	Valencia	Labourer	
5134	Cpl	Sanchez	B	20	Malaga	Shopassistant	Dems
2408	Cpl	Sanchez	J	24	Almeria	Baker	Dems
4053	Cpl	Weber	J	38	Prague	Motor designer	
2393	LCpl	Anduix	J	29	Valencia	Weaver	W/T
2591	LCpl	Bardasco	J	29	Palencia	Electrician	
2436	LCpl	Bernal	F	28	Cataluna	Tree feller	
3102	LCpl	Bonjour	J	30	Cuba	Waiter	

269

270   CHURCHILL'S SPANIARDS

Regimental Number: 1380–	Rank	Name	Initials	Age	Province of origin	Trade	Remarks
2498	LCpl	Iovine	F	21	Madrid	Soldier	
2599	LCpl	Jenfer	C	26	Madrid	Upholsterer	
2454	LCpl	Illa	A	23	Barcelona	Labourer	
2383	LCpl	Martinez	V	29	Valencia	Farmer	Dems
2382	LCpl	Munoz	F	28	Cataluna	Mason	
5134	LCpl	Sanchez	B	20	Malaga	Shopkeeper	
2603	LCpl	Solis	M	28	Asturias	Electrician	
2356	LCpl	Villa	C	21	Badajoz	Doctor	
5031	LCpl	Vidal	J	25	Valencia	Stoker	Dems
2546	Pte	Aguera	C	28	Almeria	Labourer	
2536	Pte	Alapont	C	24	Valencia	Shop assist	Excellent French
2537	Pte	Alcon	R	22	Teruel	Labourer	
5756	Pte	Sanchez	S B	25	Caceres	Shop assist	W/T, 8 years in France
2471	Pte	Alvarez	L	28	Oviedo		
2472	Pte	Amills	J	22	Cataluna	Printer	Dems
2486	Pte	Anadon	F	23	Zaragosa	Labourer	Dems
2538	Pte	Arcos	A	23	Jean	Hairdresser	Dems, Married in England
2443	Pte	Arroyo	M	26	Toledo		
7006	Pte	Aguilar	J	37	Malaga	Chauffeur	W/T, experience of N Africa
4882	Pte	Banon	P	25	Castellon	Foundry	W/T, perfect French
2539	Pte	Artal	G				
2487	Pte	Baguena	A	24	Cataluna	Mason	W/T
7116	Pte	Barberan	J	33	Bilbao	Miner	
2488	Pte	Barroso	A	22	Malaga	Labourer	
2593	Pte	Belles	V	25	Castellon	Labourer	
2445	Pte	Benitez	C	24	Badajoz	Miner	
5331	Pte	Bermejo	C	33	Salamanca	Butcher	W/T, Married England
4883	Pte	Bermejo	A	22	Tolosa	Labourer	
2489	Pte	Bielsa	C	29	Zaragosa	Labourer	Dems
5953	Pte	Blanes	F	22	Almeria	Labourer	Dems
3047	Pte	Bon	M	25	Cataluna	Foundry	

APPENDIX 1   271

Regimental Number: 1380–	Rank	Name	Initials	Age	Province of origin	Trade	Remarks
2594	Pte	Borras	E	29	Castellon	Teacher	W/T
2432	Pte	Cabrera	M	22	Cataluna	Bootmaker	
7484	Pte	Campos	A	29	Murcia	Mechanic	W/T
2397	Pte	Caceres	C	22	Madrid	Car mechanic	Dems, Married in England
2490	Pte	Campos	J	24	Cataluna	Fitter	W/T
2473	Pte	Camillieri	J	30	Alicante	Mechanic	
2438	Pte	Cano	J	24	Granada	Labourer	
2595	Pte	Cardenal	J	22	Soria	Baker	
7375	Pte	Carrero	E	27	Madrid		
2447	Pte	Carreras	J				
2418	Pte	Carron	R	28			
2491	Pte	Cases	M	25	Alicante	Mason	Dems
2372	Pte	Castellon	A	33	Huesca	Labourer	
5628	Pte	Caballo	P	30	Guadalajara	Labourer	
5877	Pte	Cepero	P	22	Granada	Chauffeur	
3007	Pte	Cervantes	J	23	Almeria	Labourer	
3099	Pte	Consque	V	27	Valencia	Pintor escernario	
5330	Pte	Corredor	J	23	Cordoba	Labourer	
3005	Pte	Cortilla	F	23	Barcelona	Shop assist	W/T
2401	Pte	Cruz	A	30	Alicante		
2410	Pte	Cuenca	D	23	Albacete	Barber	
2422	Pte	Cuevas	M	22	Malaga	Labourer	
5984	Pte	Dalmau	F	28	Barcelona	Medical assistant	W/T
2540	Pte	Delatorre	R	27	Jean	Baker	
3011	Pte	Del Rio	E	25	Malaga	Labourer	
2385	Pte	Del Rio	N	28	Valladolid		
2547	Pte	Domingo	A	24	Lerida	Cook	
2448	Pte	Dominguez	M	22	Canary Isles	Fisherman	
2492	Pte	Dura	F	23	Alicante	Labourer	
2493	Pte	Egea	I	24	Albacete		
2474	Pte	Escaso	F	28	Badajoz		

272 CHURCHILL'S SPANIARDS

Regimental Number: 1380–	Rank	Name	Initials	Age	Province of origin	Trade	Remarks
2449	Pte	Escrig	L	24	Castellon	Labourer	
3117	Pte	Fernandez	A	29	Cordoba		
2407	Pte	Fernandez	A	27	Murcia		
2515	Pte	Fernandez	B	24	Cordoba	Foundry	
2494	Pte	Fernandez	F	22	Cordoba	Labourer	
2375	Pte	Fernandez	J	21	Jean		
7483	Pte	Fernand	R	20	Vigo	Fisherman	W/T, Knows Basque coast
2450	Pte	Fernandez	M	28	Guadalajara	Labourer	
2512	Pte	Fernandez	M M	27	Granada	Labourer	
2596	Pte	Fernandez	T	25	Galicia	Labourer	
2409	Pte	Ferrer	E	32	Madrid	Labourer	
2475	Pte	Gallego	B	21	Toledo		
2495	Pte	Gallego	T				
2554	Pte	Garcia	A	38	Valencia	Labourer	
2516	Pte	Garcia	B	30	Valencia	Labourer	
2404	Pte	Garcia	R	24	Albacete	Mason	
2394	Pte	Garcia	S	24	Valencia	Labourer	
2552	Pte	Garcia	V	30	Argentine	Pedlar	
2451	Pte	Garrigas	P	23	Santander	Fisherman	Native of Vascongada
2476	Pte	Gener	R	21	Barcelona		
2497	Pte	Gil	P	20	Jaen		
2548	Pte	Gimenez	G	24	Toledo	Labourer	
2453	Pte	Gomez	M	23	Badajoz	Labourer	
2399	Pte	Gonzalez	C	24	Barcelona		
2388	Pte	Grato	J	25	Gijon	Platelayer	
2477	Pte	Gutierrez	A	29	Cordoba		
2381	Pte	Herrero	A	22	Badajos	Labourer	
2605	Pte	Herreros	P	25	Albacete	Labourer	
2517	Pte	Iniesta	J	26	Murcia		
2437	Pte	Ismer	L	26	Malaga	Foundry	
2417	Pte	Jimenez	A	23	Jaen	Labourer	Dems

APPENDIX I 273

Regimental Number: 1380–	Rank	Name	Initials	Age	Province of origin	Trade	Remarks
3383	Pte	Jimenez	J	26	Alicante	Painter	Dems, Knows Oran
5986	Pte	Jornet	A	24	Barcelona	Student Mech Eng	W/T
2389	Pte	Laiseca	S	31	Bilbao		
2369	Pte	Lara	J	28	Cordoba	Labourer	Dems
2519	Pte	Largo	U	26	Toledo	Labourer	
2600	Pte	Lasierra	F	25	Zaragosa		
2455	Pte	Latienda	A	24	San Sebastian		Native of Vascongada
2420	Pte	Lazaro	G	38	Cartagena	Labourer	
5529	Pte	Lete	J	29	Bilbao	Chauffeur	W/T, Married England, Native of Vascongada
5530	Pte	Lete	A	23	Bilbao	Labourer	Dems, Native of Vascongada
2419	Pte	Lopez	A	25	Cordoba	Labourer	
2601	Pte	Lopez	E	29	Oviedo	Labourer	
2377	Pte	Lopez	G	28	Granada	Labourer	
2499	Pte	Lopez	J	36	Murcia	Labourer	
2511	Pte	Lopez	L	24	Zaragosa	Hairdresser	W/T
5988	Pte	Lopez Llamas	J	23	Murcia	Labourer	
2373	Pte	Lopez	M	26	Oviedo	Miner	
2442	Pte	Lopez	R	24	Madrid	Soldier	Dems
2602	Pte	Lozano	M	42	Albacete	Labourer	
2500	Pte	Luque	J	33	Malaga		
2520	Pte	Luque	J	24	Cordoba		
2521	Pte	Luque	J	22	Jaen	Labourer	
5985	Pte	Llonchs	J	26	Barcelona	Weaver	W/T
2456	Pte	Mallafre	M	24	Barcelona	Chauffeur	W/T
2457	Pte	Manez	L	21	Valencia	Mason	
3002	Pte	Marco	S	25	France	Shopkeeper	
2553	Pte	Marin	R	32	Barcelona	Mason	
2458	Pte	Martin	A	36	Toledo	Butcher	
2411	Pte	Martin	G	24	Jaen		

274 CHURCHILL'S SPANIARDS

Regimental Number: 1380–	Rank	Name	Initials	Age	Province of origin	Trade	Remarks
5328	Pte	Martin	G	32	Madrid	Mason	
2439	Pte	Martin	J	23	Barcelona	Labourer	
7464	Pte	Martinez	A	18	Murcia	Cafe prop	
2368	Pte	Martinez	F	24	Almeria	Miner	
2501	Pte	Martinez	J	24	Almeria	Mason	
2441	Pte	Martinez	S	23	Jaen	Mechanic	
2374	Pte	Martenez	V	29	Valencia	Labourer	
2478	Pte	Mas	J	22	Barcelona		
2549	Pte	Masso	B	25	Barcelona		
5989	Pte	Mateo	V	22	Barcelona	Weaver	Dems
2459	Pte	Melis	L	34	Barcelona	Fisherman	
2460	Pte	Membrado	J	27	Teruel	Labourer	
2415	Pte	Molina	E	21	Ciudad Real		
1523	Pte	Montane	J	21	Tarragona		
2403	Pte	Montero	F	25	Cordoba	Mason	
2461	Pte	Monturiol	A	22	Lerida	Labourer	
7477	Pte	Murdoh	M	36	Iraq	Pedlar	
2479	Pte	Morales	C	28	Malaga	Cook	
2396	Pte	Morales	J	23	Cordoba	Labourer	
5823	Pte	Moratino	C	22	La Linea	Clerk	W/T, Lived Gibraltar, very bright/keen
2421	Pte	Moreno	J	24	Jaen	Miner	
2503	Pte	Moreno	J	34	Badajoz	Labourer	
3014	Pte	Mora	M	25	Madrid	Hairdresser	
2462	Pte	Moya	S	25	Cordoba	Labourer	
2522	Pte	Munoz	A	22	Almeria	Labourer	
2378	Pte	Munoz	J	25	Barcelona		
2524	Pte	Nadal	J	23	Alicante	Shepherd	
2480	Pte	Navarro	F	22	Barcelona		
2390	Pte	Nicolas	J	25	Barcelona		
5879	Pte	Navarro	C				
7483	Pte	Nieto	M	24	Cuba	Pedlar	

APPENDIX I 275

Regimental Number: 1380–	Rank	Name	Initials	Age	Province of origin	Trade	Remarks
2504	Pte	Nieto	T	25	Guadalajara		
2505	Pte	Orriols	J	31	Barcelona	Labourer	
2481	Pte	Ortega	A	27	Canary Isles	Labourer	
2704	Pte	Orti	M	34	Manresa	Labourer	
2525	Pte	Ostio	T	26	Malaga		
2541	Pte	Ortiz	A	25	Barcelona	Shop assist	
3017	Pte	Palanca	R	25	Valencia	Chauffeur	
2506	Pte	Palomar	J	28	Teruel		
2380	Pte	Peraferrer	F	22	Barcelona	Mason	Dems
5712	Pte	Peralta	D	22	Alicante	Painter	Dems
2526	Pte	Perez	F	25	Jaen	Labourer	
2413	Pte	Perez	J	26	Toledo	Labourer	
5329	Pte	Perez	J	26	Barcelona	Mason	
3016	Pte	Perez	V	21	Albacete	Labourer	
2463	Pte	Pina	V	25	Toledo	Labourer	
2414	Pte	Pino	A	26	Madrid	Baker	
2464	Pte	Pino	M	27	Cordoba	Labourer	
3384	Pte	Pinto	J	28	Huelva	Labourer	
2466	Pte	Planes	S	27	Zaragosa	Labourer	
2434	Pte	Pollan	L	26	Madrid		
3018	Pte	Prades	J	24	Barcelona	Fitter	
7019	Pte	Prieto	A	20	Huelva	Waiter	
2467	Pte	Puig	A	22	Murcia	Shepherd	
2542	Pte	Queralt	J	21	Tarragona		
2527	Pte	Quesada	L	29	Jaen	Mason	
2387	Pte	Quintilla	M	35	Huesca	Carpenter	Dems
5410	Pte	Ramis	B	22	Lerida	Baker	
3116	Pte	Ramira	A	27	Cadiz		
2529	Pte	Reina	F	24	Badajoz	Labourer	
2507	Pte	Rey	M	32	Barcelona	Dyer	W/T
7007	Pte	Reyes	A	33	Andalucia	Labourer	

Regimental Number: 1380–	Rank	Name	Initials	Age	Province of origin	Trade	Remarks
2427	Pte	Roca	P	26	Granada	Weaver	
5921	Pte	Robba	J	19	Malta	Labourer	
2508	Pte	Rodriguez	A	23	Granada	Mason	
2402	Pte	Rodriguez	D	21	Albacete	Mason	Dems
2550	Pte	Rodriguez	J	24	Jaen		
5132	Pte	Romeo	J	28	Toledo	Sailor	Subject to fits
2543	Pte	Romera	F	20	Granada		
2509	Pte	Romero	J	20	Valencia		
2483	Pte	Romero	M	22	Badalona	Tinsmith	
3019	Pte	Romero	R	21	Extremadura	Labourer	
2531	Pte	Rubio	V	24	Valencia	Labourer	
2379	Pte	Ruiz	F	25	Lerida		
2431	Pte	Ruiz	J	23	Cordoba	Labourer	Dems
5822	Pte	Ruiz	R	43	La Linea	Shop assist	
2532	Pte	Sabanes	F	27	Granada	Labourer	
2544	Pte	Sanabrias	F	30	Canary Isles	Stevedore	
5135	Pte	Sanchez	A	22	Malaga	Labourer	
2392	Pte	Sanchez	F	24	Jaen	Butcher	
2430	Pte	Sanchez	R	24	Cordoba		
2416	Pte	Santi	J	24	Madrid	Aviation mechanic	Dems
7553	Pte	Santana	A	29	La Linea	Labourer	
2990	Pte	Santos	M	29	Barcelona	Sailor	W/T
2424	Pte	Segura	J	27	Albacete	Labourer	
2440	Pte	Serrano	J	35	Granada	Labourer	
2590	Pte	Smil	S	35	Rumania	Stevedore	
2528	Pte	Soriano	R	22	Alicante	Carpenter	
2534	Pte	Socorro	G	31	Ciudad Real	Mason	
2469	Pte	Sorribas	R	28	Castellon	Mason	
2435	Pte	Tapia	J	22	Jaen		
2412	Pte	Tarraga	M	23	Murcia	Blacksmith	

APPENDIX I

Regimental Number: 1380–	Rank	Name	Initials	Age	Province of origin	Trade	Remarks
7425	Pte	Tchaliaken	G	37	Panama	Canal ganger	
2405	Pte	Tomas	P	23	Valencia	Labourer	
2470	Pte	Treserras	R	29	Barcelona	Labourer	
2545	Pte	Trilles	E	25	Tarragona	Radio mechanic	W/T, Married England
2986	Pte	Trujillo	F	24	Malaga		
2386	Pte	Umbo	J	25	Bilbao	Sailor	Native of Vascongada
2607	Pte	Valenzuela	J	29	Granada	Labourer	
2551	Pte	Valero	J	25	Barcelona	Shirt cutter	W/T
2535	Pte	Vallejo	R	29	Jaen	Labourer	
5983	Pte	Vaquer	J	21	Barcelona	Mechanic	W/T
2433	Pte	Verdugo	S	22	Toledo		
7020	Pte	Vilchis	M	27	La Linea	Bull fighter	
3010	Pte	Villasenor	F	28	Murcia		
2510	Pte	Virgilio	J	23	Tarragona	Shop assist	Dems

Notes:
Spellings and accents are as per the original nominal roll.
There are personnel missing from this list due to being trained as SCONCES at the time.
Dems – Demolitions trained (probably Spanish)
W/T – Wireless Training (probably Spanish)

Appendix II

List of SCONCEs

Regimental Number	Surname	First Name	Date of Birth	Enlisted at	Enlistment Centre	Date of Enlistment	Date of de-mobilisation	Notes
13802546	Aguera	Cristofol	16-Feb-14	Westward Ho	3 Centre	22-Jul-40	12-Mar-46	Class A Release / SCONCE 1
13802536	Alapont	Francisco	19-Jul-16	Westward Ho	3 Centre	17-Jul-40	14-Mar-46	Class A Release / SCONCE 5
13802471	Alvarez	Luiz	14-Jun-14	Westward Ho	3 Centre	17-Jul-40	12-Mar-46	Class A Release, CIA to ACC 1 Dec 51 / TNA HS9/27/4SCONCE 1/*
13802395	Aparicio	Baldomero	25-Dec-18	Westward Ho	3 Centre	16-Jul-40	20-Mar-46	Class A Release / SCONCE 1/*
13802443	Arroyo	Mariano	24-Mar-16	Westward Ho	3 Centre	17-Jul-40	20-Mar-46	Class A Release / SCONCE 1
13802444	Balague	Francisco	02-Jan-22	Westward Ho	3 Centre	17-Jul-40	16-Mar-46	Class A Release / SCONCE 4
13802592	Belenguer	Pedro	19-Apr-14	Westward Ho	3 Centre	24-Jul-40	03-Oct-43	TNA HS9/120/1/ SCONCE 2 *
13802593	Belles	Valeriano Bauesdo	18-Oct-16	Westward Ho	3 Centre	24-Jul-40	16-Mar-46	Class A Release/ SCONCE 5
13802852	Bernad	Jose	14-Jul-12	Liverpool	3 Centre	26-Aug-40	07-Jan-46	Class A Release SCONCE 4
13803047	Bon	Miguel	13-Jan 17	Swanwick	3 Centre	14-Sep 40	13-Mar 46	Class A Release/ SCONCE 4
13802446	Bosque	Jose	02-Jul-12	Westward Ho	3 Centre	17-Jul-40	09-Mar-42	Class W(T) Reserve 28 Feb 42, discharged Para *
13802853	Busquet Morant	Carols	08-Mar-05	Liverpool	3 Centre	26-Aug-40	27-Sep-46	Class W(T) Reseve3 13 Nov 42, re-joined 2 Oct 45, Class A Release SCONCE I
13802703	Colone	Juan	24-May-12	Westward Ho	3 Centre	06-Aug-40	07-Jan-46	Class A Release SCONCE 4
13802447	Carreras	Jose	25-Jul-16	Westward Ho	3 Centre	17-Jul-40	25-Mar-43	Para XVI (V Good) TNA HS9/271/4SCONCE 3
13802418	Carron	Ricardo	1914	Westward Ho	3 Centre	17-Jul-40	05-Nov-45	Para XVI (Good)SCONCE 5

APPENDIX II

Regimental Number	Surname	First Name	Date of Birth	Enlisted at	Enlistment Centre	Date of Enlistment	Date of de-mobilisation	Notes
13803004	Casabayo (Martinez)	Fernando	07-Aug-11	Swanwick	3 Centre	14-Sep-40	11-Feb-46	Class A Release TNA HS9/276/2 SCONCE 4
13803003	Cayuela (Salvador) Chuz	Sebastian	18-Sep-12	Swanwick	3 Centre	14-Sep-40	12-Mar-46	Class A Release TNA HS9/282/8 +photo SCONCE 3
13802703	Colome (Massalle)	Juan	24-May-12	Westward Ho	3 Centre	06-Aug-40	07-Jan-46	Class A Release
13802445	Cruz	Antonio	21-Apr-11	Westward Ho	3 Centre	16-Jul-40	15-Feb-46	Class A Release HS9/378/2
13802410	Cuenca (Henrique)	Donato	28-Apr-19	Westward Ho	3 Centre	16-Jul-40	15-Mar-46	Class A Release, transferred to RE 1 Nov 51TNA HS9/379/5SCONCE 3
13802422	Cuevas	Miguel	29-Apr-20	Westward Ho	3 Centre	17-Jul-40	06-Nov-45	Para XVI (Fair) SCONCE 5
13802391	Delgado-Martinez	Manuel	26-Jul-19	Westward Ho	3 Centre	16-Jul-40	19-Mar-46	Class A Release SCONCE 1*
13802385	Del Rio	Nicolas	13-Mar-14	Westward Ho	3 Centre	16-Jul-40	20-Mar-46	Class A Release SCONCE 1
	Del Rio	Eduardo						TNAHS9/1262/6
13802493	Egea	Ignacio	25-Apr-18	Westward Ho	3 Centre	17-Jul-40	14-Mar-46	Class A Release SCONCE 5
13802474	Escaso	Fabian	08-Jan-17	Westward Ho	3 Centre	17-Jul-40	20-Mar-46	Class A Release TNAHS9/484/85 SCONCE 5
13802514	Espallargas (Ferrer)	Manuel	26-Jan-09	Westward Ho	3 Centre	17-Jul-40	24-Jan-46	Class A Release TNA HS9/485/5 SCONCE 4
13802484	Sanfelix	Jose	15-Mar-17	Westward Ho	3 Centre	17-Jul-40	14-Mar-46	Class A Release SCONCE 5
13802407	Fernandez	Antonio	17-Nov-15	Westward Ho	3 Centre	16-Jul-40	12-Mar-46	Class A Release SCONCE 3
13802494	Fernandez	Francisco	03-Apr-20	Westward Ho	3 Centre	17-Jul-40	16-Mar-46	Class A Release SCONCE 5
13802596	Fernandez	Teodoro	01-Apr-16	Westward Ho	3 Centre	24-Jul-40	07-Sep-45	Para XVI (V Good)
13803010	Villasenor	Francisco	05-Nov-14	Swanwick	3 Centre	14-Sep-40	12-Mar-46	Class A Release
13802475	Gallego (Lozaro)	Blas	03-Feb-21	Westward Ho	3 Centre	17-Jul-40	27-Nov-45	Para XVI (V Good)SCONCE 5
	Molina Garcia	José						TNAHS9/561/3 (NOT Sconce but Republican)
13802392	Garcia	Juan	14-Feb-01	Westward Ho	3 Centre	16-Jul-40	07-Sep-44	6 HTU, Para XVIIIA (V Good) TNAHS9/561/4 SCONCE 5

Regimental Number	Surname	First Name	Date of Birth	Enlisted at	Enlistment Centre	Date of Enlistment	Date of de-mobilisation	Notes
13802496	Garcia	José	9-Feb-23	Westward Ho	3 Centre	16-Jul-40		HS9/1494/3 Transferred to R Signals 5 Aug 44 SCONCE*
13802476	Gener	Ramon	26-Jul-20	Westward Ho	3 Centre	17-Jul-40	16-Mar-46	Class A Release
	Gener	H						
13802497	Gil	Pedro	21-Apr-22	Westward Ho	3 Centre	17-Jul-40	19-Mar-46	Class A Release SCONCE 3
13802477	Guitierrez	Antonio	20-Jan-13	Westward Ho	3 Centre	17-Jul-40	11-Nov-43	DIED 11 Nov 43 SCONCE 5
13802452	Gomez	Joaquin	09-Nov-14	Westward Ho	3 Centre	17-Jul-40	12-Mar-46	Class A Release, CIA RASC Records 18 Feb 52 TNAHS9/598/3 SCONCE 5
13802399	Gonzalez (Ragal)	Comado	16-Apr-21	Westward Ho	3 Centre	16-Jul-40	17-Mar-46	Class A Release SCONCE 4
13802597	Grande (Catalan)	Antonio	28-Apr-16	Westward Ho	3 Centre	24-Jul-40	14-Mar-46	Class A Release TNA HS9/608/9 SCONCE 4
	Gutierrez	Francisco						
	Gutierrez Gallastegui	Fernando						TNAHS9/638/4 (Not SCONCE)
13803012	Gutierrez	Fernando	08-Nov-20	Swanwick	3 Centre	14-Sep-40	19-Mar-46	Class A Release SCONCE 3
	Hamira							
13802605	Herreras (Catalan)	Pedro	30-Aug-17	Westward Ho	3 Centre	24-Jul-40	12-Mar-46	Class A Release SCONCE 4
13802517	Iniesta	Juan	24-Sep-16	Westward Ho	3 Centre	17-Jul-40	13-Mar-46	Class A Release TNAHS9/777/2 SCONCE 5
13802498	Iovino	Francisco	03-Jun-21	Westward Ho	3 Centre	17-Jul-40	16-Mar-46	Class A Release *
	Iovono							
13802598	Izquierdo (Clement)	Clemente	16-Nov-16	Westward Ho	3 Centre	24-Jul-40	15-Mar-46	Class A Release HS9/781/8 SCONCE 3
13802370	Izquierdo	Vicente	12-Dec-19	Westward Ho	3 Centre	16-Jul-40	19-Mar-46	Class A Release SCONCE 3
13802518	Jurado	Jose	09-Jul-21	Westward Ho	3 Centre	17-Jul-40	20-Mar-46	Class A Release SCONCE 1
13802389	Laiseca	Sebastian	25-Dec-16	Westward Ho	3 Centre	16-Jul-40	16-Mar-46	Class A Release HS9/815/8 SCONCE 2 *
	Laiscon							

APPENDIX II 281

Regimental Number	Surname	First Name	Date of Birth	Enlisted at	Enlistment Centre	Date of Enlistment	Date of de-mobilisation	Notes
	Lassierra	Domenico						SCONCE 1*
13802455	Latienda	Angel	01-Mar-18	Westward Ho	3 Centre	17-Jul-40	15-Mar-46	Class A Release SCONCE 1
13802373	Lopez (Fernandez Salvador Garcia)	Modesto	14-Sep-16	Westward Ho	3 Centre	16-Jul-40	12-Mar-46	Class A Release SCONCE 4
13802500	Luque	Jose	21-Apr-09	Westward Ho	3 Centre	17-Jul-40	13-Feb-46	Class A Release SCONCE 3*
13802456	Mallafre	Manuel Pla	22-Nov-19	Westward Ho	3 Centre	17-Jul-40		Transferred to ACC 9 Jul 44 SCONCE 3
13803002	Marco	Silvain (Guillot)	28-Mar-19	Swanwick	3 Centre	14-Sep-40	16-Mar-46	Class A Release SCONCE 4
13802411	Martin	Guillermo	14-May-13	Westward Ho	3 Centre	16-Jul-40	12-Mar-46	Class A Release SCONCE 3
13802441	Martinez	Salvador	19-Mar-19	Westward Ho	3 Centre	17-Jul-40	15-Mar-46	Class A Release*
13802478	Mas	Jaime	06-Jul-20	Westward Ho	3 Centre	17-Jul-40	20-Mar-46	Class A Release, CIA ACC 1 Dec 51 SCONCE 3
13802549	Masso	Benito	26-Jul-17	Westward Ho	3 Centre	22-Jul-40	14-Mar-46	Class A Release SCONCE 3
13802459	Melis	Luis	24-Sep-08	Westward Ho	3 Centre	17-Jul-40	15-Jan-46	Class A Release SCONCE 5
13802460	Membrado (Juan)	Juan	15-Apr-15	Westward Ho	3 Centre	17-Jul-40		Class A Release SCONCE 3
13802415	Molina (Nieto)	Esteban	19-Nov-20	Westward Ho	3 Centre	17-Jul-40	19-Mar-46	Class A Release, CIA ACC 1 Dec 51 SCONCE 4
13802502	Montoursi	Lorenzo	20-Feb-18	Westward Ho	3 Centre	17-Jul-40	21-Mar-46	Class A Release*
13802523	Muntane	Jose	30-Jul-21	Westward Ho	3 Centre	17-Jul-40	30-Mar-46	Class A Release*
13802522	Munoz	Andres	03-Aug-20	Westward Ho	3 Centre	17-Jul-40	20-Jan-44	44 Coy, Para XVI (V Good) SCONCE 5
	Munoz	A						
13802382	Munoz	Francisco	14-Mar-14	Westward Ho	3 Centre	16-Jul-40	12-Mar-46	Class A Release TNA HS9/1075/6SCONCE 3
13802378	Munoz	Joaquim	17-Aug-17	Westward Ho	3 Centre	16-Jul-40	14-Mar-46	Class A Release SCONCE 3
13802524	Nadal	Joaquim	12-Apr-19	Westward Ho	3 Centre	17-Jul-40	15-Mar-46	Class A Release SCONCE 1
13802480	Navarro	Francisco	23-May-20	Westward Ho	3 Centre	17-Jul-40	16-Mar-46	Class A Release SCONCE 3
13802390	Nicolas	Jose	19-Feb-19	Westward Ho	3 Centre	16-Jul-40	15-Mar-46	Class A Release

Regimental Number	Surname	First Name	Date of Birth	Enlisted at	Enlistment Centre	Date of Enlistment	Date of de-mobilisation	Notes
13802504	Nieto	Teodoro	01-Apr-17	Westward Ho	3 Centre	17-Jul-40	14-Mar-46	Class A Release
13802481	Ortega	Antonio	13-Jun-12	Westward Ho	3 Centre	17-Jul-40	21-Mar-45	6 HTU, Para XVI (V Good)TNA HS9/1102/4SCONCE 1
13802541	Ortiz (Diego)	Armando	13-May-17	Westward Ho	3 Centre	17-Jul-40	14-Mar-46	Class A Release SCONCE 4
13802525	Ostio	Jose	16-Jun-16	Westward Ho	3 Centre	17-Jul-40		DESERTER 17 Oct 44TNA HS9/1128/3 SCONCE 3
13803017	Palanca	Ramon	19-Jul-17	Swanwick	3 Centre	14-Sep-40	14-Mar-46	Class A Release
13802506	Palomar	Jose	03-Jul-14	Westward Ho	3 Centre	17-Jul-40	12-Mar-46	Class A Release
13802371	Panchame (Busquet)	Fenito	25-Dec-23	Westward Ho	3 Centre	16-Jul-40		DESERTER 16 Dec 44SCONCE 4
13802851	Pardo (Garcia)	Jose	13-Mar-19	Liverpool	3 Centre	19-Aug-40	07-Jan-46	Class A Release TNA HS9/1143/8 SCONCE 4
13803015	Perez Miranda	Augusto	28-Apr-07	Swanwick	3 Centre	14-Sep-40	15-Jan-46	Class A Release SCONCE 4
13802380	Peraferrer	Francisco	20-Apr-19	Westward Ho	3 Centre	16-Jul-40	15-Mar-46	Class A Release
13802465	Planells (Ayler)	Jose	06-Sep-19	Westward Ho	3 Centre	17-Jul-40	16-Mar-46	Class A Release SCONCE 4
13802434	Pollan	Leandro	20-Jan-16	Westward Ho	3 Centre	17-Jul-40	12-Mar-46	Class A Release SCONCE 5
13803018	Prades (Molina)	Juan	17-Jun-18	Swanwick	3 Centre	14-Sep-40	15-Mar-46	Class A Release TNA HS9/1207/1 SCONCE 4
13802467	Puig	Antonio	13-Jun-20	Westward Ho	3 Centre	17-Jul-40	16-Mar-46	Class A Release
13802376	Pujol (Galvet)	Alfonso	15-Sep-16	Westward Ho	3 Centre	16-Jul-40	14-Mar-46	Class A Release TNA HS9/1217/1 SCONCE 4
	Pusol							
13802542	Queralt	Jaime	09-Feb-21	Westward Ho	3 Centre	17-Jul-40	20-Mar-46	Class A Release SCONCE 1 *
	Ramira							
13803030	Rodriguez	Jose	18-Dec-03	Swanwick	3 Centre	14-Sep-40	15-Dec-49	Later 13041649, Class A Release TNAHS9/1275/8 (+photo) SCONCE 5
	Romeo (Subirats)	Juan						HS9/1279/2
13802543	Romera	Francisco	23-Jul-21	Westward Ho	3 Centre	17-Jul-40	19-Mar-46	Class A Release SCONCE 3
13802509	Romero	Jose	05-Apr-12	Westward Ho	3 Centre	17-Jul-40	07-Jan-46	Class A Release SCONCE 4
13802379	Ruiz	Francisco	17-Jul-17	Westward Ho	3 Centre	16-Jul-40	12-Nov-45	Class B Release TNA HS9/1290/8

APPENDIX II

Regimental Number	Surname	First Name	Date of Birth	Enlisted at	Enlistment Centre	Date of Enlistment	Date of de-mobilisation	Notes
13802533	Saez	Luis	17-Mar-17	Westward Ho	3 Centre	17-Jul-40	14-Mar-46	Class A Release TNA HS9/1298/6
13803020	Roig	Angel	02-Aug-14	Swanwick	3 Centre	14-Sep-40	12-Mar-46	Class A Release
13802850	Salvador	Sebastian	25-Oct-13	Liverpool	3 Centre	19-Aug-40	20-Mar-46	Class A Release SCONCE 4
13802544	Sanabrias	Francisco	29-Mar-12	Westward Ho	3 Centre	17-Jul-40	07-Jan-46	Class A Release *
13803031	Sanchez (Berroz)	Jose	14-Feb-20	Swanwick	3 Centre	14-Sep-40	20-Mar-46	Class A Release SCONCE 4
13802430	Sanchez	Rafael	10-Jul-18	Westward Ho	3 Centre	17-Jul-40	20-Jul-46	Class A Release SCONCE 3
13802435	Tapia	Juan	10-Jan-20	Westward Ho	3 Centre	17-Jul-40		DESERTER 16 Dec 44 SCONCE 5
	Trujillo	Francois						TNAHS9/1488/1 SCONCE 5
13802425	Tuset	Juan	04-Mar-20	Westward Ho	3 Centre	17-Jul-40	01-Sep-46	Class A Release TNA HS9/1494/3
13802386	Umbo	Jose	16-Sep-17	Westward Ho	3 Centre	16-Jul-40	14-Mar-46	Class A Release TNA HS9/1497/6 SCONCE I *
13802604	Velasco	Jesus	24-Dec-15	Westward Ho	3 Centre	24-Jul-40	21-Mar-46	Class A Release SCONCE 2 *
13802551	Valero	Jose	31-Mar-17	Westward Ho	3 Centre	22-Jul-40	20-Mar-46	Class A Release SCONCE 3
13802433	Verdugo	Simeon	18-Feb-21	Westward Ho	3 Centre	17-Jul-40	19-Mar-46	Class A Release SCONCE 5
	Villaseisor							
13803010	Villasenor	Francisco	05-Nov-14	Swanwick	3 Centre	14-Sep-40	12-Mar-46	Class A Release SCONCE 4

Notes

* Selected and attended parachute training.
TNA HS/ National Archives file reference.
Class A Release Standard De-mobilisation from the Army with Reserve Liability at the end of the War.
Para XVI Medical Discharge and conduct upon release.
Class W(T) Reserve Discharge with transfer to the Reserve.
Spelling is as in the files and the nominal rolls.
Some names may be repeated due to the spelling.
This list shows a total of 119 names. It is presumed there were some twenty more but records of these have not been found, yet.

Appendix III

50 Middle East Commando List Summary

63 × Spaniards in alphabetical order as follows:

Ser	Army Number	Rank	Name	Date & Place of Birth	Enlistment Date	History
01	6100501/13808223	Pte	Alarcón Gómez, Cayo	10/04/17	23/08/40	FFL/BMVE, No. 50 ME Cdo, posted to D Bn of Layforce 24 Mar 41, escapes Crete, posted to Depot Commando & Holding Unit 17 Jul 41, confirmed in D Sqn 1 SSR* Jun 42.
02	6100503/13808266	Pte	Albadalejo, Alejandro		23/08/40	FFL/BMVE, No. 50 ME Cdo, posted to D Bn of Layforce 24 Mar 41, Crete, POW, WIA, captured, confirmed missing 2 Jun 41. Later transported to Stalag 344/8b.
03	6100504/13808238	Cpl	Álvarez, José		23/08/40	FFL/BMVE, No. 50 ME Cdo, posted to D Bn of Layforce 24 Mar 41,Crete, confirmed missing 2 Jun 41. POW Stalag 383
04	6100544 / 13806210	Pte	Arco, Luciano	20/05/18 Almeria	11/09/40	FFL/BMVE, No. 50 ME Cdo, posted to D Bn of Layforce 24 Mar 41, Not in Crete (Hospital), posted to Depot Commando & Holding Unit 17 Jul 41, receives PC number 5 Jan 42, confirmed D Sqn 1 SSR* June 42. Confirmed 362 (A) Coy PC 20 Oct 44.
05	6100502/13808211	Pte	Asenjo, Antonio	30/10/12 Puebla	23/08/40	FFL/BMVE, No. 50 ME Cdo, posted to D Bn of Layforce 24 Mar 41, escapes Crete, posted to Depot Commando & Holding Unit 17 Jul 41, receives PC number 5 Jan 42, confirmed D Sqn 1 SSR* June 42. 362 (A) Coy PC 20 Oct 44. Transferred to Army Air Corps 21 May 45.
06	6100552/13808212/ 13041866	Pte	Balerdi, Justo	26/07/20	13/10/40	FFL/BMVE, No. 50 ME Cdo, posted to D Bn of Layforce 24 Mar 41, Not in Crete (Hospital), posted to Depot Commando & Holding Unit 17 Jul 41, receives PC number 5 Jan 42, known to be in 1 SSR* Jun 42, posted PC Oct 43, 2nd SAS Dec 43, KIA 21 April 1945. Changed his name to Robert BRUCE.

APPENDIX III 285

Ser	Army Number	Rank	Name	Date & Place of Birth	Enlistment Date	History
07	6100506/13808213	Pte	Bardenas, Roberto	05/04/19	23/08/40	FFL/BMVE, No. 50 ME Cdo, posted to D Bn of Layforce 24 Mar 41, Crete, given initial PC number 5 Jan 42.
08	6100505/13808239	L Sgt	Barroso, Manuel		23/08/40	FFL/BMVE, No. 50 ME Cdo, posted to D Bn of Layforce 24 Mar 41, Crete, confirmed missing 2 Jun 41. POW Stalag 383
09	6100545/13808257	LCpl	Blasco, Vicente	25/04/17	11/09/40	FFL/BMVE, No. 50 ME Cdo, posted to D Bn of Layforce 24 Mar 41, confirmed missing 2 Jun 41. POW Stalag 3d Berlin, then Stalag 4c (labourer)
10	6100551/13808260	Pte	Bravo, José		13/10/40	FFL/BMVE, No. 50 ME Cdo, posted to D Bn of Layforce 24 Mar 41, Crete, confirmed missing 2 Jun 41. POW Stalag 8b
11	6100553/13808261	Pte	Carmona, Miguel		13/10/40	FFL/BMVE, No. 50 ME Cdo, posted to D Bn of Layforce 24 Mar 41, Crete, confirmed missing 2 Jun 41. POW Stalag 8b then 4a
12	6100507/13808267	Pte	Castellano, Francisco		23/08/40	FFL/BMVE, No. 50 ME Cdo, posted to D Bn of Layforce 24 Mar 41, Crete, confirmed missing 2 Jun 41. POW Stalag 4c
13	6100546/13808258	Pte	Cervantes, Santiago	03/08/18	11/09/40	FFL/BMVE, No. 50 ME Cdo, posted to D Bn of Layforce 24 Mar 41, Crete, confirmed missing 2 Jun 41. POW Stalag 4b. 43 (coal mining)
14	6100508/13808217	Cpl	Delgado, Andrés	06/01/20 Murcia	23/08/40	FFL/BMVE, No. 50 ME Cdo, posted to D Bn of Layforce 24 Mar 41, Crete, escapes Crete, posted to Depot Commando & Holding Unit 17 Jul 41, given PC number 5 Jan 42, confirmed 361 (A) Coy PC 20 Oct 44. De-mobbed 21-Jun-46. Class A Release.
15	6100509/13808240	Cpl	Díaz, José	01/01/18	23/08/40	FFL/BMVE, No. 50 ME Cdo, posted to D Bn of Layforce 24 Mar 41, Crete, confirmed missing 2 Jun 41. POW Stalag 3d then 383
16	6100510/13808218	L/Cpl	Esteve, Fernando	23/04/16 Vilanova	23/08/40	FFL/BMVE, No. 50 ME Cdo, posted to D Bn of Layforce 24 Mar 41, Crete, escapes Crete, posted to Depot Commando & Holding Unit 17 Jul 41, given PC number 5 Jan 42, transferred to QRR 21 Jul 43. WIA in Italy Oct 43. Awarded MiD Jan 46 for actions in Germany.
17	6100512/13808242	Pte	Fajardo, Joaquín	07/03/19 Otívar, Granada	23/08/40	FFL/BMVE, No. 50 ME Cdo, posted to D Bn of Layforce 24 Mar 41, Crete, confirmed missing 2 Jun 41. POW Stalag 383 then 4c (Tetchen on Elbe – railway worker). Once liberated returned to UK and posted to 361 (A) Coy PC.

Ser	Army Number	Rank	Name	Date & Place of Birth	Enlistment Date	History
18	6100514 /13808215	Pte	Fernández Caballero, Juan Francisco	24/07/18 Murcia	23/08/40	FFL/BMVE, No. 50 ME Cdo, posted to D Bn of Layforce 24 Mar 41, Crete, escapes Crete, posted to Depot Commando & Holding Unit 17 Jul 41, receives PC number 5 Jan 42, confirmed 1 SSR* June 42. Confirmed in 362 (A) Coy PC 20 Oct 44. Confirmed in Parachute Regiment in 1945. AAC by 31 May 45. Changed name to MORGAN.
19	6100513/13808243	Pte	Fraile Guerra, Tomás		23/08/40	FFL/BMVE, No. 50 ME Cdo, posted to D Bn of Layforce 24 Mar 41, Crete, confirmed missing 2 Jun 41. POW Stalag 4c
20	6100511/13808241	Pte	Franco García, Tomás	02/03/15 Zaragoza	23/08/40	FFL/BMVE, No. 50 ME Cdo, posted to D Bn of Layforce 24 Mar 41, Crete, confirmed missing 2 Jun 41. POW Stalag 4b/c. Escaped 28/03/45 and WIA.
21	6100517 /13808246	Pte	Galarreta Manconas, Luciano		23/08/40	FFL/BMVE, No. 50 ME Cdo, posted to D Bn of Layforce 24 Mar 41, Crete, confirmed missing 2 Jun 41. POW Stalag 4c
22	6100518 /13808247	Cpl	Galera, Enrique		23/08/40	FFL/BMVE, No. 50 ME Cdo, posted to D Bn of Layforce 24 Mar 41, Crete, confirmed missing 2 Jun 41. POW Stalag 344/8c
23	6100519	Pte	García, Abundio		11/09/40	FFL/BMVE, No. 50 ME Cdo, posted to D Bn of Layforce 24 Mar 41, Crete, escapes Crete, posted to Depot Commando & Holding Unit 17 Jul 41.
24	6100550/13808220	Pte	García, Antonio	15/08/15 Almansa	11/09/40	FFL/BMVE, No. 50 ME Cdo, posted to D Bn of Layforce 24 Mar 41, Crete, escapes Crete, posted to Depot Commando & Holding Unit 17 Jul 41, confirmed in D Sqn 1 SSR* Jun 42, given PC number 5 Jan 42, confirmed in 362 (A) Coy PC 20 Oct 44. De-mobbed 21-Jun-46. Class A Release.
25	6100515/13808244	Pte	García, Juan		23/08/40	FFL/BMVE, No. 50 ME Cdo, posted to D Bn of Layforce 24 Mar 41, Crete, confirmed missing 2 Jun 41. POW Stalag 4f
26	6100556/13808221	Pte	Garrigos, García	25/02/17	11/10/40	FFL/BMVE, No. 50 ME Cdo, posted to D Bn of Layforce 24 Mar 41, Crete, escapes Crete in 42, posted to Depot Commando & Holding Unit 17 Jul 41, confirmed in D Sqn 1 SSR* Jun 42.
27	6100555/ 13808268/ 138041867	Pte	Geronimo, Francisco	26/09/17	13/10/40	FFL/BMVE, No. 50 ME Cdo, posted to D Bn of Layforce 24 Mar 41, Crete, escapes Crete in 42, posted to Depot Commando & Holding Unit 17 Jul 41, confirmed in D Sqn 1 SSR* Jun 42. Posted PC Oct 43, 2nd SAS Dec 43 to end of war. Changed name to Frank WILLIAMS.

APPENDIX III 287

Ser	Army Number	Rank	Name	Date & Place of Birth	Enlistment Date	History
28	6100516/13808245	Sgt	Gómez, Serafín		23/08/40	FFL/BMVE, No. 50 ME Cdo, posted to D Bn of Layforce 24 Mar 41, Crete, confirmed missing 2 Jun 41. POW Stalag 344
29	6100520/13808248	Pte	Heras, Braulio		23/08/40	FFL/BMVE, No. 50 ME Cdo, posted to D Bn of Layforce 24 Mar 41, Crete, confirmed missing 2 Jun 41. POW Stalag 4c, KIA 8 May 45
30	6100557/13808263	Pte	Hidalgo, José	27/08/20 Córdoba	11/10/40	FFL/BMVE, No. 50 ME Cdo, posted to D Bn of Layforce 24 Mar 41, Crete, confirmed missing 2 Jun 41. POW Stalag 4b/c
31	6100521/13808249	Cpl	Jorda, Francisco		23/08/40	FFL/BMVE, No. 50 ME Cdo, posted to D Bn of Layforce 24 Mar 41, Crete, confirmed missing 2 Jun 41. POW Stalag 3d, 21a
32	6100523	Pte	León, J		23/08/40	FFL/BMVE, No. 50 ME Cdo, posted to D Bn of Layforce 24 Mar 41, hospitalised for Crete, Commando Holding Depot. X List. Possibly returned to QRR as annotated on QRR Enlistment Register.
33	6100558/13808264	Pte	Lillo, Julián	Abanojar, Ciudad Real	11/10/40	FFL/BMVE, No. 50 ME Cdo, posted to D Bn of Layforce 24 Mar 41, Crete, confirmed missing 2 Jun 41. POW Stalag 344/8b
34	6100522/13808270	Pte	Lloret, Carlos		23/08/40	FFL/BMVE, No. 50 ME Cdo, posted to D Bn of Layforce 24 Mar 41, Crete, confirmed missing 2 Jun 41. POW Stalag 344/8b
35	6100524/13808250	Pte	Lumbrera, Francisco	Jaén	23/08/40	FFL/BMVE, No. 50 ME Cdo, posted to D Bn of Layforce 24 Mar 41, Crete, confirmed missing 2 Jun 41. POW Stalag 4c, KIA 8 May 45
36	6100525/13808233	Pte	Luque Tirado, Antonio	20/01/11	23/08/40	FFL/BMVE, No. 50 ME Cdo, posted to D Bn of Layforce 24 Mar 41, not in Crete. Classed as a deserter 2 Dec 43.
37	6100528/13808251	Sgt	Marín, Basilio		23/08/40	FFL/BMVE, No. 50 ME Cdo, posted to D Bn of Layforce 24 Mar 41, Crete, confirmed missing 2 Jun 41. Spent 10 months on Crete escaping and evading. Captured Apr 1942. POW Stalag 3d Berlin then 383
38	6100529/13808272	Pte	Marino, Ángel	27/07/17 Bilbao	23/08/40	FFL/BMVE, No. 50 ME Cdo, posted to D Bn of Layforce 24 Mar 41, Crete, confirmed missing 2 Jun 41. POW Stalag 344/8b
39	6100561/13808265	Pte	Martínez, Aurelio		13/10/40	FFL/BMVE, No. 50 ME Cdo, posted to D Bn of Layforce 24 Mar 41, Crete, confirmed missing 2 Jun 41. POW Stalag 4b

Ser	Army Number	Rank	Name	Date & Place of Birth	Enlistment Date	History
40	6100549/13808224	Pte	Martínez, Barnabé	11/07/14 Madrid	11/09/40	FFL/BMVE, No. 50 ME Cdo, posted to D Bn of Layforce 24 Mar 41, Crete, escapes Crete, posted to Depot Commando & Holding Unit 17 Jul 41, confirmed in D Sqn 1 SSR* Jun 42. Down as a deserter 24 Oct 43. Confirmed 362 (A) Coy PC 20 Oct 44. Class A release.
41	6100559/13808259	Pte	Martínez, Francisco		11/10/40	FFL/BMVE, No. 50 ME Cdo, posted to D Bn of Layforce 24 Mar 41, Crete, confirmed missing 2 Jun 41. POW Stalag 4b
42	6100547/13808226	Pte	Martínez, Miguel	23/02/19 Or 07/03/40 Madrid	11/09/40	FFL/BMVE, No. 50 ME Cdo, posted to D Bn of Layforce 24 Mar 41, Crete, escapes Crete, posted to Depot Commando & Holding Unit 17 Jul 41, confirmed in D Sqn 1 SSR* Jun 42. Confirmed 361 (A) Coy PC 20 Oct 44. De-mobbed 21-Jun-46. Class A Release.
43	6100548/13808225	Pte	Martínez, Francisco	04/03/19 Carolina	11/09/40	FFL/BMVE, No. 50 ME Cdo, posted to D Bn of Layforce 24 Mar 41, Crete, escapes Crete in 42, posted to Depot Commando & Holding Unit 17 Jul 41, confirmed in D Sqn 1 SSR* Jun 42.
44	6100526/13808269	Pte	Mena, Juan		23/08/40	FFL/BMVE, No. 50 ME Cdo, posted to D Bn of Layforce 24 Mar 41, Crete, POW, 344/4b. Confirmed repatriated 3 Nov 1943 possibly via Barcelona.
45	6100527/13808227	Pte	Mena, Vincente	10/05/17	23/08/40	FFL/BMVE, No. 50 ME Cdo, posted to D Bn of Layforce 24 Mar 41, not in Crete, posted to Depot Commando & Holding Unit 17 Jul 41, transfers QRR 21 Jul 43, on D-Day, WIA 14 Jun 44. Medically discharged 7 Oct 44.
46	6100560/13808228	Pte	Mercado, José		13/10/40	FFL/BMVE, No. 50 ME Cdo, posted to D Bn of Layforce 24 Mar 41, Crete, escapes Crete in 42, posted to Depot Commando & Holding Unit 17 Jul 41, confirmed in D Sqn 1 SSR* Jun 42. De-mobbed 1 May 44. 12 Centre Para XVI (V Good).
47	6100530/13808252	LCpl	Navarrete, Francisco		23/08/40	FFL/BMVE, No. 50 ME Cdo, posted to D Bn of Layforce 24 Mar 41, Crete, confirmed missing 2 Jun 41. POW Stalag 344/8b
48	6100562/13808271	Pte	Pereira Martínez, Francisco	Extremadura	13/10/40	FFL/BMVE, No. 50 ME Cdo, posted to D Bn of Layforce 24 Mar 41, Crete, confirmed missing 2 Jun 41. POW Stalag 344/8c
49	6100532/13808239	Sgt	Pineira, Lorenzo	07/02/20 Vitoria	23/08/40	FFL/BMVE, No. 50 ME Cdo, posted to D Bn of Layforce 24 Mar 41, Crete, escapes Crete, posted to Depot Commando & Holding Unit 17 Jul 41, confirmed in D Sqn 1 SSR* Jun 42. Confirmed 361 (A) Coy PC 20 Oct 44. De-mobbed 21-Jun-46. Class A Release.

APPENDIX III   289

Ser	Army Number	Rank	Name	Date & Place of Birth	Enlistment Date	History
50	6100531/13808253	Pte	Postillo, Rafael		23/08/40	FFL/BMVE, No. 50 ME Cdo, posted to D Bn of Layforce 24 Mar 41, Crete, confirmed missing 2 Jun 41. POW Stalag 3d Berlin then 383
51	6100533/13808230	Pte	Redondo, José	04/04/19 or 20 Córdoba	23/08/40	FFL/BMVE, No. 50 ME Cdo, posted to D Bn of Layforce 24 Mar 41, Crete, escapes Crete, posted to Depot Commando & Holding Unit 17 Jul 41, confirmed in D Sqn 1 SSR* Jun 42. Confirmed 361 (A) Coy PC 20 Oct 44. De-mobbed 21-Jun-46. Class A Release.
52	6100563	Pte	Rodriguez, José		13/10/40	FFL/BMVE, No. 50 ME Cdo, posted to D Bn of Layforce 24 Mar 41.
53	6100534/13808254	Pte	Sánchez, Manuel	21/06/46	23/08/40	FFL/BMVE, No. 50 ME Cdo, posted to D Bn of Layforce 24 Mar 41, Crete, confirmed missing 2 Jun 41. POW Stalag 3d then Oflag 7b. De-mobbed 21 Jun 46.
54	6100554/13808262	Pte	Sánchez Monterrubio, Cleto	Azuaga	13/10/40	FFL/BMVE, No. 50 ME Cdo, posted to D Bn of Layforce 24 Mar 41, Crete, confirmed missing 2 Jun 41. POW Stalag 8b
55	6100536/13808231	Pte	Santiago, Basilio	17/07/18 Or 07/06/19 Badajoz	23/08/40	FFL/BMVE, No. 50 ME Cdo, posted to D Bn of Layforce 24 Mar 41, not in Crete, posted to Depot Commando & Holding Unit 17 Jul 41, confirmed in D Sqn 1 SSR* Jun 42 (Para training). Confirmed 20 361 (A) Coy PC Oct 44. De-mobbed 21-Jun-46. Class A Release.
56	6100535/13808232	Pte	Surera, Manuel	18/03/19 Or 05/03/19 Cordoba	23/08/40	FFL/BMVE, No. 50 ME Cdo, posted to D Bn of Layforce 24 Mar 41, escapes Crete, posted to Depot Commando & Holding Unit 17 Jul 41, confirmed in D Sqn 1 SSR* Jun 42 (Para training). Confirmed 361 (A) Coy PC 20 Oct 44. De-mobbed 21-Jun-46. Class A Release.
57	6100537/13808278	A/LCpl	Tavio, Enrique	18/11/15 Puerto Luz	23/08/40	FFL/BMVE, No. 50 ME Cdo, posted to C Bn of Layforce 16 Apr 41, posted to Cyprus, confirmed in 362 (A) Coy PC 20 Oct 44.
58	6100538 13808255	Pte	Torralbo, Miguel	08/09/07 Córdoba	23/08/40	FFL/BMVE, No. 50 ME Cdo, posted to D Bn of Layforce 24 Mar 41, Crete, confirmed missing 2 Jun 41. POW Stalag 4b.
59	6100539/13808214	Sgt	Trancho Bartolomé, Moisés	25/11/16 Barakaldo	23/08/40	FFL/BMVE, No. 50 ME Cdo, posted to D Bn of Layforce 24 Mar 41, Crete, escapes Crete, posted to Depot Commando & Holding Unit 17 Jul 41, given PC number 5 Jan 42, known to be in 1 SSR* Jun 42*, died 29 Jul 1943 (cause unknown).

Ser	Army Number	Rank	Name	Date & Place of Birth	Enlistment Date	History
60	6100540/13808256	Pte	Trill, Jaime		23/08/40	FFL/BMVE, No. 50 ME Cdo, posted to D Bn of Layforce 24 Mar 41, Crete, confirmed missing 2 Jun 41. POW Stalag 3d Berlin then 383.
61	6100541/13808222	Cpl	Valero Giménez, Antonio	13/07/14 or 14/06/13 Las Mecas	23/08/40	FFL/BMVE, No. 50 ME Cdo, posted to D Bn of Layforce 24 Mar 41, Crete, escapes Crete, posted to Depot Commando & Holding Unit 17 Jul 41. Receives PC number 5 Jan 42, confirmed in D Sqn 1 SSR* Jun 42, confirmed in 362 (A) Coy PC 20 Oct 44.
62	6100542/13808215	Pte	Vargas Crespo, Antonio	30/01/16	23/08/40	FFL/BMVE, No. 50 ME Cdo, did not go Crete. Posted to Depot Commando & Holding Unit 20 Jun 41. Given PC number 5 Jan 42.
63	6100543/13080234	Pte	Villanova, Josep	06/09/20 Costa Blanca	23/08/40	FFL/BMVE, No. 50 ME Cdo, posted to Commando Depot Crete, escapes Crete, posted to Depot Commando & Holding Unit 17 Jul 41, confirmed in D Sqn 1 SSR* Jun 42, transfers QRR 21 Jul 43, WIA in Italy Oct 43, awarded MM1. Medical discharge 20 Jun 1944.

Notes
(All spellings of names in table above have been Hispanicised as spellings in various records differ):

FFL/*BMVE*   French Foreign Legion / *Bataillon de Marche de Volontaires Étrangers*
No. 50 ME Cdo   Number 50 Middle East Commando
D Bn Layforce   D Battalion of Layforce commanded by Col "Bob" Laycock
D Sqn 1 SSR*   D Squadron of 1st Special Service Regiment
QRR   Queens Royal Regiment (West Surrey)
Para Training   Parachute Training
WIA   Wounded in Action
KIA   Killed in Action
POW   Prisoner of War
361/362 (A) Coy PC   361/362 (Alien) Company Pioneer Corps
X List   Special duties

Appendix IV

Spaniards on the Nominal Roll of D Squadron, 1st Special Service Regiment in the Summer of 1942

Regimental Number	Surname	Initial	Comments
13808223	Alarcon	C.	
13808211	Asenjo	A.	
13808211	Arco	L.	
13808213	Balerdi	J.	
138082XX	Esteve	?	
13808215	Fernandez	J.	
13808219	Garcia	A.	
13808220	Garcia	A.	
80790	Garcia	J.	Origin unknown – could have been in No.51 ME Commando
81654	Garcia	E.	Origin unknown – could have been in No.51 ME Commando
13808221	Garrigos	A.	
80644	Ismael	M.	
	Jeronimo	F.	
13808225	Martinez	F.	
13808284	Martinez	B.	
13808236	Martinez	M.	
81896	Martinez	J.	Origin unknown – could have been in No.51 ME Commando
13808228	Mercado	J.	
81648	Morales	G.	Origin unknown – could have been in No.51 ME Commando
1808229	Pineira	L.	
13808231	Santiago	?	
80907	Soriano	A.	Origin unknown – could have been in No.51 ME Commando
13808232	Surera	M.	
13808221	Trancho	M.	Down as Cpl
13808222	Valero	A.	Down as LCpl
13808234	Villanova	J.	

Notes

This nominal roll is probably dated to August 1942 since Justo Balerdi was transferred in on 11 August 1942. Five individuals on this list are not original members of No.50 ME Commando and most probably other Spaniards who joined No. 51 ME Commando from the French forces, but this cannot be currently confirmed. However, there was certainly a 'Garcia' in No.51 ME Commando.
Note that some of those who survived Crete are not on this list, e.g. Redondo.

Appendix V

Spaniards in the SAS During The Second World War

Army Number	Name	History Summary
2nd SAS		
6100555/ 13808268/ 138041867	Francisco José Gerónimo (Frank Williams)	2nd SAS From Málaga. *Légion Étrangère*, June 1940 crossed to Palestine, No.50 ME Commando, posted to D Battalion of Layforce 24 March 1941, Crete, escaped Crete in 1942, posted to Depot Commando & Holding Unit 17 July 1941, confirmed in D Squadron 1 SSR August 1942. Posted PC October 1943. Joined SAS, 2nd SAS, (3 Squadron) December 1943 until end of war. Operations – DUNHILL V, TRUEFORM 2, TOMBOLA
6100552/ 13808212/ 138041866	Justo Balerdi (Robert Bruce)	2nd SAS (3 Squadron). From Sestao, Bilbao. *Légion Étrangère*, Jun 1940 crossed to Palestine, No.50 ME Commando, posted to D Battalion of Layforce 24 March 1941, Not in Crete (Hospital), posted to Depot Commando & Holding Unit 17 July 1941, received PC number 5 January 1942, confirmed in D Squadron 1 SSR August 1942, posted PC Oct 1943. Joined 2nd SAS, 3 Squadron, December 1943. KIA 21 April 1945. Operations – RUPERT 4, TOMBOLA
13301853	Rafael Ramos Masens (Did not change name apart from Ralph)	2nd SAS. From Barcelona but brought up in Madrid. *Légion Étrangère*, then labour company in N Africa. Enlisted British Army October 1943, 363 Company, volunteered to join SAS in Algeria December 1943, 2nd SAS, 3 Squadron, awarded MM in Italy 1945 on Operation TOMBOLA. Operations – DUNHILL V, BRAKE 2, GALIA, TOMBOLA
13301854	Juan Torrents Abadia (John Colman)	2nd SAS (3 Squadron). From Barcelona. *Légion Étrangère*, then labour company in N Africa. Enlisted British Army October 1943, 363 Company, volunteered to join SAS in Algeria December 1943 – 2nd SAS, 3 Squadron. Operations – DUNHILL V, TRUEFORM, ARCHWAY, APOSTLE/DOOMSDAY
13301810	Ángel (Higinio) Camarena Espinosa (Alan Cooper)	2nd SAS (3 Squadron). From Madrid. Served in Spanish Army in 1935–1936. Imprisoned 1936–1941. Joined Pioneer Corps, 363 Company in 1943 then SAS in December 1943. Operations – LOYTON (NORTH), ARCHWAY, APOSTLE/DOOMSDAY

SPANIARDS IN THE SAS DURING THE SECOND WORLD WAR 293

Army Number	Name	History Summary
13301811	Francisco Revuelta (Robert Shaw)	2nd SAS (3 Squadron). From Santander. *Légion Étrangère*, then labour company in N Africa, then Pioneer Corps, 361 Company in 1943, then SAS in December1943. POW Stalag 9c. Emigrated to Australia after war. Operations – DUNHILL V
13301792	Francisco López Martín (Henry Martin)	2nd SAS (HQ Squadron). Enlisted into the Pioneer Corps in N Africa, 361 Company, then SAS in December1943. Operations – LOYTON (NORTH)
13301840	Carlo(s) Bovio (James Benson)	2nd SAS (3 Squadron). Enlisted into the Pioneer Corps in N Africa, 361 Company then SAS. Captured 1945. Transferred to AAC 30 May 1945. Nationality not confirmed. Operations – DEFOE, DUNHILL V, PISTOL, GALIA
13301469	Enric Boganim (Henry Hall)	2nd SAS (3 Squadron). Seems to have been *Légion Étrangère* in N Africa, then joined Pioneer Corps, 361 Company in 1943, then SAS in December1943. Nationality not confirmed. Operations – WALLACE, ARCHWAY, HARDY
3rd & 4th SAS		
–	José García	3rd SAS (HQ Squadron, 1 Squadron). From Alicante. Joined the French Free Army September 1943. Posted to *3ᵉ BIA* October 1943 then sent to UK to 3rd SAS. Parachute training in August 1944. Operations – HARROD, BARKER, AMHERST
41278	Gabriel García	3rd SAS (1 Squadron). Born Casablanca but Spanish family. Joined the Free French Army September 1943. Posted to *3ᵉ BIA* October 1943, then sent to UK. Parachute training in March 1944. Operations – HARROD, BARKER, AMHERST
–	Francisco Benítez García	3rd SAS (3 Squadron). Joined the Free French Army September 1943. Posted to *3ᵉ BIA* October 1943 then sent to UK. Parachute training January 1944. Operations – DICKENS
31655	José Ibarra	*1ᵉ BIA*. From Barakaldo. Joined Free French Army April 1941 in Santiago, Chile. Travelled from Argentina to UK April 1941. Joined *1ᵉ BIA*. By August 1943 is a Corporal *1ᵉ BIA* in Camberley.
	Manuel Velasco	4th SAS (HQ Squadron, then 3 Squadron). Operations – FRANKLIN
41495	Nicolás Franco	3rd SAS. Joined Free French Army in Oran and arrived UK May 1944. Parachute training July 1944. Operations – MOSES
35179	Julio Cerrillos	4th SAS (3 Squadron, HQ Squadron). Enlisted in the 1st Foreign Cavalry Regiment in Fez December1939. Arrived UK December1942. Assigned to the 1st Air Infantry Company July 1943. Joined *4ᵉ BIA*, 2 Squadron. Promoted to Corporal August 1943. Operations – COONEY, FRANKLIN
3161	Roma Francisco Golf	3rd SAS. From Alicante. Joined Free French Army June 1943 in Tunisia. Parachute course January 1944. Operations – DERRY, ABEL, AMHERST

Appendix VI

List of Spaniards known to have died whilst serving in the British Army, recorded by the Commonwealth War Graves Commission

Service No, Rank, Name	Unit, Regiment, Country of Service	Date of Death Age	Commemorated at Remarks
13802426 Private Jose Lopez	Pioneer Corps United Kingdom	20 March 1941	Plymouth (Weston Mill) Cemetery Sec. C. Cons. Grave 17877 United Kingdom Killed during the Plymouth Blitz
13802384 Private Elardis Zamora	Pioneer Corps United Kingdom	20/21 March 1941	Plymouth (Weston Mill) Cemetery Sec. C. Cons. Grave 17881 United Kingdom Killed during the Plymouth Blitz
13802400 Private Francisco Gomez	Pioneer Corps United Kingdom	21 March 1941 22 years old	Brookwood 1939-1945 Memorial, Panel 20. Column 3 United Kingdom Killed during the Plymouth Blitz
13802426 Private Jose Lopez	Pioneer Corps United Kingdom	24 March 1941	Plymouth (Weston Mill) Cemetery Sec. C. Cons. Grave 17877 United Kingdom Killed during the Plymouth Blitz
13805409 Private Jose Martinez	Pioneer Corps United Kingdom	11 May 1942	Tidworth Military Cemetery Sec. B. (R.C.). Grave 186 United Kingdom
13809698 Private Gonzalo Collado De La Cruz	Pioneer Corps United Kingdom	10 May 1943 26 years old	El Alia Cemetery 12. H. 5. Algeria
Me/13808214 Corporal Moses Trancho-Bartolome	Middle East Commando / Pioneer Corps United Kingdom	29 July 1943 25 years old	Ramleh War Cemetery 3. F. 10. Israel and Palestine (including Gaza) Cause of death unknown

APPENDIX VI

Service No, Rank, Name	Unit, Regiment, Country of Service	Date of Death Age	Commemorated at Remarks
13809738 Private Gumersindo R Lasuen	Pioneer Corps United Kingdom	15 October 1943	El Alia Cemetery 12. C. 21. Algeria
13802477 Private Antonio Guitierrez	Pioneer Corps United Kingdom	11 November 1943	Bodmin Cemetery Sec. T. Grave 400.
Bna/13809978 Private De Toralba	Pioneer Corps UnitedKingdom	24 March 1944	Medjez-El-Bab War Cemetery 18. F. 7. Tunisia
13301767 Private Pedro Ansola Fuentecilla	Pioneer Corps United Kingdom	7 April 1944 20 years old	Bone War Cemetery, Annaba II. A. 1. Algeria
144117556 Private Lucio Sauquillo	Parachute Regiment, AAC 12th (10 Battalion The Green Howards (Yorkshire) Battalion United Kingdom	Died 13 June 1944 21 years old	Hermanville War Cemetery 1.N. 19 France Died of wounds after defence of Breville, Normandy
13807007 Private Antonio Reyes-Martinez	Pioneer Corps United Kingdom	19 June 1944 34 years old	Chippenham (London Road) Cemetery Sec. 1. Row G. Grave 4. United Kingdom
14428239 Trooper Jose Maria Irala	Reconnaissance Corps, AAC United Kingdom	Died 22 September 1944 20 years old	Arnhem Oosterbeek War Cemetery 22.A.5 Netherlands
2719596 Private Marcial Fernandez	2nd Irish Guards United Kingdom	Died 21 September 1944 26 years old	Arnhem Oosterbeek War Cemetery 11.B.4 Netherlands Killed in fighting at Nijmegen
Me 1304186 Private Robert Bruce	2nd SAS, AAC Pioneer Corps United Kingdom	21 April 1945	Milan War Cemetery V. A. 3. Italy KIA on Operation TOMBOLA in Emilia Romagna
Me 13808248 Private Braulio Heras	Middle East Commando / Pioneer Corps United Kingdom	8 May 1945	Died in Germany but on Athens Memorial Face 9. Greece Killed during air raid/artillery attack on POW Camp
Me 13808250 Private Francisco Lumbrera	Middle East Commando / Pioneer Corps United Kingdom	8 May 1945	Died in Germany but on Athens Memorial Face 8. Greece Killed during air raid/artillery attack on POW Camp
13805134 Corporal Bartolomeo Sanchez	Pioneer Corps United Kingdom	8 July 1946 24 years old	Axford Churchyard West part. United Kingdom

Information collated from <https://www.cwgc.org/find-records/find-war-dead/>

Appendix VII

List of Enlisted Spaniards in the British Army 1939–1946

Number	Rank	Name	Initials	DOB	Enlisted	Unit	Date Tos	Discharged	Remarks
13300006		Lojo	Jose Maria	15-Jun-15	Algiers	357 Coy	19-Aug-43	20-Nov-46	Class A Release
13300007	Pte	Magana	Juan	11-Jun-23	Algiers	357 Coy	16-Jan-44	18-Sep-46	Para XVI (V Good)
13300008	Pte	Canovas	Alfonso	09-Feb-25	Algiers	357 Coy	16-Jan-44	17-Oct-45	Para XVIIIA (V Good)
13300009		Rodenas	Eulogio	15-Sep-15	Algiers	357 Coy	29-Jan-44	22-Apr-47	Class A Release
13300010		Sabate	Ricardo	25-Aug-21	Algiers	357 Coy	29-Jan-44	10-Jul-47	Alias Carlos SORIA, Class A Release
13300011		Duenas	Jose	18-May-24	Algiers	357 Coy	15-Feb-44	20-Aug-46	Class A Release, transferred to RE 5 Apr 541
13300012		Olivares	Elueterio	20-Feb-24	Algiers	357 Coy	15-Feb-44		DESERTER 21 Mar 46, Extracted to NSRW
13300014		Salguero	Gabriel	12-Sep-17	Algiers	357 Coy	05-Apr-44	31-May-47	Class A Release
13300015		Gimenez	Fernando	14-Apr-20	Algiers	357 Coy	05-Apr-44	10-Jul-47	Class A Release
13300016		Pelleja	Juan	12-Nov-13	Algiers	357 Coy	05-Apr-44	02-Feb-47	Class A Release
13300018		Perez	Tomas	03-Nov-11	Algiers	357 Coy	25-Apr-44		Transferred to Somert LI 19 Feb 46
13300019		Mur	Antoine	24-Aug-19	Algiers	357 Coy	19-May-44	10-Jul-47	Class A Release
13300020		Torres	Bartolome	30-Nov-01	Algiers	357 Coy	23-May-44	16-Aug-46	Class A Release
13300021		Moreno	Manuel	12-Mar-23	Algiers	357 Coy	03-Jun-44	07-Aug-47	Class A Release
13300022		Caballero	Juan	19-Nov-05	Algiers	357 Coy	20-Jun-44	20-Jun-44	Class A Release

APPENDIX VII 297

Number	Rank	Name	Initials	DOB	Enlisted	Unit	Date Tos	Discharged	Remarks
13301368		Larrea	Jesus	02-May-23	Hussein Dey	361 Coy	29-Jul-43	09-Jul-47	Later BarquerrFrancicso GOMEZ, Class A Release
13301369		Alonso	Francisco	06-May-18	Hussein Dey	361 Coy	29-Jul-43		Docs to North Africa Records
13301391		Ridriguez	Jose Sanchez	12-May-12	In the field	361 Coy	03-Aug-43	27-Oct-46	Class A Release
13301471		Canselvo-Martinez	M						
13301392		Gabriel	Emilio Sanchez	30-Jun-16	In the field	361 Coy	03-Aug-43	03-Jan-47	Class A Release
13301475		Alarcon	Antonio (Lopez)	01-Feb-13	Hussein Dey	361 Coy	12-Aug-43	27-Oct-46	Later Manual Martin MORAN, Class A Release
13301476		Rosales	Jose (Lopez)	17-Jun-17	Hussein Dey	361 Coy	12-Aug-43	02-Nov-47	Later Ricardo Rio MILLAN, Class A Release 2 Jan 47
13301477		Vidal	Joaquin (Requena)	12-Nov-14	Hussein Dey	361 Coy	12-Aug-43		Docs to North Africa Records
13301497		Grana-Pepez	Mauel	04-Aug-12	In the field	361 Coy	15-Aug-43	27-Oct-46	Later Felipe Garna GARCIA, Docs to North Africa Records, Class A Release
13301498		Ramos-Perez	Jose	22-Jul-16	In the field	361 Coy	15-Aug-43		Docs to North Africa Records
13301515		Ibanez	Manuel	10-Dec-19	In the field	361 Coy	20-Aug-43	01-May-47	Later Garcia Ibo YANEZ, Class A Release
13301516		Zugasti	Ramon	30-Sep-15	Tunis	361 Coy	10-Aug-43	30-Nov-46	Class A Release
13301517		Pena	Andres	10-Nov-15	Tunis	361 Coy	10-Aug-43	30-Nov-46	Class A Release
13301518		Guttierez	Francesca	29-Jul-17	Tunis	361 Coy	10-Aug-43	02-Jan-47	Class A Release
13301519		Munoz	Ensigne	16-May-22	In the field	361 Coy	20-Aug-43	14-Jan-47	Class A Release
13301520		Llorente	Vanancio Pazuelo	25-Aug-10	Tunis	361 Coy	24-Aug-43	07-Oct-46	Class A Release
13301521		Perez	Francisco Arrando	09-Jul-21	Tunis	361 Coy	24-Aug-43	20-Jan-47	Class A Release
13301522		Pallares	Juan Palan	09-Dec-19	Tunis	361 Coy	24-Aug-43		Docs to North Africa Records
13301523		Santa-Cruz	Fernando (Ortiz)	12-May-05	Hussein Dey	361 Coy	24-May-05		Docs to North Africa Records
13301524		Pico	Antonio (Celaya)	21-Sep-15	In the field	361 Coy	25-Aug-43	13-Apr-47	Class A Release

298 CHURCHILL'S SPANIARDS

Number	Rank	Name	Initials	DOB	Enlisted	Unit	Date Tos	Discharged	Remarks
13301721		Gonzalez	Carlos	19-Oct-19	Hussein Dey	361 Coy	07-Aug-43	15-Feb-47	Later Rafael Gallego SERRANO, docs to North Africa Records
13301722		Cortababia	Victoriano	21-Aug-19	Hussein Dey	361 Coy	07-Aug-43	01-May-47	Later Angel Carrillo GUERRA, Class A Release
13301741		Ramos Paris	Miguel	18-Dec-21	In the field	361 Coy	05-Sep-43	10-Jul-47	Later Jose Menedez ALONSO, Class A Release
13301742		Gascon Giron	Ricardo	08-Nov-21	In the field	361 Coy	05-Sep-43		Docs to North Africa Records
13301743		Maia	Jose	14-Dec-19	Maison Carree	362 Coy	10-Sep-43		Docs to North Africa Records
13301767		Ansola	Pedro Bocanegra	14-May-23	Algiers	361 Coy	20-Sep-43	07-Apr-44	DIED 7 Apr 44
13301776		Lopez	Antonio (Bilches)	16-Apr-15	Hussein Dey	361 Coy	27-Sep-43		Docs to North Africa Records
13301777		Garcia	Severiano Moreno	03-Dec-11	Algiers	361 Coy	28-Sep-43	27-Oct-46	Later RapaelMarionoLuez FUENTE, DESERTER 2 Feb 46–20 Mar 46, Class A Release
13301787	Pte	Muro	Desidoro Gallego	08-Apr-15	Algiers	361 Coy	20-Sep-43	22-Sep-45	Class W(T) Reserve 15 Jul 45–22 Sep 45, discharged W(T) Reserve (Indifferent)
13301788		Rey	Amador Arnais	20-Feb-24	Algiers	361 Coy	20-Sep-43	27-Feb-47	Class A Release
13301789		Lopez	Diego Aroca	26-Jul-21	Algiers	361 Coy	20-Sep-43	25-Jun-47	Class A Release
13301790		Moran	Vanzetti Iglesias	15-Oct-22	Algiers	361 Coy	20-Sep-43		Transferred to Palestine Regt 20 Sep 45, rejoined PC 19 Feb 47, Class A Release
13301791		Munoz	Mariano Gimenez	27-Dec-23	Algiers	361 Coy	20-Sep-43	10-Jul-47	Class A Release
13301792		Martin	Francisco Lopez	21-Feb-11	Algiers	361 Coy	20-Sep-43		Transferred to Army Air Corps 20 May 45
13301793		Rodriguez	Francisco Cano	12-Apr-21	Algiers	361 Coy	20-Sep-43	25-Jun-47	Docs to North Africa Records
13301801		Samuel	Antonio (Garcia)	15-Dec-14	Hussein Dey	361 Coy	04-Oct-43	30-Nov-46	Class A Release
13301802		Nunez	Emilo (Roca)	15-Oct-15	Hussein Dey	361 Coy	04-Oct-43	03-Jan-47	Class A Release
13301803		Garrido	Juan Contrevas	10-Jan-15	Hussein Dey	361 Coy	06-Oct-43	03-Jan-47	Later Demofilo Marino ALCALA, Class A Release

APPENDIX VII 299

Number	Rank	Name	Initials	DOB	Enlisted	Unit	Date Tos	Discharged	Remarks
13301804		Flores	Jose Zamara	29-Jun-23	Hussein Dey	361 Coy	06-Oct-43	10-Jul-47	Later Jose Zamora SERRANO, Class A Release
13301805	Pte	Lazar	Raimond	16-Aug-09	Algiers	362 Coy	05-Oct-43	08-Jan-44	362 Coy, Para XVIIIA
13301806		Pons	Jose C	09-May-09	In the field	361 Coy	09-Oct-43		Docs to North Africa Records
13301807		Palacios	Salvador (Zuriceta)	09-Nov-20	Hussein Dey	361 Coy	12-Oct-43		Docs to North Africa Records
13301808		Alfonso	Vitorinio (Rodriquez)	06-Mar-19	Hussein Dey	361 Coy	12-Oct-43	27-Feb-47	Class A Release
13301809		Fernandez	Frntos (Montes)	27-Dec-20	Hussein Dey	361 Coy	12-Oct-43	31-May-47	Class A Release
13301810		Camarena	Higimio (Espinosa)	11-Jan-17	Hussein Dey	361 Coy	12-Oct-43		Later Alan COOPER, Transferred to Army Air Corps 20 May 45
13301811		Revolta	Francisco (Sarabia)	02-Apr-17	Hussein Dey	361 Coy	12-Oct-43		Later Robert SHAW, docs to North Africa Records – POW Europe
13301812		Rosagro	Alfinzo (Zamora)	22-May-22	Hussein Dey	361 Coy	12-Oct-43	08-Jul-47	Class A Release
13301813		Marco	Antoines (Lozano)	24-Dec-21	Hussein Dey	361 Coy	12-Oct-43		Docs to North Africa Records
13301814		Randez	Vegueria Francisco	30-May-16	Hussein Dey	361 Coy	14-Oct-43	22-Apr-47	Class A Release
13301815		Torres	Fernando Mendoza	25-May-19	Hussein Dey	361 Coy	14-Oct-43		Docs to North Africa Records
13301834		Andres	Lion Gonzalez	05-Sep-18	Hussein Dey	361 Coy	19-Oct-43	13-Apr-47	Class A Release
13301835		Martin	Miguel San Roman	10-Dec-18	Hussein Dey	361 Coy	19-Oct-43	01-May-47	Class A Release
13301836		Valero	Antoino	08-May-15	Hussein Dey	361 Coy	19-Oct-43		Docs to North Africa Records
13301837		Quijano	Peroz Miguel	20-Jan-21	Hussein Dey	361 Coy	19-Oct-43		Docs to North Africa Records
13301838		Uribelarrea	Marcelo Manero		Hussein Dey	361 Coy	19-Oct-43	19-Nov-46	Class A Release
13301839		Bosso	Antonio	10-Apr-94	Maison Carree	363 Coy	21-Oct-43	03-May-45	Presumed KILLED IN ACTION 3 May 45
13301840		Bovio	Carlo	12-Dec-19	Maison Carree	363 Coy	03-Oct-43		Later James BENSON, docs to North Africa Records
13301853		Ramos	Maseus Rafael	05-May-19	Hussein Dey	363 Coy	16-Oct-43		Docs to North Africa Records

300 CHURCHILL'S SPANIARDS

Number	Rank	Name	Initials	DOB	Enlisted	Unit	Date Tos	Discharged	Remarks
13301854		Torrents	Abadia Juan	06-Jan-10	Hussein Dey	363 Coy	16-Oct-43		Later John COLMAN, transferred to Army Air Corps 20 may 45
13301855		Varon	Burgos Ricardo	05-Apr-16	Hussein Dey	363 Coy	16-Oct-43	28-Jun-47	Later Modesto Vicente MORA, Class A Release
13301856		Fort	Martinez Pedro	08-Sep-16	Hussein Dey	363 Coy	16-Oct-43	02-Jan-47	Class A Release
13301857		Valero	Almargo	30-Jan-18	Hussein Dey	363 Coy	16-Oct-43	31-May-47	Later Alvarez Clenterio CINTAS, Class A Release
13301859		Munoz	Antonio Martinez	30-Oct-12	Hussein Dey	363 Coy	16-Oct-43		Docs to North Africa Records
13301860		Bravo	Lezcano Julio	26-Nov-21	Hussein Dey	363 Coy	16-Oct-43		Docs to North Africa Records
13301861		Rodriguez	Felix Rafael	16-Sep-17	Hussein Dey	363 Coy	16-Oct-43		DESERTER 20 Mar 44
13301862		Roca Martinez	Antonio	14-Apr-11	Tunis	363 Coy	21-Oct-43	05-Nov-46	Class A Release
13301863		Panies Martinez	Alfonso	06-Aug-20	Tunis	363 Coy	21-Oct-43	08-Jul-47	Class A Release
13301864		Sanchez	Juan Garcia	11-Dec-19	Tunis	363 Coy	22-Oct-43	14-May-47	Class A Release
13301865		Orgaz Bravo	Angel	11-Jan-21	Tunis	363 Coy	22-Oct-43		Docs to North Africa Records
13301866		Sanchez	Conception	01-Jul-20	Tunis	363 Coy	22-Oct-43		Docs to North Africa Records
13301867		Ruiz	Francisco Seco	11-Jun-19	Tunis	363 Coy	22-Oct-43	01-May-44	DIED 1 May 44
13301868		Esteve	Joseph Pichar	21-Apr-16	Hussein Dey	361 Coy	22-Oct-43	07-Feb-47	Class A Release
13301870		Attias	Eduardo	08-Nov-95	Tunis	363 Coy	23-Oct-43	23-Jan-47	Class A Release
13301871		Lopez-Ruiz	Rafael	06-Apr-21	Maison Carree	363 Coy	28-Oct-43	12-Jun-44	DIED 12 Jun 44
13301872		Sierrano Diaz	Antiono	10-Apr-18	Maison Carree	363 Coy	28-Oct-43		Docs to North Africa Records
13301873		Ferrigno	Oniodio?	10-Oct-15	Maison Carree	363 Coy	28-Oct-43	01-Oct-46	Class A Release
13301875		Presa	Argos Antolin	28-May-14	Hussein Dey	361 Coy	02-Nov-43		Docs to North Africa Records
13301878		Artunedro-Solbes	Pedro	30-May-15	Tunis	363 Coy	26-Oct-43	04-Jan-47	Class A Release
13301879		Sanchez-Fulgencio	Francisco	27-Mar-21	Tunis	363 Coy	26-Oct-43	25-Jun-47	Class A Release
13301880		Moreno-Alfaro	Jose	24-Jun-16	Tunis	363 Coy	26-Oct-43	02-Jan-47	Class A Release
13301882	Pte	Olmoz-Gonzalez	Christobee	13-Apr-07	Tunis	363 Coy	08-Nov-43	13-Nov-45	Later Francisco Lopez ALVAREZ, Para XVI (Good)
13301883		Rovira-Balaguer	Enrique	16-May-11	Tunis	363 Coy	09-Nov-43	06-Nov-46	Class A Release

APPENDIX VII 301

Number	Rank	Name	Initials	DOB	Enlisted	Unit	Date Tos	Discharged	Remarks
13301884		Gonzalez-Laguillo	Pedro	08-Sep-11	Tunis	363 Coy	09-Nov-43		DESERTER 2 Feb 44, docs to North Africa Records
13301885		Gonzalez-Sarabia	Miguel	10-Oct-15	Tunis	363 Coy	09-Nov-43	02-Jan-47	Class A Release
13301886		Esclapez-Urbain	Manuel	15-Jun-15	Tunis	363 Coy	09-Nov-43		DESERTER 28 Apr 44
13301887		Crevs	Angel Pureta	14-Aug-21	Tunis	363 Coy	09-Nov-43	08-Jul-47	Class A Release
13301888		Garcia Frenandez	Casino	04-Mar-19	Tunis	363 Coy	09-Nov-43	31-May-47	Class A Release
13301889		Villagrasa Roy	Francisco	19-Oct-19	Tunis	363 Coy	09-Nov-43	31-May-47	Class A Release
13301890		Aloi	Salvator	11-Nov-08	Maison Carree	363 Coy	03-Nov-43	06-Dec-46	Class A Release
13301891		Martinez-Cazorla	Teodoro	09-Nov-18	Maison Carree	363 Coy	02-Nov-43		Docs to North Africa Records
13301908		Aguirre-Otermin	Miguel	28-Dec-19	Maison Carree	363 Coy	14-Nov-43	31-May-47	Class A Release
13301909		Garin-Quintero	Francisco	24-Aug-17	Maison Carree	363 Coy	14-Nov-43	19-Nov-46	Class A Release
13301910		Garcia -Sanchez	Antonio	13-Mar-19	Maison Carree	363 Coy	13-Nov-43	14-May-47	Later Moscardo Core VICENTE, Class A Release
13301911		Gutierrez-Romero	Antonio	14-Jul-14	Maison Carree	363 Coy	13-Nov-43	03-Jan-47	Later Mellado Francicso MADRID, Class A Release
13301912		Jimenez-Alvarez	Juan	24-Dec-12	Maison Carree	363 Coy	13-Nov-43	23-Dec-46	Class A Release
13301913		Llamas-Carro	Juan	14-Aug-15	Maison Carree	363 Coy	13-Nov-43	06-Nov-46	Class A Release
13301914		Moreno-Lindo	Francisco	18-Oct-15	Maison Carree	363 Coy	13-Nov-43	02-Jan-47	Later P G BATALLA, Class A Release
13301915		Moreno-Rodriguez	Jose	30-May-15	Maison Carree	363 Coy	12-Nov-43	19-Nov-46	Class A Release
13301916		Martinez-Martinez	Julio	14-Mar-16	Maison Carree	363 Coy	14-Nov-43		Docs to North Africa Records
13301917		Rocamor-Ruiziaga	Juan	22-Dec-15	Maison Carree	363 Coy	14-Nov-43	02-Jan-47	Later Juan Devesa LOPEZ, Class A Release
13301918		Rama-Rama	Gabriel	05-Nov-15	Maison Carree	363 Coy	16-Nov-43		Docs to North Africa Records
13301919		Sanchez-Gimenez	Mariano	10-May-15	Maison Carree	363 Coy	13-Nov-43	02-Jan-47	Class A Release

302 CHURCHILL'S SPANIARDS

Number	Rank	Name	Initials	DOB	Enlisted	Unit	Date Tos	Discharged	Remarks
13301920		Mora-Menarguez	Adanto	31-Aug-05	Maison Carree	363 Coy	20-Nov-43	25-Aug-46	Class A Release
13301921		Franados-Sanchez	Francisco	29-Jan-18	Maison Carree	363 Coy	19-Nov-43	14-May-47	Class A Release
13301922		Garcia-Perea	Daniel	01-Jan-16	Maison Carree	363 Coy	14-Nov-43		Docs to North Africa Records
13301925		Murgia	Fortunato Posario	22-Dec-25	Maison Carree	363 Coy	20-Nov-43		Docs to North Africa Records
13302004		Martinez	Augustin	23-Jul-23	Hussein Dey		04-Mar-44		DESERTER 4 Aug 45, Extracted to NSRW
13302006	Pte	Ramet	Sebastian Moreno	11-Jan-24	In the field		28-Jan-44	17-Nov-46	Para XVI (V Good)
13302008		Sanchez	Jose Maria	01-Sep-21	Hussein Dey		07-Mar-44		Transferred to Army Air Corps 31 May 45
13302010		Nunez	Filippe Juan	14-Jul-19	Hussein Dey		22-Feb-44	25-Jun-47	Class A Release
13302200		Diaz-Conde	Mario	10-Apr-17	In the field		19-May-44	25-Jun-47	North Africa, Class A Release
13302201		Dominguez Martin	Bartolome	20-Aug-18	In the field		19-May-44	08-Jul-47	North Africa, Class A Release
13302207		Miguel Leon	Jose	12-Feb-18	In the field		01-May-44	08-Jul-47	North Africa, Class A Release
13302208	Pte	Rosello-Riera	Esteban	03-Feb-16	In the field		01-May-44	01-Apr-47	.North Africa, Para XVI
13302209		Villacreges Perez	Miguel	28-Oct-16	In the field		01-May-44	31-May-47	North Africa, Class A Release
13302210		Ferandez Collado	Francisco	23-Feb-17	In the field		01-May-44	25-Jun-47	North Africa, Class A Release
13302211		Maissoni-Biscarro	Pedro	15-Nov-18	In the field		01-May-44	08-Jul-47	North Africa, Class A Release
13302212		Diaz-Diaz	Pedro	20-Oct-19	In the field		01-May-44	10-Jul-47	North Africa, Class A Release
13302213		Cabrerizo-Palenzuela	Juan	14-Feb-18	In the field		01-May-44	08-Jul-47	North Africa, Class A Release
13302214		Carmen Aragues	Pedro	02-Jul-11	In the field		01-May-44	02-Jan-47	North Africa, Class A Release
13302215		Montoliu Miralles	Jose	27-Nov-14	In the field		01-May-44	01-May-47	North Africa, Class A Release
13302217		Merida Perez	Henrique	14-Mar-20	In the field		01-May-44	26-Jun-47	North Africa, Class A Release

APPENDIX VII 303

Number	Rank	Name	Initials	DOB	Enlisted	Unit	Date Tos	Discharged	Remarks
13302218		Marquez Davila	Fernondo	14-Apr-40	In the field		01-May-44	13-Apr-47	North Africa, Class A Release
13302219		Punsa Fuster	Francisco	09-Jul-16	In the field		01-May-44	31-May-47	North Africa, Class A Release
13302220		Encina Martinez	Jose	05-Oct-17	In the field		01-May-44	25-Jun-47	North Africa, Class A Release
13302221		Mastimija Vall	Henrique	14-Nov-17	In the field		01-May-44	25-Jun-47	North Africa, Class A Release
13302222		Inglesias	Manuel	22-Nov-10	In the field		01-May-44	30-Nov-46	North Africa, Class A Release
13302223		Royo Mauricio	Maunel	18-Apr-10	In the field		01-May-44	30-Nov-46	North Africa, Class A Release
13302231		Oliva Moreno	Salvador	20-Dec-06	In the field		15-Jun-44	16-Oct-46	North Africa, Class A Release
13302232		Castro Ambrosio	Antonio	17-Jul-19	In the field		15-Jun-44	10-Jul-47	North Africa, Class A Release
13302233		Estirado Ruescas	Marcos	22-Oct-07	In the field		15-Jun-44	05-Nov-46	North Africa, Class A Release
13302235		Gomes Pena	Francisco	08-Jan-13	In the field		15-Jun-44	22-Apr-47	Later Sauveur Michel MARCO, North Africa, Class A Release
13302236		Lopez Camacho	Antonio	23-Feb-20	In the field		15-Jun-44	19-Nov-46	North Africa, Class A Release
13302237		Lorenzo del Valle	Maximiliano	29-May-16	In the field		15-Jun-44	27-Jun-47	North Africa, Class A Release
13302241		Martinez Lopez	Francisco	02-Jul-14	In the field		19-Jun-44	01-May-47	Later Paul Jean Gilbert FRESNEAU, North Africa, Class A Release
13302242		Tocon Ledesma	Acracio	02-Feb-15	In the field		19-Jun-44	14-May-47	North Africa, Class A Release
13302243		Botella Cerdan	Antonio	16-Jun-12	In the field		19-Jun-44	02-Jan-47	Later Jose christabal BELLOT, North Africa, Class A Release
13302246		Gimenez-Ferrar	Fernando	20-Aug-24	In the field		19-Jun-44	13-Apr-47	North Africa, Class A Release
13302247		Ruiz Amador	Abelino	04-Sep-02	In the field		19-Jun-44	06-Nov-46	North Africa, Class A Release
13302249		Fernandez Tudela	Juan	16-Oct-11	In the field		19-Jun-44	10-Dec-46	North Africa, Class A Release
13302255		Acamon	Cartonell	24-Sep-19	Algiers		29-Jun-44	10-Jul-47	Class A Release
13302256		Dorca Massip	Juan	26-Jul-17	Algiers		29-Jun-44	25-Jun-47	Class A Release
13302257		Fontanet Redon	Jean	02-Feb-15	Algiers		29-Jun-44	14-May-47	Class A Release

Number	Rank	Name	Initials	DOB	Enlisted	Unit	Date Tos	Discharged	Remarks
13302258	Pte	Ferrer Robert	Jose	03-Sep-18	Algiers		29-Jun-44	06-Oct-46	Para XVI (V Good)
13302259		Herran Verdiell	Domingo	27-Oct-10	Algiers		29-Jun-44	03-Jan-47	Class A Release
13302260		Montolla Fernandez	Roberto	15-Feb-17	Algiers		29-Jun-44	27-Feb-47	Later Raimundo San-Miguel RASINES, Class A Release
13302261	Pte	Pinardel	Ismael Pallares	04-Dec-20	Algiers		29-Jun-44	06-Oct-46	Para XVI (Exemplary)
13302262		Tejada Gonzales	Pedro	14-Nov-20	Algiers		29-Jun-44	19-Nov-46	Later Bonilla Rafael GAVILANCS, Class A Release
13302277		Jimenez Posas	Fernando	06-Nov-19	Algiers		11-Jul-44		Name changed by Statutory Declaration to Manuel SANCHEZ GOMRZ, DESERTER 37 Jun 46
13302291		Barrus	Esteban Ricardo	03-Apr-20	Algiers		25-Jul-44	13-Apr-47	Class A Release
13302299		Cabrera	Basilio Torralbo	28-Feb-15	Algiers		29-Jul-44	31-May-47	Class A Release
13302301		Navarro	Gabriel Cerezuela	31-May-18	Algiers		03-Aug-44	10-Jul-47	Class A Release
13302302		Gonzales	Valeriano de Diego	12-Sep-08	Algiers		03-Aug-44	25-Jan-47	Class A Release
13302303		Gonzales	Jose Lopez	12-Jul-29	Algiers		03-Aug-44	30-Nov-46	Class A Release
13302308		Becerra	Antonia	26-Sep-14	In the field		21-Aug-44	14-May-47	North Africa, Class A Release
13302332		Illescas	Maunel	12-May-22	In the field		21-Aug-44	17-Sep-47	Later Antonio Garcia RODRIGUEZ, North Africa, Class A Release
13302337		Maidell Estivil	Juan	25-Apr-16	In the field		21-Aug-44	25-Jun-47	North Africa, Class A Release
13302339		Marin	Pedro	04-Jul-09	In the field		21-Aug-44	30-Nov-47	Later Jean Martin FAJARDO, North Africa, Class A Release
13302340		Marintur	Emilio	12-Nov-14	In the field		21-Aug-44	14-May-47	North Africa, Class A Release
13302362		Garcia	Antonio Moreno	19-May-13	Algiers		09-Aug-44	08-Oct-46	DESERTER 13 Aug 45–2 Aug 46, Class A Release
13302364		Perez	Juan Casado	18-May-18	Algiers		09-Aug-44	10-Jul-47	Class A Release
13302365		Nieto	Domingo Santos	05-Jun-16	Algiers		09-Aug-44	25-Jun-47	Later Rey Manuel DIAZ, Class A Release
13302366		Bastarrechia	Asrensio Argengnenoa	08-Jul-12	Algiers		12-Aug-44	22-Apr-47	Class A Release

APPENDIX VII 305

Number	Rank	Name	Initials	DOB	Enlisted	Unit	Date Tos	Discharged	Remarks
13302367		Giral	Paulius Poblador	14-Feb-14	Algiers		12-Aug-44	24-May-47	Later Gregorio Guiral CALVED, Class A Release
13302368		Sans	Maximiliano Prados	23-Jan-10	Algiers		12-Aug-44	03-Jan-47	Class A Release
13302369		Ruiz	Raymond Fernandez	23-Jun-10	Algiers		22-Aug-44	27-Oct-46	Class A Release
13302370		Brun	Jose Tim	07-Sep-20	Algiers		22-Aug-44	19-Aug-47	Class A Release
13302371		Barbera	Samora Juan	10-Sep-17	Algiers		22-Aug-44	08-Jul-47	Class A Release
13302372		Romero	Planas Antonio	07-Feb-19	Algiers		22-Aug-44	08-Aug-47	Class A Release
13302373		Rodriguez	Andrei Salvatore	04-Jul-17	Algiers		22-Aug-44		DESERTER 18 Feb 45–21 Mar 45 and 29 Jul 45, Extracted to nSRW
13302379		Garcia Dione Gonzalez	Emilio	15-May-19	In the field		24-Aug-44	29-Aug-46	North Africa, DIED 29 Aug 46
13302382			D V						North Africa (no details joined Aug 44?)
13302395		Bernardino	Alfred	02-Jan-23	In the field		31-Aug-44		North Africa, transferred to Army Air Corps 31 May 45
13302396		Calvo	Soilo	17-Jun-17	In the field		29-Aug-44	20-Jan-47	North Africa, Class A Release
13302398		Dominguez Rubio	Francisco		In the field		28-Aug-44	10-Jul-47	North Africa, Class A Release
13302401		Garcia-Argrilea	Felix	05-Oct-24	In the field		01-Sep-44	08-Nov-47	North Africa, Class A Release
13302402		Giner Abad	Manuel	05-Dec-25	In the field		14-Sep-44	22-Jan-48	North Africa, Class A Release
13302403		Gonzales Huertas	Ramon	05-Aug-16	In the field		02-Sep-44	26-Nov-45	North Africa, Class A Release
13302405		Inzerillo	Armando	15-May-24	In the field		04-Sep-44	21-Feb-47	North Africa, Class A Release
13302406		Lopez Rodriguez	Valendin	29-Jan-16	In the field		29-Aug-44	25-Jun-47	North Africa, Class A Release
13302410		Moreno Cardena	Jose	24-Jan-18	In the field		30-Aug-44	10-Jul-47	North Africa, Class A Release
13302414		Ramos Y Gomes	Luis	03-Apr-26	In the field		04-Sep-44		North Africa, transferred to Army Air Corps 31 May 45
13302417		Rodriguez	Miguel						North Africa, Cypriot PC (Joined Sep 44?)

306 CHURCHILL'S SPANIARDS

Number	Rank	Name	Initials	DOB	Enlisted	Unit	Date Tos	Discharged	Remarks
13302423		Tomas-Amengual	Bernardo	31-Jul-15	In the field		30-Aug-44	06-Dec-46	North Africa, Class A Release
13302426		Verdugo Cueva	Jose	15-Feb-21	In the field		02-Sep-44	17-Sep-47	North Africa, Class A Release
13302427		Aletti	Ernest	03-Sep-26	Algiers		11-Sep-44	01-Oct-46	Class A Release
13302428		Manchon	Salvador Mas	02-Oct-24	Algiers		30-Aug-44	25-Oct-47	Class A Release
13302429		Robles	Jose	23-Apr-25	Algiers		30-Aug-44	15-Mar-47	Class A Release
13302430		Castano	Francisco Perez	03-Jun-22	Algiers		30-Aug-44	17-Sep-47	Class A Release
13302431		Parra	Jose Rondon	13-Sep-13	Algiers		02-Sep-44	14-May-47	Class A Release
13302432		Thomas	Francisco	15-Sep-19	Algiers		02-Sep-44	21-Sep-46	Later Thomas Francisco CANAS PRATS, Class A Release
13302433		Salvador	Diasdado	27-Dec-13	Algiers		02-Sep-44	14-May-47	Class A Release
13302434		Cajal	Cosme Caballero	28-Sep-07	Algiers		02-Sep-44	03-Jan-47	Class A Release
13302435		Galvez	Antonio	29-Nov-09	Algiers		02-Sep-44	07-Jan-47	Class A Release
13302436		Fabra	Rogelio	11-May-18	Algiers		02-Sep-44	08-Aug-47	Class A Release
13302437		Tejedo	Vicente Soto	24-Apr-09	Algiers		31-Aug-44	30-Nov-46	Class A Release
13302438		Martinez	Enrique Cambre	04-Oct-16	Algiers		05-Sep-44	08-Jul-47	Class A Release
13302439		Alonso	Constantin Solis	21-Feb-21	Algiers		05-Sep-44	17-Sep-47	Class A Release
13302440		Ferrer	Enrique Martinez	17-Jun-17	Algiers		05-Sep-44	10-Jul-47	Class A Release
13302441		Labadie	Manuel Fernandez	01-Feb-15	Algiers		05-Sep-44	25-Jun-47	Class A Release
13302442	Pte	Martinez	Vincente Vidal	16-Dec-22	Algiers		05-Sep-44	29-Oct-46	Para XVI (V Good)
13302443		Rubio	Manuel Martinez	18-Apr-18	Algiers		05-Sep-44	18-Aug-47	Class A Release
13302444		Vera	Cristobal Saraiba	21-Oct-03	Algiers		05-Sep-44	28-Nov-46	Class A Release
13302445		Borras	Francisco Paris	02-Dec-16	Algiers		21-Sep-44	08-Jul-47	Class A Release
13302446		Cazorla	Antonio Morales	19-Oct-19	Algiers		21-Sep-44		DESERTER 24 Mar 47, Extracted to NSRW
13302447		Godoy	Jose Puente	22-Dec-19	Algiers		21-Sep-44	19-Aug-47	Class A Release

APPENDIX VII 307

Number	Rank	Name	Initials	DOB	Enlisted	Unit	Date Tos	Discharged	Remarks
13302448		Marti	Doman	12-Aug-14	Algiers		21-Sep-44	07-Jun-47	Class A Release
13302449		Mateo	Garcia Garcia	08-Jul-14	Algiers		21-Sep-44	31-May-47	Class A Release
13302450		Mazorriaga	Manuel Alonso	23-Dec-23	Algiers		21-Sep-44	25-Oct-47	Class A Release
13302451		Villar	Diego Garcia	24-May-18	Algiers		21-Sep-44	08-Aug-47	Class A Release
13302452		Aghilocho-Soto	Francisco	05-May-24	Algiers		21-Sep-44	08-Nov-47	Class A Release
13302460		Eforgan Seregui	Miguel	19-Nov-13	In the field		05-Sep-44	20-May-47	North Africa, transferred to Palestine Regt 25 Jul 45, Class A Release
13302465	Pte	Martins Merendao	Antonio	14-Mar-07	In the field		Sep-44	08-Nov-45	North Africa, Para XVI (Good)
13302466		Mrdina Pomar	Fernando	15-May-26	In the field		04-Sep-44	09-Mar-48	North Africa, Class A Release
13302467		Medrano-Fernandez	Antonio	29-Nov-23	In the field		13-Sep-44	28-Apr-47	North Africa, Class A Release
13302468		Morales	Joseph	21-Feb-21	In the field		08-Sep-44		North Africa, att 59 DOD RASC Spanish coy 31 Mar 46
13302469		Minoz Oliva	Florentine	17-Dec-15	In the field		05-Sep-44	11-Dec-46	North Africa, Class A Release
13302471		Nieves Y Gordo	Antonio	28-Aug-21	In the field		11-Sep-44	17-Sep-47	North Africa, Class A Release
13302475		Polo Cabeza	Victor	16-Jun-23	In the field		16-Jun-23	24-Apr-47	North Africa, Class A Release
13302484		Tribes	Manuel	28-Aug-24	In the field		08-Sep-44	07-Apr-48	North Africa, Para XVI
13302486		Vinaz	Albert Jose	18-Aug-18	In the field		13-Sep-44	03-Oct-47	North Africa, Class A Release 3 Oct 47
13302488		Ballo	Sebastian	13-May-13	Algiers		25-Sep-44	31-Jan-47	Class A Release
13302489		Munoz	O						North Africa (no details, joined Sep 44?)
13302491		Mateu	Michel	01-Jan-17	Algiers		25-Sep-44	26-Jun-47	Class A Release
13302492		Munoz	Cristobal	30-Aug-18	Algiers		25-Sep-44	08-Aug-47	Class A Release
13302493		Salcedo	Francisco	03-Feb-21	Algiers		25-Sep-44	27-Feb-47	Class A Release
13302494		Solis-Fernandez	Joseph	13-Jul-17	Algiers		25-Sep-44	08-Aug-47	Class A Release
13302496		Arcaras	Jose	24-Jan-24	In the field		14-Sep-44	18-Oct-47	Later Samuel COHEN, North Africa, Class A Release
13302508		Jimenez	Rafael	15-Apr-24	In the field		14-Sep-44	08-Nov-47	Later Jack Chalom SOUSSAN, North Africa, Class A Release

308 CHURCHILL'S SPANIARDS

Number	Rank	Name	Initials	DOB	Enlisted	Unit	Date Tos	Discharged	Remarks
13302510		Mafoda Serfaty	Jose	18-Oct-18	In the field		15-Sep-44	30-Jul-47	North Africa, transferred to Palestine regt 25 Jun 45, rejoined PC date NK, Class A Release
13302513		Ruiz-Y-Lerdo de Tejada	Raymond	20-Aug-26	In the field		16-Sep-44	13-Jan-48	North Africa, Class A Release
13302531		Gonzales	Michel Monioz	03-Feb-15	Algiers		23-Sep-44	18-Sep-46	Para XVI (Fair)
13302532		Grao	Ramon	10-May-17	Algiers		23-Sep-44	10-Jul-47	Class A Release
13302629		Lopez-Parramon	Ramon						Enlisted North Africa (no details)
13302689		Fernandez-Yanez	Vincete						Enlisted North Africa (no details)
13802369		Lara	Jose	18-Jul-14	Westward Ho	3 Centre	16-Jul-40	12-Mar-46	Class A Release
13802370		Jzquierdo	Vicente	12-Dec-19	Westward Ho	3 Centre	16-Jul-40	19-Mar-46	Class A Release
13802371		Panchame	Fenito	25-Dec-23	Westward Ho	3 Centre	16-Jul-40		DESERTER 16 Dec 44
13802372		Castillon	Antonio	24-Jul-09	Westward Ho	3 Centre	16-Jul-40	24-Jan-46	Class A Release
13802373		Lopez	Modesto	14-Sep-16	Westward Ho	3 Centre	16-Jul-40	12-Mar-46	Class A Release
13802374		Martinez	Victorano	02-Dec-12	Westward Ho	3 Centre	16-Jul-40	12-Mar-46	Class A Release
13802375		Fernandez	Julian	07-Apr-18	Westward Ho	3 Centre	16-Jul-40	14-Mar-46	Class A Release
13802376		Pujol	Alfonzo	15-Sep-16	Westward Ho	3 Centre	16-Jul-40	14-Mar-46	Class A Release
13802377		Lopez	Girardo	28-Sep-14	Westward Ho	3 Centre	16-Jul-40	12-Mar-46	Class A Release
13802378		Munoz	Joaquim	17-Aug-17	Westward Ho	3 Centre	16-Jul-40	14-Mar-46	Class A Release
13802379		Puiz	Francisco	17-Jul-17	Westward Ho	3 Centre	16-Jul-40	12-Nov-45	Class B Release
13802380		Peraferrer	Francisco	20-Apr-19	Westward Ho	3 Centre	16-Jul-40	15-Mar-46	Class A Release
13802381		Herrero	Alberto	29-Sep-20	Westward Ho	3 Centre	16-Jul-40	16-Mar-46	Class A Release
13802382		Munoz	Francisco	14-Mar-14	Westward Ho	3 Centre	16-Jul-40	12-Mar-46	Class A Release
13802383		Martinez	Valentin	10-Aug-12	Westward Ho	3 Centre	16-Jul-40	07-Jan-46	Class A Release
13802384		Zamora	Eladio	17-Aug-18	Westward Ho	3 Centre	16-Jul-40	20-Mar-41	DIED night 20/21 Mar 41
13802385		Del Rio	Nicolas	13-Mar-14	Westward Ho	3 Centre	16-Jul-40	20-Mar-46	Class A Release
13802386		Umbo	Jose	16-Sep-17	Westward Ho	3 Centre	16-Jul-40	14-Mar-46	Class A Release
13802387		Quintilla	Miguel	05-Aug-07	Westward Ho	3 Centre	16-Jul-40	13-Jan-46	Class A Release
13802388		Grato	Julio	25-Mar-17	Westward Ho	3 Centre	16-Jul-40	14-Mar-46	Class A Release
13802389		Laiseca	Sebastian	25-Dec-16	Westward Ho	3 Centre	16-Jul-40	16-Mar-46	Class A Release

APPENDIX VII 309

Number	Rank	Name	Initials	DOB	Enlisted	Unit	Date Tos	Discharged	Remarks
13802390		Nicolas	Jose	19-Feb-19	Westward Ho	3 Centre	16-Jul-40	15-Mar-46	Class A Release
13802391		Delgado-Martinez	Manuel	26-Jul-19	Westward Ho	3 Centre	16-Jul-40	19-Mar-46	Class A Release
13802392	Cpl	Garcia	Juan	14-Feb-01	Westward Ho	3 Centre	16-Jul-40	07-Sep-44	6 HTU, Para XVIIIA (V Good)
13802393		Anduix	Juan	28-Apr-13	Westward Ho	3 Centre	16-Jul-40	12-Mar-46	Class A Release
13802394		Garcia	Salvador	28-Apr-18	Westward Ho	3 Centre	16-Jul-40	14-Mar-46	Class A Release
13802395		Aparicio	Baldomero	25-Dec-18	Westward Ho	3 Centre	16-Jul-40	20-Mar-46	Class A Release
13802396		Morales	Jose	25-Sep-19	Westward Ho	3 Centre	16-Jul-40		DESERTER 8 Nov 44
13802397		Caceres	Carmelo	18-Jan-20	Westward Ho	3 Centre	16-Jul-40	16-Mar-46	Class A Release
13802398		Sanchez	Felipe	28-Apr-19	Westward Ho	3 Centre	16-Jul-40	16-Mar-46	Class A Release
13802399		Gonzalez	Comado	16-Apr-21	Westward Ho	3 Centre	16-Jul-40	17-Mar-46	Class A Release
13802400		Gome	Francisco	19-Apr-18	Westward Ho	3 Centre	16-Jul-40	21-Mar-41	DIED 21 Mar 41
13802401		Cruz	Antonio	21-Apr-11	Westward Ho	3 Centre	16-Jul-40	15-Feb-46	Class A Release
13802402		Rodriguez	Deogracia	15-Oct-19	Westward Ho	3 Centre	16-Jul-40	16-Mar-46	Class A Release
13802403		Montero	Francisco	11-Nov-15	Westward Ho	3 Centre	16-Jul-40	12-Mar-46	Class A Release
13802404		Garcia	Ramon	07-Feb-18	Westward Ho	3 Centre	16-Jul-40	10-Oct-45	Class B Release
13802405		Tomas	Pascual	29-Jan-18	Westward Ho	3 Centre	16-Jul-40	15-Mar-46	Class A Release
13802407		Fernandez	Antonio	17-Nov-15	Westward Ho	3 Centre	16-Jul-40	12-Mar-46	Class A Release
13802408		Sanchez	Jose	21-Dec-17	Westward Ho	3 Centre	16-Jul-40	15-Mar-46	Class A Release
13802409		Ferrer	Emilio	01-Aug-10	Westward Ho	3 Centre	16-Jul-40	05-Dec-45	Class A Release, CIA RASC Records 18 Feb 52
13802410		Cuenca	Donato	28-Apr-19	Westward Ho	3 Centre	16-Jul-40	15-Mar-46	Class A Release, transferred to RE 1 Nov 51
13802411		Martin	Guillermo	14-May-13	Westward Ho	3 Centre	16-Jul-40	12-Mar-46	Class A Release
13802412		Tarraga	Mario	08-Feb-20	Westward Ho	3 Centre	16-Jul-40	19-Mar-46	Class A Release, CIA ACC 1 Dec 51
13802413		Perez	Jesus	16-Apr-16	Westward Ho	3 Centre	17-Jul-40	19-Mar-46	Class A Release
13802414	Pte	Pino	Angel	10-Apr-19	Westward Ho	3 Centre	17-Jul-40	06-Dec-44	6 HTU, Para XVI (V Good)
13802415		Molina	Esteban	19-Nov-20	Westward Ho	3 Centre	17-Jul-40	19-Mar-46	Class A Release, CIA ACC 1 Dec 51
13802416	Pte	Santi	Jose	15-Aug-15	Westward Ho	3 Centre	17-Jul-40	14-Mar-44	13 Pan Coy, Para XVI (Good)
13802417		Jimenez	Agostin	12-Jul-19	Westward Ho	3 Centre	17-Jul-40	15-Mar-46	Class A Release
13802418	Pte	Carron	Ricardo	1914	Westward Ho	3 Centre	17-Jul-40	05-Nov-45	Para XVI (Good)

Number	Rank	Name	Initials	DOB	Enlisted	Unit	Date Tos	Discharged	Remarks
13802419		Lopez	Angel	19-Aug-17	Westward Ho	3 Centre	17-Jul-40	14-Mar-46	Class A Release
13802420		Lazaro	Gracia	14-Jun-09	Westward Ho	3 Centre	17-Jul-40	23-Jan-46	Class A Release
13802421		Moreno-Chemorro	Juan	22-May-18	Westward Ho	3 Centre	17-Jul-40	14-Mar-46	Class A Release
13802422	Pte	Cuevas	Miguel	29-Apr-20	Westward Ho	3 Centre	17-Jul-40	06-Nov-45	Para XVI (Fair)
13802423		Haro	Rodrigo	28-Mar-10	Westward Ho	3 Centre	17-Jul-40	11-Feb-46	Class A Release
13802424		Segura	Jose Mario	13-Sep-41	Westward Ho	3 Centre	17-Jul-40	12-Mar-46	Class A Release
13802425		Tuset	Juan	04-Mar-20	Westward Ho	3 Centre	17-Jul-40	01-Sep-46	Class A Release
13802426		Lopez	Jose	10-Apr-17	Westward Ho	3 Centre	17-Jul-40	24-Mar-41	DIED 24 Mar 41
13802427		Roca	Pedro	19-Mar-16	Westward Ho	3 Centre	17-Jul-40	12-Mar-46	Class A Release
13802428	Pte	Garcia-Caballero	Juan	01-Oct-17	Westward Ho	3 Centre	17-Jul-40	09-Apr-42	1 (Sp) Coy, Para XVI (Good)
13802429		Cuenca	Enrique	08-Dec-10	Westward Ho	3 Centre	17-Jul-40	13-Feb-46	Class A Release
13802430		Sanchez	Rafael	10-Jul-18	Westward Ho	3 Centre	17-Jul-40	20-Jul-46	Class A Release
13802431		Ruiz	Juan	13-Feb-18	Westward Ho	3 Centre	17-Jul-40	15-Mar-46	Class A Release
13802432		Cabrera	Miguel	1920	Westward Ho	3 Centre	17-Jul-40	16-Mar-46	Class A Release
13802433		Verdugo	Simeon	18-Feb-21	Westward Ho	3 Centre	17-Jul-40	19-Mar-46	Class A Release
13802434		Pollan	Leandro	20-Jan-16	Westward Ho	3 Centre	17-Jul-40	12-Mar-46	Class A Release
13802435		Tapia	Juan	10-Jan-20	Westward Ho	3 Centre	17-Jul-40		DESERTER 16 Dec 44
13802436		Bernal	Francisco	19-Jul-14	Westward Ho	3 Centre	17-Jul-40	12-Mar-46	Class A Release
13802437		Ismar	Luiz	08-Jan-16	Westward Ho	3 Centre	17-Jul-40	19-Mar-46	Class A Release
13802438	Pte	Cano	Juan	24-Jun-18	Westward Ho	3 Centre	17-Jul-40	17-Apr-44	1 (Sp) Coy, Para XVI (Fair)
13802439		Martin	Juan	17-Jan-19	Westward Ho	3 Centre	17-Jul-40	15-Mar-46	Class A Release
13802440		Serano	Jose	02-Oct-06	Westward Ho	3 Centre	17-Jul-40	15-Jan-46	Class A Release
13802441		Martinez	Salvador	19-Mar-19	Westward Ho	3 Centre	17-Jul-40	15-Mar-46	Class A Release
13802442		Lopez	Bicardo	17-Apr-18	Westward Ho	3 Centre	17-Jul-40	14-Mar-46	Class A Release
13802443		Arroyo	Mariano	24-Mar-16	Westward Ho	3 Centre	17-Jul-40	20-Mar-46	Class A Release
13802444		Balague	Francisco	02-Jan-22	Westward Ho	3 Centre	17-Jul-40	16-Mar-46	Class A Release
13802445		Benitz	Cruz	06-Jul-17	Westward Ho	3 Centre	17-Jul-40	12-Mar-46	Class A Release
13802446		Bosque	Jose	02-Jul-12	Westward Ho	3 Centre	17-Jul-40	09-Mar-42	Class W(T) Reserve 28 Feb 42, discharged Para
13802447	Pte	Carreras	Jose	25-Jul-16	Westward Ho	3 Centre	17-Jul-40	25-Mar-43	Para XVI (V Good)
13802448		Dominguez	Matias	10-Dec-20	Westward Ho	3 Centre	17-Jul-40		DESERTER 16 Dec 44

APPENDIX VII

Number	Rank	Name	Initials	DOB	Enlisted	Unit	Date Tos	Discharged	Remarks
13802449		Escrig	Luis	25-Sep-18	Westward Ho	3 Centre	17-Jul-40	20-Mar-46	Class A Release
13802450		Fernandez	Mariano	06-Apr-14	Westward Ho	3 Centre	17-Jul-40	12-Mar-46	Class A Release
13802451	Pte	Garrigas	Pedro	20-Aug-18	Westward Ho	3 Centre	17-Jul-40	28-Mar-44	1 (Sp) Coy, Para XVI (V Good)
13802452		Gomez	Joaquim	09-Nov-14	Westward Ho	3 Centre	17-Jul-40	12-Mar-46	Class A Release, CIA RASC Records 18 Feb 52
13802453		Gomez	Manuel	24-May-19	Westward Ho	3 Centre	17-Jul-40	15-Mar-46	Class A Release
13802454		Jlla	Arturo	27-Oct-19	Westward Ho	3 Centre	17-Jul-40	15-Mar-46	Class A Release
13802455		Latienda	Angel	01-Mar-18	Westward Ho	3 Centre	17-Jul-40	15-Mar-46	Class A Release
13802456		Mallafre	Manuel	22-Nov-19	Westward Ho	3 Centre	17-Jul-40		Transferred to ACC 9 Jul 44
13802457		Maniez	Laureano	06-Jan-22	Westward Ho	3 Centre	17-Jul-40	09-Nov-45	Class B Release
13802458	Pte	Martin	Augustin	05-May-15	Westward Ho	3 Centre	17-Jul-40	18-Jun-45	Para XVI (Good)
13802459		Melis	Luis	24-Sep-08	Westward Ho	3 Centre	17-Jul-40	15-Jan-46	Class A Release
13802460		Membrado	Juan	15-Apr-15	Westward Ho	3 Centre	17-Jul-40		Class A Release
13802461		Montoliol	Andres	17-Feb-20	Westward Ho	3 Centre	17-Jul-40	16-Mar-46	Class A Release
13802462		Moya	Nicolas	29-Jan-14	Westward Ho	3 Centre	17-Jul-40	12-Mar-46	Class A Release
13802463		Pina	Valentin	14-Nov-17	Westward Ho	3 Centre	17-Jul-40	14-Mar-46	Class A Release
13802464		Pino	Miguel	01-Aug-18	Westward Ho	3 Centre	17-Jul-40	15-Mar-46	Class A Release
13802465		Planells	Jose	06-Sep-19	Westward Ho	3 Centre	17-Jul-40	16-Mar-46	Class A Release
13802466		Planes	Stanislao	21-Apr-17	Westward Ho	3 Centre	17-Jul-40	12-Mar-46	Class A Release
13802467		Puig	Antonio	13-Jun-20	Westward Ho	3 Centre	17-Jul-40	16-Mar-46	Class A Release
13802468		Rojano	Andres	27-Feb-19	Westward Ho	3 Centre	17-Jul-40	16-Mar-46	Class A Release, CIA RE Records 1 Feb 52
13802469		Sorribas	Rafael	24-Dec-14	Westward Ho	3 Centre	17-Jul-40	06-Aug-44	6 Centre, Para XVIII (V Good)
13802470		Tresserras	Rafael	07-Aug-13	Westward Ho	3 Centre	17-Jul-40	12-Mar-46	Class A Release
13802471		Alvarez	Luiz	14-Jun-14	Westward Ho	3 Centre	17-Jul-40	12-Mar-46	Class A Release, CIA to ACC 1 Dec 51
13802472		Amills	Jose	10-Jun-20	Westward Ho	3 Centre	17-Jul-40	16-Mar-46	Class A Release
13802473		Camilleri	Jose	16-Oct-13	Westward Ho	3 Centre	17-Jul-40	16-Mar-46	Class A Release
13802474		Escaso	Fabian	08-Jan-17	Westward Ho	3 Centre	17-Jul-40	20-Mar-46	Class A Release
13802475	Pte	Gallego	Blas	03-Feb-21	Westward Ho	3 Centre	17-Jul-40	27-Nov-45	Para XVI (V Good)
13802476		Gener	Ramon	26-Jul-20	Westward Ho	3 Centre	17-Jul-40	16-Mar-46	Class A Release
13802477		Guitierrez	Antonio	20-Jan-13	Westward Ho	3 Centre	17-Jul-40	11-Nov-43	DIED 11 Nov 43

312 CHURCHILL'S SPANIARDS

Number	Rank	Name	Initials	DOB	Enlisted	Unit	Date Tos	Discharged	Remarks
13802478		Mas	Jaime	06-Jul-20	Westward Ho	3 Centre	17-Jul-40	20-Mar-46	Class A Release, CIA ACC 1 Dec 51
13802479		Morales	Cristobal	08-Jan-13	Westward Ho	3 Centre	17-Jul-40	12-Mar-46	Class A Release
13802480		Navarro	Francisco	23-May-20	Westward Ho	3 Centre	17-Jul-40	16-Mar-46	Class A Release
13802481	Pte	Ortega	Antonio	13-Jun-12	Westward Ho	3 Centre	17-Jul-40	21-Mar-45	6 HTU, Para XVI (V Good)
13802482		Perez	Guillarmo	02-Jun-10	Westward Ho	3 Centre	17-Jul-40	13-Feb-46	Class A Release
13802483		Romero	Marcial	15-Nov-19	Westward Ho	3 Centre	17-Jul-40	16-Mar-46	Class A Release
13802484		Sanfelix	Jose	15-Mar-17	Westward Ho	3 Centre	17-Jul-40	14-Mar-46	Class A Release
13802486		Anandon	Francisco	10-Oct-19	Westward Ho	3 Centre	17-Jul-40	15-Mar-46	Class A Release, CIA to RASC Records 18 Feb 52
13802487		Baguena	Antonio	30-Jun-19	Westward Ho	3 Centre	17-Jul-40	15-Mar-46	Class A Release
13802488		Barroso	Antonio	10-Aug-20	Westward Ho	3 Centre	17-Jul-40	19-Mar-46	Class A Release
13802489		Bielsa	Cristobal	25-Dec-13	Westward Ho	3 Centre	17-Jul-40	12-Mar-46	Class A Release
13802490		Campos	Juan	19-Jan-19	Westward Ho	3 Centre	17-Jul-40	19-Jan-19	Transferred to ACC 11 Jan 46
13802491		Cases	Manuel	05-Feb-17	Westward Ho	3 Centre	17-Jul-40	19-Oct-45	Class B Release
13802492		Dura	Francisco	14-Oct-20	Westward Ho	3 Centre	17-Jul-40	20-Mar-46	Class A Release
13802493		Egea	Iguacio	25-Apr-18	Westward Ho	3 Centre	17-Jul-40	14-Mar-46	Class A Release
13802494		Fernandez	Francisco	03-Apr-20	Westward Ho	3 Centre	17-Jul-40	16-Mar-46	Class A Release
13802495	Pte	Gallego	Tomas	04-Jun-18	Westward Ho	3 Centre	17-Jul-40	05-Feb-43	Para XVI (V Good)
13802496		Garcia	Jose	09-Feb-23	Westward Ho	3 Centre	17-Jul-40		Transferred to R Signals 5 Aug 44
13802497		Gil	Pedro	21-Apr-22	Westward Ho	3 Centre	17-Jul-40	19-Mar-46	Class A Release
13802498		Iovino	Francisco	03-Jun-21	Westward Ho	3 Centre	17-Jul-40	16-Mar-46	Class A Release
13802499		Lopez	Joaquim	19-Mar-06	Westward Ho	3 Centre	17-Jul-40	15-Jan-46	Class A Release
13802500		Luque	Jose	21-Apr-09	Westward Ho	3 Centre	17-Jul-40	13-Feb-46	Class A Release
13802501		Martinez	Jose	12-Feb-16	Westward Ho	3 Centre	17-Jul-40	12-Mar-46	Class A Release
13802502		Montoursi	Lorenzo	20-Feb-18	Westward Ho	3 Centre	17-Jul-40	21-Mar-46	Class A Release
13802503		Moreno	Juan	18-Nov-09	Westward Ho	3 Centre	17-Jul-40	24-Jan-46	Class A Release
13802504		Nieto	Teodoro	01-Apr-17	Westward Ho	3 Centre	17-Jul-40	14-Mar-46	Class A Release
13802505		Orriols	Jose	27-Jan-12	Westward Ho	3 Centre	17-Jul-40	07-Jan-46	Class A Release
13802506		Palomar	Jose	03-Jul-14	Westward Ho	3 Centre	17-Jul-40	12-Mar-46	Class A Release
13802507	Pte	Rey	Manuel	27-Dec-13	Westward Ho	3 Centre	17-Jul-40	05-Nov-45	Para XVI (V Good)
13802508		Rodriguez	Anronio	25-Dec-19	Westward Ho	3 Centre	17-Jul-40	16-Mar-46	Class A Release
13802509		Romero	Jose	05-Apr-12	Westward Ho	3 Centre	17-Jul-40	07-Jan-46	Class A Release

APPENDIX VII 313

Number	Rank	Name	Initials	DOB	Enlisted	Unit	Date Tos	Discharged	Remarks
13802510		Virgili	Juan	11-Oct-20	Westward Ho	3 Centre	17-Jul-40	19-Mar-46	Class A Release
13802511		Lopez	Luiz	18-Jun-18	Westward Ho	3 Centre	17-Jul-40	14-Mar-46	Class A Release
13802512		Fernandez-Martinez	Manuel	01-Jan-16	Westward Ho	3 Centre	17-Jul-40	29-Mar-46	Class A Release
13802513		Delgado	Manuel	18-Jul-07	Westward Ho	3 Centre	17-Jul-40	15-Jan-46	Class A Release
13802514		Espallargas	Manuel	26-Jan-09	Westward Ho	3 Centre	17-Jul-40	24-Jan-46	Class A Release
13802515		Fernandez	Bartolome	17-Oct-18	Westward Ho	3 Centre	17-Jul-40	14-Mar-46	Class A Release
13802516		Garcia	Benigno	10-Oct-17	Westward Ho	3 Centre	17-Jul-40	12-Mar-46	Class A Release
13802517		Iniesta	Juan	24-Sep-16	Westward Ho	3 Centre	17-Jul-40	13-Mar-46	Class A Release
13802518		Jurado	Jose	09-Jul-21	Westward Ho	3 Centre	17-Jul-40	20-Mar-46	Class A Release
13802519		Largo	Urbano	24-Dec-15	Westward Ho	3 Centre	17-Jul-40	12-Mar-46	Class A Release
13802520		Luque	Jose	23-Jul-18	Westward Ho	3 Centre	17-Jul-40	15-Mar-46	Class A Release
13802521		Lugue	Juan	09-Mar-21	Westward Ho	3 Centre	17-Jul-40	19-Mar-46	Class A Release
13802522	Pte	Munoz	Andres	03-Aug-20	Westward Ho	3 Centre	17-Jul-40	20-Jan-44	44 Coy, Para XVI (V Good)
13802523		Muntane	Jose	30-Jul-21	Westward Ho	3 Centre	17-Jul-40	30-Mar-46	Class A Release
13802524		Nadal	Joaquim	12-Apr-19	Westward Ho	3 Centre	17-Jul-40	15-Mar-46	Class A Release
13802525		Ostio	Jose	16-Jun-16	Westward Ho	3 Centre	17-Jul-40		DESERTER 17 Oct 44
13802526	Pte	Perez	Felipe	05-Dec-17	Westward Ho	3 Centre	17-Jul-40	12-Nov-45	Para XVI (V Good)
13802527		Quesada	Louis	11-Jun-12	Westward Ho	3 Centre	17-Jul-40	17-Jan-46	Class A Release
13802528		Rafael	Soriano	01-Nov-20	Westward Ho	3 Centre	17-Jul-40	19-Mar-46	Class A Release
13802529		Reina	Francisco	31-Mar-18	Westward Ho	3 Centre	17-Jul-40	20-Mar-46	Class A Release
13802530	Pte	Ribera	Anselmo	20-Apr-15	Westward Ho	3 Centre	17-Jul-40	11-Oct-41	1 (Sp) Coy, Para XVI (Indifferent)
13802531		Rubio	Vicente	02-Jan-18	Westward Ho	3 Centre	17-Jul-40	15-Mar-46	Class A Release
13802532		Jabane	Francisco	14-Aug-15	Westward Ho	3 Centre	17-Jul-40	12-Mar-46	Class A Release
13802533		Saez	Luis	17-Mar-17	Westward Ho	3 Centre	17-Jul-40	14-Mar-46	Class A Release
13802534	Pte	Socorro	Gonzalez	21-Nov-11	Westward Ho	3 Centre	17-Jul-40	05-Feb-43	Para XVI (Good)
13802535		Vallejo	Ramon	04-May-13	Westward Ho	3 Centre	17-Jul-40	12-Mar-46	Class A Release
13802536		Alapont	Francisco	19-Jul-16	Westward Ho	3 Centre	17-Jul-40	14-Mar-46	Class A Release
13802537		Alcon	Remigio	05-Jan-20	Westward Ho	3 Centre	17-Jul-40	21-Mar-46	Class A Release
13802538		Arcos	Alfonso	18-Jul-19	Westward Ho	3 Centre	17-Jul-40		DESERTER 23 Mar 46
13802539		Arrel	Gregorio	11-May-12	Westward Ho	3 Centre	17-Jul-40	14-Mar-46	Class A Release
13802540		Delatorre	Ruiz	15-Apr-17	Westward Ho	3 Centre	17-Jul-40	12-Mar-46	Class A Release

314 CHURCHILL'S SPANIARDS

Number	Rank	Name	Initials	DOB	Enlisted	Unit	Date Tos	Discharged	Remarks
13802541		Oritz	Armando	13-May-17	Westward Ho	3 Centre	17-Jul-40	14-Mar-46	Class A Release
13802542		Queralt	Jaime	09-Feb-21	Westward Ho	3 Centre	17-Jul-40	20-Mar-46	Class A Release
13802543		Romera	Francisco	23-Jul-21	Westward Ho	3 Centre	17-Jul-40	19-Mar-46	Class A Release
13802544		Sanabrias	Francisco	29-Mar-12	Westward Ho	3 Centre	17-Jul-40	07-Jan-46	Class A Release
13802545	Pte	Trilles	Eduardo	30-Aug-17	Westward Ho	3 Centre	17-Jul-40	28-Jan-44	Para XVI (V Good)
13802546		Aguera	Cristofol	16-Feb-14	Westward Ho	3 Centre	22-Jul-40	12-Mar-46	Class A Release
13802547		Domingo	Antonio	20-Jul-18	Westward Ho	3 Centre	22-Jul-40		Class A Release
13802548		Gimenez	Gonzalo	25-Nov-17	Westward Ho	3 Centre	22-Jul-40	28-Feb-46	Class B Release
13802549		Masso	Benito	26-Jul-17	Westward Ho	3 Centre	22-Jul-40	14-Mar-46	Class A Release
13802550		Rodiguez	Jesus	01-Jun-20	Westward Ho	3 Centre	22-Jul-40	19-Mar-46	Class A Release, CIA to ACC 1 Dec 51
13802551		Valero	Jose	31-Mar-17	Westward Ho	3 Centre	22-Jul-40	20-Mar-46	Class A Release
13802552		Garcia	Valentin	12-Oct-12	Westward Ho	3 Centre	23-Jul-40	17-Jan-46	Class A Release
13802553		Marin	Ramon	14-Oct-10	Westward Ho	3 Centre	31-Jul-40	12-Feb-46	Class A Release
13802554		Garcia-Perez	Amancio	27-Sep-05	Westward Ho	3 Centre	24-Jul-40	15-Jan-46	Class A Release
13802591		Bardasco	Julian	21-Aug-13	Westward Ho	3 Centre	24-Jul-40	21-Aug-13	Class A Release
13802592		Belenguer	Pedro	19-Apr-14	Westward Ho	3 Centre	24-Jul-40	03-Oct-43	DIED 3 Oct 43
13802593		Belles	Valeriano Bauesdo	18-Oct-16	Westward Ho	3 Centre	24-Jul-40	16-Mar-46	Class A Release
13802594		Borras	Emilio	17-Jan-13	Westward Ho	3 Centre	24-Jul-40	13-Mar-46	Class A Release
13802595		Cardinal	Joaquin	26-Jul-20	Westward Ho	3 Centre	24-Jul-40	21-Mar-46	Class A Release
13802596	Pte	Fernandez	Teodoro	01-Apr-16	Westward Ho	3 Centre	24-Jul-40	07-Sep-45	Para XVI (V Good)
13802597		Grande	Antonio	28-Apr-16	Westward Ho	3 Centre	24-Jul-40	14-Mar-46	Class A Release
13802598		Izquierdo	Clemente	16-Nov-16	Westward Ho	3 Centre	24-Jul-40	15-Mar-46	Class A Release
13802599		Jenfer	Carols	02-Nov-16	Westward Ho	3 Centre	24-Jul-40	15-Mar-46	Class A Release
13802600		Lasurra	Faustino	15-Sep-17	Westward Ho	3 Centre	24-Jul-40	12-Mar-46	Class A Release
13802601		Lopez	Emilio	11-Jul-11	Westward Ho	3 Centre	24-Jul-40	15-Feb-46	Class A Release
13802602		Lozano	Miguel	09-Sep-00	Westward Ho	3 Centre	24-Jul-40	26-Oct-45	Class A Release
13802603	Pte	Solis	Manuel	06-Apr-14	Westward Ho	3 Centre	24-Jul-40	02-Dec-43	1 (Sp) Coy, Para XVI (V Good)
13802604		Velasco	Jesus	24-Dec-15	Westward Ho	3 Centre	24-Jul-40	21-Mar-46	Class A Release
13802605		Herreras	Pedro	30-Aug-17	Westward Ho	3 Centre	24-Jul-40	12-Mar-46	Class A Release
13802607		Valenzuela	Juan	15-Mar-14	Westward Ho	3 Centre	30-Jul-40	12-Mar-46	Class A Release
13802703		Colone	Juan	24-May-12	Westward Ho	3 Centre	06-Aug-40	07-Jan-46	Class A Release

APPENDIX VII 315

Number	Rank	Name	Initials	DOB	Enlisted	Unit	Date Tos	Discharged	Remarks
13802704		Orti	Miguel	16-Feb-19	Westward Ho	3 Centre	06-Aug-40	24-Jan-46	Class A Release
13802851		Pardo	Jose	13-Mar-19	Liverpool	3 Centre	19-Aug-40	07-Jan-46	Class A Release
13802852		Bernad	Jose	14-Jul-12	Liverpool	3 Centre	26-Aug-40	07-Jan-46	Class A Release
13802853		Busquet	Carols	08-Mar-05	Liverpool	3 Centre	26-Aug-40	27-Sep-46	Class W(T) Reseve3 13 Nov 42, rejoined 2 Oct 45, Class A Release
13802990	Pte	Santos	Manuel	15-Jun-13	Derby	3 Centre	14-Sep-40	09-Aug-43	Para XVI (V Good)
13803001		Rodrigues	Manuel	12-Aug-10	Swanwick	3 Centre	14-Sep-40	20-Dec-45	Later 13116608, Class A Release
13803002		Marco	Sylvain	28-Mar-19	Swanwick	3 Centre	14-Sep-40	16-Mar-46	Class A Release
13803003		Cayuela	Salvador	18-Sep-12	Swanwick	3 Centre	14-Sep-40	12-Mar-46	Class A Release
13803004		Casabayo	Fernando	07-Aug-11	Swanwick	3 Centre	14-Sep-40	11-Feb-46	Class A Release
13803005		Cortilla	Fernandez	19-Mar-19	Swanwick	3 Centre	14-Sep-40	20-Mar-46	Class A Release
13803006	Pte	Corbacho	Jose	24-Aug-18	Swanwick	3 Centre	14-Sep-40	16-May-41	Para XVI (Good)
13803007		Cervantes	Juan	22-Feb-19	Swanwick	3 Centre	14-Sep-40	16-Mar-46	Class A Release
13803009		Negueroles	Agustin	31-Jul-19	Swanwick	3 Centre	14-Sep-40	16-Mar-46	Class A Release, transferred to RASC 9 Oct 51
13803010		Villasenor	Francusco	05-Nov-14	Swanwick	3 Centre	14-Sep-40	12-Mar-46	Class A Release
13803011		Deerio	Edwardo	20-Jan-17	Swanwick	3 Centre	14-Sep-40	14-Mar-46	Class A Release
13803012		Guttierez	Fernando	08-Nov-20	Swanwick	3 Centre	14-Sep-40	19-Mar-46	Class A Release
13803013	Pte	Moya	Juan	15-Feb-19	Swanwick	3 Centre	14-Sep-40	27-Feb-42	1 (Sp) Coy, Para XVI (Good)
13803014		Mota	Manuel	16-Jul-17	Swanwick	3 Centre	14-Sep-40	16-Mar-46	Class A Release
13803015		Perez	Augusto	28-Apr-07	Swanwick	3 Centre	14-Sep-40	15-Jan-46	Class A Release
13803016		Perez	Vincent	06-Feb-20	Swanwick	3 Centre	14-Sep-40	14-Mar-46	Class A Release
13803017		Palanca	Ramon	19-Jul-17	Swanwick	3 Centre	14-Sep-40	14-Mar-46	Class A Release
13803018		Prades	Juan	17-Jun-18	Swanwick	3 Centre	14-Sep-40	15-Mar-46	Class A Release
13803019		Romero	Raphael	04-May-19	Swanwick	3 Centre	14-Sep-40	19-Mar-46	Class A Release
13803020		Roig	Angel	02-Aug-14	Swanwick	3 Centre	14-Sep-40	12-Mar-46	Class A Release
13803021		Rubio	Antonio	12-Aug-17	Swanwick	3 Centre	14-Sep-40	28-Mar-44	1 (Sp) Coy, Para XVI (V Good)
13803030		Rodriguez	Jose	18-Dec-03	Swanwick	3 Centre	14-Sep-40	15-Dec-49	Later 13041649, Class A Release
13803031		Sanchez	Jose	14-Feb-20	Swanwick	3 Centre	14-Sep-40	20-Mar-46	Class A Release
13803033		De Castro	Silvio	20-Apr-08	Swanwick	3 Centre	14-Sep-40	10-Apr-46	Class A Release
13805328		Martin	Grezorio	28-Nov-13	Euston	Spanish Coy	20-Jan-41	12-Mar-46	Class A Release

316 CHURCHILL'S SPANIARDS

Number	Rank	Name	Initials	DOB	Enlisted	Unit	Date Tos	Discharged	Remarks
13805329		Perez	Jacinto	15-Sep-16	Euston	Spanish Coy	20-Jan-41	15-Mar-40	Class A Release
13805330		Corredor	Jean	28-Aug-17	Euston	Spanish Coy	20-Jan-41	16-Mar-46	Class A Release
13805331		Bermego	Castello	29-Nov-13	Euston	Spanish Coy	20-Jan-41	12-Mar-46	Class A Release
13805529		Lete	Jose Gomez	16-May-13	Croydon	3 Centre	21-Feb-41		DESERTER 10 Aug 45
13805530		Lete	Antonio Larrenaga?	20-Jul-19	Croydon	3 Centre	21-Feb-41	19-Mar-46	Class A Release
13805983		Vaquer-Borrull	Jaime	27-Oct-20	Euston	6 Centre	27-Oct-41	20-Mar-46	Class A Release
13805984		Dalmau Norat	Francisco	24-Jul-15	Euston	6 Centre	27-Oct-41	20-Mar-46	Class A Release
13805985		Llonchs-Fontanillas	Jose	07-Aug-16	Euston	6 Centre	27-Oct-41	23-Mar-46	Class A Release
13805986		Jornet	Antonio Robert	20-Jul-19	Euston	6 Centre	27-Oct-41	23-Mar-46	Class A Release
13805988		Lopez-Llamas	Juan	03-Jan-18	Euston	6 Centre	27-Oct-41	02-Mar-46	Class A Release
13805989		Mateo	Victoriano Mates	22-Jul-20	Euston	6 Centre	27-Oct-41	20-Mar-46	Class A Release
13808212		Balerdi	Justo	25-Jul-20	Fayed		05-Jan-42		Later 13041866 Robert BRUCE, Service to reckon from 13 Oct 40, Docs to Jerusalem Records 1944
13808213		Bardenas	Roberto	05-Apr-19	Fayed		05-Jan-42		Service to reckon from 23 Aug 40, Docs to Jerusalem Records 1944
13808214		Trancho Bartholomen	Moises	25-Nov-16	Fayed		05-Jan-42	29-Jul-43	DIED 29 Jul 43, Service to reckon from 23 Aug 40, Docs to Jerusalem Records 1944
13808215		Fernandez-Caballero		24-Jul-18	Fayed		05-Jan-42		Transferred to Army Air Corps 31 May 45, Service to reckon from 23 Aug 40, Docs to Jerusalem Records 1944
13808216		Vargas Crespo	Antonio	30-Jan-16	Fayed		05-Jan-42		Service to reckon from 23 Aug 40, Docs to Jerusalem Records 1944
13808217		Delgado	Andres	06-Jan-20	Fayed		05-Jan-42	21-Jun-46	Class A Release, Service to reckon from 23 Aug 40, Docs to Jerusalem Records 1944

APPENDIX VII 317

Number	Rank	Name	Initials	DOB	Enlisted	Unit	Date Tos	Discharged	Remarks
13808218		Esteve	Fernando	23-Apr-16	Fayed		05-Jan-42		Transferred to Queen's Regt 21 Jul 43, Service to reckon from 23 Aug 40, Docs to Jerusalem Records 1944
13808219		Garcia	Antonio	15-Aug-15	Fayed		05-Jan-42	21-Jun-46	Class A Release, Service to reckon from 23 Aug 40, Docs to Jerusalem Records 1944
13808220		Garcia	Antonio	07-Jan-07	Fayed		05-Jan-42		DESERTER 24 Oct 43, Service to reckon from 11 Sep 40, Docs to Jerusalem Records 1944
13808221		Garrigos	Garcia	25-Feb-17	Fayed		05-Jan-42		Service to reckon from 13 Oct 40, Docs to Jerusalem Records 1944
13808222		Valero Gimenez	Antonio	13-Jul-14	Fayed		05-Jan-42		Service to reckon from 23 Aug 40, Docs to Jerusalem Records 1944
13808223		Alarcon Gomez	Cayo	10-Apr-17	Fayed		05-Jan-42		Service to reckon from 23 Aug 40, Docs to Jerusalem Records 1944
13808224		Martinez	Barnabe	11-Jul-14	Fayed		05-Jan-42	21-Jun-43	DESERTER 24 Oct 43, Class A Release, Service to reckon from 11 Sep 40, Docs to Jerusalem Records 1944
13808225		Martinez	Fernandez	04-Mar-19	Fayed		05-Jan-42		Service to reckon from 13 Oct 40, Docs to Jerusalem Records 1944
13808226		Martinez	Miguel	23-Feb-19	Fayed		05-Jan-42	21-Jun-46	Class A Release, Service to reckon from 11 Sep 40, Docs to Jerusalem Records 1944
13808227		Mena	Vicente	10-May-17	Fayed		05-Jan-42		Transferred to Wueen's Regt 21 Jul 43, Service to reckon from 23 Aug 40, Docs to Jerusalem Records 1944
13808228	Pte	Mercado	Joseph	22-Jan-19	Fayed		05-Jan-42	01-May-44	12 Centre Para XVI (V Good), Service to reckon from 13 Oct 40, Docs to Jerusalem Records 1944
13808229		Pineira	Lorenzo	07-Feb-20	Fayed		05-Jan-42	21-Jun-46	Class A Release, Service to reckon from 23 Aug 40, Docs to Jerusalem Records 1944

318   CHURCHILL'S SPANIARDS

Number	Rank	Name	Initials	DOB	Enlisted	Unit	Date Tos	Discharged	Remarks
13808230		Redondo	Jose	04-Apr-20	Fayed		05-Jan-42	21-Jun-46	Class A Release, Service to reckon from 23 Aug 40, Docs to Jerusalem Records 1944
13808231		Santiago	Basilio	17-Jul-18	Fayed		05-Jan-42	21-Jun-46	Class A Release, Service to reckon from 23 Aug 40, Docs to Jerusalem Records 1944
13808232		Surera	Emmanuel	18-Mar-19	Fayed		05-Jan-42	21-Jun-46	Class A Release, Service to reckon from 23 Aug 40, Docs to Jerusalem Records 1944
13808233		Lugue Tirado	Antonio	20-Jan-11	Fayed		05-Jan-42		DESERTER 2 Dec 43, Service to reckon from 23 Aug 40, Docs to Jerusalem Records 1944
13808234		Villanova	Jose	06-Sep-20	Fayed		05-Jan-42		Transferred to Queen's Regt 21 Jul 43, Service to reckon from 23 Aug 40, Docs to Jerusalem Records 1944
13808236		Simberas	Paul	Aug-17	Cairo		18-Dec-41	13-Apr-43	DESERTER 21 Sep 42–2 Nov 42, DIED 13 Apr 43, Docs to Jerusalem Records 1944
13808237		Muir	Edward Patrick	09-Nov-08	Lobatsi		22-Jan-42		Docs to Jerusalem Records 1944
13808238		Alvaresz	J		Lobatsi		23-Aug-40		Docs to Jerusalem Records 1944
13808239		Barroso	M		Lobatsi		23-Aug-40		Docs to Jerusalem Records 1944
13808240		Diaz	Y		Lobatsi		23-Aug-40		Docs to Jerusalem Records 1944
13808241		Franco	T		Lobatsi		23-Aug-40		Docs to Jerusalem Records 1944
13808242		Fajardo	J		Lobatsi		23-Aug-40		Docs to Jerusalem Records 1944
13808243		Fraili	G		Lobatsi		23-Aug-40		Docs to Jerusalem Records 1944
13808244		Garcia	John		Lobatsi		23-Aug-40		Docs to Jerusalem Records 1944
13808245		Comez	S		Lobatsi		23-Aug-40		Docs to Jerusalem Records 1944
13808246		Galarreta	M L		Lobatsi		23-Aug-40		Docs to Jerusalem Records 1944
13808247		Galera	R E		Lobatsi		23-Aug-40		Docs to Jerusalem Records 1944
13808248		Heras	B		Lobatsi		23-Aug-40		Docs to Jerusalem Records 1944
13808249		Corda	F		Lobatsi		23-Aug-40		Docs to Jerusalem Records 1944
13808250		Lumberas	F		Lobatsi		23-Aug-40		Docs to Jerusalem Records 1944

APPENDIX VII 319

Number	Rank	Name	Initials	DOB	Enlisted	Unit	Date Tos	Discharged	Remarks
13808251		Marin	B		Lobatsi		23-Aug-40		Docs to Jerusalem Records 1944
13808252		Navarette	F		Lobatsi		23-Aug-40		Docs to Jerusalem Records 1944
13808253		Postillo	R		Lobatsi		23-Aug-40		Docs to Jerusalem Records 1944
13808254		Sanchez	Manuel		Lobatsi		23-Aug-40	21-Jun-46	Class A Release, Docs to Jerusalem Records 1944
13808255		Torralbo	M		Lobatsi		23-Aug-40		Docs to Jerusalem Records 1944
13808256		Trill	T		Lobatsi		23-Aug-40		Docs to Jerusalem Records 1944
13808257		Blasco	V		Lobatsi		11-Sep-40		Docs to Jerusalem Records 1944
13808258		Cevantes	S		Lobatsi		23-Aug-40		Docs to Jerusalem Records 1944
13808259		Martinez	F		Lobatsi		11-Sep-40		Docs to Jerusalem Records 1944
13808260		Bravo	J		Lobatsi		13-Oct-40		Docs to Jerusalem Records 1944
13808261		Carmona	M		Lobatsi		13-Oct-40		Docs to Jerusalem Records 1944
13808262		Cleto	S		Lobatsi		13-Oct-40		Docs to Jerusalem Records 1944
13808263		Hidalgo	T		Lobatsi		13-Oct-40		Docs to Jerusalem Records 1944
13808264		Lillo	J		Lobatsi		13-Oct-40		Docs to Jerusalem Records 1944
13808265		Martinez	A		Lobatsi		13-Oct-40		Docs to Jerusalem Records 1944
13808266		Albaladeco	A		Lobatsi		23-Aug-40		Docs to Jerusalem Records 1944
13808267		Castellano	P F		Lobatsi		23-Aug-40		Docs to Jerusalem Records 1944
13808268		Geronimo	Francesco	26-Sep-17	Cairo		13-Jul-42		Later 13041867 Frank WILLIAMS, Service reckoned from 13 Oct 40, Docs to Jerusalem Records 1944
13808269		Mena	V		Lobatsi		23-Aug-40		Docs to Jerusalem Records 1944
13808270		Lloret	C		Lobatsi		23-Aug-40		Docs to Jerusalem Records 1944
13808271		Martinez	Pereira		Lobatsi		13-Oct-40		Docs to Jerusalem Records 1944
13808272		Marino	A		Lobatsi		23-Aug-40		Docs to Jerusalem Records 1944
13808273		Resnick	Philipos	23-Jun-12	Lobatsi		15-Oct-41		Docs to Jerusalem Records 1944
13808274		Johnson	Qwen Robert	17-May-93	Lobatsi		28-Oct-41		Docs to Jerusalem Records 1944
13808278		Tavio	Enrique	18-Nov-15	Cairo		03-Mar-42	08-Jun-46	Service reckoned from 23 Aug 40, Class A Release, Docs to Jerusalem Records 1944
13809970		Santos	Enlogio	26-Mar-18	Bonfarik	N Africa	13-Apr-43		Alias TEJERA, transferred to RASC 29 Nov 43

320 CHURCHILL'S SPANIARDS

Number	Rank	Name	Initials	DOB	Enlisted	Unit	Date Tos	Discharged	Remarks
13809471		Oronoz	Faustino	25-Oct-15	Bonfarik	N Africa	13-Apr-43	06-Nov-46	Class A Release
13809472		Saurina	Agustin	08-Apr-21	Bonfarik	N Africa	13-Apr-43		DESERTER 17 Dec 45
13809473		Lopez	Diego	07-Jul-18	Bonfarik	N Africa	13-Apr-43		Alias CARRASCO
13809474		Caparros	Juan	22-Apr-18	Bonfarik	N Africa	13-Apr-43		Alias GOMES, DESERTER 16 Oct 43
13809475		Brion	Ramon	23-Dec-15	Bonfarik	N Africa	13-Apr-43	26-Oct-46	Class A Release
13809476		Gonzalez	Armando	20-Mar-03	Bonfarik	N Africa	13-Apr-43	21-Jun-46	Class A Release
13809477		Elias	Manuel	12-Oct-13	Bonfarik	N Africa	13-Apr-43	03-Jan-47	Class A Release
13809478		Bernardez	Enrique	29-Dec-12	Bonfarik	N Africa	13-Apr-43	07-Oct-46	Class A Release
13809479		Cabanas	Jose	08-Oct-12	Bonfarik	N Africa	13-Apr-43		DESERTER 27 Aug 43–20 Oct 43, discharged 337 Coy Para XVI
13809480		Marte	Ludwig	16-May-15	Bonfarik	N Africa	15-Apr-43		Docs to N Africa Records 1944
13809481		Antonescu	Valeriu	16-Jan-20	Bonfarik	N Africa	16-Apr-43		Docs to N Africa Records 1944
13809482		Hirsch	Oskar	16-Apr-14	Bonfarik	N Africa	02-Apr-43		Docs to N Africa Records 1944
13809483		Hofbauer	Alfred	28-Apr-13	Bonfarik	N Africa	02-Apr-43		Docs to N Africa Records 1944
13809484		Horwitz	Herbert	09-Sep-03	Bonfarik	N Africa	02-Apr-43		Docs to N Africa Records 1944
13809485		Da Silva	Raimundo Manuel	16-Oct-16	Bonfarik	N Africa	02-Apr-43		Docs to N Africa Records 1944
13809486		Plaza-Agudo	Austonio	13-Jul-24	Bonfarik	N Africa	02-Apr-43	25-Jun-47	Class A Release
13809500		Garcia-Caicedo	Manuel	15-Jul-23	Hussein Dey	N Africa	09-Apr-43		Docs to N Africa Records 1944
13809501		Oviedo	Jose	16-Jun-21	Hussein Dey	N Africa	09-Apr-43	15-Feb-47	Class A Release
13809603		Sanchez	Antonio	18-Mar-18	Bonfarik	N Africa	23-Apr-43		DESERTER 3 Jul 43–5 Dec 43
13809604		Vila	Luis	30-Mar-22	Bonfarik	N Africa	23-Apr-43	14-May-47	Class A Release
13809612		Soriano	Jose Gomez	03-Jan-14	Maison Carrel	N Africa	25-Apr-43	26-Oct-46	Class A Release
13809613		Belzado	Andres	10-Feb-19	Maison Carrel	N Africa	25-Apr-43	23-Jan-17	Alias SANZ, Class A Release
13809656		Albiol	Jose Subirats	29-Jul-98	Boufarick	N Africa	29-Apr-43		Docs to N Africa Records 1944
13809657		Aldave	Rebullida Enrique	13-Aug-07	Boufarick	N Africa	29-Apr-43		Docs to N Africa Records 1944
13809658		Armancha	Jose Ripoll	01-Jan-12	Boufarick	N Africa	29-Apr-43	07-Oct-46	Class A Release
13809659		Arpal	Jose Guiral	07-Jan-13	Boufarick	N Africa	29-Apr-43		Docs to N Africa Records 1944
13809660		Arranz	Faustuio Nevol	18-Oct-01	Boufarick	N Africa	29-Apr-43		Docs to N Africa Records 1944
13809661		Ayuso	Joaquin Palas	06-Jan-98	Boufarick	N Africa	29-Apr-43	21-Jun-46	Class A Release

APPENDIX VII 321

Number	Rank	Name	Initials	DOB	Enlisted	Unit	Date Tos	Discharged	Remarks
13809662		Aza	Luis Coz	26-Jan-10	Boufarick	N Africa	29-Apr-43		Docs to N Africa Records 1944
13809663		Baldo	Martin Balzano	05-Aug-09	Boufarick	N Africa	29-Apr-43	31-Aug-46	Class A Release
13809664		Bandera	Isidoro Fueyo	06-May-14	Boufarick	N Africa	29-Apr-43		DESERTER 18 Sep 43
13809665		Barbon	Higinio Rodriquez	25-May-98	Boufarick	N Africa	29-Apr-43	21-Jun-46	Class A Release
13809666		Barcaiztegui	Angel Garmendia	28-Feb-06	Boufarick	N Africa	29-Apr-43		DESERTER 8 Oct 43
13809667		Barnada	Baye Juan	11-Jul-12	Boufarick	N Africa	29-Apr-43	07-Oct-46	Class A Release
13809668		Barnada	Jose Baye	04-Jan-16	Boufarick	N Africa	29-Apr-43	28-Nov-46	Class A Release
13809669		Barquero	Cayetano Perez	07-Aug-10	Boufarick	N Africa	29-Apr-43		DESERTER 7 Mar 44
13809670		Barrachina	Angel Llorca	08-Aug-97	Boufarick	N Africa	29-Apr-43		Docs to N Africa Records 1944
13809671		Bartra	Jaime Bartram	15-Sep-93	Boufarick	N Africa	29-Apr-43	07-Dec-45	Class A Release
13809672		Bas	Isidro Gonzalo	15-May-15	Boufarick	N Africa	29-Apr-43	27-Oct-46	Class A Release
13809673		Benedicto	Ramon Guzman	07-Jul-15	Boufarick	N Africa	29-Apr-43		DESERTER 8 Oct 43
13809674		Berrar	Santiago Laplaza	25-Jul-03	Boufarick	N Africa	29-Apr-43	21-Jun-46	Class A Release
13809675		Biensoba	Ignaris Guerrero	17-Sep-04	Boufarick	N Africa	29-Apr-43	01-Jul-45	Class A Release
13809676		Blasco	Francisco Grego	02-Jan-16	Boufarick	N Africa	29-Apr-43	28-Nov-46	Class A Release
13809677		Bori	Rafael Fernandez	13-Sep-04	Boufarick	N Africa	29-Apr-43	01-Jul-46	Class A Release
13809678		Bruns	Federico Revuiner	18-Jul-11	Boufarick	N Africa	29-Apr-43		DESERTER 1 Nov 43
13809679		Cabedo	Francisco Collado	13-Aug-08	Boufarick	N Africa	29-Apr-43		Docs to N Africa Records 1944
13809680		Calderon	Miguel Manas	06-Oct-07	Boufarick	N Africa	29-Apr-43	03-Aug-46	Class A Release
13809681		Canadell	Jose Rovira	11-Nov-08	Boufarick	N Africa	29-Apr-43	16-Aug-46	Class A Release
13809682	Pte	Cardena	Clemente Moron	24-Apr-14	Boufarick	N Africa	29-Apr-43	17-Nov-45	Para XVI (V Good)
13809683		Carmona	Josi Peria?	27-Feb-04	Boufarick	N Africa	29-Apr-43		Docs to N Africa Records 1944

322 CHURCHILL'S SPANIARDS

Number	Rank	Name	Initials	DOB	Enlisted	Unit	Date Tos	Discharged	Remarks
13809684		Carrasco	Andrew Parilla	04-Feb-13	Boufarick	N Africa	29-Apr-43	05-Nov-46	Class A Release
13809685	Pte	Carretero	Alfonso Clement?	08-Nov-11	Boufarick	N Africa	29-Apr-43	11-May-45	Para XVI (V Good)
13809686		Casado	Ramon Miras	24-May-10	Boufarick	N Africa	29-Apr-43		DESERTER 1 Aug 43
13809687		Castano	Ignacio Acsuar	24-Jun-09	Boufarick	N Africa	29-Apr-43	31-Aug-46	Class A Release
13809688		Cervera	Luis Gasulla	31-Aug-10	Boufarick	N Africa	29-Apr-43	11-Sep-46	Class A Release
13809689		Checa	Juan Alad	29-Sep-03	Boufarick	N Africa	29-Apr-43	21-Jun-46	Class A Release
13809690		Contreras	Fidel Intoria	21-Aug-00	Boufarick	N Africa	29-Apr-43		Docs to N Africa Records 1944
13809691		Corominas	Torro Benito	05-Jan-05	Boufarick	N Africa	29-Apr-43	25-Sep-46	Class A Release
13809692		Cortrs	Rafael Parra	21-Dec-13	Boufarick	N Africa	29-Apr-43	02-Jan-47	Class A Release
13809693		Cubillo	Eugenio Marcos	06-Sep-93	Boufarick	N Africa	29-Apr-43	21-Jun-46	Class A Release
13809694		Culianes	Antoino Duenas	12-Feb-17	Boufarick	N Africa	29-Apr-43	21-Jun-46	DESERTER 16 Oct 43, Class A Release
13809695		Curos	Jose Colobrans	10-Sep-04	Boufarick	N Africa	29-Apr-43		DESERTER 2 Oct 43, Docs to N Africa Records 1944
13809696		Cussi	Marcelnio Villanueva	20-Aug-00	Boufarick	N Africa	29-Apr-43		Docs to N Africa Records 2040
13809697		de La Calle	Epifanio Martin	07-Apr-13	Boufarick	N Africa	29-Apr-43	18-Dec-46	Class A Release
13809698		de La Cruz	Gonzals Colla	25-Jan-17	Boufarick	N Africa	29-Apr-43	10-May-43	DIED 10 May 43
13809699		Dominguez	Tome Lorenzo	18-Jan-06	Boufarick	N Africa	29-Apr-43		DESERTER 3 Mar 44
13809700		de Montes	Roberto Castillo	09-Jul-17	Boufarick	N Africa	29-Apr-43		DESERTER 7 Sep 43
13809701		Estlela	Vincente Mut	20-Sep-18	Boufarick	N Africa	29-Apr-43		Docs to N Africa Records 1944
13809702		Esteve	Salvador Gomez	05-Jun-14	Boufarick	N Africa	29-Apr-43		Docs to N Africa Records 1944
13809703		Fernandez	Adolfo Noval	24-Jun-00	Boufarick	N Africa	29-Apr-43	21-Jun-46	Class A Release
13809704		Fernandez	Manuel Perez	26-Aug-01	Boufarick	N Africa	29-Apr-43	03-Aug-46	Class A Release
13809705		Pareja	Francisco Navgio	31-Jan-20	Boufarick	N Africa	29-Apr-43	23-Dec-46	(Alias Christobel Bar PAREJA), Class A Release
13809706		Ferrer	Casado	12-Dec-12	Boufarick	N Africa	29-Apr-43	07-Oct-46	Class A Release
13809707		Ferrer	Juan Salas	12-Feb-13	Boufarick	N Africa	29-Apr-43		DESERTER 9 Mar 44

APPENDIX VII 323

Number	Rank	Name	Initials	DOB	Enlisted	Unit	Date Tos	Discharged	Remarks
13809708		Fernandez	Edyardo Lopez	10-Oct-14	Boufarick	N Africa	29-Apr-43		DESERTER 2 Mar 44
13809709		Figueras	Fulgencio Aig	27-Aug-18	Boufarick	N Africa	29-Apr-43	03-Jan-47	Class A Release
13809710		Figuerola	Ramon Pasalaique	18-Nov-11	Boufarick	N Africa	29-Apr-43	28-Sep-46	Class A Release
13809711		Fine Boy	Samuel	16-Sep-18	Boufarick	N Africa	29-Apr-43	03-Jan-47	Class A Release
13809712		Galiano	Jose Roman	29-Apr-92	Boufarick	N Africa	29-Apr-43		Docs to N Africa Records 1944
13809713		Gamon	Domingo Biel	08-Dec-12	Boufarick	N Africa	29-Apr-43	07-Oct-46	Class A Release
13809714		Garcia	Andres Jose	21-Mar-15	Boufarick	N Africa	29-Apr-43	27-Oct-46	Class A Release
13809715		Garcia	Angel Bazo	17-Sep-98	Boufarick	N Africa	29-Apr-43	21-Jun-46	Class A Release
13809716		Garcia	Antonio Conesa	30-Nov-16	Boufarick	N Africa	29-Apr-43		Docs to N Africa Records 1944
13809717		Garcia	Fausto Miguel	21-Jul-87	Boufarick	N Africa	29-Apr-43		Docs to N Africa Records 1944
13809718		Garcia	Florencio de la Pena	14-Oct-14	Boufarick	N Africa	29-Apr-43	27-Oct-46	Class A Release
13809719		Garcia	Jose Zamora	14-Nov-04	Boufarick	N Africa	29-Apr-43		Docs to N Africa Records 1944
13809720		Garcia	Juan Alarcon	12-Aug-06	Boufarick	N Africa	29-Apr-43	09-Oct-46	Class A Release
13809721		Garcia	Juan Morais	30-Jul-16	Boufarick	N Africa	29-Apr-43	13-Apr-47	Class A Release
13809722		Gimenez	Enrique Genienez	15-Jan-04	Boufarick	N Africa	29-Apr-43	01-Jul-46	Class A Release
13809723		Gimeno	Aalcador Monzo	03-Feb-02	Boufarick	N Africa	29-Apr-43		DESERTER 9 Mar 44
13809724		Girona	Miguel Girona	19-Feb-04	Boufarick	N Africa	29-Apr-43	01-Jul-46	Class A Release
13809725		Gomez	Celedonio Neto	12-Jan-17	Boufarick	N Africa	29-Apr-43		DESERTER 24 Jul 43
13809726		Gomez	Juan Gonzalez	05-Nov-12	Boufarick	N Africa	29-Apr-43	30-Nov-46	DESERTER 29 Aug 43–20 Dec 43, Class A Release
13809727		Gonzalez	Joaquin Martos	19-Jan-14	Boufarick	N Africa	29-Apr-43	05-Nov-46	Class A Release
13809728		Rodriguez	Martinez Juan	22-Jun-11	Boufarick	N Africa	29-Apr-43	28-Sep-46	(Alias GONZALEZ), Class A Release
13809729		Gurucchari	Felix Mendevil	09-Feb-99	Boufarick	N Africa	29-Apr-43	21-Jun-46	Class A Release
13809730		Gutierrez	Asenjo Alfonso	12-Feb-93	Boufarick	N Africa	29-Apr-43		Docs to N Africa Records 1944

Number	Rank	Name	Initials	DOB	Enlisted	Unit	Date Tos	Discharged	Remarks
13809731		Gutieraez	Tomas Ramiro	19-Jan-08	Boufarick	N Africa	29-Apr-43	16-Aug-46	Class A Release
13809732		Hermida	Alvarez Jose	08-Mar-13	Boufarick	N Africa	29-Apr-43	28-Dec-46	Class A Release
13809733		Hernandez	Manuel Fernandez	06-Jun-13	Boufarick	N Africa	29-Apr-43	17-Oct-46	Class A Release
13809734		Hidalgo	Augusto de Salas	26-Oct-06	Boufarick	N Africa	29-Apr-43		Docs to N Africa Records 1944
13809735		Iniguez	Alberto Faurdinie?	29-Sep-02	Boufarick	N Africa	29-Apr-43	21-Jun-46	Class A Release
13809736		Jorda	Enrique Rolland	20-Jan-00	Boufarick	N Africa	29-Apr-43		DESERTERR date NK
13809737		Labanda	Jose Fernandez	02-Feb-02	Boufarick	N Africa	29-Apr-43		Docs to N Africa Records 2034
13809738		Lasuen	Gunersindo	13-Jan-01	Boufarick	N Africa	29-Apr-43	15-Oct-43	DIED 15 Oct 43
13809739		Longas	Emilio Costo	21-Feb-98	Boufarick	N Africa	29-Apr-43		Docs to N Africa Records 1944
13809740		Lopez	Emilio Fernandez	07-Oct-13	Boufarick	N Africa	29-Apr-43	28-Dec-46	Class A Release
13809741		Lopez	Francisco Garcia	12-Aug-09	Boufarick	N Africa	29-Apr-43	31-Aug-46	Class A Release
13809742		Lopez	Gumersindo Lopez	21-Jul-11	Boufarick	N Africa	29-Apr-43		Docs to N Africa Records 1944
13809743		Lopez	Jesus Bartolo	02-Feb-21	Boufarick	N Africa	29-Apr-43	01-May-47	Class A Release
13809744		Lopez	Roque Ruiz	08-Apr-15	Boufarick	N Africa	29-Apr-43	27-Oct-46	Class A Release
13809745		Lopez	Silverio Aviles	02-Mar-11	Boufarick	N Africa	29-Apr-43		Docs to N Africa Records 1944
13809746		Luzon	Jose Morales	02-Jul-11	Boufarick	N Africa	29-Apr-43		DESERTER 26 May 43
13809747		Magan	Marcelino Sierra	16-Apr-06	Boufarick	N Africa	29-Apr-43	09-Oct-46	Class A Release
13809748		Marti	Milet Jose	12-Nov-99	Boufarick	N Africa	29-Apr-43	21-Jun-46	Class A Release
13809749		Martin	Fabian Martin	13-Jul-10	Boufarick	N Africa	29-Apr-43	11-Sep-46	Class A Release
13809750		Martinez	Francisco Calvo	04-Jan-97	Boufarick	N Africa	29-Apr-43	21-Jun-46	Class A Release
13809751		Mascot	Antonio Trilla	03-Dec-95	Boufarick	N Africa	29-Apr-43	09-Oct-46	Class A Release
13809752		Miron	Mariano Belmonte	21-Apr-09	Boufarick	N Africa	29-Apr-43	31-Aug-46	Class A Release
13809753	Pte	Molina	Hilario Moreno	26-Apr-17	Boufarick	N Africa	29-Apr-43	05-Feb-44	361 Coy Para XVI

APPENDIX VII 325

Number	Rank	Name	Initials	DOB	Enlisted	Unit	Date Tos	Discharged	Remarks
13809754		Montanana	Ismael Orts	06-Sep-17	Boufarick	N Africa	29-Apr-43	30-Nov-46	Class A Release
13809755		Munesa	Julien Monrel	27-Jul-13	Boufarick	N Africa	29-Apr-43	16-Oct-46	Class A Release
13809756		Navarro	Francisco Garcia	10-Nov-21	Boufarick	N Africa	29-Apr-43	01-May-47	Class A Release
13809757		Obis	Antonio Canpo	13-Mar-21	Boufarick	N Africa	29-Apr-43	01-May-47	Class A Release
13809758		Olivares	Alberto Ispizua	14-Sep-88	Boufarick	N Africa	29-Apr-43		Docs to N Africa Records 1944
13809759		Oltra	Miguel Valor	01-Jan-04	Boufarick	N Africa	29-Apr-43	01-Jul-46	Class A Release
13809760		Pairo	Jose Giralt?	02-Aug-09	Boufarick	N Africa	29-Apr-43	31-Aug-41	Class A Release
13809761		Pairo	Miguel Giralt	13-Jan-96	Boufarick	N Africa	29-Apr-43	21-Jun-46	Class A Release
13809762		Parraga	Antonio Delsas	10-May-08	Boufarick	N Africa	29-Apr-43	16-Aug-46	Class A Release
13809763		Pastor	Faustuis Vicario	18-Feb-14	Boufarick	N Africa	29-Apr-43	27-Oct-46	Class A Release
13809764		Pazos	Mariano Salamanca	28-May-09	Boufarick	N Africa	29-Apr-43	31-Aug-46	Class A Release
13809765		Pensado	Felix Bravo	24-Sep-07	Boufarick	N Africa	29-Apr-43		Docs to N Africa Records 1944
13809766		Pitarch	Joaquin Segarro	22-Jul-01	Boufarick	N Africa	29-Apr-43		Docs to N Africa Records 1944
13809767		Ponce	Francisco Ibanez	25-Feb-07	Boufarick	N Africa	29-Apr-43	03-Aug-46	Class A Release
13809768		Porcar	Joaquin Aparicio	24-Dec-09	Boufarick	N Africa	29-Apr-43	31-Aug-46	Class A Release
13809769		Prado	Jose Luis Perez	05-Jan-19	Boufarick	N Africa	29-Apr-43	01-May-47	Class A Release
13809770		Puddu	Hercules Mameli	26-Jul-10	Boufarick	N Africa	29-Apr-43		Docs to N Africa Records 1944
13809771		Puig	Vicente Domenech	04-Jun-11	Boufarick	N Africa	29-Apr-43		Docs to N Africa Records 1944
13809772		Raina	Jose Lucas	24-Jun-94	Boufarick	N Africa	29-Apr-43	21-Jun-46	Class A Release
13809773		Ramos	Sebastian Blanco	21-Jul-08	Boufarick	N Africa	29-Apr-43	25-Aug-46	Class A Release
13809774		Reventlow	Rudolfo	01-Sep-97	Boufarick	N Africa	29-Apr-43		Docs to N Africa Records 1944

326 CHURCHILL'S SPANIARDS

Number	Rank	Name	Initials	DOB	Enlisted	Unit	Date Tos	Discharged	Remarks
13809775		Ribera	Salvador Masmicha	09-Sep-17	Boufarick	N Africa	29-Apr-43	30-Nov-46	Class A Release
13809776		Roa	Ventura Augustine	03-Apr-15	Boufarick	N Africa	29-Apr-43	27-Oct-46	Class A Release
13809777		Rodriguez	Alberto Martinez	25-Aug-20	Boufarick	N Africa	29-Apr-43		DESERTER 27 Aug 43, Docs to N Africa Records 1944
13809778		Rodriguez	Pablo Peinado	15-Jan-97	Boufarick	N Africa	29-Apr-43	21-Jun-46	Class A Release
13809779		Rodriguez	Silvino Sanchez	10-Aug-10	Boufarick	N Africa	29-Apr-43	11-Sep-46	Class A Release
13809780		Roldan	Antonio Ruiz	28-Mar-93	Boufarick	N Africa	29-Apr-43	07-Dec-45	Class A Release
13809781	Pte	Roldan	Antonio Zamon	30-Jan-05	Boufarick	N Africa	29-Apr-43	05-Sep-44	Para XVI (Good)
13809782		Romero	Valentine Gil	20-Dec-07	Boufarick	N Africa	29-Apr-43		DESERTER 23 Dec 43, Docs to N Africa Records 1944
13809783		Ruie	Juan Martin	27-Nov-11	Boufarick	N Africa	29-Apr-43	28-Sep-46	Class A Release
13809784		Ruiz	Miguel Luques	12-Aug-95	Boufarick	N Africa	29-Apr-43	07-Dec-45	Class A Release
13809785		Ruiz	Serafin Donaire	14-May-11	Boufarick	N Africa	29-Apr-43	28-Sep-46	Class A Release
13809786		Sanchez	Antonio Hermandez	20-Jan-19	Boufarick	N Africa	29-Apr-43	03-Jan-47	Class A Release
13809787		Sanchez	Francisco De Hars	05-Jul-05	Boufarick	N Africa	29-Apr-43		Docs to N Africa Records 1944
13809788		Sanchez	Juan Martinez	10-Oct-13	Boufarick	N Africa	29-Apr-43		DESERTER 17 Jul 45, Docs to N Africa Records 1944
13809789	Pte	Sanchez	Torcuato Clemente	04-May-04	Boufarick	N Africa	29-Apr-43	30-Jan-47	Para XVI (Exemplary)
13809790		Sancho	Jose Royo	18-Sep-04	Boufarick	N Africa	29-Apr-43	01-Jul-46	Class A Release
13809791		Sanpedro	Jamie Frenendez	31-Mar-12	Boufarick	N Africa	29-Apr-43		DESERTER 31 Oct 43, Docs to N Africa Records 1944
13809792		Hernandez	Salvador Simenez	10-Jul-18	Boufarick	N Africa	29-Apr-43	13-Apr-47	Class A Release
13809793		Soler	Francisco Alexandre	28-Oct-16	Boufarick	N Africa	29-Apr-43		Docs to N Africa Records 1944
13809794		Solder	Jose Rodriguez	12-Apr-23	Boufarick	N Africa	29-Apr-43		Docs to N Africa Records 1944

APPENDIX VII 327

Number	Rank	Name	Initials	DOB	Enlisted	Unit	Date Tos	Discharged	Remarks
13809795		Tamarit	Edwardo Rubio	04-Apr-18	Boufarick	N Africa	29-Apr-43	03-Jan-47	Class A Release
13809796		Terron	Santiago Rueda	17-Sep-11	Boufarick	N Africa	29-Apr-43		Docs to N Africa Records 1944
13809797		Tobenas	Ramon Cirac	31-Aug-99	Boufarick	N Africa	29-Apr-43	21-Jun-46	Class A Release
13809798		Torralba	Angel Belfrau	07-Jul-14	Boufarick	N Africa	29-Apr-43		Docs to N Africa Records 1944
13809799		Torralba	Antonio Belfrau	22-Jul-17	Boufarick	N Africa	29-Apr-43	02-Jan-47	Class A Release
13809800		Torres	Dionisio Najas	06-Jun-04	Boufarick	N Africa	29-Apr-43		Docs to N Africa Records 1944
13809801		Tudela	Alfonso Ballester	19-Jun-08	Boufarick	N Africa	29-Apr-43	16-Aug-46	Class A Release
13809802		Tudo	Santiago Suner	24-Mar-00	Boufarick	N Africa	29-Apr-43		Docs to N Africa Records 1944
13809803		Urgeles	Antonio Castejon	16-Mar-12	Boufarick	N Africa	29-Apr-43	07-Oct-46	Class A Release
13809804		Urrios	Mariano Francisco	12-Oct-15	Boufarick	N Africa	29-Apr-43	27-Oct-46	DESERTER – rejoined 15 Aug 46, Class A Release
13809805		Vargas	Antonio Tribas	12-Oct-17	Boufarick	N Africa	29-Apr-43	30-Nov-46	Class A Release
13809806		Ventura	Antonio Gines	09-Feb-11	Boufarick	N Africa	29-Apr-43	15-Mar-47	Class A Release
13809807		Vicente	Domingo Gonzalez	05-Mar-98	Boufarick	N Africa	29-Apr-43		DESERTER 31 Oct 43, Docs to N Africa Records 1944
13809808		Vidal	Angel Olcina	02-Dec-02	Boufarick	N Africa	29-Apr-43	21-Jun-46	Class A Release
13809809		Vidal	Candido Calvet	02-Feb-14	Boufarick	N Africa	29-Apr-43	26-Oct-46	Class A Release
13809810		Zapata	Juan Cisneroo	08-Mar-06	Boufarick	N Africa	29-Apr-43	01-Oct-46	Class A Release
13809811		Zapater	Jose Jusen	15-Nov-20	Boufarick	N Africa	29-Apr-43	22-Apr-47	Class A Release
13809812		Melia	Libirtario	27-Sep-23	Boufarick	N Africa	29-Apr-43	31-May-47	Class A Release
13809813		Parraz	Jean Parraz	25-Mar-23	Boufarick	N Africa	29-Apr-43	31-May-47	Class A Release
13809814	Centurion	Centurion	Antonio Centurion	20-Jun-03	Boufarick	N Africa	06-May-43	16-Sep-46	Class A Release
13809815	Centurion	Centurion	Miguel Alamino	09-Oct-14	Boufarick	N Africa	06-May-43	21-Oct-46	Class A Release
13809816		Fluxa	Juan Mariano Bertamen	19-Jan-11	Boufarick	N Africa	06-May-43		Docs to N Africa Records 1944

Number	Rank	Name	Initials	DOB	Enlisted	Unit	Date Tos	Discharged	Remarks
13809817		Lopez	Miguel Barril	11-Jul-01	Boufarick	N Africa	06-May-43	21-Jun-46	Class A Release
13809818		Mata	Josi Rabot	16-Aug-17	Boufarick	N Africa	06-May-43		Docs to N Africa Records 1944
13809819		Ramos	Tomas Miralles	27-Oct-11	Boufarick	N Africa	06-May-43		Docs to N Africa Records 1944
13809820		Gonzalez	Emilio Roca	02-Feb-13	Boufarick	N Africa	10-May-43		Docs to N Africa Records 1944
13809821		Coronaido	Miguel	11-Jun-20	Algiers	N Africa	17-May-43		Docs to N Africa Records 1944
13809822		Losa	Antonio Mora	12-Mar-01	Algiers	N Africa	17-May-43		Alias Jose MARTINEZ, Docs to N Africa Records 1944
13809823		Ruiz	Hoyos Abilio	20-Nov-23	Algiers	N Africa	16-May-43	31-Jan-47	Alias Julio ARDINES, Class A Release
13809824		Medina	Jose Nogiera	05-May-17	Algiers	N Africa	16-May-43	03-Jan-47	Alias Luiz CAZORRO, Class A Release
13809825		Gomez	Bernardo Heredia	23-Jul-12	Boufarick	N Africa	29-Apr-43	07-Oct-46	Class A Release
13809826		Mena	Alfredo Sanchez	10-Aug-03	Boufarick	N Africa	29-Apr-43	21-Jun-46	Class A Release
13809827		Rodriguez	Blas Martinez	06-Dec-09	Boufarick	N Africa	29-Apr-43	31-Aug-46	Class A Release
13809828		Serrano	Mariano Herranz	05-Mar-04	Boufarick	N Africa	29-Apr-43	01-Jul-46	Class A Release
13809842		Susso	Vicente Angel	27-Jul-22	Hussein Dey	N Africa	16-May-43		DESERTER 19 Oct 43
13809843		Martinez	Mariano Lozano	04-Jan-09	Hussein Dey	N Africa	16-May-43	06-Sep-46	Class A Release
13809844		Medina	Juan Lepez	15-Apr-05	Hussein Dey	N Africa	16-May-43	16-Jul-46	Class A Release
13809845		Sanchez	Guillermo Danerro	08-May-01	Hussein Dey	N Africa	16-May-43	21-Jun-46	Class A Release
13809858		Spier	Adolfo Noval	29-May-14	Hussein Dey	N Africa	24-May-43		Docs to N Africa Records 1944
13809859	Pte	Nolla	Francisco Teigell	16-May-97	Hussein Dey	N Africa	24-May-43	05-Feb-44	Para XVI
13809860		Ruiz	Bartholome	27-Jan-11	Hussein Dey	N Africa	28-May-43	07-Oct-46	Class A Release
13809861		Gomez	Antonio Vilaverdi	22-Apr-18	Hussein Dey	N Africa	30-May-43	02-Jan-47	Class A Release
13809862		Alino	Juan Lopez	29-May-43	Algiers	N Africa	29-May-43		Docs to N Africa Records 1944
13809863		Perez	Juan Monteaguolo	06-Jan-18	Algiers	N Africa	29-May-43	02-Jan-47	Alias Santago Frenandez CAMBRIO, Class A release

APPENDIX VII 329

Number	Rank	Name	Initials	DOB	Enlisted	Unit	Date Tos	Discharged	Remarks
13809864		La Fuerte	Domingo Lopez	30-Dec-06	Algiers	N Africa	29-May-43		DESERTER 12 Oct 43–25 Nov 43, Docs to N Africa Records 1944
13809865		de la Torre	Rafael	15-Mar-24	Hussein Dey	N Africa	25-May-43	08-Jul-47	Class A Release
13809866		Baiget Farre	Joan	14-May-96	Maison Carrel	N Africa	24-May-43		Repatriated 1945
13809935		Castillon	Mariano Pascaial	22-Apr-18	Hussein Dey	N Africa	08-Jun-43	02-Jan-47	361 Coy, Class A Release
13809936		Garcia	Miguel Fernandez	06-Jun-19	Hussein Dey	N Africa	08-Jun-43	22-Apr-47	361 Coy, Class A Release
13809937		Rillo	Miguel Irazo	08-Feb-18	Hussein Dey	N Africa	08-Jun-43		361 Coy, DESERTER 14 Nov 43
13809938		Gilabert	Saaquin Chiguillo	16-Jun-22	Hussein Dey	N Africa	08-Jun-43	15-Mar-47	361 Coy, Class A Release
13809939		Lima	Salvador Garcia	15-May-10	Hussein Dey	N Africa	08-Jun-43	06-Oct-46	361 Coy, Class A Release
13809940		Gonzalez	Florial Vargas	15-May-22	Hussein Dey	N Africa	13-Jun-43	23-Apr-47	361 Coy, Class A Release
13809941		Martins Serodio	Jose	15-Nov-02	Hussein Dey	N Africa	13-Jun-43	23-Jun-46	361 Coy, Class A Release
13809942		Rosique	Francisco Resalt	08-Mar-11	Hussein Dey	N Africa	13-Jun-43	08-Oct-46	Class A Release
13809950		Lillo	Ramon Garcia	21-Dec-20	Maison Carrel	N Africa	21-Jun-43	21-Jan-47	Class A Release
13809951		Lopez	Nemecio Revingis	13-Oct-19	In the field	N Africa	22-Jun-43	22-Apr-47	361 Coy, Class A Release
13809952		Palomares	Teodora Tonias	06-Dec-18	In the field	N Africa	22-Jun-43	22-Apr-47	361 Coy, Class A Release
13809953		Pavon	Rafael Holdago	02-Mar-18	In the field	N Africa	23-Jun-43		361 Coy, DESERTER 21 Dec 43
13809954		Navarro	Elias Villalonga	07-Aug-07	In the field	N Africa	23-Jun-43		361 Coy, transferred to RASC 27 Feb 44
13809955		Rosique	Jose Solano	08-Dec-16	In the field	N Africa	23-Jun-43	30-Nov-06	361 Coy, Class A Release
13809956		Murcia	Alfonso Lopez	01-Dec-09	In the field	N Africa	23-Jun-43	11-Sep-46	361 Coy, Class A Release
13809957		Gimenez	Mariano Morell	04-May-13	In the field	N Africa	23-Jun-43		361 Coy, Docs to N Africa Records 1944
13809958		Sanchez	Josie	10-Jan-09	In the field	N Africa	23-Jun-43		361 Coy, Docs to N Africa Records 1944

330 CHURCHILL'S SPANIARDS

Number	Rank	Name	Initials	DOB	Enlisted	Unit	Date Tos	Discharged	Remarks
13809959		Hernandel	Pedro Barcelona	26-Feb-17	In the field	N Africa	23-Jun-43	03-Jan-47	361 Coy, Class A Release
13809960		Coronello	Vincent?	06-Jun-07	Maison Carrel	N Africa	23-Jun-43		362 Coy, Docs to N Africa Records 1944
13809961	Pte	Salen	Julio Bagnes	16-May-18	Hussein Dey	N Africa	25-Jun-43	01-Nov-43	337 Coy, Para XVI
13809962		Jines Basitida	Vera	09-Nov-02	In the field	N Africa	28-Jun-43	21-Jun-46	Alias Jose Veslidas MARIN, Class A Release
13809963		Jungstein	Abram	28-Dec-06	Maison Carrel	N Africa	27-Jun-43	04-Aug-46	Class A Release
13809964		Serduk	Alphons	16-Oct-99	Maison Carrel	N Africa	28-Jun-43	09-Aug-46	Class A Release
13809965		Roberts	Oscar Ballester?	20-Jun-19	In the field	N Africa	25-Jun-43		Alias Jose Ballesti VALERO, Docs to N Africa Records 1944
13809966		Lastra	Jose Suraz	17-Dec-14	Hussein Dey	N Africa	15-Jun-43	06-Dec-46	Class A Release
13809978		Torralba	Diego Ena	25-Mar-18	In the field	N Africa	07-Jul-43	24-Mar-44	DIED OF WOUNDS 24 Mar 44
13809979		Martinez	Pedro Ribes	11-Nov-22	In the field	N Africa	08-Jul-43		Docs to CMF Records 1946
13809980		Garcia	Nicolas Sanchez	30-Aug-13	In the field	N Africa	11-Jul-43	10-Feb-47	Alias MarfassCamatens ARTES, Class A Release
13809981		Gil	Santaella Antoino	03-Jan-11	In the field	N Africa	11-Jul-43	16-Oct-46	Alias Mauel Rios LOZANO (Declared 18 Jul 43), Class A release
13809982		Lopez	Amadeo Retiro	09-Jun-14	Hussein Dey	N Africa	12-Jul-43		Docs to N Africa Records 1944
13809983		Klepetar	Hans	16-Jun-19	Hussein Dey	N Africa	13-Jul-19	05-Apr-47	Class A Release
13809984		Stummer	Maximilian	30-Mar-16	Maison Carrel	N Africa	14-Jul-43		Docs to N Africa Records 1944
13809985		Tello	Perez Sebastian	08-May-14	In the field	N Africa	14-Jul-43	28-Nov-46	Alias Asensio Sebastian PEREZ, Class A Release
13809986		Garcia	Francis Juan	07-Nov-16	In the field	N Africa	14-Jul-43	18-Feb-47	Alias Juan Pereo GARCIA, Class A Release
13809987		Chueca	Alejandrmo Pasculena	28-Nov-17	In the field	N Africa	14-Jul-43	02-Jan-47	Alias Jose Aree GUTIERREZ, Class A Release
13809988	Pte	Brenner	Salomon	16-Jul-13	Hussein Dey	N Africa	15-Jul-43	08-Jan-44	362 Coy, Para XVIIIA
13809989		Gasco	Bicente Carbonell	01-Feb-09	Hussein Dey	N Africa	15-Jul-43	28-Sep-46	Class A Release
13809990		Gonzalez	Luis Guerrera	15-Apr-11	Hussein Dey	N Africa	15-Jul-32	16-Oct-46	Class A Release
13809991		Ochoa	Victorio Rico	06-Jul-16	Hussein Dey	N Africa	15-Jul-32		Docs to N Africa Records 1944

APPENDIX VII 331

Number	Rank	Name	Initials	DOB	Enlisted	Unit	Date Tos	Discharged	Remarks
13809992		Benavente	Manuel Sedaus	28-Jun-15	Hussein Dey	N Africa	15-Jul-32	30-Nov-46	Alias Manuel Cedano SANCHEZ, Class A Release
13809993		Puig	Manuel Martel	15-May-15	Hussein Dey	N Africa	15-Jul-32	26-Oct-46	Class A Release
13809994	Pte	Schiffer	Joseph	22-Oct-10	Maison Carrel	N Africa	16-Jul-43	08-Jan-44	Para XVIIIA
13809995		Perez	Alezo Perez	17-Feb-12	In the field	N Africa	19-Jul-43	23-Dec-46	Class A Release
13809996		Diaz	Aquilino Nolledo	04-Sep-08	In the field	N Africa	19-Jul-43	11-Sep-46	Class A Release

British North Africa Spanish Enlistements – Short Details Only Due to Loss of Records

	Number	Name	Initials	Notes	
BNA	13301075	Zara	V	Box 43	
BNA	13301076	Aquilina	E	Box 33	
BNA	13301078	Balzan	S	Box 33	
BNA	13301086	Calleja	J	Box 34	
BNA	13301290	Munoz	V C	Cyprus Boxes 66,67	
BNA	13301331	Vella	A	Box 43	
BNA	13301343	Iglecias	O	Box 37	
BNA	13301381	Pariente	E	Box 40	
BNA	13301382	Azan	R	Box 33	
BNA	13301506	Enriguez	V	Box 35	
BNA	13301630	Ortiz	F	Box 40	
BNA	13301776	Vega	M V	Box 43	
BNA	13301816	Zamon	M L	Box 43	
BNA	13301916	Rodriguez	A L	Box 41	
BNA	13301991	Inguanez	A N	Box 37	
BNA	13302216	Rodriguez-Mova	R	Cyprus Boxes 66,67	
BNA	13302230	Martinez-Perez	F	Cyprus Boxes 66,67	
BNA	13302234	Garcia	A	Box 36	
BNA	13302290	Sanchez Montes	R	Box 42	
BNA	13302307	Aguilar	A	Cyprus Boxes 66,67	
BNA	13302313	Canto	Manuel	Cyprus Boxes 66,67	406 Coy
BNA	13302314	Carrega	Antonio	Box 34	406 Coy
BNA	13302315	Casal	F	Box 34	
BNA	13302316	Centenera	Mariano	Box 34	406 Coy
BNA	13302317	Cordero	Raphel	Box 35	406 Coy
BNA	13302324	Ferrer	P	Cyprus Boxes 66,67	
BNA	13302329	Gomez Blanco	Juan	Box 37	406 Coy
BNA	13302331	Hernandez	Jose	Box 37	406 Coy
BNA	13302341	Martinez-Gal	Emilio	Cyprus Boxes 66,67	406 Coy
BNA	13302344	Mora Domingo	Jose Antonio	Box 39	406 Coy
BNA	13302345	Gimeno Rebelles	B	Box 37	
BNA	13302346	Navarro	Jean	Box 40	406 Coy
BNA	13302351	Quinta Nieves	Antoine	Box 41	406 Coy
BNA	13302352	Serrano	Jose	Box 42	406 Coy
BNA	13302357	Vasquez Garcia	Cristobel	Box 43	406 Coy
BNA	13302363	Serra	F V	Cyprus Boxes 66,67	
BNA	13302378	Aguilar-Garcia	Juan	Cyprus Boxes 66,67	406 Coy
BNA	13302380	Martinez	Jose	Box 38	406 Coy
BNA	13302386	Aranguena-Delapaz	Alfonso Adolfo	Cyprus Boxes 66,67	406 Coy
BNA	13302387	Arriado-y-Gimenez	Alfonso	Box 33	406 Coy
BNA	13302388	Barrachina-Montemayor	Carlos	Box 33	406 Coy
BNA	13302392	Carbillo-y-Sanchez	J	Cyprus Boxes 66,67	
BNA	13302393	Capilla	Aguilla Rafael	Box 34	406 Coy
BNA	13302399	Fernandez	Antoino	Box 36	406 Coy

APPENDIX VII 333

	Number	Name	Initials	Notes	
BNA	13302400	Fuentes	Alexandro	Cyprus Boxes 66,67	406 Coy
BNA	13302407	Martinez de Jesus	Carlos	Box 38	406 Coy
BNA	13302408	Martinez-Perez	Antonio	Cyprus Boxes 66,67	406 Coy
BNA	13302411	Osuna-Rodrigues	Ricardo	Box 40	406 Coy
BNA	13302412	Pascual Falan	C	Box 40	
BNA	13302413	Perez-Garcia	Luis	Box 40	406 Coy
BNA	13302415	Rebollo-y-Carretero	Jesus	Box 41	406 Coy
BNA	13302416	Reynes	Pedro	Cyprus Boxes 66,67	406 Coy
BNA	13302417	Rodriguez-Garcia	Michel	Box 41	406 Coy
BNA	13302418	Romero Perez	Diego	Box 41	406 Coy
BNA	13302424	Toro	Salvador	Cyprus Boxes 66,67	406 Coy
BNA	13302425	Torres Gimenez	Joseph	Box 43	406 Coy
BNA	13302456	Cavacas	Edwardo Jose	Box 34	406 Coy
BNA	13302458	Dos Santos	Joaquin Jose	Box 35	406 Coy
BNA	13302461	Gallardo-Visosa	I?	Cyprus Boxes 66,67	
BNA	13302473	Pages-Puig	Jose	Box 40	406 Coy
BNA	13302474	Perez	Mayer	Box 40	406 Coy
BNA	13302477	Reina-Loque	Rafael	Cyprus Boxes 66,67	406 Coy
BNA	13302478	Ruiz-Jimenez	Juan	Box 42	406 Coy
BNA	13302480	Soler Lopez	Juan	Box 42	406 Coy
BNA	13302481	Solino-Moya	M	Cyprus Boxes 66,67	
BNA	13302485	Viegas	Manuel Junior	Box 43	406 Coy
BNA	13302489	Ceresuela	E	Box 34	
BNA	13302498	Cereto-y-Rosa	Joso	Box 34	406 Coy
BNA	13302502	Garcia-y-Fortuoso	M	Cyprus Boxes 66,67	
BNA	13302503	Garcia-Sanchez	Jose	Box 36	406 Coy
BNA	13302505	Gonzales Fuentes	J	Box 37	
BNA	13302509	Llanos-Garcia	Manuol	Box 38	406 Coy
BNA	13302511	Navarro	C	Cyprus Boxes 66,67	406 Coy
BNA	13302516	Vidal	E	Box 43	
BNA	13302518	Menor	V	Box 39	
BNA	13302523	Santa-Cruz	F O	Box 42	
BNA	13302524	Macia-Alcaraz	R	Box 38	
BNA	13302526	Monje	M	Box 39	
BNA	13302527	Tejero	R	Box 43	
BNA	13302528	Galiano	J	Cyprus Boxes 66,67	
BNA	13302529	Montero	R	Box 39	
BNA	13302530	Turrillo	I	Cyprus Boxes 66,67	
BNA	13302536	Arteagabeitia-Goitia	C	Box 33	
BNA	13302546	Cases-Martinez	A	Box 34	
BNA	13302553	Garcia-Gonzales	F	Box 36	
BNA	13302566	Penyer	M	Box 40	
BNA	13302567	Perez	F	Cyprus Boxes 66,67	
BNA	13302569	Pulga	R J	Box 41	
BNA	13302570	Rique	A	Cyprus Boxes 66,67	
BNA	13302571	Roman-Gomez	R D	Cyprus Boxes 66,67	

	Number	Name	Initials	Notes
BNA	13302573	Vila-Romaguera	E	Box 43
BNA	13302574	Benitez-y-Carrasco	J	Box 33
BNA	13302575	Caballero	J	Cyprus Boxes 66,67
BNA	13302576	Carratala-Hernandez	J	Box 34
BNA	13302577	Elarbi	R	Cyprus Boxes 66,67
BNA	13302578	Ervite-Aranda	J	Cyprus Boxes 66,67
BNA	13302578	Perez	S	Box 40
BNA	13302579	Gomez-y-Garcia	J	Box 37
BNA	13302582	Maria	J	Box 38
BNA	13302584	San Martin-Hernandez	P	Box 42
BNA	13302585	Torrente-Larrosa	F	Box 43
BNA	13302588	Fernandez	A	Box 36
BNA	13302592	Gonzales	A	Cyprus Boxes 66,67
BNA	13302593	Reus	R	Cyprus Boxes 66,67
BNA	13302594	Sitgis-Peres	F	Cyprus Boxes 66,67
BNA	13302595	Alcocel-Diaz	J	Box 33
BNA	13302596	Devidas	I	Box 35
BNA	13302597	Gil-Lopez	C	Box 37
BNA	13302605	Ruiz-y-Cobo	J	Cyprus Boxes 66,67
BNA	13302607	Vogel	W	Box 43
BNA	13302608	Cuadros	A	Box 35
BNA	13302609	Martinez	M	Box 38
BNA	13302610	Mateus	F	Box 39
BNA	13302611	Rojo	J	Box 41
BNA	13302612	Soiza	L	Box 42
BNA	13302613	Somodevilla	S	Box 42
BNA	13302616	Anconina-Murciano	M	Box 33
BNA	13302617	Azan	S	Box 33
BNA	13302618	Bastos-Gimenez	J	Box 33
BNA	13302619	Bernardo	F	Box 33
BNA	13302623	Delgado	J	Cyprus Boxes 66,67
BNA	13302624	Diaz	A	Box 35
BNA	13302626	Fernandiz-Ibanez	J M	Box 36
BNA	13302629	Lopez-Parramon	R	Box 38
BNA	13302630	Metsis	R	Cyprus Boxes 66,67
BNA	13302631	Ohayon	M	Box 40
BNA	13302632	Padilla	F	Box 40
BNA	13302639	Valero-Espina	L	Cyprus Boxes 66,67
BNA	13302641	Villanueva-y-Balbao	J M	Box 43
BNA	13302643	Asayag Gabbay	A	Box 33
BNA	13302644	Gozal-Bencheton	R	Box 37
BNA	13302645	Harrosh-Ifrah	M	Box 37
BNA	13302646	Ruiz-Vega	I	Cyprus Boxes 66,67
BNA	13302647	Salafranca-y-Rabaja	E	Cyprus Boxes 66,67
BNA	13302651	Castro-Salguera	E	Box 34
BNA	13302652	Correa-Gonsalez	D	Cyprus Boxes 66,67

	Number	Name	Initials	Notes	
BNA	13302654	Emanuelo	J	Box 35	
BNA	13302655	Hernandez	F	Cyprus Boxes 66,67	
BNA	13302657	Moreno-Velasquez	V	Box 39	
BNA	13302658	Padro-Pasero	E	Box 40	
BNA	13302661	Triano-Garcia	R	Box 43	
BNA	13302662	Atemcia-Rodriguez	A	Box 33	
BNA	13302665	De Hernandez Sanchez	L	Box 35	
BNA	13302666	Mata-Rueda	D	Box 39	
BNA	13302672	Villegas-y-Castillo	J	Box 43	
BNA	13302674	Juan	I	Box 37	
BNA	13302676	Rodriguez	S	Cyprus Boxes 66,67	
BNA	13302677	Blasquez	V	Box 34	
BNA	13302678	Beltran-Perez	J	Box 33	
BNA	13302679	Estevan	J	Box 35	
BNA	13302680	Bragado-Cernuda	A	Cyprus Boxes 66,67	
BNA	13302683	Perez	M	Box 40	
BNA	13302684	Alvarez-Sanchez	F	Box 33	
BNA	13302687	Beltran-Seller	E	Box 33	
BNA	13302688	Carrasco-Garcia	A	Cyprus Boxes 66,67	
BNA	13302690	Garcia-Alvarez	E	Box 36	
BNA	13302691	Hernandez	J	Cyprus Boxes 66,67	
BNA	13302694	Martin	A	Box 38	
BNA	13302695	Martin-Fernandez	R	Cyprus Boxes 66,67	
BNA	13302696	Martin-Vegas	I	Cyprus Boxes 66,67	
BNA	13302697	Martinez	J	Box 38	
BNA	13302698	Nidam	J	Box 40	
BNA	13302699	Ortiz	J	Box 40	
BNA	13302701	Rosa-y-Cuesta	F	Box 41	
BNA	13302703	Rubio-Romero	C	Box 42	
BNA	13302706	Sanchez-Inyesto	C	Box 42	
BNA	13302707	Santiago-Goliano	C	Box 42	
BNA	13303635	Sanchez-Sierra	M	Cyprus Boxes 66,67	
BNA	13309719	Garcia	J	Box 36	
BNA	13809135	Alvarez	A G	Box 33	
BNA	13809473	Lopez (Carrasco)	D	Cyprus Boxes 66,67	
BNA	13809474	Caparros (Gomez)	J	Cyprus Boxes 66,67	
BNA	13809479	Cabanas	J	Cyprus Boxes 66,67	
BNA	13809603	Sanchez	A	Box 42	
BNA	13809655	Aguado	A G	Box 33	
BNA	13809656	Albiol	J S	Cyprus Boxes 66,67	
BNA	13809657	Aldave	R E	Box 33	
BNA	13809659	Arpal	J G	Cyprus Boxes 66,67	
BNA	13809660	Arranz	F N	Box 33	
BNA	13809662	Aza	L C	Cyprus Boxes 66,67	
BNA	13809664	Bandera	I F	Cyprus Boxes 66,67	
BNA	13809666	Barcaiztegui	A G	Cyprus Boxes 66,67	

	Number	Name	Initials	Notes
BNA	13809669	Barquero	C P	Cyprus Boxes 66,67
BNA	13809670	Barrachina	A L	Cyprus Boxes 66,67
BNA	13809673	Benedicto	R G	Cyprus Boxes 66,67
BNA	13809676	Cabedo	F C	Cyprus Boxes 66,67
BNA	13809678	Bruns	F R	Cyprus Boxes 66,67
BNA	13809683	Carmona	J	Box 34
BNA	13809683	Carmona	J B	Cyprus Boxes 66,67
BNA	13809686	Casado	S M	Cyprus Boxes 66,67
BNA	13809690	Contreras	F	Box 35
BNA	13809694	Culianes	A D	Cyprus Boxes 66,67
BNA	13809698	De La Cruz	G C	Box 35
BNA	13809699	Dominquez	T L	Cyprus Boxes 66,67
BNA	13809700	De Montes	R C	Cyprus Boxes 66,67
BNA	13809701	Estela	V M	Cyprus Boxes 66,67
BNA	13809702	Esteve	S G	Box 35
BNA	13809707	Ferrer	J S	Cyprus Boxes 66,67
BNA	13809708	Fernandez	E L	Cyprus Boxes 66,67
BNA	13809712	Galiano	J R	Cyprus Boxes 66,67
BNA	13809716	Garcia	A C	Cyprus Boxes 66,67
BNA	13809717	Garcia	F M	Box 36
BNA	13809723	Gimeno	S M	Cyprus Boxes 66,67
BNA	13809725	Gomez	C M	Cyprus Boxes 66,67
BNA	13809730	Gutierrez	A A	Cyprus Boxes 66,67
BNA	13809734	Hidalgo	A de S	Cyprus Boxes 66,67
BNA	13809737	Labanda	J F	Cyprus Boxes 66,67
BNA	13809738	Lasuen	G R	Box 38
BNA	13809739	Longas	E C	Cyprus Boxes 66,67
BNA	13809742	Lopez	G L	Cyprus Boxes 66,67
BNA	13809745	Lopez	S A	Box 38
BNA	13809746	Luzon	J M	Cyprus Boxes 66,67
BNA	13809753	Molina	H M	Cyprus Boxes 66,67
BNA	13809758	Olivares	A I	Box 40
BNA	13809765	Pensado	F B	Cyprus Boxes 66,67
BNA	13809771	Puig	V D	Box 41
BNA	13809777	Rodriguez	A M	Cyprus Boxes 66,67
BNA	13809781	Roldan	A Z	Box 41
BNA	13809782	Romero	V G	Cyprus Boxes 66,67
BNA	13809787	Sanchez	F D H	Box 42
BNA	13809791	Sanpedro	J F	Cyprus Boxes 66,67
BNA	13809793	Soler	F A	Cyprus Boxes 66,67
BNA	13809794	Soler	J R	Box 42
BNA	13809796	Terron	S R	Box 43
BNA	13809798	Torralba	A B	Box 43
BNA	13809800	Torres	D N	Cyprus Boxes 66,67
BNA	13809802	Tudo Suner	S	Box 43
BNA	13809807	Vicente	D G	Cyprus Boxes 66,67

	Number	**Name**	**Initials**	**Notes**	
BNA	13809816	Fluxa	J M B	Cyprus Boxes 66,67	
BNA	13809818	Mata	J R	Box 38	
BNA	13809819	Ramos	T M	Cyprus Boxes 66,67	
BNA	13809820	Gonzales	E R	Box 37	
BNA	13809821	Coronado	M	Box 35	
BNA	13809830	Latin	M	Box 38	
BNA	13809864	La Fuerte	D L	Cyprus Boxes 66,67	
BNA	13809957	Gimenez	M M	Cyprus Boxes 66,67	
BNA	13809958	Sanchez	J	Box 42	
BNA	13809978	Torralba	D E	Box 43	
BNA	13809979	Martinez	P R	Box 38	
BNA	13809982	Martinez	A L	Box 38	
BNA	13809991	Ochoa	V R	Cyprus Boxes 66,67	

Bibliography

The National Archives

DNS/4320/20, Enlistments, Queen's Royal Regiment (West Surrey)
HO213/289, Non-German Refugees, Basque Children
HO 213/289, letters updating on the Situation Regarding the Basque Refugee Children
HO 213/287, letter from Mr W. Roberts to the Home Office, 27 April 1937
HO 213/828, Return of Aliens registered as residing within Metropolitan Police District: 1942
HO 405/61458, Alien and Immigration, Applications for Naturalisation
HS3-50, SOE Africa and Middle East Group, Massingham, Prisons, internment and concentration camps, 1943
HS6/173, PHILOTUS mission
HS6/918, SOE Western Europe, Spain, General correspondence
HS6/961, Training for SCONCE
HS7/163, Iberian section history 1940–45 by Major Morris and Major Head
HS7/164, Iberian section history 1940–45 by Major Morris and Major Head
HS7/169, SOE Histories and War Diaries, MASSINGHAM
HS9-150-6, Report by Commandant Bigeard
HS9/276/2, Fernando Martínez Casabayo personal file.
HS9/649/2, Richard Everard Hambro personal file
HS9-877-5, Report by Captain Peter Lake on activities in France in 1944
HS9/1048/7, Esteban Molina personal file
NRA 44612: Queen's Royal Regiment, Register of Soldiers
WO 166/5440, The Pioneer Corps, 10 Group War Diary
WO 169, PRO 57/1637, War Diary G(R) Branch GHQ, Middle East Forces
WO 171/1245, Allied Expeditionary Force, North-West Europe (British Element): War Diaries, Second World War, ARMY AIR CORPS, Parachute Regiments, War Diary for 12 Battalion
WO 171/406, 1 Airborne Reconnaissance Squadron
WO 171/1256, 2 Irish Guards (Armoured Battalion) War Diary
WO 416/246/118, Angel Marino POW file
WO 416/304/136, German POW Record Card for Francis Revuelta
WO 361/719, France: special operations by the SAS (Special Air Service); Operation Trueform
WO 201/2597, Combined Training Centre: Middle East, 1940–44.
WO 219/2403, Special Air Service reports: operation Galia
WO 218/215, Operation Tombola: report
WO 373/13/478, Recommendation for Award for Ramos, Raphael
WO 373/4/392, Military Medal citation for Private Vilanova
WO 373/98/802, Military Medal citation for Sergeant Canovas
GR 28P4 3277, Report by Alfonso Canovas

CAB 66/59/35, Anthony Eden, *Policy Towards Spain*, Cabinet War Office Memorandum, dated 12 December 1944
CAB 129/46/34, Cabinet Office Memorandum, Title Spain
13/GEN/1954 (Demob. 5A)

Imperial War Museum Archives

Private Papers of J. Trill, Biography of a Spanish Soldier 1939 – 1946, IWM 3705
Private Papers of J. R. Snowden, IWM 12555
Interview with Wilfred George Beeson, recorded 13April 1981, IWM 4802
Interview with Leslie Wright, recorded 1983, IWM 7311
Interview with George Alan Dawson Young, recorded 12 December 1983, IWM 7328
Interview with Arthur William Joscelyne, recorded 23 April 1987, IWM 9768
Interview with Elisha Roberts, recorded 1989, IWM 11942
Interview with John Colman (Juan Torrents Abadía), recorded 27 December 1997, IWM 17730
Interview with Edward Lyster 'Tinker' Gibbon, recorded 2000, IWM 20119
Interview with Eveleigh Earle Dennis 'Dumbo' Newman, recorded 13 December 2004, IWM 27463
Photograph: Command of French Units handed to *Général* Bonjour, 2 October 1945, IWM B 15793

The British Library

013943647: *The Spanish News Sheet*; Edited by the International Commission for War Refugees in Great Britain, 1940–45, British Library. System number: 013943647. UIN: BLL01013943647.

Other Archives

Handbook of the Organisation Todt (OT), MIRS, London, dated March 1945, Ike Skelton Combined Arms Research Library Digital Library, <https://cgsc.contentdm.oclc.org/digital/collection/p4013coll8/id/1457>. Accessed 21 November 2022
Royal Engineers Museum Archive, Extracts from 295 Field Company RE (TA), 3 Sep 1939 to 2 Mar 1946
Supplement to *The London Gazette*, 2 April 1946
Surrey Heritage Centre Archive, QRWS/8/2/14, Reports of the campaigns in the Western Desert and Italy, War Diary for 1/5 Battalion
CIA-RDP13X00001R000100330006-2: SO Operation Instructions – Lieutenant Colonel W. A. Eddy USMC, 14 October 1942

Unpublished Archives, Works and Memoirs

Middle East Commando Research Group Archive. Held by the author.
Asensio Pérez, Victor, *Un Alcorisano en la II Guerra Mundial*, 2021 (manuscript in the Author's collection)
Pereira, Francisco, *Life Stories*. Held by the author.

Rose, Edward, *A Gift of Tongues*, a personal unpublished memoir. Extract provided by the Royal Pioneer Corps Archive
Sánchez Monterrubio, Cleto, *Memorias de Tres Banderas*. Copy kept by the author.
The Diary of Captain H. A. N. Cole, Pioneer Corps. Extracts provided by his grandson Richard Normington. Held by the author.
Roa Ventura, Agustín, *Los años de mi vida, , Contribución histórica sobre el proceso de los españoles fuera y dentro de España*. Personal Papers. Held by the author.
Roa Ventura, Agustín, *El Fracaso de la Victoria*. Personal Papers. Held by the author.
Tunnickliffe, Major K. O. MBE, *14th Forestry Company, New Zealand Engineers*, Private Diaries
Zapico, Jesús Velasco, *Una Vida Española, a Personal Family Memoir, 1915–1995*. Unpublished memoir. Author's collection and copyright.

Books, Theses, Articles & Documents

Anonymous, 'Fought in Spanish Civil War, French Foreign Legion and for Britain', *Henley Standard*, 29 September 1989
Allport, Alan, *Britain at Bay: The Epic Story of the Second World War: 1938–1941* (London: Profile Books, 2021)
Andújar, Tomás, 'The Wound Covered in Sand', Ayuntament de Barcelona Archive, 2006. <https://ajuntament.barcelona.cat/lavirreina/sites/default/files/2020-06/La%20herida%20cubierta%20de%20arena-en-tau%20maquetat.pdf>. Accessed 12 June 2022
Alpert, Michael, *The Spanish Civil War at Sea: Dark and Dangerous Waters* (Barnsley: Pen and Sword Books Ltd, 2021)
Arasa, Daniel, *Exiliados y Enfrentados, Los Españoles en Inglaterra de 1939 a 1945* (Barcelona: Ediciones de la Tempestad/Puntos, 1995)
Arasa, Daniel, *Los Españoles de Churchill* (Barcelona: Editorial Armonía Poética, 1991)
Atkin, Nicholas, *The Forgotten French: Exiles in the British Isles, 1940–44* (Manchester: Manchester University Press, 2003)
Beeson, George, *Five Roads to Freedom* (London: Corgi Books, Transworld Publishers, 1977)
Bertaux, Pierre, *Libération de Toulouse et de sa Région* (Paris: Hachette, 1973)
Binney, Marcus, *Secret War Heroes* (London: Hodder and Stoughton, 2006)
Brennan, Gerald, *The Spanish Labyrinth: An Account of the Social and Political Background to the Spanish Civil War* (Cambridge: Cambridge University Press, 1960)
Buchanan, Tom, 'The Truth Will Set You Free: The Making of Amnesty International,' *Journal of Contemporary History*, Vol.37, No.4 (October 2002)
Buckmaster, Maurice, *They Fought Alone* (London: The Popular Book Club, 1958)
Canessa, Eric, *They Went to War – The Story of Gibraltarians who served in His Majesty's Forces in World War II Away From their Homeland* (Gibraltar: Eric Canessa, 2004)
Carr, Raymond, *Spain 1808–1939* (Oxford: The Clarendon Press, 1966)
Carr, Raymond, *Modern Spain 1875–1980* (Oxford: Oxford University Press, 1980)
Celada, Antonio, González de la Aleja, Manuel & Pastor Garcia Daniel (eds), *La Prensa Británica y la Guerra Civil Española* (Salamanca: Amarú Ediciones, 2013)
Celaya, Diego Gaspar, 'Premature Resisters. Spanish Contribution to the French National Defence Campaign in 1939/1940,' *Journal of Modern European History*, Vol.16, 2018, Issue 2
Chamero Serena, Joaquín, *De Belalcázar al infierno de Djelfa* (Córdoba: Círculo Rojo, 2002)
Charaudeau, Anne, 'Les Réfugiés Espagnols dans les Camps d'Internement en Afrique du Nord, *Hommes et Migrations*', n°1158, octobre 1992, mémoire multiple

Childs, Martin, 'General Marcel Bigeard: Soldier who Served in Three Conflicts and Became an Expert on Counter-Insurgency,' *The Independent,* Thursday 1 July 2010, <https://www.independent.co.uk/news/obituaries/general-marcel-bigeard-soldier-who-served-in-three-conflicts-and-became-an-expert-on-counterinsurgency-2015150.html>. Accessed 12 June 2023

Cleminson, Richard, 'Spanish anti-fascist 'prisoners of war' in Lancashire, 1944–46,' *International Journal of Iberian Studies* Volume 22, Number 3 2009 Intellect Ltd, English language. DOI: <10.1386/ ijis.22.3.163/1>

Cochrane, Archibald L., *One Man's Medicine* (London: The British Medical Journal, 1989)

Comor, André-Paul, *L'Épopée de la 13e Demi-Brigade de Légion Etrangère, 1940–1945* (Paris: Nouvelles Editions Latines, 1988)

Conner, Bruce and Milano, Vince, *Normandie front: D-Day to Saint-Lô Through German Eyes* (Stroud: Spellmount, 2011)

Dalmau, John, *Slave Worker in the Channel Islands* (Guernsey: Guernsey Press Company, 1957)

Dannatt, Richard, Lyman, Robert, *Victory to Defeat: The British Army 1918–40* (Oxford: Osprey Publishing, 2023)

Davie, Michael (ed.), *The Diaries of Evelyn Waugh* (London: Weidenfeld & Nicholson, 1976)

Dickson, Archibald, Letter to the *Sunday Despatch* newspaper, dated 2/3 April 1939. <https://viewfromlavila.com/2018/03/28/the-stanbrook-story-the-unlikely-british-heroes-of-alicantes-darkest-hour/>

Dowswell, Paul, *Aliens: The Checkered History of Britain's Wartime Refugees* (London: Biteback Publishing Ltd, 2023)

Dreyfus-Armand, Geneviève, *El Exilio de los Republicanos Españoles en Francia* (Barcelona: Ediciones Crítica, 2000)

Dreyfus-Armand, Geneviève, *L'Exil des Républicains Espagnols en France: De la Guerre Civile à la Mort de Franco* (Paris: Albin Michel, 1999)

Dodds-Parker, Sir Douglas, *Setting Europe Ablaze: Some Account of Ungentlemanly Warfare* (United Kingdom: Springwood Books, 1983)

Dulphy, Anne, 'Sables d'Exil. Les Républicains Espagnols dans les Camps d'Internement au Maghreb (1939–1945)', *Exils et migrations ibériques au XXe siècle,* 2009

Edwards, Jill, *The British Government & the Spanish Civil War, 1936–1939* (London: MacMillan Press Ltd, 1979)

Fairey, John, *Remember Arnhem: Story of the First Airborne Reconnaissance Squadron at Arnhem* (Bearsden: Peaton Press, 1990)

Farran, Roy, *Winged Dagger: Adventures on Special Service* (Glasgow: Grafton Books, 1948)

Farran, Roy, *Operation Tombola* (London: Arms & Armour Press, 1960)

Fonseca Rodríguez, Diego, 'What was Franco's Role in the Deportation of 10,000 Spaniards to Nazi Camps?', *El País,* 26 April 2019 <https://english.elpais.com/elpais/2019/04/26/inenglish/1556272970_468527.html>. Accessed 12 December 2020.

Ford, Roger, *Fire from the Forest: The S.A.S. Brigade in France, 1944* (London: Cassell, 2003)

Gallagher, Mike, *With Recce at Arnhem: Recollections of Trooper Des Evans a First Airborne Division Veteran* (Barnsley: Pen and Sword Books Ltd, 2018)

Garrido Orozco, Luís, *Des Républicains Espagnols á La Chapelle-Launay. Janvier–Juillet 1940* <http://enenvor.fr/eeo_actu/wwii/des_republicains_espagnols_a_la_chapelle_launay_janvier_juillet_1940.html>. Accessed 20 November 2021

Gaspar Celaya, Diego *La Guerra Continua. Voluntarios Españoles al Servicio de la Francia Libre (1940–1945)* (Madrid: Marcial Pons Historia, 2015)

Get, Philippe, *L'Equipe du Nord, Igney 09–18 septembre 1944* (Toulouse: Cool Libri, 2021)

Gildea, Robert, *Fighters in the Shadows – A new History of French Resistance* (London: Faber & Faber, 2015)

Gildea, Robert, Tames, Ismee (eds), *Fighters Across Frontiers: Transnational Resistance in Europe, 1936–48* (Manchester: Manchester University Press, 2020)

Glover, Michael, *An Improvised War. The Abyssinian Campaign of 1940–1941* (New York: Hippocrene Books, 1987)

Grande Catalán, Antonio, *Number One Spanish Company. Memorias de Antonio Grande* (Alicante: Imprenta Gamma, 2002)

Greenacre, John, *Churchill's Spearhead: The Development of Britain's Airborne Forces during World War II* (Barnsley: Pen and Sword Books Ltd, 2010)

Hagen, Louis, *Arnhem Lift: A Fighting Glider Pilot Remembers* (Barnsley: Leo Cooper, 1993)

Hann, Robert, *SAS Operation GALIA, Bravery Behind Enemy Lines in the Second World War* (Peterborough: Fast Print Publishing, 2013)

Hart-Harris, Duff, *Man of War: The Secret Life of Captain Alan Hillgarth. Officer. Adventurer, Agent* (London: The Random House Group, 2012)

Heath, F.W. (ed.), *A Churchill Anthology, Selections from the Writings and Speeches of Sir Winston Churchill* (London: Oldhams Books Limited, 1962)

Hilliman Captain C. MC MM RPC, 'Looking Back at 51 Commando,' *The Pioneer Magazine*, No.132, September 1977

Isla, Lala (ed.), *Aventuras en la Nostalgia: Exiliados y Emigrantes Españoles en Londres* (Madrid: Ministerio de Trabajo e Inmigración, 2008)

Jackson, Julian, *The Fall of France: The Nazi Invasion of 1940* (Oxford: Oxford University Press, 2003)

Kackson, Robert, *Dunkirk, The British Evacuation, 1940* (London: Arthur Barker Ltd, 1976)

Jefferson, David, *Tobruk, A Raid too Far* (London: Robert Hale Ltd, 2013)

Jump, Jim, 'Spanish Republican exile Activism, Anguish and Assimilation,' *Theory & Struggle*, Volume 121, <https://doi.org/10.3828/ts.2020.17>

Kateb, Kamel, *Les Immigrés Espagnols Dans les Camps en Algérie (1939–1941)*, Belin, "Annales de démographie historique" (2007) 1 n° 113, pp.155 – 175. ISSN 0066-2062 ISBN 2701147086 <https://www.cairn.info/revue-annales-de-demographiehistorique-2007-1-page-155.htm>

Keene, Judith, *Fighting for Franco: International Volunteers in Nationalist Spain during the Spanish Civil War, 1936–39* (London: Hambledon Continuum, 2001)

Kemp, Peter, *Mine were of trouble* (London: Cassel and Company Ltd, 1957)

Kennedy Shaw, W. B., *Long Range Desert Group, The Story of its Work in Libya 1940–1943* (London: Wm Collins Son & Co Ltd, 1945)

Kochanski, Halik, *Resistance: The Underground War in Europe, 1939–45* (London: Penguin Random House, 2022)

Landsborough, Gordon, *Tobruk Commando* (London: Mayflower Books Ltd, 1968)

Lardner, John, 'Two Spaniards First of Troops to cross Volturno in Italy,' *North American Newspaper Alliance*, October 1944

Leroy, Stéphane, *Les Exilés Républicains Espagnols des Régiments de Marche des Volontaires Étrangers. Engagement, présence et formation militaire (janvier 1939–mai 1940)*, Cahiers de civilisation espagnole contemporaine, 6 (2010), DOI: <https://doi.org/10.4000/ccec.3285>. Accessed 10 November 2021

Lett, Brian, *The Small Scale Raiding Force* (Barnsley: Pen and Sword Books Ltd, 2013)

Liarte, Ramón, *¡Ay, de los vencedores!* (Barcelona: Ediciones Picazo, 1986)

Litherland, Sidney, *The Junak King, Life as a British POW 1941–45* (Stroud: Spellmount, 2014)

Lyman, Robert, *First Victory, Britain's Forgotten Struggle in the Middle East, 1941* (London: Constable & Robinson Ltd, 2006)

McKelvey, Peter, 'New Zealand Foresters at War,' *The New Zealand Journal of Forestry*, February 2001

Macintyre, Ben, *Colditz: Prisoners of the Castle* (London: Penguin Random House, 2022)

Mackay, Francis, *Overture to Overlord, Special Operations in Preparation for Overlord* (Barnsley: Pen and Sword Books Ltd, 2005)

Mañes Postigo, Joaquín, *La Legión Extranjera y sus Españoles 1831–2017* (Palma del Condado: Magasé Ediciones, 2018)

Marnham, Patrick, *War in the Shadows, Resistance, Deception and Betrayal in Occupied France* (London: Oneworld Publications, 2012)

Marco, J., 'Transnational Soldiers and Guerrilla Warfare from the Spanish Civil War to the Second World War', *War in History*, Vol.27, no.3, pp.387–407 <https://doi.org/10.1177/0968344518761212>. Accessed 12 June 2022

David Mathieson, David, *Frontline Madrid, Battlefield Tours of the Spanish Civil War* (Oxford: Signal Books Limited, 2014)

Mead, Richard, *Commando General: The Life of Major General Sir Robert Laycock KCMG CB DSO* (Pen & Sword Books Ltd, Barnsley, 2016)

Melka, Robert L., 'Darlan Between Britain and Germany 1940–41,' *Journal of Contemporary History*, Vol.8, No.2 (April 1973), pp.57–80

Mesquida, Evelyn, *La Nueve, 24 August 1944, The Spanish Republicans Who Liberated Paris* (Barcelona: Christie Books, 2015)

Messenger, Charles, *The Middle East Commandos* (Wellingborough: William Kimber & Co. Ltd, 1988)

Miller, David, *Mercy Ships, The Untold Story of Prisoner-of-War Exchanges in World War II* (London: Continuum UK, 2008)

Monferer Catalán, Luís, *Odisea en Albion* (Madrid: Ediciones de la Torre, 2007)

Moradiellos, Enrique, *El reñidero de Europa. Las dimensiones internacionales de la guerra civil española* (Barcelona: Ediciones Península, 2001)

Morgan, Mike, *Daggers Drawn: Real Heroes of the SAS & SBS* (Staplehurst: Spellmount, 2012)

Mortimer, Gavin, *The SAS in Occupied France: 2 SAS Operations, June to October 1944* (Barnsley: Pen and Sword Books Ltd, 2023)

Mortimer, Gavin, *Stirling's Men: The Inside Story of the SAS in World War 2* (London: Weidenfeld & Nicolson, 2004)

Murland, Jerry, *The Dunkirk Perimeter and Evacuation 1940, France and Flanders Campaign* (Barnsley: Pen and Sword Books Ltd, 2019)

Norton-Taylor, Richard, 'MI6 spent $200m bribing Spaniards in Second World War,' *The Guardian*, Thursday 23 May 2013. <https://www.theguardian.com/uk/2013/may/23/mi6-spain-200m-bribes-ww2#:~:text=At%20least%20%2414m%2C%20some,in%20banks%20in%20New%20York>. Accessed 12 April 2020

Naharro-Calderón, José María, *Ante el Horror … los Campos de Concentración Devant l'Horreur … les Camps de Concentration*. Archivo de la Frontera. (Nota de lectura, 2015), jmn@umd.edu

Neiberg, Michael S., *When France Fell, The Vichy Crisis and the Fate of the Anglo-American Alliance* (Cambridge Massachusetts: Harvard Press, 2021)

O'Connor, Bernard, *Blowing up Iberia: British, German and Italian Sabotage in Spain and Portugal during the Second World War* (Bedford: Bernard O'Connor, 2019)

Oliveira Avedaño, José, 'Españoles en la Segunda Guerra Mundial,' *Revista Historia y Vida, Magazine*, no.106

Orozco, Luís, 'La odisea de los aviadores de la 185 Compañía de Trabajadores Extranjeros (I)', *ICARO, Boletín Informativo de La Asociación de Aviadores de la República*, nº 125, abril 2018

Otway, Lieutenant Colonel T.B.H. DSO, *Official History of the Second World War, Army, Airborne Forces* (London: War Office, 1951, reprinted by The Naval & Military Press)

Parello, Vincent, 'Troisième République, 118-1, La Guerre Civile Espagnole Aujourd'Hui (1936–2016),' *Bulletin Hispanique*, 2016

Pawley, Margaret, *In Obedience to Instruction, FANY with the SOE in the Mediterranean* (Barnsley: Leo Cooper, 1999)

Playà, Josep, 'Los 9.161 Españoles Deportados a Campos Nazis: sus Nombres y sus Historias,' *La Vanguardia*, Barcelona, 5 May 2020 <https://www.lavanguardia.com/cultura/20200505/48973724359/registro-online-espanoles-campos-concentracion-nazi.html>. Accessed 5 November 2021

Pons Prades, Eduardo, *Republicanos Españoles en la Segunda Guerra Mundial* (Madrid: La Esfera de los Libros S.L., 2003)

Porch, Douglas, *The French Foreign Legion. A Complete History of the Legendary Fighting Force* (New York: Skyhorse Publishing, 2010)

Porch, Douglas, *Defeat and Division, France at War 1939–1942* (Cambridge: Cambridge University Press, 2022)

Preston, Paul, *Franco*, (London: Harper Collins, 1993)

Preston, Paul, *We Saw Spain Die: Foreign Correspondents in the Spanish Civil War* (London: Constable & Robinson, 2008)

Preston, Paul, *The Spanish Holocaust: Inquisition and Extermination in Twentieth-Century Spain* (London: Harper Press, 2013)

Preston, Paul, *A People Betrayed: A History of Corruption, Political Incompetence and Social Division in Modern Spain* (London: William Collins, 2020)

Pruszyński, Ksawery, *Polish Invasion* (Edinburgh: Birlinn Publishers, 2010)

Radford, Charlie, McKay, Francis, (ed.), *SAS Trooper: Charlie Radford's Operations in Enemy Occupied France and Italy*, Francis McKay (Barnsley: Pen and Sword Books Ltd, 2010)

Ramirez Copeiro del Villar, Jesús, *Objetivo Africa, Crónica de la Guinea Española en la II Guerra Mundial* (Huelva: Imprenta Jimenez S.L., 2004)

Ramón Roca, Juan and Reyes, Ariane, *Españoles en Argelia: Emigración y Exilio, Memoria Gráfica* (Wroclaw: Ariane Reyes Meresse, 2022 second edition)

Rawson, Andrew, *Organising Victory: The War Conferences 1941–45* (Stroud: History Press, 2013)

Rhodes-Wood, Major E. H., *A War History of The Royal Pioneer Corps 1939–1945*, (Aldershot: Gale & Polden Ltd, 1960) Converted electronically by Norman & Paul Brown <www.royal-pioneercorps.co.uk>

Richards, Ted, *Archibald Dickson – An Unsung Roath Hero* (Roath Local History Society, 2021) <https://roathlocalhistorysociety.org/2021/08/20/archibald-dickson-an-unsung-roath-hero/>. Accessed 23 July 2022

Roa Ventura, Agustín, *La Batalla de Narvik, Revista Historia y Vida*, No. 119

Roa Ventura, Agustín, *Agonía y Muerte del Franquismo (Una Memoria)* (Barcelona: Barral Editores, 1977)

St Clair, A.D. (Sandy), *The Endless War* (Canada: Turner-Warrick Publications, 1987)

Shelmerdine, Brian, *British Representations of the Spanish Civil War* (Manchester: Manchester University Press, 2006)

Simmons, Mark, *Ian Fleming and Operation GOLDEN EYE. Keeping Spain out of World War II* (Oxford: Casemate Publishers, 2018)

Smith, Colin, *England's Last War Against France, Fighting Vichy 1940–1942* (London: Weidenfeld & Nicolson, 2009)

Smyth, Denis, *Diplomacy and Strategy of Survival, British Policy and Franco's Spain 1940–41* (Cambridge: Cambridge University Press, 1986)

Steckoll, Solomon H., *The Alderney Death Camp* (St Albans: Granada Paperback, 1982)

Stein, Louis, *Beyond Death and Exile. The Spanish Republicans in France, 1939–1955* (London: Harvard University Press, 1979)
Stevens Coon, Carleton, *A North Africa Story: The Anthropologist as OSS Agent, 1941–1943* (University of Michigan: Gambit Press, 1980)
Tabernilla, Guillermo & González, Ander, *Combatientes Vascos en la Segunda Guerra Mundial, Fighting Basques Project* (Madrid: Desperta Ferro Ediciones SLNE, 2018)
Thomas, Hugh, *The Spanish Civil War* (London: Penguin Books, 2001)
Thomas, Martin, 'The Massingham Mission: SOE in French North Africa, 1941–1944', *Intelligence and National Security*, 1996, 11:4, 696-721, <https://doi.org/10.1080/02684529608432387>
Tremlett, Giles, *The International Brigades: Fascism, Freedom and the Spanish Civil War* (London: Bloomsbury Publishing, 2020)
Tucker-Jones, Anthony, *Operation Dragoon: The Liberation of Southern France 1944* (Barnsley: Pen and Sword Books Ltd, 2009)
Tudor, Malcolm, *SAS in Italy 1943–1945, Raiders in Enemy Territory* (London: Fonthill Media, 2018)
Vermesch, Olivier, *Les Espagnols de l'Opération Dynamo: Les Compagnies de Travailleurs Étrangers Dunkerque, mai-juin 1940*. 2020, pp.3–4. <https://atf40.1fr1.net/t10452-compagnies-de-travailleurs-etrangers-espagnols-1939-1940>. Accessed 12 February 2021
Vargas Rivas, Antonio, *Guerra, Revolución y Exilio de un Anarcosindicalista*, (Almería: privately published, October 2007 second edition)
Vilar, Juan B, *Ay de los Vencidos! El Exilio y los Países de Acogida* (Madrid: Ed. Eneida, 2009)
Vilar, Juan B, 'La Última Gran Emigración Política Española. Relación Nominal de los Militantes Republicanos Evacuados de Alicante en el Buque Inglés Stanbrook con Destino a Orán en 28 de Marzo de 1939,' *Anales de Historia Contemporánea*, No. 2, 1983
Wigg, Richard, *Churchill and Spain: The Survival of the Franco Regime 1940–1945* (Eastbourne: Sussex Academic Press, 2008)

Hansard

Volume 362: Refugees, debated on Wednesday 10 July 1940, <https://hansard.parliament.uk/Commons/1940-07-10/debates/513c14f4-f07b-48c8-bf14-f863b62ffa58/Refugees?highlight=spaniards%20pioneers%20corps#contribution-cfe94ba1-8e93-499e-bf95-fa0ef7663819>. Accessed 12 June 2021
Volume 362: Refugees, debated on Wednesday 10 July 1940, <https://hansard.parliament.uk/Commons/1940-07-10/debates/513c14f4-f07b-48c8-bf14-f863b62ffa58/Refugees>. Accessed 12 June 2021
Volume 392. *Disabled Prisoners of War (Exchange with Germany), debated 19 October 1943*, <https://api.parliament.uk/historic-hansard/commons/1943/oct/19/disabled-prisoners-of-war-exchange-with>. Accessed 6 August 2021
Volume 389: *North Africa (Internees)*, debated on Wednesday 12 May 1943, <https://hansard.parliament.uk/Commons/1943-05-12/debates/c65a59d3-8ff7-4853-acd5-6b6089490acf/NorthAfrica(Internees)?highlight=spaniards#contribution-e218df29-1357-45fe-a13b-7c36ab2cd051>. Accessed 12 June 2022
Volume 107: Hansard, *Refugee Children From Spain*, debated Tuesday 2 November 1937, <https://hansard.parliament.uk/Lords/1937-11-02/debates/0f5c2cde-a65d-4f2b-9915-64628ebdbd84/RefugeeChildrenFromSpain?highlight=refugee%20children%20from%20spain#contribution-f0e47155-ffeb-41cd-88aa-a50907c7a13c>. Accessed 15 August 2023

Volume 420: Debate on Pioneer Corps (Release of Aliens), debated 5 March 1946, <https://hansard.parliament.uk/Commons/1946-03-18/debates/5f3727f5-638a-4cb0-b5a7-132a370f3043/StraitsSettlements(Repeal)BillLords?highlight=release%20aliens#contribution-20dd2598-4f1e-41ae-95a7-72d568159be1>. Accessed 12 December 2022

Volume 423: Debate on Aliens (Place of Release), debated 4 June 1946, <https://hansard.parliament.uk/Commons/1946-06-04/debates/59c92b60-2336-41f9-a028-26810bc579cf/Aliens(PlaceOfRelease)>. Accessed 12 December 2022

Volume 449: Debate on Foreign Affairs, 10 December 1948, <https://hansard.parliament.uk/Commons/1948-12-10/debates/2a8b1ed1-d7e8-4922-b5d6-14e7d4c7c90c/ForeignAffairs?highlight=debate%20foreign%20affairs#contribution-b6bd55f7-b5be-4812-a717-a6c9e3bb1ff7>. Accessed 29 December 2023

Websites

Bassins des Lumieres, <www.bassins-lumieres.com/en/discover/place-of-history#3/1>. Accessed 15 August 2023

The Association for the UK Basque Children, www.basquechildren.org Accessed 12 December 2021

Basque Government Website <www.euskadi.eus/gobierno-vasco/>. Accessed 12 December 2021.

Les Pages de Livres de Guerre, Vichy: lois et mesures antisémites, Décret-loi du 12 novembre 1938 relatif à la situation et à la police des étrangers, <http://pages.livresdeguerre.net/pages/sujet.php?id=docddp&su=103&np=780>. Accessed 23 January 2022

The United Holocaust Memorial Museum, <collections.ushmm.org/search/catalog/irn504525) (25/05/2018>. Accessed 10 January 2022

Forum Armée de Terre Française, Compagnies de Travailleurs Etrangers Espagnols <atf40.1fr1.net/t10452-compagnies-de-travailleurs-etrangers-espagnols-1939-1940>. Accessed 23 January 2022

Mauthausen Concentration Camp Memorial website. <www.mauthausen-memorial.org/en/Gusen/The-Concentration-Camp-Gusen/Prisoners/Spanish-Republicans>. Accessed 29 December 2021

Royal Logistics Corps Digital Archive, <www.rlcarchive.org/ContentRPC>. Accessed 1 Sep 2020

En Revor, Des Républicains Espagnols à La Chapelle-Launay, Janvier–Juillet 1940, <enenvor.fr/eeo_actu/wwii/des_republicains_espagnols_a_la_chapelle_launay_janvier_juillet_1940>. Accessed 29 December 2021

Sixth Foreign Infantry Regiment, <foreignlegion.info/units/6th-foreign-infantry-regiment/>. Accessed 10 November 2021

ANZAC POW Free Men in Europe, Crete <www.anzacpow.com/Part-5-Other-European-Free-Men/chapter_5__crete>. Accessed 25 August 2022

Archivo Histórico de Euskadi <dokuklik.euskadi.eus/badator/visor/001/90030>. Accessed 20 March 2022

Ayuntament de Barcelona Archive <https://ajuntament.barcelona.cat/lavirreina/>. Accessed 12 June 2022

Archives Nationales D'outre-Mer, Aix-en-Provence. Harry Alexander, 'Oral History interview with Harry Alexander', <collections.ushmm.org/search/catalog/irn504525>. (25/05/2018). Accessed 10 December 2019

Memoire de Louin, <memoiredelouin.fr/index.php/patrimoine/histoire/13-patrimoine-histoire/84-1939-groupement-des-travailleurs-espagnols?showall=1>. Accessed 1 July 2019

Basque files of personnel held at Gurs Camp. <www.euskadi.eus/gobierno-vasco/-/noticia/2017/acceso-al-listado-de-las-personas-confinadas-en-el-campo-de-gurs/>. Accessed 10 August 2021, <roath-localhistorysociety.org/2021/08/20/archibald-dickson-an-unsung-roath-hero>. Accessed

12 June 2022, <pages.livresdeguerre.net/pages/sujet.php?id=docddp&su=103&np=780>. Accessed 12 June 2021

Mémoire des Hommes, Portail Culturelle du Ministère des Armées, Engagés volontaires étrangers en 1939–1940, <www.memoiredeshommes.sga.defense.gouv.fr/fr/arkotheque/client/mdh/engages_volontaires_etrangers/resus_rech.php>. Accessed 10 April 2021, <www.anzacpow.com/Part-5-Other-European-Free-Men/chapter_5_crete>. Accessed 18 June 2022

Documento de sentencia de la Causa 246–1936, recogida en: AHPSCT. Expedientes de Reclusas de La Prisión Provincial de Santa Cruz de Tenerife, Expediente nº 3798, <https://pellagofio.es/islenos/yo-fui-en-el-correillo/prisiones-flotantes-en-el-puerto-de-santa-cruz>. Accessed 9 November 2021

Three Spanish members of No.50 Middle East Commando take a rest below the Sphynx. (Miguel Martínez collection)

Other ranks in No.1 Spanish Company queue up for a meal in Belgium. (Augusto Pérez Miranda collection)

Members of the Spanish Ex-Servicemen's Association are escorted down Whitehall as they process to the Cenotaph on Sunday 19 October 1975. (Agustín Roa Ventura collection)

Index

Abadalejo, Alejandro 251
Abrial, Amiral Jean 162
Abruzzo, Italy 205
Absent Without Leave (AWOL) 107, 247
Abyssinia 132, 135, 136
Acción Nacionalista Vasca (ANV) 227
Adge 43
Adi Ugri 136
Adjutant 130, 154, 222
Agar, Olive Annie 227
Agrupación de Guerrilleros Españoles 238, 246
Aguero, Cristobal 106
Ahaus 222
Airborne Forces xxx, 99, 192, 197, 217, 226, 228, 230, 236, 342, 344
Alapont, Francisco v, 101, 270, 278, 314
Albacete 58, 271, 272, 273, 275, 276
Albania 95
Albinea Commune, Italy 209, 210
Alderney 237, 345
Aldershot 57, 58, 73, 82, 87, 247, 344
Alexander, Harry 45, 46, 347
Alfonso XIII xi, 36
Algerian Division 157
Algiers iv, xvii, xix, 45, 46, 155, 159, 161, 162, 164, 169, 170, 171–173, 176–179, 182, 190, 191, 198, 237, 296, 298, 299, 304–308, 328, 329
Alhucemas xi, 98
Alicante 41, 42, 58, 59, 61, 76, 111, 155, 158, 159, 198, 214, 271, 273–276, 293, 342, 345
Alien enlistment the British Army 74, 75, 122, 123, 226, 227, 230, 296
Alien registration card ix
Alleato Battalion vii, 208, 209
Allied POWs v, 146, 160
Almeria, Spain 47, 74, 79, 85, 87, 110, 179, 236, 251, 261, 265, 269, 270–272, 274, 284
Alsace, France 54, 161, 237
Álvarez, Luís 104, 105, 270, 278, 312
Álvarez, José 135, 145, 284
Amnesty International 259, 263, 340
Anglo-American relations 246
Annual, disaster of, xi, 36
Antwerp 159

Anzio, Italy xviii
Appeal for Amnesty 263
Aragón Front 42, 70, 123, 236
Arasa, Daniel xxiii, xxviii, xxix, 58, 59, 63, 64, 72, 112, 113, 118, 120, 126–128, 130, 134, 141, 146, 148, 150, 153, 154, 171, 174, 178, 186, 188, 189, 221, 340
Ardennes 50, 57
Ardennes Offensive xix, 85, 205
Aretxabaleta 227
Argelès-sur-Mer, France 42, 44, 45, 46, 48, 107, 153
Arias Navarro, Carlos xxix, 268
Ariège, France viii, xviii, 44, 236–241
Arles-sur-Tech, France 42
Armée du Levant 119
Arnhem vii, xxx, 217, 226, 230, 232, 233, 236, 341, 342
Arnhem Bridge 230
Askyphos, Crete 141
Asturias, Spain xii, 236, 270
Asturias miners ix, 36
Ataka Port 187
Atbara River 134
Atholl, Duchess of 39, 226
Atlantic Wall 55, 67
Atlee, Clement Richard xx, 250
Aude, France 43, 240
Auschwitz xix
Austin Motor Company 250
Australia 254, 293
Austria xiii, 56, 144
Avonmouth xv, 73
Avonmouth railway station xv, 73
Absent Without Leave (AWOL) 107, 247
Axminster 85

Baalbeck xiv, 52, 117, 119
Babali Hani, Crete 139, 141
Bacarès, France iv, 43, 44, 47, 50, 51, 115, 153
Bad Segeburg 224
Badajoz 123, 269–272, 274, 275
Badanelli 172
Bailey Bridge 236

Bailly-le-Franc, France 198
Balagué, Francisco 72, 97, 113, 278, 311
   SCONCE Training 97
   visit of De Gaulle to Trentham Park 72
Baldo, Martín 260, 321
Balearic Islands 237
Balerdi, Justo (Robert Bruce) vii, xviii, xx, 285, 317
   1 SSR 150, 188, 291
   killed in action 194, 211, 212
   name change 194
   Operation TOMBOLA 208, 211
   SAS 150, 191, 193, 292
   SAS in France 197, 198
Barakaldo 51, 153, 289, 293
Barba Nero 208
Barcelona xii, xiii, 36, 38, 40, 42, 57, 59, 63, 64, 66, 70, 72, 99, 107, 108, 112, 113, 118, 120, 126, 191, 237, 251, 256, 266
   Anarchist Movement 47
   Hispano Suiza 202
   Hospital 221
   No. 1 Spanish Company 269, 270–277, 288, 292, 340, 341
   prisoner exchanges 148, 150
Barcroft, Major 103
Bardenas Ardines, Julio 173, 286, 317
Bardia 133
Barre, Colonel Fernand 117, 119
Bartolomé Guzmán, Vicenta 251
Basilio, Santiago vii, 120, 121, 188, 289, 319
Basque
   Basque Children's Committee (BCC) 39, 226
   Basque Country xi, 100, 162, 251
   Basque refugee children xii, 162, 226–228, 244, 245, 251, 255, 338
   SS *Habana* xii, 39, 226, 227
   Southampton xii, 39, 226
Bayswater 244
Béarn 44
Beaulieu Estate 96, 100, 103
Beeson, George 145, 146, 339, 340
Beirut xiv, 51, 117, 118
Belabaye 123
Belain, René xv, 55
Beltrán, Basilio 108
Benenson, Peter (Amnesty International) 259, 261, 263
Benouville 228
Berber Tribes 36, 162
Bergan rucksack 196, 207, 208
Bergen-Belsen Concentration Camp xx, 215
Berlin xii, xix, xx, 147, 148, 237, 247
   Battle of 247
   POW Camps 146, 148, 285, 287, 289, 290
   Victory Parade vii, xxx, 223, 224, 231
Bernárdez, Enrique vi, xxv, 158, 320
Berry, Major Desmond 193
Bevin, Ernest 254, 257
Bigeard, Commandant Marcel vii, 237, 238, 239, 241, 338, 340, 341
Bir Hakeim, Battle of xvi, 119, 189
Bilbao xii, 38, 146, 153, 161, 198, 199, 228, 251, 270, 273, 277, 287, 292
Birkenau xix
Birmingham 107, 230, 250
Birmingham Post & Mail 254
Bitter Lakes v, 128, 129, 137
Bizerta Naval Base 157, 159
Blackpool 241
Blanche Couronne 59, 64
Blasco, Vicente 135, 147, 251, 285, 319
Blue Division 148, 245, 260, 261
Blundell Violett 205
Boganim, Enric (Henry Hall) 191, 194, 293
Boghari (Camp Morand) 45, 46, 159
Bois du Creux 198
Bomba, Italy 131
Bonham-Carter, Helena 261
Bonham-Carter, Lady Violet 261
Bonjour, Général Auguste-Leon 216, 339
Bonjour, Private Jacques xxviii, 74, 269
Bordeaux 35, 38, 334, 109
   SOE 109
   Submarine pens 67
Bordighera xvi, 101
Borghetto di Vara 205
Borí, Manuel 245, 260, 322
Borras Castell, Emilio 59, 246, 271, 315
   St Nazaire 59, 63
Bosque, José 103, 104, 105, 107
   retention & release Camp 020 105, 107
   SOE SCONCE 103, 104, 107
   Spanish Civil War 107
Bou Afra 160, 166
Boufarik xvii, 158, 172, 173
Bournemouth xviii
Bovio, Carlos (James Benson) 192, 194, 198, 205, 293, 300
Bracero, Luís 118, 185
Bradley, General Omar 258
Branston vi, 180, 181
Bravo, Laura 244, 255
Bremen 222
Bren Light Machine Gun 130, 196, 208, 240, 251
Breslau 148
Brest 70, 72, 73, 114

British Ambassador 95, 100
British Army iii, vi, xiv, xv, xiii, xxv, xxvi, xxviii, xxix, xxx, xxxi, 35, 36, 56, 57, 58, 73, 74, 75, 115, 183, 184, 217, 225, 230, 241, 247, 264, 266, 268, 294, 341
British Army & Commonwealth Units & Formations
  British 1st Army 174
  1st Airborne Division 230, 233
  1st Airborne Reconnaissance Squadron vii, 230
  1st Airlanding Reconnaissance Squadron 230
  2nd Irish Guards 235, 236, 338
  5th Indian Division 136
  5th Parachute Brigade 227
  6th Airborne Division 227
  7th Armoured Division 217, 218, 221, 223
  8th Army 119, 217
  8th Hussars 222
  9th Brigade 136
  10th Battalion Green Howards 227
  10th Brigade 136
  11th New Zealand Forestry Company 77
  12th (Yorkshire) Parachute Battalion xviii, 227, 228
  14 Field Company Royal Engineers 236
  14th Infantry Brigade 132
  14th New Zealand Forestry Company 77, 78
  21st Army Group 84, 192, 193
  22nd Armoured Brigade 222
  XXX Corps 218, 236
  43 (Wessex) Infantry Division 236
  50th (Northumbrian) Division 221
  57th Division 177
  99 Primary Training Corps 227
  100 Company REME 227
  231 Infantry Brigade 222
  295 Field Company Royal Engineers 221, 222, 339
  Army Air Corps 192, 216, 227, 228, 284, 298–300, 302, 305, 306, 317
  Auxiliary Military Pioneer Corps xxi, 57
  Durham Light Infantry 124, 138
  Intelligence Corps 169
  Leicestershire Regiment 126
  Queen's Royal Regiment (West Surrey) xvii, 124, 125, 126, 189, 248, 338
    1/5 Battalion Queen's Royal Regiment (West Surrey) xvii, xviii, xix, xx, 148, 154, 217, 218
    A Company 1/5 Battalion Queen's Royal Regiment (West Surrey) 219
  Pioneer Corps Records 332, 333, 334, 335, 336, 337
  Reconnaissance Corps 230
  Royal Army Medical Corps 143, 191, 221
  Royal Army Service Corps 174
  Royal Electrical and Mechanical Engineers (REME) xxii, 177, 227
  Royal Engineers xxv, 132, 174, 205, 221, 222, 236, 339
  Royal Scots Greys 131, 186
  Royal Signals ix, 112, 253
  Royal Sussex Regiment 138
  Sherwood Rangers 130, 154
British Cabinet 246, 258, 259, 339
British Chiefs of Staff 258
British Consulate, Casablanca 191
British Expeditionary Force (BEF) xiv, xxi, xxx, 49, 54, 57, 58, 59, 93, 131, 173
  BEF GHQ France 58, 61
British Trade Unions 260, 261
Brixton 252
Brock Hall 97- 99
Brodie, Captain 127
Bromsgrove Rovers Football Club 251
Brugada, José 108
Bruguera, Julián 187
Brunet de Sairigin, Lieutenant Gabriel 73
Brussels xviii, xix, 84, 86, 196
Buffalo LVT 215, 222
Buitrago 59
Buiza Fernández-Palacios, *Almirante* Miguel Republican Navy 42, 157
Burbage 77
Burgos 64, 95, 263, 300
Burma xvi, 113
Burton, Captain W.J. 138, 139
Busquets I Morant, Carles 113, 267, 278
Butler, Company Sergeant Major J. 176
Bystřice 146

Caboche, Camp Commandant Djelfa 46, 165, 169
Caen, France xviii, 221, 222, 228
Calne 77
Calvert, Brigadier Mike 216
Camarena Espinosa, Ángel Higinio (Alan Cooper) vii, ix, 292, 299
  Canaries & Franco 203
  enlistment 191
  name change 194
  post-war 254, 268
  SAS 195, 198
  SAS operations 202, 215
Camp 020 106-108
Camprodón 40

Camus, Albert xxx
Canada 76, 244
Canaries/Canary Islands 94, 101, 202, 203
Cano, Juan 79, 271, 311
Canovas Alonso, Antonio 236
Canovas, Sergeant Alfonso vii, viii, xix, 174, 236, 239, 241
    AUBE Mission 237, 238, 339
    enlistment 237
    Military Medal 240
Capua 218
Carabineros 74, 123
Cardenal Atence, Joaquín 59, 63, 271
Cardiff viii, 73, 158, 159, 254
Carlisle 182
Carnforth 182
Carnot 45, 159
Carreno, Mr v, 137, 138
Carrero Blanco, Almirante Luís xx, 265, 266
Cartagena 41, 155, 157, 161, 269, 273
Casa del Lupo 209
Casabayo, Fernando 279, 315, 338
    Camp 020 106
    Mrs Casabayo 109
    Selling secrets to Franco 107–109
    SOE SCONCE 103
Casablanca 66, 169, 191, 199, 237, 293
Casablanca Conference xvii
Casal Català xvi, 244, 245, 249
Caspe 95
Castel Sant' Angelo, Rome 214
Castelorizzo 134
Castiella, Fernando María xx, 259, 261
Castres 166
Catalunya xi, xii, xiii, 221, 236
Catholic church 36
Cator, Major H. J. 'Kid' 131, 132, 135
Catshill 250
Confederación Española de Derechas Autónomas (CEDA) xi, 36
Cenotaph, the viii, xx, xxix, 259, 260, 261, 266, 267, 349
Census 1951 243
Central Ordnance Depot 180
Centres d'Acceuil xiii, 42, 43
Centro Democrático Español 162
Cerbère 40, 42
Champs-Elysées parade 84
Channel Islands 55, 237, 341
Chapman MC, Major A.L. 'El Comandante' 82
Chard, Somerset xx, 85, 250
Charfield 350
Charleroi xix, 85

Chatto & Windus 251
Chiesa Di Rossano 205
Cherchell 45, 157, 159
Cheschem-el-Chelb 185
Chile 47, 293
Cholditz, General von iv, 84, 85
Chorley 56
Churchill, Sir Winston Leonard Spencer xviii, 93, 340, 342, 354
    becomes Prime Minister xiv, xxx, xxxi
    Franco Regime post-war 246, 257
    monarchy in Spain 245
    money laundering via Juan March 94
    Republican Spanish opinion 169
    resigns as Prime Minister xx
    SOE 110
    strengthening neutrality in Spain 93, 94, 100, 243, 245
    Victory Parade 223
Ciudad Real 112, 123, 274, 276, 287
Clark Blanch & Co 252
Clark, John 261
Clark, Lieutenant Brian 104
Closed Method 221
Club des Pins 169, 170, 237
Cochrane, Captain Archie 143, 148, 341
Cochrane Iron Works 251
Col d'Ares, france 40, 41
Colchester vii, 196, 215, 216
Cold War 257
Cole, Major Hubert vi, xxv, 175–179, 340
Collective Defence Plan (NATO) 257
Collioure 44, 45
Colomb-Béchar Camp 46, 156, 160, 165
Columna Durruti 45
Combined Training Centre 188, 338
Comisión Administrativo de Fondo de Ayuda a los Refugiados Españoles (CAFRE) xxi, 171
Commando dagger 130, 143
Commando Order xvii, 194
Commando service certificate ix
Commendation for Good Service v, 111
Committee for Help to Spanish Democrats 259
Commonwealth War Graves Commission iii, 211, 212, 294
Communist Party of Great Britain (CPGB) 263
Compagnies et Groupes de Travailleurs Espagnols (CTEs/GTEs) xv, xxi, 35, 48, 49, 55, 67, 166, 347
Compagnies et Groupes de Travailleurs Étrangers (CTEs/GTEs)
    CTEs employment, formation, organisation 47, 48, 49, 50, 54, 55, 64

French Labour Companies and Groups (CTEs and GTEs) x, xxi, 35, 47–50, 54, 55, 64–67, 153, 159, 160, 163
8e Régiment de Travailleurs Étrangers 46, 159
105e Compagnie de Travailleurs Étrangers 49, 166
117e Compagnie de Travailleurs Étrangers 166
159e Compagnie de Travailleurs Espagnols 55, 166
Compagnies et Groupes de Travailleurs Étrangers or *Compagnies de Travailleurs Espagnols*
  CTEs employment, formation, organisation 47, 48, 49, 50, 54, 55, 64
  French Labour Companies and Groups (CTE and GTE) x, xxi, 35, 47–50, 54, 55, 64–67, 153, 159, 160, 163
  8e Régiment de Travailleurs Étrangers 46, 159
  105e Compagnie de Travailleurs Étrangers 49, 166
  117e Compagnie de Travailleurs Étrangers 166
  159e Compagnie de Travailleurs Espagnols 55, 166
Companys I Jover, Lluís 56, 67, 244, 245
Concentration camps (French & Vichy) 44, 52, 167, 170, 338
Concentration camps (Nazi) xix, 54, 56, 67, 247
Concentration camps (Franco Regime) 157
Concordat (Franco's Spain and Vatican) xx, 258
Confederación Nacional de Trabajo (CNT) xxi, 47, 170, 179, 180
Constance, Juliet 253, 254
Constantine 177
Continuing the Fight xxx, xxxi, 150, 183, 216, 241, 260, 268
Cordes-sur-Ciel, france 227
Corey, Corporal George 219
Corinth 143
Corsica 169, 170
Cortesano, Armando 244
Cotleigh 85
Council of Ministers 243
Courts Martial 126
Covent Garden 253
Coventry 250, 251
Covin, Lieutenant Colonel J. B. 137
Craster, Major J.G. 174
CREFORCE 141
Crete v, vi, vii, x, xv, xvi, xix, xxv, xxix, 115, 198, 284–290, 346, 347
  Battle for Crete x, xvi, 115, 139, 142, 198
  Escape 150, 151, 152, 153, 154, 185, 186, 187, 199, 217, 250, 251, 291, 292
  Layforce 126, 127, 139, 141, 142, 184

Middle East Commando 132, 133, 134, 135, 137
POWs 120, 130, 140, 141, 143, 144, 146, 148, 149, 154, 190, 198, 199, 201, 246, 250, 251, 252
Crisis of Spain xi
Croix-de-Berny 84
Cumberledge/Saunders Group (SOE Crete) 152, 201
Cyprus 58, 289
Cyrenaica xvi
Czechoslovakia xiii, 146, 254

Dachau Concentration Camp xi, 56
Dahler 172
Dakota aircraft 205, 230
Daladier Decree 39
Daladier, Edouard xiii, 39
Dalmau i Norat, Francesc 75, 76, 245, 271, 316
Dalton, Hugh (Ministry for Economic Warfare) 110
Daly, Lieutenant Colonel D.R. 137
Damas 117
Darby, Arthur 'Tim' Claude 148
Darlan, *Amiral* François xvii, 93, 162, 167, 343
Davies, Ernest 261
D-Day xvii, xviii, 57, 82, 95, 111, 154, 192, 196, 221, 222, 226, 227, 288, 341
de Barcenas, Domingo 257
de Borbón, Don Juan xx, 245
de Gaulle, *Général* Charles André Joseph Marie xiv, xviii, xxvii, 72
  de Gaulle visit to Trentham Park xiv, 72, 73
  de Gaulle and Spanish *maquis* xxvii, 67
  de Gaulle and Britain xiv, xviii, 162
de la Mora, Constancia 43
de Lara, Major L.H. Officer Commanding No.1 Spanish Company 82, 85
de Larminat, Colonel Edgar 118, 119
de Miguel Montañés, Miguel 59, 61
Délegué Général 162
Delgado, Andrés 249, 285, 317
Deller, Lieutenant John 237
Demobilisation xxx, 57, 182, 216, 247, 250, 251
Denison smock 195, 209
Denison, Lieutenant 198
Denmark 70, 216
Dentz, *Général* Henri 119
Depot Commando Training and Holding Unit (DCTHU) 150, 152, 284, 285, 288, 289, 290, 292
Derby 180, 249, 315
Díaz, Juan 251

Díaz, Paco 157
Dickson, Captain Archibald (SS *Stanbrook*) xiii, 158, 159, 341, 344, 346
Diên Biên Phù 237
Dieppe xvii
Director Naval Intelligence 93, 94
Dives River 227, 228
División Española de Voluntarios 245
Dieudonna, Company Quartermaster Sergeant L.A.A. 75
Djavel Jaures 164
Djebel Dufeir 135
Djebel Negus 135
Djelfa Concentration Camp vi, xvii, 46, 47, 55, 162, 164, 166, 179
  accommodation 166, 167, 168
  conditions 166, 167
  liberation 169, 170, 171
  numbers/types of prisoners 47, 160, 165, 166
Djenien Bou Rezg 160
Dominican Republic 47
Donovan, Colonel William 'Wild Bill' 94
Dordogne 238
Dover 253
Dresden xvi, xix, 164
Dronne, Captain Raymond 84
Drop Zone X-ray vii, 231
Dugdale, Mr John, MP 249
Dunham House (SOE) 97
Dunkirk, France xiv, xxiii, xxx, 55, 64, 66, 93, 119, 217, 342, 343
Durée de la guerre 48, 50, 52, 54, 115, 119
Duvivier-Bône 177

Eastleigh 226
Ebro River xiii
Economic Aid (Franco's Spain) xx, 258
Eddy, Colonel William 164, 167, 169, 339
Eden, Anthony 172, 246, 339
Edinburgh 63, 70, 344
Edwards, Mr Bob MP 261
Egea, Ignacio 106, 271, 279, 313
Egypt xv, 200
  French Forces 118, 192
  Middle East Commando v, vi, xv, xvi, 115, 126, 134, 135, 136, 138, 139, 142, 151, 152
Eindhoven 236
Eisenhower, General Dwight D xviii, 104, 167
El Alamein, Battle of xvii, 217, 245
El Guerrah 177
El Hogar Español xvi, 244, 249
El polvorilla (the Tinderbox) 176
Elboeuf 201

Emnals, Davis 261
Enfield Webley pistol 195
Eritrea xv, 132, 135, 136, 188
Escape and evade 141, 150, 195, 199, 211
Espallargas Monferrer, Manuel v, xxiv, 91, 251, 265, 313
  French Foreign Legion & Narvik 68, 70
  Manuel Certificate of Good Conduct, King's Birthday Honours List 111
  SOE 97, 98, 103, 279
  Spanish Ex-Servicemen's Association 260
Esquerra Republicana 201
Esteve, Fernando v, vi, vii, viii, xxiv, 121, 130, 285, 317
  1 SSR 186, 189, 291
  Crete 133, 151
  Germany 223, 224, 225
  London 252, 253, 259
  Normandy 221, 222
  Queen's Royal Regiment (West Surrey) 218
  Volturno River 218, 219, 220
Esteve, Père 178
Ethiopia xii, 38, 13
Euskadi Ta Askatasuna (ETA) xxi, 226
Eusko-Etxea (Basque Centre) xiii, 244, 247
Evans, Colonel Arthur MP 73
Evans, Lieutenant Colonel Ivor 98
Eve, Lieutenant 219
Evetts, Major General John 137
Extremadura 40, 58, 64, 123, 276, 288

Fairburn-Sykes knife 195
Fairford 196
Fajardo, Antonio and Manuel 256
Fajardo, Joaquín v, vi, viii, ix, 126, 285, 319
  Crete 133
  end of the war 29, 248
  escaping Syria 121, 126
  Middle East Commando 126, 153
  POW 144-147, 149
Fajardo, Juan 260
Falaise Pocket xviii
Falange Española xi
Fallinbostel 222
Fanny Cap Badge 130, 151
Fanny dagger 127, 130
Far East xxix, 85, 95, 182, 241, 247
Farran, Major Roy 190, 192, 341
  Italian detachment 203, 204, 205
  Operation TOMBOLA 207, 208, 209, 211
Father of the Chapel 260
Favrel, Charles 71
Fernández, Francisco 103

Fernández, Marcial vii, 235, 236
Fernández, Teodoro 63
Fernando Po xvi, 109, 110
Ferrandiz Boj, Joaquín 59, 61, 64
Ferris, Major A.J 173
Fifth columnists 74
Fineboy, Daniel 165
Finland 70, 117
First World War xi
Fleming, Lieutenant Commander Ian xxx, 92, 94, 101, 344
Foix, France xviii, 236, 237, 240
Football iv, 75, 153, 154, 244, 247
Force 133 xvi, 152, 201
Force H 93
Force Z xv, 136
'The Forgotten Prisoners' 263
Fort William 95
Fournier, Captain 203
Fox Primary School 257
Fox-Davies, Captain Harry xv, 123, 124, 130, 132
Fraga Iribarne, Manuel 265, 268
France, 1940 Invasion of 48, 193, 237
Franceville Plage 227
Franco Bahamonde, *General* Francisco viii, xii, 36, 75, 92, 94, 95, 111, 144, 202, 203, 215, 244, 245, 256, 259, 265, 341, 342, 344
   Caudillo xii, xxix, 38, 202
   death xx. xxix, 182, 260, 268
   Franco Regime xx, xxx, 47, 70, 183, 228, 236, 237, 242, 261, 264, 266
   Franco Regime non-belligerence 93, 94, 100, 101, 114, 169, 245, 246
   Franco Regime and the Allies 245, 246, 257, 258
   Generalissimo xii, 38
   Hitler xv, 100
   Mussolini xii, xv, 100
   Spanish Civil War xiii, xxvii, 39
   survival post-war 245, 246, 256, 257, 258
   Vichy Regime 35, 56, 67
Franco-Spanish border x, 37, 50, 52
Francs-Tireurs et Partisans (FTP) xxi, xxvii, 67
Franks, Lieutenant Colonel Brian 193
Franksa Kirkegarr Cemetery iv, 71
Fraser, Peter Prime Minister of New Zealand 77
Free French Army xvi, xviii, xix, xxvii, 72, 108, 110, 119, 120, 123, 162, 184, 186, 192, 193, 198, 199, 214, 237, 293
   1e Bataillon d'Infanterie de l'Air (1e BIA) 192, 293
   3e BIA 192, 198, 214
   4e BIA 192, 193, 293

   1e Compagnie d'Infanterie de l'Air (1e CIA) 192
   1eCompagnie de Chasseurs Parachutistes 192
   2eCIA 192
   2e Division Blindée (Leclerc's 2nd Armoured Division) iv, xviii, xxvii, 84, 237, 171
   3e Régiment de Chasseurs Parachutistes (3e RCP) 192
   6e Division Française Libre 119
   501e Régiment de chars de combat 84
   La Nueve (9e Compagnie of the *Régiment de Marche du Tchad)* xviii, 82, 84, 171, 343
   Régiment de Marche du Tchad xviii, 84, 171
Free French Recruitment Office, London 108
Free Zone, France xiv
Freedom for Prisoners 259
Freedom for Spain xxx, 259, 261
French Armistice xiv, xvi, 48, 50, 51, 54, 55, 66, 67, 73, 118, 119, 190
French Interior Ministry 45
French Maghreb 159, 162, 341
French Territorial Commands 49
French West Africa 160
Frente Popular xii, 38
Freyberg VC GCMG KCB KBE DSO & 3 Bars, Lieutenant General Bernard 139

Gallego Santines, Consuelo 153
García Carrión, Juan 251
García Flores, José iv, v
   Légion Étrangère 68, 69
   No. 1 Spanish Company 75, 78
   Post war viii, ix, 253, 254, 264, 265
   SOE (SCONCE) v, 101, 102, 105, 113, 281
   Wireless training and Royal Signals 103, 112
García Garrigos, Francisco vi, 151, 187, 286
García Navarro, Antonia 236
García, Fausto Miguel vi, 161, 323
   children in Britain 161
   internment 162, 166
   Orán 161, 162, 163
García, Francisco 325
García, Gabriel (3rd SAS) 199, 293
García, José (3rd SAS) 198, 293
García, Sara xxiv, 264, 265
García, Teodosia vi, 163
García, Toni (No. 51/52 Middle East Commando) 136. 188, 291
Gardner, Selina 79, 80
Gasa Camp 46
Gaullist/Vichy struggle 52
Gedaref 134, 135
Genaifa / Geneifa xvi, 126, 127, 132, 134, 135, 137, 138, 185, 186, 187

INDEX 357

General Assembly, United Nations xx, 257
Geneva Convention 56
Germany Army
   German 6th Army xvii
   German 15th Army xix, 222
   LI German Mountain Corps vii, 209
German surrender xvii, xx, 84, 215, 222, 247
Geronimo, Francisco (Frank Williams) iv, v, xxiv, 199, 216, 320
   1 SSR 152, 187
   Crete vii
   escape from Syria 117, 118, 121, 126
   escape and evasion in Crete vi, xvi, 141, 150, 199-201
   Légion Étrangère iv, v, 52, 53, 117, 118
   marriage 244, 254, 255
   Middle East Commando v, 135, 286
   name change 193,194
   post-war viii, ix, 244, 254, 255
   SAS vii, 191, 194, 195, 292
   SAS operations France 198, 199
   SAS operations in Italy (TOMBOLA) 204, 208, 211, 213, 214
Ghent 222
GHQ Liaison Regiment 95
Giado Camp, Libya 60
Gibraltar xxix, 104, 162, 179, 258, 340
   escape/enlistment of Republican Spaniards 57, 76, 237
   GOLDEN EYE 94
   Operation FELIX xv, 94, 100, 114
   POWs (Middle East Commando & SAS) 143, 144, 198
   SOE 94, 274
Gijon xiii, 38, 153, 272
Gimeno, Pascual vii, 238
Giraud, *Général* Henri xvi, 164, 167
Glasgow xix, 75, 79, 95, 162, 179, 247
Godfrey CB, Admiral John 94
GOLD Beach 221
GOLDEN EYE (SOE/Naval Intelligence) 94, 344
Gómez, Emilio 63
Gómez, Francisco 76, 103
Gómez, Serrafín 133, 287
Gondar 134, 136
Goole 249
Gough, Major Freddie 230, 233
Governor General of Algeria (*Gouverneur Général d'Algérie*) 157
Goya 263
Graham, Lieutenant Colonel J.M. 186
Granada 250, 256, 271, 272, 273, 176, 277, 285
Grande Catalan, Antonio 57, 58

185 Labour Company 57, 58, 59
Escape from France 61, 63, 64
No. 1 Spanish Company 88, 91
SOE (SCONCE) 97, 110, 111, 280
Spanish Civil War 58
Granell, Lieutenant Armando 84
Grangeaud, Second Lieutenant 237
Greece invasion xvi, 100, 131, 132
Greenwood, Mr Anthony MP 250
Grendon Hall (SOE telegraphy) 101
Griffiths, James 261
Grittleton 77
Groupement de Travailleurs Étrangers du Levant (GTEL) 119
Guadarrama 123
Guardias de Asalto 98, 251
Guards Division 236
Guelma 169
Guerrilla groups/warfare 98, 104, 110, 127, 169, 170, 238, 256, 343
Guinea xvi, 109, 110, 344
Guinness, Lieutenant Colonel Robert 104
Gurs Camp, France xiv, 43, 44, 48, 52, 58, 347, 185
   internees (Basques, Republican Air Force) 43, 153
   Labour Company xiv, 59, 61
Guscott, Sergeant vii, 205, 207, 208, 210
Gutierrez, Antonio (death by stabbing) 79, 272

Haafjelder Peninsula, Norway 70
Hadjerat M'guil 160
Haifa 123
Haig's Motor Limited 107
Hall o' the Hill Camp and the 226 55, 56
Hambro, Lieutenant Richard 96, 338
Hamburg, Germany xix, 154, 215, 222
Harburg Forest, Germany 222
Haro, Rodrigo iv, xxiv, 79, 81, 83, 269
   marriage iv, 79, 80
   No.1 Spanish Company iv, v, 78, 90, 269, 310
   woodwork/sawmill 79
Hartenstein Hotel, Arnhem viii, 232, 233
Harvey, Lieutenant Ken 209
Haymarket, London 261
Hendaye, France 251
   meetings xv, 93, 94
   Spanish Civil War 38
Hepburn, Major J. 174
Heraklion, Crete 132
Heras, Braulio vi, 149, 287, 319
   POW & death 146, 148, 150, 295
Herault 43, 44

Hereford 247
Hermon, Captain K.E. 138
Hernández Jiménez, Salvador 165
High Commissioner of the Levant 119
Hillgarth, Commander Alan 93, 108, 342
   British Consul in Mallorca 93
   Gallipoli 93
   GOLDEN EYE 94
   Naval Attaché in Madrid 93, 94, 99, 162
   Naval Intelligence 93, 94
Himmler, Heinrich 245
Hiroshima xx, 247
Hispano-Suiza, Barcelona 201
Hitler, Adolf xi, xii, xv, xvii, xxvii, xxviii, 92, 111, 114, 123, 254
   Commando Order xviii, 194
   death xiv
   German-Spanish meetings/discussions/agreements xv, 93, 100
   invasion of Iberian Peninsula xvi, 94, 100, 114
HMS *Daring* 178
HMS *Decoy* 131
HMS *Hereward* 131
HMS *Talisman* 185
Hoare, Sir Samuel 93, 104
   British Ambassador in Madrid 94, 100, 162
   keeping Spain neutral 169, 243
Hidalgo de Cisneros, General Ignacio 43
Hoenfels 145
Hoffen 237
Hogar Español xvi, 244, 249
Holding Battery, Boroughbridge 216
Hollywood 112
Home Office (Aliens Department) 193, 226, 338
Homs, Syria 54, 117, 118, 119, 218
Horsa Glider 230
Hotchkiss machine gun 240
House of Commons xiv, 172, 226
Houses of Parliament 226, 250, 257
Hubbard, Major W.T. 174
Huesca xii, 271, 275
Hughes, Margaret Kathleen 107
Hunstanton 221
Hussars 135, 138, 222
Hussein Day, Algeria 174, 176, 191, 198, 297–231

Ibarolla, Agustín 263
Iberian Peninsula xv, 38, 92, 94, 99, 100, 104, 109
Imperial War Museum xxiv, xxvi, 35, 42, 66, 67, 120, 144, 170, 339
Improvised rafting 128
Independent Belgian Air Service Company 193
Industrialisation in Spain 36

Inter-Allied Commission 170
Inter-Allied Mission xvii
International Brigades xii, xiii, xxix, 113, 161, 345
   British watch lists 74
   in internment camps 43, 45, 47
   Internationales 45
Internment camps x, xiii, xxvii, 39, 43, 44, 54, 56, 65, 75, 98, 154, 160, 176, 183
Iovino, Francisco 103, 104, 280, 313
Irala, José María 'Joe' vii, xix, 226, 228, 230, 232, 233
Iron Curtain 257
Italian Detachment (SAS) vii, 204

Jaifa, Egypt 122
Japan xvi, xx, 241, 247
Jebel ech Chambi 158
Jedburgh Teams 99, 196
Jeger, Mr George, MP 249, 261
Jellicoe, Major the Earl 190
Jewish European refugees 160
Jews xii, 47, 131, 160, 161, 166
Jocelyne, Arthur escape from Dunkirk 66, 339
Jodl, *Generaloberst* Alfred xx, 247
John Bull Magazine 176
Jones, Captain O. 77
Jones, Major D.W. 174
Jornet, Antonio 75, 76, 273, 316
Juan Carlos I xx, 265
Judes (Septfonds) Internment Camp 43, 44
Junta de Ayuda a los Refugiados Españoles (JARE) 243
Juntas de Defensa xi
Jurado, José (Company Sergeant Major, No. 1 Spanish Company) 85, 91, 104, 269, 280, 313

Kabrit, Egypt 137, 188
Kaplowitch, Captain 100
Kasos, Greece 134, 135
Kasserine Internment Camp 46
Kasserine Pass xvii, 158, 170
Katana, Syria 117, 118
Keevil 228
Kemp, Peter 95, 99, 342
Kensal Road 260
Keren 136
Keyes, Geoffrey 185
Khor Abd-er-Razzag 134
Khor Kumar 134
Killwinning, Scotland 79
Kineton 179
King's College Cambridge 143
Kirk, Flight Sergeant 238

Kirkpatrick, Piper David 209
Knocker, Major 117, 118, 119
Koffler, Dr 166
Kosta Spirachi (Francisco Geronimo) 200, 201
Krotos 201

L'Hôtel Fourre 59
La Chapelle Launey 59
La Junquera, Spain 40
La Retirada x, xxiii, 37, 38
La Spezia, Italy 205
La Zarza, Spain 123
Labour Companies (BEF)
    No. 185 Spanish Labour Company iv, xiv, xxiii, 57, 58, 68
    No. 185 Spanish Labour Company evacuation 64
    No. 185 Spanish Labour Company formation xiv, 58, 59
    No. 185 Spanish Labour Company organisation 60, 82
    No. 31 Labour Company 59
    No. 4 Labour Group, France 59
    No. 4 Railway Labour Company 59
Labour government 169, 257
Labour Party 259, 261
Labrador, Spain 250
Ladgrove Road 251
Lagara Morillez, Alberto 110
Lagos 110
Lake, Captain Peter 238, 338
Lamsdorf, Germany 146
Lanchester sub machine gun 130
Lapie, Pierre-Olivier 70
Larkhill Camp 227
Larzac, France 50, 70, 117
Latour-de-Carol-Osseja 40
Laws, Lieutenant D.V. 198
Laycock, Robert ix, xv, 115, 136–137, 139, 141, 143, 150, 185, 243, 290, 343
    Layforce & Crete 137, 139, 141, 143, 150, 290
    Operation FLIPPER 185
Lazareno, Manolo 244
Le Bourg, France 59
Le Caprice viii, 252, 253
Le Goulet, France 59
Le Grand, B. Captain 74
Le Landron, France 54
Le Nebourg, France iv, 83
Le Perthus, France 40, 42
Le Pont de la Guillette 221
Leadenhall Street 252
League of Nations xiv

Lebanon xvi, 115, 117, 118, 119, 154
Leclerc, Général iv, xviii, xxvii, 84, 171, 237
Lee Enfield rifle 130
Lees, Captain Mike 209, 210, 211
Légion Étrangère and Volunteer Marching Units
    Légion Étrangère iv, xxvii, xxix, 35, 40, 48, 50, 52, 53, 57, 68, 69, 70, 72, 74, 98, 107, 112, 117, 118, 119, 123, 154, 155, 167, 170, 171, 172, 173, 178, 190, 198, 199, 201, 252, 292, 293, 341
    Régiments Étrangers d'Infanterie (REIs)
    1e REI 50, 68, 70
    2e REI 50, 52, 68
    3e REI 50, 68, 190
    4e REI 54
    6e REI v, 54, 117, 119, 120, 121, 123
    11e REI 54
    12e REI 52, 54
    13e Demi-Brigade de la Légion Étrangère (13e DBLE) 54, 68
    13e DBLE xvi, 54, 68, 119,120, 186, 189
    13e Demi-Brigade de Montagne de la Légion Étrangère (13e DBMLE) xxi, 54, 57, 68, 70, 107
        arrival in UK 72
        Avonmouth xv, 73
        disbandment 1940 73
        Norway xiv, 70, 107
        Trentham Park & de Gaulle xiv, 72
    Bataillons de Marche de Voluntaries Étrangers (BMVE) xiv, xxi, 35, 51, 52, 115, 117, 153, 284-290
    1e Bataillon de Marche de Volontaires Étrangers (1e BMVE) 51, 115, 117, 153
    11e Bataillon de Marche de Volontaires Étrangers (11e BMVE) 115
    Régiments de Marche de Volontaires Étrangers (RMVEs) 115
    21e RMVE 50, 54
    22e RMVE 50, 54, 115
    23e RMVE 50, 51, 54
    Dépôt Métropolitain de la Légion Étrangère de Sathonay 52
    Dépôt Commun des Régiments Étrangers (Foreign Légion Training Depot, DCRE) xxi, 52, 190, 68, 69
    Étrangers Volontaires pour la Durée de la Guerre (EVDG) 50, 115
    Regiments' Training Depot (DCRMVE) xxi, 50, 115
Lend Lease xvi
Lequerica, José Felix 246
Lett, Major Gordon 205

Lewes Bomb 195
Lewes, Jock 195
Libuše, Kodešovă vii, 255
Lille, France 64, 84
Lincolnshire 230
Linguistic difficulties 96, 173
Liverpool 76, 101, 278, 282, 283, 315
Livingston, Mr Harry 162
Llons Fontavillas, José 76
Llorens White, Antonio 59, 64
Long Rage Desert Group (LRDG) vii, xxi, xxiv, 184, 188, 189, 190, 194
Longbridge 250
López Martín, Francisco (Henry Martin) 191, 194, 202, 293
López, José 76, 294, 304
López, Manuel 64, 66
López, Private (murder of French officer) 177
Los Reclutas vii, 263, 265
Lumbrera, Francisco vi, 148, 149, 150, 287, 295
Luque, José xxiv, 103, 273, 313

Maas River 222, 230
Mac, William 104
MacArthur, General Douglas xix
Machado, Antonio 242
Macintosh, Major Charles 205
MacLeod, Brigadier Roderick 193
Madagascar 238
Madrid 58, 177, 190, 202, 203, 230, 266, 269–276, 288, 292, 301, 243
  British Embassy & Intelligence Services 93, 94, 100, 108, 162, 256
  Pact of Madrid xx, 258
  Spanish Civil War xii, xiii, 35, 36, 38, 45, 58, 64, 66, 70, 123
Maginot Line 48, 166, 237
Maison Carrée, Algeria 176, 191, 202, 298, 300, 301, 302
Maknassy Camp 46
Málaga xii, 52, 170, 199, 269 – 277, 292
Maleme, Crete 141
Malta 276
Maltese gangs 252
Manchester xviii, 96, 107, 193
Manning, Mrs Leah 226, 228
Manresa, Spain 236, 275
Montauban, France 249
Maquis 56, 67, 198, 217, 236, 238, 240
Marble Arch 259, 261
March Ordinas, Juan 93, 94
Marchelépot 54
Margate 66

Marín, Basilio v, 120, 145, 287, 319
Market Harborough 106
Marseille, France 40, 52, 70
Marshal Aid 257
Marshall, Lieutenant John 217, 232, 233
Marshills Camp 76, 77
Martinez Restaurant viii, 252, 257, 264, 265, 268
Martínez, Francisco 74
Martínez, Herminio 244
Martinez, Miguel v, vi, xxiv, 128, 129, 133, 138, 151, 180, 248, 249
Marylebone Police Court 108
Más, Jaume 266, 267, 274, 281, 312
Massiet, General 117
Mateo, Victoriano 76, 317
Matthews, Herbert 40
Mauthausen-Gusen Concentration Camp xiii, xv, xx, xxiii, 56, 247, 346
Mayhew, Christopher 257
Mayne, R.B. (Paddy) 190
McGibbon, Captain Bob commanding Spaniards in Middle East Commando 115, 126, 127, 129, 130, 131, 132, 154, 252
  Crete 138, 139, 140, 141
McGinty, Major (Farran) 208
Mediterranée-Niger (Mer-Niger) Compagnie 160
Meheri Zabbens 157
Meknassy 157
Melville, Major D.W., MC 131
Mena, Juan 148, 150, 288, 318
Mena, Vicente 218, 221, 288, 320
Meridien, England 182
Mers-el-Kebir xv, 93, 162
Merville Battery 227
Metemma-Gondar Road 134
Mexico xxvii, 47, 157, 159, 171, 172, 176, 242, 243, 250
MI5 74, 107, 109
MI6 94, 108, 343
MI9 201, 99
Middle East Commando iii, v, vi, xxiv, 115, 124, 127, 130, 131, 132, 137, 140, 141, 143, 148, 150, 151, 174, 185, 186, 187, 246, 252, 294, 295, 339
  No. 50 Middle East Commando iii, v, xiv, xv, xviii, 40, 115, 137, 179, 180, 182, 188, 190, 198, 217, 220, 221, 242, 249, 250, 251, 267, 284, 290, 348
  Crete v, 132, 133, 134
  establishment 119, 124, 125, 126
  POWs 145
  training 127, 130, 131
  No. 51 Middle East Commando xv, 131, 135, 136, 185–188

No. 52 Middle East Commando 131, 132, 134, 138, 154
No. 7 Commando 137, 148
No. 8 Commando 136, 137
No. 11 (Scottish) Commando xv, 136, 137, 165
Layforce xvi, 115, 119, 136, 137, 138, 139, 140, 141, 150, 184, 186, 187, 201, 284–290, 292
  A Battalion Layforce 137
  B Battalion Layforce 137, 138
  C Battalion Layforce 137, 150, 138
  D Battalion Layforce xvi, 119, 137–141, 290, 292
Middle East Commando Depot 131, 150, 186
Middle East Commando operations
  ABSTENTION 134, 137
  COMPASS 132
  FLIPPER xvi, 185
  WORKSHOP 136
Middle East Forces (MEF) xxi, 124, 127, 128, 129, 174, 338
Middlewich 182
Miguel de Cervantes, cruiser vi, 157, 158
Miguel de Unamuno Camp 64
Milan, Italy xix, 211, 212, 295
Military Intelligence (Research) (MI (R)) xxi, 124
Military Medal xvii, xviii, xix, xxviii, 126, 184, 210, 219, 240, 241, 338
Military Police xxi, 72, 123
Miller, Major C.D.O. 135
Mills grenades 240, 241
Mills, Lieutenant Colonel A. F. MC 174
Minaya, Spain 58
Ministry of Economic Warfare (MEW) xxi, 186
Ministry of Industrial Production and Labour 160
Miranda de Ebro Camp 64
Missing List 141
Mittelhauser, *Général* Eugène 118
Moascar xv, 124
Modena, Italy 207, 208, 211
Mola, *General* Emilio 38
Molina, Alfred 112
Molina, Esteban 97, 112, 274, 281, 310, 338
Molotov-Ribbentrop Pact xiv
Molto Stanco 204, 208, 211
Mon Pinçon 222
Monckton 193
Monte Cassino xviii
Monte Cusna 208
Montgomery, Field Marshall Sir Bernard xx, 222, 223, 230
Montgomery, Michael (Miguel Bon) ix, xxiv
Montilla, Spain 250, 186
Montoursie, Lorenzo 103

Moor Park. England 192
Moore, Henry 263
morale of Spaniards 95, 96, 97, 104, 131, 177
Morand Camp 45, 46, 159
Morgan, Fr Ricardo xxiv
Moroccan troops (*Goumiers*) 160
Morocco xi, xvii, 36, 46, 54, 64, 67, 68, 73, 94, 95, 98, 155, 159, 160, 161, 162, 164, 165, 169, 174, 190, 268
Moscow Dynamo 247
Mowlem, Peter 148
Muirhead, Major 247
Mulberry Harbour 82
Munich Agreement xiii
Muñoz, Francisco 103
Muntane, José 106, 285, 313
Murphy, Robert 162
Mussolini, Benito xii, xv, xix, xxviii, 100, 111
Mutual Defence Assistance Agreement xx, 258

Nagasaki, Japan xx, 247
Nantes, France 38, 59
Naples, Italy xvii, 218
Narvik, Norway xxviii, 68, 70, 72, 73, 98, 107, 108, 136, 344
National Joint Committee for Spanish Relief xxii, 39, 226
(Spanish) Nationalist POW Camp 198
North Atlantic Treaty Organisation (NATO) xxii, 258, 259, 261
Naturalised British ix, 160, 254
Navarrete, Francisco 120, 121, 126, 146, 267, 288
Navarro, Francisco 103, 274, 282, 312
Navy Army and Air Force Institute (NAAFI) xxi, 245, 249
Nazi Germany xiii, xiv, xv, xxvii, 38
  concentration camps 56
  Nazification 159
  Nuremberg Laws xii
  Operation BARBAROSSA xvi, 100
  Operation FELIX xv, xvi, 94, 100
Nederrijn, Netherlands 232
Negrín Committee 105
Negrín, Dr Juan, Prime Minister of Spain xii, 243, 244, 257
Nelson, Sir Frank (SOE) 93
Neutrality xi, xiv, xxvii, xxx, 36, 93, 110, 243, 245
New Forest 96
New York Times 40
New Zealand Forestry Companies xvi, 76, 77, 78
New Zealand Maori Infantry 139, 140, 141
Newman, Dumbo 168, 170, 339
News Chronicle 250

Newsweek 257
Niven, David 95
Noel-Baker, Mr Philip MP 249
Nogueroles, Agustín 267
Nogues, *Général* Charles-Auguste 162
Nones, Elwyn 261
Non-Intervention xxvii, 38, 39, 42, 226
Normandy iv, xviii, xxx, 56, 57, 82, 84, 86, 112, 153, 154, 193, 196, 198, 217, 221, 222, 227, 228
North Africa 155, 158, 165, 166, 171, 172, 174, 179, 183, 203, 249
North Stoneham 226
Norway xiv, xxix, 57, 68, 70, 71, 72, 184, 215, 230, 268
Notting Hill 257
Nuffield Orthopedic Centre 221

Oberkommando der Wehrmacht (OKW) xv, 94, 194
Obis Campo, Antonio iv, vi, viii, ix, xxv, 46, 55, 165, 166, 167, 168, 171, 179, 180, 181, 182, 251, 325
Occupied Zone, France xiv
Office for Strategic Studies (OSS) xvii, xxii, xxv, 162, 164, 169, 170, 179, 196, 345
Oliveira Avidaño, José (escape from Dunkirk) 66
Oosterbeek xix, 233
Operations
    AGREEMENT xvii, 188
    AVALANCHE xvii, 218
    BARBAROSSA xvi, 100
    BLACKCOCK xix, 222
    BLUECOAT 222
    CATAPULT xv, 93
    CHARIOT xvi, 59
    COBRA 198
    DRAGOON xviii, 345
    DYNAMO xiv, 49, 64, 66, 93, 345
    FELIX xv, xvi, 94, 100
    FLIPPER xvi, 185
    GOODWOOD 222
    HUSKY xvii, 218
    JUBILEE xvii
    MARKET GARDEN xviii, 230, 236
    MERKUR xvi
    PLUNDER 222
    SHINGLE 350
    TORCH xvii, 74, 109, 155, 164, 167, 172, 190, 193, 203
Opus Dei 265
Orán, Algeria vi, xv, 41, 42, 45, 52, 70, 117, 155, 157–163, 166, 170, 177, 293, 345

Orchudesch 172
Orléansville 45, 159
Organisation Todt 55, 67, 339
Orne River 228
Ortega, Eliane vi, xxv, 159, 166
Ouarsenis 45, 159
Ouled Hills 46
Oxford, England 36, 96, 107, 108, 221, 247
Oxford Street 261

Pack Howitzer, 75mm 204, 211
Packington Park Camp 182
Pacts of Madrid 258
Paddington, London 108, 252, 254
Pair Fishing Company Ltd 113
Palestine 117, 118, 119, 122, 123, 188, 199, 292, 294, 298, 307
Palestinian Army 144
Palmyra, Syria 117
Pamiers, France 236, 237, 99, 100, 111, 112, 182, 191, 192, 227, 230, 252
parachute training viii, xviii
    No.1 Parachute Training School (PTS), Ringway xviii, 96–100, 111, 112, 193, 214, 227, 230
    Polish Parachute Centre 192
    1 SSR 188
    SAS 191, 192, 193, 214
    SCONCEs 96, 97, 98, 99, 100, 111, 112
Pardo García, José 251
Paris xxii, 54, 56, 93, 162, 198, 199, 227, 241, 243, 252, 263
    Liberation 1944 iv, xviii, xxvii, 67, 84, 343
Parish, Captain C. 138, 140
Partido Nacional Vasco (PNV) 244
Partido Socialista Obrero Español (PSOE) xxii
Patterson, Captain Joseph 191, 192
Patton, General George S. 198, 202
Pearl Harbour xvi
Pedder, Lieutenant Colonel R.R. 137
Penicillin 221
Pentonville Prison 66
Pereira Martínez, Francisco 123, 288
Pérez Miranda, Augusto iv, v, viii, 69, 86, 90, 97, 98, 99, 256, 282, 316, 349
Parkins, Robert 59, 62
Pétain, Maréchal Henri Philippe xiv, 56, 67, 73, 162
Petts Wood, England 252, 264
Phantom (GHQ Liaison Regiment) 95
Philby, Kim xxx, 92, 95, 96
Phillippeville, Algeria 177, 193
Phoney War 54

INDEX

Pi I Sunyer, Carles 244
Picardie, France 50, 54
Piccadilly Circus 263
Pickering, Lance Corporal (SOE) 105
Pino, Miguel 260, 267, 275, 312
Pioneer Corps
  10 Group, Pioneer Corps 76, 338
  37 Group Pioneer Corps 76
  56 Group, Pioneer Corps 76
  91 Group, Pioneer Corps 174
  92 Group, Pioneer Corps 174
  No.1 Palestinian Company 131
  No.1 Spanish Company iii, iv, v, ix, xvi, xvii, xviii, xix, xx, xxiv, 57-114
    361 Pioneer Company reinforcement 179, 180
    Ardennes 57, 85
    enlistment xxvii, 74, 75, 110, 113, 278–283
    football team 75
    forestry v, xvi, 76, 77, 78, 78, 79, 84, 85, 88, 180, 340, 343
    killed in Plymouth Blitz xv, 76, 294
    Normandy 82, 84, 86, 112
    Plymouth xv, 64, 72, 75, 76, 77, 92, 93, 98, 104, 107, 109, 294
    stabbing incident November 1943 79
    standard ix, 87, 270
    Victory Parade in Taunton 87
  337 (Alien) Pioneer Company xvii, 173, 191, 320, 330
  338 (Alien) Pioneer Company 174
  361 (Alien) Pioneer Company vi, viii, xvii, xix, xx, 68, 84, 109, 153, 162, 165, 166, 167– 183, 191, 198, 202, 245, 247, 249, 250, 251, 252, 260, 267, 285, 288–290, 293, 297–330
  362 (Alien) Pioneer Company xix, 73, 74, 152, 174, 179, 182, 249, 250, 284, 286–290, 298, 299, 305, 330, 331
  363 (Alien) Pioneer Company xix, 174, 179, 182, 191, 249, 250, 292, 300–303, 332, 335
  364 (Alien) Pioneer Company 174
  406 (Alien) Pioneer Company 174, 332–335
  Pioneer Corps Base Depot (PCBD) 152
  Pioneer Corps Records Office 193
Pistolerismo xi, 36
Plymouth
  Plymouth Blitz xv, 76, 294
  Plymouth, Citadel Barracks 64
  Plymouth Millbay Station xv, 76, 92
  Plymouth Visit by king and Queen 76
  Plymouth Weston Mill cemetery 294
Plympton 98
Po Valley, Italy 209

Poland xiv, xix, 95, 117, 144, 146, 148
Polikarpov 59
Pons Prades, Pedro xxx, 43, 44, 48, 344
Pont-sur-Yonne 54
Pope-Smith, Lieutenant Colonel J. S. 174, 175
Port Ibrahim 187
Port Said 134
Port Sudan 134, 135
Port Tewfik 187
Portbou 40
Porte d'Italie 84
Portillo, Luís Gabriel 266, 267
Portillo, Michael 266
Portugal xxvii, 67, 92, 93, 94, 103, 343
Potsdam Conference xx
Prats de Mollo, Spain 40, 41, 42
Prayols, France 240
Préfecture d'Alger xiv, 159
Prestataires Militaires Étrangers (PME) xiv, xxii, 47, 58
Prestwick 193
Prestwick Airport 195
Primo de Rivera, *General* Miguel xi, xxx, 36
Primo de Rivera, José Antonio xi
Primo de Rivera, Miguel 259
Prisoner Exchange 148, 150, 343, 345
Probert, Major Bill vii, 237, 238, 240
Projectile Infantry Anti-Tank (PIAT) xii, 195
Puigcerda 40
Punta del Carnero Camp 75
Pyrenees xiii, xviii, 38, 39, 40, 42, 44, 45, 58, 74, 107, 115, 236, 250

Queen Mary 77
Quennell, Major Hugh 92, 93, 94, 100, 103

Rabat, Morocco 169, 174, 191
Radio operator vii, 112, 194
Radio Televisión Española (RTVE) xxix
Radway, England 180, 247
Ramat David, Palestine 188
Ramos Masens, Rafael (Ralph) vii, viii, xxiv, 190, 191, 194, 204, 213, 215, 292, 300
  DUNHILL V 198
  GALIA xix
  BRAKE 2 vii, xix, 205, 207, 208
  TOMBOLA vii, 208, 209, 210, 211
  TRUEFORM 201
  Military Medal xix, 210, 338
  post-war viii, 253, 254, 255
  SAS training & name 194, 195, 292
Randall, Lieutenant John 215
Ranville, France 227, 228

Reconquista de España 236
Red Cross 172, 247
Red Sea 128, 134
Redondo, José 185, 187, 249, 250, 289, 291, 318
Redruth, England xvi, 76
Regent Street, London 252, 261
Reggio Emilia 208
Regni Lagni Canal, Italy 218
Regionalist League of Catalonia xi
Reichstag, Berlin 247
Renkun, Netherlands 232
Rennes, France 72
Returned to Unit (RTU) 112
Reunions 252, 257, 264
Revuelta, Francisco (Robert Shaw) SAS vii, 191, 194, 198, 254, 293, 338
Rhine xix, 85, 198, 215, 222, 230, 236
Rhineland xii, 38, 236
Rhodes 137, 138
Rhodesia Hotel, South Kensington 95
Ribbentrop, Joachim von xiv, 93
Riccomini, Lieutenant 210
Rieucros xiii, 42, 44, 45
Rif War xi, 36, 98
Ringway, Manchester, England xviii, 96–100, 111, 112, 193, 214, 227, 230
River Jordan 121
Roa Ventura, Agustín iv, v, vi, xxvi, 41, 68, 70,71, 82, 84, 85, 86, 111, 161, 183, 268, 326, 340, 344
   361 Pioneer Company vi, 174, 176, 326
   demobilisation 182
   Djelfa 164, 165, 169, 171
   fighting to in Britain 242, 245, 247, 249, 250
   internment in France iv, v, vi, 41, 43, 44, 47, 164, 169
   Manuel Espallargas 179, 251
   protests v Franco Regime viii, ix, 259, 260, 262, 263, 264, 266, 267
   Spanish Ex-Servicemen's Association viii, ix, 260, 263, 264, 266, 267, 349
   Trafalgar Square 10 July 1960 261, 262
Roath, Wales 158, 344, 347
Robba, José 76
Robehomme, France 227
Rodriguez, Jesús v, 88, 90, 276
Rodriguez, José 189
Roer xix, 222
Roermond 222
Romedenne Chateau, Belgium v, 85, 89, 90
Rommel, *Feldmarschall* Johannes Erwin xvi, xvii, xix, 185, 186
Rooney, Major Oswald Basil 'Mickey' 198
Roosevelt, President Franklin Delano xvi, 94

Rose, Captain Edward 172, 173, 340
Rose, Lieutenant Colonel Stephen 127, 128, 132
Rossano Valley, Italy 207
Rotspanienkampfer 56
Rouen, France iv, xviii, xxiii, 82, 83, 199
Rousseau, Lieutenant Joseph Maurice 202
Royal Academy, London 263
Royal Air Force (RAF) xix, 77, 101, 196, 198
   38 Group RAF 196
   624 Squadron RAF 238
   RAF Ringway xviii, 96–100, 111, 112, 193, 214, 227, 230
   RAF Tempsford 196
   Transport Command 196
Royal Family xxx
Royal Navy xv, 101
Royo (Pascual Gimeno) 238, 240
Ruskington, England 130
Russia xvi, 70, 100, 246, 258
Russo, Lieutenant James 138, 139, 140, 141

Sagan, Poland 146
Sahara Desert 159, 160, 165
Saint Cyprien, France 42, 44, 47, 48, 153
Saint Joris Weert, Belgium 84
Saint Nazaire 38, 49, 59
Salerno, Italy xvii, 217, 218
Salisbury Plain 196
Salornaye, France 198
Saltash, England 76
Salvador, Sebastián 97, 107
Samarine, Lieutenant 199
San Francisco xx, 247
San Maria Capua Vetere 218
Sánchez Monterrubio, Cleto 40, 117, 121, 122, 126, 137, 144, 289, 340
Sánchez, Manuel v, 130, 289
Sandbach, Lieutenant 138, 140, 141
Sanjurjo, *General* xi
Santander xii, 38, 98, 100, 153, 198, 272, 293
Sarraut, Albert 40
Sathonay, France 52
Sauquillo Echevarria, Lucio vii, xviii, xix, 226, 227, 229
Sauquillo Eregaña, Luís
Saveney, France 59, 62
Savernake Forest 77
Savoy Grenadiers 136
Scarborough, england 227
Scotland Yard 243
Scott RN, Lieutenant Charles 103
Secret Intelligence Service (SIS) xxii, 92, 93, 94, 99, 101, 104, 162

Secteur Fortifié de Flandres (SFF) xxii, 64, 66
Segre River 39
Selerie, Captain Peter 130, 154
Senegalese soldiers/troops 42, 160, 52
Septfonds Camp 43, 44, 48
Seravezza, Italy 207
Serrano Suñer, Ramón xv, 36, 93, 100, 110, 245
Servicio de Evacuación de Refugiados Españoles (SERE) xxii, 243
Sevenoaks, England 264
Sevilla, Spain 250
Seward, Margery 250
Sherman, Admiral 258
Sicily xvii, 136, 162, 169, 174, 218
Sidbury, England 250
Sidi Azaz Camp Libya 160
Sidi Bel Abbès 50, 52, 54, 68, 71
Sidmouth, England 85, 250
Simpson, Colonel Adrian 124
Singapore xvi
Sint-Jansbeek 232
Small Scale Raiding Force (SSRF) 95, 110, 342
Smith and Wesson revolver 195
Smith, Major R.D. MC 58, 59, 60, 61, 74, 82
Snowden, Lieutenant J.R. 200, 201, 339
Solborg, Robert 162
Sollum Bay 132
Soltau, Germany 222
Somerville, Vice Admiral James 93
Soper, Dr Donald 261
South America 47, 101, 105, 113
South Wales 216, 254
Soviet Union xiv, xvi, xxvii, 47, 105
Spahis (French indigenous cavalry) 160
Spalding, England 230
Spanish Ambassador 56, 67, 257, 259, 265
Spanish Civil War
    Battle of Brunete xii, xxvii, 38, 74, 123
    Battle of the Ebro xiii, 39, 40, 74, 95, 100, 190, 199
    Battle of Guadalajara xii, xxvii
    Battle of Jarama xiii, 95, 123
    Battle of Teruel xiii, xxvii, 38, 39, 95, 123
    Guernica xii, 38, 39, 226
Spanish communists OSS
Spanish Embassy, London xxvi, 108, 109, 261
Spanish Ex-Servicemen's Association viii, ix, xxviii, xxix, 260, 263, 264, 266, 267, 349
    Committee 179, 242, 259, 260
    Franco's Prisoners Speak 263, ix
    newsletter 260, ix
    protests v Franco Regime viii, ix, 259, 260, 261, 262, 263, 264, 266, 267

    Trafalgar Square 10 July 1960 261, 262
Spanish Morocco xi, 95, 110, 203
Spanish neutrality 93, 203
Spanish News Sheet 76, 339
Spanish Newsletter 244
Spanish POWs 143, 145, 148, 246
Spanish Question 257
Spanish Republican News 244
Spanish Republican Armed Forces
    Popular Army of the Spanish Republic 164
    Republican Air Force 43, 59, 61
    Republican Army 35, 38, 40, 41, 45, 58, 98, 107, 170, 176, 202
    XII Army Corps 74
    56th Division 74
Spanish Republican Constitution xi, 36
Spanish Republican Fleet 157, 42, 46
Spanish Second Republic 84, 243
Spanish Sefardic Jew 157
Special Air Service xxii, 95, 115, 150, 184, 185, 193, 199, 207, 338
    1st SAS 190, 192, 193, 196, 215
    2nd SAS vii, xvii, xviii, xx, xix, 117, 118, 152, 167, 184, 189–194, 196, 198, 199, 210, 202, 203, 204, 205, 213, 216, 284, 292, 293, 295
    2nd SAS Funnies 184, 191
    2nd SAS Thanksgiving Service 216
    3rd SAS 196, 198, 203, 214, 293
    4th SAS 171, 184, 193, 214, 216, 293
    5th (Belgian) Special Air Service Regiment 193, 199, 216
    L Detachment 150, 184, 185, 190, 196
    Special Air Service Brigade 150, 185
    SAS Brigade HQ 193
    SAS disbandment 216
    SAS Operation AMHERST 199, 214, 293
    SAS Operation ARCHWAY vii, xix, 215, 292, 293
    SAS Operation BARKER 198, 199, 293
    SAS Operation BRAKE 2 vii, x, xix, 205, 206, 207, 210, 292
    SAS Operation DICKENS 203, 293
    SAS Operation DUNHILL V xviii, 198, 292, 293
    SAS Operation GALIA x, xix, 205, 206, 207, 210, 292, 293, 338, 342
    SAS Operation KEYSTONE 214
    SAS Operation LOYTON xviii, 202, 292, 293
    SAS Operation RUPERT xviii, 198, 292
    SAS Operation TOMBOLA vii, x, xix, 194, 204, 205, 206, 207, 208, 211, 213, 292, 295, 338
    SAS Operation TRUEFORM xviii, 199, 201, 292, 338

SAS Operation VARSITY 215
SAS Operations in France phases 196
SAS Tactical HQ 186
Special Auxiliary Force 192
Special Boat Service (SBS) 184
Special Boat Squadron 190
Special Duties 150, 290
Special Forces xxiv, 150, 184, 190, 192, 193, 241, 341
Special Operations Executive (SOE)
   Special Operations Executive AUBE Mission vii, xviii, 236, 237, 238
   Special Operations Executive (SOE) 23 Land 93
   Special Operations Executive (SOE) 24 Land 03
   Special Operations Executive (SOE) H Section 92, 96, 97, 99, 106
   SOE/OSS BRANDON Mission xvii, 169
   SOE MASSINGHAM Mission 167, 169, 170, 338, 345
   SOE Operation BLACKTHORN 94
   SOE Operation MAD DOG 94
   SOE Operation PANTHINO 109, 110
   SOE Operation PENNINE 109
   SOE Operation POSTMASTER xvi, 109, 110
   SOE Operation RELATOR 94, 95, 99, 100, 104
   SOE Operation SPRINKLER 96, 98, 99, 100, 101
   SOE Operation WARDEN 101
   SCONCE Training 92–106, 338
   SCONCE I xv, 95, 96, 278–283
   SCONCE II 96, 112, 278–283
   SCONCE III 96, 98, 278v283
   SCONCE IV v, xvi, 96, 97, 98, 100, 107, 110, 112, 113, 278–283
   SCONCE V 98, 101, 278–283
Special Projects Operations Centre 241
Special Raiding Squadron 190
Special Service Regiment (1 SSR) iii, vi, xvii, xxi, 150, 151, 152, 184, 187, 188, 290
   1 SSR D Squadron iii, xvii, 150, 153, 187, 188, 190, 291, 292
   1 SSR LRDG vii, xxi, xxiv, 184, 188, 189, 190, 194
Specialist Training Centre Brickenbury (STS 17) 95
Specialist Training Centre Comely Hall (STS 41) 106
Specialist Training Centre Inverairlort House (STS 25) 95
Specialist Training Centre Thame House (STS 42) v, 97, 98
Specialist Training Centre The Drokes (STS 33) 96
Specialist Training Centre The House on the Shore (STS 34) 96
Sphakia, Crete xvi, 139, 141, 143, 146, 200
SS *Habana* 226
SS *Stanbrook* xvii, 158, 159, 341, 345
St Cyprien camp 66
St Elizabeth Hospital Arnhem 233
St Jean de Luz, France 58
St Nazaire, France iv, xvi, 60, 61, 63
Staffeta 208, 209
Stafford Prison 72, 73
Stalag 344 146, 284–288
Stalag 383 120, 145, 252, 284–288
Stalag 3D 146, 284–288
Stalag 4C 146, 148, 150, 284–288
Stalag 8C 146
Stalag 9C 198, 293
Stalingrad, Battle of xvii, 111
Stamford Bridge 256
Stirling, David 137, 150, 190
Stirling, Bill 189, 193
Stockton-on-Tees, England 351
Stonehenge, England 227
Stoneybridge, England 85
Stratford-Upon-Avon, England 176
Stroehrer, Baron Berhard von 100
Suda Bay, Crete xvi, 139
Sudan 130, 134, 135, 188
Sudbury, England vi, 180, 249
Suez Canal 122
Sulingen, Germany 222
Sunday Despatch Newspaper 158, 341
Supreme Allied Commander Europe xviii
Supreme Commander of Allied Troops 167
Supreme Headquarters Allied Expeditionary Force (SHAEF) 193
Surera, Manuel iv, v, vi, vii, viii, xxviii, 51, 120, 132, 133, 134, 137, 149, 150, 151, 152, 185, 186, 187, 188, 189, 249, 250, 289, 291, 318
Suzzoni 159
Swallow Street, London 252
Swanwick, England 278 – 283, 315, 316
Swindon 77
Swiss Cottage, London 251
Switzerland 164, 237
Sykes, Manuela 261
Sykes, Private 146
Symons, Lieutenant Colonel Peter 132
Syria v, xiv, xvi, 40, 52, 54, 115, 117, 118, 119, 120, 122, 123, 154, 186, 188, 198, 199

Tamarit, Eduardo iv, vi, xxv, 49, 166, 168, 173, 178, 182, 327

Tangier 104, 164
Tarbes, France 70, 216
Tarrant Rushton 196, 230
Taunton, England 87
Tehran Conference xviii
Tewson, Mr H. 226
Thessaloniki, Greece 143
Thomas, D. V. 77
Thompson sub machine gun 130
Thoroton, Colonel Charles 93
Thorpe, Jeremy MP 263
Tilly-sur-Seulles, France 221
Tobruk, Libya xvii, 188, 342
Torre Maina, Italy 211
Torrents Abadía, Juan 42, 167, 169, 190, 191, 194, 198, 201, 202, 215, 254, 292, 300
Tosdedt, Germany 222
Toulouse, France 67, 153, 202, 236, 340
Tourcoing, France 64
Tovar, Coronel López 246
Trades Union 226, 260
Trafalgar Square viii, 113, 251, 256, 259, 261, 262
Trancho Bartolomé, Corporal Moisés vi, xxiv, 51, 128, 137, 138, 150, 153, 154, 186, 289, 291, 294, 317
Trans-Saharan Railway 46, 66, 190
Trentham Park xiv, 72, 107, 119
Tresserras, Rafael xxiv, 250, 312
Trevor-Rope, Hugh 263
Trill, Jaime v, 35, 120, 121, 145, 250, 251, 290, 319
Trueta I Raspall, Dr Josep 221, 244
Trujillo, Francisco 106, 277, 283
Truro, England 79
Tunis 45, 46, 117, 155, 157, 160, 161, 177, 297–301
Tunisia xvii, 46, 111, 136, 155, 157, 158, 159, 160, 161, 162, 169, 170, 190, 214, 293, 295
Tunnicliffe, K.O. 77
Turre, Almería 79

U-Boat 101
UGT 1 Batallón Fulgencio Mateos 153
UNESCO xx, xxii, 258
Unión General de Trabajadores (UGT) 170
United Nations xx, xxii, 246, 247, 257, 258
United States xvi, xx, 52, 160, 257, 258
United States Joint Chiefs of Staff 258
Urquhart, General 233
US Army
    US Army 195
    US 3rd Army 198, 202
    15th Army Group 202
    82nd Airborne Division 236

Val d'Aran 246
Valenciennes, France 84
Valladolid, Spain 58, 76, 271
Vallespir 42
Vancia, France 52
Varaville, France 227
Vargas Rivas, Antonio viii, ix, 85, 87, 179, 183, 252, 256, 260, 261, 264, 265, 267, 290, 345
Vázquez, Alfonso 157
Velasco Zapico, Jesús iv, v, xxiv, 57, 59, 61, 62, 63, 77, 83, 100, 101, 106, 112, 252, 253, 254, 264, 265, 283, 315
Vernet d'Arriège Camp 47, 164, 169
Via delle Forbici 203
Vichy France xiv, xv, xvi, 35, 47, 52, 55, 56, 67, 72, 73, 93, 101, 119, 131, 155, 160, 162, 164, 170, 236, 343, 345. 346
Vickers Machine Gun 195, 205, 233
Vicky the cartoonist 250
Victoria Cross 185
Victoria station 261
Victory in Europe xx
Victory Parade vii, xx, xxx, 84, 87, 223
Vidal, Marco 189
Vigo 158, 272
Vilanova, Josep vii, xvii, xxviii, 126, 218, 219, 220, 221, 285, 338
Villa Calvi 209, 210
Villa Rossi vii, 209, 210
Ville d'Argel ship 70
Vitoria, Spain 64, 227, 288
Volturno River xvii, 126, 154, 218, 219, 342

Walker-Brown, Captain Bob 205, 207
Wall Street xi, 36
Warsaw xix
Watermanship 128
Waugh, Evelyn 137, 139, 141, 341
Wavell, Major General A. P. 130
Wedgwood, Colonel 72
Wedgwood-Benn, Anthony 259
Wells, Company Sergeant Major A. T. 74
Wells, H.G. 244
Weser River 222
Westminster Abbey xii
Westminster House 108
Weston, General 139
Westward Ho xv, 57, 64, 74, 278–283, 308–315
Weygand, *Général* Maxime 162
White Mountains, Crete 199
Whitehall, London viii, xxix, 260, 266, 267, 349
Wickwar 77
Willemzagen Camp, Berlin 237

Wilson, Captain L.N.R. 138
Wiltshire xvi, 76, 77, 196, 227
Wingfield-Morris Hospital 221
Wireless operator 103, 112, 196
Wireless Training School (WTS), Fawley Court v, 100, 102
Wivenhoe, England vii, 196, 204, 213, 215
Woodward, Dorothy 107
Wright, Sergeant Lesley 136, 339
Wurm, Germany 222

Xanten, Germany xix, 222

Yalta Conference xix
Young, Lieutenant Colonel George, DSO xv, xvi, 119, 120, 123, 124, 130, 132, 138, 139, 140, 141, 143, 190, 339
Younger, Kenneth 169

Zamora, Eladio 76, 294, 309
Zaragoza xxviii, 39, 247, 286